# Southern First Ladies

# Southern First Ladies

## Culture and Place in
## White House History

Edited by Katherine A. S. Sibley

University Press of Kansas

Published by the University Press of Kansas (Lawrence, Kansas 66045),
which was organized by the Kansas Board of Regents and is operated
and funded by Emporia State University, Fort Hays State University,
Kansas State University, Pittsburg State University, the University of Kansas,
and Wichita State University.

Library of Congress Cataloging-in-Publication Data

Names: Sibley, Katherine A. S. (Katherine Amelia Siobhan), 1961– editor.
Title: Southern First Ladies : culture and place in White House history /
edited by Katherine A. S. Sibley.
Other titles: Culture and place in White House history
Description: [Lawrence] : University Press of Kansas], [2021] | Includes index.
Identifiers: LCCN 2020022376
ISBN 9780700630431 (cloth)
ISBN 9780700630448 (ebook)
Subjects: LCSH: Presidents' spouses—United States—Biography. |
Women—Southern States—Biography. | Presidents' spouses—United
States—History. | Presidents' spouses—Political activity—United
States. | Presidents' spouses—United States—Social life and customs. |
White House (Washington, D.C.)—Social aspects. | Presidents—Family.
Classification: LCC E176.2 .S68 2021 | DDC 973.09/9—dc23
LC record available at https://lccn.loc.gov/2020022376.

British Library Cataloguing-in-Publication Data is available.

Printed in the United States of America

10 9 8 7 6 5 4 3 2 1

The paper used in this publication is acid free and meets the minimum
requirements of the American National Standard for Permanence of Paper
for Printed Library Materials Z39.48-1992.

*To Randall M. Miller*

# Contents

## PART II: From the Progressive Era to the Present Century

# *Foreword*

---

There is a pattern to the story, and also a message. Dining together, or perhaps riding in a horse-drawn carriage, in a plush Pullman, or in a modern motorcade, the president of the United States turns with self-satisfaction to ask his first lady: "Aren't you glad you married me? If you were married to that (insert profession here), you'd only be the wife of (same profession)."

"If I was married to *him*," she quickly retorts, "*he* would have been president."

Humorous for sure, the vignette is not necessarily good history. I doubt, in fact, such a conversation ever took place, yet one can easily find it attributed to the Obamas, the Bushes (both generations), the Clintons, and why not the Eisenhowers and the Hardings, too? There seems a perpetual desire to cut down the great man just a little with the reminder that he did not make it alone.

Which happens to be true. Presidents do not scale such heights on their own, and nearly all found comfort, support, guidance, and a partner within their marriage. Long before the women in this book bore the title first lady, their savvy, political acumen, advocacy, and often warmth (sometimes in contrast to their husbands' chillier dispositions) formed a critical part of the presidents' rise. Those same attributes, as this volume shows, critically affected each man's presidency as well.

So, too, did they affect American culture writ large because first ladies are so much more than "merely" presidential partners. Hillary Rodham Clinton embodied a transformation of women's role in US society, but she was not the first first lady to leave her mark. One cannot tell the nation's story of the 1840s without noting Sarah Polk's political might, or the 1860s without employing Mary Todd Lincoln's travails, which reflected the broader nation's. Obviously, no retelling of the failed peace following the Great War is truly complete without reference to Edith Bolling Wilson; neither can we understand fully the US environmental movement without Lady Bird Johnson's role. Outside the United States, first ladies such as Laura Bush also left their stamp. Her ongoing initiatives include the President's Emergency Fund for AIDS Relief and the US-Afghan Women's Council, which promotes education for women and girls in Afghanistan.

The point is not that first ladies—and not so far from now, first gentlemen, too—influence their partners; it is that they are best understood as part of the broader tapestry of the country's presidential past and present. And in this case, the peculiar and particular tapestry of the South, a region whose politics, identity, and social mores resound far beyond its borders. This volume in your hands is not the first to explore first ladies or the initial exploration of the land below the Mason-Dixon Line. But it is unique in doing both at once, reflecting the manner in which first ladies have both an influence and a history of their own tied to place and context, with implications both for White House traditions and the activism in which these women engaged. The Center for Presidential History could not be prouder of the part we played in bringing this group of extraordinary scholars together. Their work is our joy and your gain.

Jeffrey A. Engel
Director, Center for Presidential History
Southern Methodist University
March 10, 2020

# Acknowledgments

This volume has been a collaboration, and I am so appreciative for the help of so many in making it possible. Without the warm welcome I received from Jeffrey A. Engel, director of the Center for Presidential History (CPH) at Southern Methodist University, to host our conference in 2018, this book likely would never have seen the light of day—and definitely would not have had such a joyful emergence. Quickly grasping the significance of place in White House history, Jeff invited me in 2017 to present a talk and then in 2018 to organize a conference at the CPH, "Southern Belles, Washington Balls, and Dixie's Reach: How Southern First Ladies Changed America's Compass," where a number of our authors first presented our work on this topic. In addition to hosting and connecting me with contributors who have enriched this book, he invited C-SPAN to broadcast our gathering. As I write this I am reminded again of that special time, and I would especially like to thank Ronna Spitz, coordinator at the CPH, who so kindly made all the arrangements. I am also most grateful to Tom Zeiler, for years my dear colleague at the Historical Advisory Committee at the US State Department's Office of the Historian, who introduced me to Jeff and the CPH.

So many of my first lady scholar colleagues have made this such an interesting and deeply satisfying ride! I want to thank most enthusiastically for their inspiration and, often, their essential editing advice, the following wonderful people: Kristin Ahlberg, Catherine Allgor, Carl Anthony, Mary Brennan, Lisa Burns, Diana Carlin, Teri Finneman, Louie Gallo, Myra Gutin, Chris Leahy and Sharon Williams Leahy, John Marszalek, Anita McBride, Jody Natalle, Valerie Palmer-Mehta, Janette Muir, Melly Scofield, Nancy Smith, Molly Wertheimer, and Nancy Beck Young, all of whom have been on this "first lady special" with me for quite some time now. For assistance with the research in my own chapter, I would also like to thank Glenn Whaley and her staff at the Central Arkansas

Library System and its Butler Center for Arkansas Studies, who so generously granted me the Jim Pledger Memorial Research Award for Use of Clinton-era Materials on Education in 2018. I gratefully extend my appreciation as well to the staff at the Lyndon Baines Johnson (LBJ) Library who welcomed me and helped me find such good resources, as did the archivists at Princeton's Seeley Mudd Library and the George W. Bush Presidential Library. While this project was developing, Anita McBride, director of the First Ladies Initiative at American University, and Natalie Gonnella-Platts, director of the Women's Initiative at the George W. Bush Presidential Center, kindly invited me to participate in their events, including the "First Ladies in Service" panel discussion at the National Archives in 2016, the "Engage: The Role of the First Lady" presentation at the George W. Bush Presidential Center in 2018, and the White House Historical Association's Presidential Sites Summit in 2019, events where I had the opportunity to meet in person our three most recent first ladies. These opportunities have all given me fresh inspiration.

I would especially like to thank the History Department, Drexel Library, and the dean's office at Saint Joseph's University for the support they have lent me over the years to attend conferences, speak and teach about the topic of first ladies, and continue my research. At the University Press of Kansas, David Congdon, a superb editor, has always been encouraging and supportive in improving this work, and a true partner in this endeavor. Any mistakes in this volume, of course, remain mine.

My siblings are among my dearest friends, and my brother George in particular always has something to say on first ladies, which makes the topic so much fun! I am lucky that he enjoys coming to my conferences and continuing to enlighten me with his deep reading on such a wide range of mold-cracking topics. My girlfriends, meanwhile, have leavened many a day while this project was under way with lots of great walks and talks. My beloved husband, Joe, has shared me with Florence and many of the other first ladies for most of our life together now. Dearest Joe, thank you for making my life so joyful and for all our good conversations on this and other topics! I look forward to spending more time with you and Jonah and Marin now that the Southern first ladies are going to be put to bed.

I am dedicating this book to Randall M. Miller, my dear colleague for the past three decades. An expert on the South, Randall has always deepened my awareness with his knowledge of the region; his work (and activism) on the issue of slavery as well as on the Civil War, African American history, religious and ethnic influences, and Southern dissent have broken new ground in our fuller understanding of US history. As a mentor and friend, he has provided me more opportunities to widely research and publish than I know where to start. From my first review in the *Pennsylvania Magazine of History and Biography* to my book on the Cold War to my *Companion to First Ladies*, Randall's support, helpful commentary, warm encouragement, and kindly assistance have been an ever-present lodestar. His humor, keen insights, and generous spirit have always brightened and inspired me, and I have been so lucky to have him across the hall. Thank you for our many years of comradeship and warm collegiality, Randall!

Katherine A. S. Sibley
Swarthmore, Pennsylvania

# Southern First Ladies

# Introduction

Catherine Allgor and Katherine A. S. Sibley

It was only in the past three or four decades that scholars began to pay serious attention to American first ladies, contextualizing them and exploring them as historical actors. Before the 1980s, works on these women depicted them largely as celebrity wives, untethered to the larger fields of women's history or political history, their stories serving as complements to their husbands' contributions. At best, they appeared as a parade of "women worthies," as in a favorite book of Julia Tyler's entitled *The Court Circles of the Republic, or, the Beauties and Celebrities of the Nation: Illustrating Life and Society under Eighteen Presidents, Describing Administrations from Washington to Grant* (1869) by Elizabeth F. Ellet; almost a century later, *The Woman in the White House: The Lives, Times, and Influence of Twelve Notable First Ladies* (1963) by Marianne Means showed that pattern of portrayal to be little altered. As Elizabeth Lorelei Thacker-Estrada has pointed out, poor Margaret Taylor fell under the shadow of her husband's horse, "Old Whitey," whose portrait was more prominent in books about her husband than her own was. That equine exemplar well illustrates Nancy Beck Young's observation that "first ladies . . . provide a barometric reading of attitudes toward women's 'proper' role in society at any given moment in time."[1]

At first glance, the relatively recent emergence of first ladies studies might seem puzzling. Surely, when the new scholars of women's lives, words, and work were casting about for historical subjects, one might have imagined that these "firsts" would be first in line. A clue to such scholarly neglect might lie paradoxically in their fame and familiarity. As the second wave of the women's movement appeared in the 1960s and 1970s, historians were determined to find "hidden figures" in history, declaring their mission to unmute long-stifled voices. The wives and hostesses of presidents, some of whom were national figures, might have seemed too obvious —too elite, as well. Thus, most works about them remained strictly biographical or condensed them into group or collective treatments.

Starting in the 1980s with books such as Sylvia Jukes Morris's pioneering study of Edith Roosevelt, biographical treatments began to explore these women with increasing depth and complexity; in collective works, too, they were given context and nuance. Since then, new analyses have explored first ladies' professional responsibilities, communication styles, marriages, relations with the press, political activism, popularity, feminist inclinations, and physiques.[2] Portraits of them now abound. All the same, an important piece of first ladies' identity in the White House has been largely overlooked: the element of place. As sociologist Dwight Billings and anthropologist Ann Kingsolver noted recently in their study of Appalachia, "Place matters, more than ever, in the construction of identity and meaning, politics and policy, citizen activism, creative expression, and in scholarship. . . . *Place*, as much as anything, is *action* more than passive context. It is about what people *do*."[3]

Through the lens of place, and most especially, the specific place of Southernness, this book explores the ways in which cultural backgrounds molded a set of influential first ladies' presentation, actions, and activism while in office. "Southernness" is a fairly recent category of analysis and a highly interdisciplinary one; recent works, for instance, have employed the term to explore white, working-class masculinity after World War II, the literature of William Faulkner and Zora Neale Hurston, and linguistic and media studies of Black Southern hip-hop and country music.[4] In this volume our authors use Southernness to define and better understand the cultural attributes, characteristics, and actions of seventeen first ladies, from Martha Washington to Laura Bush. As our contributors also suggest, these elements are not confined to the women explored here; indeed, they have adhered to the office of first lady itself in lasting ways, regardless of the regional backgrounds of successive occupants.

The seventeen first ladies defined in this volume as Southern were either born in the South—specifically, the former states of the Confederacy or their slave-holding neighbors such as Missouri—or else lived in those states for a significant portion of their adult lives (Julia Tyler, Hillary Clinton, Barbara Bush). With the exception of Julia Grant, every one of these women was also married to a Southern man and was living when her husband was in the White House (thus, Rachel Jackson and Angelica van Buren do not appear). Two mid-nineteenth-century wives, Letitia Tyler and Margaret Taylor, have been omitted because of a combination of their short spans in the office, their limited influence on the position, and scant sources on their lives.

Depending on historical context, one of the chief cultural attributes our set of first ladies has shared is certain conventions around gender roles, particularly the idea of Southern white womanhood, a concept well illuminated by Jane Turner Censer, and before her, Anne Firor Scott. As Censer notes, although this ideal connoted "self-sacrifice and duty" as well as "benevolence" in the domestic sphere, the Civil War challenged it, calling for different roles for Southern white women; they served as spies, nurses in makeshift hospitals, and heads of plantations, all of which gave them a new and emboldened cast outside the home. The ideal of Southern white womanhood thus expanded to encompass both "politically and socially conservative activities, as well as reforming ones," Censer writes.[5] Yet this kind of tension over proper gender roles did not begin with the Civil War. Southern women in the White House had wrestled with it from the beginning. As Young points out her overview chapter for Part I, "At its core the institution of the first lady has been structured around and . . . in rebellion against Southern ideas of womanhood." Although such gender conventions have only continued to change with time, as Diana Bartelli Carlin notes here in her chapter on Martha Washington, even today "many elements remain, often rooted in the colonial South, and include emphases on family, community, religious practice, and social rituals," and these remain attached as well to expectations around the position of first lady.

A second Southern cultural element these elite white women shared was their problematic relationship with questions of race. For some, this included their personal perpetuation of slavery, as every single first lady covered in the first section of this book enslaved people, and five of them—Martha Washington, Dolley Madison, Elizabeth Monroe, Julia Tyler, and Sarah Polk—brought their enslaved into the White House. And while Mary Lincoln might have served as first lady of the Union, she continued to support the slaveholding practices of her old Kentucky home. For those later Southern first ladies who grew up during the Jim Crow era, whether consciously or not, their lives were shaped by a culture that benefited them as white women. Many of them fought this systemic racism by making efforts to alleviate the results of its oppression during the long civil rights struggle that began with Reconstruction, as Ellen Wilson did; Edith Wilson, by contrast, cherished her prejudices and was active in perpetuating the myth of the lost cause. In the more recent past, first ladies such as Lady Bird Johnson, Rosalynn Carter, and Laura Bush all lived and wrestled with the legacy of segregation in their states before coming to the White House and brought their Southern-influenced advocacy to their work in Washington. Thus, the topic of race serves to illuminate how Southern first ladies were also activists, progressive or not.

At different points in time, then, along with the regional associations of their birthplaces or domiciles, elements of Southernness for the first ladies in this volume have included gender conventions regarding their presentation and behavior that they might have embraced or struggled with and notions of white supremacy that they either accepted or attempted to undermine. Meanwhile, activism on any number of fronts in the twentieth and twenty-first centuries expanded to enable these women to further engage in progressive and even transgressive conversations on issues such as girls' education, race relations, military issues, mental health, and the environment. Throughout our book, place—Southernness—influenced their selection and pursuit of activist roles, as we will discover here.

With these themes as our guiding threads, this book's organizational approach is biographical; every Southern first lady is explored in her own chapter, framed by her roots and residency and their lasting influences. The book is further divided into two chronological sections, hinging on the Progressive Era, and each of these parts contains a concluding overview chapter that highlights the activism of the women in the preceding segment. Nor does this study leave out Confederate first lady Varina Davis, whose own active effort to build a Southern nation was a short-lived and massive failure, even as its monumental legacy lives on to haunt the present moment.

The book begins with chapters on the founding first ladies, Martha Dandridge Custis Washington and Dolley Payne Todd Madison. In their era, gender roles were fixed more rigidly, and presidential wives were bound more firmly by those strictures. The dynamic of political work behind the veil was more characteristic of these women in the early years of the nation, before widespread education and suffrage enabled greater visibility for action. Nevertheless, they found ways to assert their agency by working around the expectations of Southern ladyhood or, even more intriguingly, using those very expectations—the loving wife, the devoted mother, the social hostess—to achieve their ends.

As they entertained visitors from home and abroad, performed charitable activities, and ministered to soldiers and veterans in the new Republic, Martha Washington and Dolley Madison found these occupations an avenue for their advocacy, whether to pursue their husbands' political goals or to advance their own causes. As Carlin points out in Chapter 1, Martha, who of course created the position of first lady, also "participated in the political sphere through her role as hostess to the men who eventually founded the new country." She was careful "to work behind the scenes," a model that later first ladies also found successful. Merry Ellen Scofield shows in Chapter 2 how the political entertaining continued in a more fulsome way after Dolley Madison made her home in Washington City (as it was called then), creating "Southern-inspired and Dolley-infused etiquettes that formed the backbone of a capital society." These allowed for the leading women of Washington to wield power through established social protocols regardless of party affiliation, and even years after, when Dolley returned to Washington full time in the 1840s as a widow, such patterns remained.

By shaping the style of capital entertaining along Virginia gentry lines, these first presidential wives thus made Southern culture into national culture. Washington City was undoubtedly a Southern city and has remained so. Martha's formal tea parties and drawing room receptions as well as Dolley's more frequent and crowded "squeezes" set a long-standing precedent for mixing politics and parlor talk among the genders. The gracious furnishings and decor in the grand mansion that became the setting for these gatherings were the legacy of the third Virginian first lady, Elizabeth Monroe. Her efforts transformed that building from the fiery depredations of 1812, as Mary Stockwell notes in Chapter 3, "into the elegant public space and private family home that it remains to the present day." They were also the guiding vision Jacqueline Kennedy reimagined in her reconstruction of the mansion in the early 1960s. Whereas Monroe, both because of her personality and her worsening health, was a more reticent first lady, as was her very frail Southern successor, Letitia Tyler, the next two Southerners in the office, Julia Gardiner Tyler and Sarah Childress Polk, were more active. All of these women, going back to Martha Washington, shared something else in common, too—as first ladies, their efforts benefited from the labor and support of enslaved men and women, as our chapters explore closely. One of the most avid supporters of slavery was in fact New Yorker Julia Gardiner Tyler, whose marriage in the White House was followed by a honeymoon to the Tyler plantation so the young bride could see her future as mistress of Sherwood Forest. Furthering the spread of slavery, Julia also pressed for the annexation of Texas and later defended the practice in print. After the Civil War, however, she attempted to redefine herself not as the Southern wife of the only president to renounce his US citizenship to join the Confederate government but as a former first lady of the United States and thus entitled to a pension, as Christopher J. and Sharon Williams Leahy discuss in Chapter 4.

Sarah Polk, whose term coincided with a great expansion in the US territory open to slavery, was able to shroud her very active political partnership with her husband during the Mexican American War by appearing as enforcer of the Sabbath, as Teri Finneman shows in Chapter 5. In fact, she regularly revised the president's speeches, helped him in his meetings with Congress, and provided other political advice. Though she took care to avoid the appearance of power, befitting a Southern lady concerned with domestic duties, her husband's vice president was certainly well aware of her influence. Mary Lincoln, the next wartime Southern first lady who was highly engaged with her husband's work, was chastised for her role as his adviser even as "wartime disruption encouraged and heightened women's continued political involvement," as Laura Mammina points out in Chapter 7. Many citizens mistakenly believed that as a Southerner, Mary was less than loyal to the Union; of course she supported it fully. At the same time, her relationship to her dressmaker, Elizabeth Keckly, a formerly enslaved woman whom Lincoln considered a confidante, if a trans-actional one, further reveals the complicated dynamic of race and power for women in the White House. Keckly's 1868 book on her former employer, full of intimate details and written in part to shore up the dressmaker's own reputation after Lincoln's "Old Clothes Scandal," enraged the first lady and her supporters, and, as Sylvia Hoffert shows us in Chapter 6, raised key issues about race- and class-based notions of privacy and boundaries in that era.

Down in Richmond, the "Southernness"—or not—of Varina Howell Da-vis, first lady of the Confederacy, was also a live topic during the Civil War, as Teri Finneman shows in Chapter 8. Davis herself had mixed feelings about the Confederate cause and being a Southern "first lady" and, like Lincoln, refused to be held to the model of the Southern belle. Yet in her later career, Davis wrote for Joseph Pulitzer's *New York World* as the ultimate genteel Southern lady, the very personification of the lost cause, who espoused healing the nation with sympathetic stories about former Confederates. That kind of mythology also painted Sarah Polk, who was in fact quite comfortable in her old age, as a pen-niless, lonely widow, a figure of the impoverished Old South—and aided Julia Tyler at long last to get her pension, symbolizing the restored amity of North and South, at the expense of African Americans who lost political and social rights during that era. Just this way were and are first ladies made into totems of nation-building and myth making, with a strong Southern accent of white supremacy. Years later, as Valerie Palmer-Mehta reveals in Chapter 11, Edith Wilson spent much of her long span after leaving Pennsylvania Avenue embel-lishing that very Southern myth. In a similar vein, when Woodrow Wilson's first wife, Ellen Wilson, died in the White House in 1914, not one newspaper, North or South, would acknowledge her work on behalf of impoverished Blacks in Washington, DC; as Lisa M. Burns shows in Chapter 12, this successful artist and activist was instead remembered as a "traditional Southern lady."

Whether in obituaries or in office, Southern first ladies thus became symbols for their time. Lincoln's successor, Eliza Johnson, herself also a loyal Unionist, served as a bridge between the Old and the New South. She was "no Southern belle, rather a product of the frontier," as John F. Marszalek writes in Chapter 9, but although she was "a foreshadowing of the South that was to come," she was too ill to be much of a pioneer in that regard. Other first ladies used their backgrounds (or not) when it suited them, demonstrating more autonomy in their self-definition. As Louie Gallo highlights in Chapter 10, Julia Dent Grant vehemently denied any Southern affiliation, even though she was raised in a milieu worthy of Scarlett O'Hara. She deliberately cast herself as a westerner (Missouri was her home state), but she had grown up on a plantation surrounded by enslaved African Americans and was trained and educated to be the complete belle; her husband, Ulysses, worked for a time alongside their enslaved men and women after he married her. Like Julia Tyler earlier, these women straddled the North-South divide throughout their lives; in the twentieth century, Barbara Bush and Hillary Clinton similarly found themselves pulled into such different orbits.

Two Southern first ladies in the Progressive Era who married Woodrow Wilson, Ellen Axson Wilson and Edith Bolling Wilson, showed the tension between gender roles and activism. Despite the way she was remembered upon her untimely death in the White House, Ellen Wilson was an activist reformer for the poorest in Washington, DC, as well as the first first lady who juggled her own career, as a landscape painter, with her work in the White House, as Burns tells us. Edith Wilson, however, had no interest in reform but a great deal in coloring President Wilson's health in rosy hues, all as part of her effort to preserve him in office; she became a different sort of activist. Along with his doctor, she worked assiduously to protect him (and the public) from the truth during his long months as a stroke victim from 1919 to 1921. During this crucial time after World War I, the government was "not functioning well," as Palmer-Mehta notes, and this kind of power in the hands of an unelected first lady was seen as problematic enough that (along with Kennedy's assassination) it spurred Congress to create a succession plan with the twenty-fifth amendment.

That tragic assassination also brought in our next Southern first lady, Lady Bird Johnson. Like Ellen Wilson, Johnson was a mother with a career herself, running her husband's various political offices as well as the family's radio and television stations; she, too, would be an activist in the White House. Yet as a Texan, she was very conscious of the gender role expectations still solidly in place in the 1960s for first ladies to be supportive and ladylike. Johnson's Women Doers' luncheons illuminate such tensions; acknowledging women's accomplishments in the public sphere, they couched this work in feminine terms. As Nancy Kegan Smith writes in Chapter 14, "At once a doting mother, loving wife, and a successful entrepreneur, Johnson exemplified the 'steel magnolia,'" both "gentle" *and* resolute in her work. This work included serious protection of the environment—she hated the "prissy" term "beautification"—as well as efforts to promote education for impoverished children through Head Start and advocacy for the improvement of race and regional relations, which she took directly to the South in her First Lady Special Whistle Stop Campaign of 1964.

Rosalynn Carter, discussed in Chapter 15, was another Southern activist with the benefit, like Hillary Clinton or Laura Bush later, of first having been a governor's wife. As a result, Rosalynn, Hillary, and Laura saw and acted upon problems in their own states, whether literacy, educational deficits, or mental health, and then took these to the national stage. They also took their advocacy abroad once they were in the White House. As governors' wives and as first ladies, they had to be careful about their titles in these endeavors, often working under "honorary" titles, yet they were leaders all the same. As Kristin L. Ahlberg shows us, Rosalynn's work on behalf of human rights in Latin America as well as her humanitarian efforts in Thailand involved her as a direct surrogate for her husband, who made sure that his staff equipped her with the training and materials she needed, even though some of those men were skeptical of her abilities (as were some women). Rosalynn was, of course, more than capable, and her activism with Congress also led to major new mental health legislation, unfortunately shelved in the succeeding administration.

During that administration, Ronald Reagan's, Barbara Bush was second lady for two terms before her husband, George H. W. Bush, was elected in 1988. Like her own successor, Hillary, Barbara was a Yankee who lived much of her adult life in a Southern state. She continued to return to the Bush compound in Maine each year for months at a time but remained deeply shaped by her Texas residence, which led to a love of literature and eventually vigorous activism on behalf of literacy, as Myra G. Gutin illustrates in Chapter 16. Barbara's term as first lady was just four years, but her work on literacy continued throughout her life.

Nowhere is the difficult process of constructing a regional identity clearer than that illustrated by the dramatic, contentious effort that midwestern, Wellesley- and Yale-educated Hillary Rodham Clinton underwent in her quest for political power and acceptance in Arkansas. After resisting attempts to transform her into a proper political wife under her husband's name, Hillary took on the task of remaking herself only when it became clear that was the only way for him to win. She did so selectively, struggling to satisfy her critics while preserving her own identity and values, as Janette Kenner Muir demonstrates in Chapter 17. Hillary's work abroad in promoting the causes she first adopted in the South, education and women's rights, was echoed by her Southern successor, Laura Bush, who was also driven by her exposure to the deficits of Southern schools to promote education as an important right for all children regardless of color or gender. As Anita B. McBride elaborates in Chapter 18, as the first lady Laura Bush took her advocacy in both education and health care to Afghanistan, and she continues it to this day with her global First Ladies Initiative.

Thanks to the work of scholars such as those in this volume, first ladies studies have deepened analytically in context and in historical sophistication. All the same, one of the chief reasons some historical subjects get studied and some do not come down to sources, the papers or other primary sources by and about them. Twentieth-century first ladies such as Ellen Wilson, Lady Bird Johnson, and Rosalynn Carter have letters, diaries, and even publications of their own. For

Hillary Clinton and Laura Bush, we have far more, from email correspondence to the explosion of online posts about them and by them. Even much earlier first ladies have an abundance of material—Dolley Madison's correspondence comprises thousands of letters. Others, such as Elizabeth Monroe, have little, which requires a broad reading of other contemporary accounts and imaginative use of the existing documentation. To effectively address these challenges, our authors have brought in new and compelling research in often little-used primary sources and the latest and best scholarship in this ever-evolving field.

*Southern First Ladies: Culture and Place in the White House* underlines the importance of place in contextualizing first ladies as well as in understanding the attributes associated with their gender roles, approach to race, and advocacy work. Our two concluding, overview chapters explore more deeply this theme of activism. At the end of Part I, in Chapter 11, Young looks most closely at four early first ladies—Martha Washington, Dolley Madison, Julia Tyler, and Sarah Polk—highlighting how their approaches to deportment in office, political work, entertainment, and white supremacy defined their activism in significant ways. At the end of Part II, in Chapter 19, Sibley explores the social and political activism of six modern Southern first ladies—Ellen Wilson, Lady Bird Johnson, Rosalynn Carter, Barbara Bush, Hillary Clinton, and Laura Bush—further emphasizing how these women were agents of change on such issues as housing, racial and social justice, education, conservation, health, women's concerns, and international human rights, even as they had to wrestle with constraints others placed on them.

Although the topic of first ladies is growing in context and in depth, and our study deepens it more with its focus on culture and place, in time it will be complicated still further. We might expect sooner or later that this field, which uses gender as a category of analysis, will be challenged when the spouse of a US president is a man or someone who identifies with a gender role different from that which he or she or they were assigned at birth. Such historical complexities promise to deepen the scholarly discipline, and those of us who study presidential power and the influence of presidential partners will be ready to avail ourselves of those opportunities.

## NOTES

1. See Elizabeth Lorelei Thacker-Estrada, "Margaret Taylor, Abigail Fillmore, and Jane Pierce: Three Antebellum Presidents' Ladies," in *A Companion to First Ladies*, ed. Katherine A. S. Sibley (West Sussex, UK: Wiley-Blackwell, 2016), 182; Nancy Beck Young, "The Historiography of Lou Henry Hoover," in *A Companion to First Ladies*, ed. Katherine A. S. Sibley (West Sussex, UK: Wiley-Blackwell, 2016), 423.

2. See, for example, Sylvia Jukes Morris, *Edith Kermit Roosevelt: Portrait of a First Lady* (New York: Coward, McCann, and Geoghegan, 1980); Myra Gutin, *The President's Partner: The First Lady in the Twentieth Century* (Westport, CT: Praeger, 1989); Lewis L. Gould, *American First Ladies: Their Lives and Their Legacy* (New York: Garland, 1996); Robert P. Watson, *The Presidents' Wives: Reassessing the Office of First Lady* (Boulder, CO: Lynne Rienner, 2000); Kati Marton, *Hidden Power: Presidential Marriages That Shaped Our History* (New York: Anchor, 2001); Molly Meijer Wertheimer, ed., *Leading Ladies of the White House: Communication of Notable 20th Century First Ladies* (Lanham, MD: Rowman and Littlefield, 2004); Maurine Beasley, *First Ladies and the Press: The Unfinished Partnership of the Media Age* (Evanston, IL: Northwestern University Press, 2005); MaryAnne Borrelli, *The Politics of the President's Wife* (College Station: Texas A&M University Press, 2011); Myra Gutin and Leesa E. Tobin, "'You've Come a Long Way Mr. President': Betty Ford as First Lady," in *Gerald R. Ford and the Politics of Post-Watergate America*, vol. 2, ed. Bernard J. Firestone and Alexej Ugrinsky (Westport, CT: Greenwood, 1993); Carmen R. Lugo-Lugo and Mary K. Bloodsworth-Lugo, "Bare Biceps and American (In)Security: Post–9/11 Constructions of Safety, Threat, and the First Black First Lady," *Women's Studies Quarterly* 39, nos. 1–2 (2011): 200–217. There are also many fine volumes on individual first ladies of the twentieth century in the series on modern first ladies edited by Lewis Gould and published by the University Press of Kansas.

3. Dwight B. Billings and Ann E. Kingsolver, eds., *Appalachia in Regional Context: Place Matters* (Lexington: University Press of Kentucky, 2018), Introduction.

4. Zachary J. Lechner, *The South of the Mind: American Imaginings of White Southernness, 1960–1980* (Athens: University of Georgia Press, 2018); Patricia Bradley, "Performing Southernness in Faulkner's *The Sound and the Fury* and Hurston's *Dust Tracks on a Road*," in *Faulkner and Hurston*, ed. Christopher Rieger and Andrew B. Leiter (Cape Girardeau: Southeast Missouri State University Press, 2017), 77–90; Catherine Evans Davies with Caroline Myrick, "Performing Southernness in Country Music," in *Language Variety in the New South: Contemporary Perspectives on Change and Variation*, ed. Jeffrey Reaser, Eric Wilbanks, Karissa Wojcik et al. (Chapel Hill: University of North Carolina Press, 2018), 78–96; and Regina N. Bradley, "Becoming OutKasted: Archiving Contemporary Black Southernness in a Digital Age," in *Digital Sound Studies*, ed. Mary Caton Lingold, Darren Mueller, and Whitney Trettien (Durham, NC: Duke University Press, 2018), 120–129.

5. On this topic, see, for instance, Jane Turner Censer, *The Reconstruction of White Southern Womanhood, 1865–1895* (Baton Rouge: Louisiana State University Press, 2003), 12; Anne Firor Scott, *The Southern Lady* (Chicago: University of Chicago Press, 1970).

PART I

*From the Early Republic Through
Late Reconstruction*

# CHAPTER 1

# Martha Washington
## Southern Influences in Shaping an Institution

Diana Bartelli Carlin

Martha Dandridge Custis Washington's life symbolized that of many elite white eighteenth-century Southern women, and her background helped shape her role as presidential spouse. Although she made history, the Washingtons' joint decision to burn their personal correspondence with each other makes it difficult to provide a full-blown picture of her and her influence. First lady scholar Robert P. Watson noted that she "has received surprisingly little attention" and is "a relatively enigmatic figure," with her identity "largely tied to that of her husband's."[1] The lack of attention is even more striking, he adds, because "she was the source for much of her husband's success—financially, socially, and politically; and her contributions to his achievements were significant" (19). Fortunately for this analysis of the Southern influence on the first lady role, her correspondence with family and friends, her diaries, and legal documents help fill in the gaps, as do historians' accounts of Southern landholding women in the colonial era.

Martha Washington was a product of her times, but the unique demands she faced as George Washington's wife and as the first first lady made her a trailblazer. Like other daughters of plantation-owning parents, she was prepared to be a wife, mother, estate manager, and slave owner. She fulfilled those roles at the Custis White House plantation for her first husband, Daniel Parke Custis, and then at Mount Vernon for George Washington. Managing a complex plantation and hospitality were skills that made her transition to a new and uncharted role as the first president's wife more seamless than it might have been for others. Although some of her background was not unique to Southern women, few

Martha Washington in about 1790. In Evert A. Duyckinck, *Portrait Gallery of Eminent Men and Women of Europe and America: Embracing History, Statesmanship, Naval and Military Life, Philosophy, the Drama, Science, Literature, and Art* (New York: Henry J. Johnson, 1873), 182.

were called upon to manage holdings as extensive as those of the Washingtons'. Nor were many women asked to entertain the endless streams of visitors her husband's prepresidency positions, most notably that of commander in chief of the Continental Army, attracted to their home. This chapter frames Martha Washington's story within the context of an elite, eighteenth-century, Virginia woman's life and then examines the lasting influence of the first Southern first lady on the women who followed.

## CHARACTERISTICS OF A SOUTHERN, EIGHTEENTH-CENTURY WOMAN

This book presumes that the South and its culture uniquely influenced the ways Southern women served as first lady. The words "Southern woman," however, often evoke stereotypes. Two early scholars of Southern women's history, Joanne V. Hawks and Sheila L. Skemp, wrote, "The history of Southern women is enveloped in myth and fantasy. . . . Images of Southern women are more likely to be found on the pages of *Gone with the Wind* than in history books."[2] Thus, we envision the Southern belle of the antebellum plantation as a wealthy woman of leisure concerned primarily with social gatherings and catching the right husband, or as the steel magnolia who can take whatever life throws at her and gives as well as she gets. Black Southern women's portrayals are even more circumscribed, if they are visible at all.

Despite the simplistic and incomplete picture these images provide, historians have long considered the South a distinctive region with a subculture based on ethnic and regional identity that persists to this day.[3] With an influx of transplants from across the United States and the world over the past thirty years, some of the South's distinctiveness has faded, but many elements remain, often rooted in the colonial South. These include emphases on family, community, religious practice, and social rituals.

In the late 1970s and early 1980s, when women's studies were in their infancy, scholars did not overlook Southern women and their particular attributes. Caroline Matheny Dillman noted that it is important to distinguish between "women *of* the South, that is women who not only were born and reared in the South but more importantly have a heritage of Southern culture and generations of Southerners in their family backgrounds . . . and [those] *in* the South."[4] But what constitutes a heritage *of* the South? One important distinction made between men's and women's roles in gender studies is that of spheres—public and domestic. However, in the eighteenth century, spheres were not always as clearly defined as they came to be in the nineteenth. The Southern record offers strong evidence for this, especially in elite plantation households.[5] In the plantation household, as Jacquelyn Dowd Hall confirms, boundaries were "constantly renegotiated under the pressures of social and economic change."[6] Although married women were not firmly tied to the domestic sphere, most had little or no autonomy and were under the traditional British common law, by which they "became legally bound to their husbands. . . . The law stripped married women of property rights; everything they owned automatically became the husband's property."[7] In Martha's case, her new husband was the custodian of her Custis dower inheritance during her life. These negotiations would engulf her. By the age of twenty-six, she had lost a husband, her own father, and two of her four children, and she was forced to fulfill her late husband's business obligations.

For women of any class, life was not easy, as Sally McMillen writes: "A South of magnolias, mansions, and courtly gentlemen was real for only the tiniest minority of women. Far more realistic is a view of Southern women as survivors, constantly facing the death of loved ones, living with poor health, enduring physical discomforts, and relishing only a few moments of joy or leisure. . . . They were a remarkable group, indeed a 'hardy mold'" (12). This imagery illustrates the steel magnolia archetype, which persists today for women *of* the South. And even for the plantation class, life was arduous beyond the loss of loved ones. McMillen describes the life of a white woman born into a family similar to the Dandridges', with a modest-sized plantation and a small number of enslaved people working in the fields. Women "gardened, weeded, managed the dairy, knitted, sewed and mended endlessly, nursed sick children and slaves, and . . . cooked. . . . Jobs required skill or strength or both" (131).

Because of the difficulties of colonial life and the interdependence among plantation owners, enslaved workers, and communities at large, relationships were important to survival. Family was an integral part of the Southern culture, and a wife's dedication to her husband and his pursuits was paramount. Because early death, especially in childbirth, was so common along with second or third marriages as a result of a spouse's death, the family structure was often blended in many ways. For slaveholding women, as Elizabeth Fox-Genovese has noted, "the most positive interpretation of the household lay in the metaphor 'my family, white and black,' which captured the important, if elusive, vision of an organic community."[8] Such a community required interaction and negotiation between white masters and enslaved servants, but such interactions, as Mary Jenkins Schwartz notes, "were not between equals, but, within the confines of law and custom . . . [that] created a peculiar world of their own—a world that reveals much about class, race, and gender in the early nation."[9] This was a community of interdependence, then, but not one of choice for both parts of the "family" in creating or maintaining the community and its values or standards.

Beyond their husbands and children, notes McMillen, "all women, regardless of color, enjoyed primary friendships with other females, including their mothers, daughters, relatives, neighbors, and friends."[10] For Southern white women especially, the importance of relationships put an emphasis on the need to avoid *tackiness*—which Sarah Brabant defines as a "failure to act appropriately [and] a lack of sensitivity and insight into the response of others. The Southern lady was constantly alert to what was going on around her and the implications of those events for her and for her family."[11] As indicated in the description of community, this quality applied almost exclusively to men and women of the same class and race but could be applied, as is discussed in the next section, to recipients of elite women's charitable works. Thus, the stereotype of Southern hospitality and charm is likely grounded in the colonial period.

In the rural South, Sunday gatherings before and after church were important for developing and maintaining relationships. Religion provided comfort in the face of almost certain loss of loved ones and friends. Deeply rooted religious beliefs were not unique to Southern women, nor were they class specific; however, "Southern religious values imperceptibly merged with the high culture and high politics of slaveholders, which in turn permeated Southern society," as Fox-Genovese notes.[12] For example, church officers such as Martha's father and her first husband "oversaw not only church operations but also civilian matters, including the control of slaves in the community."[13] Frederick Douglass commented scathingly on this kind of control, especially when overlaid with religious sanctimony, in his *Narrative* regarding his master's conversion: "[He] found religious sanction and support for his slaveholding cruelty. He made the greatest pretensions to piety."[14] Nevertheless, many Southern women carried out charitable efforts inspired by "their [Christian] responsibility to assist the less affluent women of their neighborhood" as well as people enslaved on their plantations.[15]

Slaveholding families also required daughters to develop social graces to navigate in society and practical skills for plantation management. This necessitated home-based instruction in the basics of reading, writing, and "ciphering." Being a *lady* required a woman to "read history and the classics and play a musical instrument" for the purposes of "entertaining her husband's friends, family, and business acquaintances."[16] Dancing was a major part of Virginians' lives, and both sexes received instruction. The social season and Williamsburg balls were important for establishing and maintaining personal, business, and political relationships and for initiating contacts for suitable marriages.[17] Genteel women, Cynthia Kierner contends, were "thought to influence the men with whom [they] interacted. . . . And to improve the manners, taste, and morals of the men who governed their society" (185). Although women were not overtly political, they had a role in the public sphere.

The ideal of the lady was not uniquely Southern; British influence also defined this ideal, but elite Southern white women's roles nonetheless elevated their stature to one of "secular sainthood."[18] Being considered a lady "constituted the highest condition to which women could aspire."[19] Jacqueline Boles and Maxine Atkinson identified common terms describing a lady: "simple, good, passive, delicate, innocent, submissive, mannerly, economical, humble, sacrificing, sympathetic, kind, weak, generous, pious, shallow, nonintellectual, hospitable, rich, and calm."[20]

This picture of elite Southern white women in the colonial era supports this book's premise that place does indeed affect one's approach to life and position. Fox-Genovese provides a natural transition to Martha's biography within a Southern context: "Gender, race, and class relations constituted the grid that defined Southern women's objective positions in their society, constituted the elements from which they fashioned their views of themselves and their world, constituted the relations of different groups of Southern women to one another. The class relations that divided and interlocked Southern women played a central role in their respective identities."[21]

## MARTHA WASHINGTON: THE PROTOTYPE OF THE SOUTHERN LADY

Martha "Patsy" Dandridge Custis Washington, as described by her biographer, Patricia Brady, "was part and parcel of English Virginia and the world of its tobacco planters"—she was definitely *of* the South. Her mother, Frances "Fanny" Jones, was a fourth-generation Virginian from "respected landowning gentry, . . . not grandees with uncounted acres."[22] Her maternal grandfather was a member of the Virginia House of Burgesses, and her great-grandfather was an Oxford graduate and Williamsburg pastor. Her father, John "Jack" Dandridge, a British merchant's son, arrived at age fifteen with his brother William. He was a deputy clerk of New Kent County, then a clerk and a colonel in the militia. But most importantly, he owned 500 acres of tobacco-producing land on the Pamunkey River. His holdings, including the house he built, Chestnut Grove, were classified as "second tier" but were adequate to enable Martha to develop the skills of a plantation mistress.[23]

Because Chestnut Grove was a relatively small plantation—with a plantation being defined as agricultural land producing a single crop primarily for export— the Dandridges did not have house servants. Jack enslaved perhaps twenty people; some were part of Fanny's dowry. Martha, known as Patsy in her childhood and to her family, most likely helped with the younger children and learned the basics of cooking, cleaning, sewing, and household management. Her education included the typical curriculum described previously. As John B. Roberts wrote, "Poor grammar and spelling plagued her throughout life, but that was little impediment to her. When she had to manage her own business affairs as a young widow, she employed a secretary to take dictation, and then copied the letters in her own hand."[24] She developed a lifelong love of reading, and several portraits of her included books in her hands or nearby. Her letters during the constitutional debates and as first lady indicate that she read newspapers and occasionally commented on political news.

A few miles down the road from Chestnut Grove sat White House, which belonged to the somewhat eccentric John Custis IV, one of Virginia's wealthiest landowners. Daniel Parke Custis oversaw his father's plantation. Like Dandridge's father, Daniel was a church vestryman who participated in community activities. Because his father had thwarted his romantic pursuits more than once, Daniel was twenty years Martha's senior when she attracted his attention. Having been in the county for eleven years, he likely watched her develop into an attractive and confident young woman. Because her father was a second-tier planter, his father railed against the engagement, publicly castigating the Dandridges as unworthy of a match and threatening his only legitimate son with disinheritance. Nonetheless a bold, seventeen-year-old Martha "audaciously pursued" Daniel, going so far as to ask for a meeting with his father (6). Although no one knows what was said, her character and willingness to face John Custis IV affected him, and he reluctantly gave his consent.

While Martha might not have had a dowry and pedigree that matched the Custis wealth or social standing, she was raised to take up the life of a Southern lady with "devotion to God, husband, and children whose training was her major responsibility."[25] The extant record of correspondence that references her includes the qualities of a lady Boles and Atkinson described. She was also an accomplished rider, regular church attendee, pianist, vocalist, and model of piety.[26] Daniel indeed found a suitable match.

Because records are scanty, details of her wedding differ. Brady and Chester Hale Sipe set the wedding at Chestnut Grove.[27] Schwartz, however, writes that the May 15, 1750, wedding took place "in the familiar, one-story brick Anglican church where both of their fathers had been vestrymen," and then the newlyweds and guests went to the Custis White House for a celebration.[28] Notice that Schwartz attributes the vestryman position to John, not Daniel, Custis—another example of a rather confused and confusing historical record.

Daniel came into a large inheritance consisting of 17,500 acres, approximately three hundred enslaved people, multiple farms, and about $100,000 when his father died shortly after the official engagement.[29] Martha proved to be a capable estate administrator and a dedicated wife who shared in their elite social life. Happiness, however, was elusive, with the deaths of two of their four young children, along with Daniel's in July 1757. She chose to manage the vast estate herself with advice from her younger brother, an attorney, and trusted friends. Her correspondence as compiled by Joseph E. Fields includes letters to her late husband's business associates in England sent within two weeks of Daniel's death.[30] She exhibited firm resolve to accept nothing but the same quality of service and goods her husband had received with the implication that if not, she could pursue other partners. She demonstrated remarkable self-confidence and devotion to her husband's legacy. Although she competently managed White House and her dower inheritance (one-third of the estate for her use for life), a second marriage was inevitable because "widows in 18th century Virginia were a sought-after commodity," and she undoubtedly wanted a father for her two young children.[31] Providence rather quickly provided an option that altered her life in unimaginable ways.

How and when George Washington and Martha Dandridge Custis met is also subject to myth and disagreement among her biographers. Her grandson wrote that it was love at first sight. Most biographers attribute their first meeting to happenstance when George stopped at an acquaintance's home to water his horse en route from Williamsburg to Mount Vernon. Eager to be on his way, he was persuaded to stay for dinner when told of other visitors at the house—the widow Custis and her two children. Here, again, biographers disagree as to whether the encounter took place at the home of the Bassetts—her relatives—or that of the Chamberlaynes—mutual friends.[32] Regardless of who initiated the introduction, George found reason to stay and continued his conversation with her the next morning before taking his leave.[33] However, George had competition from another suitor, Charles Carter, who, like Custis, was a wealthy planter. He was twenty-four years her senior and a widower with a dozen children. His letters to friends indicate he was smitten with her and pursued her aggressively, as did George, through letters and occasional visits.[34] No one will ever know why she chose a man eight months her junior with a modest estate and some notoriety as a war hero against the French, but speculation is that she might not have wanted to risk widowhood again or raise fourteen children. Watson observed, "In marrying the widow Custis, Washington gained considerable wealth, vast land holdings, and access to the upper echelons of Virginia society."[35]

Eighteen months after being widowed, Martha exchanged wedding vows with George on January 6, 1759. Again, biographers disagree as to whether the wedding took place at the chapel that allegedly was the site of her first marriage or at the Custis White House. Schwartz wrote, "Today St. Peter's Church in New Kent County acknowledges the dispute while proudly proclaiming its connection to the nation's First Lady."[36] After a brief stay at the Custis estate,

George moved his newly acquired family north to Mount Vernon, which was undergoing expansion in anticipation of his changed life status; it would expand again in 1770.

Martha's dedication to her husband's social and political aspirations meant that Mount Vernon had a revolving door for visitors before and after the Revolution, many of whom made long stays.[37] Washington described the house as a "well-resorted tavern."[38] As Brady wrote, a web of women friends "essential to Martha Washington's happiness" supported her time-consuming hospitality endeavors, and, "increasingly, these visitors were politicians."[39] Thus, she participated in the political sphere through her role as hostess to the men who eventually founded the new country.

When she married Washington, she relinquished the legal control she had over her first husband's vast estate. However, in keeping with a flexible division of responsibilities common at the time, they were locked into neither his de facto control of her property nor her subservience. As Schwartz noted, "Martha often relied on George to secure the things she wanted, [but] she also purchased items on her own, as she had done before their marriage."[40] The overlap of spheres meant that "George Washington, not Martha, for instance, had advertised for their housekeepers in Virginia."[41] This pattern of shared decision making continued during her visits to one of his winter camps during the Revolution. Washington "engaged two young carpenters to finish off one of the rooms in the top story of the building he was occupying for his wife to use. But he let Martha supervise the work," Paul Boller wrote.[42]

Martha, like many colonial women, left home alone for long periods, following her own advice to her niece Fanny Bassett Washington about the need for women to maintain some independence. Fanny oversaw Mount Vernon along with her husband—George's nephew—during the presidential years. Martha wrote to Fanny to "keep all your matters in order yourself without depending upon others as that is the only way to be happy. . . . As I wish you to be as independent as your circumstances will admit and to be so, is to exert yourself in the management of your estate if you do not no one else will—a dependence is I think a wrached [*sic*] state."[43] This certainly was Martha's approach. Her fortitude in the face of loss, her willingness to start anew with George, her management of Mount Vernon onsite and in absentia, and her winters at military camps definitely qualify her as from a "hardy mold."

Even with her independent streak, Martha was unwavering in support of her husband's decisions and his ambitions, as Brady noted: "Whether as planter, lawmaker, general, or president, George Washington relied on Martha Washington emotionally. He needed her with him, and that's where she wanted to be."[44] At the start of the Revolution, despite facing resistance to the cause from some in her extended family, "Martha [is said to have] exclaimed: 'My heart is made up; my heart is in the cause; George is right; he is always right.'"[45]

Martha, like a later first lady—Mary Lincoln—found her loyalties occasionally being questioned, possibly because of dissenting family members. Cokie Roberts described Martha's strategy after accusations of Tory sympathies: "Martha launched a public relations offensive." Bringing "her son, daughter-in-law, and nephew with her, the usually elegant plantation mistress donned homespun as she set out on the long trip north in the dead of winter" to join George in camp.[46] Roberts also noted that throughout her journey Martha "met with leaders of the patriots and so won over the doubters" (87). Her presence in camp provided moral support for her husband and the cause. She turned Mount Vernon into a clothing factory to support the war effort and to replace British manufactured goods.[47] Her efforts helped prevent desertions of poorly clothed soldiers. Roberts observed that her actions made her "truly a public figure. She wrote to a friend that she had departed from Philadelphia 'in a great pomp as if I had been a very great somebody.'"[48]

In addition to dedication to God, husband, and children, another important characteristic of a Southern lady was avoidance of tackiness. This quality reflected positively on one's spouse and family. Martha's active social life at Mount Vernon undoubtedly provided many opportunities for diplomacy and tact. Washington was attentive, listened well, and included others; in social situations, by contrast, George could be insensitive. One dinner guest wrote to his mother that "George had ignored his guests but that Martha was so gracious she deserved an 'exquisite' gift."[49] Given the importance of being a lady in Virginia society, it is not surprising that she was called Lady Washington during the Revolution. As Watson noted, "The term reflected the period's popular equivocation to royalty" even at a time when the colonies were fighting to be free of the tyranny of a monarchy and a ruling class.[50] Cokie Roberts pointed to a regiment named Lady Washington's Dragoons to further illustrate the esteem in which Martha was held.[51]

As the general's lady, Martha traveled extensively outside her provincial Virginia world. Interaction with men and women from the North and South and from all classes provided her a more expansive view of the country during its gestation. This undoubtedly helped her adapt to a republican way of thinking and acting. She reflected positively on her husband among his troops, according to many accounts, as she nursed the ill, and her "industry as a seamstress became legendary . . . supplying a warm, maternal touch."[52] Not only was she popular among the troops but she demonstrated the Christian charity of her upbringing. She engaged with women in Virginia and beyond to raise money for supplies for the ragtag army. The women collected, primarily through churches and door to door, as much as "$300,634 in paper money" in Philadelphia alone; Martha herself gave $20,000 for clothing.[53]

Finally, in exploring Martha's Southern roots, attention to her role as a slaveholder is essential. For the daughters and wives of plantation owners, the people they enslaved affected their lives in unique ways. Schwartz, who examined the impact of slavery on early first ladies, concluded that their enslaved workers "were not incidental to the First Ladies' lives but rather important constituents of their daily experiences and their hopes for the future: their own, their families', and their nation's" because they supported the "economic, social, and political world in which she and her grandchildren lived."[54] For Martha in particular, "the personal relationship she developed with slaves" was highly valued (31). When Ona Judge, the enslaved woman who served as Martha's lady's maid, ran away during the presidency, "the defection [was] shocking" to the Washingtons (106). An outraged president wrote to a friend about "the ingratitude of the girl, who was brought up and treated more like a child than a Servant."[55] They unsuccessfully pursued her return and were unable to understand that she wanted freedom. Unlike the president, who came to question the institution of slavery and whose will freed his slaves after his death, the first lady did not question the institution and considered enslaved servants a natural part of her daily life.[56] Often in her letters, Martha displayed contradictory or negative feelings toward members of her "black family" even as she ensured that they were clothed, fed, and kept as healthy as possible.[57] Although her attitudes toward the enslaved members of her "family" were decidedly racist, she considered herself a God-fearing woman whose duty was to provide for those she kept in bondage. She clearly did more for her family's livelihood and comfort than she did for the needs of the people she enslaved.

Without enslaved workers, the Washingtons could not have developed the social and political network that made their positions in the nation's founding possible. Schwartz wrote that in 1768 alone, they "had at least 130 overnight guests," not to mention 80 or more who came just for an evening meal.[58] Hospitality such as this added to their "reputation for gentility," and "the appearance and conduct of enslaved servants counted too," she noted (59–60). Martha took her enslaved entourage to winter camp, and without them to care for personal needs, she could not have carried out her work on behalf of her husband and the troops.

There is no doubt that Martha's character was shaped by her place of birth and her era. She was a woman *of* the South, but she was also a woman whose breeding and experiences made her aware that the new Republic would create change and present personal challenges. The third and fourth sections of this chapter examine how her background as a Southern woman affected her pioneering development of a new role in a new nation and her influence on future first ladies.

## LADY WASHINGTON: FORGING NEW TERRITORY WHILE ACCESSING THE FAMILIAR

Actions are powerful rhetorical tools that telegraph values and intent. When the country's first president met his wife on the New Jersey shore in a forty-seven-foot barge to take her to the presidential home in New York, he sent a clear message that "Martha Washington was an essential part of George's presidential plan."[59] The thirteen-gun salute and cheers that greeted her entry into the new nation's capital affirmed that the citizenry considered her a part of the new Republic. In keeping with their Southern origins, as Jane E. Abrams wrote, "the Washingtons . . . operated more visibly as a partnership than as a male/female binary divide."[60] Martha's unique blend of Southern lady with an independent streak and her savvy political skills gave her an edge. Carl Sferrazza Anthony said of her, "If providence itself had divinely intervened, a woman who better looked and played the part could not have been found."[61] There is no doubt that Martha's background prepared her to manage both the everyday affairs of the presidential home and her private life.

Yet Martha lacked a compass to guide her, as did her husband in creating the role of president. Richard Norton Smith observed, "The Constitution made Washington head of state as well as head of the government, and no man had a better grasp of ceremonial leadership than George III's American usurper."[62] The Constitution spelled out the executive's administrative responsibilities in broad terms, not even providing a title for the head of the executive branch. Using a twenty-first-century metaphor, George and his advisers built a plane as they piloted it at 35,000 feet. And it was a ride fraught with potential errors, missteps, and recalibration of the grand experiment. With only the reminders of oppressive monarchies and the incorporation of political theories to guide them, the founders and first officeholders in all three branches had to strike a balance between appropriating customs of their past experiences and inventing new democratic ways. For the Washingtons, "establishing the young republic's legitimacy was their chief aim, accomplished through their first presidential protocols, an uneasy blend of plebian equality and an aristocratic attention to rank."[63] Just as modern presidents have multiple audiences for their messages and actions—the physical audience and the mediated—the first president had both domestic and foreign observers watching his every step to assess the new nation's health.

The Washingtons' goal was to "envelop the new executive branch of government with the kind of decorum that would win it respect among the older countries of the world"[64] and provide accessibility to the newly minted American citizenry by opening their doors for both "plebian" and "aristocratic" activities.[65] For someone who experienced people from all classes during the war, the task was not entirely unfamiliar. Even with that experience, however, Martha learned that the job of creating a nation and establishing rituals was not going to be left to her alone. The spheres began to separate in this new Republic. Prior to Martha's arrival from Mount Vernon, the president and his advisers developed a set of protocols and formal activities that would provide what they considered balance. In order to be open but not show favoritism, they decided that the president and his wife would not accept personal invitations to dinner, and Martha would not follow the strict female code of returning visits. The first lady learned of these decisions upon arrival, when she was made aware that her first formal events were already scheduled.

The plan called for formal, men-only "levees" for the president on Tuesday afternoons and occasional dinners with the first lady present for congressional leaders and other dignitaries—domestic and foreign. Martha presided over "drawing room" receptions on Friday evenings for invited guests both male and female—with the president "laying aside his sword and cocked hat to mingle with the ladies."[66] In between, there were informal open-door times for both of them for anyone "dressed appropriately." Martha also had tea parties each week and received visitors every morning between 11:00 a.m. and 12:00 for relaxed conversation, but visitors were to leave at the stroke of noon (195). As in the South, "the social and political realms intersected on a daily basis, and political capital was built on relationships that were cemented during dinners, balls, and receptions, such as the Washingtons' popular levees."[67]

Martha did not relish her hostess duties or the fact that she was so severely restricted in her activities outside of the president's residence. She missed the freedom to visit her circle of friends. In a letter to Fanny Washington in October 1789, she confided, only half in jest, "I live a very dull life and know nothing that passes in the town. I never go to any public place. Indeed, I think I am more like a state prisoner than anything else; there are certain bounds set for me . . . and as I cannot do as I like, I am obstinate and stay at home a great deal."[68] After a year of "incarceration," the first lady convinced the president that she needed to be out and began returning social calls each day. Abigail Adams, with whom she formed a special bond, often accompanied her and was at her right side during the drawing-room receptions. Because Martha was a Southern lady, she was usually able to navigate the tightrope of demonstrating stature while being accessible. Anthony noted, "She was somehow both democratic and not so much elitist, but august. . . . [She] was as noble as George, but her naturalness seemed apparent, whereas he stayed noble."[69] Because she was reared to be sensitive to messages she sent and attuned to the nuances of those she received, she made sure her clothes were representative of a democratic leader rather than a monarch, and she was commended for her choices, including American-made clothing. Newspapers, like today, even commented on her sartorial choices, especially their "manufacture of our Country," and equated it to patriotism (38).

All of this did not mean that she escaped criticism. As political party divides developed, some Washington opponents found her too regal. She "was accused of 'aping royalty,'" especially when she would ride "about publicly in Philadelphia in a London-made yellow coach with affixed richly gilded medallions, pulled by cream-colored horses, and attended by liveried grooms in white and scarlet, the Washington colors" (46, 48). Although aware of the criticism, Martha considered her public persona important and did not change her mode of transportation. Her Southern background might have influenced her because gentry were usually transported to church and social events in liveried carriages. Conscious of the effect of such appearances, she was nonetheless determined to establish the presidency as something not completely plebian.

Although the first lady was often at the dinner table with the president when political matters were discussed, she was never overtly political. Her role, as for elite Southern women in Williamsburg, was to provide a tone of civility and "improve the manners, taste, and morals of the men who governed their society."[70] Her grandson claimed "she partook the president's 'thoughts, councils and views' and 'inspired confidence' in his politics."[71] For instance, she saw, like her husband, that "restoring good relations with England" after the Revolution was a priority and wrote in her correspondence "that it was time to put the turmoil and animosities of the Revolution to rest."[72] When others disagreed with George's policies, she made no public comment about their criticisms.

Martha did strike out on her own in a political sense in her support of veterans. Her entrenched belief in charity had her greeting these former soldiers with great regularity, and "she doled out cash" to them in her parlor, where they were "welcomed as old friends."[73] Her dedication to them was so strong that she was known to intervene with her husband to grant pardons or bestow leniency on those in legal trouble. John Roberts wrote that her concern "reveals a social consciousness that transcended the shallow life of society drawing rooms to which many women of her social standing were consigned by traditional sex roles. But Martha had never been a traditional female."[74]

The culture of charity inculcated in the South followed both the president and first lady to New York and Philadelphia, where many citizens wrote them letters or took advantage of open meetings to ask for support.[75] Although sympathetic to the needs of veterans and women, Martha chose to intervene based on individual need rather than take on a class or category specifically. She made "personal contributions to everyone from a wife raising her husband's bail to an unemployed actress, a beggar, and an insane female," as Anthony recorded and her letters demonstrated.[76]

Charity, however, starts at home, and one of Martha's primary responsibilities was to see to her husband's health and needs. Shortly after the first lady arrived, the president developed a tumor that required surgery. Martha is credited with asking that ropes be installed on streets to keep traffic and noise down so that her husband could rest (43–44). She attended a war hero's funeral while George was incapacitated, thus setting a precedent for a wife to serve as a surrogate. In performing both acts, she carved a space for the first lady to ensure continuity of presidential duties.

The Washingtons' position as elite Southern slave owners affected how they presented themselves to the world. They brought enslaved servants to New York and Philadelphia to work alongside hired staff and servants. Among them were a lady's maid, a cook, a valet, and house servants. Those enslaved at Mount Vernon were also put to work to provide supplies for the president's house that were unattainable in the city. There were criticisms of the presence of enslaved servants in the president's house, but some of the criticism related more to the aristocratic nature of having servants in a democratic country.[77] Their presence created a legal problem, however, because Pennsylvania law required that anyone bringing enslaved people into the state "would relinquish claim to them" if they were in the state for longer than six months (103). The Washingtons' solution was to send them back to Mount Vernon periodically and to have them accompany the president and Lady Washington on their summer holidays back home. This prevented Martha's dower slaves from gaining their freedom and George from having to compensate the estate. It was most likely illegal given a provision in the law regarding such a practice that exempted members of Congress but did not mention the president (103–104). Either no one learned of the plan or no one raised public awareness, but the records that exist clearly illustrate the circumvention. The Washingtons' precedent of bringing their enslaved servants to the president's house was followed by seven of the next eleven presidents. The Southern reliance on enslaved workers went on to include slave labor in building the White House with the wages for said workers going to the owners. The first African American first lady, Michelle Obama, commented on waking up every morning in a house built by slaves.[78]

The final attribute Martha brought to the position is described by Abrams as republican motherhood/wifehood. This is what we recognize today as the responsibility "to ensure that the next generation would be provided with the tools to become loyal and productive citizens."[79] A good republican wife was a woman who in "carrying out their valued domestic responsibilities . . . were also fulfilling their duty as patriotic Americans" (15). This did not mean, however, that women's work was confined to the private sphere. The hospitality Martha and her immediate successors—Abigail Adams and Dolley Madison—provided in their roles as presidential spouses built "political capital and a power base through the social realm. . . . Social and political life was often permeable and clearly intertwined in the early republic, and traditionally defined separate spheres for men and women frequently intersected" (19). Martha was tailor-made for republican motherhood. Her attention to her grandchildren—finding them good schools and tutors—and to her husband's needs and well-being contributed to the immediate and future growth of the nation. She thus set an example for other women in "fulfilling the promise of the Revolution."[80] Her emphasis on education was carried on in later centuries by first ladies such as Lady Bird Johnson, Barbara Bush, Hillary Clinton, Laura Bush, and Michelle Obama.

In sacrificing her own happiness and desired quiet life at Mount Vernon, Martha Washington created an institution that persists today. It changed with the times and with women's evolving roles, but she also set standards and established practices that continue today just as many of the roles of the president remain unchanged.

## MARTHA WASHINGTON'S LEGACY

Modern first lady scholars emphasize the partnership the presidency requires.[81] The president and first lady were consummate partners, having first forged that relationship on Virginia soil. Most of the first ladies who followed Martha were also partners—in their own way drawing both on personal characteristics and life experiences. Washington came from privilege and was *of* the South, and those factors influenced her conduct in the role and her partnership. She placed a particular stamp on the position even more deeply traced by those who followed her, especially because so many of the early first ladies were also Southerners, as Nancy Young explores further in Chapter 11. By bringing enslaved servants into the president's house and representing an institution that led to systemic racism more than two hundred years later, the Washingtons' legacy is definitely mixed, as are those of other Southern founding fathers and mothers. However, as columnist Eugene Robinson, an African American, wrote during the Black Lives Matter protests in summer 2020: "The fact that Washington, Jefferson and other early presidents owned slaves should temper our admiration for them but not erase it entirely. They gave us a nation grotesquely disfigured by slavery, but they also gave us the constitutional tools, and the high-minded ideals, with which to heal that original, near-fatal flaw."[82] Martha gave future first ladies the tools to correct the wrongs that she and others helped create over a more than four-hundred-year history beginning with the first slave ship's arrival. Her care for citizens in need and her dedication to democratic ideals are seen in the actions of first ladies such as Eleanor Roosevelt, who worked for civil rights; Lady Bird Johnson, who made a historic train trip through hostile territory in the South to promote the 1964 Civil Rights Act; and Michelle Obama, who reminded the country of its legacy of slavery but also that we could overcome it.

Beyond the issue of race, first ladies embraced causes about which they were passionate, as did Martha. Following her lead, for example, first ladies such as Mary Lincoln, Florence Harding, Eleanor Roosevelt, and Michelle Obama made military members and their families important priorities. Barbara Bush held a baby who had AIDS and showed the world not to fear the disease and to have compassion for those suffering from it. And, of course, many other first ladies have promoted myriad causes. They have a unique platform, and most have chosen to use it. Martha created a key attribute of the position in that it is rooted both in personal characteristics and life experiences that shape the first lady. As they did with Martha, race, gender, class, and place continue to influence this role.

Martha's Southern heritage shaped her unique role in the country's founding. It helped her balance the new nation's democratic aspirations with demonstrations of the presidency's status within the Republic as underlined by her role as hostess. Writing about the evolution of the first lady role since Martha's time, Bush Institute researchers Natalie Gonnella-Platts and Katherine Fritz argue that the "ceremonial hostess responsibilities have persisted. And for good reason—this type of influence may be seen to fall under what is now commonly known as co-optive, or soft, power and continues to form a critical responsibility for first ladies and presidents in the United States and other countries."[83] With the dual roles of head of government and head of state, the US president oversees the country's rituals, thus necessitating attention to soft power. The Washingtons recognized that social activities were more than superficial events to share gossip, scrutinize women's fashions, or showcase the presidential kitchen staff's talents. They understood they were establishing important precedents. Yet Martha's legacy extends beyond the traditional hostess role as indicated with the causes she and her husband promoted.

In addition to public enactment of the role, there is a private side. The notion of republican wifehood/motherhood persists today even if we do not use that term. First ladies have shown great concern for their husbands' health and well-being. A few examples include Edith Wilson, Eleanor Roosevelt, Mamie Eisenhower, and Nancy Reagan. Martha attended to her adopted children's needs by securing them a good education and taking them on outings, for example, to a circus. First ladies with children have worked to ensure them as normal a life as possible. Melania Trump delayed her departure for the White House until her son, Barron, completed his school year; Michelle Obama, the self-declared "Mom in chief," considered doing the same at one point in the transition.

Although she might have bristled at derogatory comments about her husband, Martha did not venture into politics publicly but displayed graciousness and warmth even to her husband's political opponents, thus avoiding tackiness. Most first ladies have walked just such a fine line to avoid overt interference in policy issues. When Hillary Clinton led a team to develop a plan for health-care reform, she learned there could be dangers in directly stepping into the policy realm. Wives such as Lady Bird Johnson, Rosalyn Carter, Barbara Bush, and Michelle Obama also had a role in influencing policy, but they did it by building relationships with members of Congress or by deftly guiding their husband's hand to make legislative changes. There is a clear tension between supporting a cause and directly influencing policy. Martha's approach was to work behind the scenes, and first ladies who have followed that lead saw changes made.

The Southern emphasis on being a lady led to the honorific Lady Washington during the war, which followed her to New York and Philadelphia. That undoubtedly influenced the appellation upon which the country eventually settled for presidential wives. Although the term *lady* is anachronistic in the twenty-first century, *first lady* remains in nearly universal use for the wife of a president, both in the United States and worldwide.

Many first ladies reluctantly enter politics. Martha did as well. Most, as she did, make peace with the position, growing into it and making it a platform for contributing to society in their own ways. Perhaps one of her best legacies was a philosophy echoed by others in different ways but with the same meaning: this might not be the life you thought you were getting into when you said "I do," but it can be a good life if you embrace it. As Martha wrote, "I am still determined to be cheerful and happy in whatever situation I may be, for I have also learnt from experience that the greater part of our happiness or misary [*sic*] depends upon our dispositions, and not upon our circumstances."[84] Nearly every first lady faces criticism, disappointment, and missteps on some level, but most have found ways to overcome the challenges and have even raised their stature as a result. Without a pattern, Martha designed a role for her successors to follow. Every first lady, Southern or not, has overlaid her own story to design the role uniquely, but the outline and raw materials remain the same as Martha Washington's.

NOTES

1. Robert P. Watson, "Martha Washington," in *A Companion to First Ladies*, ed. Katherine A. S. Sibley (West Sussex, UK: Wiley-Blackwell, 2016), 18.

2. Joanne V. Hawks and Sheila L. Skemp, eds., *Sex, Race, and the Role of Women in the South* (Jackson: University Press of Mississippi, 1983), xi.

3. See, for instance, Caroline Matheny Dillman, ed., *Southern Women* (New York: Hemisphere, 1988), 6.

4. Dillman, *Southern Women*, xi.

5. Sally McMillen, *Southern Women: Black and White in the Old South*, 2nd ed. (Wheeling, IL: Harlan Davidson, 2002), 120.

6. Jacquelyn Dowd Hall, "Partial Truths: Writing Southern Women's History," in *Southern Women: Histories and Identities*, ed. Virginia Bernhard, Betty Brandon, Elizabeth Fox-Genovese, and Theda Perdue (Columbia: University of Missouri Press, 1992), 17.

7. McMillen, *Southern Women*, 48.

8. Elizabeth Fox-Genovese, *Within the Plantation Household: Black and White Women of the Old South* (Chapel Hill: University of North Carolina Press, 1988), 100.

9. Marie Jenkins Schwartz, *Ties That Bound: Founding First Ladies and Slaves* (Chicago: University of Chicago Press, 2017), 2.

10. McMillen, *Southern Women*, 11.

11. Sarah Brabant, "Socialization for Change: The Cultural Heritage of White Southern Women," in *Southern Women*, ed. Caroline Matheny Dillman (New York: Hemisphere, 1988), 105.

12. Fox-Genovese, *Within the Plantation*, 44.

13. Schwartz, *Ties That Bound*, 38.

14. Frederick Douglass, *Narrative of the Life of Frederick Douglass*, Anti-Slavery Literary Project, 2005, mrbecker9.weebly.com/uploads/4/8/5/7/4857123/frederickdouglassfulltext.pdf, 36.

15. Fox-Genovese, *Within the Plantation*, 232.

16. Jacqueline Boles and Maxine P. Atkinson, "Ladies: South by Northwest," in *Southern Women*, ed. Caroline Matheny Dillman (New York: Hemisphere, 1988), 130.

17. Cynthia A. Kierner, "Genteel Balls and Republican Parades: Gender and Early Southern Civic Rituals, 1677–1826," *Virginia Magazine of History and Biography; Richmond* 104, no. 2 (Spring 1996): 185.

18. Boles and Atkinson, "Ladies," 129.

19. Fox-Genovese, *Within the Plantation*, 203.

20. Boles and Atkinson, "Ladies," 129, 130.

21. Fox-Genovese, *Within the Plantation*, 43.

22. Patricia Brady, *Martha Washington: An American Life* (New York: Viking, 2005), 14.

23. For biographical information, see Carl Sferrazza Anthony, *First Ladies: The Saga of the Presidents' Wives and Their Power, 1789–1961* (New York: William Morrow, 1990), 31–72; Brady, *Martha Washington*; Patricia Brady, "Martha Dandridge Custis Washington," in *America's First Ladies: Their Lives and Legacies*, 2nd ed., ed. Lewis L. Gould (New York: Routledge,

2001), 1–10; Watson, "Martha Washington," 6–19; Mary V. Thompson, "'An Old Fashioned Virginia House-keeper': Martha Washington at Home," presentation to Phi Upsilon Omicron, November 16, 2002 (revised November 27, 2002), University Club, Washington, DC, (accessed at the Mount Vernon Archive).

24. John B. Roberts II, *Rating the First Ladies: The Women Who Influenced the Presidency* (New York: Citadel, 2003), 6.

25. Boles and Atkinson, "Ladies," 129.

26. See Note 22 above.

27. Brady, *Martha Washington*, 32; Chester Hale Sipe, *Mount Vernon and the Washington Family: A Concise Handbook on the Ancestry, Youth, and Family of George Washington, and History of His Home*, 3rd ed. (Butler, PA: Ziegler, 1925), 25.

28. Schwartz, *Ties That Bound*, 48.

29. Brady, *Martha Washington*, 34.

30. Joseph E. Fields, comp., *"Worthy Partner": The Papers of Martha Washington* (Westport, CT: Greenwood, 1994), 5–6.

31. Thompson, "'Old Fashioned Virginia House-keeper,'" 5.

32. Ellen McCallister Clark, "The Life of Martha Washington," in *"Worthy Partner": The Papers of Martha Washington*, comp. Joseph E. Fields (Westport, CT: Greenwood, 1994), xx.

33. Mary V. Thompson, "'An Agreeable Consort for Life': The Wedding of George and Martha Washington." Presentation at the Sixth Annual Gadsby's Tavern Costume Symposium, September 29, 2001 (amended December 26, 2001), Alexandria, Virginia (accessed at Mount Vernon Archives); Brady, *Martha Washington*, 58–59; Watson, "Martha Washington," 9–10.

34. Thompson, "Agreeable Consort for Life," 5–6; Brady, *Martha Washington*, 54–55.

35. Watson, "Martha Washington," 15.

36. Schwartz, *Ties That Bound*, 54.

37. Brady, "Martha Dandridge Custis Washington," 3.

38. Richard Norton Smith, *Patriarch: George Washington and the New American Nation* (Boston: Houghton Mifflin, 1992), 64.

39. Brady, "Martha Dandridge Custis Washington," 5.

40. Schwartz, *Ties That Bound*, 59.

41. Betty Boyd Caroli, *First Ladies: From Martha Washington to Michelle Obama*, rev. ed. (New York: Oxford University Press, 2010) 6.

42. Paul F. Boller, *Presidential Wives: An Anecdotal History*, 2nd ed. (New York: Oxford University Press, 1998), 10.

43. Martha Washington to Fanny Bassett Washington, letter, September 15, 1794, in *"Worthy Partner": The Papers of Martha Washington*, comp. Joseph E. Fields (Westport, CT: Greenwood, 1994), 275.

44. Brady, *Martha Washington*, 2.

45. Boller, *Presidential Wives*, 5.

46. Cokie Roberts, *Founding Mothers: The Women Who Raised Our Nation* (New York: William Morrow, 2004), 87.

47. Brady, *Martha Washington*, 80.

48. Martha Washington to Elizabeth Ramsay, letter, December 30, 1775, in *"Worthy Partner": The Papers of Martha Washington*, comp. Joseph E. Fields (Westport, CT: Greenwood, 1994), 164.

49. Caroli, *First Ladies*, 26.

50. Watson, "Martha Washington," 10.

51. C. Roberts, *Founding Mothers*, 116.

52. Smith, *Patriarch*, 14.

53. Thompson, "'Old Fashioned Virginia House-keeper,'" 34–35.

54. Schwartz, *Ties That Bound*, 1, 17.

55. Thompson, "'Old Fashioned Virginia House-keeper,'" 19; for more on Judge, see Erica Armstrong Dunbar, *Never Caught: The Washingtons' Relentless Pursuit of Their Runaway Slave, Ona Judge* (New York: Simon and Schuster, 2017).

56. Schwartz, *Ties That Bound*, 20.

57. See Fields, *"Worthy Partner,"* 211–298, for letters from Martha Washington to Fanny Bassett Washington and others during the presidential years, often inquiring about the well-being of family and enslaved workers. Martha gave instructions for clothing and care and what she expected to see when she returned to Mount Vernon during summer visits.

58. Schwartz, *Ties That Bound*, 59.

59. Margaret Truman, *First Ladies* (New York: Random House, 1995), 17.

60. Jane E. Abrams, *First Ladies of the Republic: Martha Washington, Abigail Adams, Dolley Madison, and the Creation of an Iconic American Role* (New York: New York University Press, 2018), 7.

61. Anthony, *First Ladies*, 38.

62. Smith, *Patriarch*, 87.

63. J. Roberts, *Rating the First Ladies*, 8.

64. Boller, *Presidential Wives*, 6.

65. J. Roberts, *Rating the First Ladies*, 8.

66. Smith, *Patriarch*, 28.

67. Abrams, *First Ladies of the Republic*, 48.

68. Martha Washington to Fanny Bassett Washington, letter, October 23, 1789, in *"Worthy Partner": The Papers of Martha Washington*, comp. Joseph E. Fields (Westport, CT: Greenwood, 1994), 220.

69. Anthony, *First Ladies*, 38–40.

70. Kierner, "Genteel Balls and Republican Parades," 186.

71. Anthony, *First Ladies*, 50.

72. J. Roberts, *Rating the First Ladies*, 9.

73. Anthony, *First Ladies*, 54.

74. J. Roberts, *Rating the First Ladies*, 5–6.

75. See Fields, *"Worthy Partner,"* for letters to both Washingtons during the presidential years.

76. Anthony, *First Ladies*, 58.

77. Schwartz, *Ties That Bound*, 95.

78. Olivia B. Waxman, "Michelle Obama Reminded Us That Slaves Built the White

House. Here's What to Know," *Time*, July 26, 2016. https://time.com/4423691/michelle-obama-dnc-speech-history/

79. Abrams, *First Ladies of the Republic*, 66.

80. J. Roberts, *Rating the First Ladies*, 5.

81. Kati Marton, *Hidden Power: Presidential Marriages That Shaped Our History* (New York: Anchor, 2002); Gilbert Troy, *Mr. and Mrs. President: An Intimate Group Portrait of White House Wives*, 2nd ed. (Lawrence: University Press of Kansas, 2000); Truman, *First Ladies*.

82. Eugene Robinson, "Remove All Confederate Monuments," *Washington Post*, June 23, 2020. https://live.washingtonpost.com/opinion-focus-with-eugene-robinson-20200623.html.

83. Natalie Gonnella-Platts and Katherine Fritz, *A Role Without a Rulebook: The Influence and Leadership of Global First Ladies* (Dallas, TX: George W. Bush Institute, 2017), 10.

84. Martha Washington to Mercy Otis Warren, letter, June 12, 1790, in *"Worthy Partner": The Papers of Martha Washington*, comp. Joseph E. Fields (Westport, CT: Greenwood, 1994), 224.

# CHAPTER 2

# Dolley Madison and the Making of a Capital Etiquette

Merry Ellen Scofield

It is hard to imagine Dolley Madison not having led a hospitable life under any marital or monetary circumstances, but it need not have been a particularly Southern life or one of lasting prominence. Her marriage to James Madison gave her a Southern future (both at Montpelier and in Washington), and his political ambitions would eventually build the stage from which she would make her own history. Beginning with her years in the capital as cabinet wife and first lady and culminating with a later, decadelong return to that city, Dolley Payne Todd Madison would come to dominate social Washington with her amicable grace and Southern cordiality. Her methods would earn her immense popularity, and her reign as first lady would be the standard by which other nineteenth-century presidential spouses were judged. As importantly, she would use those same principles to lead her Washington friends in building a capital society that provided social harmony amid political contention and gave civil order to the unruly process of forming a new nation—a system of capital etiquette that would rule Washington unchallenged for half a century.

Born to Quaker parents in 1768, Dolley Payne was raised in Virginia until her fourteenth year, when she and her family moved to Philadelphia. That move and her later marriage to Quaker lawyer John Todd might have secured a more Northern life, but circumstances intervened. After two years of marriage, Dolley Todd lost her husband and one of her two children to Philadelphia's yellow fever epidemic of 1793.[1] Within a year, she had met and married James Madison. He "was short and unprepossessing of figure" (and seventeen years her senior), wrote historian Holly Shulman, "but he was brilliant and witty and he offered her security, a willingness to take on her young son, and the promise of returning to the Virginia world of her youth."[2]

James Madison at the time was a member of the House of Representatives, already renowned for his part in the Constitutional Convention of 1787 and a leading figure in the rising Democratic-Republican Party. He was also heir to Montpelier, a large plantation in Orange County, Virginia, fifty miles northwest of where the Paynes had resided. The property included an estimated five thousand acres, a stately home, and approximately one hundred enslaved individuals. Within that enslaved population, about two dozen household servants—men, women, and children—lived in close proximity to the mansion and were under the direct supervision of the new Mrs. Madison and her mother-in-law.[3]

The Madisons divided their time between the plantation and Philadelphia. As the wife of an eminent member of Congress, Dolley Madison joined the inner circles of capital society, although even before her marriage she and her friends had mingled with members of that elite community. Dolley Todd had met James Madison through her mother's former boarder, Aaron Burr. Her sister, Lucy, was married to George Washington's nephew, George Steptoe Washington, and soon after the Madisons' own wedding, Dolley's friend Eliza Collins married Virginian member of Congress Richard Bland Lee.[4] Another friend, Sally McKean, was the daughter of Justice Thomas McKean, future Pennsylvania governor, and in 1798 she wed the Spanish foreign minister, Carlos Fernando Martínez de Yrujo.[5]

The new bride watched as fellow Virginian Martha Dandridge Custis Washington created the role of first lady of the Republic. With no established precedents to guide them, the Washingtons had developed a set of social protocols they hoped would not only give dignity to their position but strike a balance between too "much state and too great [a] familiarity."[6] On Tuesdays, the president gave a public levee where great numbers of "Gentlemen" attended without invitation. On Thursdays, the couple held a formal dinner for elite members of the political community. On Fridays, Martha Washington welcomed both men and women to a formal drawing room. The couple attended the theater and certain public balls, but to avoid the perception of favoritism, President Washington did not accept dinner invitations.[7] Because it was not in Martha's nature to attend functions without her husband, she too rarely "dined or supped out."[8]

The Washingtons had also made decisions about receiving and returning formal visits. The exchange of such calls was the foundation of genteel sociability, and who called on whom first was determined by community norms. Within the government's "community," the Washingtons presumed the honor of the first visit, but the president, unable to return all of the visits made to him, decided it best to establish the protocol of returning none of them. His wife chose differently. As she explained to incoming first lady Abigail Adams, her practice had "been always to receive the first visits, and then to return them" and to repeat the process after each extended absence from the seat of government.[9]

Dolley's education in political protocol as practiced in Philadelphia ended with the Adams administration and her husband's retirement from Congress. Although the couple spent their next four years in Virginia, James Madison's focus on national politics never lessened. He was involved in then vice president Thomas Jefferson's second campaign for the presidency. He authored the Virginia resolutions against the Alien and Sedition Acts, and during the winter of 1799–1800, he represented Orange County in the state legislature. In the interval, his wife honed her social-political skills. She oversaw frequent Montpelier entertainments, and she joined her husband in the state capital of Richmond, where she complemented his legislative actions with her participation in the city's political society.[10]

Prior to his marriage, many of James Madison's political friends had considered his bachelorhood an asset. Without a wife to distract him, he, like widower Jefferson, had been able to focus completely on political matters at hand. However, in 1800, after six years of marriage, Madison was no less committed to the Republican cause than before his wedding. "I have heard every thing I could wish of [Mrs. Madison]," wrote a relieved Charles Pinckney, "for certainly if ever a man deserved a good Wife you did. Had you unfortunately got . . . in to a state of . . . petticoat Government I know no man I should have pitied more nor none I could have more sincerely wept over."[11]

As for Dolley, six years of marriage had proven that she too had chosen well. James had welcomed into his life the various and many members of her extended family, including the son he accepted as his own and a younger sister, Anna Payne, who also lived with them. His wealth provided her with material niceties, and his prominence ensured her an exalted social stature. The marriage also did what a good marriage should—made the whole greater than the sum of its parts. His learnedness influenced her learnedness; his political acumen tutored her own. Her acceptance of his reserved manner allowed him the freedom to grow as a statesman, and her sociability, although never in conflict with James's own political stance, softened the edges of both the man and his message. Together they were quickly becoming two sides of a valuable political coin, and as the eighteenth century ended, the couple moved together into what would be sixteen years of increasing political prestige and celebrity.

Jefferson had run for president in 1796 and lost. He ran again in 1800 and won. To no one's surprise, he appointed James secretary of state. After a four-year hiatus, the Madisons returned to the national seat of government, now located along the Potomac River.

The new federal capital was receiving mixed reviews. Created on land ceded by Maryland and Virginia in 1790, it was to be a planned city built from the ground up. Congress allowed ten years for preparation, but in late 1800, as the national government made its move, Washington City was still a work in process. Northern men and foreigners spoke of it with the most disdain—as a mix of muddy roads, workmen's huts, "half-starved cattle browzing among the bushes," overcrowded boardinghouses, unfinished public buildings, and running through its center a mosquito-infested creek that fed the marshes without draining them.[12]

Incoming Southerners felt more at home in Washington City, and rightly so. Congress had located its new capital in a Southern location, in which the welcoming gentry were mainly Southern-bred shipping families and planters. Those arriving from Southern states were less frustrated by the city's isolated location, its limited goods and services, and the heat of its summers. They were also more accustomed to a society exaggerated at its polar ends. An inordinate number of capital elites (mainly in the form of political imports) enjoyed the privileges of their wealth and status, while a population of poor Irish, free Blacks, and enslaved laborers struggled against poverty and disenfranchisement. Every city could claim disparate classes, but not all could claim an enslaved population or the irony of slave trading in the capital of a country that boasted of its democratic principles.

The Madisons would travel to Washington City with an entourage that included at least two enslaved servants. In contrast to Quaker belief, the mistress of Montpelier accepted her dominance over the men, women, and children she legally owned, including her right to buy and sell them as property. And although her husband's enslaved manservant, Paul Jennings, would write that she was loved by all, "white and colored," her relationship with him and the others under her control was always one of master to slave.[13] Even Dolley Madison's historic hospitality was tied to servitude. The welcoming nature of Virginians like the Madisons relied on the work of an enslaved staff. "The credit and the pleasure of entertaining a guest," recognized one Virginian, went to the masters, "while the drudgery devolves upon our slaves."[14]

Dolley disregarded much of the Quaker doctrine in favor of a more Virginian sensibility, not only in her attitude toward servitude but in her manner of dress, her enjoyment of material wealth, and her love of secular entertainments. Her father had been "disowned" by the church in 1789 for complications surrounding his failed business.[15] The church then expelled both Dolley and her sister, Lucy Washington Todd, for their marriages to non-Quakers. If meant as a punishment, the expulsion had instead released her from any obligation to those who, as she wrote her sister, "used to controle me entirely & debar me from so many advantages & pleasures."[16] But Madison held no grudge. She maintained good-natured relationships with Quaker friends and could speak lightheartedly about her past, telling former Quaker James Milnor that apparently "neither of us were very faithful representatives of that respected society."[17]

The Madisons reached the capital on May 1, 1801. Because their permanent quarters were not yet ready, Jefferson had offered them temporary lodging in the executive mansion. Thus, it would be on the grounds of today's White House that Dolley Payne Todd Madison first stepped out of her carriage and into history. A few weeks shy of her thirty-third birthday, she was "tall large and rather masculine," with a complexion "so fair and brilliant as to redeem that objection." There was "a frankness and ease to her deportment," remembered Louisa Catherine Adams, "that won golden opinions from all."[18] Dolley projected an amiability that encouraged social exchange, and she quickly reconnected with the political families she had known in Philadelphia and made immediate new friends. Together these men and women would form Washington City's first capital society.

It would be a smaller circle of political elites than in Philadelphia, and according to Jefferson, one better suited to Republican ideology. We "shall have an agreeable society here, and not too much of it," he wrote James Madison in early 1801.[19] Unlike the former capitals, Washington City lacked an entrenched upper class whose social power was often based on wealth and family name. Here, virtue and talent could hopefully shine, and almost by force of circumstances, material display and aristocratic ceremony would take a backseat. Inside the unfinished opulence of the President's House, Jefferson led by example. Gone were the formal levees of Washington and Adams. Jefferson's dress took on a form more like that of a farmer than a head of state, and he rode the streets alone on horseback. Public ceremonies were stripped of pageantry, and in place of the stiff and ceremonial affairs of his predecessors, Jefferson held his frequent and relatively small dinner parties, where, as one guest observed, "You drink as you please, and converse at your ease."[20]

The new president's pointedly relaxed style of governing effectively hid a number of similarities between his social practices and those established by Washington. His dinners might have been less formal than those of the first two presidents, but they achieved the same objective: that of entertaining high officials and "the whole of Congress, with their apendages [*sic*]" at least once a season.[21] Jefferson maintained Washington's precedent of not returning calls, and, in the same spirit, he did not accept invitations to dine or socialize in the district. During the two winters when his daughter, Martha Jefferson Randolph, spent time in Washington City (the first winter with her sister), she did not hold formal drawing rooms in the style of Martha Washington or Abigail Adams, but the ladies of society waited on her first, and then, as the first ladies had done before her, she returned the favor.[22]

The absence of a first lady's drawing room was not a point to be argued in those early years. No one in Washington held a formal drawing room at that time—not the women of the administration, not the few ladies of the foreign legations, and not the local elite—although women of their stature routinely held weekly receptions in the former capitals.[23] In contrast to Philadelphia society, the elite society of Washington was composed of fewer than a hundred women, all in constant company with each other.[24] They dined in each other's homes, danced at balls with each other's husbands, and sat for tea in homes across the city. "There is a great sameness," wrote one senator's wife of social Washington. "You see almost the same faces; with few exceptions, and the same things are acted over again."[25] In such an environment, one did not need a drawing room to mingle either with a presidential daughter or with the leading cabinet wife. Women called freely on Martha Jefferson Randolph and her sister when they were in residence, and from her home on F Street, Dolley Madison kept the most hospitable parlor in town.[26]

In a more urbane capital, Madison would have shone, but in Washington she dominated. She was not only a Southern woman in a Southern town but a wealthy Southern elite of the highest political stature whose practiced skills in sociability worked as effectively on the Potomac as they did at Montpelier. Her social standing allowed her access to every parlor in the city, and her Southern charm (in a period unfamiliar with that term) did the rest. "She seemed to combine all the qualifications requisite to adorn the station," wrote Louisa Adams, "which she filled to the satisfaction of *all*: a most difficult performance."[27]

Madison effectively led Washington's elite circle of women as they molded a civil society through their calls and entertainments and as they fostered social relationships across the city without regard to political affiliation. In return, the capital's politically elite men sought out the company of these women. Their parlors offered "pleasant places of resort," and their presence, be it at the dinner table or in the congressional galleries, meant that a certain degree of decorum would need to be maintained.[28] The women of early Washington recognized their desirability and used it. One of capital society's founding members, Margaret Bayard Smith, noted that Washington women intermingled more with men than in other cities. They often stood at parties and walked among the guests instead of staying seated, as they did in other places.[29] As they intermingled, these women raised their questions, pressed their causes, and put their husbands and fathers in a softer light with their own abilities to flatter the opposition and create harmony and civility.

On March 11, 1809, Dolley Madison moved into the executive mansion as the second presidential wife to grace its rooms.[30] She brought with her several advantages. She was surrounded by loving relations who, on and off, resided with her at the mansion. She was also an eight-year resident of Washington with an established network of local admirers and friends.

She presided over a Southern capital where the source of her wealth and her position on slavery and servitude were accepted by most of the city's elite and tolerated by the rest. She had the political savvy to understand the national and international implications of her actions and she was sure of her destiny. Moreover, her Virginian womanliness—based on hospitality, good manners, and a welcoming nature—would meld perfectly with public expectations of her new role.

As first lady, Dolley continued to exemplify the standards of civility she and the women of Washington had honed during her years as wife of the secretary of state. In the process, she returned many of the courtesies and protocols set in Philadelphia, altered somewhat to align with Republican sensibilities. Jefferson, for example, had maintained a casual and informal relationship with the foreign ministers but had frowned on their expectations of social precedence. The Madisons did better. James Madison allowed the ministers the same free access to the president his predecessor had, while his wife gave them a renewed prominence in official society. She set the tone at the inaugural ball, where the French minister led her to dinner, and then she honored them for eight more years, particularly with her friendship.

To the pleasure of a growing city, the Madisons combined the gentlemen's levee of the first two presidents with the drawing rooms of their wives to create a single weekly reception. The evenings set a precedent that lasted for generations, and although in future administrations the president, not the first lady, often took the lead role, that was far from the case during the Madison years. These Wednesday nights belonged to Queen Dolley.[31]

In many ways, Dolley's drawing room was similar to the receptions of Martha Washington and Abigail Adams. It was held regularly during the congressional season. The president attended, but more as a guest than a host; no invitations were issued, and light refreshments were served. But there were differences. The number of attendees had increased. Two hundred guests had indicated a rare and crowded drawing room during the Federalist period, whereas the Madison evenings numbered at least that many on any good night.[32] The respectability of the guests was also more in question. Benjamin Henry Latrobe complained that the Madisons' first drawing room "was very numerously attended and by none but respectable people. The second la, la. The last by a perfect rabble in beards

and boots. There is no knowing what to do . . . we are *jammed*, between our republican principles, and our aristocratic wishes."[33] Whereas Jefferson had embraced
the concept of a broad and more inclusive capital society twice a year, at a New
Year's Day reception and at his Fourth of July festivities, Dolley embraced it once
a week in a room "so throng[ed] that it amounted to a literal squeeze."[34] In so
doing, she encouraged social and political harmony, built alliances for her husband, and modeled the congeniality being promoted by women across the city.

Queen Dolley's drawing room might have been her brightest star, but it represented only a part of her efforts to create harmony between the administration
and capital gentility. As the wife of the secretary of state, she had circled the
city with visits, attended public assemblies, entertained on F Street, and, in general, represented her husband and the executive branch across Washington City
and Georgetown. As the wife of the president, neither her activities nor their
purposes lessened. Inside the President's House, she received multiple morning
visits, held her crowded drawing room, and gave large dinner parties. Off the
grounds, she returned visits and attended balls, private dinners, the horse races,
and dance assemblies. Her schedule was heavy. In 1811, she wrote her sister of
a wedding, a sleigh ride in Alexandria with more than a dozen friends (of both
Republican and Federalist persuasions), and plans to run errands about town.[35]
She expressed her disappointment that "sore ears & deafness" were keeping her
from the British minister's party and the French minister's ball.[36] A year later, the
Madisons' young houseguest, Phoebe Morris, relayed an equally hectic schedule
to her family: a "very large dining company today . . . tomorrow morning is to
be devoted to returning some of our visits; in the evening there is a party some
where." And that was only the beginning of the week: on Wednesday, there was
the drawing room, she related, and on Thursday, after a presidential dinner, "we
go to the assembly. On Friday we dine at Genl. Van Nesse's & on Saturday at
Doctor Worthingtons."[37]

The first lady ably balanced the elite protocols of Philadelphia with the ideology of the Republicans.[38] She accepted her place at the head of every prome-
nade, whether at the inaugural ball or at the many assemblies that she attended.
Nonetheless, she happily took the arm of whoever was chosen to escort her.
She worked with architect Latrobe to fashion the White House into a palace,
but she assured a visitor who had peeked into a few rooms "without leave" that
the mansion belonged as much to the public as it did to the current residents.[39]
In keeping with past protocol, Madison did not make first calls, but even here
she was disarming—once writing a new arrival to the city to hurry to the White
House so that they could begin their friendship.[40] She returned every call made
to her without complaint.[41] She conducted her weekly drawing room with a
stateliness that reinforced both her husband's political authority and her own

social authority, but with an ease and unpretentious manner that allowed her, as Margaret Bayard Smith wrote, to stand *among* as she stood *above*.[42]

The Madisons retired to Montpelier in March 1817. Their departure marked the end of what turned out to be a unique period of camaraderie between the nation's first lady and social Washington. Madison's successor, Elizabeth Monroe, would choose neither to return calls nor to participate in capital society other than in an official capacity. She, and the first ladies who followed directly after her, either lacked Dolley Madison's constitution and her willingness to participate in society off White House grounds or had tenures too short-lived to influence the precedents set by the others. Consequently, as society moved deeper into the antebellum period, it found its strength not in the leadership of any one woman but in the courtesies and protocols originally shaped by Madison and her founding sisters. These standards of etiquette gave stability to an elite society that changed faces every two, four, or eight years and provided a continual source of power to the women of Washington, who, as a unit, controlled and guarded their creation.[43]

For the next two decades, Dolley stayed in contact with Washington society through visiting friends and gossipy letters she received from the capital. The letters reveal not only the breadth of the political friendships she maintained over the years but also her confidence in an unchanging capital etiquette. She expressed that confidence in a letter written from Montpelier in 1833. Two of her nieces who had traveled to Washington wrote their aunt to complain that the French minister's wife had refused them, as visitors, the honor of a first call. Although "strangers" were granted that honor in other cities, their aunt quickly set them straight on the protocols of Washington. Surprised that they did not "know better the etiquette near courts, where ambassadors and ministers reside," she reminded them that she had "lived sixteen years in the midst of ceremonies in Washington . . . [and] . . . four years in Philadelphia." During that time, she scolded, she had been "intimate with the heads of Departments and Ministers from Europe and I never knew their ladies to visit young girls first—indeed!"[44]

James Madison died in 1836, and a year later his widow began her return to Washington, making it permanent in December 1843. At the time, Dolley was seventy-five years old and deeply in debt. In 1844, she sold Montpelier and with it, the majority of the enslaved men and women who had worked the plantation. Left under her ownership were at least four enslaved members of her Montpelier staff whom she brought with her to the capital along with her niece-companion, Anna Coles Payne.[45]

Madison returned to a city that had four times the number of foreign legations and ten times the number of congressional wives and daughters in town each season. The population was more than 30,000 (with another 20,000 by

1850), and the men in power were a mix of Whigs and Democrats with increasing political differences.[46] But Dolley also found, and apparently had never doubted, that the ladies of the city—the administrative wives, the local elite, and the visiting congressional wives—all followed the same patterns of etiquette as when she had first presided over the city.

Calls were still made at the start of each season and still completed according to protocols that honored political status above political party. The White House continued to host a scheduled reception either weekly or biweekly, but now foreign legations and cabinet wives added to the social fare by giving, if they wished, regularly scheduled drawing rooms. There were salons for invited guests held by the city's prominent wives, and there were far more public entertainments. If the tone of the entertainments had become more formal, the methods employed were still those of the Southern hostess, always mannerly, always amicable, and always highlighting social harmony.

As an icon of a past administration, Madison received a place of honor in social Washington, as did Louisa Catherine Adams and as would Elizabeth Schuyler Hamilton, widow of Alexander Hamilton, when she arrived in the 1840s. Only Dolley, though, was crowned the city's dowager queen—a coronation that paid tribute to her popularity as first lady and to a sociable spirit that had not lessened with time.[47] Letter writers of that period commonly mentioned "the venerable" Mrs. Madison.[48] "She is a *young* lady of fourscore years and upward," wrote a visiting New Yorker in 1842, who "goes to parties and receives company like the 'Queen of this new world.'"[49] She continued to sport a turban of the type that had set her style as first lady. Her wardrobe, though dated, was plush, and she dressed cleverly to show only that which had "survived old age."[50] She was "handsome & most elegant," according to one admirer, and she had not lost the charm that made her a welcome presence at any occasion.[51] "Mrs. Madison was of the party," wrote acting first lady Angelica Van Buren of a dinner in 1839, "which always contributes very much to my pleasure."[52]

Dolley Madison graced the homes of both Whigs and Democrats. She could be found one night in the parlor of Whig mayor William Seaton and another on the arm of Democratic president James Polk.[53] Her own parlor provided the city's "most attractive *salon*," where prominent local residents and members of the foreign legations mingled with families from both sides of the congressional aisle.[54] As in an earlier Washington, her actions duplicated those of the capital's other elite women. Their parlors, like that of Madison, offered pleasant retreats from "the rough edge of party violence and Republican vulgarity."[55]

Madison had returned to the capital with an unshakable conviction as to what constituted proper Washington etiquette and confidence in her standing as a social authority. When President John Tyler's daughter-in-law, Elizabeth

Priscilla Cooper Tyler, who resided in the White House, asked Madison if it were necessary to return all of her calls in person (rather than having cards delivered), the woman famous for her sociability instructed her to do so "by all means."[56] When Priscilla then sought a more agreeable opinion from another Washington matron, she learned that Mrs. Madison had, of course, been correct. "So three days in the week," wrote the young woman, "I am to spend three hours a day driving from one street to another in this city of magnificent distances."[57]

As she had in earlier years, Dolley guided by example. Although she now preferred sitting to mingling, her hospitable spirit continued to illustrate the effectiveness of Southern manners on the making of a civil society, and her conversational skills demonstrated the power behind a kind word or sincere flattery—in one case she delighted a descendant of old friends commenting that she always knew the family by their "beautiful eyes." In another, a former acquaintance that she remembered him well (when her memory had actually failed her).[58] The dowager queen made visitors feel welcome, returned their calls in a timely fashion, and made apologies when illness prevented her from doing so. Moreover, she honored the members of this later society with her charm and her presence.

During her first year back in Washington, the New York *Herald* published a piece on Madison by one of the newspaper's anonymous correspondents.[59] The gentleman, himself a bon vivant of capital society, had been asked if he would like to meet the former first lady. "'Mrs. Madison,' said [he], 'nothing would afford me so much pleasure. I am very desirous to see a lady of the old school, and of the reign of pure Virginia democracy.'" He wrote of taking a carriage to the Madison home, where he and his companion were welcomed with "great courtesy and politeness." He noted how Madison inquired kindly about the family of his companion, who was herself an older woman of the city. A number of callers appeared during their visit, and their hostess treated each of them with "attention and [a] friendly greeting." The correspondent had listened as his companion bemoaned to Dolley the "bitterness of party feelings" and how she expressed relief that it had not spoiled society, which still managed to mingle "harmoniously." The three then gossiped about the city's foreign ministers, who, said his companion, "now as in your day, [Mrs. Madison], are all the go."[60]

The reporter was delighted with Madison, praised her past achievements, and hailed her as an icon of a simpler Washington. What he failed to see —despite the clues laid before him—was that the woman who had so graciously received him was far from being a relic of the past. If the "reign of pure Virginia democracy" associated with her husband had faded with changing politics, what Dolley had brought to the city, and what she would continue to reinforce for another decade, had not. It was everywhere: in the rounds of calls that ignored political alliance, in the hospitality received indiscriminately from families on both sides of the congressional aisle, in the presidential drawing rooms, and even in the exalted social status of the foreign ministers.

Dolley Madison's social Washington would not stand the test of time. The city was already breaking into factions during her encore performance. Just being a member of the political elite no longer guaranteed an invitation to the more popular entertainments or into the best homes. One needed to have something else to offer—added wealth, a respected family name, or a singularly impressive government title. The Madisons' presidential receptions had brought in a few hundred guests; the receptions of later presidents could draw in thousands. Formal calls continued to be made and received, but it was impossible for a woman to form meaningful friendships with the four hundred or so persons on her list. The final blow came in the years immediately preceding the Civil War. During that period, capital hostesses would find that the only way to keep harmony in their parlors was with a careful selection of politically like-minded guests. Post-bellum Washington would retain many of the protocols instituted by Madison and her friends, but it retained little of that society's Southern tone and little of its heart.

Dolley Payne Todd Madison had "emerge[d] from the mediocrity" of her first marriage, wrote Northern senator Samuel L. Mitchill, to become the nation's "*queen of hearts*."[61] Her "unfailing politeness" and her determination to please would be the very definition of Southern charm, and her accomplishments as first lady would earn her a major share in the accolades paid to that sorority of women.[62] Moreover, under Dolley's guidance and by her example, social Washington would operate for decades under a set of etiquettes and protocols that favored courtesy over animosity and harmony over partisan politics. In a period of American history when the Republic was young and fragile, perhaps a civil Washington was her most important legacy.

## NOTES

1. For childhood and first marriage, see Dolley Madison, Holly Cowan Shulman, and David Maydole Matteson, *The Selected Letters of Dolley Payne Madison* (Charlottesville: University of Virginia Press, 2003), 9, 12–15.

2. Holly Cowan Shulman, "Dolley Madison's Life and Times: The Early Years," in *Dolley Madison Digital Edition*, ed. Holly C. Shulman (Charlottesville: University of Virginia Press, Rotunda, 2007), https://rotunda-upress-virginia-edu.ezproxy.princeton.edu/dmde/bio-intro.xqy. John Todd died in October 1793; the Madisons wed on September 15, 1794.

3. On Montpelier, see Ralph Ketcham, *The Madisons at Montpelier: Reflections on the Founding Couple* (Charlottesville: University of Virginia Press, 2009); James Madison, Orange County, Virginia, in the 1820 US Census.

4. Dolley Payne Todd to Eliza Collins Lee, letter, September 16, 1794, in *The Papers of James Madison*, vol. 15: *24 March 1793–20 April 1795*, ed. Thomas A. Mason, Robert A. Rutland, and Jeanne K. Sisson (Charlottesville: University of Virginia Press, 1985), 357–358.

5. Sarah (Sally) McKean Maria Theresa Martínez de Yrujo to Dolley Payne Todd Madison, letter, September 3, [1796?], in *Dolley Madison Digital Edition*, ed. Holly C. Shulman (Charlottesville: University of Virginia Press, Rotunda, 2007), http://rotunda.upress. virginia.edu/dmde/DPM0023.

6. George Washington to David Stuart, letter, June 15, 1790, in *The Papers of George Washington, Presidential Series*, vol. 5: *16 January 1790–30 June 1790*, ed. Dorothy Twohig, Mark A. Mastromarino, and Jack D. Warren (Charlottesville: University of Virginia Press, 1996), 527.

7. On Washington's schedule of dinners and receptions, see Washington to Stuart, June 15, 1790. On public balls and theater attendance, see *The Diaries of George Washington*, vol. 6: *1 January 1790–13 December 1799*, ed. Donald Jackson and Dorothy Twohig (Charlottesville: University of Virginia Press, 1979). On the declining of dinners, see George Washington to David Stuart, letter, July 26, 1789, in *The Papers of George Washington, Presidential Series*, vol. 3: *15 June 1789–5 September 1789*, ed. Dorothy Twohig (Charlottesville: University of Virginia Press, 1989), 323.

8. Martha Dandridge Custis Washington to Abigail Smith Adams, letter, February 20, 1797, in *The Adams Papers, Adams Family Correspondence*, vol. 11: *July 1795–February 1797*, ed. Margaret A. Hogan et al. (Cambridge, MA: Belknap Press of Harvard University Press, 2013), 570.

9. Washington to Adams, February 20, 1797.

10. Dolley Payne Todd Madison to Elizabeth (Eliza) Collins Lee, letter, January 12, [1800], in *The Selected Letters of Dolley Payne Madison* (Charlottesville: University of Virginia Press, 2003), 35.

11. Charles Pinckney to James Madison, letter, October 26, 1800, in *The Papers of James Madison*, vol. 17: *31 March 1797–3 March 1801 with Supplement, 22 January 1778–9 August 1795*, ed. David B. Mattern et al. (Charlottesville: University of Virginia Press, 1991), 427–429.

12. Charles William Janson, *The Stranger in America: Containing Observations . . . on the Genius, Manners and Customs of the People of the United States; with Biographical Particulars of Public Characters . . . and the Slave Trade* (London: Printed for J. Cundee, 1807), 205; Albert Gallatin to Hannah Nicholson Gallatin, letter, January 15, 1801, in Henry Adams, *The Life of Albert Gallatin* (Philadelphia: J. B. Lippincott, 1879), 252–253.

13. Paul Jennings, *Colored Man's Reminiscences of James Madison* (Orange, VA: Montpelier Foundation, 1865), 14. For enslaved servants brought to Washington, see Elizabeth Dowling Taylor, *A Slave in the White House: Paul Jennings and the Madisons* (New York: Palgrave Macmillan, 2012), 28. Regarding buying and selling, see Dolley Payne Todd Madison to Elizabeth

(Eliza) Parke Custis Law, letter, October 17, 1804, in *Dolley Madison Digital Edition*, ed. Holly C. Shulman (Charlottesville: University of Virginia Press, Rotunda, 2007), http://rotunda .upress.virginia.edu/dmde/DPM0089.

14. A Virginian, "Letters from New England—No. 2.," *Southern Literary Messenger* 1, no. 4 (December 1834): 166. See also, Anthony Szczesiul, *The Southern Hospitality Myth: Ethics, Politics, Race, and American Memory* (Athens: University of Georgia Press, 2017); Kelley Fanto Deetz, *Bound to the Fire: How Virginia's Enslaved Cooks Helped Invent American Cuisine* (Lexington: University Press of Kentucky, 2017).

15. Monthly Meeting of Friends of Philadelphia for the Southern District, February 21, 1789, Philadelphia Yearly Meeting Minutes, Haverford College Quaker Collection, Haverford, PA, 247–248.

16. Dolley Payne Madison to Anna Payne Cutts, letter, August 19, [1805], in *The Selected Letters of Dolley Payne Madison* (Charlottesville: University of Virginia Press, 2003), 64. Dolley was in Philadelphia at the time to seek medical attention for an ulcerated knee.

17. Diary of James Milnor, November 27, 1811, in John Seely Stone, *A Memoir of the Life of James Milnor, D. D.: Late Rector of St. George's Church, New York* (New York: American Tract Society, 1848), 58–59.

18. Quote from Louisa Catherine Adams, "The Adventures of a Nobody," in *Diary and Autobiographical Writings of Louisa Catherine Adams: 1778–1850*, vol. 1, ed. Judith S. Graham et al., 2 vols. (Cambridge, MA: Belknap Press of Harvard University Press, 2013), 204–205.

19. Thomas Jefferson to James Madison, letter, March 12, 1801, in *The Papers of Thomas Jefferson*, vol. 33: *17 February–30 April 1801*, ed. Barbara B. Oberg (Princeton, NJ: Princeton University Press, 2006), 256.

20. Samuel L. Mitchill to Catharine Akerly Cook Mitchill, letter, January 10, 1802, "Dr. Mitchill's Letters from Washington: 1801–1813," *Harper's New Monthly Magazine* 58, no. 347 (April 1879): 744.

21. Abigail Adams to Mary Smith Cranch, letter, June 23, 1797, in *The Adams Papers, Adams Family Correspondence*, vol. 12: *March 1797–April 1798*, ed. Sara Martin et al. (Cambridge, MA: Harvard University Press, 2015), 171.

22. "Etiquette," Philadelphia *Aurora General Advertiser*, February 13, 1804. Jefferson's younger daughter, Mary (Maria) Jefferson Eppes, died from complications of childbirth in April 1804.

23. Abigail Smith Adams to Mary Smith Cranch, letter, January 24, 1789, in *New Letters of Abigail Adams, 1788–1801*, ed. Stewart Mitchell (Boston: Houghton Mifflin, 1947), 8; Henrietta Marchant Liston to James Jackson, letter, January 15, 1797, in Bradford Perkins, "A Diplomat's Wife in Philadelphia: Letters of Henrietta Liston, 1796–1800," *William and Mary Quarterly* 11, no. 4 (October 1954): 607.

24. During summer 1802, Albert Gallatin wrote that Washington society consisted of about a hundred and fifty people, "all the city—ladies and gentlemen" (Gallatin to Hannah Nicholson Gallatin, letter, July 7, 1802, in Henry Adams, *Life of Albert Gallatin*, 304). Anna Thornton counted thirty ladies at a Georgetown ball held before the national government relocated to the Potomac, and at a similar ball after the move, fifty-seven ladies (entries for February 6 and December 19, 1800, in Anna Maria Brodeau Thornton and Worthington

C. Ford, "Diary of Mrs. William Thornton, 1800–1863," *Records of the Columbia Historical Society* 10 [1907]: 103, 223). To that, one could add a dozen or so congressional wives who joined their husbands during the congressional season (Thomas Jefferson to Martha Jefferson Randolph, letter, December 3, 1804, in Thomas Jefferson, *The Family Letters of Thomas Jefferson*, ed. James Adam Bear Jr. and Edwin Morris Betts [Charlottesville: University of Virginia Press, 1966], 265).

25. Catharine Akerly Cook Mitchill to Margaretta Akerly Miller, letter, April 8, 1806, in Catherine [*sic*] Akerly Cock Mitchill Family Papers, 1806–1936, Library of Congress.

26. [Margaret Bayard Smith], "Mrs. Madison," in James Herring and James Barton Longacre, *The National Portrait Gallery of Distinguished Americans*, vol. 3 (New York: Hermon Bancroft, 1836), 374; see also Thomas Jefferson's Dinner Records, January 17–20, 1806, best viewed as scans in Charles T. Cullen, "Jefferson's White House Dinner Guests," *White House* 17 (Winter 2006): 30–37.

27. Adams, "Adventures of a Nobody," 219.

28. Entry for March 15, 1842, in Philip Hone and Bayard Tuckerman, *The Diary of Philip Hone, 1828–1851*, vol. 2. (New York: Dodd, Mead, 1889), 121.

29. Margaret Bayard Smith to Jane Bayard Kirkpatrick, letter, March 13, 1814, in Margaret Bayard Smith and Gaillard Hunt, *First Forty Years of Washington Society* (New York: Scribner's, 1906), 97.

30. The inauguration was March 4, but Jefferson needed time to get his affairs in order. Thomas Jefferson to Charles Willson Peale, letter, March 10, 1809; Isaac Coles to Thomas Jefferson, letter, March 13, 1809, in *The Papers of Thomas Jefferson, Retirement Series*, vol. 1: *4 March 1809–15 November 1809*, ed. J. Jefferson Looney (Princeton, NJ: Princeton University Press, 2004), 45, 53–54.

31. For a contemporary use of "Queen Dolley," see William T. Barry to Catherine Armistead Mason Barry, letter, February 24, 1815, in William T. Barry, "Letters of William T. Barry 1," *William and Mary Quarterly* 13, no. 4 (April 1905): 237.

32. Abigail Adams to Mary Smith Cranch, letter, May 3, 1800, in *New Letters of Abigail Adams*, ed. Stewart Mitchell (Boston: Houghton Mifflin, 1947), 250; Ebenezer Sage to his niece, letter, January 24, 1810, Ebenezer Sage Correspondence, 1810, Manuscript Division, Library of Congress; Margaret Bayard Smith to Jane Bayard Kirkpatrick, letter, March 13, 1814, in Margaret Bayard Smith and Gaillard Hunt, *First Forty Years of Washington Society* (New York: Scribner's, 1906), 95.

33. Benjamin Henry Latrobe to George Harrison, letter, June 20, 1809, in Benjamin Henry Latrobe, *The Correspondence and Miscellaneous Papers of Benjamin Henry Latrobe*, vol. 2: *1805–1810*, ed. John C. Van Horne (New Haven, CT: Yale University Press, 1986), 731. Italics in transcription.

34. William Darlington, February 9, 1816, in Papers of William Darlington, 1800–1863, New York Historical Society, New York. *Squeeze* was nineteenth-century slang for a crowded house party.

35. Dolly Payne Todd Madison to Anna Payne Cutts, letter, December 22, [1811], in *Dolley Madison Digital Edition*, http://rotunda.upress.virginia.edu/dmde/DPM0301.

36. Madison to Cutts, December 22, 1811.

37. Phoebe Morris, letter, January 6, 1812, Dolley Madison Collection, Dumbarton House, Washington, DC.

38. On Dolley Madison's ability to mollify Republicans and Federalists: Republican Jonathan Roberts to Matthew Roberts, letter, December 2, 1811, in *The Papers of James Madison, Presidential Series*, vol. 4: *5 November 1811–9 July 1812 and Supplement 5 March 1809–19 October 1811*, ed. J. C. A. Stagg (Charlottesville: University of Virginia Press, 1999), 45n; Federalist Josiah Quincy, quoted in Edmund Quincy, *Life of Josiah Quincy of Massachusetts* (Boston: Fields, Osgood, 1869), 193.

39. Eliza Susan Morton Quincy to Mary Storer, letter, December 20, 1809, in Eliza Susan Morton Quincy and Eliza Susan Quincy, *Memoir of the Life of Eliza S. M. Quincy* (Boston: John Wilson, 1861), 129.

40. Mary Boardman Crowninshield to Mary Hodges Boardman, letter, November 11, 1815, in Mary Boardman Crowninshield and Francis Boardman Crowninshield, *Letters of Mary Boardman Crowninshield, 1815–1816* (Cambridge, MA: Riverside, 1905), 15–16.

41. "The Drawing Room," Washington *National Register*, December 13, 1817.

42. Paraphrased from Margaret Bayard Smith, *Winter in Washington*, vol. 1, 44.

43. Dolley Madison and her friends had assumed that a condition of gentility was virtue (and thus a condition of admittance into their circles), an aspect of their society not discussed in this chapter but played out during her absence from Washington in what became known as the Eaton Affair.

44. Quoting Dolley Payne Madison to Mary E. E. Cutts, letter, November 4, 1833, in *The Selected Letters of Dolley Payne Madison* (Charlottesville: University of Virginia Press, 2003), 301.

45. Ketcham, *Madisons at Montpelier*, 178–179; Paul Jennings to Sukey, letter, May 13, 1844, in *Dolley Madison Digital Edition*, http://rotunda.upress.virginia.edu/dmde/DPM3370.

46. William Q. Force, *Picture of Washington and Its Vicinity, for 1848, with Twenty Embellishments on Wood, by Gilbert & Gihon, and Eighteen on Steel, and an Introduction by Rev. R. R. Gurley; also, the Washington Guide, Containing a Congressional Directory, and much other Useful Information* (Washington, DC: W. Q. Force, 1848), 151–161, 176–178.

47. Holly Cowan Shulman, "Dolley Madison's Life and Times: Widowhood," in *Dolley Madison Digital Edition*, https://rotunda-upress-virginia-edu.ezproxy.princeton.edu/dmde/bio-intro.xqy. Dolley Madison fit the informal definition of *dowager*, that of a dignified elderly woman, but she would not become a widow until 1848.

48. Entry for February 7, 1849, in James K. Polk, *The Diary of James K. Polk During His Presidency, 1845 to 1849, Now First Printed from the Original Manuscript in the Collections of the Chicago Historical Society*, vol. 4 (Chicago: A. C. McClurg, 1910), 326.

49. Entry for March 15, 1842, in Philip Hone and Bayard Tuckerman, *The Diary of Philip Hone, 1828–1851*, vol. 2 (New York: Dodd, Mead, 1889), 119.

50. Emily Virginia Mason to Kate Mason Rowland, letter, January 2, 1844, transcription in "MA" Finding Aid Binder: James Madison, Burton Historical Collection, Detroit Public Library, Michigan.

51. Mason to Rowland, January 2, 1844.

52. Angelica Singleton Van Buren to her sister, letter, February 14, 1839, in Marion Hall Fisher and Howard T. Fisher, *Frances Calderón de la Barca Née Frances Erskine Inglis: A Biography of the Author of Life in Mexico and the Attaché in Madrid* (Bloomington, IN: Xlibris, 2016), 187. Angelica Singleton's mother was Dolley Madison's cousin, and she would introduce the young woman to her future husband, Abraham Van Buren. After her marriage in 1838, Angelica served as first lady for her widower father-in-law, Martin Van Buren (Allen Culling Clark, *Life and Letters of Dolly Madison* [Washington, DC: W. F. Roberts, 1914], 291; Shulman, "Dolley Madison's Life and Times: Widowhood."

53. Entry for February 10, 1847, in Elizabeth Lord Cogswell Dixon, "Journal written during a Residence in Washington during the 29th Congress Commencing with the first of December 1845," ed. Caroline Welling Van Deusen, *White House History* 33 (Summer 2013): 97; entry for December 10, 1846, in James K. Polk, *Diary of James K. Polk During His Presidency*, vol. 2, 271.

54. Quoted in Marian Campbell Gouverneur, *As I Remember; Recollections of American Society During the Nineteenth Century* (New York: D. Appleton, 1911), 178; description of Dolley Madison's elite company in a letter from her grandniece, Adele Cutts Williams, no date, quoted in Allen Culling Clark, *Life and Letters of Dolly Madison* (Washington, DC: W. F. Roberts, 1914), 461–463.

55. Entry for March 15, 1842, Hone and Tuckerman, *Diary of Philip Hone*.

56. Priscilla Cooper Tyler, letter, 1841, in Allen Culling Clark, *Life and Letters of Dolly Madison* (Washington, DC: W. F. Roberts, 1914), 307.

57. Tyler letter, 1841.

58. Mason to Kate Mason Rowland, January 2, 1844; Dixon, entries for January 10, 1846, and December 6, 1845, respectively, in Dixon, "Journal written during a Residence in Washington," 58–59, 38.

59. Article on Dolley Madison, "From our correspondent *Moliere* . . . Washington, Nov. 6, 1837," New York *Morning Herald*, November 10, 1837. Regarding the correspondent's anonymity, "From our correspondent *Moliere* . . . Washington, Sept. 27th, 1837," New York *Morning Herald*, September 29, 1837.

60. Quoted from "From our correspondent *Moliere* . . . Washington, Nov. 6, 1837," New York *Morning Herald*, November 10, 1837.

61. Samuel L. Mitchill to Catharine Akerly Cook Mitchill, January 3, 1802, in "Dr. Mitchill's Letters from Washington, 1801–1813," *Harper's New Monthly Magazine* 58, no. 347 (April 1879): 743.

62. Craig Claiborne, *Essentials of Etiquette: A Guide to Table Manners in an Imperfect World* (New York: William Morrow, 1992), 103.

# CHAPTER 3

# Elizabeth Kortright Monroe
## La Belle Americaine

Mary Stockwell

From the moment Elizabeth Kortright, a socialite from New York City, married James Monroe, an up-and-coming politician from Virginia, she molded her life to match his every ambition. She rode with him through the rolling countryside around Charlottesville as he built his law practice. She entertained his wealthy and powerful friends at the plantation he built in the shadow of Monticello. She travelled with him to Paris and London when he took up diplomatic posts there. Finally, when he was elected president, she served as his first lady. Drawing on her varied personal experiences, including her time as the mistress of the Highland Plantation, in Albemarle County, Virginia, she transformed the American executive mansion into the elegant public space and private family home that it remains to the present day.

### A BEAUTIFUL WOMAN

Throughout her life, the word most frequently used to describe Elizabeth was beautiful. Suitors flocked to her side when she attended the theater as a young girl in New York. Just five feet tall, she beguiled the men who swirled about her with her dark eyes, flawless complexion, and brown curls piled high atop her head. When her husband was the ambassador to France, she dazzled the Parisians. They marveled at her stunning dresses made from the finest materials, her coral and amethyst tiaras, and her charming conversation in perfect French. Later, when she entertained visitors at the White House, dressed in silk gowns trimmed with ermine, her guests remarked that she looked as young as her daughters and surely was as beautiful as the day she married the president.[1]

Two surviving portraits of Elizabeth give some hint of the beauty that

52

impressed her contemporaries. In a miniature painted in Paris when she was twenty-six, she is dressed like a Greek goddess in the height of revolutionary fashion. In a second portrait, painted some twenty years later when she was the first lady, she seems statelier but still beautiful. A handful of her surviving gowns also give a sense of her beauty. Two taffeta dresses sewn in the late colonial style are from her trousseau. One is white and covered with multicolored flowers, and the other, probably her wedding dress, is bright pink. She wore a gold velvet gown in the empire style to the coronation of Emperor Napoleon. Along with these dresses, her citrine and aquamarine jewelry, her embroidered high-heeled shoes with rhinestone buckles, and her shawls of fine silk netting attest to a beautiful woman's love of beautiful things.[2]

### Only One Letter Survives

Although many of Elizabeth's personal possessions have survived, most of her letters have not. Upon her death, at the age of sixty-two in 1830, James Monroe destroyed all of his correspondence with her and directed his two daughters, Eliza and Maria, to do the same. However, one letter survived. Written to her husband in February 1794, it reveals something of Elizabeth's character. She described how she travelled from Virginia to New York City to be at her dying father's side. With steely determination, she questioned him about his property and who in the family would inherit it. She took down his words like a lawyer taking a deposition so she could report every detail back to her husband. What would her brother, John, inherit? A cottage, a commission, some slaves, and a township north of Manhattan against which he had already taken out a loan from their father, but none of this had ever been written down. What would she and her three sisters, Hester, Maria, and Sarah, inherit? She worried they would receive little if anything. Though she pressed her father to write a will, she confessed to her husband, "I fear he will put it off too late." If only her father had ordered his finances more carefully, he could have provided quite nicely for his children, but given "the wretched management of his affairs," they would probably "not receive a farthing."[3]

### THREE STRANDS OF A LIFE

With few surviving words from Elizabeth herself, how can we ever truly know her as a person and, more specifically, how can we ever understand what experiences shaped her as the first lady? The answers can be found in the three main strands of her life: first as a beautiful New York socialite, later as the mistress of a Southern plantation, and finally as the wife of an American diplomat before she became first lady.

First Lady Elizabeth Kortright Monroe. Courtesy of the Library
of Congress Prints and Photographs Division. Reproduction Number:
LC-USZ62-25771 (b&w film copy neg.).

*Society Belle*

In addition to describing Elizabeth as beautiful, people who knew her frequently
mentioned her aloofness. She spoke with a slight English accent and carried herself with a formality more European than American. People who commented on
her "hauteur" and "exclusiveness" surmised these traits came from her upbringing in New York City's wealthy merchant class.[4] Her father, Lawrence Kortright,
a British Army captain during the Seven Years' War, made a fortune during the

conflict as part owner of several privateers that sailed against the French. He met his wife, Hannah Aspinwall, while fighting in the war in upstate New York. After his marriage, Kortright made even more money trading goods with the West Indies. He purchased a home on Manhattan's Great Queen Street, where he and his wife raised their five children, including Elizabeth, who was born on June 30, 1768.[5]

Elizabeth's polite demeanor belied the fact that she had suffered several tragedies in her youth. Her mother died in 1777, shortly after giving birth to a child who also died. One year later, her family's home was severely damaged in a fire, luckily with no loss of life. By the late 1780s, her father's fortune had been greatly reduced after Great Britain closed the West Indies to trade with the United States. With little extra money to spare, he turned the education of his daughters over to his mother, Hester Kortright. She was a powerful woman who had run her own business after her husband's death. She trained her granddaughters in sewing, playing the pianoforte, and singing but also instructed them in history, literature, and philosophy. Elizabeth was especially interested in the latest political developments in the United States and Europe. She studied French and soon mastered the language.

Even under his family's straitened circumstances, Lawrence was determined that his daughters make good marriages. He entertained frequently, throwing open the doors of his Manhattan townhouse to merchants, diplomats, and politicians, all potential suitors. Daughters Hester and Maria married into prominent merchant families, the Gouvernors and Knoxes, respectively, and Sarah married John Heyliger, the former grand chamberlain of the king of Denmark. Only Elizabeth seemed intent on making a marriage beneath her station.[6]

On January 12, 1786, she met James Monroe at the wedding of Ann Thompson, another New York socialite, and Elbridge Gerry, a Confederation Congress member from Massachusetts. Monroe, a Confederation Congress member from Virginia who was ten years Elizabeth Kortright's senior, attended the wedding as Elbridge's best man. From the moment she met him, she was taken by the tall and rather shy politician who had no fortune and few prospects. He had made a name for himself as a soldier fighting at George Washington's side in the Revolution, later studied law in Williamsburg, and was running for reelection to the Congress from his home district in Prince George's County. He was fascinated by the beautiful and intelligent young woman who enjoyed discussing politics.

The couple married at the Kortright home on February 16, 1786, and then left for a monthlong honeymoon on Long Island. Many in New York society gossiped that she could have done so much better for herself when choosing a husband. For his part, James was somewhat embarrassed that he had married a New Yorker. He confessed to his friend James Madison that he hoped his young wife would be welcomed as an adopted citizen of his state. When Monroe lost his reelection bid in May 1786, Madison mused to their mutual friend Thomas Jefferson that the young member of Congress had lingered too long up North. His constituents might have assumed that he would never return after marrying a Yankee.[7]

But James had no intention of abandoning Virginia. He instead made plans to return there in October 1786 and set up a law practice in Fredericksburg. Elizabeth, who had turned eighteen and was now pregnant with her first child, followed her husband to Virginia, where she would spend most of the rest of her life. To the end of her days, one of the greatest insults to be hurled at Elizabeth Monroe was the suspicion that, even after her many years of living as a Southerner in Virginia, she remained a "little too much of New York."[8]

*Plantation Mistress*

In October 1786, the Monroes moved into a small house in Fredericksburg that served both as a law office and a family home. Two months later, Elizabeth gave birth to a daughter named Eliza. James affectionately called his firstborn child the "little monkey." But the young family was soon separated when James, now supporting his wife and daughter as a practicing attorney, had to spend most of 1787 in Richmond. He could not bring Elizabeth and Eliza to live with him because he had no money.[9]

Living apart from her husband was difficult for her as seen in the one surviving letter of his to her, written in February 1787. She did not feel well after the birth of their daughter and complained to him of sharp pains in her breast. He attributed her illness to a lack of exercise and the many agues and fevers common in Virginia. Knowing she missed him, he reminded her that he must be away from his family to rebuild his fortune in the state. Urging her to have fortitude, he reminded her that their separation would not last forever.

Reunited with her husband within the year, she, along with Eliza, travelled with him as he argued cases throughout the state and slowly recovered his finances. There were times, however, when she and Eliza stayed behind with family friends, most notably Jefferson's daughter Martha at Monticello. Jefferson, who considered James his protégé, urged him to move closer to Monticello. James purchased a house in Charlottesville in 1789, but in the following year, when he was elected to the US Senate, he moved his family to Philadelphia. In 1793 he purchased the Highland Plantation, just south of Monticello, but did not move his family there because he was soon on his way to France as the US ambassador. Instead, he directed twenty-five of the enslaved men and women at Highland to cultivate tobacco. He would use the yearly profits from the sale of the cash crop to build his family's house there. It was not until November 1799 that the Monroe family, which now included six-month-old James Spence Monroe, finally moved into Highland.[10]

Although her husband's political career would take him in the coming years to Richmond as Virginia's governor, back to Europe as the minister to Great Britain, and finally to Washington, DC, as the secretary of state, Elizabeth considered Highland her true home for the next twenty-five years of her life. She even used the inheritance she finally won from her father's estate to help pay for the property. At Highland, she raised her adolescent daughter, Eliza, cared for her son, James, who died of whooping cough in September 1800, and gave birth to her youngest child, Maria Hester, in May 1802.[11]

The original home at Highland was a one-story, wooden-frame structure with a second-floor dormer added later. For many years, historians believed this was Highland's main house and therefore proved that the Monroes preferred living more modestly than Jefferson at Monticello or Madison at Montpelier. However, archaeologists have recently discovered the foundation of a much larger home on the estate. This "commodious dwelling house," as James Monroe described it years later when he put Highland up for sale, was seventy feet in length and would have been far grander than the small house historians now recognize as Highland's guesthouse. As yet, no descriptions of the large main house, which burned down after James sold the plantation, have been discovered.[12]

However, historians do know that the Monroes, like other Southern planters, considered their home a showplace. Here they displayed the many fine objects they had acquired through their travels in Europe and through the profits from the sale of the tobacco, corn, and wheat raised at Highland. At the time of her marriage, Elizabeth purchased several expensive pieces in New York, including a Hepplewhite dining table. The Monroes also brought furniture, china, and silverware back from their first trip to France in the 1790s, but all these items were sold to finance their second trip in 1803. They returned with many neoclassical pieces, including a larger-than-life bust of Napoleon that the emperor had presented to James in person. They also brought back eagle-back chairs and a bow-front china cabinet from England.

As Highland's mistress, Elizabeth was responsible for entertaining her husband's wealthy friends. Letters written by James and Dolley Madison show they were especially close to the Monroes and often exchanged vegetables, jams, pickles, and other foods between Montpelier and Highland. Although no letters survive from Elizabeth describing her life as a planter's wife, her duties would have included managing the kitchen. Monroe family recipes show a combination of Southern and French cuisines. She would also have maintained the wine cellar, the smokehouse, and the gardens, which provided vegetables, herbs for cooking and medicine, and flowers, the latter of which people frequently noted when visiting the Monroes.

Elizabeth would have also managed the enslaved workers in the main house, kitchen, and gardens. There is no direct evidence describing her interaction with Highland's nearly fifty enslaved persons. Slavery was not a new experience for her because her father enslaved several people. In her only surviving letter to her husband, she seemed to accept the institution without question. She was only upset that her brother would inherit their father's enslaved workers instead of herself or her sisters inheriting them. Likewise, there is no evidence of her reaction to the rebellion of Gabriel Prosser during her husband's time as governor, an event that occurred in the same month that her infant son died. Nor is there any surviving testimony on whether she came to share her husband's opinion that slavery must end and that manumitted persons must be settled in Africa.[13]

Evidence does exist, however, showing how carefully she brought up her daughters. Visitors to Highland remember seeing six-year-old Maria, just returned from England with her parents, playing with her new spaniel puppy and dressed in the latest European fashion of a short frock worn over pantaloons. A surviving sampler made by Maria shows that Elizabeth taught her daughters how to embroider. She also trained them in music. Like their mother, both girls played the pianoforte, and Eliza also played the harp. Elizabeth and her daughters played pieces by Mozart and Clementi, popular Scottish tunes, and military marches as seen in the family's music books. Through all this training, Elizabeth's goal was to make sure her daughters married well just as she had done. James would make certain that his daughters, after they were married, always had homes and land in Virginia, where they could bring up their children as they had been brought up at Highland.[14]

### Diplomat's Wife

Although the exact details of Elizabeth's life as a plantation mistress remain hidden, like the foundation of her house at Highland, her life as a diplomat's wife can be seen more clearly. She remained steadfastly at her husband's side when he travelled to Europe on behalf of the United States. Her first trip took her to Paris, when James served as Washington's minister to France from 1794 to 1797. She returned to France in 1803 when her husband was appointed Jefferson's special envoy, specifically to negotiate the Louisiana Purchase, and later lived with James in London when he served as the minister to Great Britain from 1804 to 1807.

During her first stay in Paris, Elizabeth made a striking impression on the French. Dressed in the latest fashions and speaking the language effortlessly, she was applauded as "La Belle Americaine" when she attended cultural events throughout the city. She, in turn, entertained politicians and diplomats along with foreign visitors at the house her husband purchased on Rue de Clichy. Her most memorable parties were held every Fourth of July in tents set up in the garden of her new home. Here she encouraged her guests to celebrate not just the American Revolution but the French Revolution. Showing even more appreciation for French culture, she sent her daughter Eliza to a boarding school run by Madame Jeanne Campan, a former lady-in-waiting to Marie Antoinette, where Eliza formed a lifelong friendship with Hortense Beauharnais, the daughter of Josephine Bonaparte.[15]

Elizabeth did more than entertain dignitaries as part of her husband's diplomatic mission. She actively participated in the rescue of Adrienne Motier, the wife of the marquis de Lafayette. Worried that French officials would execute Madame Lafayette if he demanded her release, James asked his wife to pay a visit to the imprisoned woman, knowing this would cause a sensation among the Parisians. He secured one of the few remaining carriages in the city, dressed the coachmen in the finest livery, and loaded the carriage with food, wine, and other gifts. With the scene now perfectly set, Elizabeth stepped into the carriage and ordered the coachman to drive swiftly to the prison. Upon arriving there, she bravely made her way to the terrified Madame Lafayette. She calmed her with kind words in fluent French. Soon everyone in Paris was talking about La Belle Americaine's visit to Madame Lafayette. A short time later, French officials, under pressure from their own citizens, released the prisoner. James won a passport for Madame Lafayette to travel to Austria, where she could be with her husband, who was imprisoned at Olmutz.[16]

During Elizabeth's second stay in Europe, she again enjoyed her time in Paris. Now feted by Emperor Napoleon and his courtiers, she was cheered every time she set foot into a theater with the orchestra playing "Yankee Doodle Dandy." But the three years she spent in Great Britain were not happy ones. She was often snubbed by British politicians and their wives, who failed to invite her to receptions even as they refused to attend parties she had carefully planned. Society matrons confessed to her that their public disdain for her was nothing personal. They were simply retaliating against her for President Jefferson's uncouth behavior toward British officials and their wives in Washington, during a time when Britain's war with France had led to impressment of American sailors and eventually to a US trade embargo.

Elizabeth might have been miserable in London, but she would always remember Paris fondly. She incorporated her love of French culture into her life as a plantation mistress by filling her house at Highland with furnishings and artwork from France, and even more importantly into her life as the first lady, where she brought a formality to social events not heretofore seen. This formality was supported by the assistance of a staff of six servants, including, according to the 1820 census, four who were enslaved—one female and three males—and two free males. More enslaved men and free workers were also employed improving the grounds of the White House, an effort that went on through James Monroe's presidency.[17]

## A SOPHISTICATED FIRST LADY

All the strands of Elizabeth's life came together in her time as the first lady. She remained the beauty who had captivated New York society. She welcomed visitors to the White House as she once invited guests to Highland. She dressed in exquisite fashions, treating everyone politely, if rather distantly, and calmly weathering complaints from Washington's society matrons that the president's house now seemed more French than American.

Her actions as first lady should not have come as a surprise to the capital's political class. She had given a hint of how she might behave as the first lady when her husband served as Madison's secretary of state from 1811 to 1817. The Monroes purchased a townhouse on I Street and invited politicians, diplomats, and their families to enjoy quiet evenings there. Guests were welcomed into richly decorated rooms filled with fresh flowers and a dignified atmosphere that greatly contrasted with the lively celebrations of First Lady Dolley Madison. Monroe brought several enslaved women from Highland to prepare the house for her family's arrival and later to cook, clean, and attend to the many needs of her guests.[18]

### The White House as a Showplace

Although her husband was inaugurated in March 1817, Elizabeth and her family remained at the house on I Street until the following September because the Executive Mansion, which the British had burned in August 1814, was still being repaired. Now called the White House for the whitewash on its outer walls, it stood cavernous and empty with unvarnished pine floors and wet plaster in every room. Only one silver candelabra and Gilbert Stuart's portrait of George Washington had survived the fire during the War of 1812.

The new first lady was determined to transform the White House into a stunning showplace decorated like her house at Highland. On her behalf, the president ordered his agents in Paris to buy as much furniture, china, and silverware as possible. Ninety-three crates packed with treasures from Napoleon's reign made their way to the White House. Elizabeth used these items to decorate the Oval Room, later named the Blue Room for its wallpaper color, and the

Gilded Minerva clock. Courtesy of the Library of Congress Prints and Photographs Division. Reproduction Number: LC-DIG-det-4a11669 (digital file from original).

State Dining Room, the two spaces she planned to use for public receptions. The most stunning pieces included beechwood chairs covered with crimson silk and eagle carvings, a bronze and crystal chandelier holding thirty candles that once belonged to the now exiled emperor, a gold mantel clock with a statue of the Goddess Minerva, and a glittering bronze plateau to hold centerpieces on the dining room table.

There were still many rooms to fill on the first floor, but the Monroes had already spent more than $18,000 of the $20,000 Congress had allocated for the entire White House. The president pressed Congress to authorize another $30,000, which Elizabeth quickly spent on more furnishings. She was finally ready to open the White House for a public reception at 3:00 in the afternoon on New Year's Day 1818. For the hundreds of visitors who crowded into the mansion, the beauty of the rooms, filled with the finest furniture and the most elegant fixtures including porcelain urns, gilded mirrors, and delicate china was matched only by the beauty of the first lady, who greeted them dressed in a stunning gown of white and gold.[19]

*The White House as a Magnet for Visitors*

Elizabeth made equally important changes to White House protocol. She held fewer drawing rooms, themselves more sedate affairs than the celebrations of the previous administration. Following a practice she had learned in France, she also decided not to call on the wives of top government officials or seek out important visitors to the capital, whether Americans or foreigners. She expected these individuals to visit her first at the Executive Mansion. Instead of being one home among many, the White House would now become the center of Washington society.

The wives of the city's many politicians were highly offended. They had loved Dolley Madison's frequent drawing rooms at the Executive Mansion and greatly enjoyed her visits to their homes. They demanded that Elizabeth maintain these customs and even threatened to boycott the few receptions that the first lady did hold if she refused. The outcry was so great that at one point James was forced to hold a cabinet meeting on the matter. The first lady turned to her friend Louisa Adams, wife of the secretary of state, John Quincy Adams, for help. She hoped that Louisa, who had lived most of her life in Europe, would understand the need for greater formality in the White House.[20]

She asked Louisa to visit Washington's society dames on her behalf, but her friend refused, probably because her mother-in-law, Abigail Adams, a former first lady, considered the changes undemocratic. Elizabeth then asked her daughter Eliza, who had married the prominent Virginia lawyer George Hay in 1808, to make courtesy calls for her. This only made the situation worse because Eliza's highhanded personality offended nearly everyone she met. When her mother was ill, Eliza also stepped in to host events at the White House, again annoying guests with her arrogant manner and cutting remarks.[21]

Elizabeth's poor health had contributed to her decision to change White House protocol. She simply did not have the stamina to keep up the round of festivities as her friend Dolley had done. She had suffered from rheumatoid arthritis for years, with the condition worsening during her second ocean crossing in 1803. When she lived in London, she suffered from both arthritis and severe headaches. She found some relief in the healing spas of Bath, and during her husband's first presidential term, she visited the mineral waters at Sweet Springs, White Sulphur Springs, and Warm Springs in western Virginia. In her final year in the White House, she showed clear signs of late-onset epilepsy.[22]

*The White House as a Family Home*

Elizabeth did something else that ruffled the feathers of Washington society. Even as she transformed the White House into a more formal public space, she was determined to maintain her family's privacy. This new attitude was most clearly seen in the wedding she held in the East Room for her daughter Maria to Samuel Gouvernor, her twenty-one-year-old cousin, the son of Elizabeth's sister Hester. Like her mother, Maria was seventeen when she married. Maria was a pleasant young woman, much more popular in Washington than her sister Eliza was. Her husband, the personal secretary to the president, was also well liked. Their wedding was held on the evening of Thursday, March 9, 1820, with only the immediate family and a small group of friends in attendance. Even the cabinet members and their families were not invited.

The first lady hoped to keep the wedding a small, private affair just like the one she had held at Highland for her daughter Eliza. But there was such an outcry in Washington that she decided to hold a larger reception after Maria and Samuel returned from their honeymoon a week later. The celebration was memorable for the fact that Elizabeth left the receiving line and went freely among her guests, chatting with everyone. She even agreed that more celebrations could be held for her daughter and son-in-law throughout the city.

On March 20, a ball in the couple's honor took place at the house of Commodore Stephen Decatur and his wife on Lafayette Square. But when Decatur was killed in a duel just two days later, all further celebrations were cancelled. Elizabeth had done her best to balance the needs of her family and demands of the public. But fate had intervened, allowing her to maintain her family's privacy.[23]

### A Refuge from the White House

Elizabeth found a way to escape from the pressures of living in the White House. She helped her husband design a retreat at Oak Hill, a plantation in Loudon County some thirty miles northwest of the capital. James had inherited the estate from his uncle in 1805. The original plantation included a small cottage and a farm where at least twenty-five enslaved people worked. In 1820, the Monroes planned a grander house for Oak Hill. Working with designs Jefferson had sent to them and with the help of White House architect James Hoban, they decided to build an imposing mansion, ninety feet wide and fifty feet deep, with a square central section that was framed by seven Doric columns, each thirty feet high, and flanked by equal wings.[24]

The Monroes moved into their new mansion in 1823, with the president spending most of his time there when Congress was out of session. He retired there permanently after he left office in 1825. In August of that year, the marquis de Lafayette, accompanied by President John Quincy Adams, paid a memorable call. Forever grateful to the Monroes for their daring rescue of his wife, Lafayette later sent white marble mantels from Italy for the fireplaces in Oak Hill's drawing and dining rooms.

Main house of the Oak Hill Plantation. Courtesy of the Library of Congress Prints and Photographs Division. Reproduction Number: HABS VA-1423-1 (CT).

Oak Hill did not remain a refuge for the Monroes for long. In 1826, Elizabeth lost consciousness, probably from an epileptic seizure, and fell into one of the home's fireplaces. She suffered serious burns before she was finally rescued. She was treated with laudanum and recovered but continued to suffer from arthritis, epilepsy, and gastrointestinal troubles. She also came down with serious bouts of influenza and fevers. On September 23, 1830, after suffering from a lung infection, she died in the presence of her grieving husband.

After burying Elizabeth at Oak Hill, and now saddled with debts even after the sale of Highland and its enslaved workers, who were transported to the Casa Blanca plantation in Florida, James moved into the home of his daughter Maria in New York City. He did not survive his wife for long, dying on July 4, 1831, five years to the day both Jefferson and John Adams passed away.[25]

## ELIZABETH MONROE'S LEGACY

In his *Autobiography*, James Monroe paid tribute to his wife of more than forty years, writing, "It is improbable for any female to have fulfilled all the duties of the partner of such cares, and of a wife and parent, with more attention, delicacy and propriety than she has done." But there is another fitting tribute to the first lady who wove together her experiences as a society belle, a plantation mistress, and a diplomat's wife in service to her nation. That tribute is the White House itself, which stands as a beautifully decorated public space, a magnet for visitors from near and far, and a private home where the president's family tries to live as normal a life as possible. There is still one more tribute to Elizabeth Monroe's legacy. When Jacqueline Kennedy, a twentieth-century first lady who also had ties to New York, Virginia, and France, redecorated the White House, she restored it to the way it had looked when the Monroes lived there. To this day, when people visit 1600 Pennsylvania Avenue, they see the house that Elizabeth Kortright Monroe imagined.[26]

## BIBLIOGRAPHICAL ESSAY

Note: Because the sources on Elizabeth Monroe are sparse, I offer this bibliographical essay as a guideline for historians, biographers, and the general public interested in her life and legacy.

The only full-length study of Monroe to date is James E. Wootman's short biography, *Elizabeth Kortright Monroe*. Major biographies of James, including Harry Ammon, *James Monroe: The Quest for Personal Identity*, and Harlow Giles Unger, *The Last Founding Father: James Monroe and a Nation's Call to Greatness*, trace the outlines of Monroe's life and cite the surviving primary sources related to her. The few references to her in the president's correspondence can be accessed in the Papers of James Monroe on the University of Mary Washington website. His *Autobiography* is most relevant for its tribute to his wife and its description of the rescue of Madame Lafayette. Another excellent online site for President Monroe and his friends Madison and Jefferson is the National Archive's Founders Online website.

Contemporary historians writing about Elizabeth Monroe now have access online to out-of-print books such as Howard Abbot, *The Courtright (Kortright) Family*, as well as newspapers such as New York City's *Independent Journal* that provide details missed by earlier biographers. Articles on the Monroes can also be found in lesser-known journals, such as Patricia P. Norwood, "Historians' Corner: Salon Music of President Monroe's Family," *American Music* 26, no. 1 (Spring 2008): 104–113, and Gerard W. Gawait, "James Monroe: Presidential Planter," *Virginia Magazine of History and Biography*. There are also passing references to Elizabeth Monroe in the biographies of contemporaries who knew her. Cynthia A. Kierner, *Martha Jefferson Randolph, Daughter of Monticello: Her Life and Times*, is a good example.

Historic sites and their websites related to the Monroe family are excellent sources of information. These include the James Monroe Memorial Museum and Library in Fredericksburg, Virginia; James Monroe's Highland in Albemarle County, Virginia; the Arts Club of Washington (James's home when he was the secretary of state); Oak Hill in Loudon County, Virginia (a private home periodically opened to the public); and the White House Historical Association website. Scholars and museum personnel at these sites have produced excellent publications and exhibits. The *Encyclopedia Virginia* is also an excellent source on the Monroes, with extensive related primary sources linked to the site. Meghan Budinger, *Our Face to the World: The Clothing of James and Elizabeth Monroe*, and Judith E. Kosik, *Monroe Family Recipes*, are examples of publications produced at the Highland Plantation and the James Monroe Memorial Museum and Library in Fredericksburg, respectively. Modern studies of the wives of Southern planters, starting with Catherine Clinton, *The Plantation Mistress: Woman's World in the Old South*, help place Monroe's life at Highland Plantation within a wider historical context. Recent archaeological findings at Highland, along with stories of enslaved families who worked there and their descendants, have been tracked in *Archaeology Magazine* (July/August 2017) and in major newspapers, including the *Washington Post* and *New York Times*.

Some of the first US histories written by women about women were on the topic of first ladies. Examples include Anne Hollingsworth Wharton, *Social Life in the Early Republic*, which provides one of the earliest descriptions of Monroe's entertaining style; Mary Caroline Crawford, *Romantic Days in the Early Republic*; and

Ohio suffragist Harriet Taylor Upton, *Our Early Presidents: Their Wives and Children from Washington to Jackson*. Another interesting early work is Marian Campbell Gouverneur, *As I Remember: Recollections of American Society in the Nineteenth Century*. Marian was the wife of Monroe's grandson Samuel Gouverneur. Although some of her facts are incorrect, she relays interesting stories passed down in the family about Monroe and her daughter Maria, Marian's mother-in-law. Popular modern works such as Cokie Roberts, *Ladies of Liberty: The Women Who Shaped Our Nation*, draw heavily on these older works and the primary sources upon which they were based, such as the letters of Margaret Bayard Smith, collected in *The First Forty Years of Washington Society*.

Contemporary studies of the White House and its occupants, including Paul Brandu, *Under This Roof: The White House and the Presidency—21 Presidents, 21 Rooms, 21 Inside Stories*; Ludwig M. Deppisch, *The Health of the First Ladies: Medical Histories from Martha Washington to Michelle Obama*; and Lawrence L. Knutson, *Away from the White House: Presidential Escapes, Retreats, and Vacations* often mention Monroe. The White House Historical Association website is an excellent source for images of the many purchases the Monroes made for the White House during their time there. Books on Jacqueline Kennedy, specifically her restoration of the White House to its early nineteenth-century appearance, such as James A. Abbott and Elaine M. Rice, *Designing Camelot: The Kennedy White House Restoration*, also provide insights into the life of First Lady Elizabeth Monroe, sadly, however, without acknowledging her contributions.

## NOTES

1. James E. Wootman, *Elizabeth Kortright Monroe*, rev. with additions by Daniel Preston and David B. Voelkel (Charlottesville/Fredericksburg, VA: Ash Lawn–Highland/James Monroe Museum and Memorial Library, 1987, rev. 2002), 1–26.

2. Meghan Budinger, *Our Face to the World: The Clothing of James and Elizabeth Monroe* (Fredericksburg, VA: James Monroe Museum and Memorial Library, 2009), 11–12, 17–20, 27–29, 30–31.

3. Elizabeth Monroe to James Monroe, letter, February 1794, in the Papers of James Monroe, University of Mary Washington, https://academics.umw.edu/jamesmonroe papers.

4. Harriet Taylor Upton, *Our Early Presidents: Their Wives and Children from Washington to Jackson* (Boston: D. Lothrop, 1891), 243.

5. John Howard Abbot, *The Courtright (Kortright) Family: Descendants of Bastian Van Kortryck, A Native of Belgium Who Emigrated to Holland about 1615* (New York: Tobias A. Wright, 1922), 42. There are conflicting accounts of the birth order of the Kortright daughters. John was the oldest child, but sources vary on whether Elizabeth was the oldest, second oldest, or youngest daughter.

6. Wootman, *Elizabeth Kortright Monroe*, 3–5; Harlow Giles Unger, *The Last Founding Father: James Monroe and a Nation's Call to Greatness*, rep. ed. (New York: Da Capo, 2010), 61–63.

7. James Monroe's biographers usually write that he was married in Trinity Church on Broadway, but an announcement of the marriage in New York City's *Independent Journal* on February 18, 1786, states that the marriage took place at the Kortright home. For Monroe's announcement of his marriage, see James Madison to Thomas Jefferson, letter, May 12, 1786, *Founders Online*, National Archives, http://founders.archives.gov/documents/Madison/01-09-02-0007. The original source is James Madison, *The Papers of James Madison*, vol. 9: *9 April 1786–24 May 1787 and Supplement 1781–1784*, ed. Robert A. Rutland and William M. E. Rachal (Chicago: University of Chicago Press, 1975), 48–54.

8. This statement, "too much of New York," often quoted in biographies of the Monroes, was made by William Wirt, later President Monroe's attorney general. See Harry Ammon, *James Monroe: The Quest for Personal Identity* (Boston: McGraw-Hill, 1971), 163.

9. James Monroe to Elizabeth Monroe, letter, April 13, 1787, in *The Papers of James Monroe*, vol. 2: *Selected Correspondence and Papers, 1776–1794*, ed. Daniel Preston (Westport, CT: Greenwood, 2006), 377–378. The Monroes' home in Fredericksburg is now the James Monroe Museum and Memorial Library and can be viewed online at https://jamesmonroemuseum.umw.edu.

10. James Monroe's relationship with Thomas Jefferson is covered in major biographies of Monroe, including those by Ammon and Unger. For Elizabeth's visits to Monticello, see Cynthia A. Kierner, *Martha Jefferson Randolph, Daughter of Monticello: Her Life and Times* (Chapel Hill: University of North Carolina Press, 2014), 37. Regarding Elizabeth's payment for Highland, see Wootman, *Elizabeth Kortright Monroe*, 4. For information on enslaved workers growing tobacco at Highland, see Unger, *Last Founding Father*, Chapter 8.

11. Biographers have listed varying dates for the death of James Spence Monroe and the birth of Maria Hester Monroe. The correct dates can be found in Wooten, *Elizabeth Kortright Monroe*, 7, 17, 19.

12. The best source on Highland is the James Monroe's Highland website at http://highland.org. Another excellent source with specific details on Highland and Monroe's other properties is the Ash Lawn–Highland and History of James Monroe's Land Holdings website, created by Christopher Fennel, at www.histarch.illinois.edu/highland/. For more on Monroe's Virginia properties, see Gerard W. Gawait, "James Monroe: Presidential Planter," *Virginia Magazine of History and Biography* 101, no. 2 (April 1993): 251–272. Information on the recent archaeological discovery at Highland can be found at the James Monroe's Highland website. See Traci Watson, "A Home Fit for a President," *Archaeology Magazine* (July/August 2017); Hawes Spencer, "James Monroe's Home May Not Have Been So Humble After All," *New York Times* (May 10, 2016); and T. Reese Shapiro, "At Virginia Home of President Monroe, a Sizable Revision of History," *Washington Post*, April 28, 2016, also provide descriptions of the discovery.

13. Catherine Clinton, *The Plantation Mistress: Woman's World in the Old South* (New York: Pantheon, 1982), 6–7, 17–32. Also see Judith E. Kosik, *Monroe Family Recipes*, rev. ed. (Charlottesville, VA: Ash Lawn–Highland, August 1994). An excellent source for Gabriel Prosser's

revolt can be found online at "Gabriel's Conspiracy" on the Encyclopedia Virginia website (https://www.encyclopediavirginia.org/Gabriel_s_Conspiracy_1800).

14. The account of Maria dressed in the height of fashion and playing with a spaniel, cited in major biographies of the Monroes, comes from a December 18, 1807, letter from Judge St. George Tucker to his daughter Anne Frances Bland. For an excellent study of music in the Monroe family, see Patricia P. Norwood, "Historians' Corner: Salon Music of President Monroe's Family," *American Music* 26, no. 1 (Spring 2008): 104–113.

15. Wooten, *Elizabeth Kortright Monroe*, 11–14.

16. James Monroe provided the best description of the rescue of Madame Lafayette in *The Autobiography of James Monroe*, ed. Stuart Gerry Brown (Syracuse, NY: Syracuse University Press, 2017), 82–83.

17. Wooten, *Elizabeth Kortright Monroe*, 19–21; for details on the enslaved staff at the White House during the Monroe presidency, see Matthew Costello, "The Enslaved Households of President James Monroe," on the White House Historical Association (WHHA) website (https://www.whitehousehistory.org/the-enslaved-households-of-president-james-monroe). The WHHA is working with the staffs of the James Monroe Papers and Highland to determine the identities of the enslaved people who worked for the Monroes. Surviving household records of the White House have provided the names of at least seven people who worked there at varying times: three women (Sucky, Eve, and Betsey) and four men (Daniel, Tom, Peter, and Hartford).

18. For information on the Monroe home on I Street, now the Arts Club of Washington, including Mrs. Benjamin Crowninshield's description of a party held there in December 1815 (she was the wife of President James Madison's secretary of the navy), see https://artsclubofwashington.org/history/monroe-house/. See also Costello, "Enslaved Households of President James Monroe," for more details.

19. Paul Brandus, *Under This Roof: The White House and the Presidency—21 Presidents, 21 Rooms, 21 Inside Stories* (Guilford, CT: National Book Network), 44.

20. Margaret Bayard Smith provided some of the best eyewitness accounts of Elizabeth's time as first lady. See Smith, *The First Forty Years of Washington Society, Portrayed by the Family Letters of Mrs. Samuel Harrison Smith (Margaret Bayard) from the Collection of Her Grandson, J. Henley* (New York: Scribner's, 1906).

21. Anne Hollingsworth Wharton, *Social Life in the Early Republic* (Philadelphia: J. B. Lippincott, 1902), 135–136, 184–191. Also see Mary Caroline Crawford, *Romantic Days in the Early Republic* (Boston: Little, Brown, 1912), 196–201. For a more modern work, see Cokie Roberts, *Ladies of Liberty: The Women Who Shaped Our Nation* (New York: William Morrow, 2008), 332–336.

22. Ludwig M. Deppisch, *The Health of the First Ladies: Medical Histories from Martha Washington to Michelle Obama* (Jefferson, NC: McFarland, 2015), 39–44.

23. For one of the best accounts of Maria's wedding, see Marian Campbell Gouverneur, *As I Remember: Recollections of American Society in the Nineteenth Century* (New York: D. Appleton, 1911), 256–261. Also see Upton, *Our Early Presidents*, 261–267.

24. Thomas Jefferson's designs were included in a letter he wrote to James Monroe on

June 17, 1820 (Virginia Historical Society). The Ash Lawn–Highland and History of James Monroe's Land Holdings website has information on Oak Hill. See also https://www .nps.gov/nr/travel/presidents/monroe_oak_hill.html.

25. Lawrence L. Knutson, *Away from the White House: Presidential Escapes, Retreats, and Vacations* (Washington, DC: White House Historical Association, 2013), 35–39; for information on the descendants of Monroe's slaves at Highland and Casa Bianca, see Audra D. S. Burch, "James Monroe Enslaved Hundreds: Their Descendants Still Live Next Door," *New York Times* (July 7, 2019).

26. Monroe, *Autobiography*, 56–57; see also James A. Abbott and Elaine M. Rice, *Designing Camelot: The Kennedy White House Restoration* (New York: Van Nostrand Reinhold, 1997).

# CHAPTER 4

# Reclamation of a First Lady
## Julia Gardiner Tyler's Pursuit of a Federal Government Pension

Christopher J. Leahy and Sharon Williams Leahy

"We look upon you in the South as one of our own possessions," C. F. Walker wrote to Julia Gardiner Tyler in January 1864, just after the former first lady fled Sherwood Forest, her home in war-torn Charles City County, Virginia, for the safety of her mother's house on Staten Island. At forty-three years of age, Julia was considered thoroughly Southern. After all, she *had* lived the majority of her adult life in the Tidewater region of the Old Dominion. Nearly twenty years earlier, she had married the much older John Tyler, tenth president of the United States and slaveholding owner of a wheat plantation. The charming and strikingly beautiful twenty-four-year-old "reigned" over the social functions at the White House for the last eight months of her husband's term. At the close of Tyler's presidency, the two embraced their position at the apex of Southern plantation society. Although her life with John did not quite match the financial affluence into which the New York native was born, Julia's marriage assured her, in her mind, a more important benefit—the lifelong social prominence and status that came from being the wife of a president.[1]

The couple's sudden and quiet wedding in New York City on June 26, 1844, took the press and the public by surprise. The thirty-year difference in age between the president and his young bride was an aspect of their union that settled in the minds of their contemporaries and even prompted ridicule in some quarters. George Templeton Strong, a New York lawyer Julia's age, expressed his disapproval of the president in colorful fashion, albeit privately. "Poor, unfortunate, deluded old jackass," he sniffed to his diary. "It's positively painful to think of his situation, and the trials that lie before him." The happy couple, of course, preferred the congratulations of friends, who toasted them as "The Union of the Useful and the Beautiful."[2]

After she was ensconced as first lady, the Northern-born Julia amplified the Southern cordiality her husband exhibited toward visitors to the Executive Mansion by willingly engaging the public and creating a "court" during social occasions that many observers in Washington compared favorably with the finest of Europe. Partisan newspapers, however, motivated by their animus toward the unpopular president, often took shots at Julia, exaggerating or mischaracterizing what went on at the White House. They ridiculed what they interpreted as her pretensions to royalty. "Mrs. Tyler appeared with a muslin cap in the shape of a crown!" one paper gleefully exclaimed, adding its refrain to what soon became a tired narrative. Julia actually avoided ostentation and dressed tastefully in either white or black because she was still in mourning for her father, who had died in the February 1844 *Princeton* explosion, which took the lives of two cabinet officials and several others. The young first lady grumbled privately about her press coverage in letters to her family but took her cue from her husband and became gracious and hospitable to all who attended her functions. After the Tylers left Washington in March 1845, Julia looked forward to establishing Sherwood Forest as an extension of that Southern hospitality and quickly adapted to the culture, customs, and political ideology that made Virginia society so different from that of New York.[3]

Julia's youth was undoubtedly one reason for her adaptability, but it was certainly not the only one. Perhaps more importantly, she possessed a natural elasticity of mind. She did not dwell on things she could not change. If she was to be the wife of a president, mistress of a plantation, mother of seven children, and later an impoverished widow, she made the best of each situation in which she found herself. She thought *executively*. Right or wrong, after she made a decision, she carried it out with almost military purpose, without regard to the opinion of others or what was expected of women at the time. Even at a young age, she barked orders to family and friends alike, marshalling the forces to think, say, and do all she required and would sometimes, for good measure, conclude her instructions with an imperious "Do you hear?"[4]

So, when Julia suggested to President Andrew Johnson on a visit to the White House in 1868 that not only should there be portraits of presidents adorning the walls of the mansion but also likenesses of their wives, it was no surprise she acted upon the idea directly. She had the perfect portrait in mind—one of herself. Julia felt strongly that the public would find portraits of the "ladies who had helped to dispense the hospitalities of the Executive residence" both "interesting and proper." She believed the ladies who preceded and followed her would be pleased with the idea and would, in time, add their own portraits to the White House collection.[5]

Just before Johnson left office in March 1869, Julia shipped her portrait to the White House, expecting that it would be hung on the wall right away; she even directed him to hang the portrait in one of the first-floor reception rooms. These were the rooms Julia believed most appropriate for a portrait of a former president's wife. The Blue and Green Rooms were the locations of her greatest triumphs as first lady, where she played the role of "principal actor" while her husband was president and where a crowd of people visiting the White House on July 4, 1844, demanded to see her. "Where is the bride?" they asked the president. "We have come to see Mrs. Tyler!"[6]

Julia donated this particular portrait not solely for the purpose of adding to the White House collection; it was not merely an act of benevolent generosity. She wanted to reinforce the point that her marriage to a sitting president in June 1844 made her first lady. Donating the portrait, then, represented a shrewd first step of her strategy in a ten-year quest for Mrs. Ex-President Tyler to reclaim her standing as first lady and later to obtain a pension from the federal government.[7]

Unfortunately, the portrait did not immediately grace the White House wall, as Julia had in mind. Johnson left the task of hanging her portrait to his administrative clerks. They found the three-quarter-length portrait by Francesco Anelli in its packing crate, but instead of hanging it in one of the easily accessible first-floor reception rooms, the clerks relegated the portrait to the attic "next to some rubbish."[8]

After the birth of her first child, Julia had wanted a portrait to commemorate her time as the "Bride of the White House." Therefore, she chose to wear her smooth, ivory wedding gown for the painting. Instead of the wedding veil crowned with the wreath of orange blossoms she wore on her head in June 1844, Julia wore the diamond Feronia her father had given her before his death. In her hand she held an exquisite ivory fan. Anelli's critics had noted his unfortunate penchant for portraying his subjects as "doughy," and his less-than-superior technique is evident in Julia's somewhat thick arms. Nevertheless, the portrait showed Julia as she would have liked to have been pictured two years after her marriage: as a young mother; a glowing, healthy woman; and the bride of a former US president. It had taken Anelli two years to complete the portrait (in 1848), and he signed the back of the canvas using the Italian spelling of Julia's first name, "Mrs. Giulia Gardiner Tyler in her twenty-sixth year." Johnson's staff was clearly unconcerned with displaying the portrait, however, and thus unwittingly thwarted Julia's opening salvo in her effort to reclaim her status as a first lady.[9]

Why did Julia need to reclaim that status? For one thing, the short duration

Julia Gardiner Tyler in her wedding gown, painted by Francesco Anelli, 1848. Julia sent
this painting to President Andrew Johnson in February 1869 with instructions to hang
it in one of the first-floor reception rooms of the White House, but it was not displayed
until Julia Grant hung it in her parlor in 1871, the first portrait of a first lady to adorn the
walls of the Executive Mansion. Courtesy of the White House Collection, White House
Historical Association, Washington, DC.

of her tenure as first lady no doubt made her forgettable to some. But there was more to it than that. Put bluntly, by 1869, many Americans did not care about her—or *for* her. In the view of much of the public as well as much of official Washington, she had lost her standing as first lady because of her association with the South. Her marriage to the only US president to renounce his citizenship and join the Confederate government; her own overt support for the slavery system, which underlay the Confederacy; and her approval of Southern independence all had marginalized her and placed her into the difficult position of having to campaign for financial benefits she believed were rightly hers. She was forced to recast herself and shed the stigma of being on the losing side of history.

Julia's Southern identity began to take shape soon after she married President Tyler, as she became a willing partner in his efforts to secure the annexation of Texas. Having abandoned any hope of winning a term in his own right by June 1844, Tyler pursued annexation in large part because he wanted a legacy as president that would overshadow the ignominy of having been read out of the Whig Party. By the time Julia became first lady, the annexation of Texas had become a sectional issue in addition to a partisan one. Secretary of State John C. Calhoun had tied Texas directly to the South with his infamous Pakenham letters in April 1844, which, in the words of one scholar, made clear that "annexation equaled defense of slavery."[10] Julia revealed no discomfort with this fact and even went out of her way to aid her husband's campaign to bring Texas into the Union by lobbying politicians on behalf of this objective at White House levees and dinners. She recognized how important annexation was to her husband and took it upon herself to craft an active role of first lady that made the most of what historian Catherine Allgor refers to as the "unofficial space" of Washington. A treaty that would have provided for Texas annexation had failed in the US Senate before President Tyler married Julia, so he used a joint resolution of Congress to finally accomplish what he always maintained was his masterwork. Annexation, of course, exacerbated sectional tension, led—indirectly—to the Mexican American War, and ultimately placed the nation on the road to the Civil War. President Tyler bore some of the blame for that disastrous outcome; Julia was tarnished by association. Her time as first lady had "Southernized" her and transformed her sectional allegiance—all to her detriment, at least in the court of public opinion.[11]

President Tyler aided this transformation by traveling with his young wife to Charles City County, Virginia, and taking her to Sherwood Forest for a five-day visit during the couple's honeymoon in July 1844. Eager to show off his new estate, which he had purchased two years earlier and partially renovated to make it suitable for his retirement from public life, Tyler was especially keen to make the first lady aware of her future role as a plantation mistress, including close responsibility for the more than sixty enslaved people who lived and worked on the farm. He recognized that becoming accustomed to slavery entailed the most difficult transition Julia would have to undertake after marrying into a prominent Southern family. He also likely hoped that her daily interactions with the enslaved people in the White House—notably an older woman named "Aunt Fanny" Hall—would make her more comfortable with the institution. Julia initially expressed unease with the new role she would ultimately play, however, writing to her mother that she would make Sherwood Forest "as pleasant as I can *under the circumstances.*" When the couple returned to the plantation for good after leaving Washington, the former president made clear he would defer to his wife on household matters and gave her the latitude to instruct the enslaved people as she saw fit. She eventually put aside her misgivings about slavery and accepted the institution's central place in her life as a transplanted Southerner. No doubt, her association with Fanny Hall, who returned to Virginia with the Tylers, eased her transition.[12]

Indeed, as time went by, any moral qualms Julia might have entertained about slavery seemed to trouble her less and less. Moreover, she adopted John's view—fairly typical in the antebellum South—that Southerners alone should determine the fate of their peculiar institution. In 1853, Julia penned a lengthy rejoinder to Great Britain's duchess of Sutherland. The duchess, along with several other prominent women in her circle, had signed an open letter calling on women in the American South to use their superior moral qualifications and the spirit of Christian charity to press for the abolition of slavery. For one week, Julia agonized over successive drafts of a response, using her husband as a sounding board. The *Richmond Enquirer* published the final version of Julia's open letter, which was soon reprinted in the *Southern Literary Messenger,* with its wide readership. Julia took the duchess of Sutherland to task for meddling in Southern affairs and shot back that if the British aristocracy really wanted to bring about moral reform, they should look no farther than the laboring poor in their own country or in Ireland. Those wretched souls, she argued, were far worse off than the enslaved people living and working on plantations like hers.[13]

Julia received hearty congratulations for her letter from Southerners, many of whom also no doubt enjoyed the fact that she had put women from Britain in their place. Of course, there was a different response in the North. Julia did not subscribe to the "positive good" defense of slavery many Southerners found appealing as abolitionist assaults became more militant during the 1830s. Her view instead seemed to be that slavery was a necessary evil, a view that comported with that of her husband. Most Northerners made no such distinction. By taking a public stance and by immortalizing that stance in writing—that is, by providing evidence that would live on—Julia subjected herself to invective from people in the North. In their eyes, she had defended the South and slavery—and many would hold it against her long after the fact. Northern memories of the letter made her uphill climb to regain her status as first lady even steeper.

There was more to it than that, however. During her marriage, Julia willingly adopted her husband's values as her own and took steps of her own volition to solidify her status as a Southerner. What perhaps most damaged her reputation, though, and what became the most difficult part of her history to overcome as she sought to reclaim her status as first lady and pursued a federal pension was something over which she actually had no control. In April 1861, her husband voted with the majority in Virginia's secession convention to sever the Old Dominion's connection to the Union he had once led. Julia Tyler supported this fateful step after it became apparent Tyler believed there was no alternative. A short time later, he became a member of the provisional Confederate Congress, again with her endorsement. The former president was in Richmond—with Julia and their baby daughter, Pearl—on January 18, 1862, preparing to take his seat in the regular Confederate Congress, when he died.[14]

The Northern public thus remembered John Tyler as the "traitor" president. The disdain ran deep. Northern newspapers barely mentioned his death. President Abraham Lincoln kept flags in Washington flying at full mast in the days after Tyler's passing, refusing to honor his predecessor and punishing him for his connection to the rebellion. The consequences of what her husband had done were nearly catastrophic for his wife. Had he simply stayed out of politics and let younger men take up the Confederate banner, he would have spared her unnecessary hardship. By selfishly entering the political game one more time, he had unwittingly fashioned an indelible image that stuck to the former first lady long after he—and the Confederacy—vanished from the scene.

Julia Tyler compounded the damage. She spent the years of the Civil War as a Southern partisan, a position she maintained even after moving back to New York at the conclusion of the war. Her Confederate sympathies poisoned her relationship with her brother, David, who was pro-Union, and played a role in a bitter legal dispute between the two siblings over their mother's will. Moreover, a highly publicized incident that occurred in the wake of President Lincoln's assassination in April 1865 further solidified Julia's reputation as a staunch Southerner. One rainy evening, three Staten Island young men forced their way inside her mother's home and demanded the rebel flag they believed was hanging somewhere in the house. After terrorizing Julia's children, the hoodlums made off with a piece of bunting hanging over the mantel in the parlor. The offensive fabric was not a Confederate flag but merely a piece of cloth Julia's late sister, Margaret, had fashioned into a colorful design years before.

Newspaper accounts of the incident tended to skip over this detail, however, choosing instead to portray what had happened as the justifiable persecution of a secessionist. Julia countered the claims of the young men who had invaded her home by appealing to some highly placed connections in the Union Army, but the negative image of her in the public mind lingered, and she realized that her status as a former president's widow—*that* president's widow—afforded her little clout and offered her no protection. It was as if people did not care to remember that she had been first lady at all. She really was a Southern "possession," just as C. F. Walker had said, and nobody else wanted her.[15]

There were other indications she had lost the status and social standing she had enjoyed as first lady. Reporting her visit to Washington in July 1868—the one that took her to the White House and an interview with President Johnson—a capital newspaper gloated that Tyler "demeans herself in private and public." Her presence in Washington still merited attention, but her motives for being there were suspect. Another newspaper reported with gratification that Julia was the only widow of a president not awarded the benefit of sending mail with free franking. Congress conferred the privilege on Sarah Polk, Mary Lincoln, and other widowed first ladies before them but conspicuously ignored Julia. One smug article later noted that she had never been granted the privilege, "her husband having died during the rebellion, to which he was lending his aid." As an avid reader of four to five newspapers a day, Julia no doubt catalogued all of the insults and concluded that many people believed that because she was a Southerner and Confederate sympathizer, she deserved only pity, or worse, derision. "The widow and the fatherless are only remembered and regarded it seems in the Litany of the Prayer Book, or in times of prosperity and peace," she complained at one point to William Cullen Bryant, editor of the New York *Evening Post.*[16]

Her allusion to prosperity is significant because Julia also realized that her poverty diminished her in the eyes of many people and further contributed to her loss of status. She had counted on an infusion of cash from the settlement of her mother's will, but mounting legal bills and her brother David's unwillingness to give quarter to her or her children forestalled that possibility. Squaring off in court "against the brutality of a worthless brother," Julia had the misfortune of seeing her name in the papers as her case made its way through the New York state legal system. The financial losses that accompanied the case were devastating. Even the court's final decision to award Julia three-eighths of her mother's real estate in New York City became little more than a pyrrhic victory, as a hefty mortgage, past-due rents, and maintenance costs on the properties chipped away at the financial benefits and but "faintly supplie[d] [her] necessities."[17]

The situation concerning her properties in Virginia was no better. The war had left Julia and most other planter families in the South in straitened circumstances. As historian Bruce Levine put it, their "vaunted world of privilege and power had come crashing down around them." Vast property holdings before 1861 did not guarantee financial solvency. Julia clearly understood this. "It seems to me the more a person has of land in Va. at present the worse he is off," she lamented in 1868. "You cannot imagine the depression there in every respect," she wrote to her lawyer, William Evarts. Sherwood Forest had been mortgaged several times—some by her husband and some during her widowhood. Julia was sued for unpaid taxes. Indeed, she almost lost the property to creditors. Her summer house near Hampton, Virginia—Villa Margaret—which she had purchased with her own funds in 1858, had been commandeered by the American Missionary Society. Under terms established by the postwar Confiscation Act, the society used the property to shelter Northern women who had come to the Old Dominion to teach people who had been enslaved in the area to read and write. Julia tried in vain to force the society to pay a fair rent for the property. The US War Department, which had overseen the operation, agreed to pay four dollars per month, a sum Julia found insulting. She sold the six-acre property in 1874 at a considerable loss.[18]

Then there was the cost of educating her sons. Julia struggled to provide for her seven children and took seriously her obligation to place the boys, especially Gardie and Aleck, the two oldest, in the best possible position to succeed in the world. In fall 1865, the boys (along with their cousin Harry Beeckman) traveled to Germany as expatriates and enrolled in school there. Julia sent what little money she could but found herself stretched thin. Aleck thrived in Germany despite the financial challenges, however. He eventually volunteered to fight on the German side in the Franco-Prussian War. Gardie found little to interest him academically in Germany and returned to the United States before his brother, enrolling in Washington College (shortly thereafter Washington and Lee) in Lexington, Virginia, in spring 1868. He graduated one year later. Somehow, Julia had cobbled together enough funds to accomplish what she had set out to do: give her sons a favorable start.[19]

Her efforts continued as the boys sought to establish themselves in their careers. Julia used her connections to prominent people—mostly politicians—to place her sons into positions of gainful employment. Her success at cultivating these connections indicates that she had not completely lost her status. Apparently, even a tarnished first lady had *some* clout. She had not entirely squandered her social currency—and she aimed to use what little she had for good effect. Julia embarked on a systematic campaign of correspondence with sympathetic politicians to enlist them to work on her behalf. Her lawyer, Evarts, was the most prominent of these men. A powerful and well-respected figure in Washington and a true insider, he had been President Johnson's attorney general and the chief lawyer for his defense during his impeachment trial. He eventually championed Julia's cause as she sought the federal pension. He also did what he could to aid her sons Lyon and Lachlan. She relied on him and was not above stroking his ego. "One word from you . . . would go much farther [*sic*]," she wrote in a letter seeking a reference from Evarts for Lachlan. Julia possessed a unique gift for flattering people—especially men—without appearing obsequious. Equally effective was her ability to enlist their help without formally asking for it. "A few kind friends to urge my cause before Congress would doubtless ensure my success," she wrote to US Representative Alexander H. Stephens of Georgia during her campaign for the pension, "and your kindness and eloquence I trust I may depend upon." Her way with words usually had the desired effect, and her political allies went to bat for her almost without giving it a second thought.[20]

Shrewdly, Julia enlisted help from both sides of the partisan divide. Evarts was a Republican. Stephens, a Democrat, had of course been vice president of the Confederacy, a fact that offers its own irony. Julia herself was no partisan. Indeed, although her allegiance remained with the South, she had no time for either side's effort to refight the Civil War through the politics of Reconstruction. She also recognized that Northerners who "waved the bloody shirt" stood in her way and served as a barrier to her winning a pension.

Her reclamation project received a boost in 1869, when Mrs. E. F. Ellet published *Court Circles of the Republic*, a book that chronicled Washington society and provided anecdotes of the first ladies. The section of the work devoted to Julia was brief, befitting the eight short months of her tenure as official hostess, but Ellet praised the "elegance and refinement" of her White House receptions. Ellet also mentioned Julia's letter to the duchess of Sutherland, writing that it "met with universal commendation," a comment that subtly made the point that what Julia had done in 1853 in defending slavery had been within the mainstream of pre–Civil War US society.

Julia certainly recognized that Ellet's book would remind readers of her time at the pinnacle of Washington society. But she sought to drive the point home by sending the Anelli portrait of herself and $100 to an engraver named Hall, whose expert rendering of Julia's likeness adorned the pages of *Court Circles of the Republic*. The visual reminder of her marriage to a sitting president neatly complemented Ellet's text. Moreover, the near simultaneous release of the Ellet book and Julia's decision to send the portrait to President Johnson demonstrates that she took proactive steps to reclaim her status as first lady.[21]

A short time later, a woman named Laura Holloway began a writing project that aimed to flesh out the stories of the first ladies. Sensing an opportunity to help shape the record, Julia provided Holloway a detailed written account of her life she thought would serve as the basis for the book's coverage of her. But the book that resulted, *The Ladies of the White House*, first published in 1870, devoted all of one sentence to Julia's stint as first lady and did little credit to either author or subject. The sparse treatment remained in subsequent editions of the book. Despite Julia's best efforts in this case to shape the public's impression of her, Holloway's book added little to her campaign to reclaim her status as first lady. The work did not damage Julia's reputation any further, but she must have been disappointed that more was not done to enhance her image.[22]

Always one to take the world as she found it, Julia did not dwell on her disappointment. She also made a conscious effort to discipline herself against becoming bitter in the face of slights and criticism that made rehabilitating her image so difficult. She was determined to "make the best of it." Imparting this life lesson to her son Lyon, Julia wrote that doing so would "be the means of satisfying your feelings much better than by showing your dislike and opposition. That is the way to *triumph*—to make your enemies even speak well of you."[23]

Dealing with her situation philosophically only went so far, however. Julia looked for other opportunities to be proactive in her quest to reclaim her status as first lady. Accepting invitations to social events in Washington became a potent weapon in her arsenal, and it was all the easier to do after she moved to Georgetown for a bit in the early 1870s. On one occasion, she received an invitation to lunch with Laura Cooke, the wife of Henry Cooke, the governor of the District of Columbia, and several other notable Washington women. To Julia's delight, when Laura introduced her as "Mrs. Ex-President Tyler," some of these capital denizens stepped forward and told her that they had met her years before at White House receptions. "I was enthusiastically received," Julia related to Lyon and "was taken by surprise" at the "warmth of my old acquaintances." She attended a party in January 1873 in the company of the Union's foremost military hero (and current president), Ulysses S. Grant, and his wife, Julia, demonstrating that she had followed her own advice in making "an enemy think well of you." Deliberately engaging the Washington social scene forced society to forget her Southern sympathies from a decade before. Even better was an invitation President Rutherford B. Hayes's wife, Lucy, tendered in spring 1878. Standing beside Lucy and receiving guests at a White House levee, Julia told a reporter she "felt like Mrs. Madison," and she made a point to tell the scribe she "never forgot or neglected to formally invite Dolley [Madison] to assist at my receptions," a comment meant for Lucy's ears as much as for those of the reporter. Dolley, Julia added, "never failed to formally accept" her invitations and always referred to Julia in her notes as "Fair Bride." Requests for her to appear at these social functions pleased Julia immensely, and they helped—slowly—to raise her profile in Washington in a positive way.[24]

Julia recognized the benefits of her reentry into Washington society. Ultimately, she perceived that in order to secure the pension, she would have to make it more compelling for people to remember that she had been first lady than for them to recall that her husband had turned against the United States and that she had supported the Confederacy. The annual payment would serve as the best evidence that she had finally succeeded in her reclamation project—that her name and status had been restored.

Ironically, the plight of the widow of the foremost symbol of the Union and the Northern war effort spurred Julia to pursue the pension in the first place. In fall 1867, Mary Lincoln attempted to sell the clothing and jewelry she had worn as first lady to make up for a severe shortfall in her finances. Her wardrobe went on public display at a store on Broadway in New York City. The result was a disaster. A gleeful press excoriated Mary for her "second-hand clothing sale." The ensuing scandal was further inflamed by the book Lincoln's seamstress, Elizabeth Keckly, published in 1868—*Behind the Scenes, or Thirty Years a Slave, and Four Years in the White House*. Julia took to the newspapers to defend the unpopular Mary, expressing her mortification in a letter to the editor that the former first lady had been "made the butt and object of ridicule because she chose to improve her low pecuniary condition by the sale of her useless wardrobe and ornaments." Julia also noted that Mary "had appealed in vain for aid to the admirers of her deceased husband, who should only have been too glad to have given it."[25]

Julia's sensitivity to the ill treatment accorded Mary reflected her own "low pecuniary condition" in 1868, and through her defense of the Great Emancipator's widow, Julia first began to toy with the idea of pursuing her own pension from the US government. Ironically, her husband had established the precedent of awarding widowed first ladies money from the federal coffers. In summer 1841, just months after his assuming the presidency, President Tyler signed a bill into law that granted William Henry Harrison's widow, Anna, a one-time payment of her husband's yearly salary of $25,000. Zachary Taylor's widow, Margaret, received a similar payment in 1850. Continuing the practice, Congress actually awarded Mary Lincoln a slightly prorated lump sum of her husband's 1865 salary, which she quickly spent.[26]

Julia increasingly came to believe that as a former first lady, she was entitled to federal largesse. In 1868, when she was defending Mary, she had no dollar amount in mind; she had not yet begun to think in specific terms. Her inchoate thoughts about a pension began to crystallize one year later, however, as Congress awarded Mary an annual sum of $3,000. By 1870, Julia had decided to pursue her own pension, and she pressed her case with Evarts, Stephens, and US Representative John Goode of Virginia. Making oblique reference to the tenor of debate in the United States over Reconstruction and the readmittance of the

Southern states back into the Union, she argued that there "would certainly be no sincerity in the assurances of justice and impartiality" prevalent at the time "if my appeal is not responded to in the same manner as Mrs. Lincoln's, for whom a pension was without difficulty agreed upon."[27]

Yet, Mary did not return Julia's favor and made clear she believed her counterpart deserved no pension. Julia's secessionist identity was the principal reason, though Mary's misapprehension that Gardiner money was still plentiful also played a role. "A woman who was so bitter against our cause during the War," Mary declared, who had access to "much Northern property and money," and who was "so *fearful* a Secessionist—Our Republican leaders will, I am sure, remember ALL THIS and the Country will not have fallen upon such evil times as to grant her impudent request." Although most members of Congress probably paid little heed to Mary's sour grapes, Evarts gauged the timing for Julia's pension application considerably less than propitious. In the midst of the battle over Radical Reconstruction, and with the Civil War still an open wound to most Americans, sectional antagonisms likely meant Congress would look unfavorably upon a Southern first lady's claim to a pension. Evarts therefore advised Julia to shelve her plans for the time being. Disappointed, Julia nevertheless duly complied. "Of course I shall withdraw the Petition *in toto*," she wrote to Evarts.[28]

The former first lady had another reason for withdrawing her petition for a pension at that time: the opposition of her two oldest sons. In a letter to Goode, she mentioned that one of her sons (probably Gardie) expressed "himself so strenuously against such a step that I will recall it for his satisfaction." Gardie and Aleck resented their mother's pursuit of a pension because they believed she was supplicating herself before the people who had defeated the South in the war. The young men did not adopt Julia's attitude that it would be better to bury the hatchet and put sectional animosities aside. However, they were not yet in a position to help alleviate her financial difficulties. Thinking strategically, Julia bided her time until she could submit the pension petition again.[29]

In the meantime, the rehabilitation of her image continued apace. Julia attended social functions in Washington whenever she could, and she continued to display her customary assertiveness. At one point, she did so with a creative flourish, dispatching a letter to the editor of the *Washington Post* she signed only as "Lady Subscriber." Julia quoted with approval a recent article in the paper that proclaimed, "The Government in honoring and protecting those ladies who shared the honors and privileges of *its highest* office honors itself." She then continued with her own suggestion—again, proffered pseudonymously—that the widows of presidents should receive pensions of at least $10,000 per year "so that they might be placed above want, and enabled in some measure to meet the requirements their actual position in the society the country imposes upon them." Pointing out that there were four such widows—herself, Sarah Polk, Mary Lincoln, and Lucretia Garfield—"Lady Subscriber" argued that there should be "no invidious distinctions" made between the women; all four deserved the pension.[30]

Julia's letter to the newspaper editor captures the essential elements in her simultaneous campaign to reclaim her status as first lady and win a pension from the federal government. She alluded to how important a pension would be in alleviating her (and the other presidential widows') financial difficulties. She referenced the "position" society imposed upon her as a former first lady, a station, indeed, that required money to carry out properly. Perhaps most importantly, in warning against "invidious distinctions" that might be made between the widows, she subtly urged people to put aside sectional animosities. Calling for a pension of $10,000 per year (roughly equivalent to $233,000 in 2019 dollars) was ambitious, of course.

Julia made at least one other overt move to remind Washington society of her status as a former first lady. In February 1877, she sat conspicuously in the capitol's Old Senate Chamber watching the deliberations of the special commission convened to determine the outcome of the 1876 Hayes-Tilden presidential election. After Ohio Republican Hayes emerged as the winner in the so-called Compromise of 1877, a female artist, Cornelia Adele Fassett, immortalized the commission on canvas. She embarked on an ambitious two-year project to replicate one day of the proceedings by painting all 256 people who attended and placing them in the appropriate position around one of the speakers—none other than Julia's friend and lawyer, Evarts. One of sixty women whose likenesses were captured in the magnificent artwork, Julia is listed as number 53 on the key below the painting. Her attendance at the commission meeting represented more than a mere social activity for her; she deliberately sought to be noticed. Furthermore, she doggedly ensured that her likeness would be found in the painting. According to Fassett's daughter, her mother spent "many weary months" on the work, giving sittings to "every person in the picture," some of them three or four times. Julia would have had to travel from Georgetown to the Fassett studio at 925 Pennsylvania Avenue for her sittings, which shows her determination to be among the prominent people in Washington featured in the painting.[31]

Julia's determination to reclaim her status as first lady ultimately paid off. By spring 1879, she felt she had waited long enough and made plans to resubmit her pension petition to Congress. Evarts gave his approval and maintained that the timing was right. Julia had not entirely convinced her sons that pursuing the pension was a wise idea, but she did convey to them that her financial difficulties required her to do so. Nearly nine years had passed since Congress had awarded

Mary Lincoln a pension of $3,000 per year. Reconstruction was over. By this time, too, Julia had enlisted the support of another well-placed politician—Senator Robert E. Withers of Virginia. "I am encouraged to hope for success from the precedent afforded in the case of Mrs. Lincoln, the universal prevalence of the policy of conciliation and the number of friends I possess in both houses," she wrote.[32]

Her optimism was well founded. Still, naysayers in some quarters were determined to quash her chances at winning the pension and aimed barbs in her direction. Reporting that Withers had presented Julia's petition to the US Senate in January 1880, one newspaper resurrected the animus so long directed toward the memory of her late husband. "John Tyler's widow asks Congress for a pension on the grounds that she hasn't anything to live on, and speaks of the pension given to Mrs. Lincoln as a precedent. The difference between a traitor and a patriot-martyr does not seem to present itself to Mrs. Tyler's mind." US Representative William Robinson, a Republican from New York, later remarked on the floor that Julia evidently did not suffer from a lack of funds, as she had been "a brilliant light at receptions in Washington Society." Robinson obviously failed to grasp that Julia believed she had to *act* like she had been first lady before she could be *treated* like one—that is, awarded a pension.[33]

In December 1880, Congress awarded her a yearly pension of $1,200. It was a start. In late 1881, the Forty-Seventh Congress passed a bill granting Mary Lincoln a pension of $5,000. On March 29, 1882—the ninety-second anniversary of John Tyler's birth—the House of Representatives unanimously granted Julia, Sarah Polk, and Lucretia Garfield their own $5,000 pensions, ratifying a measure that had passed the Senate unanimously a short time before. Perhaps not surprisingly, Julia received additional invitations from Washington society and favorable coverage in the newspapers. In 1883, the Washington *Evening Star* lauded a ball given by General Beale that featured "three ladies who have in times past or present, held the coveted position of 'lady of the White House.'" Alongside Mary Chester McElroy (sister of President Chester Arthur) and Julia Grant, Julia Tyler was described in the paper as the "bride" who came to the Executive Mansion in her youth and who was "still a beautiful woman." This public allusion to her as a former first lady demonstrates that her strategy and patience were finally gratified. She had at last triumphed in her quest both to reclaim her status as first lady and win congressional sanction for a noteworthy federal pension.[34]

Julia's victory was of course enormously significant for her personally. She had persevered in the face of deep-seated and long-lasting animosity toward her and her husband—and their connection to the South and the Confederacy—and had ensured her financial solvency for the last years of her life. Moreover, she had been linked with the other presidential widows, and Congress had made "no invidious distinctions" between them. She was now a first lady in good standing once again.

The symbolism of Congress awarding equal pensions to the Southern widows of US presidents—Julia Tyler and Sarah Polk—and to Lucretia Garfield, the widow of a major general in the Union Army, is revealing. Historians have pointed out that the process of reunifying the nation after the Civil War and the sectional reconciliation that brought North and South together again began in earnest after Reconstruction and had been largely completed by the first decade of the twentieth century. Perhaps members of Congress had been cognizant of the need to play their part in this process and looked at the pensions as a way to do so. Reconciliation got another boost one year later, as the US Supreme Court ruled in favor of Robert E. Lee's family in the Arlington case, in which they sought just compensation from the federal government for the loss of their estate during the Civil War. The High Court's decision demonstrated that former Confederates would be treated fairly in the nation's judicial system.[35]

Outside the halls of the federal government, however, another battle was looming—this one over the memory of the war itself. In his fine study of this topic, historian David Blight wrote that the "Lost Cause took root in Southern culture awash in an admixture of physical destruction, the psychological trauma of defeat, a Democratic Party resisting Reconstruction, racial violence, and with time, an abiding sentimentalism." More broadly, the mythology of the cause "came to represent a mood, or an attitude toward the past." Shaping this mood, Blight argues, were three ingredients: "the movement's efforts to write and control the *history* of the war and its aftermath; its use of *white supremacy* as both means and ends; and the place of *women* in its development." Julia refused involvement in the lost cause mythology. She chose to look forward and did not remain wedded to the past. She did not run from her history or repudiate her life or her actions as a Southern woman; she never rejected slavery or the system that had promoted it. But neither would she embrace a memory of the war that increasingly became a racially charged source of comfort to white Southerners.[36]

What happened to the Anelli portrait Julia donated in 1869? On September 7, 1871, an article appeared in a Pennsylvania newspaper. Recounting a recent visit to the White House, a reporter gave readers a glimpse of the daily lives of President Grant and his family. After describing the newly upholstered, light-blue satin furniture in the family sitting room on the second floor, the reporter revealed a remarkable discovery he had made: Julia's portrait. "In this room hangs the only Mrs. President," he wrote. It struck him as terribly unfair to have "one single female representative" adorning a wall of the White House. He wondered why women like Julia were considered of such "little consequence" despite the fact that they "may have exerted the widest and best influence in the real concerns of the times in which they lived." The reporter's rhetorical question of why Congress did not "make appropriations [for the portraits of wives of the presidents] as they do for [the portraits of] Presidents" was just the kind of speculation Julia had wanted to spark.[37]

We do not know if she read that particular article. Five months later, however, she got to see for herself what had happened to her portrait. On Saturday, February 24, 1872, Tyler packed her daughter Pearl and young granddaughter Julia Spencer into a carriage and drove to the White House to call on the "Executives." Julia handed her card to Fred (his last name is unknown), the White House steward, and asked that it be taken up to Julia Grant, along with her request for an audience with the first lady. In the meantime, she and the girls would tour the East Room. Mrs. Grant immediately consented to the request and asked that food be brought up to her rooms so the ladies could "have a nice little luncheon." When Julia appeared in the family parlor, the two first ladies shook hands. Julia discovered how "amiable and kindly" Mrs. Grant was and appreciated her graciousness. After their repast, Mrs. Grant showed her predecessor her old rooms and, at last, revealed the location of Julia's portrait; the magnificent painting hung over the piano in Mrs. Grant's parlor. Julia had not seen it in nearly three years. She "looked a long time" at the portrait of herself dressed as she appeared twenty-eight years before on her wedding day to President John Tyler. How happy were her prospects at that time? The sight of the portrait finally hanging in the White House "moved her to tears."[38]

"How sad," Mrs. Grant thought, for her predecessor to come back "unknown" to the White House, where she had once been its most honored mistress. Mrs. Grant wanted to "make her feel thoroughly at home." To embrace a woman at one time on the opposite side of the political spectrum showed great sensitivity and generosity. When Mrs. Grant had discovered the portrait in the White House attic soon after she and her family arrived, she sent the "splendid painting" to be cleaned and had it hung "where it should have been" all along. Mrs. Grant understood the significance of the role of first lady, and she realized that acknowledgment of the position's demands was important. Displaying the portrait, of course, also paved the way for recognition of Julia Tyler's time as first lady and fortified her for her reclamation project and her pursuit of a pension. As the wife of the only president buried in a Confederate flag and as the first lady whose likeness first hung on a White House wall, the soon-to-be-pensioned Julia Tyler exemplified as few others did the way in which Northern and Southern whites had swallowed the Civil War's conflicts to embrace a new unity that only pushed off to the future a much-needed reckoning with a deeply troubled past.[39]

## NOTES

1. C. F. Walker to Julia Gardiner Tyler (hereafter cited as JGT), letter, January 10, 1864, in "Letters from a Tyler Collection," *Tyler's Quarterly Historical and Genealogical Magazine* (hereafter cited as *TQ*) 30, no. 2 (October 1948): 97.

2. Allan Nevins and Milton Halsey Thomas, eds., *The Diary of George Templeton Strong: Young Man in New York, 1835–1849* (New York: Macmillan, 1952), 238 (first quotation); *TQ* 18 (January 1937), 158 (second quotation).

3. Lancaster (Pennsylvania) *Examiner,* February 12, 1845. On the *Princeton* explosion and its implications for the Tyler administration, see Christopher J. Leahy, *President without a Party: The Life of John Tyler* (Baton Rouge: Louisiana State University Press, 2020), chap. 17.

4. JGT to Margaret Gardiner, letter, June 19, 1845, Tyler Family Papers (hereafter cited as TFP), Earl Gregg Swem Library, College of William and Mary.

5. JGT to Julia Grant, letter, n.d. [after 1870?] (incomplete), TFP.

6. JGT to Andrew Johnson, letter, February 26, 1869, in Paul H. Bergeron, ed., *The Papers of Andrew Johnson,* vol. 15 (Knoxville: University of Tennessee Press, 1999), 483; JGT to Juliana Gardiner, letter, n.d. [July 1844], Gardiner-Tyler Family Papers (hereafter cited GTFP), Sterling Memorial Library, Yale University.

7. Theodore C. Delaney, "Surviving Defeat: The Trials of 'Mrs. Ex-President Tyler,'" in *Virginia's Civil War,* ed. Peter Wallenstein and Bertram Wyatt-Brown (Charlottesville: University of Virginia Press, 2005), 230–242, addresses Julia's pursuit of a pension in a more general way.

8. Julia Grant, quoted in *Chicago Tribune,* November 4, 1888.

9. Katherine McCook Knox, *The Story of the Frick Art Reference Library: The Early Years* (New York: Frick Art Reference Library, 1979), 139; "How President Tyler Escaped," *Inter Ocean* (Chicago, IL), October 15, 1887; JGT to Juliana Gardiner, letter, December 28, 1846, TFP; "The Executive Mansion Easily Managed," *Chicago Tribune,* November 4, 1888.

10. William J. Cooper Jr., *The South and the Politics of Slavery, 1828–1856* (Baton Rouge: Louisiana State University Press, 1978), 192.

11. On Tyler and Texas, in addition to Cooper, *South and the Politics of Slavery,* see William W. Freehling, *The Road to Disunion,* vol. 1: *Secessionists at Bay* (New York: Oxford University Press, 1990), chap. 22; Michael A. Morrison, *Slavery and the American West: The Eclipse of Manifest Destiny and the Coming of the Civil War* (Chapel Hill: University of North Carolina Press, 1997), chap. 1. On Julia's efforts to lobby for Texas annexation, see "Reminiscences of Mrs. Julia G. Tyler," in *Letters and Times of the Tylers,* vol. 3 (Richmond, VA: Whittet and Shepperson, 1884–1885, 1896), 198–199; Catherine Allgor, *Parlor Politics: In Which the Ladies of Washington Help Build a City and a Government* (Charlottesville: University of Virginia Press, 2000); for JGT as an "active" first lady, see Christopher J. Leahy and Sharon Williams Leahy, "The Ladies of Tippecanoe, and Tyler Too," in *A Companion to First Ladies,* ed. Katherine A. S. Sibley (Hoboken, NJ: Wiley-Blackwell, 2016), 152.

12. JGT to Juliana Gardiner, letter, July 13, 1844, GTFP; on Southern women's acceptance that slavery undergirded their social position and privilege, see Laura F. Edwards, *Scarlett Doesn't Live Here Anymore: Southern Women in the Civil War Era* (Urbana: University of

Illinois Press, 2000), 23. A more recent book examines the extent to which females who enslaved people actually participated in the slavery system. See Stephanie E. Jones-Rogers, *They Were Her Property: White Women as Slaveowners in the American South* (New Haven, CT: Yale University Press, 2019).

13. JGT, "To the Duchess of Sutherland and the Ladies of England," *Southern Literary Messenger* 19 (February 1853): 120–126; for analysis of the letter, see Evelyn Pugh, "Women and Slavery: Julia Gardiner Tyler and the Duchess of Sutherland," *Virginia Magazine of History and Biography* 88 (April 1980): 186–202. Elizabeth Fox-Genovese and Eugene D. Genovese, *The Mind of the Master Class: History and Faith in the Southern Slaveholders' Worldview* (Cambridge, UK: Cambridge University Press, 2005), 384–385, argue that Julia's letter was a political act and places it into the larger context of Southern women's participation in the political realm.

14. Leahy, *President without a Party*, chap. 20.

15. In some ways, JGT's experience as a female head of household during the Civil War reflected larger trends in the South, and her many responsibilities while she remained at Sherwood Forest mirrored those of women whose husbands had gone off to fight in the war. See Drew Gilpin Faust, *Mothers of Invention: Women of the Slaveholding South in the American Civil War* (Chapel Hill: University of North Carolina Press, 1996), chap. 2; see also George C. Rable, *Civil Wars: Women and the Crisis of Southern Nationalism* (Urbana: University of Illinois Press, 1989), chap. 2; on the home invasion incident, see Robert Seager II, *And Tyler Too: A Biography of John and Julia Gardiner Tyler* (New York: McGraw-Hill, 1963), 508–509.

16. Washington *National Republican*, July 24, 1868 (first quotation), December 11, 1878 (final quotation); *New Orleans Crescent*, August 12, 1868; JGT to William Cullen Bryant, letter, June 27, 1864, GTFP (second quotation).

17. JGT to Editor, letter, n.d. [1868], GTFP (first quotation); JGT to Peter Cooper, n.d. [1875 typescript], TFP (second quotation).

18. JGT to William Evarts, letter, n.d. [1868 typescript], TFP (first quotation); JGT, sale ad for Villa Margaret, n.d. [1874], TFP (second quotation); Bruce Levine, *The Fall of the House of Dixie: The Civil War and the Social Revolution That Transformed the South* (New York: Random House, 2013), 289; Rable, *Civil Wars*, 240; Seager, *And Tyler Too*, 515–516; on the Confiscation Act of 1862, which authorized the Freedmen's Bureau to gain control of more than 850,000 acres of Southern land by war's end, see Eric Foner, *Reconstruction: America's Unfinished Revolution, 1863–1877* (New York: Harper and Row, 1988), 158.

19. Seager, *And Tyler Too*, 520–530.

20. JGT to William Evarts, letter, January 29, 1879, William Evarts Papers, Division of Manuscripts, Library of Congress (first quotation); JGT to Alexander H. Stephens, letter, October 4, 1877, TFP.

21. E. F. Ellet, *Court Circles of the Republic, of the Beauties and Celebrities of the Nation* (Hartford, CT: Hartford, 1869), 361.

22. JGT to Laura C. Holloway, letter, June 15, 1886, Brooklyn Public Library; Laura C. Holloway, *The Ladies of the White House; or, in the Home of the Presidents* (1870; reprint Cincinnati, OH: Forshee and McMakin, 1881), 397–399.

23. JGT to Lyon Gardiner Tyler, letter, January 18, 1873 [typescript], TFP.

24. JGT to Lyon Gardiner Tyler, letter, January 18, 1873 [typescript], TFP; *Pittsburgh Post-Gazette*, April 19, 1878; Washington *Evening Star*, January 21, 1873.

25. Jean H. Baker, *Mary Todd Lincoln: A Biography* (New York: Norton, 1987), 267–280; JGT to Editor, n.d. [1868], GTFP.

26. John Tyler to Mrs. [William Henry] Harrison, letter, June 13, 1841, TFP; Baker, *Mary Todd Lincoln*, 263. Mary Lincoln received $22,025 of her husband's $25,000 salary.

27. JGT to Alexander H. Stephens, letter, n.d. [1870 typescript], TFP.

28. Mary Lincoln, quoted in Baker, *Mary Todd Lincoln*, 361; JGT to William Evarts, letter, n.d. [1870 typescript], TFP.

29. JGT to William Evarts, letter, n.d. [1870 typescript], TFP.

30. Lady Subscriber [JGT] to Editor of the *Washington Post*, n.d. [1875?], GTFP.

31. Cornelia Adele Strong Fassett, *Painting of the Florida Case Before the Electoral Commission*, oil on canvas, 1879, Cat. No. 33.00006, www.senate.gov/artandhistory/art/artifact/painting_33_00006.htm; Mrs. Myron A. Pearce, quoted in *Chicago Tribune*, January 6, 1898; Washington *Evening Star*, March 22, 1878. On the election of 1876, see Michael F. Holt, *By One Vote: The Disputed Election of 1876* (Lawrence: University Press of Kansas, 2008).

32. JGT to John Goode, letter, n.d. [1879], GTFP.

33. Jonesborough (Tennessee) *Herald and Tribune*, January 29, 1880; *Congressional Record*, 48th Cong., 1st sess., 1909.

34. *Congressional Record*, 48th Cong., 1st sess., 1909; Washington *Evening Star*, January 24, 1883.

35. For the process of reconciliation, see Gaines M. Foster, *Ghosts of the Confederacy: Defeat, the Lost Cause, and the Emergence of the New South* (New York: Oxford University Press, 1987), chap. 5; for the Arlington case, see Anthony J. Gaughan, *The Last Battle of the Civil War: United States versus Lee, 1861–1883* (Baton Rouge: Louisiana State University Press, 2011).

36. David W. Blight, *Race and Reunion: The Civil War in American Memory* (Cambridge, MA: Belknap Press of Harvard University Press, 2001), 258–259; Foster, *Ghosts of the Confederacy*, chap. 9. Caroline E. Janney, "'The Right to Love and to Mourn': The Origins of Virginia's Ladies' Memorial Associations, 1865–1867," in *Crucible of the Civil War: Virginia from Secession to Commemoration*, ed. Edward L. Ayers, Gary W. Gallagher, and Andrew J. Torget (Charlottesville: University of Virginia Press, 2006), 165–188, argues that a "solid core of dedicated women emerged as early as 1865 and 1866 to serve as guardians of the sacred past" (quotation on 169). JGT was not among them.

37. "How the President Lives," Carlisle (Pennsylvania) *Weekly Herald*, September 7, 1871.

38. JGT to Lyon G. Tyler, letter, February 29, 1872, TFP; "The Executive Mansion Easily Managed," *Chicago Tribune*, November 4, 1888.

39. "The Executive Mansion Easily Managed," *Chicago Tribune*, November 4, 1888.

# CHAPTER 5

# A First Lady, a Funeral, and a Legacy
## Press Coverage of the Death of Sarah Polk

Teri Finneman

In April 2018, the office of George H. W. Bush released a statement announcing that former first lady Barbara Bush was ending medical care and transitioning to palliative care. She died two days later, setting off a week of media coverage focused on the first lady's life and legacy.[1] This coverage raises questions about how the media frame the legacy of first ladies, some of whom are decades removed from office at the time of death. How a first lady is memorialized in the press provides insight not only into how she will be remembered as a historical figure but also into how collective memory and American ideals have shifted from her time in office to the time of her death.

To explore this concept further, this chapter focuses on obituary coverage of Sarah Polk, the first lady from 1845–1849. Long before Eleanor Roosevelt and Hillary Clinton, there was Polk, "well-educated, shrewdly ambitious, and politically savvy."[2] Polk also had one of the longest retirements of any first lady when she died in 1891, forty-two years after leaving office. How did the press cover a Southern first lady who had served in the pre–Civil War years and had ceased to be relevant for four decades? What insight into Reconciliation and white Southern ideals can be found in the coverage of her death? Before exploring how she was framed in death, it is important to understand how Polk lived: where she came from, how she became first lady, what she accomplished, and how she spent her post–White House years.

Sarah Childress Polk. Portrait by George Dury. Courtesy of the Library of Congress Prints and Photographs Division. Reproduction Number: LC-USZ62-25782 (b&w film copy neg.).

## AN EDUCATED AND POLITICALLY SAVVY CHILDHOOD

Sarah Childress was born September 4, 1803, and grew up near Murfreesboro, Tennessee, the third of six children of Joel and Elizabeth Childress. Her family's connections and emphasis on her education were critical not only for her own future success as a political wife but also for the future presidency of James Knox Polk. Her father was a wealthy planter, merchant, and land speculator, and her uncle John Childress was a judge. Therefore, she grew up with prominent Tennessee political figures such as Andrew Jackson attending her family's social events and becoming lifelong allies. As a result, she "became well versed in political dialogues of the day, [and] understood the complexity of issues and the stakes involved in the political game of winning and holding power."[3]

A childhood that introduced Sarah Childress to the customs of politics and political entertaining was enhanced with a formal education. Joel Childress arranged for his daughters to receive private tutoring from the principal of the all-boys school their older brother, Anderson, attended. Sarah and her sister Susan also received schooling at Abercrombie's Boarding School in Nashville before traveling 500 miles on horseback to register at the Moravian Female Academy in Salem, North Carolina, in 1817.[4] The academy was well known for its prestige as a center for higher education for women, even though such an opportunity was rare at the time. Education beyond basic reading, writing, and math for girls was considered, as Anson and Fanny Nelson note, "absolutely hurtful, disqualifying her for the obvious duties of her station—the care of the household."[5] However, the Childresses "desired their daughters to have the advantage of a large school, not only in its more comprehensive course of study, but in that deeper, keener, intellectual quickening that comes from fellowship in culture."[6] This unique opportunity ended in August 1819, when the girls received word of their father's death. Shortly before Sarah's sixteenth birthday, they were called back to Tennessee, where she and her three surviving siblings cared for their mother and shared their father's wealth, which included ownership of hundreds of acres and thirty-four enslaved workers.[7] With her school years now over, Sarah returned to the social scene in Murfreesboro, which took on new life with the city's recent designation as the state capital of Tennessee. At one of those political receptions, she might have caught the eye of James Polk.

James, eight years older than his future wife, was born in North Carolina before his family settled in Columbia, Tennessee. His father, Samuel Polk, had become a wealthy land speculator, businessman, and county judge who also mingled with the influential Andrew Jackson.[8] James's early years were encumbered with health issues until he had an operation to remove bladder stones when he was sixteen.[9] The procedure is believed to have left him sterile because he and his wife were childless throughout their marriage.[10] However, with his health improved, James studied at the University of North Carolina and then returned to Tennessee to practice law and begin his political career.

Accounts of the courtship of Sarah Childress and James Polk vary. Some believe they first met while her brother Anderson and James were classmates at the same school where she received after-hours tutoring.[11] Others question this story and whether a young adult James would have encountered a preteen.[12] Another account has Anderson introducing the couple at a political reception in the early 1820s.[13] An additional popular tale has James asking Andrew Jackson for advice on how to advance his political career and being advised to marry her.[14] One of Polk's biographers questions the latter account, however, calling it an "oft-told story of dubious veracity."[15] Regardless of how their relationship began, the couple married January 1, 1824, and—as James Polk himself would joke—his wife's expectations for him to rise politically were clear.[16]

## ADVANCING THEIR AGENDA

The Polks spent the early years of their marriage in Columbia, Tennessee, where his family resided. Like their parents, the couple also enslaved men and women on their plantations, which they managed from Columbia.[17] In 1835, the Polks moved thirty-six of these enslaved people to a cotton plantation near Grenada, Mississippi; their operation later expanded to more than nine hundred acres with fifty-five enslaved workers.[18] Like others of their time, they justified slavery as religiously predestined.[19] James Polk—and likely also his wife—further believed that slavery was not just about property rights but also "ascends far higher and involves the domestic peace and security of every [Southern] family."[20] The Polks enslaved people in their home, as well, and brought some of them to the White House.[21] Like other Southern women, Sarah believed herself a good mistress, although evidence exists of overseer brutality, poor conditions, and a rebellion at the Polk plantation in Mississippi during her ownership.[22] For Southern women at the time, this practice was considered part of doing business in the quest for higher plantation profits, not the human rights problem it actually was. The fact that Sarah did not live on the plantation on a daily basis made the matter even more abstract to her, though death rates of enslaved people on her property were higher than those at other plantations.[23]

The plantation and the toil from enslaved labor provided the financial support that allowed the Polks to focus on politics. James started his political career in the Tennessee legislature before moving on to the US House of Representatives from 1825 to 1839, the last four years of which the Democrat served as speaker.

He also served a single two-year term as Tennessee's governor between 1839 and 1841 before his unexpected, dark-horse candidacy for president in 1844. From the beginning, Sarah took an active role in her husband's work by entertaining political allies in their home, updating her husband with news, arranging speaking appearances, mailing campaign literature, and handling correspondence, a role unheard of for a woman of her era with its expectations for them to focus on the care of their home and family.[24] A Polk biographer noted that she "took her job seriously and was willing to work every bit as hard as her husband to advance their agenda."[25] She bypassed gender norms by excusing herself from after-dinner conversations with women and instead joining the men's discussions.[26] Despite this unusual move, she was considered "a favorite among the political class."[27] Her confidence, social skills, and appearance "impressed virtually everyone" in Washington and served her husband well.[28] To help cover for her personal ambition or opinions, the first lady would situate arguments with "Mr. Polk believes" or say she was helping her husband to protect his fragile health, thereby adding a feminine touch of family care.[29] A devout Presbyterian, she was adamant about going to church on Sundays and respecting the Sabbath, which she also saw as an opportunity for rest for her overworked husband.[30]

Without children or much housework in their initial Washington house—a hotel/boardinghouse shared with other members of Congress—Sarah's attention could focus solely on their joint career. The couple also found aid from their old friend President Jackson, who supported James's rise to House speaker.[31] Following Jackson's tenure as president, the Polks returned to Tennessee, where James turned his attention in 1839 to running for governor to boost his state's Democratic Party and add to his credentials as a potential future candidate for vice president.[32] During his gubernatorial races—only the first of which would be successful—Sarah sent letters to him at his campaign stops with the latest political news and expressed concerns about his health. In a letter from April 10, 1841, she assured her husband there was not anything in the newspapers that would affect his campaign.[33] A few weeks later, she expressed anxiety over his health and whether he could stand the fatigue of the campaign, writing, "It makes me unhappy to think of what you must suffer."[34] In July, she complained in another letter about a houseful of relatives she had to tend to who "made me nothing more than a servant" and kept her from working political angles on his behalf.[35] The extent of her involvement in her husband's campaigns was not widely known at the time or, as Jayne Crumpler DeFiore wrote, "she would have been subjected to ridicule."[36] Nevertheless, they worked as a political team. Their gubernatorial efforts were not enough, however, because James lost his reelection bids in 1841 and 1843.

The tide turned in 1844, when the still-prominent Jackson grew irked with

Martin Van Buren, who was making a return run for the presidency, over his lack of support for annexing Texas. Jackson shifted Democratic Party support to Polk as a compromise presidential candidate.[37] Polk faced Henry Clay, a prominent Whig and former secretary of state. Although Polk lost in his home state of Tennessee, which had shifted in recent years to a Whig state, the Polks were headed back to Washington.

### "ONE OF THE MOST POWERFUL FIRST LADIES"

After learning of their victory, Sarah Polk opened their home to well-wishers, ignoring friends' concerns that her carpet and furniture could get ruined.[38] James had promised to be a one-term president, so they knew their time in Washington was limited. At forty-one, she was one of the nation's youngest first ladies and would provide the first stable, full-term presence in that post since Louisa Adams did nearly two decades before.[39] Although they did not have children, the Polks remained close with their extended families, including niece Joanna Rucker and nephew Marshall T. Polk, both of whom enjoyed long stays at the White House.[40]

As first lady, Sarah Polk devoted much of her time to serving as her husband's private secretary by helping with letters, speech revisions, meetings with members of Congress, and political advice, continuing the political assistance she had long provided.[41] Polk biographers argue that her contributions as first lady have been largely overlooked. Amy Greenberg noted that both Polks often worked twelve- to fourteen-hour days. She highlights the first lady's ability to challenge gender norms with her political activity, calling her "one of the most powerful first ladies in history."[42] Greenberg explains that Sarah played a critical role in shaping the Democratic Party's agenda in the late 1840s and created the role of an activist first lady, becoming "the first politically effective partisan first lady, in a period when the role of women was strictly circumscribed."[43] First lady scholar Carl Anthony also noted that Vice President George Dallas felt "as if the president's wife, not he, was the second most important political leader of the nation."[44] Biographer John Bumgarner wrote that she "was perhaps better versed in the game of politics than any first lady at any time, but she never made herself offensive by a display of this attribute."[45]

To be sure, Polk received some criticism for her political interest and lack of attention to domestic matters. Some female guests at her parties complained when she left to talk with the men.[46] The most frequently cited criticism came from a woman complaining to one of Sarah's friends. The unnamed woman "hoped Mr. Clay would be elected to the presidency because his wife was a good housekeeper and made fine butter."[47] After hearing of this, Sarah reportedly replied, "Tell her I said that if I should be so fortunate as to reach the White House, I expect to live on $25,000 a year, and I will neither keep house nor make butter."[48] This story perhaps more than any other illustrates the wit and confidence of Sarah Polk.

In addition to helping her husband with official business, Polk fulfilled typical first lady requirements by hosting weekly receptions and formal dinners and wearing fashionable clothes from Paris.[49] As first lady of the Democratic Party, then staunchly Southern and in favor of limited government, she emphasized her economy with money and accepted only half of the congressional stipend for White House renovations.[50] Still, she never embraced the smaller details of White House hostessing, such as planning dinners or directing the enslaved servants, whom she said already knew their duties.[51] The four enslaved people at the White House included Paul Jennings, mentioned in Chapter 2, whom a then-impoverished Dolley Madison lent out to the Polks in spring 1845, keeping his earnings herself.[52]

An avid conversationalist, Polk reportedly recalled that during dinners with guests, "I was often so much interested in the stream of discourse that the steward thought I ate too little, and he would put away some dish he knew I liked, hoping I might enjoy it afterward."[53] Knowing the political value of entertaining, Polk frequently hosted events at the White House; abiding by her religious beliefs, however, she banned hard liquor, dancing, and card playing, which generated consternation among the Washington political elite.[54] Still, her charm and ability to be "affable and gracious to all" made her a popular first lady.[55] Although she was political, "her femininity, sociality, and virtue conformed to traditional expectations,"[56] and she continued to make a point to give all credit to her husband to appease gender conventions.[57]

That is not to say the Polk administration was not without its criticism. As a first lady during the Mexican American War (1846–1848), Polk received letters begging for her assistance and telling her of its horrors. Yet she stood firmly with her husband on the concept of Manifest Destiny and believed the acquisition of Texas, California, and New Mexico were critical achievements in US history.[58] Like other white Christian women of the time, she imagined that land acquisition was "God's work," or a religious mission to civilize "the wilderness" of the frontier and its people, again illustrating a lack of regard for the rights of people of color in what was Mexican territory.[59] She also likely understood at the time the value of additional plantation land in the South. During the war, Polk downplayed critical press reports and antiwar public opinion, dismissing it as "there is always somebody opposed to everything."[60] Her husband, meanwhile, kept quiet his continued purchases of nineteen enslaved people while in office, in part because a large number of them were children separated from their families, several as young as eleven.[61]

Overall, press coverage during Polk's first lady years offered positive reviews, undoubtedly because the public was unaware of the extent of her involvement in her husband's controversial policies. Soon after the election, the *Richmond Enquirer* ran a story headlined "Who Is Mrs. James K. Polk?" The article noted she "possesses rare cultivation of mind" and was an "amiable and attractive character."[62] A few months into her term, the *New York Herald* wrote that "her conversation is exceedingly interesting, and her manners of that affable, gentle nature, so pleasing to persons of every degree. She is intellectual, too."[63] An anonymous clergyman told the press he had heard much about her but was even more impressed after meeting Polk because "I have rarely seen a lady in whom so much personal beauty, so much dignity and grace of manners, so much ease and kindness, were blended."[64] One gossip columnist scoffed that Polk "over-dresses,"[65] but another source thought she had "excellent taste in dress" in addition to being "a kind hostess and accomplished gentlewoman."[66]

Despite all of his wife's work, James rarely mentioned Sarah in his diary during his presidency beyond noting church attendance and illnesses. Still, his affection for her was clear. He wrote how "very anxious" he was to see her when she was delayed after spending several weeks in Tennessee during summer 1847.[67] A few months after her return, when she suffered a serious illness with a chill and high fever, he expressed fear she would have "a severe attack," and he remained in her room to watch over her.[68] In a more lighthearted entry in February 1848, he made note of a social engagement with his former presidential opponent, Clay, who praised Sarah by saying he had heard good opinions of her administration and then joked that opinions of her husband were mixed. The president recorded a moment of laughter when the first lady "replied pleasantly that she was happy to hear from him that her administration was approved and added if a political opponent of my husband is to succeed him I have always said I prefer you, Mr. Clay."[69]

For her part, the first lady frequently worried about her husband's health and the strain of the presidency.[70] Both were relieved when it was time to leave the White House and believed they had accomplished what they intended.[71] With Sarah integral to his success, James's presidential record included doubling the nation through gaining Texas, the Oregon Territory, New Mexico, and California—albeit through the controversial means of the Mexican American War, which served to inflame the national tension over slavery that erupted into the Civil War a decade later. The administration also reduced tariffs and reestablished an independent federal treasury.

After the Polks completed their tenure in March 1849, their exhaustion did not stop them from a retirement tour across the South and meeting "a throng of Polk admirers" at every stop.[72] Throughout the journey, other passengers died of cholera and James became ill, but the Polks made it to Nashville in early April 1849.[73] However, soon after visiting a sick nephew, James died from the illness himself on June 15, 1849, just three months after leaving office. Sarah was now a widow at age forty-five.

### WIDOWHOOD AT POLK PLACE

She was suddenly alone in Polk Place, the home specifically bought and renovated for their retirement. The *Columbia* (Tennessee) *Daily Herald* reported the house "was practically a palace in frontier Nashville, and the grounds consisted of a full city block. It would suit the Polks' needs for entertaining, conducting business, and as a refined place for resting."[74] Sarah left her husband's study as it was the day he died, struggling with her grief until her mother came up with a solution. The granddaughter of her older brother, Anderson, needed a home and a mother figure, and Elizabeth Childress thought little Sallie Jetton could solve the widow's loneliness. Indeed, she did, as Sallie remained at Polk Place for the remainder of Sarah Polk's life, growing the family to include Sallie's husband George Fall and daughter, Saidee.[75]

Throughout the rest of her life, Polk rarely left home except to visit her mother or go to church.[76] Part of her reluctance to return social calls dated back to her years in politics, when she learned she could not possibly call on everyone who visited her, thereby risking offending those she did not go see.[77] However, she also stayed home so she would be there if anyone came by "to honor the character of my husband."[78] Visitors found her still up to date on the latest news, her personality unchanged, with its "rapid flow of thought; the vivacity of expression; her animation throughout; the quick wit; the rapid comprehending of what is said, and the ready answer."[79] Polk continued to wear black mourning clothes and devoted her life to preserving her husband's legacy by answering letters and sharing stories of his life.[80] She received frequent visitors at Polk Place, including Rutherford and Lucy Hayes and Grover and Frances Cleveland. Each New Year's, members of the Tennessee legislature visited, and parades marched by her house.[81] Rumors in the press in 1856 suggested Polk would marry president-elect James Buchanan, who served as President Polk's secretary of state.[82] This, of course, was false but illustrated continued interest in her.

After James Polk died, Sarah Polk took primary control of their plantation's management, which she continued to do from a distance in Nashville.[83] She was reported to have remained neutral during the Civil War and respectful of visiting Union and Confederate soldiers. All the same, ten of her enslaved workers left when Union forces came in August 1863, and more than half of them would join the Union forces. Polk, meanwhile, did not hesitate to write for favors for her Confederate relatives and asked Abraham Lincoln himself to reprieve four other Confederate soldiers from death sentences, a request he granted.[84]

In an 1864 story that ran in a South Carolina newspaper, Polk was quoted as refuting assertions that she was a secessionist and insisting instead she was for a restored Union; "I do not deny . . . that my womanly sympathies are with the South and that I often catch myself exulting over the success of the Confederate arms, but this is only when my reason is taken prisoner and my judgment temporarily suspended at the bidding of my sympathies, prejudices, and affections."[85] She had been advised by officials to leave Nashville as the war worsened but refused; as her friends and biographers the Nelsons wrote, "She told them that she was at home, and intended to stay at home, and that if her house should be blown up or burned up, she would pitch a tent on the lawn beside Mr. Polk's tomb and stay there."[86] Polk Place survived the war, but Nashville faced significant reconstruction. Polk, like other Southerners, now needed to adjust to life without the sacrifices made by enslaved people to support her and the finances of the plantation she had known.[87]

After the war, Polk remained a role model "for a generation of deeply religious female activists who praised her humility, her piety, and her 'clinging love and single-hearted devotion' to her husband."[88] As Greenberg notes, this Southern Christian persona was idealized by women "who believed their society was rapidly degenerating" during the rise of industrialization in the late 1800s.[89] Every now and then, reporters arrived to write stories about her, with one calling her "one of the mothers of the nation."[90] At seventy-six, Polk told the reporter, laughing, "People call every day to see me . . . to see how a woman lives that lived in the White House once, and I value the attention very highly." In 1882, that status earned her, along with Julia Tyler and Lucretia Garfield, an annual pension of $5,000, as noted in Chapter 4. In a widely shared 1884 interview with a New York *Telegram* correspondent, Polk seemed in "perfect health" at eighty-one as she reminisced about her husband's election forty years earlier.[91] The story highlighted that the first lady was her husband's "prime minister" during his administration, an interesting public acknowledgment of a first lady's involvement in presidential business that would be repeated in her obituaries, showing a shifting acceptance of women's growing roles in the 1880s.

With a better understanding of Polk's life, we delve next into exploring how the press covered her death. This requires further explanation of collective memory, the "lost cause," American journalism, and obituaries to recognize the broader context and significance of how her legacy was formed.

## COLLECTIVE MEMORY

Collective memory is a social construction of the past influenced by "the beliefs, interests, and aspirations of the present."[92] For example, after the Civil War, mythology took hold that framed the "old plantation days" in the South as more idyllic than they actually were as a means for white Southerners to cope with the instability and change that followed the war.[93] This nostalgia for an antebellum South that never existed, often abbreviated as the "lost cause," had consequences because it influenced various aspects of the culture and economy of the late nineteenth century and became accepted as "factual" history.[94] Historians Janice Hume and Amber Roessner found that Southerners similarly invented or exaggerated "salvation stories" following Union General Sherman's 1864 March to the Sea to help demoralized Confederates cope with defeat.[95] Therefore, collective memory challenges the notion of a definitive past by arguing that "tales of the past are routinely and systematically altered to fit the agendas of those recycling them into the present."[96] Collective memory benefits societies by establishing a link to the past and offering a sense of continuity and identification.[97] However, it also privileges certain accounts of the past—specifically those most agreeable to prominent influencers—over others' versions of events.[98] The extent to which historical moments are accurately recorded at the time also shapes how future generations might make sense of or alter memory.[99] The role of the media in historical preservation is also important to consider, especially because media accounts of historical events have not always been accurate.[100] With these various factors at play, distortion and alterations of history occur.[101]

At the time of Polk's death and publication of obituaries in the late 1800s, journalism had moved into its "yellow," or sensational, era influenced by the likes of newspaper publishers Joseph Pulitzer and William Randolph Hearst. With this wave of sensationalism came further interest in the current president and first lady, as evidenced by reporters who in 1886 "camped around the Clevelands' honeymoon cottage in western Maryland and spied on the couple with binoculars."[102] Women became a new key demographic for newspapers, magazines, and advertisers, prompting more inclusion of "women's news" and society pages.[103] Therefore, coverage of the first lady "intensified substantially."[104] Newspaper and magazine readers "avidly perused stories on first ladies and their families, who were glorified as idealized representations of the American spirit."[105] Increasingly, journalists also framed first ladies as icons of American womanhood because of their prominence in society and the gendered expectations of their role.[106]

How Polk's death was covered in the press is of interest both because of how many years had passed since her time as first lady and how much the nation had changed in those four decades. Studying obituaries offers insight into collective memory and can provide a "truly intimate portrait of the 'ideal American' in any era."[107] In other words, obituaries illustrate what "society values and wants to remember about that person's history."[108] Legitimizing certain characteristics over others helps determine what societies will remember about their past, and the media are thus instrumental in "creating unrealistic public illusions about America's past and present" as a result.[109] In Polk's case, the obituaries provide insight into how people of the 1890s remembered the Old South, the qualities of American womanhood embraced in the late nineteenth century, and the defining characteristics of a "successful" first lady.

## AN "HONORED AND BELOVED LADY"

This chapter examines news articles from August 14, 1891, to September 14, 1891, the first month of news coverage after Polk's death.[110] Primarily small newspapers from across the country are used here because the majority of Americans at the time read such papers.[111] Before examining the themes evident in the obituary coverage, an overview of the circumstances surrounding Polk's death and the initial public reaction as reported in the press is useful to consider.

Polk had been in "perfect health," but after going for a short drive, she became ill and died a few days later, at age eighty-seven, on August 14, 1891.[112] Readers were told she had "full possession of her mental faculties" and assured her doctors that she was ready for death and what heavenly reward came to her afterward because she had "been all my life ready to obey the summons of my Master."[113] Newspapers reported that her death was "that of a Christian" because she offered a prayer and blessing to a few relatives in her sickroom, including Sallie and Saidee, before she died.[114]

As news of her death spread throughout Nashville and bells tolled, sympathy and regret were "heard from the masses" as the city filled with "inexpressible sorrow" for the "honored and beloved lady who spent her years among the people she loved so well."[115] A Delaware newspaper reflected that her death "cuts an important link in the chain that connects the present with the past," pointing out that Polk had lived under twenty presidents dating back to Thomas Jefferson and had herself served as "an important part in the history of this great nation."[116]

Obituaries also praised Polk's moral qualities. Ohio readers were told of the "beauty and strength of her character" and that "contemporary histories and magazines are full of her praise."[117] The physician attending her was quoted as saying he "had never known a grander character,"[118] and the *Indianapolis Journal* obituary called her "an example worthy of emulation."[119] The *Fort Worth Gazette*'s story featured her "gentleness and grace and the goodness and simplicity of her life" and her "lofty exemplification of Christian womanhood."[120]

It is important to note that some newspapers printed inaccurate information. This included that Sarah Childress married James Polk when she was in her teens (she was twenty), that she had only lived in Washington and Nashville during their marriage (they lived in Columbia, Tennessee, early in their marriage), and that she met James in Columbia, South Carolina, in 1824 (they were married January 1, 1824, and attended different schools in North Carolina).[121] These instances provide examples of how some historical records and memory are amiss.

Beyond the initial explanation and reaction to Polk's death, the three main themes that emerged in obituaries of her were widespread agreement that she was one of the nation's best first ladies, a nostalgia for pre–Civil War times, and reflection on a widowhood reportedly spent in seclusion and poverty. We will explore these themes individually below before reflecting on their relevance to collective memory, American obituary culture, and first lady studies.

### "A RARE TYPE OF BEAUTY"

Obituary coverage in 1891 that centered on Polk's years as first lady emphasized her appearance, declared her one of the nation's best first ladies, and called attention to her active role in her husband's administration. The commentary about her appearance not only underscored the importance of beauty but also seemed to turn the role of first lady into a beauty contest. One North Carolina obituary described her as "extremely handsome," and another noted that "her beauty and intelligence gave her distinction among the wives and daughters of the statesmen of that day."[122] Michigan readers were told Polk was "one of the handsomest women who ever graced the White House," and Tennesseans read similar praise calling her "one of the most beautiful and dignified women that ever graced the White House."[123] She was again declared "one of the handsomest, if not the very handsomest woman" to serve as first lady.[124] An Ohio newspaper called her the "most talented and beautiful uncrowned queen of the United States."[125] This exaggerated emphasis on her beauty, which went so far as to suggest a Spanish heritage she did not possess, indicates that—already in 1891—appearance was embedded as a critical factor of American womanhood and successful role fulfillment as first lady.[126]

Obituaries did go beyond Polk's appearance to also praise her intellect and performance, further illustrating that hostess skills are an important component for a successful first lady. The *New York Times* called her a polished woman and brilliant conversationalist "beloved by every one [*sic*] who had ever met her and held in the highest respect and esteem by the nation."[127] A North Dakota newspaper obituary recalled her "rare conversational powers, keen repartee, easy grace, and kind hospitality."[128] Stories often noted that she banned dancing and refreshments in the White House but retained her popularity with weekly receptions.[129] She had "charm of manner and tact which has never been exceled by her successors."[130] All of this made her "well qualified" to be first lady.[131] Newspapers also repeated the story of Clay praising her work as first lady and the story of the guest who jokingly told her there was affliction pronounced against her in the bible, referencing Luke 6:26: "Woe unto you when all men shall speak well of you."[132] The *Seattle Post-Intelligencer* obituary noted that Polk did not have children, so she "devoted herself entirely to her duties as mistress of the White House."[133] Overall, Polk was said to be "one of the most popular and gracious women that ever presided" in that mansion.[134]

Several versions of Polk's obituary were clear about the role she played helping her husband's administration. Although, as previously discussed, obituaries in American culture are usually positive in nature, it is still notable that her "full partnership" approach to the first lady role was so revered in the 1890s. This is particularly interesting considering that Eleanor Roosevelt, Nancy Reagan, and Hillary Clinton were criticized decades later for the same approach. An Ohio newspaper said Polk was her husband's "confidant and chief counselor and did much to add to his popularity and success."[135] A North Carolina newspaper noted she was not a woman politician but "was thoroughly conversant with national matters and was interested in public questions," which, it said, contributed to her place in public esteem.[136] She was a "lady of education and charming manners" who helped her husband by marking newspaper articles for him.[137] The *Delaware Gazette and State Journal* obituary noted that Polk was "interested in all that related to her husband [and] she took pains to inform herself fully in political affairs and read all the news and disclosures of the day" and was thus "a valuable assistant."[138] Another obituary noted, "The great political success of her husband was due in a large part to the council [*sic*] of his wife."[139] Whether it was the increased focus on women as consumers, workers, and activists in the 1890s, the fact that four decades had passed, thus lessening the threat of an active wife, the politeness deemed customary for obituaries, or some other factor, Polk's published eulogies still served as a remarkable example of an American womanhood that encouraged women to be intellectual, political, and involved in "male" careers. Strikingly, this progressive framing of her first lady years contrasts with another common theme found in her obituaries: a romantic reflection of her Old South past.

## "A RELIC FROM A GLORIOUS PAST"

Most references to Polk's antebellum Southern ties were subtle, yet still alluded to this period in nostalgic tones. This often occurred with references to her father, described as a "wealthy, cultured, and hospitable planter," "a farmer in easy circumstance . . . considered rich for those days," "a prosperous farmer," a "country gentleman," and a "cultured and generous entertainer," unlike many Southerners of the 1890s.[140]

Other obituaries reflected more directly on her relationship with the Confederacy, with some claiming that she sympathized with the South during the war. The *Delaware Gazette and State Journal* told readers in an unverified account that Polk welcomed Confederate officers into her home and hoped for their success because she had "the humiliation of seeing Nashville occupied by the Union troops."[141] As for her early life, her Tennessee upbringing had been in "that beautiful portion of the South, almost a wilderness then," and hers had been a childhood filled with "contentment and tranquil happiness."[142] This editorializing provides further evidence of collective memory of a golden era in the South, as does a North Carolina newspaper headline referring to Polk as "A Relic from a Glorious Past."[143] Similarly, a Connecticut obituary alluded to the legends of Southern belles by saying Polk's death "removes one of the last surviving examples of what was best in the womanhood of an almost forgotten generation."[144] The same day, the *Pittsburg Dispatch* obituary said her death removed "a lady whose national prominence belongs to an epoch of our national history entirely distinct from the present one," and a Kansas obituary distinguished her as the last of the antebellum occupants of the White House.[145] This nostalgic phrasing about the antebellum days even from Northern newspapers contributed to buttressing Southern collective memory of the "lost cause" by mourning the end of an era that people of the more recent time did not believe could be recaptured, an era that celebrated white supremacy and the racial hierarchy of the plantation.

## "OBSCURITY AND COMPARATIVE POVERTY"

Obituaries were consistent in their descriptions of Polk's widowhood, with summaries revolving around two main points: she lived in seclusion and poverty. Some exaggerated the extent of her seclusion by noting she spent "the past 50 years" or "the past 60 years" alone, and others noted 20 years or just "the last years of her life."[146] Yet less than half a century (42 years to be precise) had passed since she was in the White House; moreover, along with Sallie's family, who lived with her, she had a steady stream of visitors with whom she actively socialized.

Stories also emphasized that Polk was "well nigh penniless" as recently as six years before her death until Congress granted a widow's pension.[147] This timeline is also inaccurate (Congress had approved the pension nine years previously).[148] Furthermore, Polk frequently entertained guests and hosted society events for Sallie and Saidee after the Civil War, thereby suggesting she had some financial reserves, although it appears money might have been scarcer by the early 1880s as evidenced by the renovations needed at Polk Place.[149] Still, this theme of obscurity and poverty persisted with writeups of how Polk lived a quiet life to the point that except for a "stray newspaper paragraph" from time to time, many Americans heard little about her or "were only reminded of her existence by her death."[150] The pitiful framing of her being broke and alone in the postwar years fits into the broader collective memory of white Americans of a grand South once in its prime now rendered desolate.

## REINVENTING THE POLK MEMORY

The obituary coverage of Polk is a fascinating mix of both progressivism and nostalgia, which served to connect her to the present and the past. The praise for her achievements as first lady, as a beautiful charming hostess, a faithful Christian who also made a significant working contribution to her husband's administration, framed her as a fitting model for her own era. This narrative reflected the 1890s with its progressivism, the first wave of feminism, and newspapers' increased interest in women readers as consumers, workers, and activists. Indeed, these illustrate how obituaries do provide "a truly intimate portrait of the 'ideal American' in any era."[151] To be sure, these descriptions of her were centered around an accurate picture. However, it is questionable if the emphasis on her political role would have been as prominent or even discussed in obituaries had she been the one to die in 1849 instead of James.

Yet the most enlightening theme to emerge from the obituaries is that Sarah's story melded with the broader collective memory story of the Old South: she was a grand woman from a romanticized time that could never be recaptured, the desolate end of which contrasted with her (and its) former glory. This perhaps helps explain how she was deemed one of the nation's best first ladies in the 1890s yet is primarily forgotten today. At the time, her story offered support for a nostalgic myth embraced by a Civil War generation fading away, at a time when Confederate monuments were being erected to reaffirm that white supremacy. Recall that collective memory is a social construction of the past influenced by "the beliefs, interests, and aspirations of the present."[152] This likely aided her legacy-building in the press at the time of her death. However, because her story was just one of many others like it, her legacy was arguably engulfed over time into this broader memory of the South rather than standing on its own.

Yet Polk's legacy should not end there. As one of the first political first ladies, her story deserves to be reexamined in the context of a trailblazer for the prominent women politicians and first ladies who came after her. The story of Polk is a complex one, to be sure. As first lady in 1848, she made no public acknowledgment of the launch of the suffragist movement in Seneca Falls, accepting her own privilege in political spheres yet not advocating it for others.[153] Her role in enslaving people also affects her legacy and needs further examination in future studies. But the significance of her political role this early in US history is an important story to tell in an era that still considers it novel for a woman to have power in the White House. For long before Edith Wilson, Eleanor Roosevelt, and Hillary Clinton, there was indeed Sarah Polk.

## NOTES

1. See, for instance, "Legacy: Barbara Bush's Approach to Policy and Politics," *NPR Morning Edition*, April 18, 2018, https://www.npr.org/2018/04/18/603476064/legacy -barbara-bushs-approach-to-policy-and-politics.

2. John Bumgarner, *Sarah Childress Polk: A Biography of the Remarkable First Lady* (London: McFarland, 1997), 11.

3. Quote from Barbara Bennett Peterson, *Sarah Childress Polk, First Lady of Tennessee and Washington* (New York: Nova History, 2002), 1; also see Jayne Crumpler DeFiore, "Sarah Polk," in *American First Ladies: Their Lives and Their Legacy*, ed. Lewis Gould (New York: Routledge, 2001), 130–144; Bumgarner, *Sarah Childress Polk*.

4. Anson and Fanny Nelson, *Memorials of Sarah Childress Polk* (New York: Anson D. F. Randolph, 1892).

5. Nelson, *Memorials of Sarah Childress Polk*, 4.

6. Nelson, 5.

7. Nelson, *Memorials of Sarah Childress Polk*; Bumgarner, *Sarah Childress Polk*; Amy Greenberg, *Lady First: The World of First Lady Sarah Polk* (New York: Alfred A. Knopf, 2019).

8. Walter R. Borneman, *Polk: The Man Who Transformed the Presidency and America* (New York: Random House, 2008).

9. Borneman, *Polk*; DeFiore, "Sarah Polk."

10. DeFiore, "Sarah Polk."

11. Bumgarner, *Sarah Childress Polk*; Greenberg, *Lady First*.

12. Borneman, *Polk*; Bumgarner, *Sarah Childress Polk*.

13. Bumgarner, *Sarah Childress Polk*.

14. Valerie Palmer-Mehta, "Sarah Polk: Ideas of Her Own," in *A Companion to First Ladies*, ed. Katherine A. S. Sibley (West Sussex, UK: Wiley-Blackwell, 2016), 159–175.

15. Borneman, *Polk*, 13.

16. Nelson, *Memorials of Sarah Childress Polk*.

17. Palmer-Mehta, "Sarah Polk"; Elizabeth Lorelei Thacker-Estrada, "True Women: The Roles and Lives of Antebellum Presidential Wives," in *The Presidential Companion: Readings on the First Ladies*, ed. Robert P. Watson and Anthony J. Eksterowicz (Columbia: University of South Carolina Press, 2003), 77–101.

18. Polk Memorial Association Collection of James Knox Polk (1795–1849), Papers 1780–1972, Tennessee State Library and Archives, https://tnsos.net/TSLA/finding aids/71-228.pdf; Greenberg, *Lady First*.

19. Bumgarner, *Sarah Childress Polk*.

20. Borneman, *Polk*, 324–325.

21. Amy Greenberg, *A Wicked War* (New York: Vintage, 2012).

22. Greenberg, *Lady First*.

23. Greenberg, *Lady First*.

24. Bumgarner, *Sarah Childress Polk*; Borneman, *Polk*.

25. Greenberg, *Wicked War*, 72.

26. Peterson, *Sarah Childress Polk*.

27. Greenberg, *Wicked War*, 72.

28. Greenberg, *Wicked War*.

29. Marianne Means, *The Woman in the White House* (New York: Random House, 1963), 79; Betty Boyd Caroli, *First Ladies*, 2nd ed. (Garden City, NY: Guild America, 1997); Bumgarner, *Sarah Childress Polk*.

30. Palmer-Mehta, "Sarah Polk."

31. Nelson, *Memorials of Sarah Childress Polk*; Palmer-Mehta, "Sarah Polk"; Caroli, *First Ladies*; Thacker-Estrada, "True Women."

32. Greenberg, *Lady First*.

33. Sarah Agnes Wallace, "Letters of Mrs. James K. Polk to Her Husband," *Tennessee Historical Quarterly* 11, no. 2 (1952): 184.

34. James K. Polk Papers: Series 2, General Correspondence and Related Items, March 31, 1841–January 9, 1842, manuscript/mixed material, https://www.loc.gov/item/mss36 5090022/.

35. Wallace, "Letters of Mrs. James K. Polk to Her Husband," 190.

36. DeFiore, "Sarah Polk," 138.

37. Palmer-Mehta, "Sarah Polk"; Means, *Woman in the White House*; Bumgarner, *Sarah Childress Polk*.

38. Palmer-Mehta, "Sarah Polk."

39. Greenberg, *Lady First*.

40. James Polk, *The Diary of James K. Polk During His Presidency, 1845–1849* (Bellevue, WA: Big Byte, 2014).

41. Bumgarner, *Sarah Childress Polk*.

42. Greenberg, *Wicked War*, 75.

43. Greenberg, *Lady First*, xiii.

44. Carl Sferrazza Anthony, *First Ladies: The Saga of the Presidents' Wives and Their Power, 1789–1961* (New York: William Morrow, 1990), 140.

45. Bumgarner, *Sarah Childress Polk*, 59.

46. Bumgarner, *Sarah Childress Polk*; Means, *Woman in the White House*.

47. Nelson, *Memorials of Sarah Childress Polk*, 79; Palmer-Mehta, "Sarah Polk."

48. Nelson, *Memorials of Sarah Childress Polk*, 80.

49. Greenberg, *Lady First*; Bumgarner, *Sarah Childress Polk*, Polk Memorial Association Collection, https://tnsos.net/TSLA/findingaids/71-228.pdf.

50. Greenberg, *Lady First*.

51. Nelson, *Memorials of Sarah Childress Polk*; Bumgarner, *Sarah Childress Polk*.

52. Elizabeth Dowling Taylor, *A Slave in the White House: Paul Jennings and the Madisons* (New York: St. Martins Griffin, 2013), 153–155, cited in Lina Mann, "The Enslaved Households of President James K. Polk," White House Historical Association, https://www.white househistory.org/the-enslaved-households-of-james-k-polk.

53. Nelson, *Memorials of Sarah Childress Polk*, 112.

54. Greenberg, *Lady First*; Caroli, *First Ladies*.

55. Nelson, *Memorials of Sarah Childress Polk*, 83.

56. Palmer-Mehta, "Sarah Polk," 169.

57. Means, *Woman in the White House*.

58. Greenberg, *Lady First*.

59. Greenberg, 142.

60. Greenberg, 154.

61. William Dusinberre, *Slavemaster President: The Double Career of James Polk* (New York: Oxford University Press, 2003), 17–20, cited in Mann, "Enslaved Households of President James K. Polk."

62. "Who Is Mrs. James K. Polk?" *Richmond Enquirer*, December 7, 1844, 4.

63. *New York Herald*, May 2, 1845, 4.

64. "The People's Palace and the People's President," *Wilmington Journal*, January 9, 1846, 1.

65. "Washington Gossip," *Voice of Freedom*, March 20, 1845, 2.

66. "The Wife of the President," *Indiana State Sentinel*, June 8, 1848, 4.

67. Polk, *Diary*, 511, 530.

68. Polk, 568.

69. Polk, 634.

70. Nelson, *Memorials of Sarah Childress Polk*; Bumgarner, *Sarah Childress Polk*.

71. Means, *Woman in the White House*.

72. Borneman, *Polk*; Bumgarner, *Sarah Childress Polk*.

73. Nelson, *Memorials of Sarah Childress Polk*.

74. "Exhibit Features 'Polk Place: Presidential Legacy Lost?'" *Columbia Daily Herald*, October 12, 2015, https://www.columbiadailyherald.com/news/local-news/exhibit-features -polk-place-presidential-legacy-lost.

75. DeFiore, "Sarah Polk"; Nelson, *Memorials of Sarah Childress Polk*.

76. Bumgarner, *Sarah Childress Polk*; Caroli, *First Ladies*; Nelson, *Memorials of Sarah Childress Polk*.

77. Nelson, *Memorials of Sarah Childress Polk*.

78. Nelson, 269.

79. Nelson, 192.

80. Thacker-Estrada, "True Women"; Bumgarner, *Sarah Childress Polk*.

81. Bumgarner, *Sarah Childress Polk*; *Semi-Weekly Standard*, May 1, 1858; *Public Ledger*, September 20, 1877, 2; "Down in Tennessee," *Salt Lake Herald*, October 18, 1887, 5.

82. "President Buchanan's Marriage," *Orleans Independent Standard*, December 5, 1856, 3.

83. Box 6, Folder 10 of the Polk Memorial Association Collection of the James Knox Polk Papers 1780–1972; Greenberg, *Lady First*.

84. Greenberg, *Lady First*, 228, 234–237.

85. "Interview with the Widow of Ex-President Polk," *New South*, March 26, 1864, 4.

86. Nelson, *Memorials of Sarah Childress Polk*, 170.

87. Nelson, *Memorials of Sarah Childress Polk*; Bumgarner, *Sarah Childress Polk*.

88. Greenberg, *Lady First*, xvii.

89. Greenberg, *Lady First*.

90. "President Polk's Widow," *Louisiana Democrat*, November 25, 1874, 1.

91. "Mrs. Polk," *Memphis Daily Appeal*, November 11, 1884, 2.

92. Maurice Halbwachs, *On Collective Memory* (Chicago: University of Chicago Press, 1992), 25.

93. Lee Glazer and Susan Key, "Carry Me Back: Nostalgia for the Old South in Nineteenth-Century Popular Culture," *Journal of American Studies* 30, no. 1 (1996): 23.

94. Glazer and Key, "Carry Me Back."

95. Janice Hume and Amber Roessner, "Surviving Sherman's March: Press, Public Memory, and Georgia's Salvation Mythology," *Journalism and Mass Communication Quarterly* 86, no. 1 (2009): 119–137.

96. Barbie Zelizer, "Journalism in the Service of Communication," *Journal of Communication* 61, no. 1 (2011): 2.

97. Barry Schwartz, "Social Change and Collective Memory: The Democratization of George Washington," *American Sociological Review* 56, no. 2 (1991): 221–236.

98. Zelizer, "Journalism in the Service of Communication."

99. Schwartz, "Social Change and Collective Memory."

100. Janice Hume, "Memory Matters: The Evolution of Scholarship in Collective Memory and Mass Communication," *Review of Communication* 10, no. 3 (2010): 181–196.

101. Howard Schuman and Jacqueline Scott, "Generations and Collective Memories," *American Sociological Review* 54, no. 3 (1989): 359–381.

102. Maurine Beasley, *First Ladies and the Press: The Unfinished Partnership of the Media Age* (Evanston, IL: Northwestern University Press, 2005), 47.

103. Beasley, *First Ladies and the Press*; Sidney Kobre, *The Yellow Press and Gilded Age Journalism* (Tallahassee: Florida State University Press, 1964).

104. Lisa Burns, *First Ladies and the Fourth Estate* (DeKalb: Northern Illinois University Press, 2008), 35.

105. Beasley, *First Ladies and the Press*, 47.

106. Burns, *First Ladies and the Fourth Estate*.

107. Janice Hume, *Obituaries in American Culture* (Jackson: University Press of Mississippi, 2000), 154.

108. Hume, *Obituaries in American Culture*, 12.

109. Hume, 18; Daniel J. Boorstin, *The Image: A Guide to Pseudo-Events in America* (New York: Atheneum, 1971).

110. I used the archive in Chronicling America, the Library of Congress online database of digitized local and regional newspapers A search of "Mrs. Polk" provided a sample of 238 articles from thirty-six states and Washington, DC, that I analyzed.

111. Frank Luther Mott, *American Journalism: A History, 1690–1960*, 3rd ed. (New York: Macmillan, 1962).

112. "Mrs. Polk Dead," *Perrysburg Journal*, August 22, 1891, 2; "Mrs. James K. Polk," *Fort Worth Gazette*, August 15, 1891, 1.

113. "Aged Christian Woman Gone," *Indianapolis Journal*, August 15, 1891, 1; "Death of Mrs. Polk," *Los Angeles Herald*, August 15, 1891, 1; "A Noble Woman Dies," *St. Paul Daily Globe*, August 15, 1891, 1.

114. "Mrs. James K. Polk," *Bolivar Bulletin*, August 21, 1891, 1; "Aged Christian Woman Gone." *Indianapolis Journal*; "Mrs. James K. Polk," *Iron County Register*, August 20, 1891, 2.

115. "Mrs. James K. Polk," *Bolivar Bulletin*; "A Noble Woman Dies," *St. Paul Daily Globe*; "Death of Mrs. Polk," *Griggs Courier*, August 21, 1891, 7; "Mrs. Sarah Polk," *Bismarck Weekly Tribune*, August 21, 1891, 2.

116. *Wilmington Daily Republican*, August 15, 1891, 2.

117. "Mrs. Polk Dead," *Perrysburg Journal*, August 22, 1891, 2.

118. "Death of Mrs. Polk," *Los Angeles Herald*; "Mrs. James K. Polk," *Caldwell Tribune*, August 22, 1891, 7.

119. "Aged Christian Woman Gone," *Indianapolis Journal*.

120. "Mrs. James K. Polk," *Fort Worth Gazette*.

121. "Mrs. Polk Dead," *Perrysburg Journal*; "Death of Mrs. Polk," *Los Angeles Herald*; "Mrs. James K. Polk Dead," *Fisherman and Farmer*, August 28, 1891, 3.

122. "Mrs. Polk's Life," *Asheville Daily Citizen*, August 14, 1891, 1; "A Relic from a Glorious Past," *Progressive Farmer*, September 8, 1891, 8.

123. "Mrs. J. K. Polk Is Dead." *Diamond Drill*, August 22, 1891, 2; "Mrs. James K. Polk," *Bolivar Bulletin*; "Mrs. James K. Polk," *Iron County Register*.

124. "A Noted Widow Dead," *Watertown Republican*, August 19, 1891, 2; "Mrs. Polk Dying," *Rock Island Daily Argus*, August 14, 1891, 8.

125. "Mrs. Polk Dead," *Perrysburg Journal*.

126. "Mrs. James K. Polk," *Caldwell Tribune*, August 28, 1891, 4; "Death of Mrs. Polk," *Griggs Courier*.

127. "Obituary Sarah Childress Polk," *New York Times*, August 15, 1891, 5.

128. "Death of Mrs. Polk," *Griggs Courier*.

129. "A Noted Widow Dead," *Watertown Republican*; "Mrs. Polk Dying," *Rock Island Daily Argus*; "Death of Mrs. James K. Polk," *Bolivar Bulletin*.

130. "Mrs. James K. Polk," *Bolivar Bulletin*; "Mrs. James K. Polk," *Iron County Register*; "Mrs. J. K. Polk Is Dead," *Diamond Drill*.

131. "Mrs. Polk Dead," *Evening Bulletin*, August 15, 1891, 1; "Mrs. Polk Dead," *Daily Tobacco Leaf Chronicle*, August 15, 1891, 1.

132. "Ex-President Polk's Widow," *Delaware Gazette and State Journal*, August 20, 1891, 6; "Aged Christian Woman Gone," *Indianapolis Journal*; "Mrs. J. K. Polk," *Pierre Weekly Free Press*, August 20, 1891, 2.

133. "Mrs. Polk Is Dead," *Seattle Post-Intelligencer*, August 15, 1891, 2.

134. *Iola Register*, August 21, 1891, 1.

135. "Mrs. Polk Dead," *Perrysburg Journal*.

136. "She Deserved Distinction," *State Chronicle*, August 18, 1891, 2.

137. "She Deserved Distinction," *State Chronicle*.

138. "Ex-President Polk's Widow," *Delaware Gazette and State Journal*.

139. "Interesting to Note," *Western Sentinel*, August 20, 1891, 3.

140. "Mrs. Polk Dead," *Perrysburg Journal*; "Ex-President Polk's Widow," *Delaware Gazette and State Journal*; "Mrs. James K. Polk," *Iron County Register*; "Mrs. J. K. Polk Is Dead," *Diamond Drill*, 2.

141. "Ex-President Polk's Widow," *Delaware Gazette and State Journal*.

142. "Ex-President Polk's Widow," *Delaware Gazette and State Journal*.

143. "A Relic from a Glorious Past," *Progressive Farmer*.

144. "Mrs. James K. Polk," *Morning Journal and Courier*, August 15, 1891, 3.

145. This is the correct spelling even though the newspaper was in Pittsburgh. "Mrs. Polk Is No More," *Pittsburg Dispatch*, August 15, 1891, 4; *Wichita Daily Eagle*, August 16, 1891, 4.

146. "Death of Mrs. J. K. Polk," *Butler Weekly Times*, August 19, 1891, 1; "Mrs. James K. Polk," *Caldwell Tribune*; "Death of Mrs. Polk," *Los Angeles Herald*; "Mrs. Polk Is No More," *Pittsburg Dispatch*; *Iola Register*, August 21, 1891, 1.

147. "Mrs. James K. Polk," *Caldwell Tribune*; "Mrs. Polk Dead," *Perrysburg Journal*; "Mrs. Polk Is No More," *Pittsburg Dispatch*.

148. *Fairfield News and Herald*, April 5, 1882, 2.

149. Greenberg, *Lady First*.

150. "Mrs. James K. Polk," *Bolivar Bulletin*; *Iola Register*, August 21, 1891, 1; "Mrs. Polk Is No More," *Pittsburg Dispatch*; "Death of Mrs. James K. Polk," *Wheeling Daily Intelligencer*.

151. Hume, *Obituaries in American Culture*, 154.

152. Halbwachs, *On Collective Memory*, 25.

153. Greenberg, *Lady First*.

# CHAPTER 6

# Mary Lincoln, Elizabeth Keckly, and the Perils of White House Friendship

Sylvia D. Hoffert

The day after Abraham Lincoln's first inauguration in 1861, an ambitious and accomplished African American dressmaker named Elizabeth Keckly arrived at 8:00 a.m. at the Executive Mansion for an interview with the first lady. "Ever since arriving in Washington," Keckly wrote in her memoir, "I had a great desire to work for the ladies of the White House, and to accomplish this end I was ready to make almost any sacrifice consistent with propriety." Impressed by Keckly's demeanor, credentials, and references, Mary Lincoln began the negotiations necessary to hire her. She assured the mantua maker that the amount of work she would be able to give her would depend on her prices. "I trust that your terms are reasonable," Keckly remembered her saying. "If you do not charge too much, I shall be able to give you all my work."[1]

During the next few years, the relationship between Lincoln and Keckly grew more intimate. Basking in her dressmaker's deference and attention, the emotionally insecure Lincoln welcomed her into the private quarters of the White House, allowed her to observe and participate in the domestic life of her family, and made her a close confidante.[2] When it came to the amount of money the first lady owed to shopkeepers and home furnishing merchants, Keckly knew more about Lincoln's affairs than did the president of the United States. Lincoln turned to Keckly for solace after the murder of her husband. And she wanted Keckly by her side as she maneuvered her way through the early stages of widowhood. By 1867, the Southern-born Lincoln was referring to Keckly as her "best living friend."[3]

Elizabeth Keckly, 1861, dressmaker to Mary Todd Lincoln. Courtesy of the
Moorland-Spingarn Research Center, Howard University.

A formerly enslaved woman, Keckly was a shrewd entrepreneur whose personal and professional reputation and economic success as a modiste depended on understanding and accommodating the personal needs and social expectations of her upper-class customers.[4] Privy to Lincoln's anxieties and aspirations, Keckly valued her patronage and was proud of the gestures of friendship the first lady bestowed upon her.

Their association lasted until 1868. That spring Keckly published her memoir, *Behind the Scenes, or Thirty Years a Slave, and Four Years in the White House*, exposing to public view the intimate details of the Lincolns' private affairs.[5] Lincoln broke off her relationship with Keckly, dismissed her contemptuously as "the *colored* historian," and never spoke to her again.[6]

As a variety of scholars has pointed out, friendship is a culturally constructed relationship that is time and place specific and has different meanings for different people.[7] At the very least, friendship relies on freedom of choice and equality between the parties as well as mutuality of interests.[8] In the case of Lincoln and Keckly, considerations of race and class stood as almost insurmountable barriers to friendship. Indeed, as Thavolia Glymph has pointed out, the world of Black/white domestic relations among antebellum Southerners could be characterized as "a kind of warring intimacy."[9] But of equal importance in explaining the demise of their relationship was the persistent transactional nature of their association, their differing attitudes toward privacy, and the role that the culture of celebrity played in their lives. Lincoln's refusal or inability to appreciate the true nature of their association as much as Keckly's betrayal of her trust led to its unraveling.

The emotional centrality of female friends to the lives of white, middle-class women in the nineteenth-century United States is well documented.[10] As historians Carroll Smith-Rosenberg and Nancy Cott have pointed out, these women created a social world in which the shared destiny of housekeeping and child-bearing, combined with their reliance on each other for assistance in times of need, bound them together in a sisterhood characterized by close emotional relationships.[11] There might have been regional differences, however. According to Cott, women living in the towns and cities of the North created their relationships in an environment where ideas about class and deference were slowly being undermined by those emphasizing human equality and the importance of individual achievement.[12] Such ideas would have had less relevance in the South, where whites of all social classes based their sense of self on the social and economic benefits to be derived from slavery. In the slaveholding South, ideas about human inequality and the need to preserve class and racial boundaries as well as a determination to maintain patriarchal authority based on deference provided

the cultural framework within which white Kentuckians such as Lincoln structured their friendships.

Lincoln left no record of her childhood friendships.[13] But the three extant
letters she wrote to Mercy Ann Levering in 1840 and 1841 show that she was
capable of expressing great affection for other women and taking an intense
interest in their affairs. She met Levering in Springfield, Illinois, in 1837. During winter 1839–1840, the two young women became inseparable. When they
parted, Lincoln attempted to sustain their relationship through correspondence.
Referring to Levering as "dearest" and the "one I love so well," she longed for
the companionship they had once enjoyed. "How much I wish you were near,
ever have I found yours a congenial heart," she wrote, signing herself "your
most attached friend."[14] The memory of their affection for each other helped to
sustain Lincoln as time passed. "We were *dearer* to each other than friends," she
wrote in June 1841.[15]

Mary Lincoln relied on the emotional support of female friends throughout
her adult life. But her demand that they give her their undivided attention and
loyalty, combined with her propensity to view as an enemy anyone who did
not protect and advance her interests, meant those relationships were fragile.[16]
Her friendship with Mary Jane Welles, wife of President Lincoln's secretary of
the navy, Gideon Welles, serves as a case in point. Their association was based
on physical proximity, the similarity of their socioeconomic and educational
backgrounds, their mutual interest in spiritualism, and their grief for their dead
children. Mary Jane Welles lived in the White House when Tad Lincoln was critically ill and was one of the women who tended Lincoln after the assassination.[17]
Gideon Welles remained in his post when Andrew Johnson became president.
Mary Lincoln despised Johnson and considered the Welleses' continuing association with the new president a betrayal of their friendship. When the Welleses
accompanied President Johnson on a speaking tour through the Midwest in
August and September 1866, Mary snubbed them by making a point of being
out of town when the delegation visited Chicago.[18] Writing to Charles Sumner,
she said: "I remember Mrs [*sic*] Welles with sincere affection and gratitude during my . . . fearful bereavement in Washington. . . . *Her* heart is all right, yet the
desire of some persons [her husband's] to be in office, will cause them to bend
the knee."[19]

Keckly's first friends were those in the slave quarters. Their first names were
whatever the people who enslaved them chose to call them. Their last names are
lost to history. According to historian Deborah Gray White, friendships among
enslaved women tended to be hierarchically structured around kinship ties,
age, occupation, personal achievement, and association with the master class.

Friendship and the need for mutual support served to mitigate the brutality of slavery and the dehumanizing nature of everyday life.[20]

When Keckly moved to Washington after she purchased her freedom, she looked for friends among the elite in the African American community, many of whom were working in the White House.[21] Hannah Brooks and Rosetta Wells, who did plain sewing for the Lincolns; William Slade, the steward, and his wife, Josephine; Cornelia Mitchell, the cook; and Peter Brown, the butler, were her colleagues.[22] She boarded with the family of Walker Lewis, one of the leading caterers in the city and a trustee of the Fifteenth Street Presbyterian Church, pastored by Reverend Henry Highland Garnet, who also became a close associate. The Lewises, she wrote, were "friends in the truest sense of the word."[23] The Fifteenth Street church eventually become the focus of her social life. "She was a leader in nearly all of the church activities," Laura Fisher, a church member, remembered. "The church was her life, and she always attended its meetings as long as she could do so, which was nearly fifty years."[24] From Keckly's Black friends, we learn what became of her after 1868, when she published her much-maligned memoir.[25]

Given her background, it is not surprising that Keckly's relationships with white women were fraught with ambivalence. That did not mean, however, that they were necessarily devoid of affection. Her fondness for the white patrons who loaned her the money to buy her freedom in St. Louis is completely understandable.[26] That she described a former mistress and her children in such terms is somewhat surprising.

The Garlands held Keckly in slavery in St. Louis until she was able to buy her freedom in 1855. She lost contact with them shortly thereafter, but she and what was left of their family reunited after the Civil War. When she arrived at their plantation, the Garland women greeted her with enthusiasm, escorted her to the house "in triumph," and prepared her breakfast themselves, much to the surprise of their cook. "I was comfortably quartered," Keckly wrote, and "was shown every attention." She described the time she spent with them as "five of the most delightful weeks of my life." In her memoir she referred to them as "Old Friends."[27]

As literary critic William L. Andrews has pointed out, postbellum slave narratives such as Keckly's were motivated by a complex set of psychological, sociopolitical, and literary desires and often described reconciliation with white masters and mistresses as evidence of both the potential for self-advancement that freedom offered and progress in race relations.[28] Keckly clearly enjoyed her reunion with the Garlands, an event that offered her the opportunity to reinforce her claim to newly acquired social respectability to both her former owners and her literary audience. If what Andrews has suggested is true, portraying the Garlands as friends might have been less a description of their actual relationship than an attempt to convince her white readers that Reconstruction offered an unprecedented opportunity to establish a nation based on principles of racial harmony.

The evidence suggests that Keckly never stopped regarding her relationship with Lincoln as a transactional one. The space they occupied together was typically Lincoln's space, and the time they spent together was at Lincoln's invitation. The fact that Keckly insisted on fitting dresses in her customers' homes rather than in her boardinghouse room or workshop suggests that she was careful to keep her private life in the Black community separate from her professional one. On the one occasion Lincoln arrived on her doorstep to discuss the construction of a new garment, Keckly took exception to the visit. "I never approved of ladies attached to the President's household coming to my rooms," she wrote. "I always thought it would be more consistent with their dignity to send for me."[29]

As a young woman who grew up with enslaved people in her family's household, Mary Lincoln exploited the labor of Black women, accepted the affection of those willing to give it, and confided in those who had no choice but to listen. As first lady, she took advantage of what she perceived as the prerogatives of her exalted station, making confidantes of White House servants such as Mary Ann Cuthbert, the housekeeper, and Edward McManus, the doorkeeper, sending them on private errands and exacting personal service beyond their prescribed duties. Always feeling short of money, she was similarly prone to expect deference, favors, and sometimes gifts from those in her inner circle without any thought of compensating them financially.[30] So it is not surprising that when she found that the ladies' maid and seamstress she had brought with her to Washington was not accomplished at "arranging or dressing a lady," she called upon Keckly to perform that ancillary service.[31]

It is not clear that Lincoln paid Keckly for her services as a ladies' maid. Keckly might have performed that service gratis as a way of guaranteeing the continuation of Lincoln's goodwill and future patronage. Whatever the case, as their association continued, Keckly discovered there were various intangible benefits to be derived from her association with the first lady. She accompanied Lincoln on a trip to New York City in late fall 1862 so that she could contact potential donors for the Contraband Relief Society, an organization she had established to help care for the thousands of previously enslaved people who flooded into Washington seeking refuge during the Civil War. After persuading Lincoln to use her influence to procure $200 from a humanitarian aid fund established by the federal government, she used Lincoln's name as leverage to solicit more money from other donors. She even borrowed money from the first lady.[32] And, just before the end of the war, Keckly used her association with Lincoln to claim a place in the president's entourage when it traveled into Virginia so that she could visit her former home in Petersburg.[33]

After Lincoln's husband was killed, she continued to exploit Keckly's services by demanding her complete devotion and insisting that she abandon her customers in Washington and accompany Mary to Chicago. "I have determined that you shall go to Chicago with me, and you *must* go," Keckly remembered Mary saying.[34] The modiste remained with Lincoln in Chicago for six weeks. When Lincoln sent her back to Washington without paying her a salary, Keckly submitted a bill to the federal government, and she eventually received $210 for her services, $100 in traveling and incidental expenses, and the cost of mourning clothes.[35]

While Keckly tried to reestablish her business, Lincoln continued to place demands on her time, asking her to deliver messages to her friends and placing orders for new clothes. Perhaps because Keckly feared nonpayment, she was uncharacteristically dilatory in sending the completed garments to Chicago. A similar concern about reimbursement might account for her refusal to leave Washington and travel to the Midwest to accompany the former first lady when she went to visit her husband's tomb in Springfield on the anniversary of his death.[36]

In September 1867, Lincoln concluded that her dire financial situation required that she go to New York to sell her clothes, and she asked Keckly to close her business for an undetermined length of time and join her. Keckly eventually agreed but not out of feelings of friendship. She went to New York, she wrote, out of a sense of obligation to the widow of "the man who had done so much for my race."[37] Unarticulated but implicit in their arrangements was the assumption that Keckly would eventually be reimbursed for her efforts.

Having failed to raise money from the sale of her personal belongings, Lincoln returned to Chicago in October, leaving Keckly behind in New York to settle her affairs.[38] Unable to send Keckly money to pay for her expenses, she assured her former dressmaker that her intentions were honorable. She dearly wished, she said, that she could place Keckly "in more pleasant circumstances" and hoped "the day *may* arrive when I can return your kindness in *more* than words." Lincoln suggested that in the meantime Keckly find employment sewing for the ladies in New York and assured her that if she ever got any money, she would send some to her.[39]

Lincoln received part of her inheritance of a little more than $36,000 in mid-November 1867 but did not make any effort to pay her dressmaker what she owed her.[40] Instead, she offered to use some of the money she hoped could be raised from grateful members of the Black community to reimburse the woman she claimed was her only friend. If $50,000 was raised, she wrote, "you shall have $5,000 at my death. . . . If $25,000, you shall have the same. . . . In either event, . . . I will give you $300 a year, and the promised sum at my death. It will make your life easier."[41] A week later, Lincoln offered to send Keckly some of the dresses not sold in New York so that she could sell them to raise the money she needed.[42] "Mrs. Lincoln's venture proved so disastrous," Keckly wrote in her memoir, "that she was unable to reward me for my services, and I was compelled to take in sewing to pay for my daily bread."[43]

In need of income and fearing that what became known as the "Old Clothes Scandal" might have seriously damaged her reputation, Keckly decided to publish her memoir. In it, she exposed to public view details concerning the Lincolns' private life in the White House, including the amount of money Mary Lincoln owed to her creditors and the content of some of their most intimate conversations, one of which involved the president's threat to send his wife to an insane asylum. And when *Behind the Scenes* appeared in spring 1868, letters from Mary appeared in the Appendix without her approval.[44] Editors of periodicals and newspapers large and small published scathingly critical reviews of Keckly's book, describing it as "scandalous" and "indecent."[45] Much of the criticism of her memoir focused on the belief that she had betrayed Mary's friendship by violating her privacy. The idea of privacy did not carry the same weight for Keckly as it did either for Mary or for the reviewers of her book, who were almost certainly white and male. According to historian Mary P. Ryan, the notion of privacy originated in the early nineteenth century in the towns and cities of the North among members of the emerging middle class able to separate the domestic sphere from the workplace. In places such as Oneida County, New York, success in professional and white-collar work that increasingly depended upon individual effort rather than community associations, the prevalence of small middle-class households separated from those of their extended families, and family lives increasingly centered on nurture rather than production all buttressed the concept of privacy.[46]

Acceptance of such personal boundaries was slow to come to the South, however, which remained largely rural and agricultural during the antebellum period. Most Southern households were beehives of production. In families who enslaved people, exploiting the community effort of those workers rather than depending on individual initiative was necessary to ensure economic prosperity. Protecting privacy was not practical in an environment where those in bondage provided the most basic personal services, and security concerns demanded that enslaved people live under the watchful eyes of their owners or their surrogates.

Mary Todd Lincoln grew up in a large Southern household. The Todd house in Lexington, Kentucky, contained nine people, three of whom were enslaved,

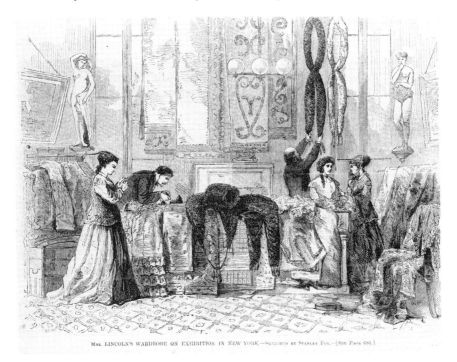

MRS. LINCOLN'S WARDROBE ON EXHIBITION IN NEW YORK.—Sketched by Stanley Fox.—[See Page 686.]

*Harper's Weekly* drawing of the "Old Clothes Scandal," October 26, 1867. Artist: Stanley Fox, with the description: "Mrs. Lincoln's wardrobe on exhibition in New York." Courtesy of the Library of Congress Prints and Photographs Division. Reproduction Number: LC-USZ62-132451 (b&w film copy neg.).

in 1820; it had grown to twenty, including eight enslaved people, in 1830; and by 1840, when Mary Todd had already moved in with her married sister in Springfield, Illinois, totaled seventeen, including five enslaved people.[47] When she married Abraham Lincoln in 1843, they settled in Springfield, and she became a middle-class housewife. With her husband away much of the time, Lincoln remained at home with her children. She did much of her own housework, partly because good help was hard to find and partly because she was unwilling to pay the going rate for household assistance.[48] Without the perpetual scrutiny of servants, she experienced for the first time the benefits of privacy.

Slavery denied Keckly that opportunity. The Burwell plantation in Virginia, where she was born, contained thirty-two people including eighteen enslaved people and three free Blacks in 1820 and grew to accommodate seventy-four people by 1830. In 1840, Keckly was living in Hillsborough, North Carolina, in a boarding school containing seventeen whites, six enslaved people, and twenty-seven scholars. After she was taken to St. Louis, she and nine others, enslaved as she was, provided the labor needed to support the eleven members of the Garland household.[49]

In rural areas and small towns, enslaved people who did not live in the big house were usually crowded together in small, one-room cabins, although on large plantations they sometimes lived in dormitories. In either case, they lived in close quarters, and their personal lives were closely supervised.[50] The geography of housing and its architecture in cities such as St. Louis encouraged a different kind of intimacy between people who enslaved Blacks and those they held in bondage. There, slave owners built compounds surrounded by walls designed to focus the attention of enslaved people on the households where they lived rather than the community beyond them.[51] Whatever Keckly's living arrangements, she would have spent her days in an environment where she had little claim to personal space and where others were free to constantly monitor the most intimate aspects of her daily life, however much she might have resisted their efforts.[52]

Her status as an enslaved woman meant that she could lay no claim to corporeal privacy and was subjected to physical and sexual abuse. Reverend Robert Burwell, who enslaved her in North Carolina, ordered the local schoolmaster, William Bingham, to discipline Keckly when Burwell's wife complained about what she considered Keckly's recalcitrance. Bingham took Keckly into his office and ordered her to take down her dress. "Recollect," Keckly wrote in her memoir, "I was eighteen years of age, was a woman fully developed, and yet this man coolly bade me take down my dress." When she refused, he bound her hands, tore her dress from her back, and picked up a rawhide whip. The beatings continued until, as Keckly put it, it became clear that nothing could be done to subdue her "proud, rebellious spirit." The violation of her bodily privacy did not end with beatings. Alexander Kirkland, the dissolute son of a local planter, raped her. "He persecuted me for four years," she wrote, "and I—I became a mother."[53]

Further complicating Keckly's sense of the private and the nonprivate was that by virtue of her vocation as a modiste, she was privy to the private affairs of her patrons. Keckly spent long hours in the company of her customers fitting the garments they had commissioned her to make. According to historian Wendy Gamber, while they stood for hours being measured, poked, and prodded, it was common for a dressmaker's patrons to relieve the tedium by talking about the most intimate aspects of their personal lives, divulging information they would never have shared with their friends and family. Keckly had no choice but to accept the role of confidante. It was part of her job to engage in what sociologists have called "emotional labor" by listening sympathetically to their confessions and complaints while she fitted their dresses. *Suggestions for Dressmakers*, a manual published at the end of Keckly's career, summed it up nicely: A dressmaker, it said, was "supposed to have a brain large enough to remember all the foibles and fads of all her customers, and a heart sensitive and loving enough to bathe each one in sympathy for all the troubles and trials to the unbosoming of which the fitting of a dress somehow leads."[54] As far as patrons were concerned, there was no expectation of reciprocity in their relationship with their dressmakers. They typically felt no compulsion to endear themselves to these women or take an interest in their personal affairs. The unarticulated assumption that dressmakers appreciated the need for discretion as one of the variety of services for which they were being paid, combined with the social distance that separated customers from those who made their clothes, encouraged patrons to consider their dressmakers a safe repository for their secrets.[55]

Keckly's lack of appreciation for Lincoln's privacy was also influenced by the fact that from the moment she entered the White House, she observed the president's wife shamelessly seeking notoriety and embracing the culture of celebrity. As Lincoln's biographer Jean Baker has pointed out, drawing attention to herself was something of an obsession for the new first lady. Lincoln was convinced that "there was no better way to certify her importance than to find herself discussed in newspapers."[56]

Celebrity was not a new phenomenon in American life. Although George Washington was well known in the Early Republic, it took the efforts of Parson Weems to embellish his already established celebrity.[57] But by the 1830s, notions about the importance of the individual and his or her potential for greatness, the rise of literacy, the availability of leisure time, and the emerging entertainment industry—combined with the growth of the mass media with their focus on human interest stories, advances in communication technology, and systematic image management—all helped accelerate the celebrity-making process.[58] All it took to expedite the process was the willingness of newspaper editors such as James Gordon Bennett, image makers such as Mathew Brady, and impresarios such as P. T. Barnum to exploit the opportunities offered by these economic, technological, and cultural changes.

Bennett was the editor of the *New York Herald*, a man determined to adapt any strategy and mine any source of news likely to increase circulation and to do what he could to feed the public's insatiable desire for insider information.[59] Brady democratized the human image by taking it out of the hands of painters, engravers, and their wealthy clients and placing it at the disposal of anyone who could afford a relatively inexpensive daguerreotype.[60] Barnum used his genius for public display to feed the public's curiosity, desire for entertainment, and love of spectacle. A showman who successfully promoted the career of the immensely talented singer Jenny Lind, he was equally adept at facilitating the celebrity of Tom Thumb (Charles S. Stratton), a man with dwarfism he found in Bridgeport, Connecticut, and indentured so that he could put him on exhibit.[61]

The culture of celebrity that Bennett, Brady, and Barnum were trying to promote appealed to both of the Lincolns. Throughout her husband's presidency, Lincoln solicited Bennett's support in an effort to make a place for herself in the public eye. When on October 21, 1861, Bennett published an editorial condemning Northern newspapers for their attacks on the president's wife, Lincoln responded with a letter of thanks and as much flattery as she could muster. "It is with feelings of more than ordinary gratitude, that I venture to address you, a note, expressive of my thanks for the kind support and consideration, extended towards the Administration, by you, at a time when your powerful influence would be sensibly felt," she wrote from the Executive Mansion.[62] She understood that propriety demanded she deny any unwomanly desire for newspaper notoriety, but she was determined that Bennett appreciate the potential power she wielded in shaping public policy. "I have great terror of *strong* minded Ladies," she wrote, "yet if a word fitly spoken and in due season, can be urged, in a time like this, we should not withhold it."[63] Throughout her husband's presidency, she continued to be solicitous of Bennett in order to ensure his continual attention and political support.[64]

Image projection was crucial to the Lincolns for both personal and political reasons. The day after Abraham Lincoln arrived in the capital for his inauguration, the new president made a trip to Brady's Washington branch to have his picture taken.[65] His wife followed suit, commissioning Brady to take her picture a few months later.[66] Mary Lincoln also exploited the celebrity of others to draw attention to herself. On February 13, 1863, she hosted a White House reception to introduce the remarkable Tom Thumb and his new wife, Lavinia Warren Stratton, like Tom also a little person, to Washington society. It was a spectacle that would have made Barnum proud. Keckly saw nothing wrong with this. "Tom Thumb had been caressed by royalty in the Old World," she wrote. "Why should not the wife of the President of his native country smile upon him also?"[67]

Embracing the culture of celebrity served Keckly's interests as well, even before she knew Lincoln. In order to build her dressmaking business, she used her connections to obtain commissions from the most prominent society matrons in Washington, whose patronage helped lay the groundwork for establishing her reputation as a celebrity mantua maker. She had only been in Washington for a few months when Varina Davis, wife of Senator Jefferson Davis, hired her. Keckly's connections with Davis and Lincoln provided her the opportunity to work for Anna Mason Lee, Robert E. Lee's sister-in-law; Margaret McLean, daughter of General Edwin V. Sumner; Adele Cutts Douglas, wife of Senator Stephen Douglas; Ann Eliza Harlan, wife of Senator James Harlan; Mary Jane Welles, wife of Secretary of the Navy Welles; and Ellen Stanton, wife of Secretary of War Edwin Stanton.[68] Her employment by such prominent society matrons ensured her a secure place at the pinnacle of her profession. By 1865 she employed a roomful of seamstresses and paid taxes on a business assessed at $2,000.[69]

Given Keckly's observation that Lincoln had willingly sacrificed her claim to privacy by pursuing celebrity status, and the dressmaker's own appreciation of the commercial opportunities the culture of celebrity made possible, it is not surprising that she welcomed the prospect of easing the pecuniary embarrassment Lincoln had caused her in the "Old Clothes Scandal" by deliberately using her association with the first lady to cultivate an audience for her own life story. Her slave narrative by itself could not have been expected to be of interest to the reading public, which was finding it difficult to deal with the social, economic, and political ramifications of the Civil War and Reconstruction. But her exposure of the intimate details of the Lincolns' life in the White House and her vivid description of the scandal had great marketing potential.

Because Keckly knew she was overstepping the bounds of propriety in publishing her story, she tried to rationalize her actions by arguing that Mary had abdicated her right to privacy by relentlessly seeking public acclaim and intentionally subjecting her affairs to public scrutiny. "Mrs. Lincoln, by her own acts, forced herself into notoriety," Keckly wrote. "She stepped beyond the formal lines which hedge about a private life and invited public criticism." Keckly also claimed that nothing she had written could "place Mrs. Lincoln in a worse light before the world than the light in which she now stands, therefore the secret history that I publish can do her no harm." And finally, Keckly argued that because her own reputation for integrity, honesty, and good sense had served as the foundation of her successful business, she felt compelled to try to redeem it. "My own character, as well as the character of Mrs. Lincoln, is at stake, since I have been intimately associated with that lady in the most eventful periods of her life," she wrote. "I have been her confidante, and if evil charges are laid at her door, they also must be laid at mine since I have been a party to all her movements. To defend myself I must defend the lady that I have served."[70]

Keckly scholars agree that whatever her motives, she violated white social conventions governing friendship and privacy as well as those pertaining to race, gender, and class relations.[71] Thus, despite a public thirsty for further scandal-mongering around Lincoln's name, the negative response to *Behind the Scenes* was as predictable as the loss of the former first lady's patronage. Keckly's memoir sold few copies, and those that did sell had little apparent influence on public opinion.[72] As Aisha Francis has so aptly put it, "The harsh backlash was a difficult lesson in the limitations of her status as a privileged and independent Black woman in the Reconstruction era."[73]

The story of Mary Lincoln's final years is well known. When her behavior became intolerably erratic, her son Robert had her committed to the Bellevue Place Sanatorium in Batavia, Illinois, in May 1875. She was released a few months later and went to live with her sister in Springfield. After spending some time in Europe, she returned to Springfield, where, half blind and partially paralyzed, she died of a stroke on July 16, 1882.[74]

Keckly lived for another twenty-five years. After she returned from New York to Washington in fall 1868, she found her prospects limited by changes long in the making and beyond her control. During and after the Civil War, the number of dressmakers trying to make a living in Washington had expanded, thus increasing competition for customers.[75] Moreover, women who might otherwise have hired her to design and construct their clothes were now making their own clothes with the help of new and reasonably priced sewing machines.[76] After Lincoln had left town in 1865, President Johnson's daughters, Martha Johnson Patterson and Mary Johnson Stover, hired Keckly to make their dresses. One day she called at the White House in connection with some work she was doing for them and was surprised to find Patterson at work at a sewing machine. Subsequently, Patterson asked Keckly to cut and fit a dress for her, implying that she intended to finish it herself. "I replied that I never cut and fitted work to be made up outside of my work-room," Keckly wrote. "This brought our business relations to an abrupt end."[77] By the time Keckly returned from New York, however, the practice of self-finishing was becoming so commonplace that she could not refuse to accommodate the practice. In October, E. Lenzberg & Co. in Washington announced the employment of the "well-known Mrs. E. Keckley" and advised any ladies interested in "making up" their own fabric to come into her dress- and cloak-making department and have their garments cut and fit to their specifications.[78]

Keckly made a modest living as a dressmaker and seamstress in Washington before she left in 1892 to teach dressmaking at Wilberforce University in Xenia, Ohio.[79] After she returned to the capital in 1897, she eventually took a room at the National Home for Destitute Colored Women and Children. She died there in May 1907 and was buried in the Columbian Harmony Cemetery in Washington.[80]

The perils inherent in Lincoln's attempt to bestow her friendship on her dressmaker are to be found in the asymmetry of power inherent in their racial, social, and economic positions. However broadminded Lincoln might have been, and however much she was willing to selectively ignore well-established boundaries between whites and Blacks, Lincoln was a Southern white woman and the first lady, and she held the power of patronage in her hands. Keckly was a formerly enslaved businesswoman whose success was dependent on her creativity, needlework skills, and emotional labor as well as the social status, recommendations, and continued support of her customers. However much time they spent together, and however much affection and goodwill they felt for each other, their association was essentially an exploitive one in which both women expected a return on their investment of time and emotional capital. For Lincoln, Keckly existed to spend time with her, make her dresses, serve as her lady's maid, listen to her concerns and complaints, provide solace in her bereavement, and help her in her efforts to adjust to the demands of widowhood. Given her many insecurities as well as her race and class assumptions, it was easy for Lincoln to misinterpret her dressmaker's deference, attentiveness, and expressions of sympathy as more than they were intended to be.

Keckly had no expectations of befriending the president's wife when she knocked on the White House door in spring 1861. Her intent was to arrange a business contract with a woman whose celebrity could help her gain even greater entrée into the dressing rooms of Washington's most prestigious families. She was willing to spend a great deal of time in Lincoln's company, comfort her in her grief, and acknowledge her gestures of friendship, but her willingness to fulfill the obligations associated with that relationship was complicated by the fact that it was in her business interest to provide these services and to be compensated for them. She claimed to have published the story of her life to help redeem Lincoln's reputation. But self-interest also prompted her to exploit Lincoln's celebrity and expose the most private aspects of her life for financial gain. Ignoring the degree to which she had stripped herself of the right to privacy in her relentless pursuit of celebrity status, Lincoln found it impossible to forgive Keckly.

## NOTES

1. Elizabeth Keckley, *Behind the Scenes, or Thirty Years a Slave, and Four Years in the White House* (New York: G. W. Carleton, 1868), 76–85, quotations on 76 and 85. With the exception of references to her book, I have used the spelling Keckly, the one she used when she signed her name.

2. Keckley, *Behind the Scenes*, xiv; Justin G. Turner and Linda Leavitt Turner, eds., *Mary Todd Lincoln: Her Life and Letters* (New York: Knopf, 1972), 113; Carl Sandburg, *Mary Lincoln: Wife and Widow* (New York: Harcourt, Brace, 1932), 263.

3. Mary Lincoln to Elizabeth Keckly, letter, October 6, [1867], in Turner and Turner, *Mary Todd Lincoln*, 440, and Keckley, *Behind the Scenes*, 301. For letters from Lincoln to Keckly signed "your friend," see Keckley, *Behind the Scenes*, 333, 339, 344, 358, 366.

4. The term *modiste* is a nineteenth-century French word for a skilled dressmaker whose knowledge of fashion and sewing allowed her both to design and to construct women's clothing in the latest style.

5. Keckly was neither the first nor the last person to publish a memoir of her time in the White House. The first was written by a man James Madison enslaved. See Paul Jennings, *A Colored Man's Reminiscences of James Madison* (Brooklyn, NY: George C. Beadle, 1865). Artist Francis B. Carpenter published his memoir of the Lincoln White House, *Six Months at the White House with Abraham Lincoln: The Story of a Picture* (New York: Hurd and Houghton), in 1866. A wide variety of White House memoirs has been published in the twentieth century, including one by a chief usher, Irwin Hood Hoover, *Forty-Two Years in the White House* (Boston: Houghton Mifflin, 1934); one by a maid and seamstress, Lillian Rogers Parks, *My Thirty Years Backstairs at the White House* (New York: Fleet, 1961); and one by a dog sitter, Traphes Bryant, *Dog Days at the White House: The Outrageous Memoirs of the Presidential Kennel Keeper* (New York: Macmillan, 1974).

6. Mary Lincoln to Rhoda White, letter, May 2, 1868, in Turner and Turner, *Mary Todd Lincoln*, 476.

7. See the online *Oxford English Dictionary* for a survey of the multiple meanings of the word "friend," www.oed.com.lib.unc.edu/view/entry/74646. James O. Grunebaum, *Friendship: Liberty, Equality, and Utility* (Albany: State University of New York Press, 2003), 58; Alan Bray, *The Friend* (Chicago: University of Chicago Press, 2003), 2; Cassandra A. Good, *Founding Friendships: Friendships Between Men and Women in the Early American Republic* (New York: Oxford University Press, 2015), 2–3.

8. William E. Wiethoff, *The Insolent Slave* (Columbia: University of South Carolina Press, 2002), 144.

9. Thavolia Glymph, *Out of the House of Bondage: The Transformation of the Plantation Household* (New York: Cambridge University Press, 2006), 37.

10. Carroll Smith-Rosenberg, "The Female World of Love and Ritual: Relations Between Women in Nineteenth-Century America," *Signs* 1, no. 1 (Autumn 1975): 1–29; Nancy F. Cott, *The Bonds of Womanhood: "Woman's Sphere" in New England, 1780–1835* (New Haven, CT: Yale University Press, 1977), 160–196; Nancy Hewitt, "Feminist Friends: Agrarian Quakers and the Emergence of Woman's Rights in America," *Feminist Studies* 12, no. 1 (Spring 1986): 27–49; Carol Lasser, "'Let Us Be Sisters Forever': The Sororal Model of Nineteenth-Century Female Friendship," *Signs* 14, no. 4 (Autumn 1988): 158–181; Christie Anne Farnham, *The Education of the Southern Belle: Higher Education and Socialization in the Antebellum South* (New York: New York University Press, 1994), 155–167; Joan Cashin, "'Decidedly Opposed to the Union': Women's Culture, Marriage, and Politics in Antebellum South Carolina," *Georgia Historical Quarterly* 78, no. 4 (Winter 1994): 735–759.

11. Cott, *Bonds of Womanhood*, 188, 194; Smith-Rosenberg, "Female World of Love and Ritual," 9.

12. Cott, *Bonds of Womanhood*, 187.

13. For characterizations of the kind of schoolgirl friendships Lincoln might have had, see Anya Jabour, *Scarlett's Sisters: Young Women in the Old South* (Chapel Hill: University of North Carolina Press, 2007), 64–76; Farnham, *Education of the Southern Belle*, 155–167.

14. Jean H. Baker, *Mary Todd Lincoln: A Biography* (New York: Norton, 1987), 77–82; Turner and Turner, *Mary Todd Lincoln*, 12. Quotation in Mary Lincoln to Mercy Ann Levering, letter, July 23, 1840, in Turner and Turner, *Mary Todd Lincoln*, 14–19.

15. Mary Lincoln to Mercy Ann Levering, letter, June 1841, in Turner and Turner, *Mary Todd Lincoln*, 25–28. Their friendship lasted for years. See Mary Lincoln to Mercy Ann Levering Conkling, letter, July 29, [1864] and November 19, [1864], in Turner and Turner, *Mary Todd Lincoln*, 178 and 187–188.

16. Baker, *Mary Todd Lincoln*, 150–151.

17. Baker, 212, 219, 230, 247–248.

18. Turner and Turner, *Mary Todd Lincoln*, 379; Mary Lincoln to Alexander Williamson, letter, August 19 and September 7, [1866], in Turner and Turner, *Mary Todd Lincoln*, 382–383 and 385–386, respectively.

19. Mary Lincoln to Charles Sumner, letter, September 10, 1866, in Turner and Turner, *Mary Todd Lincoln*, 386–387. Lincoln's friendship with Julia Jayne Trumbull had ended for much the same reason when Trumbull's husband defeated Abraham Lincoln in his bid for the Senate in 1855. Baker, *Mary Todd Lincoln*, 148–150.

20. Deborah Gray White, *Ar'n't I a Woman? Female Slaves in the Plantation South* (New York: Norton, 1985), 119–141.

21. Francis Smith Foster, "Autobiography after Emancipation: The Example of Elizabeth Keckley," in *The Elizabeth Keckley Reader*, ed. Sheila Smith McCoy, vol. 1: *Writing Self, Writing Nation* (Hillsborough, NC: Eno, 2016), 39; John E. Washington, *They Knew Lincoln* (New York: E. P. Dutton, 1842), 107.

22. Washington, *They Knew Lincoln*, 105–126, 133; Catherine Clinton, *Mrs. Lincoln: A Life* (New York: HarperCollins, 2009), 157.

23. Washington, *They Knew Lincoln*, 212; Keckley, *Behind the Scenes*, 182.

24. Washington, *They Knew Lincoln*, 218–219.

25. See, for example, Alberta Elizabeth Lewis Savoy typescript, Lincoln Financial Foundation Collection Archives, Allen County Public Library, Fort Wayne, Indiana; Washington, *They Knew Lincoln*, 215–221.

26. Keckley, *Behind the Scenes*, 54–55.

27. Keckley, 59–60, 238–258, quotations on 250, 253, 258, respectively.

28. William L. Andrews, "Reunion in the Postbellum Slave Narrative," in *The Elizabeth Keckley Reader*, ed. Sheila Smith McCoy, vol. 1: *Writing Self, Writing Nation* (Hillsborough, NC: Eno, 2016), 21–23.

29. Keckley, *Behind the Scenes*, 152.

30. Turner and Turner, *Mary Todd Lincoln*, 99; Baker, *Mary Todd Lincoln*, 166, 194, 200–201; Sandburg, *Mary Lincoln*, 89.

31. Mary Lincoln to Mary Brayman, letter, June 17, [1861], in Turner and Turner, *Mary Todd Lincoln*, 90. For references to dressing Lincoln and arranging her hair, see Keckley, *Behind the Scenes*, 87–88, 158, 161, 175.

32. Mary Lincoln to Abraham Lincoln, letters, November 2 and November 3, 1862, in Turner and Turner, *Mary Todd Lincoln*, 139–140 and 140–141, respectively; Keckley, *Behind the Scenes*, 114.

33. Keckley, *Behind the Scenes*, 169.

34. Keckley, 210.

35. Baker, *Mary Todd Lincoln*, 254; Washington, *They Knew Lincoln*, 225.

36. Mary Lincoln to Elizabeth Blair Lee, letter, July 11, 1865, in Turner and Turner, *Mary Todd Lincoln*, 258–259. See also Mary Lincoln to Mary Jane Welles, letter, July 11, 1865, in Turner and Turner, *Mary Todd Lincoln*, 256–257; Mary Lincoln to Alexander Williamson, letters, November 28, December 15, December 16, December 26, and December 31, 1865, in Turner and Turner, *Mary Todd Lincoln*, 287–288, 306–307, 308–309, 314, and 320, respectively; Keckley, *Behind the Scenes*, 226.

37. Keckley, 268–269.

38. Turner and Turner, *Mary Todd Lincoln*, 433.

39. Mary Lincoln to Elizabeth Keckly, letters, November 9, November 15, and November 21 [1867], in Turner and Turner, *Mary Todd Lincoln*, 448–449, 453–455, and 459, respectively.

40. Baker, *Mary Todd Lincoln*, 279. The amount of $36,000 would have been worth $653,000 in 2018; see https://westegg.com/inflation/infl.cgi.

41. Mary Lincoln to Elizabeth Keckly, letter, November 17, [1867], in Turner and Turner, *Mary Todd Lincoln*, 455–456.

42. Mary Lincoln to Elizabeth Keckly, letter, November 23, [1867], in Turner and Turner, *Mary Todd Lincoln*, 460–461.

43. Keckley, *Behind the Scenes*, 326.

44. Keckley, 104–105, 204, 332–371.

45. Memphis (Tennessee) *Public Ledger*, April 25, 1868, 4 (from the *Pittsburg Commercial*). See also "Review of *Behind the Scenes*," *Putnam's Magazine* (July 1868): 119; "New Publications," [San Francisco] *Daily Evening Bulletin*, May 23, 1868; "New Publications," *New York Times*, April 19, 1868, 10; "Review of *Behind the Scenes*," (Rock Island, Illinois) *Evening Argus*, April 22, 1868, 2; "Miscellany," (Bellows Falls) *Vermont Chronicle*, May 9, 1868, 4; "Reviews," *New-York Citizen*, April 18, 1868; "An Indecent Book," *New-York Citizen*, April 24, 1868, 4; "Behind the Scenes," *Atlantic Monthly* 22 (July 1868): 128. The most vicious response was a parody written by D[aniel]. Ottolengul, *Behind the Seems by a Nigger Woman Who Took in Work from Mrs. Lincoln and Mrs. Davis* (New York: National News, 1868).

46. Mary P. Ryan, *Cradle of the Middle Class: The Family in Oneida County, New York, 1790–1865* (Cambridge, UK: Cambridge University Press, 1981), 147, 153, 154, 155.

47. US Federal Manuscript Census of 1820, Fayette County, Kentucky; US Federal Manuscript Census of 1830, Lexington, Fayette County, Kentucky; US Federal Manuscript Census of 1840, Lexington, Fayette County, Kentucky.

48. Baker, *Mary Todd Lincoln*, 105–108. Mary Johnson and Mariah Vance worked for the Lincolns in Springfield. Richard Lawrence Miller, "Life at Eighth and Jackson," in *The Mary Lincoln Enigma: Historians on America's Most Controversial First Lady*, ed. Frank J. Williams and Michael Burkhimer (Edwardsville: Southern Illinois University Press, 2012), 73. Ruth Stanton, a Black woman who worked for the Lincolns in Springfield in 1848, remembered Lincoln doing most of her own housework. See Washington, *They Knew Lincoln*, 242–243.

49. US Federal Manuscript Census of 1820, Dinwiddie, Virginia; US Federal Manuscript Census of 1830, Prince Edward, Virginia; US Federal Manuscript Census of 1840, Southern Division, Orange County, North Carolina; US Federal Manuscript Census of

1850, St. Louis County, Missouri; US Federal Manuscript Slave Census of 1850, St. Louis County, Missouri.

50. Elizabeth Fox-Genovese, *Within the Plantation Household: Black and White Women of the Old South* (Chapel Hill: University of North Carolina Press, 1988), 149–151; White, *Ar'n't I a Woman?*, 124.

51. Richard Wade, *Slavery in the Cities: The South, 1820–1860* (New York: Oxford University Press, 1967), 59–60.

52. For a discussion of the resistance of enslaved women to their mistresses' authority and oversight, see Glymph, *Out of the House*, 66–96.

53. Keckley, *Behind the Scenes*, 32–39, quotations on 33, 38, and 39.

54. Wendy Gamber, *The Female Economy: The Millinery and Dressmaking Trades, 1860–1930* (Urbana: University of Illinois Press, 1997), 97, 111–113, quotation on 102. Arlie Hochschild coined the term *emotional labor* in *The Managed Heart: Commercialization of Human Feeling* (Berkeley: University of California Press, 1983), 20. She suggests that workers such as Keckly manipulate their feelings to satisfy the perceived requirements of their jobs. For explorations of this concept, see Rebecca J. Erikson, "Why Emotion Work Matters: Sex, Gender, and the Division of Household Labor," *Journal of Marriage and the Family* 67, no. 2 (May 2005): 337–351; Louwanda Evans, *Cabin Pressure: African-American Pilots, Flight Attendants, and Emotional Labor* (Lanham, MD: Rowman and Littlefield, 2013).

55. Gamber, *Female Economy*, 103. In this sense, they were much like domestic servants as discussed in Judith Rollins, *Between Women: Domestics and Their Employers* (Philadelphia, PA: Temple University Press, 1985), 166–167.

56. Baker, *Mary Todd Lincoln*, 180.

57. Lewis Gaston Leary, *The Book-Peddling Parson* (Chapel Hill, NC: Algonquin, 1984).

58. Joshua Gamson, *Claims to Fame: Celebrity in Contemporary America* (Berkeley: University of California Press, 1994), 17–23; Richard Schickel, *Intimate Strangers: The Culture of Celebrity* (Garden City, NY: Doubleday, 1985), 28; Charles L. Ponce de Leon, *Self-Exposure: Human Interest Journalism and the Emergence of Celebrity in America, 1890–1940* (Chapel Hill: University of North Carolina Press), 4–5, 18–30, 42–75, 81; Leo Braudy, *The Frenzy of Renown: Fame and Its History* (New York: Oxford University Press, 1986), 13; Thomas N. Baker, *Sentiment and Celebrity: Nathaniel Parker Willis and the Trials of Literary Fame* (New York: Oxford University Press, 1999), 5–7.

59. James L. Crouthamel, *Bennett's* New York Herald *and the Rise of the Popular Press* (Syracuse, NY: Syracuse University Press, 1989); Baker, *Sentiment and Celebrity*, 6.

60. Braudy, *Frenzy of Renown*, 492–494; Robert Wilson, *Mathew Brady, Portraits of a Nation* (New York: Bloomsbury, 2013).

61. Braudy, *Frenzy of Renown*, 498–500; Neil Harris, *Humbug: The Art of P. T. Barnum* (Chapel Hill, NC: Algonquin, 1984), 43, 49–52, 93–102, 113–141.

62. Mary Lincoln to James Gordon Bennett, letter, October 25, 1861, in Turner and Turner, *Mary Todd Lincoln*, 110–111n6.

63. Mary Lincoln to James Gordon Bennett, letter, October 4, 1862, in Turner and Turner, *Mary Todd Lincoln*, 138.

64. Mary Lincoln to Abram Wakeman, letter, September 23, [1864], and March 20, [1865], in Turner and Turner, *Mary Todd Lincoln*, 180 and 205, respectively.

65. Braudy, *Frenzy of Renown*, 496.

66. Baker, *Mary Todd Lincoln*, 195.

67. "From Washington," *Chicago Daily Tribune*, February 14, 1863, 1. Quotation in Keckley, *Behind the Scenes*, 122–123.

68. Keckley, *Behind the Scenes*, 66, 76–77, 78, 90, 161; Jennifer Fleischner, *Mrs. Lincoln and Mrs. Keckly: The Remarkable Story of the Friendship Between a First Lady and a Former Slave* (New York: Broadway, 2003), 200; Virginia E. Reynolds, "Slaves to Fashion, Not Society: Elizabeth Keckly and Washington, DC's African-American Dressmakers, 1860–1870," *Washington History* 26, no. 2 (Fall 2014): 12.

69. Keckley, *Behind the Scenes*, 162; Reynolds, "Slaves to Fashion, Not Society," 11. The $2,000 of 1865 was worth approximately $31,000 in 2016; see https://westegg.com/infla tion/infl.cgi.

70. Keckley, *Behind the Scenes*, xiii, xiv.

71. Fleischner, *Mrs. Lincoln and Mrs. Keckly*, 317; Turner and Turner, *Mary Todd Lincoln*, 472; Ishbel Ross, *The President's Wife: Mary Todd Lincoln, a Biography* (New York: Putnam, 1973), 267; Lisa Shawn Hogan, "Exposing Mary Lincoln: Elizabeth Keckley and the Rhetoric of Intimate Disclosure," in *The Elizabeth Keckley Reader*, ed. Sheila Smith McCoy, vol. 2: *Artistry, Culture, and Commerce* (Hillsborough, NC: Eno, 2017), 188, 191; Stacy Pratt McDermott, *Mary Lincoln: Southern Girl, Northern Woman* (New York: Routledge, 2015), 140.

72. Turner and Turner, *Mary Todd Lincoln*, 472.

73. Aisha Francis, "Stepping Beyond the Formal Lines: Elizabeth Keckley, Gertrude Mossell, and the Cost of Transgression," in *The Elizabeth Keckley Reader*, ed. Sheila Smith McCoy, vol. 1: *Writing Self, Writing Nation* (Hillsborough, NC: Eno, 2017), 150.

74. Baker, *Mary Todd Lincoln*, 327, 342, 352, 365, 366, 368.

75. Reynolds, "Slaves to Fashion, Not Society," 5, 10.

76. Gamber, *Female Economy*, 137.

77. Keckley, *Behind the Scenes*, 222–225, quotation on 225.

78. "Dressmaking," *Daily National Intelligencer*, October 27, 1868, 3.

79. Catalogs of Wilberforce University for 1892–1893 through 1896–1897, https://books.google.com/books?id=1ahGAQAAMAAJ&pg=RA2-PA68&lp g=RA2-PA68&dq=the+keckley+stitch&source=bl&ots=hARyCs0Idx&sig=aY hjLXtmaF8wSQIf4apfNNJAoFA&hl=en&sa=X&ved=0ahUKEwjKn6LBw6n SAhUFeSYKHdMtAYI4ChDoAQg-MAY#v=onepage&q=the%20keckley%20 stitch&f=false.

80. Washington, *They Knew Lincoln*, 214, 222; Lewis Savoy typescript; Dolen Perkins-Valdez; "Introduction," in Keckley, *Behind the Scenes* (Hillsborough, NC: Eno, 2016), xvi. She was reburied in the National Harmony Memorial Park in Landover, Maryland. Perkins-Valdez, "Introduction," xvi.

# CHAPTER 7

# Southern Woman, Republican Partisan
## Mary Lincoln's Wartime Identity

Laura Mammina

A little more than three months after becoming first lady, Mary Lincoln sent an extraordinary gift to her home state of Kentucky: weapons. On the eve of the Civil War, Lincoln found herself in an unusual position as a Southerner, a Unionist, a Republican—and the wife of the president of the United States. Her gift, meant to help white Kentuckians defend themselves against a Confederate invasion, sent a message about the preeminence of the Union and the importance of the Border States in a conflict that she asserted was about preserving the Union rather than ending slavery.

In the letter accompanying the gift, Lincoln told of her "fond and filial pride" for her "native State," making no mention of its deep and abiding interests in slavery and the domestic slave trade. Instead, Lincoln focused on the challenges Kentucky faced. She asserted that "the institutions to whose fostering care we owe all we have of happiness and glory are rudely assailed by ungrateful and paricidal hands." Framing Confederates as the aggressors, Lincoln insisted that Kentucky could remain in the Union, keeping its "institutions" (including the institution of slavery) intact. Because she embraced these limited war aims, Lincoln expressed her confidence in "the ultimate loyalty of [Kentucky's] people, who, while never forgetting the homage which their Beloved State may justly claim, still remember the higher and grander allegiance due to our common country."[1] During a time of competing loyalties and choosing sides, Lincoln framed the Civil War as a conflict between white Americans, allowing her to argue that devotion to the Union—rather than to state or sectional concerns—was the duty of all Kentuckians and all white citizens.

Lincoln's letter makes clear that at the beginning of the Civil War, her preeminent principle, like that of many white Americans, was devotion to the Union in its current form. This was no accident. Lincoln benefited throughout her life from her privilege as a white woman. Her privilege rested on her marriage to a rising star in the Republican Party and on her ability to command the labor of Black men and women, continuing a tradition of first ladies who were either enslavers or had ties to slavery and who devoted themselves to the interests of their husbands and their political parties.[2] But the Civil War created unique challenges for Lincoln—as a Kentuckian who grew up in a family that enslaved people, as a resident of a western state, as a longtime Whig who came to the Republican Party only a few years prior to the war, and as a Unionist who did not embrace abolishing slavery. Although many Americans faced difficult choices in the wake of secession and the Civil War, Lincoln's identity—and her prominence—demonstrated the competing sectional and national loyalties of some white women. Lincoln refused to distance herself from Kentucky or from her Confederate family, and she strongly defended Unionism, advocated narrow war aims that would leave slavery intact, and embraced and enhanced the status of the Republican Party.[3] Indeed, her letter makes clear her position that one could be a white Southerner, a Unionist, and a Republican all while supporting the conservative vision that the war was one in which enslaved and free Black people had no say. Lincoln asserted throughout the war that all white Americans owed their full allegiance to the federal government and the federal Union because that government and that Union supported and maintained white supremacy.[4]

Examining Lincoln's wartime political identity and political sympathies demonstrates how she navigated her own complex background in the midst of restrictive wartime ideas about white women's loyalties and women's service. These ideas, broadly speaking, emphasized either devotion to the Confederacy for white Southern women or roles as partisan mediators for white Union women, whom many expected to help curb sectional tensions by negotiating between increasingly uncompromising Northern and Southern white men. But as Civil War race and gender scholars have pointed out, such restrictive roles entirely exclude Black women from Unionism and also do not reflect the experience of white Northern and Southern women.[5] Yet these simplistic characterizations of white women's experiences abound, particularly in biographical treatments of Lincoln. Even though Lincoln clearly articulated her wartime principles, she remained beset by contemporaries who doubted her allegiances and historians who have misinterpreted her positions. Biographers have traditionally portrayed Lincoln as a conflicted, meddlesome, vengeful, or abolitionist wartime first lady. Reading Lincoln's biographers in light of recent scholarship on U.S. women's political sympathies reveals that Lincoln created a hybrid wartime role for herself as a partisan Southern Republican Unionist whose ultimate goal was the preservation of the Union and the success of the Union Army, the Republican Party, and her husband. The influence of Early Republic to Civil War race and gender scholarship illuminates that she played a role both more subtle and strategic. Lincoln sought to influence friends and relatives in the Confederacy by advocating narrow war aims in order to ensure her husband's—and the army's—success, while she treaded carefully on the issue of slavery and expanded her role as a wartime first lady. Lincoln was able to accomplish these objectives by upholding the superiority of white women and exploiting the labor of Black men and women.

Lincoln's first biographer, her niece Katherine Helm, portrays her as a woman caught between several colliding worlds. Helm believed that Lincoln struggled with "divided loyalties" to Kentucky and the Union because she was the daughter of a Kentucky family that enslaved African Americans and the wife of a Republican from the West. Yet, as Justin G. Turner and Linda Levitt Turner noted more recently, Lincoln sympathized with her home state of Kentucky not because she was unsure which side to take but because she worried about a Confederate takeover. Instead of being divided in her wartime sympathies, Lincoln maintained that she could sympathize with her home state and remain loyal to the Union. In fact, her Unionist sympathies, loyalty to the Republican Party, and belief that the United States could best protect the interests of enslavers ran so deep that she viewed the decision of her own brother, Alexander Todd, to join the Confederate Army as a personal slight. As she told her dressmaker and confidante Elizabeth Keckly, "[Todd] decided against my husband, and through him against me. He has been fighting against us; and . . . [chose] to be our bitter enemy."[6]

Lincoln's ties to Kentucky and to her Confederate family should not be read as her supporting both the Confederacy and the Union. As Elizabeth R. Varon points out in her study of white Virginia women during secession, the question of disunion often caused conflict not within women but among them, with younger white women tending to be for secession and older white women for the Union. Lincoln follows the pattern of these older white women who "had experienced the political developments of the 1840s and 1850s as adults" and remained "attach[ed] to the argument that it was woman's nature and her duty to love the Union."[7] For Lincoln and many other Southern white women of her generation, the Union took precedence.

Lincoln's status as a prominent white woman made her Unionism acceptable and possible. In fact, her devotion to the Union *as it was* rested explicitly on her racial and gender status. She made this clear in an 1856 letter to her sister Emilie Todd Helm (Katherine Helm's mother), stating, "My weak woman's heart was too Southern in feeling, to sympathise with any but Fillmore" in that year's presidential election. Fillmore, the candidate of the American (Know-Nothing) Party, appealed to "the remnants of the white Party and tapped racism, nativism, class tensions, and a resilient strain of Unionism," as Varon notes. These are precisely the reasons Lincoln supported Fillmore. Lincoln informed her sister about "the *necessity* of keeping foreigners, within bounds." Her only comment in the letter about the issue of slavery was to assure her family that her husband was not an abolitionist. As Lincoln's own words make clear, Helm's characterization of the first lady is revisionist history that seeks to make, if not all white Southern women Confederates, then all white Southern women conflicted about whether to support the Confederacy. Many white Americans found it entirely possible to support the Union and espouse racist and nativist views.[8] The country had been founded on white supremacy, and many white Americans, Lincoln included, hoped to keep it that way. Where white Southerners disagreed was over whether the United States or the Confederacy would better protect white hegemony.

Lincoln's outspoken devotion to the Union became a liability in Carl Sandburg's 1932 *Mary Lincoln: Wife and Widow*. Relying heavily on reminiscences, Sandburg peddled the idea that Lincoln inserted herself too much into political matters. Indeed, he asserted that Lincoln overstepped her bounds from the start, believing that her position as first lady was not merely to "wife, comfort, cherish the new President and help him carry the load" but also to be "an adviser, an ex-officio cabinet officer, an auxiliary First Magistrate." "From the first," Sandburg argued, "she suggested appointments and was vehement as to who should fill this or that place."[9] Sandburg here drew on the views of President Lincoln's first biographer, William H. Herndon, whose scathing portrait of the first lady in his 1888 book included the assertion that her extreme sensitivity and inability to overlook perceived slights made her a political liability. As Herndon noted, "Ordinarily she was affable and even charming in her manners; but when offended or antagonized, her agreeable qualities instantly disappeared beneath a wave of stinging satire or sarcastic bitterness, and her entire better nature was submerged."[10] Although Herndon and Sandburg both found Lincoln's behavior and temperament problematic, her actions were in keeping with both white enslaving women's insistence upon mastery and control and the long-standing tradition of Whig womanhood; they were, furthermore, also consistent with white women's political activities in the wartime North. In this context, Lincoln's behavior is neither scandalous nor surprising but is instead an extension of her background in a slave-owning family and as a politician's wife who ascended to the highest role for a white woman in the nation.

As the daughter of a prominent Lexington enslaver and politician, Lincoln expected to command labor and to voice opinions on political matters. Despite the inequalities she experienced as a woman, she could count on being both obeyed by enslaved people and treasured by her family. Her political interests were a logical outflow of her privileged social position. "Whig women" such as Lincoln imbued politics with a supposedly superior morality while cloaking philanthropic activities under the guise of women's roles as wives and mothers. Although these women Whigs expanded their roles outward from the home, few if any of them challenged the enslavement of human beings or Black women's subordinate status because they benefited from these very systems.[11] In these ways, Lincoln's outspoken opinions and temperament were not the aberration Sandburg and Herndon made them out to be but were intimately tied to her identity as a white woman from an enslaving family.

That Lincoln expressed political views and served as an advisor to her husband is even more understandable in the context of the Civil War North. Historian Nina Silber notes that the Civil War brought "Northern women more clearly into the political arena, and it compelled a keener awareness and expression of their political views." The letters Northern women wrote to the president are of most interest and clearly show this pattern. These women approached President Lincoln "as fellow partisans," and "some asked for political appointments" for their husbands or male relatives. Just as perfect strangers felt it acceptable to write to the president to give him their views on the war and their requests for political office, so the president's wife saw advising her own husband as well in alignment with wartime standards for women's behavior. As scholar Judith Giesberg asserted, "The North's military victory was made possible by the willingness . . . of the public to tolerate the evidence of a profound disruption to domestic relations."[12] Both white and Black women raised supplies and funds for soldiers; in addition, Black women protested segregation on streetcars or organized contraband relief, and white women worked in arsenals or advised the president on political matters. Thus, wartime disruption encouraged and heightened Northern women's continued political involvement.

Yet the first lady received an inordinate amount of criticism during the war for her political engagement. Writing in 1953, Ruth Painter Randall attempted to contextualize this criticism, admitting that Lincoln "unwisely took a hand in political matters" and "shock[ed] . . . the public mind" by "getting out of woman's sphere," but Randall interpreted much of the public criticism of the first lady as a thinly veiled attack on the president.[13] In doing so, Randall did not reckon with the ways in which Lincoln's political sympathies and Southern background created great difficulties in a wartime United States newly obsessed with white women's political identities. In fact, the criticism Lincoln received from both Republicans and Democrats—critiques that went so far as to accuse her of spying for the Confederacy—clearly reveals Northern anxieties over white women's roles, especially during this era of the cult of true womanhood. Although Southern white women had slowly transitioned from sectional mediators to sectional partisans between 1840 and 1860, Northern white women (and white Southern Unionists) clung to their identities as partisan mediators, equating devotion to the Union with remaining a neutral and moderating force during political crises. Their devotion to the Union seemed to subsume and even transcend sectional concerns over the expansion of slavery, meaning that they favored compromise rather than the eradication of slavery. During the war, however, widespread devotion to the Confederacy on the part of white Southern women alongside dissent to Washington's demands from working-class and immigrant Northern white women, particularly during the draft riots, caused a reckoning among Northerners. With white women's loyalty to the Union no longer ensured, Northerners faced difficult questions about which women were loyal and how loyalty could be ascertained.[14]

In this context, white Civil War Northerners questioned the first lady's commitment to the Union as anyone with direct ties to the South or to the Confederacy became suspect. Given the specter of partisan Confederate womanhood, both Republicans and Democrats doubted the loyalty of a first lady from a Kentucky family who enslaved African Americans and whose brothers fought in the Confederate Army.[15] Both political parties declared that wartime allowed for no gray area: Radical Republicans questioned how Lincoln could possibly be committed to Republican abolitionist policies; Democrats wondered how, with close family supporting the Confederacy, she could possibly be a committed Unionist. Wartime white Northerners' obsession with Lincoln's slave-owning and Confederate ties reveals a reductionist view of Unionism and abolition. Recent scholarship has demonstrated that even white women who were not from enslaving families benefited from slavery, and it was certainly possible for women with extended family in the Confederate Army to be Unionists. Few if any white women during the Civil War era dedicated themselves to "a politics of radical antislavery" because the nation's entire economic system was implicated in this institution.[16] Black men and women abolitionists' calls that the entire nation needed to reckon with its involvement in the sin of slavery went unheeded. Instead, the preoccupation with Lincoln's Southern ties allowed white Northerners to pursue narrow war aims focused on preserving the nation as it had been prior to 1860.

Even when they acknowledge her achievements, Lincoln's biographers do not always do her endeavors justice. Turner and Turner's 1972 edited collection of Lincoln's letters recognized that some of the criticism of her was a result of wartime hysteria. But in other areas, particularly in her refurbishing of the White House, they attributed the massive undertaking to her desire to turn "a

national monument and public meeting place into a livable home for her family," a project in which she engaged as a way to "forget her fears" about the impending war. Continuing this line of argument, Turner and Turner argued that
"she had always sought security in possessions and found shopping an excellent
morale booster" but noted Lincoln's poor timing: "She dismissed the fact that
the government now had to defray the huge expense of arming, clothing, and
feeding tens of thousands of men" because she reasoned that "the President's
family could not under any circumstances be expected to live like transients in a
rundown hotel."[17] Lincoln certainly loved luxury goods, and her timing—even
though she had an appropriation from Congress—might have been better. But
to characterize Lincoln's overhaul of the White House as merely a distraction
done solely to benefit her family does her a disservice. Such criticisms of Lincoln's political opinions, actions, and sympathies by her contemporaries, then
repeated by her early biographers, conceal how much she accomplished as first
lady and also ignore the role played by Black labor in her efforts.

Scholar Catherine Allgor, writing about Dolley Madison's renovation of the
White House in the early nineteenth century, defends improvements to the Executive Mansion as more than mere vanity. "Style not only dictates what comprises
substance, it is substance. . . . Style . . . creates symbols and institutions that bind
people to the political system and to a government." Much like her predecessor,
Lincoln focused her efforts not only on improving the family quarters but also
those in which official state business was done. She remodeled the East and Blue
Rooms, which before boasted "threadbare rugs and curtains," and completely
updated the Green Room, outfitting it with "heavy gold-fringed draperies with
loops and tassels." Similar to Madison, Lincoln understood that the White
House was "a national symbol, a focus for the local Washington communities
and the people of the United States." This notion was lost on Turner and Turner
and on President Lincoln as well, who commented on his wife's overspending
by protesting that "the house was furnished well enough . . . better than any one
we ever lived in." But presidents require more than houses suitable to members
of Congress from a frontier state. As Allgor observes of Madison, "Successful
governors accomplish [ruling well] through persuasion rather than force. Such
efforts require the use of symbols and other visual statements." Lincoln's White
House renovation represented to the nation not only a new political party in
power but also the preeminence of the Union. Perhaps none of Lincoln's purchases demonstrated this more clearly than one of her most expensive: a set of
fine china for official dinners, featuring the US seal on each piece, with a "gold
border [entwined] with two lines signifying the union of North and South."[18]
Because Lincoln recognized the importance of symbols as a form of soft power,
state dinners officially reminded all White House guests of national power and

the indissolubility of the Union during the time of the Civil War. Even so, Lincoln did not accomplish these objectives on her own. Like all the Southern first ladies who preceded her, she followed the long-established pattern of commanding the labor of Black men and women to support and beautify a symbol of a federal government that denied equal rights to African Americans. By focusing so closely on Lincoln's overspending, historians miss the significance of the renovation and erase the contributions of Black labor.[19]

Later biographers recognize the ways in which Lincoln expanded the first lady's role at a moment when white and Black women's public participation was more visible. Even so, these biographers give Lincoln much of the credit, ignoring the ways in which her adherence to standards of true womanhood rested on the labor of Black men and women. Jean H. Baker argued that Lincoln played an integral role as a wartime (and Republican) first lady by continuing traditional activities, broadening the first lady's sphere of influence, and setting precedents for her successors. Even during a time of war, Lincoln understood the important social activities of first ladies. Maintaining a long-standing tradition of holding receptions, Lincoln indicated to Washington that the Civil War would not interrupt the normal functions of government or restrict public access to the president and first lady. Indeed, Baker noted that Lincoln held "twice-a-week winter and spring receptions when as many as 4,000 citizens crowded in the East Room" and "levees" on "New Year's Day and holidays." In this way Lincoln furthered the legacy of other prominent first ladies, most notably Madison, who promptly resumed her "drawing rooms" after the US government returned to Washington during the War of 1812.[20] In addition, Lincoln expanded the first lady's influence. Believing that the president should control the social functions of government, she seized control of diplomatic dinners from the secretary of state. As Baker observed, Lincoln "considered Secretary Seward her husband's rival," and so "unable to challenge the secretary in the cabinet room, she intended to deny him her dining room," telling her sister Elizabeth Edwards that "[President] Lincoln, not some minion at the State Department, was in charge of th[e] administration's social events." In this way, Lincoln enlarged the reach of the first lady and cemented the president's preeminence among members of his own party. Lincoln had learned well the lessons of Whig womanhood: by cloaking partisan actions under the mantle of women's domestic duties and moral imperatives, white women furthered their political agendas without seeming to step outside the bounds of their "proper" sphere.

While these receptions and state dinners expanded the first lady's influence, they also supported traditional hierarchies because Black Americans could not attend. Elizabeth Keckly noted that at the reception after President Lincoln's second inauguration, "orders were issued" that African Americans would not

Abraham (and Mary) Lincoln's last reception, 1865. Artist: Anton Hohenstein, Courtesy of the Library of Congress Prints and Photographs Division. Reproduction Number: LC-USZC4-2438 (color film copy transparency), LC-USZ62-12824 (b&w film copy neg.).

be admitted. Through the assistance of a friend, however, Frederick Douglass was given special access by the president. While formal events remained exclusively white affairs, both the president and first lady received African American visitors, including Douglass, Sojourner Truth, and an unnamed African American teacher. Even so, these and other social functions at the White House were possible because of the labor of free Black men and women. Because the first lady was committed to saving as much of the president's salary as possible, she discharged some members of the White House staff, employing a few Black men and women who could be paid less than their white counterparts. In this way, Lincoln drew on her background in an enslaving family and as an exacting employer of Black men and women in order to expand the role of first lady and ensure a comfortable retirement for herself and the president. And while the Lincolns did permit certain Black leaders to visit the White House, the only African Americans with unrestricted access to it were those who worked there.[21]

Lincoln's visits to soldiers' hospitals set further precedent for the functions of first ladies and demonstrated how her role as the president's wife was inseparable from her identity as a white woman. By choosing to put her energy into visiting wounded soldiers, Lincoln avoided involvement in the controversial issues of the day: ending slavery and supporting African American soldiers. Civil War historian and Lincoln biographer Catherine Clinton recognizes the importance of these visits, particularly because they mirrored the actions of many Northern and Southern white women during the war. By summer 1861, Lincoln and the president "began the first of what was to be a regular parade of hospital visits . . . together and separately over the next few years." By mid-July 1862, just five months after her son Willie's death, Lincoln "embarked on a program of ministering to soldiers" and "conducted a rigorous campaign of regular visitation," handing wounded soldiers fresh fruit and flowers and writing letters home for them. "By January 1863," Clinton argues, "Mary's hospital work had become her most zealous campaign . . . she visited the hospitals two or three times a week." Another flurry of visits took place in summer 1864. These visits were corroborated by accounts in various newspapers from Washington to New York City—papers that, as Clinton and others note, usually restricted their coverage of Lincoln to "gossip and . . . partisan reports."[22] More than any of her other activities, Lincoln's wartime service to the wounded illustrates the ways in which she interpreted her role as the most prominent woman in the United States while the country was at war. Through her hospital visits, Lincoln put her own stamp on the position of first lady, insisting that the nation needed more than mere lip service to the Union from its first lady. Lincoln's hospital visits demonstrated that she was not only the wife of the president but herself a citizen of the nation. And during a time of war, the cult of true womanhood maintained, women citizens owed their country a duty of service. White Confederates and white and Black Unionists labored for their countries throughout the conflict. Lincoln, through her service to wounded soldiers, demonstrated that the first lady was no exception.[23]

While Lincoln's wartime service set a new precedent for first ladies, it also kept her safely within the bounds of acceptable war work for wealthy white women—particularly those who did not want to be associated with radical antislavery work. White middle- and upper-class Northern and Southern women visited wounded soldiers in hospitals throughout the war as an extension of women's duty to care for the sick. Lincoln might have selected this particular form of service precisely because it did not transgress proper boundaries for white women's activities and because it did not wade into any of the divisive issues of the day, including African American soldiers, relief for freedpeople, and Black citizenship.[24] Only one very narrow aspect of Lincoln's wartime involvement touched on providing support for African Americans. Her dressmaker, Keckly, intended to do something to provide financial support for freedpeople and subsequently founded the Contraband Relief Association. As Keckly stated, Lincoln was the first to donate to the association, and she and the president gave more money during the war. Even so, Keckly made clear that more important contributions came from white and Black abolitionists and working-class African Americans. In addition, Keckly appears to have met these sympathetic people in spite of Lincoln, noting that she fit in her relief efforts around different trips on which she accompanied Lincoln. Keckly's account demonstrates the limits of Lincoln's involvement: she donated money but not her time or introductions to powerful people.[25] These actions seem entirely consistent with Lincoln's behavior as first lady. While she might have supported the interests of those who worked for her and contributed to the needs of those less fortunate, her goals first and foremost were to expand her role as first lady and ensure her husband's legacy as a formidable president.

Ironically enough, the most complete account of Lincoln's own view of her role as first lady survives in the biography most critical of her: Herndon's work. Because Herndon relied on others to supply him information on periods of the president's life that he did not directly witness, Mary Lincoln's statement during an interview with Herndon in September 1866 laid the foundation for his account of her time in the White House.[26] In her own words, Lincoln painted herself as a supportive—albeit opinionated—first lady. Rather than hiding her political opinions, Lincoln foregrounded them, asserting that her husband "placed great reliance on [her] knowledge of human nature" and often told her, "when about to make some important appointment, that he had no knowledge of men and their motives." Even so, she argued that her influence only went so far because "no man or woman, could rule him after he had once fully made up his mind." In this account, Lincoln complicated notions of domesticity by portraying herself as the opposite of a pure and moral creature who remained in the home so as not to be tainted by the sinful world of work and politics. Instead, Lincoln highlighted her political bona fides—her Whig womanhood and her Republican partisanship—setting her reputation as the cunning and worldly wise partner always on the lookout for her husband's best interests. In contrast, she gave the president feminine virtues as a leader who was kind, unsuspecting, and long suffering.[27] By portraying herself and her husband in this way in her interview with Herndon, Lincoln achieved two objectives. Ascribing her husband feminine virtues and yet a strong will and a mind of his own, a leader who "rose grandly with the circumstances," she cemented her husband's legacy as a lion of a president, a leader truly too good for this world. Claiming her own greater knowledge of human beings at the same time, Lincoln partially credited herself for her husband's success.[28] In so doing, she revealed that white women's political identities and sympathies were not as simplistic as many of her contemporaries or many of her biographers claimed. By fully acknowledging her political opinions, asserting a political partnership with her husband, and maintaining that she played a role even at the highest level of politics, Lincoln made clear that restrictive roles for women did not hamper privileged white Northern or Southern women from active involvement in politics, particularly as the first lady.

Biographers of Lincoln, and even some of her contemporaries, erred in viewing her activities as first lady as controversial or aberrant. Instead, her opinions and activities must be read together and put in the larger context of wealthy, enslaving white women's political identities and opinions from the Early Republic to the Civil War era. Examining Lincoln as a first lady in this light reveals her complicated legacy. This is evident in such attributes and practices as her fervent support for the preservation of the Union as it was, her involvement in persuading the Border States not to secede, her advice on political appointments, her refusal to shy away from her Southern background and Confederate connections in the wake of criticism, her insistence on the first lady's role as the leader of the capital city's social scene, her wartime service in soldiers' hospitals, and her reliance on the labor of Black men and women to achieve her goals. As this list suggests, Lincoln fully displayed the complexities in ideas about true womanhood, Whig womanhood, Republican partisanship, and white women's wartime service. Rather than a woman who stepped out of her appropriate sphere, Lincoln expected that her opinions would be respected and used her status as an upper-class white woman and her training in the tools and techniques of owning slaves to continue long-standing traditions of both first ladies and Whig women. These women, all of them wealthy and many of them enslavers, viewed themselves not as oppressed by the patriarchal society in which they lived but as having immense power and privilege and as important actors in the political realm because of their male relatives, even if their actions occurred outside of the formal political process. Whereas the wartime North struggled to come to terms with white women's political allegiance, Lincoln embraced the path of many of her predecessors while innovating in her own ways. In her unapologetic white supremacy, Southernness, devotion to the Union, and insistence on the preeminence of the presidency, she did not innovate her role but instead built on the examples of first ladies such as Madison, reshaping these women's legacies for a new era. In her words and actions as a Southern white woman and a Republican partisan, Lincoln articulated a distinctive and conservative vision of what a first lady and a white female citizen owed to her state, her political party, and ultimately to her country.

NOTES

This chapter benefited from an enormous amount of help from many people. I would like to thank George Rable for his advice on how to write something new about Mary Lincoln, a difficult task for any historian. Katherine A. S. Sibley also deserves thanks for her insightful questions and comments, as well as Teri Finneman, Sylvia Hoffert, and the rest of the contributors to this book. Last but not least, Brandon L. Lopez and Addie Dancer, student workers in the history program at Kalamazoo College during the 2017–2018 school year, helped immensely not only with research but also with their encouragement and wise questions about how best to empathetically approach the lives of people in the past and present.

1. Mary Lincoln to John Fry, letter, June 20, 1861, in Justin G. Turner and Linda Levitt Turner, *Mary Todd Lincoln: Her Life and Letters* (New York: Knopf, 1972), 91.

2. The vast scholarship of Black feminists is particularly useful here. See Audre Lorde, "The Master's Tools Will Never Dismantle the Master's House," *Sister Outsider: Essays and Speeches by Audre Lorde*, rev. ed. (New York: Ten Speed Press, 2007), 110–113.

3. There is much disagreement over Mary Lincoln's views on slavery, abolition, and emancipation. While Jean H. Baker regards the Todd family as antislavery because of its embrace of gradual emancipation, she believes Mary Lincoln agreed with her husband in favoring that slavery only be prevented from expanding, whereas Justin G. Turner, Linda Levitt Turner, and Catherine Clinton believe she eventually became an abolitionist, almost solely basing their opinion on the posthumous assessment of white abolitionist Jane Grey Swisshelm. The most nuanced opinion of Lincoln's views comes from the Mary Todd Lincoln House, https://www.mtlhouse.org/slavery. Historians should reevaluate Lincoln's positions based on the scholarship of Thavolia Glymph, who argues that "very few Americans at the time or since have questioned much about [wealthy white women's] ascent [and] how their wealth enabled their politics." Although Glymph's comments refer to wealthy white abolitionists, I see something similar happening with Lincoln. Jean H. Baker, *Mary Todd Lincoln: A Biography* (New York: Norton, 1987), 68, 150–151; Turner and Turner, *Mary Todd Lincoln*, 145–146; Catherine Clinton, *Mrs. Lincoln: A Life* (New York: HarperCollins, 2009), 199; Mary Todd Lincoln House, "Mary Todd Lincoln's Position on Slavery," 2020. For quotation, see Glymph, *The Women's Fight: The Civil War's Battles for Home, Freedom, and Nation* (Chapel Hill: University of North Carolina Press, 2020), 151–162. Regarding recent scholarship, see Tamika Nunley, "'I Know What Liberty Is': Elizabeth Keckly's Union War," in *New Perspectives on the Union War*, ed. Gary Gallagher and Elizabeth Varon (New York: Fordham University Press, 2019); Janet Neary, "'Behind the Scenes' and Inside Out: Elizabeth Keckly's Revision of the Slave Narrative Form," *African American Review* 47, no. 4 (2014): 555–573, esp. 567; Eric Foner, *The Fiery Trial: Abraham Lincoln and American Slavery* (New York: Norton, 2010). Regarding Southern Unionists and Confederate women, see Glymph, *Women's Fight*; Elizabeth R. Varon, *We Mean to Be Counted: White Women and Politics in Antebellum Virginia* (Chapel Hill: University of North Carolina Press, 1998), 138, 152; Stephanie McCurry, *Confederate Reckoning: Power and Politics in the Civil War South* (Cambridge, MA: Harvard University Press, 2010), 117–132; Anya Jabour, *Scarlett's Sisters: Young Women in the Old South* (Chapel Hill: University of North Carolina Press, 2007), 246–251; Victoria

E. Ott, *Confederate Daughters: Coming of Age During the Civil War* (Carbondale: Southern Illinois University Press, 2008), 45–60. Regarding Northern women, see Glymph, *Women's Fight*; Jeanie Attie, *Patriotic Toil: Northern Women and the American Civil War* (Ithaca, NY: Cornell University Press, 1998), 1–5; Judith Giesberg, *Army at Home: Women and the Civil War on the Northern Home Front* (Chapel Hill: University of North Carolina Press, 2009), 10–13, 23–40; Nina Silber, *Daughters of the Union: Southern Women Fight the Civil War* (Cambridge, MA: Harvard University Press, 2005), 25–40.

4. Regarding first ladies and slavery, see the White House Historical Association, *Slavery in the President's Neighborhood*, https://www.whitehousehistory.org/spn/introduction. Regarding enslaved African Americans in the White House, see Jesse J. Holland, *The Invisibles: The Untold Story of African American Slaves in the White House* (New York: Lyons Press, 2016); Clarence Lusane, *The Black History of the White House* (San Francisco: City Lights, 2011). Regarding the federal government maintaining white supremacy, see Don E. Fehrenbacher, *The Slaveholding Republic: An Account of the United States Government's Relations to Slavery*, ed. Ward M. McAfee (Oxford, UK: Oxford University Press, 2001); Foner, *Fiery Trial.*

5. Attie, *Patriotic Toil*, 30–37; Giesberg, *Army at Home*, 17–22; Silber, *Daughters of the Union*, 124–125; McCurry, *Confederate Reckoning*, 117–132.

6. Katherine Helm, *The True Story of Mary, Wife of Lincoln* (New York: Harper and Brothers, 1928), 160, 164, 171–172, 183–187, 193–195, 208–209; Turner and Turner, *Mary Todd Lincoln*, 91, 101; Elizabeth Keckley, *Behind the Scenes, or Thirty Years a Slave, and Four Years in the White House* (New York: G. W. Carleton, 1868), 135–136.

7. See Varon, *We Mean to Be Counted*, 152, and 137–168 for white Virginia women's views on secession and Civil War. White Unionist women remain woefully understudied, particularly those from the Border States, but examples of white Southern women for whom the choice between Union and disunion was clear abound. See Josie Underwood, *Josie Underwood's Civil War Diary*, ed. Nancy Disher Baird (Lexington: University Press of Kentucky, 2009); Frances Peter, *A Union Woman in Civil War Kentucky: The Diary of Frances Peter*, ed. John David Smith and William Cooper Jr. (Lexington: University Press of Kentucky, 2000); Elizabeth A. Getz, "Between the Lines: The Diary of a Unionist Woman at the Battle of Spotsylvania Court House," *Fredericksburg History and Biography*, vol. 1 (2002), 56–90. See also Laura Mammina, "'In the Midst of Fire and Blood': Union Soldiers, Unionist Women, Military Policy, and Intimate Space During the American Civil War," *Civil War History* 64, no. 2 (2018): 146–175. Regarding Helm's view and the "Lost Cause," see Ott, *Confederate Daughters*, 157–166; Caroline E. Janney, *Burying the Dead but Not the Past: Ladies' Memorial Associations and the Lost Cause* (Chapel Hill: University of North Carolina Press, 2008), 170–173. For the stark choice white Northern women faced, see Silber, *Daughters of the Union*, 145.

8. Mary Lincoln to Emilie Todd Helm, letter, November 23, 1856, in Turner and Turner, *Mary Todd Lincoln*, 46; Elizabeth R. Varon, *Disunion! The Coming of the American Civil War, 1789–1859* (Chapel Hill: University of North Carolina Press, 2008), 258. Regarding lost cause mythology, see Gaines M. Foster, *Ghosts of the Confederacy: Defeat, the Lost Cause, and the Emergence of the New South, 1865–1913* (Oxford, UK: Oxford University Press, 1987). Regarding the US commitment to white supremacy, see Fehrenbacher, *Slaveholding Republic.* Regarding Unionists' debate on whether the United States or the Confederacy would

better support slavery, see Daniel Crofts, *Reluctant Confederates: Upper South Unionists in the Secession Crisis* (Chapel Hill: University of North Carolina Press, 1989); McCurry, *Confederate Reckoning*.

9.  Carl Sandburg and Paul M. Angle, *Mary Lincoln, Wife and Widow* (New York: Harcourt, Brace, 1932), 80, 90. For Lincoln scholars who agree with Sandburg's view, see Ruth Painter Randall, *Mary Lincoln: Biography of a Marriage* (Boston: Little, Brown, 1953), 249–252; Michael Burlingame, *Abraham Lincoln: A Life*, vol. 2 (Baltimore: Johns Hopkins University Press, 2008), 262–263; William H. Herndon and Jesse W. Weik, *Herndon's Lincoln*, ed. Douglas L. Wilson and Rodney O. Davis (Urbana: University of Illinois Press, 2006), 132–134, 257–258. For an exception to this view that closely examines Lincoln's early life, see Kenneth J. Winkle, "'An Unladylike Profession': Mary Lincoln's Preparation for Greatness," in *The Mary Lincoln Enigma: Historians on America's Most Controversial First Lady*, ed. Frank J. Williams and Michael Burkhimer (Carbondale: Southern Illinois University Press, 2012), 82–111.

10.  Herndon and Weik, *Herndon's Lincoln*, 132–134.

11.  Baker, *Mary Todd Lincoln*, 8–9, 18, 62, 66, 78; Stephanie Jones-Roberts, "Mistresses in the Making," in *Women's America: Refocusing the Past*, 9th ed., ed. Linda K. Kerber et al. (Oxford, UK: Oxford University Press, 2015), 145; Jones-Roberts, *They Were Her Property: White Women as Slave Owners in the American South* (New Haven, CT: Yale University Press, 2020). Regarding Whig womanhood, see Varon, *We Mean to Be Counted*, 73–102. Regarding Mary Lincoln as a Whig woman, see Winkle, "'Unladylike Profession,'" 86–92.

12.  Silber cites the dissertation of Rachel Seidman, which estimates that women wrote 30,000 letters to the federal government during the Civil War; see Seidman, "Beyond Sacrifice: Women and Politics on the Pennsylvania Home Front During the Civil War," PhD diss., Yale University, 1996. Regarding the political involvement of white and Black working-class women, see Giesberg, *Army at Home*, 68–142, 177; Glymph, *Women's Fight*, 127–195. White Southern women also expressed their views to wartime officials: see George C. Rable, *Civil Wars: Women and the Crisis of Southern Nationalism* (Urbana: University of Illinois Press, 1989); McCurry, *Confederate Reckoning*.

13.  Randall, *Mary Lincoln*, 218, 249, 252, 253–254, 306–318.

14.  Both white Northerners and white Southerners largely ignored the wartime contributions of Black women. See Glymph, *Women's Fight*; Erica L. Ball, *To Live an Antislavery Life: Personal Politics and the Antebellum Black Middle Class* (Athens: University of Georgia Press, 2012). Regarding the links between Republican motherhood and the cult of true womanhood, see Linda K. Kerber, *Women of the Republic: Intellect and Ideology in Revolutionary America* (Chapel Hill: University of North Carolina Press, 1980); Nancy F. Cott, *The Bonds of Womanhood: "Woman's Sphere" in New England, 1780–1835* (New Haven, CT: Yale University Press, 1977), 24–43, 46, 58. Regarding Northerners assuming white women's devotion to the Union and role as partisan mediators, see Reid Mitchell, *The Vacant Chair: The Northern Soldier Leaves Home* (Oxford, UK: Oxford University Press, 1993); 72–74, 90, 91–96; Attie, *Patriotic Toil*, 4, 7, 11–12. On the term *true womanhood*, see Barbara Welter, "The Cult of True Womanhood: 1820–1860," *American Quarterly* 18, no. 2, pt. 1 (Summer 1966): 151–174. Regarding white working-class and immigrant women's wartime dissent, see Giesberg, *Army at*

*Home*, 119–142. Regarding Northerners viewing white Southern women as united behind the Confederacy, see Mitchell, *Vacant Chair*, 89–133; Silber, "The Northern Myth of the Rebel Girl," in *Women of the American South: A Multicultural Reader*, ed. Christie Anne Farnham (New York: New York University Press, 1997), 120–132.

15. For these ideas, see Varon, *We Mean to Be Counted*, 72, 79–80, 102. Regarding how white Republican women balanced increased political action with appearing "above the partisan fray," see Silber, *Daughters of the Union*, 139–149.

16. Glymph, *Women's Fight*, 12, 127–162.

17. Turner and Turner, *Mary Todd Lincoln*, 80, 87.

18. Turner and Turner, 80, 87, 89; Catherine Allgor, *Parlor Politics: In Which the Ladies of Washington Help Build a City and a Government* (Charlottesville: University of Virginia Press, 2000), 54, 59, 63; Baker, *Mary Todd Lincoln*, 181–182, 186–187, 190–191.

19. There is ample opportunity for future scholars to build on the work of Erica Armstrong Dunbar in examining the relationship of first ladies to Black laborers in the White House, particularly enslaving first ladies and enslaved men and women. Erica Armstrong Dunbar, *Never Caught: The Washingtons' Relentless Pursuit of Their Runaway Slave, Ona Judge* (New York: 37 Ink, 2017); Callie Hopkins, "The Enslaved Household of President James Madison," White House Historical Association, https://www.whitehousehistory.org/spn /introduction; James B. Conroy, "Slavery's Mark on Lincoln's White House," *Slavery in the President's Neighborhood*, White House Historical Association, https://www.whitehouse history.org/spn/introduction. Regarding free Black men and women workers in the Lincoln White House, see Baker, *Mary Todd Lincoln*, 190–191; Lusane, *Black History of the White House*, 169–218.

20. Baker, *Mary Todd Lincoln*, 190–191, 196–200; Allgor, *Parlor Politics*, 73–77, 98; Varon, *We Mean to Be Counted*, 72. For other first ladies who used social activities to achieve political objectives, see Allgor, *Parlor Politics*, 78–87, 241.

21. Keckley, *Behind the Scenes*, 158–160; Clinton, *Mrs. Lincoln*, 171; Lusane, *Black History of the White House*, 200–215; Nell Irvin Painter, *Sojourner Truth: A Life, a Symbol* (New York: Norton, 1996), 203–207; Baker, *Mary Todd Lincoln*, 190–191. Regarding Lincoln's history of exploiting the labor of Black women, see Baker, *Mary Todd Lincoln*, 105–108.

22. Clinton, *Mrs. Lincoln*, 140–142, 142–145, 174, 180–182, 194–196, 221–222; for newspaper accounts, see her notes for pages 143, 145, 174, 180–181, 196, 221, 222. What is striking about these visits is how little other biographers, either of the president or the first lady, have had to say about them. Herndon mentions them not at all, David Herbert Donald mentions them in passing, and Michael Burlingame devotes a small paragraph. Baker's coverage is more extensive, given that her focus is solely on Mary Lincoln.

23. Varon, *We Mean to Be Counted*, 164; Silber, *Daughters of the Union*, 194–221; Attie, *Patriotic Toil*, 31, 33, 52, 95, 198; Giesberg, *Army at Home*, 145.

24. Painter, *Sojourner Truth*, 207; Foner, *Fiery Trial*, 204, 214–215, 222, 234–235, 290–302; Glymph, *Women's Fight*, 158–159; Glenn David Brasher, "Debating Black Manhood: The Northern Press Reports on the 54th Massachusetts at Fort Wagner," in *American Discord: The Republic and Its People in the Civil War Era*, ed. Megan Bever et. al (Baton Rouge: Louisiana State University Press, 2020), 22–44. Regarding Northern white women who

opposed emancipation and Black citizenship, see Silber, *Daughters of the Union*, 132–133; the majority of support for freedpeople and for African American soldiers came from the Black community because of the localized (and racist) attitudes of many white Northern women: see Glymph, *Women's Fight*, 159–161; Silber, *Daughters of the Union*, 160–161, 224, 232–235.

25. Regarding white Northern and Southern women's work caring for soldiers, see Lisa Tendrich Frank, "'With Hearts Nerved by the Necessity for Prompt Action': Southern Women, Mobilization, and the Wartime State"; and Jeanie Attie, "Real Women and Mythical Womanhood: War Relief at the Northern Homefront," in *Women and the American Civil War*, ed. Judith Giesberg and Randall M. Miller (Kent, OH: Kent State University Press, 2018), 48–49, 160–161. Regarding Keckly's Contraband Relief Association, see Baker, *Mary Todd Lincoln*, 230–231; Keckley, *Behind the Scenes*, 111–116.

26. See Herndon and Weik, *Herndon's Lincoln*, 145, 252–253, for two examples of the way in which Herndon presents the president much more favorably than he does the first lady. Regarding Herndon on Abraham Lincoln's time as president, see Herndon and Weik, *Herndon's Lincoln*, 298–305, 307–311, 312–338.

27. Herndon and Weik, *Herndon's Lincoln*, 306–307. Regarding the separation between home and work (and/or politics) and white women's duty to create a refuge from the world (rather than being involved in it), see Cott, *Bonds of Womanhood*, 64–72; Julie Roy Jeffrey, *Frontier Women: "Civilizing" the West?*, rev. ed. (New York: Hill and Wang, 1998), 14–17.

28. The first lady attributing female virtues to the president to cement his reputation was not a new tactic. Catherine Allgor argues that Margaret Bayard Smith similarly described former president Thomas Jefferson, highlighting his domestic, feminine virtues to counter charges that he was a "power-made despot" and also to "showcase [his] manhood and citizenship," ultimately using the domestic world to "package and project power." See Allgor, "Margaret Bayard Smith's 1809 Journey to Monticello and Montpelier: The Politics of Performance in the Early Republic," *Early American Studies* 10, no. 1 (2012): 47–55; Cynthia A. Kierner, *Martha Jefferson Randolph, Daughter of Monticello: Her Life and Times* (Chapel Hill: University of North Carolina Press, 2012), chap. 4.

# CHAPTER 8

# Press and Propaganda
## Examining War Coverage of the Confederate First Lady

Teri Finneman

Varina Howell Davis's role as first lady has rendered her so controversial in US history that she is often left out of scholarship altogether. Her position as representative of a traitorous would-be nation, one organized in support of white supremacy and the institution of slavery, makes this eminently understandable. Yet the story of the Confederate first lady deserves to be told to gain a better understanding of her and her role during this most contentious time in US history—a defining moment that remains contested in historical memory as well, as evidenced in the recent debate over Confederate monuments. As novelist Charles Frazier has noted, "The Civil War keeps rearing its head. . . . We never resolved the issues that rose from the ownership of human beings: the issues of race, [the] aftermath of slavery, all those things that we're still carrying with us."[1]

This chapter does not memorialize Davis like a monument might; instead, as an act of historical transparency, I seek to understand her as representative of the South's enduring cultural legacy on the office and institution of the first lady. Many first ladies shared Davis's views about slavery and white supremacy, of course, and the cultural norms that produced her also influenced the inhabitants of the White House both before and after. Indeed, after the Union defeated the Confederacy and reabsorbed it, many Confederate views and ideals remained, as we see with the "lost cause" mythology, which obsessed first ladies such as Edith Wilson and continues to reverberate today. The Union and the Confederacy might have been distinct political entities, but they shared deep sociocultural harmony, as emblematized by the statues and bases that continue to dot the Southern United States (and extending North as well). These cultural norms have been themes this book aims to interrogate.

Like her first lady counterparts in Washington, Davis was a national symbol for her countrymen and -women as Confederate first lady. Even if the nation-building attempt with which she was associated failed—and she did not always enthusiastically back her husband's government, as we shall see here—she served to represent her nation just as the official first ladies did. Her role thus further illuminates aspects of the Southern first lady this book seeks to explore, including that region's enduring cultural legacy on this office and institution.

Raised in Mississippi and later a plantation mistress and a Mississippi senator's wife, Davis nonetheless would face criticism during the Civil War as to how Southern she was. Her devotion to the Confederate cause was questioned in part because of her continued connections with friends and relatives in the North and published interviews with people she formerly enslaved, as this chapter highlights. Antislavery newspapers in particular emphasized her lack of commitment to the cause and to slavery itself. The latter was inaccurate but underlines the importance of her post as lending itself to others' propaganda purposes. Mostly, during the war years and beyond, her family symbolized Southern rights and pride for both Southerners and Northerners. In the years after Reconstruction, she played a role similar to that of Julia Tyler and Sarah Polk—a Southern white wife who served to "redeem" the South. In Davis's case, her journalism openly perpetuated the myth of the lost cause. This chapter explores press coverage of Davis during the Civil War to learn how both Northern and Southern newspapers framed the most prominent woman in the Confederacy and explores her life and work after the war as well. First, however, it is important to understand how Davis rose to her infamous role in history.

## NORTHERN AND SOUTHERN ROOTS

Davis was just thirty-four when she became Confederate first lady, and she had an unusual background for the most prominent woman in the South. Born on May 7, 1826, at her wealthy maternal grandfather's plantation in Louisiana, she was the second of eleven children of William and Margaret Kempe Howell, who raised their family in Natchez, Mississippi.[2] From the beginning, she also had Northern ties that influenced her life. Her paternal grandfather, Richard Howell, had been a prominent politician in the North, serving as New Jersey's governor from 1793 to 1801. Even though she never met her Northern grandfather, Davis liked to tell stories about him passed down through the family.[3]

Her father moved to the South in 1815, after serving in the War of 1812, in hopes of earning a fortune from plantation life.[4] One of the first friends he made after arriving in Mississippi was Joseph Davis, the much older brother of Jefferson Davis. Although Howell's move to the South sealed Varina's future because this was where she met Jefferson, the same cannot be said for her father. A mixture of poor business decisions and the Panic of 1837 led to her family filing for bankruptcy and having their possessions sold at auction in 1838.[5] For Varina, just twelve years old at the time, the bankruptcy "was one of the most painful moments" of her life, and she was "haunted forever after by the spectacle of a man going broke and taking his family down with him," as Joan E. Cashin wrote.[6] If not for the frequent aid of her mother's relatives, who also bought back the family's possessions, the Howell family would have been in even more precarious financial straits. Still, Varina felt the burden of the family's tight finances because she was expected to become more involved in homemaking and caring for her growing number of siblings, further alienating her from the planter elite's Southern belle ideal, which took hold in American culture in the 1830s to symbolize status.[7] Unlike other young Southern women of her time, Varina did not have a ball marking her official debut, the luxury of parties, or a cast of potential suitors.[8]

Beyond her family's class status, she differed in other ways from her peers. With her olive complexion from her Welsh ancestors, she did not look the part of a Southern belle with "milk-white skin," either.[9] Her personality also set her apart thanks to two childhood role models: her Southern grandmother, Margaret Kempe, and her Northern tutor, George Winchester. From Kempe, she learned Southern social skills, but she also inherited her grandmother's unladylike "biting wit and temperamental vigor."[10] This was a blessing and a curse. Varina benefited from an outgoing personality in her future social roles but at times would alienate those around her, such as when a dinner guest did not understand a joke she made and thought she was insulting the guest's marriage.[11] Her education from Madame Grelaud's academy in Philadelphia, likely financially supported by a godfather or an uncle, and her years of tutoring from Winchester also set her apart.[12] Winchester, whom she referred to as a "saintly man," was a Yale graduate, judge, Whig political figure, and close family friend.[13] Although it was common for Southern belles to receive an education, as Christie Anne Farnham noted, "being an intellectual was inconceivable. A belle could be silly but not serious—at least not serious over her studies" because she ultimately deferred to the "superior knowledge" of men.[14] Varina, in contrast, thrived in her studies and knew firsthand from her father's financial failure that men were not always wiser.[15]

She was seventeen when Joseph Davis invited her to visit his plantation seventy miles away in 1843; she had declined a prior invitation so she could finish her schoolwork.[16] During her visit, she became acquainted with Jefferson Davis, a widower more than twice her age previously married to Sarah Knox Taylor, daughter of future president Zachary Taylor. Jefferson had spent the previous eight years as a bachelor after his first wife died from malaria just months into their marriage.[17] Varina Howell described her first impression of Jefferson Davis in a letter to her mother, an artifact that foreshadows the future ups and downs of their marriage: "He impresses me as a remarkable kind of man, but of uncertain temper, and has a way of taking for granted that everybody agrees with him when he expresses an opinion, which offends me; yet he is most agreeable and has a peculiarly sweet voice and a winning manner of asserting himself."[18]

The couple married February 26, 1845, and settled into life at Davis's plantation, Brierfield. The honeymoon was short-lived because Jefferson launched his political career that summer, resulting in the first of many long separations throughout their lifetimes. The new teenage bride was not happy with her husband's decision to run for a Democratic seat in the US House of Representatives: "Then I began to know the bitterness of being a politician's wife, and that it meant long absences, pecuniary depletion from ruinous [plantation] absenteeism, illness from exposure, misconceptions, defamation of character; everything which darkens the sunlight and contracts the happy sphere of home."[19]

As Jefferson Davis bounced from life as a US representative in Washington to a soldier in the Mexican American War to life back in Washington as a US senator during the early years of their marriage, his wife struggled to adapt. Not only did she have insecurity about being his second wife, but the couple remained childless during the first seven years of their marriage. In addition, Varina missed her own family, particularly during long periods home alone.[20] She initially was unclear about what was expected of her as a plantation mistress overseeing seventy-four enslaved men and women and "expressed surprise that the slaves required so much of her time" in providing food, clothing, and medical care.[21] Furthermore, she chafed at gender norms of the time and wanted a more equal partnership with her husband with more say over her own rights and home.[22] Yet Jefferson, as Carol Berkin writes, "made it abundantly clear that he disapproved of her willfulness, her stubbornness, and what he considered her unfeminine insistence on independent judgement."[23] When he left his wife behind in Mississippi to return to Washington as a senator in November 1847, she had no choice but to bend to his wishes and declared herself a "thoughtless, dependent wife" to smooth things over.[24]

Although Varina had lived in Washington during his brief stint as a US representative, she became more engaged after he became a senator and then secretary of war for Franklin Pierce from 1853 to 1857. She thrived in the Washington social scene.[25] She became a frequent White House visitor and developed friendships with first ladies Margaret Taylor and Jane Pierce while maintaining a strong entertainment schedule in her own home.[26] She also supported her husband by assisting with his work and visiting the Senate gallery to listen to floor speeches; he was back in the Senate during the Buchanan administration.[27] Although Davis had accepted the subservience attached to her role as a wife, her personality remained unchanged, and her "judgments could be cutting and her opinions always were freely expressed."[28] As a result, she tended to connect better with the serious conversations of the men than with society women, who found her "haughty and aloof." She considered their gossip "frivolous" and "inane."[29]

By this time, the Davises had also settled into family life. Their first son, Samuel, died from measles before his second birthday. His siblings, Margaret, Jefferson Jr., and Joseph followed, with two more—William and Varina Anne (known as Winnie)—born during the war. Some of Varina Davis's siblings also lived with the family in those years.[30] As tensions grew between the North and South, the turning point for the Davis family came on January 9, 1861, when Mississippi withdrew from the Union. Twelve days later, Jefferson resigned from the Senate and packed up his family to return to their home state. Decades later, while writing his biography, Varina recalled her feelings of that time, writing that they left Washington "exceedingly sorrowful" and "mourned in secret over the severance of tender ties both of relationship and friendship."[31] Washington had become home for Davis—where her first four children were born, her friends lived, and her status and security were acquired.[32] Therefore, her feelings about secession were contradictory, not surprisingly for someone with a lifetime of strong ties to both the North and the South. She supported both the Union and slavery.[33] She knew the South did not have the population or resources to win the war.[34] However, she believed in both the "constitutional guarantees and legal obligations" of slavery, as she wrote later, and argued, as her husband did, that they cared for those they enslaved, thereby perpetuating the myth that their enslaved people were content in this role.[35]

Within weeks of Jefferson Davis's resignation, a messenger arrived at the Brierfield plantation in early February 1861 with the news that he was elected provisional Confederate president.[36] The choice was not surprising because he was a longtime Southern Democratic leader whose name had been suggested as a presidential candidate in 1860.[37] Years after the war, Varina recalled that her husband, upon hearing of his election, "looked so grieved that I feared some evil had befallen our family. After a few minutes' painful silence, he told me, as a man might speak of a sentence of death. As he neither desired nor expected the position, he was more deeply depressed than before."[38] Despite her new, elevated status as first lady, she later wrote that she "could not rally or be buoyed up," anticipating the battles ahead.[39] In a letter to her mother in June 1861, Davis complained about the exhausting constant attention from the public and stated her belief that the South could not win the war.[40] As we have seen, going back to Martha Washington, American first ladies have been closely involved in the project of building a national culture and in serving as defining symbols for their country. Varina Davis was now required to be such a builder of her nation, albeit a reluctant one.

## CIVIL WAR JOURNALISM

Before examining the news coverage specific to the Confederate first lady, it is important to understand what the newspaper industry was like during the Civil War. Significant changes in the 1800s resulted in the press becoming a "political, social, and economic force" by the time the war began.[41] Technical advances in printing paved the way for the penny press era, when newspapers were quickly produced and affordable to a mass audience at the cost of 1 cent per paper.[42] In addition, the extension of the railroads provided for greater distribution of news across the nation, as did the invention of the telegraph in 1844.[43] By the start of the war, nearly four thousand newspapers operated in the United States, with some cities served by multiple papers.[44]

Despite the new technological advances, providing news coverage of the Civil War was difficult. Finding people willing to serve as war reporters was a challenge, particularly in the South, where nearly three-fourths of printers left their businesses to serve in the military.[45] As the war progressed, limited supplies of paper, type, and ink created problems for Southern newspapers, not to mention the advertising revenue lost as a result of the economic toll of the war.[46] Shortages of paper were so extreme that a ream costing $3 to $5 at the start of the war spiked to $50 to $60 by 1864, resulting in a soaring cost for subscriptions.[47] The expense of sending dispatches via telegraph and the strenuous process of mailing reports back to newspaper offices added other hurdles. The quality of reporting was also mixed. In this era before journalism schools, reporters lacked proper training, and many reports came from what would now be referred to as citizen journalists.[48] Furthermore, like the soldiers they were covering, journalists were susceptible to being killed on the battlefield or dying from diseases that spread through camps.[49] Therefore, gathering, reporting, and publishing news during the war years was remarkably difficult at a time when demand for news escalated. In the South, Confederate newspapers tried to use their platform to rally support and convince Southerners that the struggle for the cause was worth it.[50] Their effectiveness was debatable, particularly when three-fourths of newspapers were based in the North and when Jefferson Davis was not as interested in talking to the press as Abraham Lincoln was.[51] Still, an anxious public on both sides clamored for news, with crowds gathering around newspaper bulletin boards and going to reading rooms to get updates.[52]

The rise of a second first lady in 1861 created an unparalleled twist with both Mary Lincoln and Varina Davis thrust into the roles of leading female political figures during a time of national turmoil unlike any other. How would the press react to this alternate first lady, this first lady of the Confederacy? Would she be treated as legitimate? Would she be mocked in the North and revered in the South? How would each woman come to symbolize her government's claim to sovereign nationhood, and how would the press portray their respective nation-building (as well as nation-sundering) efforts? News reports not only influence members of society at the time of publication but also capture and preserve the political and social cultures of a particular era.[53] Press constructions of first ladies are important because news reports are often the sole source of information the public has about these women.[54] As national celebrities who exercise varying levels of political and social influence, first ladies are prime subjects to better understand such cultural phenomena.[55]

An analysis of newspaper coverage of Davis between 1861 and 1865 found that she received generally positive news coverage in Southern papers and mixed coverage in the North.[56] Most notable were the Northern reports that called into question her dedication to the South. Furthermore, even though coverage of her appeared in newspapers across the country, the amount of original reporting tended to be limited. In other words, it was common to see the same story in multiple newspapers—which added to the numerical count of how often she was in the media—yet original content about her was sparse.

## CONFEDERATE SCHEMER AND NORTHERN SYMPATHIZER

During her initial days as first lady, Davis generated publicity when newspapers reported in March 1861 that she stopped in New Orleans to see her parents, who now lived there, before joining her husband in the temporary Confederate capital of Montgomery, Alabama. A news story described her as a "most estimable and gifted lady" who hosted a reception and received a serenade from Southern soldiers during her stay. The article originated in the *New Orleans Picayune* but was picked up by Northern papers, including those in Chicago, Boston, and New York.[57] Davis remembered this event years later, writing that the enthusiasm of the men "depressed me dreadfully" because she feared for their fates.[58] The contrasting perspectives of this one event foreshadowed Davis's press coverage throughout the rest of the war. Within two months, anonymous rumblings began that contradictorily framed her as both a Confederate schemer and a Northern sympathizer, depending upon the story.

In one of the first instances, a Republican newspaper in Pennsylvania ran a story claiming that Davis told a woman in Montgomery of her plans to take over the White House. The story cited a letter from a "gentleman of high position in Washington" who alleged that Davis expected to receive social calls at the Executive Mansion within two months. This prompted the reporter to write, "This is very elaborate trifling, or unsurpassed castle building."[59] Within weeks, other media outlets retracted the story by citing a letter that Davis wrote to a friend in Washington that called the claim "erroneous and unjust." One journalist added a line to the story noting, "It was very kind of Mrs. Davis to contradict such an alarming report."[60] Yet a similar story resurfaced in Northern papers several months later in which Davis reportedly told one of the women she enslaved that the Confederate government would take over Washington, and she would be mistress of the White House.[61] This coverage illustrates not only the level of editorializing present in journalism during that time but also a lack of verification techniques, such as direct interviewing, that did not become more standard until a decade later.[62] Whether purposely intended as propaganda, these stories of Davis's purported ambitions of Northern dominance potentially served as a motivating tool for the Unionists to resist the South in the early days of the war. For many Americans, the figure of the first lady as a defining symbol of national identity, especially in her role as mistress of the nation's house, was powerful enough that even the rumor of Davis's arrival at Pennsylvania Avenue caused alarm. Southern newspapers such as the *Western Democrat* in North Carolina carried the same story claiming Davis expected to occupy the White House, likely for the same propaganda reasons to motivate the public.[63]

The publication of this type of story continued on occasion throughout the war. For example, a similar story that originated in the pro-Lincoln *New York Tribune*, "Sentiments of a Traitor's Wife," recalled a day in summer 1860 when a group looked at a relic that had belonged to George Washington. Varina allegedly "refused to look at it, saying she was sick and tired of hearing so much about Washington," certainly a fitting narrative of what a "traitor's wife" should say.[64] This story is highly unlikely because Davis's grandfather Howell served under Washington in the Revolutionary War.[65] Furthermore, many Southerners identified with the Revolutionary War and saw the Confederacy as the extension of that cause, going as far as to put Washington—a Virginian—on the Confederate national seal and a postage stamp.[66] Another story in the Northern press that cited a "Mrs. A." from New York claimed Davis committed treason before the war even began. It quoted Davis as saying, "The fort [Sumter] belongs to

South Carolina and she will have it, let the consequences be what they may."[67] In what was a common critique of Confederate women by the Union military, Davis was also accused of trying to "seduce" the son of a Union general to join the Confederate cause by using "the flatteries and cajoleries that women know so well how to use."[68] As a woman and as first lady of the Confederacy, Davis's status made her a threat to Northerners—she could exert "soft power" and deploy other subtle arts Confederate men could not. The fact that these articles appeared both at the beginning of the war in 1861 and during the intense battle year of 1864 is likely not a coincidence because these were key periods for growing and maintaining war support.

On the other end of the spectrum, newspapers also published stories that Davis was not as committed to the Southern cause as a Confederate first lady was expected to be. Those rumors were already spreading by June 1861, the same month Davis wrote the letter to her mother with her doubts about the South's ability to win the war. It is unknown whether there was a direct connection—a leaking of the letter's contents—or whether the press was just using its knowledge of her Northern family ties to spark controversy. Regardless, the antislavery *Cleveland Morning Leader* was among the papers to run an article noting that Davis was "really anti-slavery in sentiment" and had once said, "If the women of the South could be consulted in this matter, slavery would be speedily abolished. As for myself, I would rather do the menial service of my family than have the responsibility and care of slaves."[69] Davis was allegedly overheard saying this after the passage of the Kansas-Nebraska Act in 1854, which allowed both territories to decide whether to be free or slave states. Considering Davis had grown up in a family that enslaved people and continued this practice during her adult life, it is not likely she said this, especially when she was still defending the institution in her writings in the 1890s and early 1900s.[70] Yet Northern papers continued to run articles that emphasized the Confederate first lady had Northern sympathies. When Northern messengers were caught delivering letters to the South, a widely run story noted there was a letter for Davis in the contraband.[71] Considering it was illegal in the South to maintain ties with the North and to sympathize with the Union, Davis's continued correspondence with friends in Washington and relatives in the North was even more striking as flagrant disregard of Confederate authority, of which she was supposed to serve as a national symbol.[72]

Perhaps the most scandalous story about her ambivalence for the Southern cause hit in mid-1862, however. Prominent newspapers across the North ran a story about Jefferson Davis's formerly enslaved coachman, who was ready to talk after escaping. He claimed the first lady had said "the Confederacy was about played out," and "she had no longer any interest in the matter" if New Orleans had been lost to the Union.[73] The Confederate loss at New Orleans was a major

Southern setback that occurred two weeks prior to the story's publication and that was of particular concern to Davis because her parents lived there.[74] In 1862, this was the most dominant story about Varina in the Northern press, no doubt a powerful piece of propaganda to boost morale and illustrate that even one of the biggest figures in the Confederacy felt the Southern cause was hopeless. This story, however, was not found in the sample of Southern newspapers analyzed here.

Throughout 1863, other stories in Northern newspapers also emphasized her ties to the Union. Yet another article noted the seizure of mail from the North with gifts intended for the Davis family.[75] An anonymous source cited a conversation before the war between the Confederate first lady and a Pennsylvania friend in which she allegedly referred to Northern states as "our natural allies."[76] In 1864, another formerly enslaved person from her plantation talked to the press, saying that Davis "sighs and pines all the time over the lost pleasures of those good old days in Washington."[77] A more in-depth version of the story in the antislavery *Smoky Hill and Republican Union* newspaper in Kansas said she "frequently talks of the Confederacy as hopeless."[78] Was the intent of these stories to capture the "truth" of who the first lady was? To run sensational material? To illustrate that the South was not as impenetrable as feared in order to raise Northern morale? As history is always complex, likely all of the above were factors. Again, because interviews were not a common or expected practice of the time, journalists did not ask Davis herself for comment about whether the stories were true. Yet, after three years of war, it is not surprising if she indeed pined for the more carefree times she had enjoyed earlier.

### AN "ESTIMABLE LADY"

Meanwhile, in the South, editors made an effort to write flattering commentary about "the president's lady."[79] A story in the *Oxford Intelligencer*, in Davis's home state of Mississippi, described her this way:

> A well-born lady, a most marked degree of personal character and strength of judgment, Mrs. Davis is singularly fitted to be the wife of a public man and to mix in the society of a capital. . . . We cannot but congratulate the new government in having a lady so peculiarly qualified to preside over and exercise the amenities of their first presidential household and particularly one who embodies in so marked a manner the lofty elements of the Southern feminine character."[80]

As a longtime figure in Washington, Davis had served as "one of the representative women of the land—as one of those who gives shape to the character of American womanhood," the article also noted. The fact that the article described Davis this way is striking because—as previously noted—her personality and physical appearance did not match the typical characteristics of white Southern femininity at the time. Yet she was a first lady now and, like American first ladies before and after her time, she took on the expectations of serving as a symbol of American womanhood.[81] This particularly came across in one article that ran in Northern papers, including the anti-Union *Daily Ohio Statesman*, and that likely ran in the Southern press as well. The story cites a letter from Davis thanking Richmond women for gifting her a "workbox," or an embroidery box. Davis wanted to "congratulate you upon the secession of Virginia" and hoped that "we have united peace to independence in our Southern Confederacy."[82] This news came within the first few months of her tenure as first lady, when she undoubtedly was most determined to perform her role as expected and to integrate with society women in the new Southern capital. However, Davis picked up early on that the Richmond elite considered her "coarse and unpolished," an outsider without a prestigious family who usurped status and did not fit expectations.[83] Her dark skin tone in a region obsessed with skin color was noted, as was her "commanding" height, her intelligence, and her bluntness "in an environment where blandness was at a premium."[84] Furthermore, as Cashin wrote, "white Richmonders reviled Northerners and suspected whites of espionage if they were born in the North or had relatives there," and Davis's continued relationships with friends and relatives on the other side of the Mason-Dixon Line were not a secret.[85]

Still, other Southern sources gave her favorable coverage. The Democratic *Nashville Union and American* cited a letter from a Georgia soldier who described Davis as "pleasant in manner and vivacious in conversation."[86] When Davis and her children temporarily escaped to Raleigh in 1862 after concern about the war's advancement into Richmond, the press there called her "the amiable and estimable lady of President Davis," who "has already become quite a favorite amongst us" with her young family.[87] The Confederate loyalist *Wilmington* (North Carolina) *Journal* referred to her "beauty, wit, and talent" and highlighted the prestigious aspects of her background: her New Jersey governor grandfather, her father's military service, and her other grandfather's "very large fortune." The story also mentioned her father being "unfortunate in business" but emphasized that her parents had succeeded because Davis was "one of the most accomplished and intellectual women of the age."[88] Justifying the credentials of the Confederate first lady was perhaps a strategy of legitimizing the Confederacy as a whole because whites in the South "were, in fact, strikingly self-conscious about the need to undertake this introspection and to publicly define the foundations of their unity."[89] This again illustrates Davis's symbolic importance as a nation-builder.

One story set out to demonstrate that the Confederate first lady was preferable to her Union counterpart. A Richmond visitor praised Varina Davis's simple style of dressing plainly, attending church, avoiding places of amusement, and usually walking when she went out. The visitor concluded "that the Richmond style is much more seemly and much more to our liking."[90] The headline, "The Rulers at Washington Might Learn," clearly alludes to the more extravagant tastes of Mary Lincoln and provides a surprisingly rare public comparison between the two competing first ladies.

Even as the war ravaged on, as the Confederate cause became more precarious, and as rumors about her commitment swirled, Davis continued to receive positive news coverage in the South. A story in the pro-Confederate *Richmond Daily Dispatch* citing "Richmond correspondence" noted Davis "is by no means an ordinary woman." The writer described her as "a stately woman, with brunette complexion, and eyes full of brilliance, tenderness, and intelligence. Her manners are very agreeable but touched with a repose that, even though carried to almost sadness, savors very much of the grand."[91] The Davises' visitors regarded the couple "with a warmth and heartiness that were maintained in perfect harmony with an air of profound respect," the story continued. Coming in the midst of low Southern morale and hardship in the Confederate military, the story gives the feel of a deliberate public relations effort to bolster confidence in the Confederate first couple.[92] Although Davis was not as invested in her role as Confederate first lady as she was her prior roles, she did perform many of its standard tasks, such as hosting dinners, receptions, and holiday parties; visiting hospitals; and responding to requests for help from relatives, friends, and strangers.[93]

She also received occasional positive personal coverage in Northern papers. A story that ran in the *Republican Ohio* newspaper described Davis as "a very worthy woman who knows how to behave."[94] A *New York Herald* article referred to her as a "comely, sprightly woman, verging on matronhood, of good figure and manners, well dressed, ladylike and clever."[95] As war-weary 1863 wore on, however, news articles in the North were not as personally flattering. One writer called her a "not pretty" woman who "dresses badly" and was said to control her husband.[96] Another story that ran in Indiana alleged that she had a fake battle fought in Richmond "in order that the regal lady might see how they did it in the army," suggesting she was war obsessed.[97] The Confederate president and first lady were both mocked for gathering up their property and preparing to leave Richmond in summer 1863 after hearing the enemy was advancing. This

"caused much unnecessary alarm to the good citizens of Richmond and no little irritation. . . . This was not considered a becoming example of the firmness
and magnanimity expected from the elected head of the Confederacy."[98] Yet
again, Varina was framed in the press as lacking appropriate commitment to
the Confederacy.

Three major stories related to her made the news toward the end of the
war, yet each was covered only briefly—a stark contrast to the massive news
coverage each would warrant today. One story that ran in pro-Union Northern
and Southern papers accused the Confederate president of fathering a son with
a woman he had enslaved named Catherine. The press cited "a letter from a
gentleman occupying a high position in the United States" who claimed that "a
batch of quarrelsome epistles" (letters) between husband and wife were found
after Union troops raided their Mississippi home. She "unbraided [*sic*] her husband bitterly" in these letters, said the source, who also cited as evidence for his
story "one of the highest officers in the squadron, who had the negro Jeff on
board his gunboat."[99] This story was likely intended for sensationalism to point
out lack of morality and to highlight the symbolic victory of Union troops in-
vading the personal home of the Confederate leader.

The second of the three major stories involving the Davises late in the war
also related to their personal lives: the death of their five-year-old son, Joseph.
One story cited a Confederate officer's private letter that described the accident
scene after the child fell from the Confederate White House balcony to the brick
pavement below. When they arrived, Varina Davis burst into "a flood of tears
and wild lamentations."[100] She did not record her own reaction, but only his, in
her biography of her husband but used the book to explain her absence at the
time of the accident: "Mr. Davis's health declined from loss of sleep so that he
forgot to eat, and I resumed the practice of carrying him something at 1 o'clock.
I left my children quite well, playing in my room, and had just uncovered my
basket in his office when a servant came for me."[101] The press noted that Varina
Davis did not attend church two weeks after the child's death but that Jefferson
Davis arrived "clad in deep mourning and looking more sad and depressed than
usual."[102] No other coverage related to her and to the accident was found in the
articles analyzed.

The final major story relating to her wartime coverage came in early 1865.
The Northern press portrayed Davis as a woman ready for the war to end,
with numerous papers running a story about a peace mission visit from Francis
Preston Blair, a former Democratic Party newspaper editor in Washington then
serving as a Republican adviser to President Lincoln. Papers emphasized that
she "went into ecstasies the moment that she saw" Blair and "threw her arms
around his neck and kissed him again and again."[103] This provided yet another

piece of propaganda for the North to illustrate that a Southern surrender was imminent because even the Confederate leader's wife reportedly was ready to give up.

THE PRESS AND PROPAGANDA

Davis most certainly was aware of her press coverage because news constantly flowed to the Confederate White House. At times, she became upset about attacks on her husband.[104] Yet neither of the Davises made an effort to work with the press to their advantage.[105] For Varina Davis, whose rise in prominence did little to curb her personality, pretending to be someone she was not in the press was not a feasible option anyway. Overall, it is not surprising that the South gave her more positive coverage that praised her womanhood, Southern femininity, and accomplishments. The press played a role in helping shape Confederate nationalism; creating confidence in government figures was critical.[106] Meanwhile, the North also used Davis as a propaganda tool by contradictorily framing her as a schemer and traitor to both sides. Northerners considered Confederate belles "she-devils" who were "hysterical, irrational, and treacherous" and who misused their feminine influence to encourage the rebellion.[107] This stereotype came into play in some coverage of Davis, with her alleged traitorous comments about the North, yet she was also portrayed as a Northern sympathizer, depending upon the particular story. Both strategies aimed to motivate Northerners to continue their resistance to the South either by reinforcing the South's treasonous nature or attempting to expose its weakness. Overall, her role as first lady and as a national symbol for the rebellion set her up as an instrument for vilification no matter what she did, a fact of which she was likely aware.

Still, Davis was treated as a legitimate public figure and generated some hospitable coverage on both sides of the Mason-Dixon Line that primarily focused on her positive qualities as a Southern white woman. Her own reluctance to actively embrace the nation-building role she was thrust into illustrates the difficulties that other American first ladies have faced in living up to the (often unrealistic) expectations the public has for them, which do not always align with the women themselves. Although Davis had friendships with former first ladies such as Margaret Taylor and Jane Pierce and firsthand insight into what the role involved, serving as the "first" first lady of a new nation created a level of pressure and expectation only previously experienced by Martha Washington. As someone who was "too well-read, too smart, and too blunt," Davis did not choose to conform to the ideal of a Southern belle first lady despite the "great pressures to follow conventional gender roles."[108] She could have enhanced her image in the South by adopting at least a public persona of firm support for the

Confederate cause, but she instead chose an approach more authentic to herself, even though it was less popular.

Ironically, but perhaps not surprisingly considering the influence of the lost cause ideology in the postwar period, Davis embraced her role as a *former* first lady more than she did when she actually held the role. Although she remained contradictory about her support of the Confederacy, she arguably became more of a symbol for that cause in the postwar years. Tourists and letters poured into the Davis home in Mississippi, leaving her to constantly perform the role of hostess for what became the Confederate fan club headquarters, and she accompanied her husband on some public appearances with Confederate supporters.[109] After he died in 1889, she wrote his lengthy biography, which served as a tribute on his behalf to the Confederacy. She also used her status as Confederate first lady to her advantage during her widowhood when she became a journalist herself and used her own power of the press to frame herself as the ultimate Southern insider.[110] After years of financial instability following the war and without any surviving sons to care for her, Davis moved to New York City in 1891 to write articles for Joseph Pulitzer's *New York World*. Pulitzer's wife, Kate, was a distant cousin of Jefferson Davis's, and Pulitzer no doubt saw the benefit of the Confederate first lady writing for his paper in the age of yellow, or sensational, journalism. In addition to writing sympathetic pieces about Confederate families and women to humanize the South to Northern readers, Davis also provided Southern manners advice in etiquette columns.[111] In the 1890s and early 1900s, she was considered one of the "few remaining links connecting the old South with the new," becoming swept up in the pervasive romanticizing of the Old South.[112] Had she learned and accepted the importance and influence of public relations earlier, her tenure as first lady would no doubt be more fully remembered today. Although she is now on the wrong side of history—an ultimate symbol of the Old South—her tenure illustrates a first lady who for too long has been collectively remembered as one-dimensional rather than as the complex Southern woman she actually was.

## NOTES

The author would like to thank Katherine A. S. Sibley for her assistance with this chapter.

1. Steve Inskeep, "In 'Varina,' a Confederate Contemplates Her Complicity," *NPR Morning Edition*, April 20, 2018, https://www.npr.org/2018/04/10/599425714/in-varina-a-confederate-contemplates-her-complicity.

2. Ishbel Ross, *First Lady of the South* (New York: Harper and Brothers, 1958).

3. Ross, *First Lady of the South.*

4. Ross, *First Lady of the South.*

5. Joan E. Cashin, *First Lady of the Confederacy: Varina Davis's Civil War* (Cambridge, MA: Belknap Press of Harvard University Press, 2006).

6. Cashin, *First Lady of the Confederacy*, 22.

7. Cashin, *First Lady of the Confederacy*.

8. Anya Jabour, *Scarlett's Sisters: Young Women in the Old South* (Chapel Hill: University of North Carolina Press, 2007); Cashin, *First Lady of the Confederacy*.

9. Lois Banner, *American Beauty* (New York: Knopf, 1983), 48.

10. Ross, *First Lady of the South*, 15.

11. Carol Berkin, *Civil War Wives: The Lives and Times of Angelina Grimké Weld, Varina Howell Davis, and Julia Dent Grant* (New York: Knopf, 2009); Cashin, *First Lady of the Confederacy.*

12. Cashin, *First Lady of the Confederacy*.

13. Varina Davis, *Jefferson Davis: A Memoir by His Wife*, vol. 1 (Baltimore: Nautical and Aviation, 1990), 188.

14. Christie Ann Farnham, *The Education of the Southern Belle* (New York: New York University Press, 1994), 127.

15. Cashin, *First Lady of the Confederacy*.

16. Cashin, *First Lady of the Confederacy*.

17. Berkin, *Civil War Wives*; Gerry Van Der Heuvel, *Crowns of Thorns and Glory* (New York: E. P. Dutton, 1988).

18. Davis, *Jefferson Davis*, vol. 1, 191.

19. Davis, *Jefferson Davis*, vol. 1, 206.

20. Berkin, *Civil War Wives*; Ross, *First Lady of the South*.

21. Cashin, *First Lady of the Confederacy*, 38.

22. Berkin, *Civil War Wives;* Cashin, *First Lady of the Confederacy*.

23. Berkin, *Civil War Wives*, 129.

24. Cashin, *First Lady of the Confederacy*, 52.

25. Ross, *First Lady of the South*; Cashin, *First Lady of the Confederacy*.

26. Van Der Heuvel, *Crowns of Thorns and Glory*.

27. Davis, *Jefferson Davis*; Van Der Heuvel, *Crowns of Thorns and Glory*.

28. Ross, *First Lady of the South*, 71.

29. Berkin, *Civil War Wives*, 143–144.

30. Cashin, *First Lady of the Confederacy*.

31. Davis, *Jefferson Davis*, 697.

32. Van Der Heuvel, *Crowns of Thorns and Glory*.

33. Cashin, *First Lady of the Confederacy*; Berkin, *Civil War Wives*.

34. Varina Davis, *Jefferson Davis: A Memoir by His Wife*, vol. 2 (Baltimore: Nautical and Aviation, 1990).

35. Davis, *Jefferson Davis*, vol. 1, 424, 479.

36. Cashin, *First Lady of the Confederacy*.

37. Cashin, *First Lady of the Confederacy*.

38. Davis, *Jefferson Davis*, vol. 2, 19.

39. Davis, *Jefferson Davis*, vol. 2, 34.

40. Cashin, *First Lady of the Confederacy.*

41. Ford Risley, *Civil War Journalism* (Santa Barbara, CA: Praeger, 2012), xii.

42. William David Sloan, *The Media in America: A History* (Northport, AL: Vision, 2017).

43. Risley, *Civil War Journalism*; David W. Bulla and Gregory A. Brochard, *Journalism in the Civil War Era* (New York: Peter Lang, 2010).

44. Risley, *Civil War Journalism*.

45. Sloan, *Media in America*; Debra Reddin Van Tuyll, "Knights of the Quill: A Brief History of the Confederate Press," in *Words at War: The Civil War and American Journalism*, ed. David Sachsman, S. Kittrell Rushing, and Roy Morris Jr. (West Lafayette, IN: Purdue University Press, 2008), 135–147.

46. Risley, *Civil War Journalism*.

47. J. Cutler Andrews, *The South Reports the Civil War* (Princeton, NJ: Princeton University Press, 1970).

48. Sloan, *Media in America*; Van Tuyll, "Knights of the Quill."

49. Sloan, *Media in America*; Van Tuyll, "Knights of the Quill."

50. Dianne Bragg, "An Affair of Words: Tennessee's Civil War Press and the Confederate Nation," in *Words at War: The Civil War and American Journalism*, ed. David Sachsman, S. Kittrell Rushing, and Roy Morris Jr. (West Lafayette, IN: Purdue University Press, 2008), 115–140.

51. Risley, *Civil War Journalism*.

52. Van Tuyll, "Knights of the Quill"; Andrews, *South Reports the Civil War*.

53. Allan Bell, "The Discourse Structure of News Stories," in *Approaches to Media Discourse*, ed. Allan Bell and Peter Garrett (Oxford, UK: Blackwell, 1998), 64–104.

54. Lisa Burns, *First Ladies and the Fourth Estate* (DeKalb: Northern Illinois University Press, 2008); Molly Meijer Wertheimer, "First Ladies' Fundamental Rhetorical Choices," in *Inventing a Voice: The Rhetoric of American First Ladies of the Twentieth Century*, ed. Molly Meijer Wertheimer (Lanham, MD: Rowman and Littlefield, 2004), 1–15.

55. Robert P. Watson and Anthony J. Eksterowicz, eds., *The Presidential Companion: Readings on the First Ladies* (Columbia: University of South Carolina Press, 2003).

56. News articles for this analysis came from Chronicling America, the Historical *New York Times*, NewspaperArchive.com, and Newspapers.com. The search timeline was February 9, 1861, to March 31, 1865, to encompass Varina Davis's time as Confederate first lady. I searched the phrase "Mrs. Davis" because of the social and press standards of the time referring to women by their married names. I analyzed a total of 216 articles from twenty-one states and Washington, DC. The United States consisted of thirty-six states during the war. A majority of the articles in the search results came from Union newspapers, with fifty-one articles from Confederate or Border States.

57. "Hon. Mrs. Jefferson Davis," *Chicago Daily Tribune*, March 2, 1861, 2; "All Sorts of Paragraphs," *Boston Post*, March 6, 1861, 2; "Serenade to Mrs. Jefferson Davis," *New York Herald*, March 11, 1861, 8.

58. Davis, *Jefferson Davis*, vol. 2, 34.

59. "Contemplated Seizure of the Federal Capital," *Alleghanian*, April 11, 1861, 2.

60. *Daily Green Mountain Freeman*, May 10, 1861, 2; *Boston Post*, May 10, 1861, 2.

61. "A Letter from Mrs. Jeff Davis," *Belmont Chronicle*, October 17, 1861, 2; *Alleghanian*, October 24, 1861, 2.

62. Michael Schudson, "Question Authority: A History of the News Interview in American Journalism, 1860s–1930s," *Media, Culture, and Society* 16, no. 4 (1994): 565–587.

63. "Old Abe in Danger," *Western Democrat*, April 16, 1861, 2.

64. "Sentiments of a Traitor's Wife," *Worthington White River Gazette*, May 17, 1861, 1; originated in *New York Tribune*.

65. Ross, *First Lady of the South*.

66. Drew Gilpin Faust, *The Creation of Confederate Nationalism* (Baton Rouge: Louisiana State University Press, 1988).

67. "Mrs. Jeff Davis and Fort Sumter," *Philadelphia Inquirer*, January 7, 1864, 2; *Boston Post*, February 5, 1864, 2.

68. Reid Mitchell, *The Vacant Chair: The Northern Soldier Leaves Home* (New York: Oxford University Press, 1993); "A Sad Case of Seduction," *Sandusky Daily Commercial Register*, November 26, 1864, 2.

69. "A House Divided Against Itself," *Cleveland Morning Leader*, June 3, 1861, 1; *National Republican*, June 8, 1861, 2.

70. Teri Finneman, "The Forgotten First Lady: Reinventing Varina Davis Through Her Journalism," *Nineteenth Century Gender Studies* 10, no. 2 (2014).

71. "Important Arrests at Baltimore," *Philadelphia Inquirer*, September 9, 1861, 1; "More Arrests in Baltimore," *New York Times*, September 9, 1861, 1; *Boston Post*, October 11, 1861, 2.

72. Cashin, *First Lady of the Confederacy*.

73. "The Situation," *New York Herald*, May 6, 1862, 6; "The Beginning of Revelations," *Chicago Daily Tribune*, May 6, 1862, 1; "Jeff Davis' Negro Coachman Escapes," *National Republican*, May 6, 1862, 2

74. "Union Captures New Orleans," http://www.history.com/this-day-in-history /union-captures-new-orleans; Ross, *First Lady of the South*.

75. "Intercepted Presents for the Jeff Davis Family," *Philadelphia Inquirer*, March 31, 1863, 1.

76. *Marshall County Republican*, April 2, 1863, 1.

77. "Attempt to Burn Out Jeff Davis," *New York Herald*, January 27, 1864, 4; "Jeff Davis' Body Servant," *American Citizen*, February 3, 1864, 2.

78. "Narrative of an Intelligent Contraband," *Smoky Hill and Republican Union*, February 20, 1864, 1.

79. "The President's Lady," *Weekly Standard*, May 14, 1862, 3.

80. "Mrs. Jefferson Davis," *Oxford Intelligencer*, April 10, 1864, 4.

81. Wertheimer, "First Ladies' Fundamental Rhetorical Choices."

82. "What Mrs. Davis Has to Say about It," *Daily Ohio Statesman*, May 29, 1861, 2; "Letter from Mrs. Davis," *Boston Post*, May 22, 1861, 1.

83. Berkin, *Civil War Wives*, 161; Ross, *First Lady of the South*; Cashin, *First Lady of the Confederacy*; Davis, *Jefferson Davis*, vol 2.

84. Cashin, *First Lady of the Confederacy*, 112.

85. Cashin, 114.

86. "The President and His Lady," *Democratic Nashville Union and American*, August 6, 1861, 2.

87. "Distinguished Visitors," *Lancaster Ledger*, May 21, 1862, 2.

88. "Correspondence of the Telegraph," *Wilmington Journal*, October 22, 1863, 4.

89. Faust, *Creation of Confederate Nationalism*, 7.

90. "The Rulers at Washington Might Learn," *Dubuque Democratic Herald*, November 18, 1863, 2.

91. "Extract from the Richmond Correspondence," *Richmond Daily Dispatch*, January 26, 1864, 1.

92. James McPherson, *Battle Cry of Freedom: The Civil War Era* (Oxford, UK: Oxford University Press, 1988).

93. Cashin, *First Lady of the Confederacy*.

94. "Mrs. Jeff Davis," *Steubenville Weekly Herald*, January 6, 1864, 2.

95. "Bull Run Russell's Diary North and South," *New York Herald*, January 26, 1863, 4.

96. "Life in the Rebel Capital," *Philadelphia Inquirer*, April 10, 1863, 2; "Second Letter," *New Albany Daily Ledger*, April 15, 1863, 1.

97. "From the Southwest," *Crown Point Register*, August 13, 1863, 2.

98. "Alarm of Jeff Davis Family," *Eau Claire Daily Free Press*, August 20, 1863, 2.

99. "Jeff Davis' Son in the National Service," *Burlington Weekly Hawkeye*, February 20, 1864, 6; *Richmond Palladium*, February 17, 1864, 4; "Jeff Davis' Son in the Federal Service," *Nashville Daily Union*, February 6, 1864, 2.

100. "The President's Household," *Memphis Daily Appeal*, May 21, 1864, 2.

101. Davis, *Jefferson Davis*, vol. 2, 496.

102. "News from Richmond," *Memphis Daily Appeal*, May 21, 1864, 2.

103. "Washington," *New York Herald*, January 23, 1865, 5; "The Peace Question," *Wheeling Daily Register*, January 24, 1865, 2.

104. Ross, *First Lady of the South*.

105. Risley, *Civil War Journalism*; Cashin, *First Lady of the Confederacy*.

106. Faust, *Creation of Confederate Nationalism*.

107. Mitchell, *Vacant Chair*, 100.

108. Cashin, *First Lady of the Confederacy*, 112, 111.

109. Cashin, *First Lady of the Confederacy*.

110. Finneman, "Forgotten First Lady."

111. Finneman, "Forgotten First Lady."

112. "News of Death Will Cause Grief Throughout South," (Richmond, Virginia) *Times Dispatch*, October 17, 1906, 1.

# CHAPTER 9

# Eliza Johnson, First Lady of the Tennessee Hill Country

John F. Marszalek

It was a beautiful fall day in 1826 as a group of teenage girls walked down the main street of Greenville, Tennessee, county seat of Greene County, a small town of less than five hundred people.[1] As they talked, they saw a wagon filled with ramshackle furniture and pots and pans, pulled by a blind horse and led by an eighteen-year-old, dark-haired boy. An older woman and man onboard the wagon, mother and father of the young man, looked worn out, having traveled through the rough country from Raleigh, North Carolina, hoping for a fresh start in this small town. Unknown to the girls was the fact that two years previously, the young man had joined three other work apprentices in Raleigh in maliciously stoning an old woman's house and then running away to avoid prosecution.[2]

The teenagers were students at a local school, and they watched with interest the scene before them. A sixteen-year-old in their midst, whose mother was often considered the prettiest woman in the county, looked as attractive as her mother was reputed to be. She was frequently described as "the purest type of a southern beauty." She had "nut brown hair . . . [with] soft hazel eyes . . . [an] unusually long Greek nose, . . . a generous mouth and a tall shapely figure." When the attractive Eliza McCardle saw Andrew Johnson pulling that blind horse, the story is told, she immediately said to a friend, "There goes my beau." On May 17, 1827, the young man, only eighteen years old himself and destined to be a future president of the United States, and his bride, at sixteen years old still the youngest first lady at the time of her marriage, exchanged their vows. The justice of the peace was Mordecai Lincoln, cousin to Abraham Lincoln's father.[3]

The young couple invested in a marriage that benefited both. Robert Steele, an 1868 biographer of President Johnson, said Eliza was "patient, gentle, forbearing," in contrast to her husband, who was "passionate, ambitious, and belligerent." Those who knew the two young people said she had an ability to calm her volcanic husband simply by gently tapping him on his shoulder. The president's bodyguard said the first lady's "influence was a strong one, and it was exerted in the direction of toleration and gentleness." The Johnsons "seemed as two souls and minds merged as one," a Greenville acquaintance said.[4]

Andrew Johnson had already served as an apprentice to tailors in several towns, so he had no trouble setting up a shop in his new community. He also rose rapidly in politics, with his shop becoming the local center for political discussion. Aided by his wife, who had a better education than he did, Andrew worked hard at gaining speaking skills and the ability to read and write effectively. In 1828, he began his political career by being elected to the first of three terms on the town council, and then he became mayor for a four-year term. In 1831, with a growing income, he purchased a building in the center of the city that he used both as a tailor shop and a house. The Johnsons were doing well. He proudly put up a sign on their new home: "A. Johnson, Tailor."[5]

Andrew was an ambitious man, determined to improve his position. In fact, a myth developed that Eliza taught him how to read and write. This was not true. He had learned these skills before he arrived in Greenville, but his wife still played an important role in his intellectual development. For example, she read to him while he tailored clothes. As one of their daughters later insisted, "She was the stepping stone to all the honor and fame my father attained."[6]

Like most women in that era, Eliza Johnson oversaw a large family. They had five children: Martha (born in 1828), Mary (1830), Charles (1832), Robert (1834), and Andrew Jr. ("Frank," 1852). Eliza also managed the household, kept track of the family's finances, taught the children the basics of their education, and maintained her husband's tailoring shop. The one thing she apparently did not do was help her husband in his campaigns for office.[7] She was no Southern belle but rather a product of the frontier; educated like a white Southern girl but more like a denizen of a small town. She was willing and able to help her husband make a success of himself in small town politics and entrepreneurship.

In 1835 Andrew Johnson expanded his horizons by moving from local politics to election to the state legislature. Starting a pattern they continued for the rest of their lives, Eliza did not travel with him to Nashville. She stayed in Greenville and kept watch over the family's fortunes, which now included a farm, and, in September 1851, a large home on the main street. Displaying their ties to the South, the family also enslaved some eight or nine people, a status symbol for them and a sign of their growing wealth. In short, he held office, and she took care of the family's financial needs and property, including the enslaved workers. Demonstrating her limited authority in the household, however, and their location in the mountain South and not the plantation South, Eliza once had an argument with an enslaved man named Sam, who felt confident enough to contest her order to have him cut some wood for the family.[8] Clearly the Johnsons were hardly of the Southern planter class, although they fully supported and benefited from the system of slavery.

Sometime during this period, Eliza contracted what was then known as *consumption*; today called *tuberculosis*. She attempted to continue helping her husband and the family, but she grew increasingly ill. By the time he was elected governor of Tennessee in 1853, she was dangerously feeble. Increasingly, she became less and less able to deal with her illness, although family correspondence indicates that her health modulated between well to weak. Adding to her problems and her chores, two of her sons were alcoholics; her mother died in 1854; and during that time too, their oldest daughter, Martha, and the younger daughter Mary were both married. By 1853, though, Andrew was worth around $50,000, or more than $3 million in 2019 dollars. Thanks to her hard work as well as his, their tailor business was going well, and Eliza made sure that their general net worth grew, too—the result of his and her small-town abilities.[9]

At the same time, Andrew's political career continued to advance. He was elected to serve two terms as governor of Tennessee (1853–1857), and then he won election as a US senator in 1858. Eliza could not travel to Nashville or Washington most of these years. Like most women in that era and that section of the country, she bore the burden of the children and the home and more and more his shop in Greenville. Her illness also made it virtually impossible for her to go far from home.

In 1858, the senator returned to Greenville, where he spent the summer with Eliza and the family. He and his wife took long walks together when she felt up to it, and they tended the gardens behind the house. Some days the Johnsons would have their adult children over to dinner, but Eliza would have to leave the cooking to others, relying more on her enslaved servants because her illness limited her energy.[10]

After the Civil War began, Andrew Johnson became the only non-Northern senator to remain in Washington and speak boldly in support of the Union. Greenville was strongly Confederate and looked askance at his pro-Union views. He was considered a traitor to his region, but his family suffered the most from his Union leanings, and life only grew more difficult for the rest of the Johnsons as he became more and more openly Unionist. As early as November 27, 1861, the Confederate government, which controlled Tennessee, served Eliza and their sons and sons-in-law with a Notice of Sequestration Proceedings to try to prevent them from selling any of Andrew's assets until proceedings took place to name him an "alien enemy." On January 18, 1862, Eliza Johnson was actually sequestered; she found herself in the clutches of the Confederate government though she was married to the former Tennessee governor, still a US senator (1859–1862).[11]

In response, she and Frank, her nine-year-old son, stayed out of Greenville and off their properties, living with married daughter Mary Stover outside the city. Her husband could do little but complain to fellow Tennessee Unionists. "After my wife, with her child . . . had fled . . . and while confined to a bed of sickness, the act of sequestration was enforced to wrest her dwelling, leaving her houseless and the unguarded victim of insult." Andrew was angry, but, as a Unionist in a Confederate state, he could do little to protect either his wife or his property.[12]

On April 24, 1862, General Kirby Smith ordered Eliza and her family to leave Tennessee. Because she could not travel, she responded politely but emphatically, "In my present state of health, I know I can not undergo the fatigues of such a journey: my health is quite feeble, a greater portion of the time being unable to leave my bed." General Smith gave her several months to get better and, on September 19, 1862, she told him that she was ready to travel and asked for the necessary passports to allow her family to cross into Union territory. These were granted, but the Confederates confiscated Eliza's Greenville home in the summer of 1862, thereafter turning it into a military hospital. They also froze all the Johnsons' assets.[13]

Still ill, Eliza made it to Union-controlled Nashville in October 1862, leaving the people they enslaved in Greenville. She remained there for two months with her husband, then traveled to Indiana Springs, which she hoped would be restorative for her illness. The consumption remained a problem, however. Abraham Lincoln had appointed Andrew Johnson war governor of Tennessee in mid-1862, based in Nashville, and Unionists believed he did a good job in that position. Yet he constantly worried about his wife and family. Along with the prospect of her illness, his sons Charles and Robert could not overcome their alcoholism. Andrew himself suffered from the effects of a prewar broken arm, stomach ills, and a variety of other ailments. He received a letter from his son Charles in October 1862 telling him how the family, traveling together by wagon and railroad and now with Martha Patterson and Mary Stover's children, was suffering from Confederate harassment. The news only made him feel more anxious. Fortunately, Confederate Army officer Nathan Bedford Forrest, who at first told the family during a forced meeting that "Jesus Christ [himself] could not cross his [my] lines," arranged a flag of truce for the family.[14]

As the family's travels continued to Louisville, Eliza Johnson worried that Confederate sympathizers would assassinate her husband. At this point he wrote a letter to her clearly expressing his despondency and telling her of his own physical problems. These words could only have depressed her more. At the same time he urged her to remain hopeful. The letter rambled over a variety of topics, but a key theme was Andrew's advice to Eliza on how to handle their children. Finally he ended, "Give my love to all and accept for yourself the best wishes of a devoted husband's heart."[15]

Of course, with a war on and the ravages of drink unabated, there was only so much the two could do to protect their children. In 1863, the couple suffered the death of their son Charles, a surgeon in the Union Army. He fell from his horse and crushed his skull. At the same time, son Robert, a colonel in that same army, continued having major physical difficulties and, as a result, increased his consumption of alcohol. Andrew Johnson was so worried about Robert that he ordered him to come to Nashville so he could watch over him. Daughter Mary Stover's husband, Daniel Stover, also a Union soldier, died from tuberculosis in 1864. The only thing Andrew could enjoy was news of his youngest son, Frank. He seemed to be doing well and stayed with his sick mother.[16]

Eliza Johnson continued her nomadic ways into August 1864, still accompanied by her sons Robert and Frank. They traveled as far as New England, either to deal with her illness or to try to cure Robert of his alcoholism. What they did there is unclear, but, by March 1865, she was back in Nashville. Her husband's staunch pro-Unionism as a Southerner had led to his nomination as vice president on Lincoln's ticket. He and Lincoln won, so he moved to Washington. Eliza, however remained in Nashville. She, a Unionist, lived with Lizinka Ewell, wife of General Richard S. Ewell, a Confederate. Eliza found this woman insufferable; however, she had no choice but to remain in the Confederate's house. She was just too feeble to move.[17]

Then Eliza Johnson's world, already difficult, grew worse. Lincoln was assassinated on April 14, 1865, and her husband was suddenly elevated to the presidency. These events only increased her worries. Daughter Martha Patterson wrote to her father in Washington and exclaimed, "I never felt so sad, in all my life, and poor mother she is almost deranged fearing that you will be assassinated." His wife certainly did not want to become first lady.[18]

Despite the threat, the new president was safe; his would-be assassin, George Andrew Atzerodt, had other thoughts. Still, he could not move into the White House because Mary Lincoln continued living there, grief-stricken over her husband's murder. Andrew stayed in the Soldiers Home for most of the summer, even after Lincoln left the White House. Under tremendous political strain, President Johnson made it clear to his family members that he expected them to come to Washington and live with him as soon as they could.[19]

The family left Nashville in early June 1865, reached Cincinnati, Ohio, and continued toward the nation's capital. In mid-July, Andrew received a letter from Lizinka Ewell, asking him to pardon her Confederate husband and apologizing for her treatment of the Johnson family in Nashville. As the president had the right to do, he issued the pardon, and the former landlady, who had so antagonized the family, sank out of view.[20]

Some of the Johnsons arrived in Washington in June 1865, and the rest came in August. The White House quickly filled with young people and activity. In addition to the first lady and her two sons, Robert and Frank, there were daughter Martha Patterson and her husband, David, now a US senator, and their two children. Daughter Mary Stover, now a widow, and her three offspring lived there, too. One of these children was named Eliza Johnson Stover, known as Lillie. Having his wife and family around him made the president much happier and more relaxed.[21]

Yet the first lady's illness remained a problem. She settled into the south corner, second-floor room in the White House, rarely leaving it on even the most festive occasions. From this post, at least, she could keep a close watch on Andrew because he had his office across the hall from her room. She made sure he dressed appropriately and also attempted to check his fiery temper. Every morning, the president would stop by to see her, and in the afternoons the grandchildren joyfully ran in to see their grandmother. In that way she kept her close connection to her family.[22]

However, she was in no shape to be the nation's first lady. That task devolved to Martha. Fortunately, as a child, she had gone to a boarding school in Washington and, despite her father's long-held political animosity toward his fellow Tennessean, President James Polk, she had frequently visited the White House and developed a friendship with First Lady Sarah Polk, so she was familiar with the house and its customs. Excited about Martha's residence in the White House, Sarah planned a visit to see her.[23]

Martha gained great praise for all her work in refurbishing the White House after the wear and tear of Lincoln's funeral. She not only used wisely the $30,000 that Congress appropriated for its renewal but also put on work clothes every morning to help with the cleanup. She even purchased some cows for the White House lawn and milked them every morning so that the family might have fresh milk and butter. She was a talented substitute for her ill mother, and she maintained her hill country experience from the rural South in the White House.[24] The first lady, meanwhile, spent almost all of her time in her room, even eating breakfast there by herself. Yet Eliza and her husband met each morning to discuss his schedule, and then she toured his office to make sure everything he needed was in its place. She regularly spoke to the staff, which included two of the Johnsons' former enslaved servants: William Johnson, the president's valet, and Florence Johnson, who served as a maid. Eliza also read her mail, which usually included pleas for patronage; in the afternoon, she read newspapers and a variety of other public documents. She clipped articles from the press that she passed along to her husband, always making sure that she dressed well for him.[25]

Even though she was often behind the scenes, the first lady was not overlooked at the White House. As biographer Kenneth Rayner noted in 1866, "I have not the honor of personally knowing her, but, having made most respectful mention of her name in the book, I wish to offer this humble tribute to the virtues of her character, as wife, mother, and friend."[26] She attended White House functions only a few times, however, to the point that she was nicknamed "almost a myth." In fact, she might have appeared in public only twice. In August 1866, when Queen Emma of Hawai'i visited the White House, Eliza stood at her husband's side but quickly called for a chair so she could sit down. In 1868, she helped organize and attended a children's ball. At that event, she greeted the young guests from a chair, apologetically saying repeatedly, "My dears, I am an invalid."[27]

Most of the time, then, Martha, with help from her sister Mary Stover, acted as first lady of the Johnson administration. Martha Patterson was the first senator's wife and daughter of a president to do that. Unlike her mother, Patterson was in the public eye all the time, yet soon after arriving in Washington, she expressed a feeling her mother shared: "We are plain people from the mountains of Tennessee, called here for a short time by a national calamity. I trust too much will not be expected of us." Johnson family members saw their time in Washington as brief, occasioned only by Lincoln's assassination.[28]

Thanks to Patterson's talents, however, the White House social events during the Johnson presidency were hailed as tasteful and appealing. The Johnson women, the public noted, did not "expose as much flesh as possible," as was the fashion in those days. They buttoned up their evening clothes to their necks, and this "lack of chic seemed only to add to their popularity." Secretary of the Navy Gideon Welles, an acerbic critic of most things, was ecstatic in his praise of the family. "No better persons have occupied the Executive Mansion," he said.[29] Patterson had learned from the Polk White House and in boarding school how to make sure social functions were conducted properly. The first reception took place on New Year's Day 1866, even though the White House was still in ramshackle shape. Unconcerned, she spruced it up with flowers and had children liven the proceedings with their energy and laughter. In this instance, at least, her hill country experience was especially helpful to her.[30] Overall, Martha Patterson's role underlines the importance of surrogate first ladies, often overlooked in studies of the office, even as they made frequent appearances in the role from Andrew Jackson's time to Grover Cleveland's.

The positive feelings for President Johnson's family could not mask growing unrest, however. He was considered a Southerner and a Democrat acting as president of a nation that remained victoriously Northern and Republican. He did not understand his Radical Republican opponents, and because he was not elected, his refusal to compromise with them caused a multitude of problems. Lincoln's death, the public knew, had gained his vice president the highest office in the land. Unfortunately, he did not know how to use this power in the most effective way.[31] He seemed always to be in some argument with his political opponents. His Southern attitudes toward the formerly enslaved people and his recalcitrance about them, including his refusal to assist Blacks in any way, was a real liability for him as well as for the nation. It was an attitude shared by his wife and family.

This weakness became especially obvious when his impeachment was debated in Congress from March through May 1868. The president and Congress argued over each other's rights and duties, especially the Tenure of Office Act and the powers of Secretary of War Edwin M. Stanton. The president's attorneys kept telling him to keep silent, and it is said that the first lady insisted, "We're just going to go ahead with business as usual." Receptions continued, and she kept reading and clipping the newspapers. Eliza also kept believing that her husband would be acquitted in any impeachment trial, and when one of the White House staff ran from Congress to the White House to tell her that good news, she responded, "I knew he would be acquitted. I knew it."[32]

The first lady continued to believe in her husband's innocence, but with only ten months left in his presidential term, he had to face a future with practically no political power. As a lame duck president, he regularly took his grandchildren on rides in the countryside outside Washington. Sometimes he went off by himself with only his bodyguard accompanying him. Meanwhile, Eliza's illness kept her in her room. Both she and the president lived separate lives, frequently by themselves, more the result of her illness than any North-South animosity.[33]

Mercifully, to many sighs of relief from inside and outside the White House, President Johnson's term came to an end in March 1869. Eliza left the building several days before the inauguration of his successor, Ulysses S. Grant. The Stover family went straight to Greenville to prepare the Johnson home. Like most presidents do, Andrew kept signing bills until the last moment, although none of significance. At noon, however, he stopped, shook hands with his cabinet, and got into a waiting carriage. He met his wife at the home of John F. Coyle, one of the owners of the *National Intelligencer* newspaper and probably Johnson's best friend in the capital city. There, the couple stayed for two weeks, unwinding from their days in the White House.

They then headed to their home in Greenville. Eliza's bedroom, really her sickroom, was on the second floor, and Andrew's bedroom was on the first, near the front door. He found Greenville "dull and flat," and he could not wait for the spring to come, "when I will be set free from this place for ever I hope." Still, he wasted little time before going on a tour to mend fences with the politicians in the state. As always, Eliza stayed home, so she was living alone when son Robert succumbed to his alcoholism and died by suicide.[34]

Andrew Johnson wanted to become a senator again to rescue his reputation after the near impeachment. At first, he ran for the US House of Representatives, then for the Senate, until finally in 1875, the Tennessee legislature elected him one of its US senators, on the fifty-fifth ballot. Among the many letters the Johnsons received was one to Eliza that praised her for the fact that her husband "attributed to your influence his success in life." As for Greenville's reaction to the election, son Frank announced triumphantly, "Greenville still moves along in the same dull old way, but on Tuesday when the news of your election reached us it presented more the appearance of an Indian village dancing their scalp dance; everything and everybody seemed wild."[35]

Buoyed by such a raucous sendoff from his friends and neighbors, the new senator traveled to Washington, but his still ill wife remained in Greenville. Unfortunately, Andrew served only briefly because he had a massive stroke, and he died on July 31, 1875, with Eliza holding his hand. He requested that he be wrapped in a US flag and that a copy of the Constitution be placed under his head. Eliza died less than six months later, on January 15, 1876, and she was buried next to him in the Greenville Cemetery. Ill as she was, her life span was almost as long as his.[36]

President Grant had nothing good to say about his predecessor. Julia Dent Grant, for her part, remembered the former first lady fondly. In her memoirs, she said Eliza Johnson "was a retiring, kind, gentle, old lady, too much of an invalid . . . but she always came into the drawing room after the long state dinners to take coffee and receive the greetings of her husband's guests. She was always dressed elegantly and appropriately."[37]

In fact, Julia Grant was too kind. As Nancy Beck Young has noted, Andrew Johnson's wife "had little contact with the general public or government officials during her husband's administration . . . [and so] ultimately, Eliza Johnson had little impact on the development of the [office of] First Lady." She described this herself: "It's all very well for those who like it, but I do not like this public life at all. I often wish the time would come when we could return to where I feel we best belong." Her role as first lady was a difficult one, affected less by her region of birth than by her battle with tuberculosis.[38]

Eliza and Andrew Johnson were hill country people from Tennessee who, although they enslaved workers, did not live on a large plantation as so many elite

Southerners did. They saw themselves as Unionists and smaller farmers and entrepreneurs who battled the large slaveholders who dominated Southern society even as they benefited from that system. They proved to be the foundation of the new industrial South, where plantations and slavery were less important than was interest in post–Civil War era expansion, despite the nostalgic myths about the antebellum period that continued to sway the reputations and mindsets of Southern first ladies from Sarah Polk to Edith Wilson. Eliza Johnson, as titular first lady, and Martha Patterson as her surrogate, demonstrated the conflict between the changing South and the modernizing North. Caught in the middle, Eliza, beaten down by illness, never influenced the nation. Though she was not a Southerner of the old school but more a foreshadower of the South yet to come, she had little influence in that role; she experienced a life largely of physical struggle rather than one as a trailblazer.

## NOTES

1. Hans L. Trefousse, *Andrew Johnson: A Biography* (New York: Norton, 1991), 29.

2. Leroy P. Graf, Ralph W. Haskins, and Paul Bergeron, eds., *The Papers of Andrew Johnson*, vol. 1 (Knoxville: University of Tennessee Press, 1967–2000), 4n.

3. Laura C. Holloway, *The Ladies of the White House* (Philadelphia: Bradley, 1880), 488; Robert W. Winston, *Andrew Johnson, Plebeian and Patriot* (New York: Henry Holt, 1928), 20; Marriage License and Certificate, May 17, 1827; Graf, Haskins, and Bergeron, *Papers of Andrew Johnson*, 1, 4–5; Trefousse, *Andrew Johnson*, 29.

4. Leslie W. Dunlap, *Our Vice Presidents and Second Ladies* (Metuchen, NJ: Scarecrow, 1988), 101; Margarita Spalding Merry, comp. and ed., *Through Five Administrations of Colonel William H. Crook* (New York: Harper and Brothers, 1910), 87; Carl Sferrazza Anthony, *First Ladies: The Saga of the Presidents' Wives and Their Powers, 1789–1961* (New York: Morrow, 1990), 205.

5. "Andrew Johnson," *North Carolina Encyclopedia*, www.ncpedia.org-johnson-andrew; *Burke's Presidential Families of the United States of America*, 2nd ed. (London: Burke's, 1981), 300; Jean Choate, *Eliza Johnson: Unknown First Lady* (New York: Nova, 2004), 14.

6. Choate, *Eliza Johnson*, 11; Nancy Beck Young, "Eliza (McCardle) Johnson (1810–1876): First Lady—1865–1869," in *America's First Ladies: Their Lives and Their Legacies*, ed. Lewis L. Gould (New York: Garland, 1996), 193.

7. Pamela K. Sanfilippo, "Eliza McCardle Johnson and Julia Dent Grant," in *A Companion to First Ladies*, ed. Katherine A. S. Sibley (Hoboken, NJ: Wiley-Blackwell, 2016), 231–232.

8. Young, "Eliza (McCardle) Johnson," 193–194; "Slaves of Andrew Johnson" (Washington, DC: National Park Service, 2015), 2.

9. Young, "Eliza (McCardle) Johnson," 194; Lately Thomas, *The Three Lives of the Seventeenth President of the United States of America* (New York: Morrow, 1968), 86. See Bureau of Labor Statistics, Consumer Price Index, Inflation Calculator, www.officialdata.org.

10. Choate, *Eliza Johnson*, 50–51.

11. Notice of Sequestration Proceedings, November 27, 1861; Writ of Attachment, January 18, 1862, in Graf, Haskins, and Bergeron, *Papers of Andrew Johnson*, vol. 5, 37, 37n, 107–108, respectively.

12. Andrew Johnson, "Speech to David County Citizens," March 1862, in Graf, Haskins, and Bergeron, *Papers of Andrew Johnson*, vol. 5, 240n, 235, respectively.

13. Graf, Haskins, and Bergeron, *Papers of Andrew Johnson*, 352n–353n; Lynne E. Ford, *Encyclopedia of Women and American Politics* (Detroit, MI: Facts on File, 2008), 259.

14. Graf, Haskins, and Bergeron, *Papers of Andrew Johnson*," vol. 6, 23, 23n.

15. John Grant Wilson and John Fiske, eds., "Eliza McCardle," in *Appleton's Cyclopedia of American Biography* (New York: D. Appleton, 1888), 439; Graf, Haskins, and Bergeron, *Papers of Andrew Johnson*," vol. 16, 197n.

16. Trefousse, *Andrew Johnson*, 168; Susan Sawyer, *More Than Petticoats: Remarkable Tennessee Women* (Helena, MT: Falcon, 2000), 43; Young, "Eliza (McCardle) Johnson," 195.

17. Graf, Haskins, and Bergeron, *Papers of Andrew Johnson*," vol. 7, 124; "Cabinet and Vice Presidents: Andrew Johnson, 1808–1875," in Lehrman Institute, *Mr. Lincoln's White House*.

18. Graf, Haskins, and Bergeron, *Papers of Andrew Johnson*, vol. 7, 560.

19. Graf, Haskins, and Bergeron, *Papers of Andrew Johnson*, vol. 8, 32, 38.

20. Graf, Haskins, and Bergeron, *Papers of Andrew Johnson*, vol. 8, 198, 403, 404n.

21. Young, "Eliza (McCardle) Johnson," 196; Choate, *Eliza Johnson*, 50; Albert Castel, *The Presidency of Andrew Johnson* (Lawrence: University Press of Kansas, 1979), 36.

22. Thomas, *Three Lives of the Seventeenth President*, 170; Anthony, *First Ladies*, 204–205.

23. Graf, Haskins, and Bergeron, *Papers of Andrew Johnson*, vol. 9, 442, and vol. 10, 570, respectively.

24. Mary Clemens Ames, *Ten Years in Washington* (Hartford, CT: A. D. Washington, 1874), 245–247.

25. Anthony, *First Ladies*, 204–205; Sarah Fling, "The Formerly Enslaved Households of President Andrew Johnson," https://www.whitehousehistory.org/the-formerly-enslaved -households-of-president-andrew-johnson.

26. Graf, Haskins, and Bergeron, *Papers of Andrew Johnson*, vol. 10, 648–649, 649n.

27. Ann Bausum, *Our Country's First Ladies* (Washington, DC: National Geographic, 2007), 55; Thomas, *Three Lives of the Seventeenth President*, 478; Paul F. Boller Jr., *Presidential Wives* (New York: Oxford University Press, 1988), 131.

28. Holloway, *Ladies of the White House*, 516; Ames, *Ten Years in Washington*, 245.

29. Amy LaFollette Jensen, *The White House and Its Thirty-Five Families* (New York: McGraw-Hill, 1970), 97–98; Gideon Welles, *Diary of Gideon Welles*, vol. 3 (Boston: Houghton Mifflin, 1911), 556.

30. Holloway, *Ladies of the White House*, 511.

31. Castel, *Presidency of Andrew Johnson*, 36; Henry Graff, ed., *The Presidents: A Reference History*, 2nd ed. (New York: Scribner's, 1996), 243–244.

32. Choate, *Eliza Johnson*, 137.

33. Susan Swan and C-SPAN, *First Ladies: Presidential Historians on the Lives of 45 Iconic American Women* (New York: 2015), 137–138; Choate, *Eliza Johnson*, 137.

34.  Choate, *Eliza Johnson*, 128–139; Merry, *Through Five Administrations of Colonel William A. Crook*, 148.

35.  Choate, *Eliza Johnson*, 142–144; Graf, Haskins, and Bergeron, *Papers of Andrew Johnson*, vol. 16, 282.

36.  Choate, *Eliza Johnson*, 145–149; Thomas, *Three Lives of the Seventeenth President*, 303; Graf, Haskins, and Bergeron, *Papers of Andrew Johnson*, vol. 16, 694.

37.  Julia Dent Grant, *The Personal Memoirs of Julia Dent Grant (Mrs. Ulysses S. Grant)*, ed. John Y. Simon (New York: Putnam's, 1975), 164.

38.  Young, "Eliza (McCardle) Johnson," 200; "Eliza Johnson," National First Ladies Library, www.firstladies.org/biographies/.

# CHAPTER 10

# *Julia Dent Grant*
## *Aspiring Southerner*

Louie P. Gallo

"You are Southern, are you not?" was a question that seemed to follow Julia Dent Grant. In one instance, it was asked by a lady with whom she was conversing while staying in Holly Springs, Mississippi, in 1863, at the height of the Civil War. She responded vehemently, "No, I am from the West. Missouri is my native state." The lady retorted, "Yes, we know, but Missouri is a Southern state. Surely, you are Southern in feeling and principle?" She again exclaimed, "No, indeed, I am the most loyal of the loyal."[1] It was clear that she equated being Southern with being in support of the rebellion. To counter that association, Julia portrayed herself as a Westerner during the war and during her time as first lady from 1869 to 1876. However, despite her objections to the label, there was a noticeably Southern air about her in her manners and overall customs.

Julia Dent was born in 1826 on a plantation of more than eight hundred acres known as White Haven, located on the outskirts of St. Louis. The owner, her father, Frederick Fayette Dent, used the informal title of "Colonel" to project his image as a landowning gentleman in the traditional Southern sense. Although Julia attempted to distance herself from her Southern identity, she, by all measure, fits the romanticized version of the Southern belle. Growing up, she was given a formal education, the finest clothing, and enslaved servants. She also participated in prestigious social engagements and was expected to marry a prosperous gentleman and fully execute her motherly duties at home while supporting her husband. The one trait of stereotypical Southern belles from the era she did not possess was that of physical beauty. She was plagued with

Portrait of Julia Grant. Courtesy of the Library of Congress Prints and Photographs Division. Reproduction Number: LC-USZ62-25791 (b&w film copy neg. of detail).

strabismus—a condition that causes the eyes to cross or wander—which affected not only her appearance but also her vision.[2]

Her overall description of her childhood conformed to a Southern worldview. She began to write her autobiography in the 1890s, a few years after the death of her famed husband, Ulysses S. Grant, in 1885. She described the grandeur of White Haven, from its sprawling orchards of various fruit trees to the vast amount of space where the Dent children played. She wrote in wonderful detail about watching her older brothers exercise and play games in the fields and about how they fished in the nearby stream. She defined her English-born mother, Ellen Wrenshall Dent, who migrated to the United States at a young age, as an intelligent, kind, and beautiful "western pioneer's wife." Julia also boasted about the types of people who visited the plantation, including governors, military leaders, and family friends. According to her, White Haven was the "showplace of the county."[3]

This plantation might have been a magnificent place for a white girl and her family, but that was not the case for the dozens of enslaved people forced to live there. When discussing the subject in her memoirs, she perpetuated the myth of the enslaved workers' contentment. She claimed that the people her family enslaved were treated with care and affection. She wrote, "Papa used to buy for them great barrels of fish-herring from that part of the country. Molasses, tobacco, and some whiskey (on cold, raw days) were issued regularly to them from the storehouse, and then they had everything the farm produced. . . . I think our people were very happy." Julia also stated that she would give the "menservants" a "little tobacco, whiskey, or money" when they asked her for it (34–35).

As a child, she had her own group of enslaved girls, whom she called her "maids" and "nurses." She stated, "We always had a dusky train of from eight to ten little colored girls of all hues, and these little colored girls were allowed to accompany us if they were very neat" (36). The mere fact that she controlled a group of enslaved children lends credence to the notion of young Julia Dent being the typical antebellum Southern belle. Her exculpatory references to that era tell us even more about the 1890s, when Southern white myth making (and nostalgic Confederate monument building) peaked.[4]

Julia's Southern identity was only reinforced by the formal schooling she received. Her primary school was located near White Haven, and its cofounder was her father. She thoroughly enjoyed her elementary education because she was treated so well and was rarely reprimanded. Her brothers, and sometimes one of her enslaved women named Kitty, would literally carry her to the schoolhouse. Her mother even sent a special armchair for her, when the other students had to sit in chairs with no backs.[5]

After she completed her primary schooling, she was transferred to the Academy for Young Women at Fifth and Market Streets in St. Louis. Major Philip Mauro, a veteran of the War of 1812, his daughters, and his wife founded this prestigious school for elite young ladies.[6] Here, the teachers did not treat Julia with the same kindness her elementary school teachers did, but she made friends with her classmates and could travel home on the weekends. She loved to read novels during her time at the academy, but she claimed (or confessed) that she was "below the standard" in every course except philosophy, mythology, and history.[7]

Her formal education was over when she graduated from the academy in 1843. During the winter of that year, she spent her time socializing and getting to know the young military men in St. Louis, often introduced by her brother, Frederick, stationed at Jefferson Barracks, just a few miles from White Haven. When her brother visited in spring 1844, he brought along his West Point Military Academy roommate, Ulysses Grant, who began to make daily visits to White Haven and steadily escorted Julia Dent around the city.[8] In April 1844, before taking a leave of absence to visit his family in Ohio, Ulysses offered to give her his class ring. She refused, stating, "Oh, no, mamma would not approve of my accepting a gift from a gentleman."[9] In fact, she was surprised by the offer because she did not see him as a potential suitor. According to contemporary etiquette books, an elite Southern lady should only accept presents of jewelry from a man "to whom she has promised her hand."[10]

Ulysses acceded to her denial, but during his absence, Julia began to understand that her affection for him was rooted in more than just friendship; it was love. She stated, "I, child that I was, never for a moment thought of him as a lover. I was very happy when he was near, but that was all. Oh! How lonely it was without him." And to her surprise, he visited again before being shipped off to fight in the Mexican American War. In May 1844, during his last week in Missouri, Ulysses proposed to her, and this time she accepted. For the next two years, he fought in nearly every major battle of the war. The couple was connected only by the occasional letter. To this day, only Ulysses Grant's side of the correspondence remains, but it reveals a deep and passionate love between the two.[11]

They were married in August 1848, shortly after Ulysses returned home from the war. In true Southern tradition, the newlyweds were showered with bouquets of flowers.[12] However, members of his family did not attend the wedding because of their adamant opposition to slavery. He came from a staunch abolitionist family. His own father, Jesse Root Grant, even lived with the notable abolitionist John Brown when he was a child.[13] Despite their objections, Ulysses was dedicated to Julia and was ready to settle down, start a family with her, and begin his career as a farmer. But, first, he needed to complete his tenure in the military. After their wedding, he was stationed in Detroit, Michigan, and Sackett's

Harbor, New York. Julia was with him until early 1850, when she moved back to St. Louis to give birth to their first child, Frederick. Everything appeared to be going smoothly for the young couple until Grant was transferred to California in July 1852. Then pregnant with their second child, she stayed in Ohio.

While Ulysses Grant and his party were crossing the treacherous Panama isthmus, full of physical hazards and risks of disease, Julia gave birth to Ulysses Jr., affectionately given the nickname Buck because he was born in Ohio, the "Buckeye State." Because Ulysses Sr. was on the West Coast, he did not get to see Buck until the boy was almost two years old. This was a difficult time for him because he was separated from his family. But it was an even more difficult time for her, essentially raising two small children on her own, a far cry from the expected life of a Southern lady. To help her with this burden, she moved back to St. Louis with her family, counting as well on their enslaved servants. She received some letters from him during this time, but they were usually filled with sadness or bad news from the West Coast. Aside from a few anecdotes about the children in her memoirs, she did not provide many details of that time in St. Louis.

By summer 1854, depressed and greatly missing Julia, Ulysses allegedly began to drink heavily; he was forced to resign from the military and moved back home to his wife and young family.[14] Soon after, Julia's father gave them some land for a house and farming purposes. They had two more children, a girl named Ellen, nicknamed Nellie, and a boy named Jesse.

The subsequent years were not ideal for the family. Although Ulysses was finally able to begin supporting his wife and children by farming, he did not have much success. Not surprisingly, Julia's assessment of her husband's agrarian abilities differed from the actual results. She wrote, "Ulys was really very successful at farming. His crops yielded well—that is, much better than papa's, but not as much as he anticipated from his calculations on paper."[15] Emphasizing the image of a Western pioneer, she wrote, "I was a splendid farmer's wife."[16] During this time his father-in-law gave him an enslaved man, William Jones. Ulysses earned the disdain of his neighbors as he worked in the fields alongside Jones and other African American men he hired. This arrangement lasted only a year because he freed Jones in March 1859.[17]

In fact, within four years of obtaining his farm, Ulysses had to sell off all his agricultural assets. He then tried his hand at real estate, and at one point he even resorted to selling firewood on the streets of St. Louis.[18] Eventually, the family was forced to move to Galena, Illinois, where Ulysses worked as a clerk in his father's leather goods store. This was a low point for Julia and her family, but circumstances soon provided them a chance to improve their lot.

In 1861, when the Civil War broke out, Grant was able to use his military skills, with his wife's support. During the first two years of the war, he rose through the ranks of the Union Army. He fought battles in Missouri and Kentucky before being promoted to major general in February 1862. After a difficult victory at Shiloh, Tennessee, he was tasked with capturing the Confederate stronghold at Vicksburg, Mississippi. Julia Grant visited her husband while he pushed the troops through Mississippi. She was so close to the action, in fact, that she was present during the running of the batteries at Vicksburg in April 1863.[19]

She did not make this trip alone. She was accompanied by her youngest son, Jesse, and an enslaved woman named Jules who served as her nurse and maid. Jules, who was born at White Haven, accompanied Julia anytime she visited Ulysses during the war. The Southern women with whom Julia interacted during these visits must have understood the irony of a Union general's wife bringing an enslaved person with her to Mississippi.[20]

After witnessing this Vicksburg scene, she returned to Missouri with her three youngest children.[21] Upon arriving in St. Louis, Julia's regional identity was once again questioned. All her neighbors saw themselves as Southerners, and they could not believe she did not follow suit. They exclaimed, "It is right for you to say you are Union, Julia, but we know better, my child; it is not in human nature for you to be anything but Southern." Her skeptical neighbors also jokingly accused her of alerting the authorities about the mail they were sending South. They would quip, "We know you will not. We know how you have been brought up and an oath would not be more binding than the sanctity of your roof."[22] As the wife of a leading Union general, Julia began to overtly distance herself from any association with the Southern rebellion but not necessarily with her aspirations of being a Southern lady. She continued to enjoy the life afforded her while staying on her father's Southern plantation, and her father's affinity for the Southern cause and slavery made it more difficult for her to completely abandon her Southern roots.

Ulysses Grant was ultimately able to capture Vicksburg, then Chattanooga, Tennessee, before being promoted to head of the entire Union Army. He defeated Robert E. Lee in Virginia to effectively bring an end to the war. These successes catapulted him to the national stage in the United States. Next to the martyred Abraham Lincoln, he was the best-known American at the time.

The end of the war signified that Julia Grant's life as a slave owner was over. Even the enslaved woman Jules, who accompanied her on her trip to Mississippi, escaped to her freedom in 1864. Because Julia was the wife of the war's most successful general, she did not feel the full financial and social impact of losing her slave power. During this period, the Grants were given the full star treatment. The people of Philadelphia gifted the family a large house in the city, and soon after, in February 1866, Major General Daniel Butterfield gave the family $105,000 as a gift from New York City financiers to help pay for a new house in Washington.[23] Ulysses's fame easily made him the Republican candidate in the presidential election of 1868. His campaign slogan of "Let Us Have Peace" unified the country and helped to secure his election victory.

As the newly minted first lady on March 4, 1869, Julia emphasized her role as a loyal patriot, but she did not entirely let go of her Southern customs. She was always dressed in the finest clothes and made sure that she served as hostess of the social gatherings at the White House. At the start of her first White House reception, Julia was doubtful of her capability to handle her duties as first lady, so she decided to follow the lessons she learned while observing the ladies from the previous administration.[24] She wrote, "I followed their example and stationed myself back of a white marble table, on which lay a large bouquet." To her surprise, the guests did not come in until she was urged to meet them at the door. This slight misstep was corrected, and Julia quickly became an excellent hostess. In her memoirs, she described the White House as being "in utter confusion" when she first arrived; the Johnsons' tenure had been fraught with disarray because of First Lady Eliza Johnson's illness. Julia brought along some of her now paid Black servants to fix the problem.[25] She (and they) quickly got to work. She had each room furnished, the carpets replaced, and the reception room to the right of the front entrance renovated. She enforced a dress code for the workers and even had the gates closed all around the property to keep the public from wandering onto the grounds. As she explained, "Order soon came out of chaos." She organized the White House in a hierarchical Southern style and commented, "It . . . seems as much like home to me as the old farm in Missouri, White Haven" (174).

By this time, the Grant children were becoming adults, and their mother rarely was able to visit with them. The younger ones were in school, and the eldest, Fred, was travelling throughout Europe with the notable General William T. Sherman. As a mother who took pride in raising her children, Julia was saddened by the inevitable reality of their going out on their own. She stated, "During our first four years at the Executive Mansion, we saw little or nothing of the children." To counter this sense of loss, Julia focused on her formal duties as first lady, and she even became involved in her husband's political dealings (178–180).

The most noteworthy political issue she dealt with as first lady was the "Gold Ring Scandal." In 1869, President Grant's brother-in-law Abel Corbin, along with Jay Gould and Jim Fisk, attempted to corner the gold market by buying the precious metal at a low cost and selling it after the price increased. They deviously tried to convince the president to hire an inside man as the assistant treasurer. Ultimately, the scheme failed because the first lady informed the president of the strange attention Corbin and his wife, Grant's sister Virginia, were devoting to the market. The president subverted the conspirators' attempts to make a profit, but the damage had already been done to the economic markets. Countless people lost an immense amount of money on their gold investments.[26]

The Gold Ring Scandal appeared to be a turning point for the first lady. It was the first time she was involved in the politics of her husband's presidency, but it certainly was not the last. President Grant might not have taken all of Julia's political advice, but she regularly voiced her opinions on policy proposals and administrative decisions anyway. She even appeared at Senate hearings and cabinet meetings, and on occasion, she helped to determine who the president would meet. During the entire eight years of her husband's administration, Julia made sure that she greeted every world leader and diplomat who visited the White House. Her social grace with public figures and her active partnership with her husband were an extension of the same characteristics exhibited by previous Southern first ladies such as Sarah Polk and Julia Tyler.[27]

There was no doubt, however, that Julia's most memorable moments in the White House involved her family. She was instrumental in organizing the famous wedding of her only daughter, Nellie, to Englishman Algernon Sartoris. The ceremony, with more than two hundred people in attendance, occurred in the East Room of the White House in May 1874. The event was so well publicized that the Oliver Ditson Company published a collection of dance music for the wedding that included "Nellie Grant's Wedding March." The first lady was pleased with the ceremony, but she was saddened by the fact that her young daughter would be moving to England.[28] Fortunately, her eldest son, Fred, and his wife, Ida Honoré Grant, had a child in the White House in 1876. The infant was named after her grandmother: Julia Dent Grant. Little Julia, as she was known to the family, would later grow up to marry Russian Prince Michael Cantacuzene.[29]

As Julia's time in the White House ended, she reflected on how much she had enjoyed the experience. Even after being away from St. Louis for years, Julia could not forget her rural roots. She said, "My life at the White House was like a bright and beautiful dream, and we were immeasurably happy. It was quite the happiest period of my life. I suppose I might say with touching effect that the quiet tranquility of the farm and its home associations were sweeter to me than the gayety and excitement of the Executive Mansion, but it wouldn't be true."[30]

After leaving the White House in 1877, the couple decided to keep collecting fond memories. Along with two of their sons, they embarked on a two-year trip around the world, where they met with world leaders, artists, and even their beloved daughter, Nellie. During the trip, the former first lady was well received by the elite and common folk alike. She purchased valuable items such as opera shawls from France and fine china from Asia. She even kept a scrapbook with photos of all the famous people she had met during their trip, which took them from the diamond deserts of Egypt's historic ruins to the golden valleys of the Bonanza Mine in Virginia City, Nevada.[31]

After they returned from their journey, there was talk of Ulysses Grant running for a third term as president. The prospect of him pursuing the presidency again filled Julia with what she described as "suspense." In her memoirs, she claimed that she did not believe he would be the Republican nominee. She was correct in her assessment; James Garfield ultimately received the Republican nod.[32] After the failed attempt at a third term, the family lived in New York City until disaster struck in 1884. The investment firm Grant and Ward, a partnership between Ulysses Grant Jr. and Ferdinand Ward, collapsed. Ward had set up what is referred to today as a Ponzi scheme, which left the Grant family utterly penniless.[33] According to the former first lady, "the failure of Grant and Ward came like a thunderclap. It was a great shock to my family, as they all believed they were not only prosperous but wealthy."[34] Soon after the collapse of Grant and Ward, the family received even more terrible news. The former president was diagnosed with advanced throat and mouth cancer. During the final months of his life, he rushed to finish writing his personal memoirs so that he could leave his wife a substantial income. In June 1885, the family moved to the calm, quiet, rural community of Mount McGregor, New York, for his final days. He was able to finish his memoirs before his death on July 23, 1885. The two volumes went on to be among the best-sellers of nineteenth-century American literature.[35]

Julia would ultimately receive approximately $400,000 in royalty payments from the sale of her husband's memoirs.[36] She spent her final years living in comfort in Washington, where she advocated for soldiers and war veterans, promoted the significance of her husband's legacy, and interacted with the wives of politicians.[37] During this period Julia began to write her autobiography. She meticulously planned and organized the manuscript, even making a folder of personal photographs she wanted included in the book. Unfortunately, Julia could not find anyone to publish her manuscript before her death in December 1902. Her personal account of her evolving social identity would stay hidden for decades until the renowned documentary editor and executive director of the Ulysses S. Grant Association, John Y. Simon, published an annotated edition of the manuscript in 1975.

Julia was the first first lady born west of the Mississippi River, technically making her a Westerner because that area of the country was considered the frontier in her era. However, her back story reveals a complex cultural identity clearly influenced by Southern customs.[38] As she grew older, she attempted to distance herself from those parts of her identity she associated with the South and secession, especially after she was thrust into the roles of wife of a leading Union general and the nation's first lady. Nevertheless, her well-written autobiography shows that she spent most of her early life ascribing to Southern norms, values, traditions, and stereotypes. In many ways, in her later life, she continued to aspire to the lifestyle of a traditional Southern lady. She never renounced slavery and seemed to have always excused how she benefited personally from the enslavement of others. As historians continue to grapple with the truth and horrors of the country's original sin of slavery, Julia's failure to atone for her participation in the institution remains to define her legacy.

## NOTES

1. Julia Dent Grant, *The Personal Memoirs of Julia Dent Grant (Mrs. Ulysses S. Grant)*, ed. John Y. Simon (New York: Putnam's, 1975), 106.

2. Daniel Bennett St. John Roosa, *A Clinical Manual of Diseases of the Eye: Including a Sketch of Its Anatomy* (New York: William Wood, 1894), 546–549.

3. Grant, *Personal Memoirs of Julia Dent Grant*, 33, 40.

4. Lee Glazer and Susan Key, "Carry Me Back: Nostalgia for the Old South in Nineteenth-Century Popular Culture," *Journal of American Studies* 30, no. 1 (1996): 1–24.

5. Grant, *Personal Memoirs of Julia Dent Grant*, 37; Pamela K. Sanfilippo, "Elizabeth McCardle Johnson and Julia Dent Grant," in *A Companion to First Ladies*, ed. Katherine A. S. Sibley (West Sussex, UK: Wiley-Blackwell, 2016), 237; Carol Berkin, *Civil War Wives: The Lives and Times of Angelina Grimké Weld, Varina Howell Davis, and Julia Dent Grant* (New York: Knopf, 2009), 224.

6. Berkin, *Civil War Wives*, 224; Grant, *Personal Memoirs of Julia Dent Grant*, 62; *The Caduceus of Kappa Sigma*, vol. 19 (Philadelphia: Franklin., 1904), 265.

7. Grant, *Personal Memoirs of Julia Dent Grant*, 38.

8. Ronald C. White, *American Ulysses: A Life of Ulysses S. Grant* (New York: Random House, 2016), 47.

9. Grant, *Personal Memoirs of Julia Dent Grant*, 49.

10. Mary Elizabeth Wilson Sherwood, *Etiquette, the American Code of Manners: A Study of the Usages, Laws, and Observances, Which Govern Intercourse in the Best Circles of American Society* (New York: Routledge, 1834), 44.

11. Grant, *Personal Memoirs of Julia Dent Grant*, 49–50; Ulysses S. Grant, *The Papers of Ulysses S. Grant*, ed. John Y. Simon, vol. 1 (Carbondale: Southern Illinois University Press, 1967), xxxvii. For the correspondence between Julia Dent and Ulysses Grant during the Mexican American War, see Grant, *Papers of Ulysses S. Grant*, vol. 1, 23–164.

12. Ishbel Ross, *The General's Wife: The Life of Mrs. Ulysses S. Grant* (New York: Dodd, Mead, 1959), 49.

13. Ron Chernow, *Grant* (New York: Penguin Books, 2017), 5.

14. Ron Chernow claims that Fort Humboldt was awash in liquor and that Grant had a hard time resisting it; see Chernow, *Grant*, 84–85. However, official military records of the time are silent regarding accusations of Ulysses's drinking while he was stationed on the West Coast.

15. "Ulys" was the nickname she gave Ulysses Grant.

16. Grant, *Personal Memoirs of Julia Dent Grant*, 77.

17. Brooks D. Simpson, *Ulysses S. Grant: Triumph over Adversity, 1822–1865* (Boston: Houghton Mifflin, 2000), 67; Chernow, *Grant*, 101; John F. Marszalek, David Nolen, and Louie Gallo, *Hold On with a Bulldog Grip: A Short Study of Ulysses S. Grant* (Jackson: University Press of Mississippi, 2019), 33.

18. Chernow, *Grant*, 102, 104.

19. Grant, *Personal Memoirs of Julia Dent Grant*, 112.

20. Candice Shy Hooper, *Lincoln's Generals' Wives* (Kent, OH: Kent State University Press, 2016), 312; Grant, *Personal Memoirs of Julia Dent Grant*, 83, 105.

21. The eldest child, Fred, stayed with his father during the rest of the Vicksburg campaign.

22. Grant, *Personal Memoirs of Julia Dent Grant*, 113.

23. Grant, *Personal Memoirs of Julia Dent Grant*, 157, 167n.

24. In part because of illness, Eliza Johnson was unable to handle most of her duties as first lady. The responsibilities of first lady were managed by her eldest child, Martha Johnson Patterson. See Sanfilippo, "Elizabeth McCardle Johnson and Julia Dent Grant," 233.

25. Grant, *Personal Memoirs of Julia Dent Grant*, 173, 175.

26. Berkin, *Civil War Wives*, 284–285.

27. See Christopher J. Leahy and Sharon Williams Leahy, "The Ladies of Tippecanoe, and Tyler Too," in *A Companion to First Ladies*, ed. Katherine A. S. Sibley (West Sussex, UK: Wiley-Blackwell, 2016); Valerie Palmer-Mehta, "Sarah Polk: Ideas of Her Own," in *A Companion to First Ladies*, ed. Katherine A. S. Sibley (West Sussex, UK: Wiley-Blackwell, 2016), 151, 168; Ross, *General's Wife*, 213, 226–227; Sanfilippo, "Elizabeth McCardle Johnson and Julia Dent Grant," 241–242.

28. Grant, *Personal Memoirs of Julia Dent Grant*, 181.

29. Gilson Willets, *Inside History of the White House: The Complete History of the Domestic and Official Life in Washington of the Nation's Presidents and Their Families* (New York: Christian Herald, 1908), 228, 281–285.

30. Willets, *Inside History of the White House*, 138.

31. Edwina S. Campbell, *Citizen of a Wider Commonwealth: Ulysses S. Grant's Postpresidential Diplomacy* (Carbondale: Southern Illinois University Press, 2016), 202–203.

32. Grant, *Personal Memoirs of Julia Dent Grant*, 321–322.

33. Charles Bracelen Flood, *Grant's Final Victory: Ulysses S. Grant's Heroic Last Year* (New York: Da Capo, 2011), 35–36.

34. Grant, *Personal Memoirs of Julia Dent Grant*, 327.

35. See Ulysses S. Grant, *The Personal Memoirs of Ulysses S. Grant: The Complete Annotated Edition*, ed. John F. Marszalek, with David S. Nolen and Louie P. Gallo (Cambridge, MA: Belknap Press of Harvard University Press, 2017).

36. Mark Perry, *Grant and Twain: The Story of an American Friendship* (New York: Random House, 2005), 118.

37. Sanfilippo, "Elizabeth McCardle Johnson and Julia Dent Grant," 244.

38. Campbell, *Citizen of a Wider Commonwealth*, 202.

# CHAPTER 11

# Southern Roots of Activism

Nancy Beck Young

"The office of the first spouse is a rancid barrel of presidential pork that has outlived its usefulness"—so said Jack Shafer, a writer for *Politico Magazine*, in late November 2016. This commentary implied a criticism of all the public functions Americans have come to expect from first ladies: entertaining foreign and domestic government officials, adopting a political cause, and lobbying on behalf of the president are key examples. Shafer disliked the nepotistic power given to presidential spouses, historically wives, for reasons of marriage and not talent or professional accomplishment. He complained that the first lady's East Wing office employed approximately twenty-five people and operated with an annual budget of $1.5 million in federal spending.[1]

Shafer insinuated that eliminating the office itself would end first lady activism, a consequence he welcomed, but an examination of the history of first lady advocacy suggests otherwise. Public engagement by presidential spouses preceded the bureaucracy that now supports such endeavors. Still, Shafer's exposition indicates an unease about presidential wives, figures who mostly have garnered tremendous public acclaim. To understand that anxiety requires grappling with the early history of first lady activism. The East Wing bureaucracy Shafer disdained had not always been thus. Not until the Theodore Roosevelt administration did the federal government employ a social secretary for the first lady. Prior to the twentieth century, presidential spouses relied on relatives and friends to assist with correspondence and entertaining. This ad hoc relationship did not mean eighteenth- and nineteenth-century first ladies were traditional in their behavior; rather, it shows the lag time between the gradual acceptance of first lady activism and the development of institutional support structures for such work.[2]

What, then, were the roots of first lady activism if not the bureaucracy? Part of the answer comes from exploring the concept of political marriage, and part comes from a regional analysis of the earliest first ladies. In our democratic society, the evolution of political marriage has had hierarchical and grassroots sources. To understand this complex and convoluted process, examination of the earliest and most prominent American political marriages is necessary. The United States, born in a revolution against monarchy, nonetheless bestowed certain pseudoroyal elements upon the president and his family, not the least of which was the designation of "first lady" for the president's wife and the formal hostess obligations she assumed. Presidents' wives have also transcended these expectations by adopting individually unique modes of activism, atypically in the nineteenth century and somewhat more commonly in the twentieth.[3]

Several notable early first ladies did function politically in precedent-setting fashion—and their actions helped frame the office of first lady from the beginning. As this chapter will emphasize, the most important source of first lady activism emanates from perhaps the most unlikely region of the country: the South. Indeed, Southern-born and Southern-identified women helped construct the parameters of being a first lady and authored the earliest examples of first lady activism. They did so within the confines of their marriages, making political marriage a key component of the Southern-constructed role of activist first ladies.[4] Indeed, the public act of defining a woman through her marriage (a designation affirmed by the term "lady") as opposed to defining her through independent accomplishments has demarcated acceptable and unacceptable choices for first ladies. We may also consider the role of presidential marriage in national politics. For example, scholars of the early national period have explored how political wives, many of them Southern, played a significant role in creating the social and cultural context for governance in Washington, and a few historians have looked as well at twentieth-century presidential partnerships.[5]

The activist Southern women who were also first ladies contrasted sharply with the more passive images associated with proper womanhood—the cult of domesticity—that prevailed in the nineteenth century. Many first ladies accorded well with the cult of domesticity and its emphasis on piety, purity, submissiveness, and domesticity; they embraced their privacy. Few first ladies from the nineteenth century sought the public spotlight, let alone an activist policy agenda. For a good number of them, of course, illness made it impossible to enter the public sphere, and they relied on relatives (often daughters and daughters-in-law) to perform their ritualistic hostess duties. These duties became the default for proper first lady behavior, rather than activism, even as the abolitionist and suffrage movements were emerging.[6]

Activist Southern first ladies, nevertheless, form an important link with more contemporary iterations of the office. In this closing chapter to Part I of the book, I concentrate on four first ladies of the Early Republic and antebellum years—Martha Washington, Dolley Madison, Julia Tyler, and Sarah Polk—to understand the Southern origins of first lady activism. I conclude with a consideration of reactions against first lady activism, also often rooted in the South. This part of the chapter extends as well into the twentieth century and looks at Southern criticism of Lou Henry Hoover, Eleanor Roosevelt, and Lady Bird Johnson for taking public stances in favor of racial equality.

Martha Washington defined the position of first lady with a Southern flair, and although her immediate successors did not entirely mimic her, she and her early Southern successors played an important role in originally conceiving what it has meant to be first lady. It could not have been otherwise given the prominence and prevalence of Southern men as president in the antebellum United States. Four of the first five presidents were Southern, and of the fifteen antebellum presidents, eight were Southern. Thus, the earliest first ladies hailed from the South, and most were activists, at least according to the standards of their era.

Our first first lady Martha Washington had been well regarded among George Washington's male colleagues for her diplomacy and activist style as a public, political wife.[7] But when her husband became president, there was no direction or definition or budget or even inkling that an office of the first lady would emerge over the next two-plus centuries. As new and radical as was the concept of an elected president, none even conceived that the spouse of the chief executive would play a noncodified, yet semiofficial and uncompensated role in national governance because none had thought about the concept of political marriage. The process by which the office of the first lady was constructed, let alone the concept of the first lady itself, was slow, iterative, and biographical, meaning that presidential wives over time wrote and rewrote their position and their power.

Because Washington, DC, was a new capital in a new nation, the social mores were fluid in a way unlike those of European capitals, where the public roles for men and women were determined by their fixed positions among royal hierarchies. This fluidity meant that the earliest women to hold the office would sketch out its roles and responsibilities. For example, monarchs never entertained visiting ministers over a meal. The different circumstances in the United States resulted in part from electoral realities that constantly shifted the government personnel and in part because lawmakers typically did not bring their families to Washington. The first lady thus enjoyed tremendous flexibility to define her role in the government. Madison was the first first lady to work for any length of time out of the new national capital in Washington, and as two scholars observed, "When Dolley took up the role of First Lady in Washington, she was, in a very significant way, the first 'First Lady' of the new American nation. She was a blank slate upon which people could write their wishes and anxieties. Some adored her. Others loathed her. Many exaggerated her power."[8]

As Washington and Madison's experiences illuminate, then, at its core the institution of the first lady has both been structured around and at other times in rebellion against Southern ideas of womanhood. As historians of Southern women have noted, the earliest concepts of Southern womanhood—that elite, white women belong on a pedestal—is complex, based as much in mythology as in reality.[9] Indeed, the most well-known Southern first ladies were more often in rebellion against societal expectations of how they should behave than in agreement with established norms. Looking for the Southern roots of the office of first lady thus requires two approaches: first, illumination of the precedents Southern presidential spouses established during their husbands' administrations, and, second, analysis of Southern-authored and Southern-framed critiques of first ladies—regardless of regional identity—for not following the established mores. This latter point builds upon Southern notions of proper female behavior, a concept derived from national assumptions about gender roles but notably layered with racial constructs. There are several key areas in which Southern first ladies established the overall parameters of the office and showed how presidential spouses could become activists: through demeanor, politics, entertaining, and white supremacy.

The South as a place also shaped the evolution of the first lady for reasons of divisive national politics. In the nineteenth century, slavery—its expansion and its continuation—became a determining issue of national life, leading up to the Civil War, and after the war race and racism proved equally significant. Although neither the Civil War nor race and racism were exclusively Southern, both issues loomed large over the evolving idea of the first lady. And, just as significant, the earliest widespread reactions against first lady activism would also come from the South.

## DEMEANOR AND ACTIVISM

Southern women constructed the office of first lady by using attitude and activism to fashion the most important executive branch office not named in the Constitution or conceived by the founders as necessary to the success of the United States. Through demeanor and carriage, first ladies could be both traditional and activist at the same time. Indeed, a traditional mode of comportment could be used to mask or at least counterbalance activist challenges to the status quo. Demeanor proved crucial to Martha Washington's efforts as first lady, and the same can be said for many of her successors. Numerous contemporaries commented on her attitudinal fitness to assist her husband's presidency. A Polish politician and writer who had visited Mount Vernon called Washington a "worthy wife." Mercy Otis Warren observed to Abigail Adams in 1776, "I think the Complacency of her Manners speaks at once the Benevolence of her Heart, and her affability, Candor and Gentleness Quallify her to soften the hours of private Live or to sweeten the Cares of the Hero and smooth the Rugged scenes of War." Further, she possessed the cultural sophistication associated with successful presidential spouses. For example, in 1765 Washington took piano lessons. She had an appreciation for the leading artistic talents of the new nation, attending an exhibition of paintings by Jonathan Trumbull.[10]

For Dolley Madison also, "hospitality and graciousness of deportment" were perhaps the most important political arrows in her quiver. She used these "female" traits to exert tremendous influence over Washington affairs. For eight years before her husband's presidency, she had learned the mores of the national capital while he served as secretary of state for President Thomas Jefferson. Because Jefferson was a widower, Madison oversaw many social affairs during his administration. The Jefferson approach to entertaining was not a good model for her, though. According to one student of the era, he had been too "extreme" and "radical" in his republicanism. As first lady, Madison saw her job as bringing together Republicans and Federalists so the business of the government could go forward. She did so from day one, attending the first inaugural ball with her husband. Both Madisons chose a wardrobe emphasizing the republican values of the people. Her ballgown was velvet, modest in cut, and less ornate than was stylish in Europe. Moreover, she wore pearls, not the diamonds popular with European aristocrats. After the Madison presidency ended, the Portuguese-born wife of a Swedish diplomat told the former first lady, "You were loved by all your country men and country women, and as the Wife of their President, you honored his elevated post, and were respected for your judicious conduct, and affable kind manner."[11]

Her successor, Elizabeth Monroe, was another Southern first lady who contributed both to décor in the Executive Mansion (thanks to furniture gleaned from her residency in France) and to presidential gatherings. Throughout, she displayed an "exceedingly gracious" manner. Her fragile health, though, blunted her activism, leading her to rely increasingly on her daughter Eliza to carry out official functions.[12]

For other Southern first ladies after Madison, religion became the foundation for their bearing in the world and their activism. As one example, Sarah Polk's religious values became a leading recommendation for her husband's presidency. To that point, former president Andrew Jackson wrote to president-elect James K. Polk, whose career he had mentored: "With all our kind salutations to Mrs. Polk, say to her how much we approve her conduct in putting down the desecration of the Sabath near Smithland." Jackson was referring to Sarah Polk's prohibition of music aboard the steamboat her husband's inaugural party took on its journey to Washington. Because the party continued its travels on a Sunday, she had decreed that no music be played, in part to counter potential criticism for not honoring the sabbath. "Say to her carry this thro' your whole administration," Jackson intoned, "& god will smile upon you & her, and the whole United States will approve & rejoice." He recommended that his protégé use the incident to his advantage to set a tone of reasonable religious obser-vation for his presidency—one that would garner him continued public sup-port—and to use religious mores to accumulate protection from expectations for public availability on Sundays. Explained Jackson, if a friendly newspaper editor "would publish a short Journal of your trip with this incident it would relieve you from visits on the Sabath."[13] Sarah Polk needed no encouragement to protect her husband's peace on the sabbath, however, which fit well her own inclinations and this era of the cult of domesticity.

## POLITICS AND ACTIVISM

For antebellum Southern first ladies, an acceptable, female demeanor proved essential to successful political engagement. Indeed, the former provided a safe penumbra that often shielded political activism from criticism. In the context of late-eighteenth-century mores, Martha Washington charted an activist course other presidential spouses followed. On August 13, 1790, she appeared at a trea-ty-signing ceremony between the US government and the Creek Nation. She also attended the inaugural law lectures given by Associate Justice of the US Su-preme Court James Wilson just a few days later, on August 17, 1790. Moreover, Washington sometimes appeared with her husband when he inspected industry. For example, she toured a cotton manufactory in Philadelphia in 1792. Finally, she corresponded with a widow of a Revolutionary War soldier to explain she lacked the power to provide assistance, though not the desire to do so. Abigail Adams, who followed Washington as first lady, expanded these precedents for political engagement, revealing that the roots of first lady activism were not ex-clusively Southern but also biographical. Adams had throughout her marriage chastised her husband John to consider female rights, most famously asking him to "remember the ladies" when he participated in drafting the Declaration of Independence.[14]

The Southern women who succeeded Washington and Adams pushed fur-ther their political activism. Madison practiced it in large and small ways, rang-ing from her manner of decorating the Executive Mansion to her management of political discourse. Working with Benjamin Henry Latrobe to furnish the president's house, Dolley Madison wanted to make the official residence a symbol of republican values. She sought furniture made by American craftsmen, for instance, and used Greco-Roman design to show the United States as a new Greece.[15] In this way the feminine sphere of housekeeping took on significant political import.

Political influence came with a price. The toll of being first lady revealed itself in Madison's correspondence, which included much less about her personal life and concerns than that which she wrote before and after her husband's presidency, and much more about her official duties. Her correspondence for these years is full of requests for favors that could be granted only by the spouse of a high-ranking public official. For example, Abigail Adams wrote her seeking a federal appointment for her grandson. Explaining she had "never had the pleasure of a personal acquaintance with you," Adams indicated that because she was "unaccustomed to ask favors of this nature for Friends or connections," she preferred writing the first lady rather than President Madison. In so doing, Adams conformed with the etiquette of letter writing among the governing elites because she wrote to a woman and not the male officeholder.[16]

Madison's political work in this regard drew criticism from novelist George Watterston. He made a veiled, satirical attack on Madison in *The Wanderer in Washington,* calling out her work on behalf of government job seekers. Although she did help friends and family looking for positions, the number of requests she received was minuscule compared with the overall number sent to the Madison administration. Moreover, a notable part of her work fell wholly within the feminine realm in that she helped younger female relatives and family friends find eligible and socially acceptable marriage partners (including, much later, Angelica Singleton, whom she introduced to Abraham van Buren, son of President Martin van Buren). Indeed, Dolley Madison as first lady was frequently called a "queen" both by those who disliked her public activities and those who celebrated the work she undertook.[17]

Political discord in Washington, though, made matters difficult for Madison. When the president fired Robert Smith as secretary of state, Smith and his wife used Washington society to retaliate. Smith even published a pamphlet in which he lambasted the president. Dolley Madison told her sister, "We expect too Mr S—s book [will be] opening the eyes of the world on all our sins &. &." Smith was not alone in attacking both Madisons. US Representative Josiah Quincy, a Massachusetts Federalist, pilloried the first lady in Congress for mixing politics with entertainment. He eviscerated her Executive Mansion parties because they provided an environment in which "little men who sigh after great offices" could engage in the partisan behavior he believed detrimental to good governance.

Dolley Madison, he contended, enabled the "toads that live upon the vapor of the palace [and] that swallow great men's spittle at the levees."[18]

Madison's activism took on entirely new characteristics during the War of 1812, when she evacuated the Executive Mansion. She recounted her experiences to her sister: "At this late hour a wagon has been procured, I have had it filled with the plate and most valuable portable articles belonging to the house; whether it will reach its destination; the Bank of Maryland, or fall into the hands of British soldiery, events must determine." At the same time, Madison annoyed a male friend who "c[a]me to hasten my departure, and is in a very bad humor with me because I insist on waiting until the large picture of Gen. Washington is secured, and it requires to be unscrewed from the wall. This process was found too tedious for these perilous moments." Instead, Madison "ordered the frame to be broken, and the canvass taken out" before handing it over to "two gentlemen of New York, for safe keeping." Enslaved people in the Executive Mansion were key to this rushed clearing out, including fifteen-year-old Paul Jennings. She closed, telling her sister, "I must leave this house, or the retreating army will make me a prisoner in it, by filling up the road I am directed to take. When I shall again write you, or where I shall be tomorrow, I cannot tell!!"[19]

Madison's childhood friend Eliza Collins Lee wrote her at the conclusion of her husband's presidency about her record, celebrating exactly how important Madison's work as first lady had been for the country and explaining that Madison would not escape public responsibilities with her departure from Washington. "Talents such as yours were never intended to remain inactive on retiring from public life."[20]

Between Madison's years as first lady and 1844, when Julia Gardiner married the recently widowed John Tyler, the first lady had either not been Southern— Louisa Adams and Anna Harrison—or like Elizabeth Monroe and Letitia Tyler, had arranged for female surrogates to handle the basic responsibilities accruing to presidential wives. All had embraced domesticity over activism. Julia Gardiner Tyler made for a different brand of Southerner in the Executive Mansion. She had been born and bred in the North, but when she married President Tyler during his administration, she also married his region, the South, adopting the mores and preferences of her husband's home state. Just as importantly, she married the idea of being a politician's wife. In the process, she revealed just how political marriage could be for those who sought alliance with powerful men. She savored the idea and reality of activism because she had wanted the life that came with being spouse of the president. She proved herself an assiduous student of politics and usually with a Southern accent that involved supporting the expansion of slavery. To ensure her favorable reception in Washington, Tyler encouraged a New York journalist to facilitate flattering coverage in the national newspapers. As a result, she came to be known as "Mrs. Presidentress," a term of affection for some and criticism for others. A detractor of hers intimated that with Sarah Polk, whose husband ran in 1844, "*We can beat that.*" Ironically, Polk proved that she herself was quite an activist; she had been known in the 1830s as "Membress of Congress-elect."[21]

Tyler, like her husband, eagerly wanted to see the admission of Texas as a slave state. She defended her husband's interest in the issue as that of a "patriot" who sought to guarantee the "vital interest to the whole Union." To effect her desired ends, she used her position as hostess for administrative social functions. At an early dinner, Secretary of State John C. Calhoun sat to the right of the first lady. They discussed Texas and who would vote for its admission to the Union. Julia Tyler stressed the importance of honor in ensuring Texas's admission. Calhoun, a strong supporter of annexation, nonetheless told her, "There is no honor in politics." She replied, "We will see" before writing on a piece of paper "Texas and John Tyler." She passed the note across the table to Supreme Court Justice John McLean, also her former suitor. McLean adhered to Tyler's request and offered the toast, much to Calhoun's (and President Tyler's) chagrin.[22]

Later, she wrote her sister praising a message the president issued, stressing "Oh! if it will only have the effect of admitting Texas!" Julia Tyler remained focused on the Texas question, noting on February 23, just days before they left office, "The Texas question looks very encouraging. It is confidently expected to be passed this week. The prospect is quite bewildering; for it is the President's last remaining desire." She regularly visited the Capitol, where she lobbied as many senators as she could.[23]

Tyler's political interests did not end when her husband left the presidency. Instead she revealed herself as an astute, but also problematic, observer of secessionist politics during the Civil War era. At this juncture, Tyler's activism occurred in her correspondence and conversations with friends, family, and political acquaintances and in her encouragement of her husband's last hurrah on the political stage. Such active engagement with the major political issues of the 1850s contrasts sharply with the overall political disengagement of her first lady successors: Margaret Taylor, Abigail Fillmore, and Jane Pierce. On February 3, 1861, Tyler wrote her mother of her experiences at the Washington Peace Conference, an unsuccessful effort to resolve the sectional crisis short of civil war, observing, "Perhaps I am here during the last days of the Republic." The next day she observed that her husband was "the great centre of attraction. Everybody says he is looked to to save the Union." During these last days before the Civil War she displayed a naive optimism that slavery and the Union could be preserved. She discussed these matters with a number of male politicians and considered how the former president "would achieve for himself" nothing short of "immortality" should he "bring all the discordant elements together." Her husband, though, was ambivalent about the question of preserving the Union versus secession. A week later Julia Tyler reported deteriorating conditions that she blamed on Northerners: "The New York and Massachusetts delegation will no doubt perform all the mischief they can; and it may be, will defeat this patriotic effort at pacification."[24]

With the passage of time and the worsening of conditions in the North and South, Tyler grew more strident in her defense of slavery. In April she argued that President Abraham Lincoln would be well advised to "acknowledge the Southern Confederacy. It rests with him to prevent or urge a most unnatural and bloody war. The idea of *any* State meeting his demand! It is disgraceful." A month later, after Fort Sumter, she contended, "The South is merely defending itself against them in the just maintenance of her rights." Tyler attacked her native North for being unwilling to work with the South. She concluded, "For my part, I am utterly ashamed of the State in which I was born, and its people. All soul and magnanimity have departed from them—'patriotism' indeed!"[25] Not surprisingly, her husband willingly served in the Confederate Congress until his death in January 1862.

The one antebellum first lady after Tyler who enjoyed politics and expanded the precedents for first lady engagement was Sarah Polk. Though little of her correspondence exists within her husband's papers, Polk early on exhibited tremendous interest in national politics. Indeed, there were no shadows for her. A colleague of her husband's remarked in 1835, "I am glad a certain lady is in good spirits, and engaged in the *amusement* of politics, though from my heart I could wish that she had some more *amusing amusements* to *amuse* herself with—something more domestic for instance." When James K. Polk was elected speaker of the House of Representatives, H. B. Kelsey told him, "Give my best respects, especially, to Mrs. *Speaker* Polk."[26]

Later, when he was elected president, commentators mixed their support for Sarah from feminine arguments to political arguments. One described her as the "nation's mother." Multiple individuals wrote the Executive Mansion indicating their plans to name a new baby after her; she herself bore no children, although she later adopted her niece, Sarah "Sallie" Jetton. A family associate, however, observed that Sarah Polk was "a little power behind the Throne." This strange admixture resulted from the strained legacy that had emerged around the first lady position. For example, a friend of the president's observed, "All the men of wealth . . . laud Mrs. Polk, no small matter by the way in that White House . . . where the democrats have always held since Jefferson's day that a wife is a *bad* thing."[27]

ENTERTAINING AND ACTIVISM

These antebellum Southern first ladies were just as important in determining the parameters for entertaining, an effort sometimes infused with political import. After her husband became president, Martha Washington found herself drawn to other strong women, such as Abigail Adams, and she relied on their contributions to official entertaining. Adams explained, "We live upon terms of much Friendship & visit each other often." The two women were allies in the conduct of social affairs in the new nation. In her own way, Martha Washington thus began the precedent nineteenth-century first ladies solidified of relying on surrogates to assist with social responsibilities. For Washington this arrangement extended her activist entertaining, yet for first ladies uninterested in politics or physically frail, the precedent afforded an opportunity to eschew activism in all forms. Indeed, many first ladies in the nineteenth century used surrogates to shield themselves from public responsibilities altogether.[28]

Martha Washington, however, understood how to mix entertaining with politics. By all indications, as noted frequently in President Washington's diary, she was a popular and well-regarded hostess. That had been true before her husband's presidency, and it remained the case during his time in office. In the years prior to the Revolutionary War, she exhorted a group of Virginia politicians who had dined with her family that they must resist the British position. As first lady her entertaining regularly included large groups of men and women. At one dinner during the Washington administration, though, she hosted as the only woman in attendance. William Maclay, who chronicled the evening, asserted that it took place "without any remarkable occurrences" in "a very crouded drawing Room" on February 17, 1797, poignantly at the end of her husband's presidency.[29]

At her Friday evening levees, which lasted about three hours, Martha Washington served "Tea, Coffee, Cake, Lemonade & Ice Creams." Abigail Adams noted that the servants would announce the guests. Then male surrogates Colonel David Humphries or Tobias Lear received them. Ladies then made "a most Respectfull courtesy" to Martha Washington. After the arrival of all the guests, the "Pressident then comes up and speaks to the Lady, which he does with a grace dignity & ease, that leaves Royal George far behind him." Lear noted that the guest lists for these Friday evening affairs had grown to fill the size of the house. He worriedly told the president, "All these things combine to swell the bills."[30]

Some scholars have argued that Americans were more excited about the prospects of Dolley Madison presiding over the nation's social affairs than they were about her husband assuming the presidency. Madison brought the same political and activist philosophy to her work as Executive Mansion hostess Washington had. She changed the name of the weekly gatherings from "levees," a formal and hierarchical style of entertaining associated with the Federalist Party, to "drawing rooms" to convey a sense of welcome to Americans regardless of social class, although not of race—everyone in attendance was white. Madison's gatherings were so popular they were dubbed "squeezes" because of the crowds. Said one guest, "Such a crowd I was never in. It took us ten minutes to push and shove ourselves through the dining room; at the upper part of it stood the President and his lady, all standing, and a continual moving in and out." A member of the British legation in Washington complained about Madison's social style as simplistic and lacking sufficient entertainment. A Republican lawmaker, though, feared he might be snubbed for not being elite enough. After he attended one of Madison's drawing rooms, he decided otherwise, terming the first lady "a democrat." Watterston wrote of the first lady, "Her memory was so tenacious, that after a single introduction she could, like Cato, name every gentleman and lady that had been introduced to her; and strangers have often been surprised at the facility with which she could address them by name, when they had no expectation of being known."[31]

Rejecting the style of the levee meant the responsibilities of entertaining intensified for Dolley Madison compared with those of Martha Washington. Whereas Washington sat on a raised platform and never had to mingle with her guests, Madison, employing purposefully republican-themed methods of entertaining, chatted with her guests as she moved throughout the room. Indeed, Madison worked the room like a politician; in doing so she consolidated the Southern standard for mixing politics with entertaining activism Martha Washington had first established. A Federalist newspaper editor explained, "She glided into a stream of conversation and accommodated herself to its endless variety. In the art of conversation she is said to be distinguished." Knowing her primary political task was neutrality, Madison typically carried a copy of *Don Quixote* at social gatherings. She explained, "I have this book in my hand . . . to have something not ungraceful to say, and, if need be, to supply a word of talk."[32]

Several decades later, Julia Tyler told her mother of her accomplishments in Washington society, perhaps with Dolley Madison's example in mind. To ensure the success of President Tyler's accidental presidency, the first lady took seriously the entertaining for which she was already gifted. For example, she understood that her husband must have a solid working relationship with Congress, and she did her part by receiving the necessary social calls from other Washington wives. Indeed, social expectations were not limited to the first lady but also extended to the wives of other governmental officials. Making social calls in this way was integral to the female social infrastructure. For some wives the work was tedious, requiring as many as fifty visits in just one day, and netted few immediate, tangible results. For others, it was a highlight of being a political spouse. During her Washington years, Julia Tyler relished the social world of the government. She once remarked to her mother, "Not to have all the company and in the very way that I do would disappoint me very much." Moreover, in late December 1844 she hosted a reception attended by the British minister, Sir Richard Pakenham. Unlike previous Southern first ladies, however, Tyler's focus was both personal and political. She bragged, "At least fifty members of Congress paid their respects to me, and all at one time. I did not enter the room until they had assembled. It really presented an array; and it was imposing to see them all brought forward, and introduced one by one."[33]

## WHITE SUPREMACY AND ACTIVISM

The roots of first lady activism were not entirely positive because they included white supremacy, with multiple Southern first ladies using their voices and positions to reinforce exclusionary racial bias. When later generations of first ladies confronted white supremacy, they faced hostile reactions. Indeed, in the twentieth century, first ladies' responses to race and racism led traditionalists to suggest politically engaged first ladies were flouting social mores by advocating civil rights. Doing so, traditionalists held, placed these first ladies out of bounds with what was acceptable for presidential spouses. What, then, were the sources of such traditionalism? The answer is found in the same early national era when first lady activism took root. Put simply, it involved the seamless weaving of enslaved labor into the running of the president's house and the economic livelihood of Southern presidential families. Indeed, concepts of entertaining, from the earliest days of the Republic, were based on the unexamined expectation of enslaved labor. Martha Washington established this precedent by bringing enslaved people to the president's house first in New York City and later in Philadelphia, when the national capital was moved. She put much thought into determining whom she would bring with her and how they as enslaved workers would interface with the running of the government. The Washingtons' actions were especially egregious in Philadelphia because they swapped out the enslaved people between that city and Mount Vernon every six months to limit the terms of service in the capital (there was a Pennsylvania law that if they stayed any longer, they could seek freedom in the courts). To solve the problem of the optics associated with slavery, the Washingtons also employed free labor in the president's house, but they found those workers less satisfactory in comparison with enslaved persons.[34] A total of seven first ladies—Martha Washington, Dolley Madison, Elizabeth Monroe, Letitia Tyler, Julia Tyler, Sarah Polk, and Julia Taylor—relied on those they held in bondage for work during their husbands' presidencies (enslaved persons also worked in the Executive Mansion during two additional presidential administrations, when there were surrogates: those of Thomas Jefferson and Andrew Jackson).

Just as important, what little of Washington's correspondence remains shows that she played a vital role in the management of enslaved persons at Mount Vernon. She criticized those who had less daunting work assignments, such as sewing garments, for not meeting quota. Through her husband, she directed that those who could not keep up would be returned to less desirable field-work. Washington certainly was adamant about keeping these enslaved persons productive even when she was first lady and not living in Mount Vernon, advising relatives on the management of both her plantation's natural resources and its human, enslaved ones, seeing them all as commodities necessary for the estate's output. Thus, she told Frances Washington in 1793 to take "every precaution . . . to prevent waste of the timber, or the cutting down too much thereof—and no abuse of either the land or negroes, be permitted."[35]

Of the precedent-setting antebellum first ladies, Dolley Madison was the only one to demonstrate a trace of humanity toward those she held in bondage, revealing just how intrinsically linked racial subjugation and first lady comportment could be during the foundational years of the new government. That said, Madison still relied on her enslaved workers to run the Executive Mansion. She required enslaved men to hold torches during some of her receptions, in essence turning them into human candlesticks. Enslaved persons were ever present as servants at all of Madison's social engagements. Thus, in the words of one historian, she "imposed slavery on her guests and by implication helped to impose it upon the nation."[36]

Perhaps because of her Quaker background, in the 1830s Dolley Madison wrote in self-congratulatory terms of her efforts to care for the medical needs of the African Americans she held in bondage. She also negotiated with men over the sale of enslaved persons in her possession. Such was necessary because she needed resources to pay her debts. Ultimately, though, she preferred to deed her remaining enslaved persons to her son and freed none of them. Examples from other first ladies abound. Upon Sarah Polk's urging, for example, her husband negotiated to buy back an enslaved man he had earlier sold for being "unruly." The first lady wanted the man back because, according to the president, "we own his mother."[37]

Other first ladies could be quite outspoken in public in defense of slavery. Following the publication of *Uncle Tom's Cabin* by Harriet Beecher Stowe, a number of titled Englishwomen wrote an open appeal to Southern women calling for abolition. Julia Tyler, now back in Virginia, replied on behalf of her adopted region in a published letter dated January 24, 1853. Tyler told the duchess of

Sutherland and ladies of England, "The women of the South, especially, have not received your address in the kindest spirit." She stressed that Northern women knew no more of the South than did Englishwomen; Southern women should be trusted to manage affairs in their region without outside interference, she claimed. She further described in detail England's complicity in the spread of slavery in the Americas. "England," asserted Tyler, "when she had the power to prevent the introduction of negroes into the United States, most obstinately refused to do it." She then remonstrated that the Englishwomen would be wise to tend to abuses within their own borders, namely "the unsupplied wants of your own people. . . . In view of your palaces, there is misery and suffering enough to excite your most active sympathies." A decade later Tyler even wrote to President Lincoln, seeking mercy for a Southern Confederate being whipped by enslaved persons he had purported to own for his past cruelties to them. As the widow herself of the only US president who had also been a member of the Confederate Congress, Julia Tyler discounted these reports and instead contended the man was honorable, respected, and not a participant in the war.[38] This white supremacy, so deeply enmeshed in the eighteenth- and nineteenth-century Southern roots of first lady activism, left a legacy for later first ladies who sought to take their activism in a different direction.

Multiple examples exist of Southerners in the twentieth century who castigated activist first ladies for not behaving "properly" regarding racial issues and highlight the irony of this turn in activism. Three particularly salient case studies involve both Southern *and* non-Southern women in the White House. Lou Henry Hoover, Iowa born and a global citizen as an adult, experienced severe excoriation for hosting Jessie DePriest—wife of the first African American to serve in Congress since the end of Reconstruction, US Representative Oscar Stanton DePriest (R-IL), and an African American woman from Chicago—at a White House tea for congressional spouses. Eleanor Roosevelt, the first lady who followed Hoover and who expanded many of the precedents she had set, also endured copious criticism for her civil rights advocacy. Finally, Lady Bird Johnson earned the enmity of her native Southerners when she made pro–civil rights arguments while campaigning for her husband in the Deep South in 1964.

The DePriest tea was a carefully orchestrated affair in 1929. Hoover screened the guest list to guarantee that all the women entertained alongside DePriest would accord her the courtesy and dignity befitting the wife of a lawmaker. The first lady ensured that no publicity was given to the event before it was staged, but afterward the uproar was deafening. The Texas legislature passed a resolution condemning her. Margie Neal, a member of the Texas State Senate and the first woman elected to that body, authored the resolution, which argued, "Social recognition . . . of a member of the negro race" caused Texans and Southerners to "bow our heads in shame and regret." The *Christian Century*, though, wrote critically about Lone Star State lawmakers, questioning their professed Christianity: "One wonders what conception these Texas politicians, some of them presumably members of Christian churches, have of the Founder of their faith and his doctrine of human brotherhood."[39]

Another Texan told the first lady the tea would only "bring harm to the negroes of the South" because "that kind of treatment of the negro does not set well with those of the southland, who love the negro in his place, but not at our dinner table." Other Southerners complained that the timing of the tea alongside the anniversary of the delivery of the Emancipation Proclamation in many of the Southern states was especially insulting. A Texas man questioned "whether or not you realize the deep chagrin which you have brought upon all self-respecting white citizens of the south by your entertainment in the nation's White House on a basis of social equality of a member of that race who celebrate this as their natal day, or do you care?" Non-Southerners demonstrated their ability to be equally boorish and hateful, but when they did so, they were playing on a terrain of racism and Jim Crow segregation Southern at its core. Indeed, a Chicago woman was vituperative in her unsigned comments: "You should be ashamed of yourself for entertaining a *nigger wench* at the White House."[40]

Hoover's challenge to white supremacy abated because of the reaction to the DePriest tea, but Eleanor Roosevelt proved a constant, if moderate, disparager of segregation throughout her husband's presidency. In 1936, a Virginia newspaper criticized Roosevelt for using the word "equality" twelve times in one speech to African Americans. At the 1938 meeting of the Southern Conference for Human Welfare in Birmingham, Alabama, Roosevelt rejected segregation by sitting with African Americans. The following year, she aggravated white racism when she challenged the Daughters of the American Revolution for denying Marian Anderson, an African American contralto, the right to sing in Constitution Hall. Roosevelt resigned her membership in the DAR, and she helped secure an alternate venue for Anderson: the Lincoln Memorial.[41]

By World War II Southerners were disgusted with Roosevelt's advocacy for racial justice. During the war years real economic change came to the South, and defenders of the status quo looked for a scapegoat. Complaints about Roosevelt escalated as the war progressed. An Arkansas farmer told her, "The negroes are refusing to work on the farms and in the houses. . . . We of the South believe that you are using your high position to stir up racial trouble." Prosperous white Southern women showed their conspiratorial thinking by blaming the decreasing number of African American women willing to work as domestic servants on Roosevelt. They claimed that Eleanor Clubs were the culprit, but no such entities have ever been discovered. Although white Southern women alleged the first lady was "ruin[ing] the niggers," careful analysis of Eleanor Roosevelt's rhetoric proves she was cautious and prudent in her advocacy for equality, aware that her husband's political prospects depended on her circumspection. Her most vociferous critics were not so cautious. A Mississippi senator introduced into Congress legislation calling for African Americans to be sent back to Africa and for Eleanor Roosevelt to be made their queen.[42]

The condemnation of Lady Bird Johnson in 1964 by Southerners was of a piece with what Hoover experienced in 1929 and Roosevelt throughout her husband's administration. Both women had attempted to challenge white Southern norms of racial hierarchy. Both did so under the imprimatur of being first lady, so the criticism also was about who they were and the role they played in the federal government. In fall 1964, Lady Bird Johnson went on the hustings to support her husband's campaign for the presidency in his race against Arizona senator Barry Goldwater. Although she made multiple solo trips around the country, her most notable effort was an old-fashioned whistle stop tour of the South. Her train took her from Alexandria, Virginia, to New Orleans, Louisiana, and she did not avoid the deepest, most intransigent white supremacist parts of the South. Nor did she ignore the recently enacted Civil Rights Act of 1964, endorsing its necessity to the future success of the country.[43]

Doing so brought disparagement of her efforts. At one stop anti-Johnson white pulled the fire alarm to disrupt her remarks. Moreover, pro-Goldwater signs were commonplace throughout the Deep South, and some were tinged with racism. The one reading "Black Bird Go Home" was ironic because Lady Bird Johnson was a proud Southerner with familial roots in the Deep South. At a stop in Columbia, South Carolina, Goldwater partisans chanted "We Want Barry!" while Johnson was speaking. They were so loud that the crowd could not hear her remarks. She fell back on the mores of Southern white womanhood, raising her white-gloved hand and asking the crowd to respect her freedom of speech. When the crowd was even more hostile at another stop, Johnson's use of the white glove to signal the need for Southern chivalry did not work. A male politician traveling with her called the crowd "a Nazi gathering."[44] Hoover, Roosevelt, and Johnson all pushed the boundaries of first lady activism because of racism *and* faced white supremacist backlash as a result.

CONCLUSION

Just as Southern women played an integral role in constructing the complicated but important office of the first lady, so too did the original sin of the South—racism—shape critiques of first ladies who challenged the status quo. This reality became most vivid during Michelle Obama's tenure as first lady. Her very existence as the first African American first lady—and an activist, at that—elicited horrific racist gibes on the internet, right-wing talk radio, and cable news. This noxious racism further informed critiques of her first lady activism, which from this perspective rendered Obama as an "angry Black woman" when she tackled issues such as the nutritious value of school lunches and encouraged exercise. Among the criticisms raised were that she did pushups, wore shorts, was overweight, harmed the cause of feminism by focusing on her family, lacked class, lacked patriotism, wore a sweater to Buckingham Palace, sat with her elbow on the table, had a "gorilla face," and was actually a man who murdered Joan Rivers to prevent the comedienne from joking that she (Obama) was transgender.[45]

Looking at this problem of racism juxtaposed against the Southern architecture of the institution of the first lady adds nuance that otherwise would not be apparent. Southern women built the role of first lady with their Southern worldviews, which shaped beliefs in the wider populace about what first ladies could do. Part II of this book will explore this theme further in the lives of the seven Southern women in the White House from 1913 to the present. The political power first ladies claimed thus proved contingent, and in constant jeopardy of revocation, by a society uncomfortable with gendered activism and by other first ladies complacent with a shadowed existence. It also was subject to critique based on the restriction and denial of equality for people of color. No wonder, then, that it proved easy for a media writer to call for the end of first lady activism in the early twenty-first century. The power of first ladies has historically been both problematic and limited. This power and the women who wield it discomfit Americans across the political spectrum. Predictably, those conservatives who want less fluidity and more rigidity, ensuring power stays gendered male, are too often ready to criticize first ladies who bend or break the binds of their position. Ironically, feminists who want more fluidity and less fortuity in expanding the gendering of power have found first lady power disconcerting. For them, a woman's power that exists only because of her husband's position cannot be satisfying. Given the historical antecedents behind the creation of the position, there is no foreseeable end to the complex contradictions surrounding first lady power, other than, perhaps, the election of a female president and the ascent of a first gentleman in the East Wing.

## NOTES

1. Jack Shafer, "Abolish the Office of the First Lady," *Politico Magazine*, November 22, 2016, https://www.politico.com/magazine/story/2016/11/abolish-the-office-of-the-first-lady-214471.

2. Carl Anthony, "The White House Staff of First Ladies," National First Ladies' Library, August 24, 2016, http://www.firstladies.org/blog/the-white-house-staff-of-first-ladies/.

3. Some good general histories of American first ladies include Carl Sferrazza Anthony, *First Ladies: The Saga of the President's Wives and Their Power, 1789–1961* (New York: William Morrow, 1990); Betty Boyd Caroli, *First Ladies* (New York: Oxford University Press, 1986); Myra G. Gutin, *The President's Partner: The First Lady in the Twentieth Century* (Westport, CT: Greenwood, 1991); Gil Troy, *Affairs of State: The Rise and Rejection of the Presidential Couple since World War II* (New York: Free Press, 1997). For an excellent and innovative discussion of gender and early American politics, see Catherine Allgor, *Parlor Politics: In Which the Ladies of Washington Help Build a City and a Government* (Charlottesville: University of Virginia Press, 2000).

4. Nancy F. Cott, *Public Vows: A History of Marriage and the Nation* (Cambridge, MA: Harvard University Press, 2000); Hendrik Hartog, *Man and Wife in America: A History* (Cambridge, MA: Harvard University Press, 2000); Elaine Tyler May, *Great Expectations: Marriage and Divorce in Post-Victorian America* (Chicago: University of Chicago Press, 1980); Marilyn Yalom, *A History of the Wife* (New York: HarperCollins, 2001); Gil Troy, *Mr. and Mrs. President: From the Trumans to the Clintons*, 2nd ed., rev. (Lawrence: University Press of Kansas, 2000).

5. Allgor, *Parlor Politics*; John F. Marszalek, *The Petticoat Affair: Manners, Mutiny, and Sex in Andrew Jackson's White House* (Baton Rouge: Louisiana State University Press, 2000); Troy, *Mr. and Mrs. President*; Anthony, *First Ladies*; Carl Sferrazza Anthony, *America's First Families: An Inside View of 200 Years of Private Life in the White House* (New York: Touchstone, 2000). Examples of scholarly inquiry into twentieth-century marital partnerships include Katherine A. S. Sibley, *First Lady Florence Harding: Behind the Tragedy and Controversy* (Lawrence: University Press of Kansas, 2009); Nancy Beck Young, *Lou Henry Hoover: Activist First Lady* (Lawrence: University Press of Kansas, 2004).

6. Regarding nineteenth-century gender roles, see Nancy F. Cott, *The Bonds of Womanhood: "Woman's Sphere" in New England, 1780–1835* (New Haven, CT: Yale University Press, 1977). For first ladies in the nineteenth century, see Caroli, *First Ladies*, 33–83; Lewis L. Gould, ed., *American First Ladies: Their Lives and Legacies*, 2nd ed. (New York: Routledge, 2001).

7. Andrew Burnaby to George Washington, letter, April 9, 1778, in *The Papers of George Washington, Revolutionary War Series*, vol. 14: *March–April 1778*, ed. David R. Hoth (Charlottesville: University of Virginia Press, 2004), 433.

8. Dolley Payne Madison, *The Selected Letters of Dolley Payne Madison*, ed. David B. Mattern and Holly C. Shulman (Charlottesville: University of Virginia Press, 2003), 90, 100–102.

9. Jane Turner Censer, *The Reconstruction of White Southern Womanhood, 1865–1895* (Baton Rouge: Louisiana State University Press, 2003); Catherine Clinton, *Tara Revisited: Women, War and the Plantation Legend* (New York: Abbeville, 1995); Laura F. Edwards, *Gendered Strife and Confusion: The Political Culture of Reconstruction* (Urbana: University of Illinois Press, 1997); Laura F. Edwards, *Scarlett Doesn't Live Here Anymore: Southern Women in the Civil War Era* (Urbana: University of Illinois Press, 2000); Anne Firor Scott, *Making the Invisible Woman Visible* (Urbana: University of Illinois Press, 1984); Anne Firor Scott, *The Southern Lady: From Pedestal to Politics, 1830–1930* (Chicago: University of Chicago Press, 1970); Marjorie Spruill

Wheeler, *New Women of the New South: The Leaders of the Woman Suffrage Movement in the Southern States* (New York: Oxford University Press, 1993).

10. George Washington, *The Diaries of George Washington*, vol. 6: *January 1790–December 1799*, ed. Donald Jackson and Dorothy Twohig (Charlottesville: University of Virginia Press, 1979), 301 (first quote), 13; Mercy Otis Warren to Abigail Adams, letter, April 17, 1776, in *The Papers of George Washington, Revolutionary War Series*, vol. 3: *January–March 1776*, ed. Philander D. Chase (Charlottesville: University of Virginia Press, 2004), 75 (second quote); Washington, *Diaries of George Washington*, vol. 2, *1766–1770*, ed. Donald Jackson and Dorothy Twohig (Charlottesville: University of Virginia Press, 1976), 40.

11. Madison, *Selected Letters*, 92–93 (first three quotes); Lucia Alice von Kantzow to Dolley Payne Madison, letter, June 26, 1818, in Madison, *Selected Letters*, 230 (last quote).

12. Harrison Gray Otis quoted in H. Ammon, *James Monroe: The Quest for National Identity* (Boston: McGraw-Hill, 1971), 403, cited in Finn Pollard, "Elizabeth Monroe," in *A Companion to First Ladies*, ed. Katherine A. S. Sibley (West Sussex, UK: Wiley-Blackwell, 2016), 83. In this chapter, I avoid calling the official presidential residence in Washington, DC, the White House. Although the structure itself first housed the Adamses at the very end of John Adams's tenure in office, it was not known as the White House officially until Theodore Roosevelt's administration. Instead, I use the terms Executive Mansion and official residence interchangeably to refer to the structure known today as the White House.

13. Alfred Balch to James K. Polk, letter, January 4, 1845, in *Correspondence of James K. Polk*, vol. 9: *January–June 1845*, ed. Wayne Cutler and Robert G. Hall II (Nashville, TN: Vanderbilt University Press, 1996), 17; Andrew Jackson to James K. Polk, letter, February 8, 1845, in *Correspondence of James K. Polk*, vol. 9: *January–June 1845*, ed. Wayne Cutler and Robert G. Hall II (Nashville, TN: Vanderbilt University Press, 1996), 93.

14. George Washington, *The Papers of George Washington, Presidential Series*, Vol. 6: *July–November 1790*, ed. Mark A. Mastromarino (Charlottesville: University of Virginia Press, 1996), 249, 578, 113; Washington, *The Papers of George Washington, Presidential Series*, vol. 1: *September 1788–March 1789*, ed. Dorothy Twohig (Charlottesville: University of Virginia Press, 1987), 171. For some of the best treatments of Abigail Adams, see G. J. Barker-Benfield, *Abigail and John Adams: The Americanization of Sensibility* (Chicago: University of Chicago Press, 2010); Joseph J. Ellis, *First Family: Abigail and John* (New York: Knopf, 2010); Woody Holton, *Abigail Adams* (New York: Free Press, 2009); Phyllis Lee Levin, *Abigail Adams: A Biography* (New York: St. Martin's, 1987), 82 (quote).

15. Madison, *Selected Letters*, 94–97.

16. Madison, 90–91, 109, 110, 114, 117, 131, 134, 200, 210, 213; Abigail Adams to Dolley Payne Madison, letter, May 14, 1815, in Madison, *Selected Letters*, 200–201 (quotes).

17. Madison, *Selected Letters*, 91 (quote), 97–99.

18. Madison, 100–102.

19. Dolley Payne Madison to Lucy Payne Washington Todd, letter, August 23, 1814, in Madison, *Selected Letters*, 193–194; Marie Jenkins Schwartz, *Ties That Bound: Founding First Ladies and Slaves* (Chicago: University of Chicago Press, 2017), 276–280; "Summer 1814: Dolley Madison Saves Washington's Portrait, with Some Help," https://www.nps.gov/articles/dolley-madison-washingtons-portrait.htm.

20. Eliza Collins Lee to Dolley Payne Madison, letter, March 2, 1809, in Madison, *Selected Letters*, 214–215.

21. Edward P. Crapol, *John Tyler: The Accidental President* (Chapel Hill: University of North Carolina Press, 2012), 219–220 (first quote); Aaron V. Brown to James K. Polk, January 1, [1845], in *Correspondence of James K. Polk*, vol. 9 *January–June 1845*, ed. Wayne Cutler and Robert G. Hall II (Nashville, TN: Vanderbilt University Press, 1996), 6–7 (second quote); Amy S. Greenberg, *Lady First: The World of First Lady Sarah Polk* (New York: Random House, 2019), 52 (last quote).

22. "Reminiscences of Mrs. Julia G. Tyler," c. June 25, 1887, in *The Letters and Times of the Tylers*, vol. 2, ed. Lyon G. Tyler (New York: Da Capo, 1970), 194–201.

23. Julia Gardiner Tyler to Margaret Gardiner, letter, December 5, 1844, in *Letters and Times of the Tylers*, vol. 2, ed. Lyon G. Tyler (New York: Da Capo, 1970), 358 (first quote), 361 (second quote); Gary May, *John Tyler* (New York: Times, 2008), 123.

24. Julia Gardiner Tyler to Mrs. Gardiner, letter, February 3, 1861, in *Letters and Times of the Tylers*, vol. 2, 596–598 (first quote); Julia Gardiner Tyler to Mrs. Gardiner, letter, February 4, 1861, in *Letters and Times of the Tylers*, vol. 2, 596–598 (next four quotes), and Julia Gardiner Tyler to Mrs. Gardiner, letter, February 13, 1861, in *Letters and Times of the Tylers*, vol. 2, 612–613 (last quote); Crapol, *John Tyler*, 261.

25. Julia Gardiner Tyler to Mrs. Gardiner, letter, April 18, 1861, in *Letters and Times of the Tylers*, vol. 2, 646–647 (first quote); Julia Gardiner Tyler to Mrs. Gardiner, letter, May 4, 1861, in *Letters and Times of the Tylers*, vol. 2, 649 (second quote); Julia Gardiner Tyler to Mrs. Gardiner, letter, May 7, 1861 (last quote), in *Letters and Times of the Tylers*, vol. 2, 650.

26. Samuel H. Laughlin to James K. Polk, letter, May 30, 1835, in *Correspondence of James K. Polk*, vol. 3: *1835–1836*, ed. Herbert Weaver and Kermit L. Hall (Nashville, TN: Vanderbilt University Press, 1975), 209 (first quote); Henry B. Kelsey to James K. Polk, letter, December 23, 1835, in *Correspondence of James K. Polk*, vol. 3, 410 (second quote).

27. Robert Butler to James K. Polk, letter, March 15, 1845, in *Correspondence of James K. Polk*, vol. 9: *January–June 1845*, 510c (first quote); see, for example, Franklin B. Carpenter to James K. Polk, letter, May 24, 1845, in *Correspondence of James K. Polk*, vol. 9, 557c; John W. Rucker to James K. Polk, letter, April 15, 1845, in *Correspondence of James K. Polk*, vol. 9, 531c, (second quote); John Catron to James K. Polk, letter, May 20, 1845, in *Correspondence of James K. Polk*, vol. 9, 397 (last quote).

28. George Washington, *The Diaries of George Washington*, vol. 5: *July 1786–December 1789*, ed. Donald Jackson and Dorothy Twohig (Charlottesville: University of Virginia Press, 1979), 456 (quote); Washington, *The Papers of George Washington, Presidential Series*, vol. 4: *September 1789–January 1790*, ed. Dorothy Twohig (Charlottesville: University of Virginia Press, 1993), 423. For more on the use of surrogates, see Caroli, *First Ladies*, 35.

29. Washington, *Diaries of George Washington*, vol. 6, 1, 4, 9, 12, 24, 31, 37, 45, 59, 62, 72, 75, 77, 84, 90 (first quote), 91, 234 (second quote); Washington, *Diaries of George Washington*, vol. 3: *1771–1775, 1780–1781*, ed. Donald Jackson and Dorothy Twohig (Charlottesville: University of Virginia Press, 1978), 272.

30. Washington, *Diaries of George Washington*, vol. 5, 451 (first three quotes); Tobias Lear

to George Washington, letter, September 12, 1790, in Washington, *Papers of George Washington, Presidential Series*, vol. 6, 422 (last quote); Schwartz, *Ties That Bound*, 94–95.

31. Madison, *Selected Letters*, 90, 94–97.

32. Madison, 100–102.

33. Burton W. Peretti, *The Leading Man: Hollywood and the Presidential Image* (New Brunswick, NJ: Rutgers University Press, 2012), 25; Rachel A. Sheldon, *Washington Brotherhood: Politics, Social Life, and the Coming of the Civil War* (Chapel Hill: University of North Carolina Press, 2013), 69–70 (first quote); Julia Gardiner Tyler to Mrs. Gardiner, letter, December 6, 1844, in *Letters and Times of the Tylers*, 358 (last quote).

34. Schwartz, *Ties That Bound*, 94–116.

35. George Washington to Anthony Whitting, letter, December 23, 1792, in Washington, *Papers of George Washington, Presidential Series*, vol. 11: *August 1792–January 1793*, ed. Christine Sternberg Patrick (Charlottesville: University of Virginia Press, 2002), 545; Schwartz, *Ties That Bound*, 82–93; Martha Washington to Frances Washington, letter, June 2, 1793, in George Washington Family Letters, Library of Congress, American Memory Project accessed in North American Women's Letters and Diaries, Colonial to 1950, https://nwld-alexanderstreet-com.ezproxy.lib.uh.edu/cgi-bin/asp/philo/nwld/getdoc.pl?S2019-D004 (quote).

36. Schwartz, *Ties That Bound*, 268 (quote), 283.

37. Madison, *Selected Letters*, 348–349, 361, 372, 374–375; Schwartz, *Ties That Bound*, 340–341; James K. Polk to Gideon J. Pillow, letter, April 20, 1846, in *Correspondence of James K. Polk*, vol. 11: *1846*, ed. Wayne Cutler, James L. Rogers II, and Benjamin H. Severance (Nashville, TN: Vanderbilt University Press, 2009), 132–133 (quotes).

38. *Letters and Times of the Tylers*, vol. 2, 519–520; Julia Gardiner Tyler, "To the Duchess of Sutherland and Ladies of England," letter, February 2, 1853, in *Southern Literary Messenger; Devoted to Every Department of Literature and the Fine Arts* 19 (February 1853): 120–126 (quotes); Julia Gardiner Tyler to Abraham Lincoln, letter, May 21, 1864, in *Private and Official Correspondence of Gen. Benjamin F. Butler, During the Period of the Civil War*, vol. 4. (Norwood, MA: Plimpton, 1917), 628, accessed in North American Women's Letters and Diaries, Colonial to 1950, https://nwld-alexanderstreet-com.ezproxy.lib.uh.edu/cgi-bin/asp/philo/nwld /getdoc.pl?S1988-D527.

39. Young, *Lou Henry Hoover*, 65–72; S.C.R. 11, in *Journal of the State of Texas Being the Second Called Session of the Forty-First Legislature Begun and Held at the City of Austin, June 3, 1929* (Austin: A.C. Baldwin, 1929), 195 (first two quotes); "Texas Solons Bow Their Heads in Shame," *Christian Century* 46 (July 3, 1929): 860 (last quote).

40. W. C. Jennings to Lou Henry Hoover, letter, June 15, 1929, in "DePriest Incident, Critical of Mrs. Hoover," Box 49, Subject Files, Lou Henry Hoover Papers, Herbert Hoover Presidential Library, West Branch, Iowa (first two quotes); H. B. Davis to Lou Henry Hoover, letter, June 19, 1929, in "DePriest Incident, Critical of Mrs. Hoover" (third quote), and One of the Club to Lou Henry Hoover, letter, June 23, 1929 (last quote), in "DePriest Incident, Critical of Mrs. Hoover."

41. Pamela Tyler, "'Blood on Your Hands': White Southerners' Criticism of Eleanor

Roosevelt During World War II," in *Before* Brown: *Civil Rights and White Backlash in the Modern South*, ed. Glenn Feldman (Tuscaloosa: University of Alabama Press, 2004), 96–115.

42. Tyler, "'Blood on Your Hands,'" 96–115; William E. Leuchtenburg, *The White House Looks South: Franklin D. Roosevelt, Harry S. Truman, Lyndon B. Johnson* (Baton Rouge: Louisiana State University Press, 2005), 139.

43. McGovern: Lady Bird Visit, September 17, 1964, 118–120, in File 2, Box 79, Katie Louchheim Papers, 1997 Addition, Library of Congress, Manuscript Division, Washington, DC; "'Lady Bird' Boosters," *Baltimore Afro-American*, October 17, 1964; Randall Woods, *LBJ: Architect of American Ambition* (New York: Simon and Schuster, 2006), 542; Remarks by Lady Bird Johnson, Rock Hill, South Carolina, October 7, 1964, in "South Carolina, October 7, 1964," Box 79, White House Social Files—Liz Carpenter Files, Lyndon B. Johnson Library, Austin, Texas.

44. "Story of the Lady Bird Special," n.d., in "TR1/Johnson, Mrs.," Box 2, White House Central Files, Lyndon B. Johnson Library; Gary Donaldson, *Liberalism's Last Hurrah: The Presidential Campaign of 1964* (Armonk, NY: M. E. Sharpe, 2003), 274 (quotes); Jonathan Darman, *Landslide: LBJ and Ronald Reagan at the Dawn of a New America* (New York: Random House, 2014), 210; Recording of Telephone Conversation Between Lyndon B. Johnson, Lynda Bird Johnson, and Johnson, October 7, 1964, 9:40PM, Tape WH6410.04 PNO 1, Citation #5842, Recordings of Telephone Conversations—White House Series, Recordings and Transcripts of Conversations and Meetings, Lyndon B. Johnson Library; Woods, *LBJ*, 543; Aboard the Lady Bird Special, in File 5, Box 11, Louchheim Papers, LC.

45. Mikki Kendall, "22 Times Michelle Obama Endured Rude, Racist, Sexist, or Plain Ridiculous Attacks," *Washington Post*, November 16, 2016.

# From the Progressive Era to the Present Century

# CHAPTER 12

# Ellen Axson Wilson
## A Progressive Southern First Lady

Lisa M. Burns

First lady scholarship emerged as a discipline in the 1980s, when researchers moved beyond treating first ladies as famous wives and instead studied them as influential political figures in their own right who reflected and affected their historical eras. One of these early works was Frances Wright Saunders's perceptive study of Ellen Axson Wilson. She noted that Wilson was a woman living "between two worlds" who, "while playing an essential role in Woodrow Wilson's private and professional life, manifestly expanded the expected Victorian woman's role beyond the bounds of domesticity." Ellen Wilson was "editor, counselor, teacher, politician, artist, landscape designer, and latent feminist."[1] Indeed, she embraced the true womanhood ideal of her era by placing her husband's and children's needs first, yet she also embodied the spirit of the new woman in her social advocacy work and when she decided later in life to pursue a career as an artist. Because of her husband's career ambitions, which she actively promoted, Wilson learned foreign languages, researched books, and hosted gatherings of scholars and civic leaders, acting as both a helpmate and a shrewd adviser to her husband, blurring the lines between personal and political.

Less emphasized by Saunders, however, was a certain strand that connected Wilson's two worlds—her Southern background. She was a Georgian born on the eve of the Civil War who spent most of her adult life living in Northern cities and towns. Although her personal belief in racial segregation reflected her Southern upbringing, this prejudice did not stop her from advocating for improved living and working conditions for African Americans. Wilson was thus a "progressive" Southern first lady in two respects. First, she embraced the spirit

Portrait of Ellen Louise Axson Wilson. Courtesy of the Woodrow Wilson Presidential Library. Photo Identifier: WWPL 1248.

of social reform that characterized Progressive Era politics, becoming actively involved in efforts to improve housing conditions for poor minority residents in Washington, DC, still very much a Southern city, and to create healthier workplace conditions for female government employees, many of whom were Black. Yet her advocacy at times was problematic, with proposed reforms promoting racial and social segregation, reflecting the dark side of progressive politics. Second, she personified the progressive values of the new woman by pursuing a career as a professional artist, which she continued during her time as first lady, making her the first working first lady in the White House. Although she was not a working woman in the traditional sense, she pursued her own career as an artist and advocated for improved working conditions, and in some cases suffrage, for women.[2] Wilson served as first lady for just seventeen months before her untimely death, yet she accomplished a great deal during her brief tenure, paving the way for a more activist approach to the first lady position. Interestingly, Southern and Northern newspapers remembered her very differently upon her death, showing the divide she had to carefully bridge in her life. This chapter examines how Wilson both embraced and challenged the conventions of her Southern upbringing to become the embodiment of Progressive Era ideals.

## THE PROGRESSIVE ERA'S INFLUENCE ON ELLEN WILSON

Wilson lived during a time that saw a cultural shift from the Victorian Era, with its emphasis on strict social hierarchies and clear divisions between gender roles, to a period focused on social reform and activism that attracted a diverse following, including Republicans and Democrats, workers and wealthy philanthropists, and men and women. The Progressive Era spanned from the end of the economic depression of the 1890s to the US involvement in World War I. The unifying element in the Progressive Era was a sense of social responsibility. According to Lewis L. Gould, "In response to diverse pressures of industrialization, urban growth, and ethnic tension, American society embarked on a myriad of reform movements that, taken together, set the terms for debate on public policy for the succeeding half century."[3] Much of what was accomplished in the Progressive Era was a culmination of years of effort, such as the enfranchisement of women and legal protections for industrial workers. Yet, as Gould noted, progressive ideals would continue to influence politics for years to come, including the work of presidential couples Franklin and Eleanor Roosevelt and Lyndon and Lady Bird Johnson.

But progressivism also had its flaws, frequently promoting racist, classist, and nativist sentiments, sometimes unintentionally and other times deliberately. Most of the reformers were upper-class white men and women who sought to fix the problems facing the lower classes, comprising mainly immigrants and racial minorities, without truly understanding or addressing the underlying causes of poverty and inequality. Charlotte Rich notes, "Despite the optimistic discourse of this political era, and its undeniable improvements in many Americans' quality of life through seeking to regulate the excesses of rampant capitalism, these years also saw the legalization of the practice of racial segregation, the growth of nativist sentiments that led to immigration restrictions, and widespread efforts to assimilate both immigrants and Native Americans in ways that were well intentioned but nonetheless classist and ethnocentric."[4] Thus, the social reforms of the Progressive Era often had both positive and negative outcomes.

The Progressive Era created a climate in which social reform efforts were commended. In the process, it made women's participation in such movements more acceptable, bringing for many their first socially sanctioned experience in the public sphere. According to historian Glenda Riley, "Thousands of women flocked to the various reform causes. . . . Women worked individually, joined organizations of men and women, and became members of women's voluntary associations. . . . Almost all were encouraged to believe that the traditional image of women as domestic and passive beings, uninvolved in the larger society outside of their own homes, was about to undergo extensive revision."[5]

Progressive Era reform movements brought many privileged white women in both the North and South out of the private sphere of the home and into the public sphere for the first time.[6] This social activity challenged the prevailing notions of women's roles while simultaneously reinforcing boundaries based on class and race. Although this is a critique of progressivism in general, Southern women, in particular, found themselves grappling with these issues. Margaret Ripley Wolfe claims, "Southern female activists reflected their times, places, and personal values. Class and race served as omnipresent reminders of the distinctions between the reformers and those whose lives they were attempting to change."[7]

For many years, the social place of upper-class white women was confined to the private, domestic sphere. In the mid-nineteenth century, a strong surge of rhetoric appeared extolling the virtues of the private sphere and what is now referred to as the cult of true womanhood.[8] Barbara Welter, who helped coin the term, explained, "The attributes of True Womanhood, by which a woman judged herself and was judged by her husband, her neighbors, and society could be divided into four cardinal virtues—piety, purity, submissiveness, and domesticity. . . . With them she was promised happiness and power."[9] But this ideal was unattainable for most women, especially when social forces such as the Civil War, westward migration, industrialism, the depression of the 1890s, and progressivism forced women to reconsider their roles. Yet the rhetoric of true womanhood was still prominent, especially in women's magazines.[10] According to Welter, "The stereotype, the 'mystique' . . . of what woman was and ought to be persisted, bringing guilt and confusion in the midst of opportunity."[11] This was particularly true for Southern women "haunted by the specter of the 'Southern Lady,'" an extreme version of true womanhood that placed white women on a pedestal where they could be revered and protected, safely within the confines of the private sphere.[12] This notion of white Southern womanhood lasted well into the Progressive Era, as evidenced by the language used to describe Wilson in several of her obituaries from Southern newspapers.

The Progressive Era aided in the birth of a new cultural trend, the new woman. According to Beverly Sanders, the new woman was "the educated young single woman in rebellion against the exclusively domestic role of the nineteenth century woman."[13] As Riley describes the term, "The 'new women' were asking for their rights and were also willing to fulfill their social responsibilities by contributing their resources and energies to reform activities."[14] These new women, who were mostly white but also included Black activists such as Ida B. Wells-Barnett and Mary Church Terrell, sought the expansion of their roles to include both the private and public spheres, but not all agreed on the extent or degree of change necessary. Although some supported suffrage, others did not. Whereas true women remained solely in the private sphere and suffragists encouraged women to act in the public sphere, new women functioned in both the private and public spheres. This standpoint seemed to appeal especially to many mature women such as Wilson who were reared to believe in the ideal of true womanhood but felt they had more to contribute to society. During the Progressive Era, women thus achieved "a new kind of public power." According to Glenna Matthews, "They began to win electoral office, they saw the enactment of major public policy for which they had struggled, and they enjoyed an increasing public presence." However, she noted, "Women's power and women's access to public influence still fell far short of that exercised by men."[15] As Rich concluded, "The New Woman was an earnest crusader, assuming a public role to fight injustices against women, children, and the poor, even if the changes she advocated might not restructure the conditions that perpetuated such inequality."[16] Indeed, some white women activists themselves undermined the advances of Black women also seeking change.

The Progressive Era helped to shape Wilson's life and influenced her performance of the first lady role. Her religious background, which stressed charity and service to others, as well as her headstrong and independent nature, allowed her to embrace the spirit of progressivism and the new woman. But these movements were often at odds with the ideals of the white Southern lady, strongly grounded in the true woman tradition. In her pursuit of a career as a professional artist and her social activism, primarily on behalf of African Americans, Wilson was progressive compared with other white Southern women. Yet she would never forget her Southern roots.

## ARTISTIC CAREER

Ellen Axson grew up in Rome, Georgia, a small market town nestled in the foothills of the Appalachian Mountains, in the state's northwest corner.[17] Hers was a deeply religious family. Her father, Edward Axson, was a Presbyterian minister like his father before him. Her mother, Janie, was also the daughter of a Presbyterian pastor. Ellie Lou, as Ellen was called then, lived a comfortable life. Her family was well known and respected in Rome because of her father's vocation.[18] Her mother was an avid reader who shared her love of literature with her daughter and encouraged Ellen's intellectual development and artistic talent, which emerged at a young age.[19] However, her father thought his daughter "obstreperous" and "entirely too much inclined to have her own opinions."[20] At Rome Female College, Ellen was an eager student, excelling in literature, composition, math, and foreign language classes and demonstrating exceptional artistic talent under the tutelage of Helen Fairchild, who had studied at the prestigious National Academy of Design in New York City.[21] Fairchild was so impressed with her pupil that she submitted her work to the Paris International Exposition, which awarded the eighteen-year-old a bronze medal for excellence in freehand drawing.[22]

Painting and drawing were long considered acceptable pastimes for young society ladies. But Ellen Axson saw art as a career path that would take her from her quiet hometown to the cosmopolitan city of New York. Inspired by her teacher and her award, she began charging a small fee for portraits she drew from photographs and in a short time was earning enough money to support herself, and she earned quite a reputation in her home state of Georgia.[23] According to her brother Stockton, "She had fully made up her mind to be a professional portrait painter. . . . When she was perhaps twenty-two years of age she really contrived to earn a tidy sum of money each year."[24] Ellen planned to use the money she earned as a portraitist to move to New York to study art and pursue a career. But her plans were put on hold when her mother died in 1881, leaving her to care for her younger siblings and father, who suffered from depression throughout his life. In her father's church just two years later, she was first spotted by her future husband and US president Woodrow Wilson, also a minister's son. They were engaged within six months.[25]

Ellen Axson and Woodrow Wilson spent most of their engagement apart. While she remained in Georgia caring for her family, he was in graduate school at Johns Hopkins University. When her father, then in a mental institution, died in 1884 under questionable circumstances, she suggested breaking off the engagement, but Woodrow refused. And when he offered to drop out of school to take a teaching position in order to support her and her brothers, she instead encouraged him to finish his degree. She argued "that she wanted to be self-sufficient, if necessary. Woodrow laughed that Ellen 'was preparing to be my widow.'"[26] Yet her father's passing actually gave her the freedom to pursue her dream of studying art in New York because he left her a substantial inheritance. Saunders claimed that she said to her brother Stockton "with unabashed enthusiasm, 'Now that we are rich, you can go to college and I can go to the Art League.'"[27] Her decision embodied the spirit of the new woman, who was independent, self-reliant, and wanted to pursue opportunities beyond the domestic sphere.[28] Unlike most women of her era, who would have turned to their fiancé for support, Ellen used her inheritance to move to New York City alone and enroll at the liberal Art Students League.

The Art Students League was a student-run organization that did not discriminate based on gender or race, considered fairly radical for the period.[29] Some of the top American impressionists of the period taught at the Art Students League. Ellen Axson excelled in her classes, earning praise from her instructors and winning a spot in the League's exclusive life class, which employed live models, some nude and some draped. Eager to learn more, she started taking classes at the Metropolitan Museum of Art as well.[30] When she was not in class, she spent her time touring museums, attending lectures, and going to the theater, often without an escort, much to her fiancé's dismay.[31] She even attended burlesque shows, something "unthinkable in Georgia."[32]

Kristie Miller, one of Ellen's biographers, argued that New York helped the Georgia native "shed her provincialism." She tried to lessen her Southern accent, asking her fiancé for assistance because he had successfully dropped his own Southern drawl. She also experimented with attending different churches and was exposed to liberal viewpoints, even if she did not embrace them herself.[33] Historian Sina Dubovoy claimed that Ellen eventually became disillusioned with the Art Students League because of its students' widespread feminism and an "atmosphere of radical freethinking and the championing of radical lifestyles that profoundly disturbed her."[34] Even though she was not as bohemian as some of her colleagues, in part because of her Southern upbringing as a minister's daughter, her frequenting summer artists' colonies in Old Lyme, Connecticut, and Cornish, New Hampshire, throughout her life suggests in fact that she felt comfortable in such surroundings. She enjoyed her independence and did not mind doing things on her own, whether it was attending lectures on controversial topics unaccompanied or spending hours sketching.

When Woodrow Wilson finished his graduate studies, Ellen Axson left New York and the couple was married, putting the brakes on her art pursuits. He was concerned that he was being selfish in asking her to give up her art career. She assured him that she did not want to offer her husband "a divided allegiance" and that giving up her art would be "no sacrifice in exchange for a love as his."[35] She also knew that the life of a professional artist was filled with uncertainty. In a candid letter to him discussing her talent, Wilson admitted that she was "above the average among the art-students," yet, "it is *barely* possible that my talent for art combined with my talent for work *might*, after many years, win me a place among the first rank among American artists—who don't amount to much *anyhow*, you know!"[36] She instead decided to invest her energy in her husband's career.[37] Following her marriage, she focused on her roles as wife to him and mother to daughters Margaret, Jessie, and Eleanor (Nell). However, as Dubovoy noted, "While Ellen expected to give up the professional pursuit of art after her marriage, she never for a moment considered her training in New York to be a waste of time or money."[38]

Wilson did not completely abandon her art, but she once explained that "three daughters take more time than three canvases."[39] When her daughters were older, her husband encouraged her to pursue her artistic career. Following the 1905 death of her younger brother Eddie and his family in an accident, Ellen was deeply depressed. Woodrow thought a summer in Old Lyme, Connecticut, home to a well-known artists' colony, might lift her spirits. She began painting landscapes, adopting the style of the American impressionist movement. She met several famous American painters, some of whom had also trained at the Art Students League.[40] Encouraged by the feedback she received that summer, she started to pursue a career as a professional artist.

From that point on, Ellen and her daughters spent the summers in the artists' communities of Old Lyme and Cornish. She took classes from artists including Frank DuMond, who arranged for her to have her own studio, and stayed at places such as Florence Griswold's boardinghouse, the summer retreat of American impressionist painters.[41] She "plunged back into the art world, developing the side of her life that was not entwined with Woodrow's."[42] After several summers, she started showing the original paintings, mostly landscapes, she had amassed over that period.[43] She won a spot in her first New York show under the name "W. Wilson" in an effort to remain anonymous.[44] In spring 1912, she hired prominent New York gallery owner William Macbeth to be her agent. He sent her best works to various competitions, and they won places at several shows, including the Art Institute of Chicago, the National Academy of Design in New York, the John Herron Art Institute of Indianapolis, and the Pennsylvania Academy of the Fine Arts. Several paintings were sold.[45] The Association of Women

Painters and Sculptors also exhibited five of her landscapes and invited her to join the organization. The Pen and Brush Club, an organization for professional women artists and writers, made her a member as well.[46] At age fifty-two, Wilson had "at last 'arrived' as a professional artist in her own right."[47]

Another sign of Wilson's professional success was her first solo exhibition of fifty landscapes in February 1913, just before her husband's inauguration, at the Arts and Crafts Guild in Philadelphia. She sold twenty-four paintings and donated the proceeds to the Martha Berry Schools, which served needy rural children in her hometown of Rome, Georgia.[48] She continued to paint and sell her artwork while in the White House, pursuing an independent career as she performed the duties of the first lady position. She even turned part of the unused third floor of the White House into an art studio.[49] And she continued to donate all of the money she earned to the Martha Berry Schools.

Wilson's decision to continue working at her profession after entering the White House is emblematic of the new woman, who fulfilled her own interests while still performing the roles of wife and mother. She was developing her own identity as an artist separate from her husband or her role as first lady and was on the verge of making her mark on the art world before her premature death.[50] Continuing to pursue an independent career, even on a part-time basis, is a feat yet to be matched by any other first lady. Even though Eleanor Roosevelt wrote newspaper and magazine columns and hosted her own radio show, her work was still connected to her role as first lady.[51] In contrast, Wilson's artwork was in no way related to her first lady duties, giving her a level of independence despite the demands and constraints of the first lady institution.[52]

Wilson's artistic talent also allowed her to move beyond the confines of her small Southern hometown. She first moved North to pursue her studies in New York City, where she was exposed to a more bohemian lifestyle—quite the contrast from the life of a minister's daughter. Later, she would spend her summers in New England artist colonies rather than visiting her Southern relatives. In fact, she rarely travelled south of the Mason-Dixon Line after she resumed her art career. However, she always remained connected to the South, as evidenced by her decision to donate the proceeds of her artwork to fund scholarships for rural children in Georgia. She also decorated the White House with Southern handicrafts when she just as easily could have featured the paintings of her famous friends, who were among the leading American impressionists.[53]

## SOCIAL ACTIVISM

Social reform was a hallmark of the Progressive Era. As Nancy S. Dye noted, "Women filled the progressive landscape," focusing on a wide variety of causes, including the improvement of working conditions especially for women and children, clean water, pure food and milk, adequate sanitation, and improved housing and schools.[54] Wilson's interest in helping others, particularly the less fortunate, might have initially been grounded in her Christian upbringing as a minister's daughter. But, as her husband's political involvement increased, so did her advocacy of various progressive reform efforts. Although the president was more focused on effecting policy, the first lady concentrated on social change, reflecting the different approaches taken by men and women involved in the Progressive movement.[55]

According to Wilson's cousin Mary Hoyt, she never could "keep herself away from some kind of social work."[56] The first lady's interest in social reform developed during her time in New York City at the Art Students League. She volunteered at a mission school in one of the city's poor neighborhoods, where she taught African American children basic reading, writing, and math along with bible studies every Sunday. After her first visit to the mission, she wrote to her fiancé, "I was rather pleased with my first experience of a city mission. It is a big room—full of noisy bright very clean and respectable looking little darkies—did I tell you it was a colored school?"[57] Her Southern roots are evident in her use of the term "darkies," which she also used to describe one of the models at the Art Students League in another letter.[58] But, based on her phrasing, it seems that she had "forgotten" to mention previously to her fiancé that she was working with African American students, likely because she knew he might object. And he did, asserting that he thought she was "exposed to risks. . . . I can't help questioning the wisdom of the arrangement."[59] Ellen countered that it was "her duty" to teach at the school. In one letter, she told Woodrow, "To think first of any small risk or unpleasantness connected with teaching there does not seem right. . . . The mere possibility should not keep me from *trying* to do something."[60] In spite of his concerns, she worked at the mission throughout her stay in New York. This insistence on working outside the home was a vital part of Wilson's new woman persona. Her commitment to working at the mission and her independence would later inspire her daughter Jessie to become involved in the settlement house movement. It would also be an important foundation for her own work later in assisting the poor residents of Washington, DC.

Just two weeks after her husband's inauguration, the first lady learned of the project that would become a primary focus of her brief time in the White House. On March 20, she attended a lecture sponsored by the National Civic Federation's (NCF) Woman's Department. According to the *New York Times*, she asked many questions "in regard to the housing conditions in Washington and the improvement in alley dwellings, in which this section of the Federation is deeply interested."[61] A few days later, she toured the alleys near Capitol Hill for the first time accompanied by Charlotte Hopkins, chair of the NCF's Woman's Department, and Grace Bicknell, chair of the group's Housing Committee. The primarily African American residents lived in "the most shocking conditions" in run-down shacks and converted barns with no running water or sanitation.[62] After visiting the alleys, the first lady was presented with the NCF's plan to build more than a hundred two-family dwellings. The so-called "sanitary" housing would be rented at affordable rates and supervised by a social worker, similar to the settlement house movement model. She immediately committed herself to the cause, becoming a stockholder in the newly organized Sanitary Housing Company.[63]

Wilson started taking political leaders and their wives on tours of the alleys to lobby for support of the NCF's plans to clear the alleys and move families into sanitary housing complexes. She even designated a White House automobile for the alley inspections. One of those tours included the wife of the assistant secretary of the navy, future First Lady Eleanor Roosevelt.[64] Wilson joined a group of progressive reformers known as the Committee of Fifty, responsible for drafting legislation addressing the alley problem. Her name is listed in the *Congressional Record* as a member of the committee responsible for this proposal.[65] She held several lobbying and fund-raising events at the White House, urging members of Congress to support the alley bill, introduced in February 1914 and nicknamed "Mrs. Wilson's bill."[66] It was the first legislation to be named for a first lady. It was passed six months later by both the House and Senate just hours before she died. Newspapers reported that she told her husband she would "go away more cheerfully" if the bill was passed.[67] Unfortunately, the bill was never successfully enacted because of lack of funding and the outbreak of World War I. However, Wilson's advocacy is still significant for being the first time a first lady was so publicly involved in policymaking and in lobbying for legislation. When the housing projects envisioned by the NCF were finally constructed in the 1930s, one of them was named the Ellen Wilson Dwelling.[68]

Wilson's advocacy on behalf of housing reform reflected Progressive Era values, but her activism generated some criticism. Her own social secretary, Belle Hagner, condescendingly called the White House lobbying events "slumming parties." One newspaper said, "Just what Mrs. Wilson is to gain by driving through these alleys quite baffles Washington."[69] A May 16, 1913, *New York Times* article, "Mrs. Wilson Slumming" addressed that question, stating that the first lady was "seeking first-hand information for the movement to improve the living conditions of the poor in Washington." However, the use of the word "slumming" in the title reflected a sarcastic tone that can be interpreted as a critique of Wilson's involvement in alley clearance.[70] The bill also faced opposition on the Hill, particularly from Southern lawmakers, because it threatened vested property interests and involved whites, including white women, advocating on behalf of African Americans for improved (albeit segregated) living conditions.[71] This criticism of Wilson's efforts was similar to what other white Southern female reformers faced. According to Jean E. Friedman, "The Southern lady who defied class convention and ideology to champion blacks, workers, and the poor nonetheless confronted a world divided by race, class, and gender."[72]

The alley bill was not Wilson's only advocacy work. She started conducting informal inspection trips of public offices to review workplace conditions, continuing the work of her first lady predecessor, Helen Taft.[73] In October 1913, she visited the US Post Office and was appalled to find no bathrooms for the low-paid female clerks, along with unsanitary conditions that could lead to diseases such as tuberculosis. She brought her concerns to Postmaster General Albert S. Burleson but received no response.[74] So, at a White House luncheon, she asked her husband's chief adviser, Colonel Edward Mandell House, to look into the situation. When he tried to dismiss her concerns, the two got into a heated exchange that caught the attention of the entire table. House then promised to "take it up and see that something is done."[75] In his memoirs, House described Wilson's forcefulness in pursuing the matter with him, observing that she was as much of a political force in the White House as her husband was and felt free to discuss political matters with the president's closest advisers.

Later in October, Wilson conducted an unannounced tour of the Government Printing Office. A *New York Times* article said it was part of her plan to inspect working conditions in government offices, stating, "She is interested in social welfare work and wants to know for herself just how the government treats its employees in the way of space, light, and air and other things essential to their health and comfort." The article also mentioned her visit to the US Post Office.[76] In November 1913, Wilson became the honorary vice chair of the Woman's Department of the NCF, whose main focus was "to improve the working conditions of Government employees."[77] According to the *New York Times*, she informed the organization that in accepting the position, "she was acting, not as the President's wife but as a woman whose heart was in the social welfare movement."[78] The story went on to reference her inspection visits to government offices and her housing reform efforts.

However, Wilson's inspection tours have been tied to speculation that she influenced her husband's decision to segregate government offices. In April 1913, the NCF's Hopkins accompanied her to the Bureau of Engraving and Printing to investigate the working conditions of female employees. Wilson observed Black and white women working side by side. Shortly after her visit, it was suggested that the African American women sit at separate tables in the lunchroom. The *Washington Bee*, an African American newspaper, reported that the recommendation did not appear to have "any connection with the visit of the first lady," but, "many people assert that the two things are related to each other as cause and effect."[79] Hopkins came to the first lady's defense, telling the *Washington Post* that she "did remark on the fact that the whites and negroes were working together, and was informed that no distinctions were made with regard to color in government departments, and that was all there was to the matter." Hopkins went on to state that Wilson was "too kind" to all of the workers and that the newspapers should not let "anything like these rumors to get out."[80]

Yet historians noted that President Wilson systematically reimposed segregation in government offices by his first summer in office, raising the question of what role, if any, Ellen might have played in the matter, given that she was well known for serving as one of Woodrow's trusted advisers. Their daughter Jessie told Wilson biographer Ray Stannard Baker that her mother felt "much more strongly about the color line" than her father did. Kristie Miller pointed out that Ellen was "a Southern woman" and seemed to have no Black friends. But Miller concluded that, even if she agreed with her husband's position on segregation, it is doubtful she was "the sole or predominant influence in his decision to re-segregate the federal offices." Miller also claimed that although she likely never condoned complete equality between the races, "there is no evidence of her actively trying to thwart the progress of African Americans, and many examples of her trying to improve their lives."[81] Even the African American newspaper the *Washington Bee*, which questioned whether the first lady might have played a role in the resegregation of federal offices, would ultimately praise her work on behalf of the capital's African American residents, proclaiming that she had "established a precedent that was foreign to many in her race."[82]

Other biographers agree that, in spite of her views on segregation, Wilson was genuinely committed to progressive reforms aimed at benefitting the African American community. Dubovoy notes that, while the Wilsons were "thorough-going segregationists," neither one ever felt or exhibited personal animus toward persons of color. As an example of this, she recounts the first lady's willingness to address "the disgraceful living conditions of poor blacks in the nation's capital," even in the face of a "barrage of criticism from southern lawmakers and their spouses that all but killed her efforts for improvement."[83] Still, Dubovoy argues that she "did not intellectualize too deeply about the causes of their plight; to blame it on segregation or discrimination would have been alien to her who saw misery not at all from an intellectual standpoint but from the heart."[84] This interpretation seems to underestimate Wilson's intellect as well as overlook her Southern background. Hopkins of the NCF, who introduced her to the alley issue, wrote to President Wilson after his wife's death praising her tireless commitment to helping Washington's African American residents. She claimed, "Mrs. Wilson understood the general situation, grasping at a glance the fact that with 96,000 Negroes, a third of the population, the great crying need was improved living conditions. . . . Mrs. Wilson never made any secret to any of the men she took in the alleys that the work she was trying to do in passing the bill was to improve the conditions of the Negroes. Only 2,000 whites live in these alleys." In this connection, Hopkins also mentioned her financial support of the District's Colored Social Settlement.[85] Hopkins characterized the first lady's reform efforts as consciously focused on helping African Americans, which countered Dubovoy's claim that she saw misery from "the heart" and not from an "intellectual standpoint." Miller suggests that her interest in the alleys "may have been less motivated by concern for her black neighbors than by her ongoing interest in Progressive causes."[86] Yet she also mentioned that Wilson "felt a particular responsibility for African Americans, explaining that her mother and grandmother, both slaveholders, had taught her that it was the duty of southern Christian women to 'work for the good of the Negroes.'"[87] Wilson's Southern Christian upbringing, coupled with her support of progressive causes, emboldened her to advocate on behalf of African Americans while continuing to believe in racial segregation, much like other Southern women involved in the Progressive movement.[88]

In discussing her reform efforts, Wilson was often humble. In a letter to a cousin about the activists she worked with, she said, "The women are so grateful that it is embarrassing. Here they have worked for years and years and could get nothing. I have done so little—only been interested."[89] But she was clearly aware that her advocacy had an impact. She mentioned to her husband that the leaders of the NCF claimed she "had done more good in Washington in four months than any other President's wife had *ever* done in four years—had completely changed the conditions of life for 12,000 people, or was it 12,000 alleys?"[90] Some in her own family downplayed her advocacy efforts, perhaps because they conflicted with ideas of "proper" Southern womanhood. Her brother Stockton said that she was compassionate, "less given to reform than to quietly performed acts of mercy."[91] Yet there was nothing quiet about her public support of the Slum Clearance Act, including her lobbying of members of Congress and her role in drafting the legislation. Meanwhile, newspaper coverage of her alley tours and her government office inspections pointed out her interest in social reform. Dubovoy argues, "That Ellen would take on the conspicuous role of social crusader indicates that she was far from shy and, though ladylike, far from docile. She knew how to pull political strings as well as her husband, and influence people even better than he."[92] Indeed, she embodied the Progressive Era's commitment to social reform in a public way even when it was contradictory to her Southern upbringing and contrary to the typical performance expected of a first lady.

## LEGACY

In October 1914, Wilson had been scheduled to return to her childhood hometown of Rome, Georgia, where town leaders were planning a grand celebration for their famous former resident. Sadly, her homecoming came two months early; her family returned her to Rome to be buried beside her parents after she died in August from Bright's disease. Rome's residents lined the streets in the pouring rain to pay their respects.[93] An article in the local newspaper proclaimed, "She's come home to Dixie to lie down and peacefully sleep 'mid the flowers and friends she loved so well."[94]

Following her unexpected death, newspapers paid tribute to Wilson in obituaries that discussed her life and praised her performance of the first lady role. But there were noticeable differences in the way she was remembered in national publications compared with Southern newspapers. Two of the most prominent newspapers of the era, the *New York Times* and the *Washington Post*, published lengthy articles reviewing her final hours and detailing her accomplishments. The *New York Times* called her an "earnest welfare worker," recounting her inspection of federal offices and her alley tours. The article mentioned that she told her husband she would "pass away more contentedly" if she knew Congress had passed the Slum Clearance Bill, noting that "before she lost consciousness Mrs. Wilson had the satisfaction of knowing that the measure had been passed by the Senate and that the House would follow suit." Her deathbed request was repeated by a number of news outlets, along with the story that she asked her doctor and family friend to "take good care of my husband." The article called her "the chief aid and inspiration" of the president, noting her role as his trusted adviser. Along with detailing her family life, the story also mentioned her artistic talent, referring to her time at the Art Students League and adding that her paintings had been shown the previous year at a prestigious national exhibition. Her Southern roots were mentioned; the paper remarking that "friends regarded Mrs. Wilson as distinctively a Southern woman in many ways" but offered no details other than a flattering description of her appearance.[95]

Similarly, the *Washington Post* discussed her deep interest in "the social welfare of the community." The article mentioned that the White House received flowers "from many humble homes . . . as Mrs. Wilson had made many friends in the slums and city generally in her endeavors to help the friendless and poverty-stricken."[96] A separate article in the *Washington Post* talked about her advisory role and noted her support of housing reform, calling her "a friend of the poor and lowly to whose needs she devoted time and strength." In addition, the story acknowledged her artistic accomplishments and her time at the artists' commune in Cornish, New Hampshire.[97] Both the *New York Times* and *Washington Post* praised Ellen primarily for her progressive ideals and her active performance of the first lady role.

Wilson's life was remembered somewhat differently in Southern accounts of her passing. In the Woodrow Wilson Papers at the Library of Congress, there is an interesting collection of clippings of obituaries from Southern newspapers. Of the thirty-eight articles, twenty-one are from Georgia newspapers. There is no note indicating why these specific clippings were saved or who collected them, but clearly someone thought that the Southern obituaries were particularly noteworthy. In more than half of the articles, Wilson is remembered as a paragon of true womanhood and a model white Southern lady. Fourteen of the articles framed her exclusively as an exemplar of true womanhood, with no references to her more progressive characteristics. One Alabama newspaper claimed, "Mrs. Wilson represented the highest and best of the educated, cultured, and talented type of Southern Christian womanhood."[98] A Louisiana publication noted that the Georgia native "embodied in her personality all of the best qualities of her sex. . . . She presided over the domestic side of the White House with an unostentatious grace and charm."[99] According to one Georgia paper, "She eloquently proclaimed the highest type of American womanhood," which held to the "traditions and ideals . . . of her cavalier heritage."[100] Another article said, "She had the simple love of home that makes wifehood and motherhood so divine an ideal."[101] The few stories that did reference her advocacy characterized it as Christian charity. One Georgia newspaper observed, "She was continually looking for some place where she might help relieve the poor and suffering."[102] Another publication referred to her deathbed request that the alley bill be passed but implied that she supported the cause because "her heart was ever warm and her hands ever busied in service for the poor."[103]

A handful of Southern newspapers recognized Wilson's roles as advocate, adviser, and artist. An article called "How She Wished to Be Remembered" focused solely on her support of the alley bill and concluded that support of the legislation was the best way to honor her legacy.[104] The obituary in the Dublin, Georgia, paper referred to essays written by the first lady on behalf of social advocacy efforts, noting, "Her most beautiful and forceful passages occur in the papers read before the various civic and charitable institutions of which she was a most enthusiastic and active member."[105] Unfortunately, these essays have apparently been lost, and this lone obituary is the only reference to their existence. Another Georgia newspaper claimed that Wilson's alley tours helped to "inspire burdened mothers with hope to gladden the darkened lives of the children of the slums, to make the weak and discouraged to grow strong in the comforting thought that somebody cared."[106] A detailed article in an Alabama paper referred to her as an "ardent social worker" whose dying request was passage of the alley bill. The story also praised her artistic talents.[107] And in Mississippi, one newspaper stated that the problems of the District's poorest residents were "scarcely known to the public at large until Mrs. Wilson's several trips through the alleys of that city was [*sic*] given publicity through the newspapers."[108] However, none of the newspapers, including the *New York Times* and *Washington Post*, mentioned that her social reform work was primarily aimed at assisting African Americans. In these obituaries, the clash of Southern and Northern gender norms and racial conventions was highlighted as Wilson was remembered as both a traditional Southern lady and a model Progressive Era new woman.

## CONCLUSION

When considered collectively, these obituaries painted a picture of a complex and fascinating woman who found a way to live between two worlds. In some ways, she was a traditional white Southern woman who devoted her life to home and family. Yet she was so much more. She was a true helpmate to her husband, but that entailed being knowledgeable about politics and being willing to take on a public role. She shared his progressive political views, which championed social reform and required women to expand their roles beyond the domestic sphere. She also shared her husband's belief in racial segregation, a common facet of progressivism, but she still focused much of her advocacy on improving the lives of African Americans. She embodied the spirit of the new woman, finding a way to straddle the public and private spheres and balance the roles of wife and mother with those of social reformer and professional artist. She expanded the role of the first lady with her advocacy and art career, yet she continued to perform the traditional hostess duties, overseeing her two daughters' White House weddings and numerous other social occasions during her short seventeen months in the position.

However, Wilson's progressive nature was not without its problems, much like the Progressive movement itself, when middle- and upper-class reformers were sometimes out of touch with the true needs of those they were trying to help.[109] There is not enough evidence to determine what influence, if any, Wilson had on her husband's decision to enforce segregation in federal offices, which might have been linked to her workplace inspections. There is also the problematic legacy of her slum clearance work. Wilson and the women of the NCF meant well in their efforts to improve the living conditions of Washington's poorest residents. The proposed sanitary housing complexes were much healthier and welcoming spaces than the alley shacks. Yet many of the alleys were cleared before the complexes were built, forcing residents to relocate. And the housing projects eventually constructed in the 1930s had their own problems. They essentially segregated a city's poorest residents, often persons of color, into neighborhoods where they could be contained. The people in these projects formed their own tightknit communities, but they were still separate from the larger, majority white communities and treated as such. There is no indication from the historical record that Wilson or her NCF colleagues viewed slum clearance as a form of segregation. Instead, many of these white women viewed it as social reform or charity. But, according to Rich, other progressive reformers promoted racial segregation as a way to stabilize race relations "so that the work of uplift and as-similation of various nonwhite or non-middle-class 'Others' (in this case, African Americans) could continue."[110]

Regardless of their intentions, the actions of Ellen Wilson and her colleagues still had consequences that linger to this day. In an interesting twist of fate, the housing project named in Wilson's honor, once a thriving Black neighborhood in the District's Capitol Hill area, succumbed to crime and drugs and a lack of city resources before it was condemned in the late 1980s, and residents were forced to leave without being offered alternative housing, much like the original alley dwellers.[111] The site was later converted into the District's first mixed-in-come housing co-op, which still bears the name Ellen Wilson Place. However, of the 134 refurbished townhomes, only 33 were reserved for the lowest-income families, who are the majority of public housing residents. Still, according to a 2013 *Washington Post* article, "the city's first social experiment with mixed-in-come housing has become a model for other developments, even if it made only a modest contribution toward solving the District's affordable housing prob-lem."[112] The story noted that more than six hundred families were on a waiting list for the development's subsidized units. One wonders whether the current residents, regardless of income bracket, know much about the namesake of their neighborhood.

In a letter to her husband from October 1913, Wilson stated her belief that no one should "rest on the laurels of another person, but must grow to the limits of . . . her own spirit, mind, and ability."[113] This passage captures the essence of Ellen Axson Wilson. The obstreperous minister's daughter from Rome, Georgia, seemed to know no limits until her physical body finally gave out. She juggled many roles—wife, mother, adviser, artist, advocate, and first lady. She embraced the spirit of the Progressive Era without forsaking her white Southern femininity, making her a truly progressive, yet complicated, Southern first lady.

## NOTES

1. Francis Wright Saunders, *First Lady Between Two Worlds: Ellen Axson Wilson* (Chapel Hill: University of North Carolina Press, 1985), xiii.

2. Lisa M. Burns, "Ellen Axson Wilson: A Rhetorical Reassessment of a Forgotten First Lady," in *Inventing a Voice: The Rhetoric of American First Ladies of the Twentieth Century*, ed. Molly M. Wertheimer (Lanham, MD: Rowman and Littlefield, 2004), 93.

3. Lewis L. Gould, *The Progressive Era* (Syracuse, NY: Syracuse University Press, 1974), 1.

4. Charlotte Rich, *Transcending the New Woman: Multiethnic Narratives in the Progressive Era* (Columbia: University of Missouri Press, 2009), 3–4.

5. Glenda Riley, *Inventing the American Woman: A Perspective on Women's History, 1865 to the Present*, vol. 2 (Arlington Heights, IL: Harlan Davidson, 1986), 37.

6. Noralee Frankel and Nancy S. Dye, eds., *Gender, Class, Race, and Reform in the Progressive Era* (Lexington: University Press of Kentucky, 1991), 3.

7. Margaret Ripley Wolfe, *Daughters of Canaan: A Saga of Southern Women* (Lexington: University Press of Kentucky, 2015), 139–140.

8. This image permeated the women's magazines, books of etiquette, and religious literature of the nineteenth century. Magazines such as *Godey's Magazine and Lady's Book, Ladies' Companion,* and *Mother's Magazine* were immensely popular in the mid-1800s, and they continued to prize domesticity above all for many years to come. And for those who disagreed with these views, there was sharp rebuke and criticism.

9. Barbara Welter, "The Cult of True Womanhood: 1820–1860," in *The American Family in Social-Historical Perspective*, ed. Michael Gordon (New York: St. Martin's, 1973), 225.

10. For a detailed look at the iconography of true womanhood and new womanhood in women's magazines, see Carolyn Kitch, *The Girl on the Magazine Cover: The Origins of Visual Stereotypes in American Mass Media* (Chapel Hill: University of North Carolina Press, 2001).

11. Welter, "Cult of True Womanhood," 242. Welter's article, initially published in the late 1960s, has been critiqued for its limitations (see Mary Louise Roberts, "True Womanhood Revisited," *Journal of Women's History* 14, no. 1 [2002]: 150–155), and many authors have expanded on her work. However, the concept is still widely used in discussing the Victorian ideals of womanhood promoted in the popular media of the era.

12. Wolfe, *Daughters of Canaan*, 134.

13. Beverly Sanders, *Women in the Progressive Era: 1890–1920* (Newton, MA: Educational Development Center, 1979), 47.

14. Riley, *Inventing the American Woman*, 63.

15. Glenna Matthews, *The Rise of Public Woman: Woman's Power and Place in the United States, 1630–1970* (New York: Oxford University Press, 1992), 172.

16. Rich, *Transcending the New Woman*, 19.

17. Sina Dubovoy, *Ellen A. Wilson: The Woman Who Made a President* (New York: Nova, 2011), 1; Homepage, RomeGeorgia.com, accessed January 27, 2018, http://www.rome georgia.com/.

18. Dubovoy, *Ellen A. Wilson*, 11.

19. Saunders, *First Lady Between Two Worlds*, 22–23.

20. Saunders, 18.

21. Saunders, 14.

22. Saunders, 15.

23. Dubovoy, *Ellen A. Wilson*, 18.

24. Stockton Axson, *Brother Woodrow: A Memoir of Woodrow Wilson*, ed. Arthur S. Link (Princeton, NJ: Princeton University Press, 1993), 90.

25. George Osborn, "The Romance of Woodrow Wilson and Ellen Axson," *North Carolina Historical Review* 39, no. 2 (Winter 1962): 33.

26. Kristie Miller, *Ellen and Edith: Woodrow Wilson's First Ladies* (Lawrence: University Press of Kansas, 2010), 13.

27. Saunders, *First Lady Between Two Worlds*, 47.

28. See Burns, "Ellen Axson Wilson," 82.

29. Miller, *Ellen and Edith*, 14.

30. Dubovoy, *Ellen A. Wilson*, 52.

31. Miller, *Ellen and Edith*, 14.

32. Dubovoy, *Ellen A. Wilson*, 55.

33. Miller, *Ellen and Edith*, 14–15.

34. Dubovoy, *Ellen A. Wilson*, 58.

35. Miller, *Ellen and Edith*, 15.

36. Dubovoy, *Ellen A. Wilson*, 50.

37. Miller, *Ellen and Edith*, 15.

38. Dubovoy, *Ellen A. Wilson*, 51.

39. Carl S. Anthony, *First Ladies: The Saga of the Presidents' Wives and Their Power, 1961–1990* (New York: Morrow, 1990), 343.

40. Saunders, *First Lady Between Two Worlds*, 163.

41. Saunders, 192.

42. Miller, *Ellen and Edith*, 39.

43. Burns, " Ellen Axson Wilson," 85.

44. Saunders, *First Lady Between Two Worlds*, 256.

45. Dubovoy, *Ellen A. Wilson*, 235.

46. Burns, "Ellen Axson Wilson," 86.

47. Dubovoy, *Ellen A. Wilson*, 235.

48. Saunders, *First Lady Between Two Worlds*, 257.

49. Burns, "Ellen Axson Wilson," 84.

50. Miller, *Ellen and Edith*, 93; Dubovoy, *Ellen A. Wilson*, xiv.

51. For more, see Maurine Beasley, *First Ladies and the Press: The Unfinished Partnership of the Media Age* (Evanston, IL: Northwestern University Press, 2005), 20–21.

52. Burns, "Ellen Axson Wilson," 94–96.

53. Saunders, *First Lady Between Two Worlds*, 243.

54. Nancy S. Dye, "Introduction," in *Gender, Class, Race, and Reform in the Progressive Era*, ed. Noralee Frankel and Nancy S. Dye (Lexington: University Press of Kentucky, 1991), 1.

55. Dye, "Introduction," 2.

56. Miller, *Ellen and Edith*, 74.

57. Dubovoy, *Ellen A. Wilson*, 58.

58. Dubovoy, 58.

59. Woodrow Wilson to Ellen Axson Wilson, letter, February 9, 1885, in *The Priceless Gift*, ed. Eleanor Wilson McAdoo (New York: McGraw-Hill, 1962), 122.

60. Arthur S. Link, David W. Hirst, and John Little, eds., *The Papers of Woodrow Wilson* (Princeton, NJ: Princeton University Press, 1966), 233–234.

61. "Mrs. Wilson in Civic Work," *New York Times*, March 20, 1913, 11.

62. Miller, *Ellen and Edith*, 75.

63. Saunders, *First Lady Between Two Worlds*, 245.

64. Miller, *Ellen and Edith*, 79.

65. House of Representatives, 63rd Congress, 2nd Session, *Certain Alleys in the District of Columbia, Hearing Before the Committee on the District of Columbia on H.R. 13219, March 13 and 18, 1914* (Washington, DC: Government Printing Office, 1914), 37. The names of the Committee of Fifty for Improvement of Housing and Alley Conditions were officially entered into the *Congressional Record* during this hearing.

66. Saunders, *First Lady Between Two Worlds*, 246.

67. Burns, "Ellen Axson Wilson," 91.

68. Laura Lang, "Dream City," *Washington City Paper*, April 16, 1999, 1.

69. Miller, *Ellen and Edith*, 79.

70. Burns, "Ellen Axson Wilson," 59.

71. Ray Stannard Baker, *Woodrow Wilson: Life and Letters*, vol. 4: *President 1913–1914* (New York: Doubleday, Doran, 1931), 467.

72. Jean E. Friedman, "Review: *The Southern Lady: From Pedestal to Politics, 1830–1930*," *Journal of Southern History* 63, no. 1 (1997): 216–217.

73. For more on Helen Taft's advocacy work, see "First Lady Biography: Helen Taft," National First Ladies Library, http://www.firstladies.org/biographies/firstladies .aspx?biography=27.

74. Saunders, *First Lady Between Two Worlds*, 246.

75. Saunders, 246.

76. "Broke Office Rule for Mrs. Wilson," *New York Times*, October 31, 1913, 3.

77. "Mrs. Wilson to Aid," *New York Times*, November 3, 1913, 1.

78. "Mrs. Wilson to Aid," 1.

79. Miller, *Ellen and Edith*, 76.

80. Miller, 76.

81. Miller, 77.

82. Miller, 77.

83. Dubovoy, *Ellen A. Wilson*, 56, 228.

84. Dubovoy, 228.

85. Mrs. (Charlotte) Archibald Hopkins to Woodrow Wilson, letter, June 21, 1915, Woodrow Wilson Papers, Library of Congress, Washington, DC.

86. Miller, *Ellen and Edith*, 77.

87. Miller, 74.

88. Wolfe, *Daughters of Canaan*, 139.

89. Baker, *Woodrow Wilson*, 467.

90. Saunders, *First Lady Between Two Worlds*, 247.

91. Dubovoy, *Ellen A. Wilson*, 58.

92. Dubovoy, 228.

93. "Mrs. Wilson Buried Beside Her Parents," *New York Times*, August 12, 1914, 9.

94. "Coming Home," *Rome Tribune Herald*, August 11, 1914.

95. "Mrs. Wilson Dies in White House," *New York Times*, August 7, 1914, 1.

96. "Mrs. Wilson Dies after Long Period of Illness," *Washington Post*, August 7, 1914, 1.

97. "Death of White House Chatelaine Brings Gloom to Nation's Capital," *Washington Post*, August 7, 1914, 7.

98. "National Calamity," *Huntsville Morning Courier*, August 7, 1914.

99. "Death of Mrs. Wilson," *New Orleans Statesman*, August 7, 1914.

100. "Mrs. Woodrow Wilson," *Moultrie Observer*, August 10, 1914.

101. "The Nation's Sorrow," *Fitzgerald Leader Enterprise*, August 10, 1914.

102. "Death of Mrs. Wilson," *Sparks Eagle*, August 7, 1914.

103. "Nation's Sorrow."

104. "How She Wished to Be Remembered," *Brunswick News*, August 12, 1914.

105. "Mrs. Wilson," *Dublin Courier Herald*, August 10, 1914, Woodrow Wilson Papers, Library of Congress, Washington, DC.

106. "Tribute to Mrs. Helen Axson Wilson," *Dawson News*, August 14, 1914.

107. "Mrs. Wilson Was the Highest Type of American Woman," *Gadoden Journal*, August 10, 1914.

108. "Wife of President Wilson Dead," *Meridian Star*, August 7, 1914.

109. Molly Ladd-Taylor, "Hull House Goes to Washington: Women and the Children's Bureau," in *Gender, Class, Race, and Reform in the Progressive Era*, ed. Noralee Frankel and Nancy S. Dye (Lexington: University Press of Kentucky, 1991), 123.

110. Rich, *Transcending the New Woman*, 31.

111. Lang, "Dream City," 1.

112. Jessica Schulberg, "Built to Replace Ellen Wilson Housing Project, Townhouses Are a Mixed-Income Model," *Washington Post*, November 3, 2013.

113. Saunders, *First Lady Between Two Worlds*, 258.

# CHAPTER 13

# Edith Bolling Wilson
## A "Southern" New Woman

Valerie Palmer-Mehta

Edith Bolling Wilson (1872–1961), second wife of Woodrow Wilson, has been called, with equal parts awe and displeasure, our "first woman president."[1] Although she engaged in what Anne Scott called the "Sisyphean task" of living up to the demands of Southern womanhood,[2] her actions indicated that she desired to chart her own course in life, an attribute Ruth Bordin described as emblematic of the new woman of the Progressive Era.[3] And, while she lacked the formal education and professional status of the new woman, Edith consistently exhibited a penchant for enlarged opportunities and independence of spirit even as she confirmed Southern traditions. Indeed, she was a figure who simultaneously broke with convention while also making efforts to uphold it.

In her memoir, Edith gestured toward this complex blend of attributes as she nostalgically recounted an "exciting and unexpected trip" she embarked upon with her mother's half-sister, Elizabeth Logwood, to witness the 1890 unveiling of the equestrian statue of General Robert E. Lee, the first statue built on Virginia's controversial Monument Avenue.[4] Though she had not planned on voyaging to Richmond, Edith was enthralled by the excitement at the train station as she saw her uncle, General James G. Field, off to the event. Untroubled in her assumptions, she stated, "It seemed that the entire South was going to pay tribute to its loved leader." Thus, when her young aunt suggested that they should not miss this historical occasion, Edith quickly agreed and, without preparation or hesitation, she boarded the train. Signaling both her independence and her loyalty to the Old South, she stated, "All I needed was a word, and in another minute we were off. She got a seat on the train, but I stood up all the way."[5]

Edith's affinity for autonomy and mobility also was exhibited years later when she became the first woman in Washington, DC, to obtain a license to drive an electric car. Her efforts to learn how to ride a bicycle in the White House basement were no less significant.[6] Although her car could reach a top speed of only thirteen miles an hour, and she did not entirely master biking, such forms of mobility symbolized for women at the beginning of the twentieth century meaningful autonomy and courage.[7] Gesturing toward mobility's political significance, Susan Hanson wrote that the bicycle was central to broadening a woman's sense of enterprise and access to opportunity at that time: "More than 'just' a means to regain . . . lost mobility after too many years of being trapped in decorous middle-class womanhood," the bicycle's "freedom of movement" was "bound up with an exhilarating feeling of confidence" and "a sense of expanded possibilities, aspirations."[8]

A desire for enlarged opportunities can similarly be identified in Edith Wilson's experiences as first lady. Foreshadowing the power that later would be ascribed to her and broadening the first lady role, she was the first to stand behind her husband as he took the oath of office, the first to sit next to the chief justice during the president's inaugural address, and the first to travel abroad with the president.[9] She also engaged in nontraditional tasks and had an unusual presence in vital meetings; she was tasked by President Wilson to serve as a cryptologist during the war, and she sat in on conferences with advisers, undoubtedly to their displeasure.[10] When President Wilson delivered the covenant charter of the League of Nations to an all-male peace conference at the Quai D'Orsay, the first lady cleverly negotiated permission to attend; A. Scott Berg states that Prime Minister Georges Clemenceau of France granted this request with the condition that she remain hidden behind a curtain so that "the wives of other delegates would not pester" him for similar considerations.[11] No feminist, Edith likely remained unaware of the value of these activities beyond their personal import, but Barbara Klaczynska suggested that her "modeling of later first lady activities . . . [was] significant."[12]

In the months following President Wilson's devastating stroke in October 1919, the independence and authority the first lady exhibited while acting as "steward" of his health caused considerable controversy that lingers today.[13] At the time, Senator Albert Fall from New Mexico famously declaimed, "We have a petticoat government!"[14] Although scholars have largely provided more tempered assessments, many continue to believe Edith exercised meaningful influence. August Heckscher posited, "A major share in the governance of the country fell to this woman."[15] In a circumspect observation, Gregg Phifer maintained that her "selection, timing, and manner of presentation of issues . . . inevitably influenced presidential choices."[16] Others have viewed her power as much more limited; Judith Weaver, for example, argued that she merely "either rubber stamped suggestions by Cabinet members or ignored their requests."[17] Few doubt, however, that her interpersonal sway transformed "the dynamics of Woodrow Wilson's presidency," and James McCallops further asserted that "old friends and key advisors were pushed out of favor and replaced by Edith, although she denied any influence over her husband."[18] Perhaps the greatest evidence of her perceived influence might be gleaned from the structural change her actions as first lady prompted. Although it took some decades, the specter of the power she might have wielded in place of her disabled husband, combined with the assassination of President John F. Kennedy, served as impetus for the creation of the twenty-fifth amendment, which provides for a succession process in the face of a president's death, resignation, or inability to serve.

Such power has rarely been imputed to a first lady; Edith, indeed, embodied in her actions the agency suffragists promoted for all women through the nineteenth amendment. Even so, she was not a vigorous champion of expanding the scope of possibilities for others of her gender. She evinced an active hostility toward some suffragists and did not publicly advocate for women's suffrage until after the equivocating President Wilson sought a federal amendment for the cause. As a lost heir to a planter aristocracy, it is perhaps unsurprising that she failed to be a swift friend to a movement that grew out of abolitionist efforts. That the suffrage movement had its roots in abolition, with, as Marjorie Spruill Wheeler stated, its attendant "belief in . . . equality" and "disregard for vital social distinctions" rendered it anathema to those who sought to protect the postbellum South from the "'ravages' of Northern culture."[19] Of course, those roots did not prevent the movement itself from becoming increasingly racist in the late nineteenth century, in line with Jim Crow legislation, which had disenfranchised so many Southern Black men by the 1890s.

Edith's perspective on race relations evinces both a propensity to whitewash the institution of slavery common to her time and a paternalistic perspective on African Americans that speaks to her upbringing as a descendant of a Virginia planter family. Indeed, the unreflective, bigoted comments she unself-consciously shared in her memoir and her lifelong efforts to preserve the memory of General Lee, whom Gary Gallagher identified as "the preeminent Lost Cause hero," exemplified her stance.[20] Both progressive in some senses and conservative in others, Edith was an enigmatic and, as Arthur Link averred, "indomitable" first lady whose negotiation of complex personal and political challenges both inside and outside the White House warrants closer examination.[21]

## SOUTHERN ROOTS AND THE LOST CAUSE

One of eleven children, Edith Bolling was born in Wytheville, Virginia, on October 15, 1872, to Sallie Spiers White Bolling (1843–1925) and William Holcombe Bolling (1837–1899), a descendant of the Powhatan princess Pocahontas. The Bolling family, members of the Virginia planter class, deeply valued their Southern roots long before the shadow of Civil War stoked tensions between the North and South.[22] Her family members' attachment to a distinctly Southern way of life persisted subsequent to the Civil War while their feelings toward the North hardened. Born during the turbulent Reconstruction era, Edith was regaled with romanticized stories of the Old South as she grew up, cultivating, as Phyllis Lee Levin wrote, "her allegiance with tales of antebellum glory and of devastation during the Civil War."[23] There is little doubt her Southern roots made an indelible mark, as her later commemorative efforts show. Levin aptly called her "supremely Virginian" and "a southerner by birth, tradition, loyalty, and ancestry."[24]

After emancipation, the Bollings eventually lost the ability to maintain their Bedford County plantation. Knowledge of their financial and social privations was significant and formative for Edith Bolling Wilson. Indeed, she commenced her 1938 memoir by elaborating upon her father's account of the plantation's dismantling, illuminating her family's dire economic conditions subsequent to the war and their resentment of the North. She recalled that her father advised the formerly enslaved members of his plantation that they were free and would now "have to work to provide for [them]selves;" however, some "stayed on after emancipation and looked to him to provide for them just as before. . . . The poor things could not comprehend and stood silent." Given the destruction of the war, the Bollings had scarce supplies. William Bolling was compelled to travel to Lynchburg and ask "for food for 'the wards of the nation'" from officers of the federal government. Edith pointed out that the Union soldiers had taken all their horses, so her father was reduced to hitching a mule to his wagon for the trip. When he returned with food, "there was great rejoicing in the [formerly enslaved people's] cabins," she stated, "but neither my grandmother nor my mother nor my aunt would touch it"; not even the postwar delicacy of coffee "would tempt these unreconstructed ladies, who said that Yankee coffee would choke them."[25]

Gallagher's proclamation that "White Southerners emerged from the Civil War thoroughly beaten but largely unrepentant" finds form and meaning in this family narrative.[26] Edith's recollection and her memory of a formerly enslaved person who begged to remain with the Bollings—a request "hard to refuse" but refused nonetheless—show how she idealized and gravely distorted life under bondage by presenting it as a form of pleasant relations between kindly owners who "provided for" the people they enslaved.[27] Her remarks denied the barbaric and oppressive force of slavery, her family of origin's complicity in perpetuating it, and the fact that the enslaved workers' labor actually "provided for" the Bollings.

Edith rounded out this sobering opening narrative by advising her memoir readers that enthusiasm for the Confederacy fostered the relationship between her Aunt Mary Jefferson Bolling and her Uncle Rudolf Tuesler. She stated, "The fact that he espoused the Confederate cause appealed to her, for she was a Rebel, as we were called, to the end of her life. This, and his suffering for the cause, made a romantic combination she was unable to resist."[28] Considering her vastly provocative life, it is interesting that Edith elected to convey these particular stories to commence her memoir. In so doing, she demonstrated her personal embrace of the Lost Cause ideology as she affirmed her family's solidarity with the Confederacy and the Old South. In the picture Edith paints, the women in her family most vigorously championed these perspectives. Karen Cox agreed in her pivotal study: not only were white women the "first southerners to engage in activities with the Lost Cause" but also they "founded the Confederate tradition," taking on positions of leadership in "commemorating and preserving the southern past" as they wished to perceive it.[29]

The ideology of the *Lost Cause*—a term bestowed by Edward Pollard in 1866—was a form of revisionist history that worked to restore the self-perception of white Southerners and maintain white supremacy in the midst of overwhelming defeat.[30] This belief was grounded, as Cox noted, in an inevitable but always "benevolent" portrayal of racialized socioeconomic hierarchy.[31] Sidestepping slavery as the impetus of the Civil War and instead positing it as a conflict of states' rights—and of Northern intrusion—the war was framed as an unjust imposition on the Southern way of life, and its leaders and fallen were cast as sacred heroes. This ideology was spread throughout the South during the years Edith Bolling came of age through all manner of popular and intellectual culture, including literature, artwork, textbooks, oratory, flags, and Confederate organizations, monuments, and activities.[32]

Edith imbibed the Lost Cause ideology with relish. As the story that began this chapter indicates, she displayed great enthusiasm in traveling to Richmond when she was seventeen to witness the unveiling of the statue of Lee. More than three decades later, in 1924, she affirmed her commitment to the preservation of Confederate memory when changes were proposed to the Robert E. Lee Chapel on the campus of Washington and Lee University in Lexington, Virginia. General Lee had been appointed president of what was then named Washington College from 1865 until his death in 1870. During his tenure, he oversaw the design and construction of a chapel that also housed his office. Lee, his wife, parents, and seven children were subsequently entombed beneath the chapel. Pamela Simpson advised that this chapel became known as the "Shrine of the South."[33]

When university president Henry Louis Smith proposed plans in the early 1920s to demolish and replace the building because of its limited space and poor construction, a furor ensued.[34] Edith and Woodrow Wilson contributed to the cacophony of Southern voices opposing the renovations as a "desecration" in a published letter to Smith.[35] Although both sides of the Lee Chapel controversy viewed Lee's memory as hallowed, they ardently disagreed on which specific objects and edifices best represented and preserved that memory.[36] The Wilsons were both listed as the signatories on the typed protest to Smith, but other evidence, including a handwritten note, suggests Edith Wilson's authorship of the letter.[37] Smith's response also indicates that he saw the former first lady as influencing its content and tone, referring to "loyal and impulsive womanhood" as behind the missive.[38] Smith's characterization of Edith and her allies in the local Mary Custis Lee Chapter of the United Daughters of the Confederacy was part of a larger rhetorical strategy the university aimed at the women's campaign. Simpson argued that the potency of this "subversive" and "willful" group of women took the university by surprise, yet their efforts could not be described as feminist: "What they defended was not their right to challenge authority but instead the conservative position we have come to know as the Lost Cause."[39] As someone who enjoyed influencing her social world and who was committed to the Old South, Edith undoubtedly took pride in participating in this successful campaign.[40]

Edith Wilson's devotion to Lee drew other Virginia clubs and associations to enlist her assistance and her fervor in maintaining the Confederate general's memory. In 1930, she sent a note to the Garden Club of Virginia, whose members were preserving the gardens at Lee's birthplace in Stratford. Her words again failed to register Lee's divisive role in US history, and she assumed, just as she did forty years earlier, a universal Southern stance on the general: "I think not only we Virginians but all the South are eager to honour our great leader in any possible way."[41] In August 1932, Edith kicked off the Greenbrier Resort's first Lee Week celebration, designed to promote the resort's historical legacy as the "Saratoga of the South," complete with "Old South balls" and Confederate imagery; Lee Week continued annually until World War II. After the war, the former first lady's dedication to the general continued to be affirmed, when Edward C. VanDeventer, president of the Alexandria Association of Virginia, sent her an eight-page, single-spaced speech on Lee for her perusal.[42] Delivered to the association on Lee's birthday in 1948, the speech contended that Lee believed

Edith Wilson at the opening of the President's Cottage Museum at the Greenbrier, August 22, 1932. She is standing with the president of the United Daughters of the Confederacy, Amanda Austin Byrne (Byrne is at Wilson's left, slightly in front of her), and a number of other members of the UDC. The man standing behind Wilson is Henry Waters Taft, the brother of President Taft, who with her served as a dignitary at the dedication ceremony for the museum. Courtesy of the Greenbrier Resort, White Sulphur Springs, West Virginia, and the Woodrow Wilson Presidential Library. Photo Identifier WWPL0743.

"he could have won Gettysburg if Stonewall Jackson had been with him."[43] As this correspondence attests, Edith Wilson—who had not even been alive under slavery—was invested in all manner of preservation of Confederate memory, particularly as it related to Lee.

## EARLY YEARS

Although the Lost Cause ideology helped ease the psychological discomfort of the Civil War for white Southerners in the midst of their defeat by affirming their pride and maintaining white supremacy, it did little to ameliorate their material conditions subsequent to the war. Thus, in the midst of far-reaching economic and social adjustments common to the postbellum South, Edith's paternal grandmother, Anne Wigginton Bolling, sold their Rose Cottage Plantation in 1873.[44] Baby Edith's parents, siblings, both grandmothers, two paternal aunts, and other members of the extended family all made their home in a crumbling brick commercial building in Wytheville, once used as a Confederate hospital, purchased by her father and grandmother in 1860.[45] After it was fixed up and cleaned, her large family occupied the second floor of the building, and the first floor housed three storefronts that provided rental income.

Cox argued that although many white Southern women devoted themselves to disseminating the Lost Cause ideology, white Southern men "were more committed to their own business and political success than to the success of the Confederate tradition."[46] The Bolling family followed this tradition when her father, William Bolling, a graduate of the University of Virginia, joined his uncle, General William Terry, former first lieutenant of the Wythe Grays and commander of the Stonewall Brigade, in his law practice in Wytheville. Edith claimed in her memoir that her father had saved his uncle from impending Union capture during the war. However, she glossed over the fact that an African American driver—to whom she unashamedly referred to as "the old darky driver"—was central to the commander's rescue because the driver expertly steered the old carriage while the cavalrymen were in hot pursuit.[47] Bolling would eventually become circuit court judge of Pulaski and Wythe Counties, and General Terry was twice elected to the US House of Representatives, joining other Confederate officers elected or appointed to high positions subsequent to the war.

As a young girl, Edith was selected from among her siblings to become the primary caregiver for her bedridden paternal grandmother, who had suffered a spinal cord injury after falling from a horse in her youth. The girl was responsible for handling all of her grandmother's physical needs in addition to tending to her extensive collection of canaries. She stated, "I used to make a game of counting the times she would call me to wait on her, and sometimes it was thirty-nine or forty in a night."[48] In return, her grandmother provided Edith her first, informal education, reading to her from the bible and teaching her to read, write, knit, sew, embroider, and crochet; her father, meanwhile, took responsibility for teaching her arithmetic. She also gained exposure to the classics, such as Shakespeare and Dickens, when her father read to the family.[49] In Edith's description of her grandmother's mercurial temperament, one can see ominous echoes of the future first lady's interpersonal proclivities, particularly with President Wilson's advisers, as she remembered, "She simply did, or did not, like you . . . no compromise."[50]

Although Edith Bolling's sisters engaged formal learning outside the home, she continued her home studies with her grandmother.[51] Her parents allowed this arrangement to continue until she was fifteen, at which time she enrolled in Martha Washington College in Abingdon, Virginia, with the aim of studying music. Opening its doors in 1860, the school offered an education that Levin called "positively visionary."[52] However, unused to an exacting schedule, Edith did not adjust well. She would not return, ostensibly because of illness. Subsequently, she stayed almost a year at Powell's School in Richmond until the beloved headmaster, Mr. Powell, was injured in a streetcar accident, closing the school. At a time when women's education was neither valued nor prioritized, and with three brothers requiring instruction, her own education was considered complete after a mere two years of formal schooling.[53]

## COURTSHIP AND MARRIAGE

Blossoming into womanhood, Edith attracted the attention of many suitors, the first of which was a nearly forty-year-old Northerner who initially claimed an interest in her older sister. Edith, only fifteen, recognized that she was "on the threshold of my first serious love affair." However, at such a tender age, she was not capable of fully comprehending, as this older man clearly did, the nature of his designs on her, even as they shared romantic late-night dates in the mountains.[54] Considering her family's feelings toward the North, such a marital arrangement was likely predestined to fail.

Edith evinced a similar naiveté in her initial meetings with the man who would become her first husband. She met Norman Galt, a native of Washington, DC, through Gertrude and Alexander Galt, her sister and brother-in-law, with whom she stayed for several months. The cousin of Alexander, Norman was an eligible bachelor—from a region likely more palatable to her—in the jewelry and silversmithing business. At first, Edith claimed, "It did not occur to me that Norman Galt's frequent visits were in any way due to his interest in me." However, eventually they began courting, and she agreed to marry Galt in 1896. Although it is impossible to know the true nature of their bond, her recollection of the circumstances surrounding their nuptials suggests that theirs might have been a relation of friendship and financial stability: "We were the best of friends, and I liked him immensely, but did not want to marry anyone. However, his patience and persistence overcame me."[55] Although Edith initially expressed an interest in not marrying, a progressive stance at the time, it would have been difficult for her to resist the offer considering contemporary gender conventions and the financial hardships the Bolling family faced. She fashioned Galt in her memoir as a kindly man who was attentive to her needs, but it is notable that she painted her relational life prior to Woodrow Wilson as bleak in her early courtship letters to him.[56] Some biographers, like Kristie Miller, have suggested the marriage was pleasant but "loveless."[57] Sadly, their only child died within days of his premature birth.[58]

After twelve years of marriage, Norman Galt passed away on January 28, 1908, with Edith identified in his will, as noted in the *Washington Herald*, as his sole devisee, legatee, and executrix.[59] Although she could have immediately relieved herself of the responsibilities of Galt & Bro. Jewelers by selling it outright, Edith decided to make Henry Christian Bergheimer, a long-term employee, manager of the daily operations, and she sought additional input from her lawyer, Nathaniel Wilson, in keeping the business going until it was more profitable to sell.[60] Through their combined efforts and her prudent management of her personal finances, she managed to live a life of relative comfort, underscoring her independence after becoming a widow.

That Edith lived a life of some means and pleasure subsequent to the death of her first husband can be gleaned from the long sojourns she made to Europe with family and friends. Writing from Salzburg, Austria, she and her sister Bertha told of their trip to Bozen via the Brenner Pass: "We went for a delightful drive . . . and the driver we had was the best looking fellow—tall and dark with glorious eyes and a perfect mop of curly hair"; they enthusiastically enlisted his services for the next day because he "promised to yodel for us when we get up in the mountain."[61] Edith made two such additional trips with Alice Gertrude (Altrude) Gordon, the daughter of a friend, James Gordon. Prior to his death from cancer, James Gordon had asked Edith to look after his motherless daughter.[62] Although she and Altrude barely knew each other, they embarked on their first five-month tour of Europe in 1911. It is interesting to note that although scholars often emphasize her lack of education, when Edith wrote to her sister Bertha about her adventures abroad with Altrude, she communicated her pleasure in reading: "Altrude and I go way out on the bow and take our rugs and read aloud."[63] The relationship the women forged would eventually lead Edith Bolling Galt to Woodrow Wilson, when her friend began dating, and eventually married, Cary Grayson, the president's personal doctor.

Learning from Altrude Gordon that Edith Galt was fond of long walks, Grayson suggested that she spend time with President Wilson's cousin, Helen Woodrow Bones, who was living at the White House. Grayson had advised walking to Bones to aid her poor health because she had had limited exercise while tending to the needs of the late Ellen Axson Wilson, the president's first wife. After one such walk in March 1915, Helen Bones invited Edith Galt to the White House for tea. She initially declined, indicating that her footwear was not appropriate for such an occasion, but she consented when Bones advised her that no one would be there. Much to Edith's surprise, however, the pair ran directly into Grayson and President Wilson upon their return from a golf outing, and the four agreed to gather for refreshments.[64] Berg argued, "Dr. Grayson had clearly arranged the 'chance encounter'"; indeed, the president had noticed, and remarked upon, Edith's beauty during a chance sighting on the streets of Washington, DC, while out on a drive with Grayson.[65] Betty Boyd Caroli advised that there was an "immediate attraction" between President Wilson and the widow, who "combined a good measure of exuberant independence with sufficient amounts of subservience that . . . Wilson found essential in all women."[66]

This tea commenced a rapidly progressing romance. Although the president was highly educated, having earned a doctorate in history and political science from John Hopkins University, he assured Edith that this disparity in their backgrounds would not be an issue because he was not interested in a "bluestocking."[67] They also shared in common their Southern heritage. That Woodrow was born and raised within the traditions of the South and had an understanding of the ravages of, and hardships after, the Civil War, likely appealed to Edith. For his part, he was thoroughly taken with her. In a letter dated May 5, 1915, he wrote, "God had indeed been good to me to bring such a creature as you into my life. Every glimpse I am permitted to get of the secret depths of you I find them deeper and purer and more beautiful than I knew or had dreamed of."[68]

Edith declined his first marriage proposal on May 4, which she deemed too soon to be suitable after Ellen Wilson's death on August 6, 1914. However, she accepted his subsequent proposal, and their engagement was announced on October 6, 1915, despite the disapproval of his advisers, who thought news of the swift remarriage would be a liability in the coming reelection year. John Roberts pointed out, "If President Wilson's staff had had their way, he would never have married Edith Bolling Galt."[69] But the public was intrigued with the president's new paramour, as one magazine attested: "Nothing since the news that Fort Sumter had been fired on has attracted so much attention in Washington society as the romance of the President and Mrs. Galt. Everywhere it is the absorbing topic of conversation."[70] The couple was wed in a small ceremony in her Dupont Circle townhome on December 18, 1915, in the company of family.

## EDITH WILSON'S WHITE HOUSE

Edith Wilson was popular with the public during her early years as first lady; William Eaton and Harry Read referred to her as "a great favorite."[71] Perhaps her presence even helped President Wilson's reelection the next year, when he ran on the slogan "He Kept Us Out of War." In spite of Woodrow Wilson's personal advocacy of peace, however, the United States was compelled to enter World War I on April 6, 1917. The first lady's actions in support of the war effort further assisted her public image. In July 1917, the *New York Times* reported that she was displaying in the White House dining room window her Food Administration card, pledging to engage in food conservation efforts.[72] She observed "meatless Mondays" and "wheatless Wednesdays"; setting aside her fondness for driving, the Wilsons observed "gasless Sundays" as well.[73]

The first lady supported the war effort in other ways. Amy Slagell and Susan Zaeske noted that Wilson wrote an open missive with Anna Howard Shaw in the *New York Times* entreating mothers of the entente to urge their sons and daughters to resist the moral corruption that attends war.[74] In addition to promoting the sexual health of the Allied nations, she joined celebrities Charlie Chaplin and Mary Pickford in promoting war bonds, and she volunteered with the Red Cross as the honorary chair of the DC branch of its Women's Volunteer Aid Committee.[75] The National Superintendent of Surgical Dressings of the Red Cross stated that Edith, dismissing any special treatment, "was willing to do menial tasks, and washed dishes and carried heavy coffee urns with apparent enjoyment."[76] Finally, ostensibly to avoid imposing on a limited workforce, she arranged for sheep to graze the White House lawn—a move that ultimately served to "keep away visitors"[77] during her husband's later illness and whose elimination by Florence Harding was met with "jubilation."[78] Nonetheless, it is notable that the sale of the sheep's wool raised nearly $100,000 for the Red Cross.[79]

While war raged abroad, women's struggle to achieve the vote was ablaze at home. President Wilson's reputation for being a strong leader in his party with an ability to mobilize legislation, Belinda Stillion Southward has contended, led National Woman's Party (NWP) leaders Alice Paul and Lucy Burns to seek his support for suffrage.[80] After repeated meetings with him between 1913 and 1916 resulted in no meaningful movement on a federal woman suffrage amendment, however, the NWP determined that "Wilson's willingness to listen functioned as a substitute for political action."[81] The NWP was right to question his motives; his opposition to, and equivocation on, women's suffrage has been well documented.[82] President Wilson eventually supported suffrage on the state level, but Klaczynska noted that his stance simply served to "justify his opposition" to a federal amendment by positioning it "as a states' rights issue."[83] Consequently, the NWP adopted more insistent tactics, including picketing in front of the White House from January 1917 to June 1919. Arrested on specious charges of impeding foot traffic, the picketers were imprisoned at the Occoquan Workhouse, where the conditions were deplorable.[84] As the struggle persisted, sentences became longer, and the women resorted to hunger strikes to bring attention to their plight.[85] On November 10, 1917, thirty-three suffragists were arrested on what has been termed the Night of Terror; police beat the incarcerated suffragists mercilessly.[86] Two weeks later the women would be released, and their imprisonment would subsequently be deemed unconstitutional.[87]

Edith's ability to connect her personal desire for expanded opportunities with the NWP's collective struggle to broaden women's sociopolitical role was initially unclear, as she remained publicly silent during the NWP's highly visible protests and their disturbing incarcerations. She later made her feelings transparent in her memoir. Capitalizing on the Russian Republic's enfranchisement of women, the NWP had displayed a banner outside the White House highlighting the hypocrisy of the United States and its leader in June 1917, and the former first lady was still seething two decades later.[88] The visiting Russian delegation had to pass picketers holding a banner stating that President Wilson was deceiving the Russians. A country that denied women the right to vote was no democracy and did not deserve "free" Russia as an ally, the suffragists declared. "I was indignant, but apparently no less so than a crowd of onlookers who tore the picketers' banner down," Edith recalled.[89] Additionally, when the president and she were returning from Elizabeth Harding's wedding, the first lady justified the activists' incarceration as she did the aggression they endured, invoking what was then considered a pejorative term for them: "The Suffragettes displayed a banner so outrageous that the police arrested them."[90] Karlyn Kohrs Campbell reminded us that, during this period in the United States, "only their opponents called them 'suffragettes,' . . . whereas in Great Britain, the radical wing of the movement . . . adopted this epithet as their own."[91] When President Wilson granted a pardon to sixteen incarcerated suffragists on July 19, 1917,[92] Edith still would not lend her compassion, believing that granting reprieve to "'those devils in the work house' was a 'mistake.'"[93] Moreover, she revealed that she was furious that Collector Dudley Field Malone of the Port of New York "defended these women."[94] She saw Malone's resignation to serve as the suffragists' lawyer as such an offense that Edith became enraged when she learned that Wilson's secretary, Joseph Tumulty, had socialized with Malone in a theater subsequent to his departure.[95]

Thus, despite her drive and capacity to expand her own role in life, biographers of Edith, including Hatch, Levin, Klaczynska, and Miller, agreed that she was opposed to women's suffrage. However, at the time, as Klaczynska noted, the public incorrectly assumed the first lady was in support of the cause. Earlier, when their engagement was announced, Woodrow Wilson had endorsed an unsuccessful New Jersey suffrage effort, and Edith was incorrectly identified as the impetus for this stance. However, suffragists remained attuned to her real position: "Activists . . . were not fooled by Edith's reputation as a supporter and, understanding the couple's joint opposition, taunted them for it."[96] Caroli provided a particularly pointed perspective on this issue, comparing the first lady's stance during the suffrage effort with her actions during President Wilson's disability: "In neither case did she express the slightest interest in . . . setting an example for strong and independent women. In both instances, her concern centered on how the issue affected her husband's well-being," which of course, was also vital for her own.[97]

That Edith was concerned with her husband's well-being and, by extension, his public image, was certain; she went to great lengths to ensure his positive image in life as well as death. She and her brother Randolph Bolling, who served as her secretary, reached out repeatedly to Senator Carter Glass of Virginia to enlist his assistance in preventing other entities from trademarking the president's portrait, name, and signature after his passing.[98] Similarly, when a public high school in New York erected a portrait of him, Edith called it the "very worst likeness" she "had ever seen" and tried to get the portrait replaced.[99] She similarly disliked the portrait of him showcased in the White House and worked assiduously to get it replaced with a portrait by Frank Graham Cootes, who learned later that his only remuneration would be the honor of having his painting displayed in the Executive Mansion. Edith then failed to include the artist's name on the accompanying plaque.[100] These incidents symbolize how the former first lady was painstakingly focused when considering the quality of President Wilson's public image but was not similarly attuned to the needs and reputations of others.

Edith Wilson's dedication to her husband's public image and her Southern heritage undoubtedly influenced her reaction to the suffragists as well. As Hatch asserted, "What really made her frothing mad was the[ir] 'unladylike' conduct," which worked in opposition to her Southern rearing, where "women traditionally deferred to men and gained their purpose in subtly managing them."[101] Edith might have embraced subtlety to secure her way throughout her life, but her temper also is well documented; Klaczynska noted the president appreciated her "fury . . . on his behalf."[102] That she privately transgressed some norms of Southern femininity did not mean she was comfortable with such public violations by others, however, particularly when they opposed her husband. Edith thus found the NWP's radical actions offensive; counter to Southern expectations for femininity; and, most importantly, disrespectful to her husband, to whom she was doggedly loyal.[103]

Wheeler argued that the "South was distinctive—indeed notorious . . . as the region that afforded the movement the greatest resistance and the least success."[104] Opposition to women's suffrage was intricately intertwined with the Lost Cause because the "Southern lady" was cast as the "guardian and symbol of Southern virtue."[105] Her "indirect influence" was a sign "of the superior morality of Southern society" for those whites who subscribed to this notion;

the "ideal Southern woman relied upon chivalrous Southern men to represent her interests in the outside world," a role particularly important given Southern males' tenuous positioning subsequent to the war.[106] That the women's suffrage movement had roots in abolition was of course another of its drawbacks from the perspective of some white people.[107] Given the strength of the Lost Cause ideology, it is not surprising that Southern women such as Wilson did not take up the mantle of women's suffrage, or, if they did, commonly promoted it as a method to maintain white supremacy (as did some of their Northern counterparts).

After political pressure commanded it, President Wilson eventually placed his support behind the federal women's suffrage amendment and urged ratification by the states. The Wilsons' home state of Virginia subsequently voted against ratification on February 12, 1920, and did not support the amendment until 1952. However, the state's vote was not needed. Ratification was completed on August 18, 1920, with Tennessee's Harry T. Burn casting the controversial tie-breaking vote after some urging from his mother, who advised him: "Hurrah and vote for suffrage!"[108] Despite the enormity of this political victory as well as its meaning for the broader culture and the women who labored for the cause, President Wilson did not mark the occasion with ceremony.[109] All the same, Secretary of State Bainbridge Colby sent Edith a memento of the historic occasion—one of the pens he used in signing the certificate of ratification of the Nineteenth Amendment.[110] When she was able to do so, and despite all her disparagement of the movement, she exercised her right to vote.[111]

President Wilson was responsible for managing significant social change at home, but he also chose to take a major role in negotiating the terms of peace abroad. Despite meaningful opposition, he made the unusual step of traveling to Europe himself with top advisers, from December 1918 to February 1919 and from March to June 1919, to participate in the negotiation of the Treaty of Versailles and to advance his own vision for peace. Left out of the deliberations were key Republicans, a move that later would undercut his efforts to gain approval in the US Senate for the treaty and the League of Nations.[112] After the Paris Peace Conference began in January 1919, it would be marked by protracted discussions and draining days.

When the Wilsons returned home in late February 1919, Woodrow Wilson had been away, as Berg stated, "longer than any President in history."[113] He was immediately confronted with the hardships that faced the postwar United States and harsh criticism from those who viewed his trip abroad as abandonment of the American people, especially because he had refused to include a broad base of political representation in his Paris contingent. Not surprisingly, when President Wilson revealed his plan for the League of Nations, he met strong resistance from Henry Cabot Lodge and other Republicans in the Senate. Returning to

Paris in March 1919, he faced additional pressure because "Colonel" Edward Mandell House, his trusted adviser, had made compromises at the conference, undermining, in President Wilson's mind, his plan to achieve enduring peace and leaving him furious.[114] House had already become a target of the first lady's hostility, and this enabled her to undercut his influence. The long and pressure-filled hours, mercurial tempers, and lack of physical exercise took their toll. On April 3, 1919, Woodrow became very ill. Grayson advised the public that the president had influenza, but it appears that he had suffered a viral infection *and* a small stroke, portending future difficulties.[115] It would not be the last time Grayson would deceive the public, with Edith's ready agreement.

After Germany signed the Treaty of Versailles, President Wilson felt he must convince the US public to accept the treaty and the League of Nations, if the Republicans in the Senate would not. He embarked on a speaking tour of the United States in September 1919. McCallops maintained that Wilson, already weakened, "pushed himself mercilessly by delivering thirty-two speeches in twenty-two days."[116] Exhausted and stricken with illness and pain, he collapsed. The first lady and Grayson compelled him to abandon his tour, and they returned to Washington, DC, hoping that rest would allow him to recover his health. In spite of their efforts, Woodrow suffered a shattering stroke on October 2, 1919, that would effectively render him incapacitated for months and from which he would never fully recover.[117]

Although the president was now clearly disabled, the first lady, along with Grayson and Tumulty, worked to conceal the depths of his illness from the public. When, a few days after his stroke, Secretary of State Robert Lansing approached Grayson and Tumulty with the prospect of certifying his disability, they refused. As Berg stated, "And so began the greatest conspiracy that ever engulfed the White House."[118] The president was not able to sit up in his wheelchair until November 17, 1919, and was unable to attend cabinet meetings until April 14, 1920.

In the intervening months, Edith became "de facto the President."[119] Heckscher noted, "A major share in the governance of the country fell to this woman of strong natural intelligence (but with no more than two years of formal schooling); of prejudices and preferences deeply rooted in her nature; and, not least, of passionate devotion to her husband."[120] First ladies have long wielded meaningful influence, despite societal pressure to limit their role and their own strategic striving to dismiss such allegations. Although this first lady had no discernible commitment to politics, she was interested in all manner of relational attachments regarding her husband.[121] Echoing her Southern grandmother's approach to relationships, Edith formed strong and inflexible opinions regarding those closest to President Wilson. This feature of her personality had meaningful consequences for the nation when the president fell gravely ill.

At that time Edith's interpersonal jealousies and penchant toward grudges became more problematic, especially because, as Weaver pointed out, "Woodrow Wilson's . . . tendency to idealize the women in his life made him peculiarly receptive to his wife's entreaties."[122] President Wilson had worked closely with House and Tumulty, but they both had made the political miscalculation of interfering with the Wilsons' early relationship.[123] Edith would always remember their efforts to impede the progress of her relationship with the president as she worked to chip away at their influence. Although she was compelled to work with Tumulty, particularly upon President Wilson's disability, she had long believed him "common," and the fact that he admired the president's first wife had only further worsened her opinion of him.[124] Because Edith wanted to be the person who held the most sway in her husband's life, she also was not fond of the strong influence of House, who made the unfortunate recommendation that she leave political affairs to him and President Wilson; as Weaver wrote, "Edith did not swallow this advice easily. She in fact loved working with Wilson."[125] House was a skilled statesman who made few enemies, but the first lady was chief among them, and she assiduously urged her husband to view him with the skepticism she possessed.

Although Tumulty and House were the most obvious targets of her interpersonal aggression, few escaped her withering gaze. After Lansing approached Tumulty and Grayson with questions as to whether to declare the president disabled in light of his devastating stroke, Edith considered him a traitor. Subsequently, President Wilson requested, and received, Lansing's resignation, ostensibly because the secretary of state had held unauthorized cabinet meetings during the president's incapacitation; however, other members of those meetings remained unscathed.[126] When Sir Edward Grey came to the United States to aid President Wilson in resolving the US political conflict over the League of Nations, he waited in vain for months to speak to the president. It is believed the first lady would not let Grey visit Woodrow while he was incapacitated because she found offense with his refusal to send home a British army officer, Major Charles Kennedy Craufurd-Stuart, who had previously "expressed a vulgar dislike" for her.[127] Klaczynska noted that a bawdy joke made at Edith's expense made Craufurd-Stuart the subject of her ire.[128]

There are varying perspectives on the first lady's power at the time, but most agree that her actions, combined with subsequent events, cultivated support later for the implementation of a succession process in the event of a president's disability or death. Diminishing her own role, however, Edith famously stated,

"The only decision that was mine was what was important and what was not, and the *very* important decision of when to present matters to my husband."[129] Yet Heckscher reminded us that "her power, derived from determining what issues would come before her husband and what visitors would be admitted to the sickroom, was obviously very great."[130] Although the government kept functioning, for all intents and purposes, it was not functioning well—and sometimes not at all. Through time, the first lady had isolated President Wilson from his top advisers, and with his disability, this practice of hers was exacerbated. In the absence of President Wilson's leadership, US-Mexican relations deteriorated, Attorney General Mitchell Palmer and his agents engaged in civil liberty violations in their zealous repression of communist radicals, appointments were not made, and even negotiations to further the president's beloved League of Nations faltered.[131] Edith's decision to shield him from hearing alternative perspectives, combined with Woodrow's own unwillingness to compromise on the issue, set the stage for the Senate's failure to ratify the Treaty of Versailles. The United States would never join the League of Nations.[132]

Despite his limitations, President Wilson had considered a third term. However, this prospect was not well received by his advisers or the larger Democratic establishment. Upon completion of his second term, the Wilsons moved to a house on S Street in Washington, DC, where he passed away just three short years later, in 1924; the former first lady bequeathed this home to the National Trust for Historic Preservation upon her death in 1961. Noting that her "desires and fears were all too human," Klaczynska asserted that Edith's "main 'cause' . . . was Woodrow."[133]

## A "SOUTHERN" NEW WOMAN

There is no doubt that Edith Wilson negotiated a challenging role at a pivotal moment in US history. She came of age during a period of substantial social and economic change in the postbellum South and spent her middle years navigating World War I, peace after the war, women's suffrage, and her husband's diminished health. Perhaps as a result of living through dizzying periods of change and transition, she both reified and subverted social convention. Edith remained committed to her Southern roots throughout her life, giving her planter origins primacy in her memoir and enthusiastically affirming the place of General Lee in Confederate history. She also engaged Southern tradition in her deep loyalty to her husband and her attention to his public image and memory. At the same time, it is clear she enjoyed exercising control over her own life as well as her husband's and charting her own course. By distancing President Wilson from the advisers pivotal to him, Edith began to exert the influence they once had. She

Edith Wilson unveiling Robert E. Lee painting, 1932. This picture was also taken at the Greenbrier Resort's inaugural Lee Week; Edith was unveiling the portrait at the Lee Monument Ball. The Resort was reviving a series of balls given back in the 1870s at White Sulphur Springs to raise money for the Lee statue on Monument Avenue. Courtesy of the Greenbrier Resort, White Sulphur Springs, West Virginia.

enjoyed freedom of movement and being free from male control except that of her husband, with whom she negotiated power. In interesting ways, Edith was a complex amalgam of the Southern and new woman—although she performed neither identity fully, she adopted each in some way.

Similarly to Sarah Polk, wife of the eleventh president, James Polk, Edith Wilson outlived her husband by nearly four decades. In the intervening years, she too pressed herself into the service of shaping her husband's legacy, maintaining the rights to his papers and possessing control of the script for the 1944 film *Wilson*. However, unlike Sarah Polk, whose personal thoughts remain a mystery— even as her identity as a white Southern widow in the late nineteenth century was pressed into service as an exemplification of the Lost Cause, as Chapter 5 notes—we have a deliberate record of Edith Wilson's perspectives in her memoir. Perhaps inspired by far-reaching efforts to shape the national memory of the antebellum South, of whose monuments and commemorative activities she wrote, Edith found value in shaping the public memory of her husband and her actions on his behalf. Although her memoir is a rhetorical re-presentation of the facts, some incorrect, it reveals to readers much more about its author, what she wanted us to know about her activities and thoughts as first lady, and the social conventions and prejudices of the time.

Unlike Sarah Polk, Edith Wilson did not fade from public life. She continued to represent her husband in public activities and was considered a potential contender in the 1928 presidential election,[134] at whose Democratic National Convention she "received marked tribute."[135] When President Franklin Delano Roosevelt issued his declaration of war to Congress, she was at Eleanor Roosevelt's side. After supporting John F. Kennedy's candidacy, she attended his inauguration, riding in his parade. When President Kennedy announced his newly founded Freedom from Hunger Foundation in November 1961, Edith was enlisted as a founding member.[136] The next month, on December 28, 1961, Edith passed away on Woodrow Wilson's birthday, the same day she had been scheduled to attend a dedication ceremony for the Woodrow Wilson Bridge.[137] To the end, she remained tirelessly committed to promoting his life and legacy. Although they both made history in their own notable ways, perhaps most striking about the pair is their loyalty to each other, a complicated loyalty forged in Southern tradition and identity; as Tumulty stated, "No public man ever had a more devoted helpmeet, and no wife a husband more dependent upon her sympathetic understanding of his problems."[138]

## NOTES

1. William Hazelgrove, *Madam President: The Secret Presidency of Edith Wilson* (Washington, DC: Regnery, 2016), xi.

2. Anne Firor Scott, *The Southern Lady: From Pedestal to Politics, 1830–1930* (Chicago: University of Chicago Press, 1970), 21.

3. Ruth Bordin, *Alice Freeman Palmer: The Evolution of a New Woman* (Ann Arbor: University of Michigan Press, 1993), 2–3.

4. Edith Bolling Wilson, *My Memoir* (1938, rpt., New York: Arno Press, 1980), 14.

5. Wilson, *My Memoir*, 14.

6. Wilson, 146.

7. Edith Bolling Wilson Birthplace Foundation and Museum, "Edith Bolling Wilson's 1904 Automobile Operator's Permit Listed on Virginia's 2017 Top 10 Endangered Artifacts," EdithBollingWilson.org, https://www.edithbollingwilson.org/news/edith-bolling-wilsons-1904-automobile-operators-permit-listed-on-virginias-2017-top-10-endangered-artifacts-list.

8. Susan Hanson, "Gender and Mobility: New Approaches for Informing Sustainability," *Gender, Place, and Culture* 17, no. 1 (2010): 6.

9. Associated Press, "Mrs. Woodrow Wilson, 89, Dies on the Birthday of Her Husband," *New York Times*, December 29, 1961, 1; Barbara Klaczynska, "Edith Wilson: The First

Lady in Charge," in *A Companion to First Ladies*, ed. Katherine A. S. Sibley (West Sussex, UK: Wiley-Blackwell, 2016), 364; Amy Slagell and Susan Zaeske, "Edith Bolling Galt Wilson: Actions Speak Louder Than Words," in *Inventing a Voice: The Rhetoric of American First Ladies of the Twentieth Century*, ed. Molly Wertheimer (Lanham, MD: Rowman and Littlefield, 2004), 113.

10. A. Scott Berg, *Wilson* (New York: Berkeley, 2013), 433; Klacynska, "Edith Wilson," 365; Gregg Phifer, "Edith Bolling Wilson: Gatekeeper Extraordinary," *Speech Monographs* 38, no. 4 (1971); 280.

11. Berg, *Wilson*, 542.

12. Klaczynska, "Edith Wilson," 377.

13. Edith Wilson famously identified herself as Woodrow Wilson's "steward." Wilson, *My Memoir*, 289.

14. Slagell and Zaeske, "Edith Bolling Galt Wilson," 103.

15. August Heckscher, *Woodrow Wilson: A Biography* (New York: Collier, 1991), 616.

16. Phifer, "Edith Bolling Wilson," 281.

17. Judith Weaver, "Edith Bolling Wilson as First Lady: A Study in the Power of Personality, 1919–1920," *Presidential Studies Quarterly* 15, no. 1 (1985): 56.

18. James McCallops, "Edith Bolling Galt Wilson: The Protective Steward," in *The Presidential Companion: Readings on the First Ladies*, ed. Robert Watson and Anthony Eksterowicz (Columbia: University of South Carolina Press, 2003), 102.

19. Marjorie Spruill Wheeler, *New Women of the New South: The Leaders of the Woman Suffrage Movement in the Southern States* (New York: Oxford University Press, 1993), 5.

20. Gary Gallagher, "Introduction," in *The Myth of the Lost Cause and Civil War History*, ed. Gary Gallagher and Alan Nolan (Bloomington: Indiana University Press, 2010), 2.

21. Arthur Link, "President's Helpmate: Edith Bolling Wilson—First Lady Extraordinary," *New York Times*, December 10, 1961.

22. See, for example, the correspondence from Archibold Bolling to Ann Bolling, December 6, 1833, Box 1, Edith Bolling Galt Wilson [EBGW] Papers, Library of Congress, Washington, DC.

23. Phyllis Lee Levin, *Edith and Woodrow: The Wilson White House* (New York: Scribner's, 2001), 58.

24. Levin, *Edith and Woodrow*, 58.

25. Wilson, *My Memoir*, 1–2.

26. Gallagher, "Introduction," 1.

27. Wilson, *My Memoir*, 2.

28. Wilson, 2.

29. Karen L. Cox, *Dixie's Daughters: The United Daughters of the Confederacy and the Preservation of Confederate Culture* (Gainesville: University Press of Florida, 2003), 2–3.

30. Edward A. Pollard, *The Lost Cause* (1866, rpt., Whitefish, MT: Kessinger, 2010).

31. Cox, *Dixie's Daughters*, 2.

32. To draw this sketch of the Lost Cause, I draw mainly upon Cox, *Dixie's Daughter's*, 1–5; Gaines M. Foster, *Ghosts of the Confederacy: Defeat, the Lost Cause and the Emergence of the New South, 1865–1913* (Oxford, UK: Oxford University Press, 1987), 4–8; Gallagher, "Introduction," 1–4.

33. Pamela H. Simpson, "The Great Lee Chapel Controversy and the 'Little Group of Willful Women' Who Saved the Shrine of the South," in *Monuments to the Lost Cause: Women, Art, and the Landscapes of Southern Memory*, ed. Cynthia Mills and Pamela H. Simpson (Knoxville: University of Tennessee Press, 2003), 85.

34. Simpson, "Great Lee Chapel Controversy," 91–92.

35. Edith and Woodrow Wilson to Henry Louis Smith, letter, December 9, 1923, Lee Chapel Papers 1923–1924, University of Virginia Library, Charlottesville, Virginia.

36. Simpson, "Great Lee Chapel Controversy," 94.

37. Edith Wilson to Mrs. Maurice Moore, letter, December 11, 1923, Lee Chapel Papers 1923–1924, University of Virginia Library, Charlottesville, Virginia.

38. Henry Louis Smith, "Dr. Smith Replies to President Wilson," *Rockbridge County News*, December 20, 1923, Lee Chapel Papers 1923–1924, University of Virginia Library, Charlottesville, Virginia.

39. Simpson, "Great Lee Chapel Controversy," 95.

40. The chapel remains controversial in present times; see "W&L Won't Move Events from Lee Chapel," https://www.insidehighered.com/news/2018/08/29/washington -and-lee-rejects-plan-move-events-out-lee-chapel.

41. Edith Wilson to Hetty Cary Harrison, letter, January 16, 1930, Box 19, EBGW Papers, Library of Congress, Washington, DC.

42. The author is very grateful to Katherine Sibley for her work in locating and tracking down information regarding the two photos included in this chapter and to Robert Conte, historian of the Greenbrier Resort, for providing these details on Lee Week; also see Edward C. VanDeventer to Edith Wilson, letter, February 12, 1948, Box 34, EBGW Papers, Library of Congress, Washington, DC.

43. *Alexandria Gazette* as quoted in William H. Nichols, untitled speech, January 19, 1948, delivered before the Alexandria Association, Alexandria, Virginia. The speech is included in VanDeventer to Wilson, February 12, 1948.

44. Levin, *Edith and Woodrow*, 524.

45. Levin, 59–60; Wilson, *My Memoir*, 1.

46. Cox, *Dixie's Daughters*, 5.

47. Wilson, *My Memoir*, 3.

48. Wilson, 10.

49. Wilson, 6, 10, 19.

50. Wilson, 5.

51. Wilson, 10.

52. Levin, *Edith and Woodrow*, 63.

53. Wilson, *My Memoir*, 13–16.

54. Wilson, 14.

55. Wilson, 17–18.

56. See Woodrow Wilson as quoted in Edwin Tribble, ed., *A President in Love: The Courtship Leters of Woodrow Wilson and Edith Bolling Galt* (Boston: Houghton Mifflin, 1981), 16.

57. Kristie Miller, *Ellen and Edith: Woodrow Wilson's First Ladies* (Lawrence: University Press of Kansas, 2010), 104, 111.

58. Miller, *Ellen and Edith*, 103–104.

59. "Notice," *Washington Herald*, February 22, 1908, 3.

60. Wilson, *My Memoir*, 22.

61. Edith Bolling Galt, with her sister Bertha Bolling, to Vi[ola] and Junebug, letter, September 4, 1910, Box 1, EBGW Papers, Library of Congress, Washington, DC.

62. Wilson, *My Memoir*, 29.

63. Edith Wilson to Bertha Bolling, letter, August 16, 1913, Box 1, EBGW Papers, Library of Congress, Washington, DC.

64. Berg, *Wilson*, 356–358.

65. Berg, 358, 355.

66. Betty Boyd Caroli, *First Ladies: From Martha Washington to Michelle Obama* (Oxford, UK: Oxford University Press, 2010), 145.

67. Klaczynska, "Edith Wilson," 360.

68. Woodrow Wilson as quoted in Tribble, *President in Love*, 11.

69. John B. Roberts II, *Rating the First Ladies* (New York: Citadel, 2003), 200.

70. "Washington Fashionable Society in Dismay," *Omaha Sunday Bee Magazine*, November 14, 1915.

71. William Dunseath Eaton and Harry C. Read, *Woodrow Wilson: His Life and Work* (C.E. Thomas, 1919), 219.

72. "Mrs. Wilson Posts Pledge: Food Card Displayed in Window of White House Dining Room," *New York Times*, July 7, 1917, 2.

73. Berg, *Wilson*, 448.

74. Slagell and Zaeske, "Edith Bolling Galt Wilson," 112–113. Although this coauthored missive was written with a suffrage figurehead, Slagell and Zaeske noted that the content "reinforced traditional ideas about women's concerns" and mirrored "Wilson's idea of appropriate womanly behavior" (113).

75. Roberts, *Rating the First Ladies*, 203.

76. "Wife Guard to President: Mrs. Wilson Thought Presence Might Foil Assassin," *New York Times*, February 18, 1920.

77. Katherine A. S. Sibley, *First Lady Florence Harding: Behind the Tragedy and Controversy* (Lawrence: University Press of Kansas, 2009), 74.

78. Katherine A. S. Sibley, "Florence Kling Harding: Celebrity and Activist," in *A Companion to First Ladies*, ed. Katherine A. S. Sibley (West Sussex, UK: Wiley-Blackwell, 2016), 385.

79. Berg, *Wilson*, 449.

80. Belinda A. Stillion Southard, *Militant Citizenship: Rhetorical Strategies of the National Woman's Party, 1913–1920* (College Station: Texas A&M University Press, 2012), 129.

81. Southard, *Militant Citizenship*, 132–133.

82. See Levin, *Edith and Woodrow*, 181–182; Klaczynska, "Edith Wilson," 365–367.

83. Klaczynska, "Edith Wilson," 366.

84. See, for example, Ellen Maury Slayden's account in Levin, *Edith and Woodrow*, 184.

85. Terence McArdle, "'Night of Terror': The Suffragists Who Were Beaten and Tortured for Seeking the Vote," *Washington Post*, November 10, 2017.

86. Julia Mickenberg, "Suffragettes and Soviets: American Feminists and the Specter of Revolutionary Russia," *Journal of American History* 100, no. 4 (March 2014): 1041.

87. McArdle, "'Night of Terror.'"

88. Southard, *Militant Citizenship*, 141–142; Sally Hunter Graham, "Woodrow Wilson, Alice Paul, and the Woman Suffrage Movement," *Political Science Quarterly* 98, no. 4 (Winter 1983–1984): 667–668.

89. Wilson, *My Memoir*, 138.

90. Elizabeth Harding was the daughter of William P. G. Harding, chair of the Federal Reserve. Wilson, *My Memoir*, 138.

91. Karlyn Korhs Campbell, *Man Cannot Speak for Her,* vol. 1: *A Critical Study of Early Feminist Rhetoric* (Westport, CT: Praeger, 1989), 3.

92. "Suffragists Weep for Joy on Pardon by Wilson," *Los Angeles Herald,* July 19, 1917.

93. Southard, *Militant Citizenship*, 145.

94. Wilson, *My Memoir*, 138.

95. Weaver, "Edith," 61.

96. Klaczynska, "Edith Wilson," 366.

97. Caroli, *First Ladies*, 150.

98. Randolph Bolling (on behalf of Edith Wilson) to Carter Glass, letter, May 7, 1924; Carter Glass to Randolph Bolling, letter, May 16, 1924; Chauncey P. Carter to John Randolph Bolling (on behalf of Edith Wilson), letter, November 5, 1942; Edith Wilson to Carter Glass, November 7, 1942; Rixey Smith to Edith Wilson, November 16, 1942; all in Box 19, EBGW Papers, Library of Congress, Washington, DC.

99. Edith Wilson/secretary to F. Graham Cootes, letters, March 4, 1936, and March 5, 1936, both in Box 12, EBGW Papers, Library of Congress, Washington, DC.

100. Edith Wilson/secretary to F. Graham Cootes, March 4, 1936; March 5, 1936; May 27, 1936; January 29, 1937; November 18, 1937; F. Graham Cootes to Edith Wilson/secretary, November 10, 1937, all in Box 12, EBGW Papers, Library of Congress, Washington, DC.

101. Alden Hatch, *Edith Bolling Wilson: First Lady Extraordinary* (New York: Dodd, Mead, 1961), 80.

102. Klacyznska, "Edith Wilson," 364.

103. Hatch, *Edith,* 79–80; Slagell and Zaeske, "Edith Bolling Galt Wilson," 108–109.

104. Wheeler, *New Women of the New South*, 4.

105. Wheeler, 4.

106. Wheeler, 7.

107. Wheeler, 5.

108. Febb Ensminger Burn to Harry T. Burn, letter, August 1920, Calvin M. McClung Historical Digital Collection, Knox County Public Library, 2, http://cmdc.knoxlib.org/cdm/ref/collection/p265301c0118/id/699.

109. Klaczynska, "Edith Wilson," 367.

110. Bainbridge Colby to Edith Wilson, February 10, 1921, Box 12, EBGW Papers, Library of Congress, Washington, DC.

111. Slagell and Zaeske, "Edith Bolling Galt Wilson," 109. Residents of the District of Columbia could not vote for president until 1964.

112. Berg, *Wilson*, 515–518.

113. Berg, 547.

114. Berg, 556; McCallops, "Edith Bolling Galt Wilson," 112–113.

115. Varying perspectives on his illness are offered by Berg, *Wilson*, 569–569; Hazelgrove, *Madam President*, 228–229; Levin, *Edith and Woodrow*, 291–292; McCallops, "Edith Bolling Galt Wilson," 114.

116. McCallops, "Edith Bolling Galt Wilson," 114–115.

117. McCallops, 115–116.

118. Berg, *Wilson*, 642–645.

119. John Dos Passos, *Mr. Wilson's War: From the Assassination of McKinley to the Defeat of the League of Nations* (New York: Doubleday, 2013), 492.

120. Heckscher, *Woodrow Wilson*, 616.

121. See, for example, Weaver, "Edith," 60, 69–70.

122. Weaver, 63.

123. See, for example, Berg, *Wilson*, 374–375; Heckscher, *Woodrow Wilson*, 354–355; Levin, *Edith and Woodrow*, 109–110, 113–115; Miller, *Ellen and Edith*, 120–122.

124. Miller, *Ellen and Edith*, 119.

125. Weaver, "Edith," 53.

126. Weaver, 64–65.

127. Phifer, "Edith Bolling Wilson," 287.

128. Klacynska, "Edith Wilson," 372.

129. Wilson, *My Memoir*, 289 (emphasis in original).

130. Heckscher, *Woodrow Wilson*, 616.

131. See, for example, Berg, *Wilson*, 670–672; Weaver, "Edith," 57–59.

132. Berg, *Wilson*, 653–655.

133. Klazcynska, "Edith Wilson," 377.

134. "Will Try to Name Mrs. Wilson to Run for Vice Presidency," *New York Times*, September 4, 1927, 1.

135. Winifred Mallon, "Women of Note Share Opening Day: An Honored Guest at the Convention," *New York Times*, June 27, 1928, 3.

136. Felix Belair Jr., "Group to Combat Hunger in the World: Kennedy Asks All to Support New Foundation," *New York Times*, November 23, 1961, 1.

137. Associated Press, "Mrs. Woodrow Wilson," 1.

138. Joseph Patrick Tumulty, *Woodrow Wilson as I Know Him* (New York: Double Day, 1921), 436.

# CHAPTER 14

# Lady Bird Johnson
## First Lady of Deeds

Nancy Kegan Smith

I am proud that I am part of the South.[1]

Each of [our] actions sprang from what nurtures us, and what
nurtured me was walking through the piney woods in my own deep
East Texas.[2]

Lady Bird Johnson did not know as she became first lady what her focus
would be because of the tragic and unexpected way in which she assumed her
role. However, she most certainly brought her strong Texas and Southern roots.
She also brought her years of experience and savvy from living her whole adult
life with Lyndon Baines Johnson (LBJ) in the political arena, when he represented Texas in Congress and then in the vice presidency. As Press Secretary
Bill Moyers said when LBJ became president, "Like her beloved flowers in the
field, she was a woman of many hues. A strong manager, a canny investor, a
shrewd judge of people." But even more striking than that, Moyers added, was
"her courage."[3]

Claudia Alta "Lady Bird" Taylor Johnson was born and raised in Texas, a
state with a long and proud tradition of strong, independent, and accomplished
women including Governors Ma Ferguson and Ann Richards; other politically
prominent women included Oveta Culp Hobby, Sarah Tilghman Hughes, Kay
Bailey Hutchison, Barbara Jordan, and Laura Bush. Along with Lady Bird, these
Texas women, as Phyllis McKenzie wrote, "have been women of courage. They
willingly shouldered responsibilities. They took actions that they did not have
to take. They stepped forward from deep convictions and held fast to belief in

Portrait of Lady Bird Johnson, White House grounds, October 20, 1967. Courtesy of the Lyndon B. Johnson Presidential Library. Serial Number C7029-18.

themselves."[4] Congresswoman Jordan helped us understand the importance of being Texan when she said: "I get from the soil and spirit of Texas the feeling that I, as an individual, can accomplish whatever I want to, and that there are no limits, that you can just keep going, just keep soaring."[5]

Together with her Texas heritage, Lady Bird brought a deep Southern legacy. She spent every summer in Alabama with her mother's relatives; both her parents were originally from there. After her mother died, she was primarily raised by her Aunt Effie Pattillo, who moved from Alabama to Texas. There is a Southern term, *steel magnolia*, that Lady Bird embodied, a combination of both her traditional femininity and her uncommon fortitude—contrasting images of hard steel and soft magnolia. If ever a woman met this definition, it was Lady Bird. Two excellent and vivid examples of the meaning of steel magnolia in Mary Beth Brown's book *Condi: The Life of a Steel Magnolia* detail how this term is construed. As a young girl in 1961, Condoleezza Rice had to confront demeaning treatment when shopping in her hometown of Birmingham, Alabama; luckily, her mother, Angelena Rice, a high school math teacher, set for her a particularly powerful example of a steel magnolia's poise and firmness in response to Jim Crow insults. When Condi Rice was told she could not use the whites-only dressing room, her mother responded calmly, "My daughter will try on this dress in a dressing room, or I am spending my money elsewhere!" The clerk reluctantly agreed. In another shopping incident, when Condi Rice touched a pretty hat and was told gruffly to get her hands off it, Angelena Rice told the clerk, "Don't talk to my daughter that way" and then instructed the girl, "Condoleezza, do touch every hat in this store."[6] Like Condi Rice's mother, Lady Bird, too, was definitely a steel magnolia and had many occasions in her life that required the contrasting qualities of hard steel conviction delivered in a soft magnolia way. This chapter examines just how much her background from the South, and particularly from Texas, influenced her and how these influences can be seen in both her approach to people and to the programs and activities she chose to highlight as first lady.

## CLAUDIA ALTA TAYLOR: GROWING UP IN TEXAS AND SUMMERING IN ALABAMA

Claudia Alta Taylor was born December 22, 1912, in Karnack, Texas, where she was also raised. Karnack is in a rural part of East Texas, near the Louisiana border, amid lakes and cypress trees. Both her parents were originally from Alabama and moved to Texas as young adults. Her father, Thomas Jefferson Taylor, did not come from a rich family and was following the thinking of the time, as his daughter told an interviewer, when he left Alabama to "go West, young man . . . [having] heard that Texas had great opportunities and lots of land, and you could make money."[7] Indeed, he became a wealthy landowner who also ran a general store; he was known as "The Boss" and declared himself a "dealer of everything." The family lived in a white antebellum home called the Brick House, originally built by enslaved workers. Taylor's employment and fair treatment of African Americans raised the ire of the Ku Klux Klan, who wrote him a note, as Lady Bird recalled: "I do not think my daddy was ever cruel. I think he was just about as just as he could be in those times and in that setting with black people."[8]

Her mother, Minnie Pattillo Taylor, came from a wealthier background than her father did. Lady Bird remembered her as "a sort of woman whom apparently many people remembered as distinctive . . . she was not one who melted into the background."[9] Lady Bird recalled that not only did her mother campaign for a local politician but also, in spite of the time and place, she had "lots of good black friends, and they believed in her. But they believed in my daddy, too; they liked him mighty well."[10] Her mother died when Claudia was five, and as a result, she was raised by her mother's unmarried sister, Effie, her nurse, and her father. She had two older brothers, Tommy and Tony, but they were off at boarding school, so she often spent her time alone.

Interestingly, the origins of her nickname, Lady Bird, tell us something about the culture of the South and the way in which the Jim Crow line could be murky. The accepted and oft-told story is that her African American nurse, Alice Tittle, called her "pretty as a Lady Bird." When asked, this was how Johnson explained the nickname she tried to kick in her youth. However, years later when reminiscing about her childhood, she told Mike Gillette, "The nickname had actually come from two black childhood playmates who themselves were nicknamed 'Stuff' and 'Doodlebug.'" As Gillette noted, "It was later deemed more respectable to assign credit to the nurse and thereby avoid the impression of interracial socialization."[11]

Johnson's memories of her early years seemed fond. From both her mother and later her aunt, she inherited a love of reading and the arts. From her father she learned independence and picked up business and financial savvy. Most of all, though, she loved being outside. She attended a one-room school in Karnack and then Marshall High School, about fifteen miles away. In her reminiscence about one of her favorite picnic spots, Caddo Lake, for her fiftieth high school reunion in May 1978, Lady Bird's love of nature was evident: "The lake is so vivid in my thoughts, with Spanish moss draped from the age-old cypress, dark enchanting lagoons where occasionally you would see an alligator slithering from a muddy bank. . . . How many lazy Sunday afternoons we spent floating along in a bateau under those feathery trees and pulling in among the gnarled old roots! Time stood still and we loved it that way."[12] From the age of six until she married, she also spent every summer in Alabama, visiting with her mother's relatives, which included many long family dinners. She remembered in a speech at the University of Alabama in 1966 "laughing hayrides and watermelon suppers, learning to swim in Mulberry Creek, the lazy curl of a cousin's fishing line flickering in the sun, church on Sunday and then the long Sunday dinner with kinfolks—endless kinfolk—discussing the endless family gossip around the table."[13]

Sometimes she attended local Black churches with her nurse, including Mount Sinai Missionary Baptist Church and Peter's Chapel. "I felt very much at home there," she recalled. "They always had a lot of emotion in their services and a lot of singing. . . . I felt a part of them, and I liked it."[14] As this childhood memory suggests, if Lady Bird had led a rather secluded life, she was open to new experiences. She also had a great desire for adventure and for travel. After graduating from high school at only fifteen, she convinced her father and Aunt Effie that she should attend the exclusive Saint Mary's Episcopal School for Girls in Dallas, a junior college, where she had stayed from 1928 to 1930. Her formative years had given her a great love and appreciation of nature, reading, education, and business. She had earlier visited Austin and decided that she would go to the University of Texas, where she began her studies in 1930. She graduated in only three years with her bachelor of arts; in 1934, she earned a bachelor of journalism. Cecille Harrison Marshall, her college roommate, remembered that Lady Bird was interested both in the politics of the campus and in having fun and that she "always seemed to know who she was and that she had a sense of her own being."[15]

In 1934 Lady Bird met Lyndon Johnson, then a legislative aide to Congressman Richard M. Kleberg (D-TX). The intriguing young man who captured her heart was a Texan who grew up in the Hill Country outside of Austin. His father was a farmer and a state representative, and his mother taught elocution. Money was extremely tight, and Lyndon went to public schools and worked his way through the local Southwest Texas State Teachers College in San Marcos. After graduation, he taught at a Mexican American school in the small Texas town of Cotulla. Lyndon developed great fondness for the children, who came from economically deprived backgrounds and faced discrimination because of their Mexican American heritage. He encouraged them to use education as a way to better their lives. He would never forget this experience or his own background, which made him a champion of civil rights and education during his presidency.

Theirs was a quick courtship—he asked her to marry him the day after he met her. Eager and impatient, Lyndon wrote to Lady Bird, "This morning I'm ambitious, proud, energetic and very madly in love with you." This quick proposal concerned her; she was also in love but did not care for politics. She wrote back, "Lyndon, please tell me as soon as you can what the deal is. . . . I am afraid it's politics. . . . I would hate for you to go into politics."[16] A similar concern and dislike of politics was later expressed by another first lady, Michelle Obama, who said to Barack Obama when she first learned of his desire to run for state office, "I married you because you're cute and you're smart, but this is the dumbest thing you could have ever asked me to do."[17]

All the same, in November 1934 Claudia Alta Taylor and Lyndon Baines Johnson married, and soon she became immersed in the profession of which she had once been so wary. Within months, Lyndon was named head of the Texas National Youth Administration; in 1937, he was elected to Congress in a special election. His campaign echoed a New Deal platform. He maintained the seat for a dozen years, and in 1942 his wife seemed to have embraced the political life, writing, "Lyndon, this has been a marvelous experience, this campaign. I wouldn't trade it for a million dollars."[18]

Lady Bird Johnson was a huge asset for Lyndon when he was elected to Congress. She had aided him in his campaigns and funded his effort using some of her inheritance from her mother's estate. She ran his office when he joined the US Navy as a lieutenant commander three days after the attack on Pearl Harbor, and while he worked on supply issues and as an observer on bomber missions in the South Pacific. She wrote his aunt and uncle in Austin in 1942: "We are all working hard to keep up Lyndon's standards and I do want both of you to drop me a line whenever you think of anything, big or trivial, that Lyndon's office could be doing to be of service to his friends in Austin and the district."[19]

The same year, the Johnsons finally bought a permanent home in Washington, DC, the culmination of a long process of multiple moves. How Lady Bird got the house demonstrates her Texas spirit and strength in her beliefs and is one of the few times on record when she actually lost her temper. When the Johnsons first went to look at the house, Lyndon told her he did not want to buy it. She burst into tears and said, "'All I've got to look forward to is one more damn campaign!' And I really let him know what I thought of the fourteen moves or so we had made in eight years of marriage. So he looked shocked. John [Connally] looked at him and kind of grinned and said, 'I think you better go back and buy that house.'"[20]

Not too long after buying their Washington home, she had another wish fulfilled with the births of her daughters Lynda and Luci, in 1944 and 1947, respectively. Meanwhile, she and LBJ had made a significant decision. They had invested some of her inheritance in her first radio station in Austin, KTBC, in 1943. She was a hands-on owner—from cleaning the station to hiring the staff. She was a boss in a time few women were, and thanks to her efficient

management, the station was successful, allowing the Johnsons to buy more outlets. In 1951, Lady Bird decided to add a television station. Her investments
later ensured the couple's financial comfort. Her ownership and management of
radio and television stations was something she would always treasure. Demonstrating her outstanding business acumen, they also underlined her Texas confidence and independence. At once a doting mother, loving wife, and successful
entrepreneur, Lady Bird exemplified the steel magnolia.

At the same time, she continued to keep a busy political schedule. LBJ had
decided after six terms in the House to run for the Senate in a hotly contested
election in 1948. Successfully elected, just four years into his term he became the
youngest minority leader in US Senate history in 1953. The following year, when
the Democrats won control of the Senate, he became majority leader, and his
effective negotiation and leadership skills in that post became legendary.

When John F. Kennedy unexpectedly asked LBJ to be his vice-presidential
running mate in the 1960 campaign, Lady Bird Johnson had been a congressional and senatorial spouse for almost thirty years. Once fearful of making presentations, she had taken a course with Hester Provensen, a well-known Washington
speech teacher, and by 1960 had become an eloquent and thoughtful speaker
and a seasoned campaigner with a good understanding of politics. Regardless,
the Kennedy organization used her in a traditional woman's campaign role. She
was asked to campaign in Texas with Ethel Kennedy and Eunice Shriver Kennedy because she was a political asset in the state, which the candidate needed
to win. She could also act as a surrogate for the pregnant Jacqueline Kennedy.
Lady Bird mainly attended ladies' teas, shaking hands along with the Kennedy
women. Liz Carpenter, who was with her on these trips, remembers that sometimes the Kennedy advance women would complain that Lady Bird was taking
too long in the receiving line, but Lady Bird would just smile sweetly and tell
Carpenter, "But this is my state," and she would continue visiting. This was
another clear indication of her upbringing—her gracious and warm Southern
charm. Even Robert Kennedy, no fan of LBJ, complimented Lady Bird on her
campaigning, saying "Lady Bird carried Texas."[21]

While campaigning in Dallas on November 4, 1960, Lady Bird Johnson faced
an unexpected, ugly event with her typical courage, calm, and grace. A reaction-
ary Congressman from Dallas, Bruce Alger, had organized a protest outside of
the Adolphus Hotel, which suddenly turned into an angry mob of well-dressed
Republican women waving signs calling LBJ a turncoat and telling him to go
home. Lady Bird was spat upon, and her hat was knocked off her head by a sign.
She recalled, "I just had to keep on walking and suppress all emotions . . . and be
just like Marie Antoinette in the tumbrel."[22] Thus, as the Johnsons walked arm
in arm, she remained calm, continuing to smile and nod to the crowd. Moyers,

who was with them on this trip, later remembered his own reaction at the time: "Her very demeanor create[d] a small zone of grace in the midst of that tumultuous throng."[23]

## FIRST LADY OF "DEEDS, NOT WORDS"

Reflecting on her time in the White House in her *White House Diary* in 1970, Lady Bird said: "As I look back on those five years of turmoil and achievement, of triumph and pain, I feel amazement that it happened to me, and gratitude that I had the opportunity to live them, and strongest of all . . . a deep, roaring faith and love for this country."[24]

Turmoil and pain indeed characterized the start of her role as first lady— with the tragic assassination of a young and popular president on November 22, 1963. The horror of that day always stayed with Lady Bird. Years later when she spoke of the assassination it was with emotion in her voice. In an oral history interview I did with her, she commented on becoming first lady: "You will remember the hideous [circumstances that brought] us into the presidency. Nothing had been contemplated or prepared for—[it was] just the most violent and awful beginning, and I sensed that I had walked on a stage for a role I had never rehearsed."[25]

Lady Bird's tenure as first lady and the many historic achievements she accomplished stand out against the backdrop of the ongoing turbulent and tragic events of the 1960s. There was racial strife throughout the nation, including riots in cities, and protests of President Johnson's policies that escalated the Vietnam War, part of a younger generation's challenge to the role of the government and the agenda of its leaders. The last year of the Johnson administration saw the assassinations of Robert F. Kennedy and Martin Luther King Jr. Yet as Moyers said of Lady Bird, "She seemed to grow calmer as the world around her grew more furious."[26] As first lady, she brought her Southern/Southwestern background of poise and charm and kept her focus on achieving her goals. Whether confronted by racists on her groundbreaking 1964 Whistle Stop campaign or heckled by war protesters, she responded graciously, trying to listen to the concern and the message but stay true to what she believed.

For the first few months after she became first lady, her main concern was to make a peaceful and welcoming home for her husband and daughters and to do what she could to help Jackie Kennedy; as she noted, "And then beyond that you find your niche."[27] By the election of 1964, Lady Bird was beginning to define herself, and her niche would be substantive. When asked repeatedly by reporters how she viewed her role as first lady, she would respond, "My role as first lady will emerge in deeds, not words."[28]

She emerged as a successful first lady, focusing her considerable talents on many different causes. She revived, renewed, and modernized the activist model of first lady created by Eleanor Roosevelt both by being an effective champion for her projects and by being directly involved with the legislative agenda when necessary. Having largely surmounted her fear of public speaking, she gave more than 160 speeches. She quickly realized how effectively she could support and campaign for President Johnson's civil rights legislation and bring a special touch to this issue as a Southerner. She also founded and chaired the First Lady's Committee for a More Beautiful Nation's Capital, which focused on beautifying both public areas and lower-income areas in the District, including public housing projects and schools. She served as honorary chair of Head Start, an early education program for underprivileged children, and traveled both with and without President Johnson throughout the country in support of War on Poverty programs. She campaigned and worked tirelessly for highway beautification, addressing the blight of billboards and other eyesores on interstates, and her work led directly to the passage of the Highway Beautification Act of 1965. Her conservation efforts were also evident in her support for President Johnson's See the U.S.A. program, for which she made numerous trips to visit and promote the national parks. It was important to her to further Jackie Kennedy's Committee for the Preservation of the White House, too, on which she served as a member. At a time when women's rights were rising on the national agenda, she established the Women Doer Luncheons, focusing on and discussing key societal issues. Dictating her thoughts daily into a tape recorder, Lady Bird became the first first lady to create a formal record of her time in office, in her *White House Diary*. She hired Liz Carpenter as her press secretary, and formalized staffing for the first lady's office. Throughout Lady Bird's time there, she presided over countless White House dinners, luncheons, receptions, tours, and presentations and accompanied the president on foreign visits. She both supported and gave her honest input to her husband on many complex issues, including whether he should run for president in 1964 and 1968, his treatment of the Walter Jenkins scandal, and how he should handle the press. Drawing on her Southern/Southwestern roots for her backbone, courage, grace, and conviction as first lady, she became a leader of her times—not just a mirror.

One of her earliest initiatives occurred during the 1964 campaign when she decided she would campaign solo for LBJ in the South. Civil rights efforts were a major focus of theirs, and she remarked on how difficult this stand was for them both:

> His position in the Southwest did not make him a deeply rooted typical southerner by any means. He wasn't. He was a southwesterner. But Texas

was one of the Confederate states, and he strongly aligned with a lot of those senators and cared greatly for them. . . . I did feel an acute separation from a lot of my friends, particularly southern friends, because we were really flying right in their teeth with civil rights. . . . Lyndon was just as anxious to do it for the white man as for the black man, because he thought it left a burden on his shoulder, on his heart, that he just wanted to be rid of, wanted all people to be rid of.[29]

Not only was this a unique campaign trip but it was totally organized and planned by women at a time when politics was still run by men. Along with Lady Bird, two key women organizers of the trip, also from the South, were Press Secretary Liz Carpenter and Social Secretary Bess Abell. Liz reminisced years later about how women planning a trip did not go over well with Kenny O'Donnell, a close aide to President Kennedy who still worked for President Johnson:

This is why you love Lyndon Johnson. I tried and tried to meet with Kenny O'Donnell about this campaign. Kenny O'Donnell had no respect for any women in politics whatsoever. The whole attitude of the Kennedy men who worked in this operation was to keep women barefooted and have them on their feet, preferably pregnant, on election day—but nothing beyond that. Kenny O'Donnell wouldn't even meet with Bess and me to talk about this until I laid the whole plan in front of the President. The President yanked him up there on the second floor of the White House and we got out maps and the President was obviously so enthusiastic about what Mrs. Johnson could do on a train trip that we sat there and planned it. I enjoyed watching Kenny O'Donnell being brought around by the President of the United States on the value of women, and he had to suffer three of them—Mrs. Johnson, Bess, and me, for that period.[30]

In October 1964, Lady Bird Johnson set out on a unique campaign trip: the Whistle-Stop Campaign. This was the most public exposure she had experienced in her political life and, at the outset, conditions did not promise a favorable reception. The Civil Rights Act of 1964 had passed in July, and she was travelling by train through the South for four days from Alexandria, Virginia, to New Orleans, Louisiana. Years later, she emphasized her reason for making this trip: "I have a strong sentimental, family, deep tie to the South, and I thought the South was getting a bad rap from the nation and indeed the world. It was painted as a bastion of ignorance and all sorts of ugly things. It was my country, and although I knew I couldn't be that persuasive to them, at least I could talk to them in language they would understand."[31]

Lady Bird Johnson aboard the Lady Bird Special, Whistle-Stop Campaign: October 6, 1964, Alexandria, Virginia. Courtesy of the Lyndon B. Johnson Presidential Library. Serial Number FM5-10.

Liz Carpenter's files at the LBJ Library contain notes from a tape Lady Bird Johnson recorded about her Whistle Stop speeches. The transcriptions gave rare and detailed insight into her thinking before she departed:

> I want to go because I am proud of the South and I am proud that I am part of the South. . . . I am proud of what the South has contributed to the fabric of our national life. . . . And yet now in this decade, there is a shearing apart of the South from the national life. And every time the rest of the nation makes one more snide joke about corn-pone or red-necks, the defenses of the South go up angrily. . . . It is partly the South wanting to pull away and partly the rest of the nation misunderstanding—yes even

laughing—in a way. . . . What do I think I and my little trip down into the South can do about it? . . . To say . . . the South, to this Democratic candidate for President, and to his wife—is a respected and valued and beloved part of the country.[32]

Years later, Moyers eloquently described and summarized how courageous, dangerous, and important the Whistle Stop trip was, along with Lady Bird's reasons for taking it, in a eulogy:

These were her people, here were her roots. And she is not ready to sever them. So she sets out on a whistle-stop journey of nearly seventeen hundred miles through the heart of her past. She is on her own now—campaigning independently—across the Mason-Dixon line down the buckle of the Bible Belt. . . . The boos, the jeers, the hecklers, the crude signs and cruder gestures, the insults and the threats . . . the air has become so menacing we run a separate engine fifteen minutes ahead of her in case of a bomb. . . . She never flinches. . . . In Columbia [SC] she answers hecklers with . . . "This is a country of many viewpoints. I respect your right to express your own. Now is my turn to express mine." An advance man called me back at the White House. . . . He was choking back the tears. "As long as I live, I will thank God I was here today, so that I can tell my children the difference courage makes."[33]

The trip turned out to be tremendously successful despite the rough treatment Lady Bird faced. It marked her emergence as an active and activist first lady; to use one of her favorite phrases, she was a "can do" person. It showed she was going to do the things she felt strongly about—regardless of whether they might involve controversy. She was going to use her podium as first lady. Her approach to tackling issues was very much Southern—trying not to ruffle feathers and being carefully politic behind the scenes, always in a calm, courteous, and polite way. But it also demonstrated her steel magnolia side and her Texan confidence, courage, and independence. The trip was credited with helping garner Southern support for LBJ, who won three Southern states in the 1964 election at a time when it was feared that Southern Democrats would bolt the party. It was estimated that more than a half million people heard her message, and with national television coverage, she both elevated the dialogue and furthered support for implementation of civil rights.[34]

After the successful 1964 campaign, she began to think about what other issues she would like to spotlight as first lady. One of her choices was Head Start. She made numerous trips in support of this program as well as for President

Johnson's War on Poverty. On these trips, her Southern charm and warmth was evident. On a trip to Appalachia in March 1967, Lady Bird met with the owner of a small house in an isolated town and talked easily with this woman about the War on Poverty programs and the Teacher Corps. She discussed the growing of tomatoes, corn, cabbage, and beans and gave the woman a present of preserves and honey from the Johnsons' Texas ranch.[35]

The cause that became one of her best known was *beautification*. Although this term became identified with her efforts to preserve the natural beauty of the United States in myriad places including along highways, in the gardens of the capital, and in national parks—to name just a few—Lady Bird actually disliked the word. As she said in an interview with Barbara Klaw in 1980, "It sounds cosmetic and trivial and it's prissy, but try as we would we couldn't come up with anything better."[36]

In my oral history interview with her, she explained her process for picking projects:

> What was there so evident on the nation's agenda that particularly struck a responsive chord in me? What made my heart sing? . . .
>
> This was sort of the beginning of the great wave of interest in the environment: clean air, clean rivers, wilderness, inner city parks, just the whole big ball of interwoven skeins. . . . It was right down my alley because nature had given me more joy and serenity and happy memories. So I decided that this was certainly going to be one of my projects, and it found its expression in the beautification program in Washington simply because that's where we lived. . . . You begin where you are, and you hope it has a ripple effect, set[s] some kind of chain reaction, some kind of standards, maybe.[37]

Liz Carpenter also highlighted the importance of the first lady's love of nature in her choice to focus on beautification:

> It really was born in Lady Bird Johnson in Karnack, Texas, when she was a child. She loved beauty; she loved those piney woods; she loves going out in a bateau on Caddo Lake and seeing the cypress trees and their gnarled roots. Those were the things that she really carried with her all her life, and she spoke of it in a speech. . . . "Each of [our] actions sprang from what nurtures us, and what nurtured me was walking through the piney woods in my own deep East Texas."[38]

In November 1964, President Johnson's Task Force on Natural Beauty submitted its report to him, stating, "The time was never better for action to conserve

Lady Bird Johnson planting a cherry tree, Cherry Blossom Festival, April 6, 1965, Washington, DC. Courtesy of the Lyndon B. Johnson Presidential Library. Serial Number 34199-11.

the natural beauty of this land."[39] That winter, the Johnsons met at their ranch with Secretary of the Interior Stewart Udall, who suggested that Lady Bird think about the idea of concentrating on conservation, focusing her efforts on making Washington, DC, "a garden city."

By January 1965, the idea had evolved into a Committee for a More Beautiful Capital, with a membership that included Udall and other key people from the Department of the Interior, urban planners, Mayor Walter Washington, friends of the Johnsons, and other ardent supporters of beautification. It focused on addressing two main areas: first, to beautify those parts of the city most visited by tourists and locals, and second to tackle the poorer neighborhoods by beauti-fying public housing projects and schools, echoing themes of the Great Society. On February 11, 1965, the committee's first meeting was held in a typically Southern way; as Lady Bird commented, "How many things are launched un-der the name of a tea!"[40]

This work proceeded across the nation as well, as the first lady pushed for key legislation to limit the number of roadside billboards. The Highway Beautifica-tion Act thus became known as "Lady Bird's Bill." Its passage was in large part attributed to her careful politicking, strongly opposed by the well-funded and politically powerful Outdoor Advertising Association. Despite this opposition, President Johnson told his cabinet and staff, "You know I love that woman and she wants that Highway Beautification Act," and "by God, we're going to get it for her."[41] Although it fell somewhat short of all its original aims in its final ver-sion, the act was nonetheless passed by Congress in October 1965 and became a landmark piece of legislation.

Lady Bird implemented her desire to promote beautification and Presi-dent Johnson's See the U.S.A. program by visiting many national parks with the press. Perhaps the trip best illustrating her Southwestern/Texas roots and love of nature was in April 1966 to see Big Bend National Park. This trip be-came legendary—as she hiked in jeans and a red-checkered shirt and cowboy hat with Secretary Udall, Liz Carpenter, and a hundred press representatives. The trip featured one reporter in bright red britches carrying a matching um-brella while she climbed up mountains. The next day the entourage enjoyed an eleven-mile passage down the Rio Grande River on rafts, some of which overturned. The first lady paddled her own raft for part of the way. President Johnson wryly remarked to Liz when she asked him about the press coverage, "Well, it's good. You have a five-column picture on page one of the *New York Times*. Lady Bird looks like the Lone Ranger, and Stewart Udall looks like Tonto."[42]

By the end of the Johnson administration, the first lady's desire to promote and protect the environment had resulted in a broad and effective series of

Lady Bird Johnson tours Big Bend National Park, Texas, 1966. Courtesy of the Lyndon B. Johnson Presidential Library. Serial Number C1616-9A.

programs. With her committee, she had beautified Washington, DC, both in heavily visited public spaces, often with flowers, and in its poorer urban areas; led a national campaign for highway beautification; championed and campaigned for conservation programs throughout the nation; and led trips in support of the national parks. Lady Bird best defined what beautification meant to her and its importance to society in a speech she gave at Williams College: "We are talking about more than 'beautification.' We are talking, really, about one of the most fateful questions of the time: whether the physical setting of American life will be pleasant or squalid."[43]

### "THE FIRST LADY IS, AND ALWAYS HAS BEEN, AN UNPAID PUBLIC SERVANT ELECTED BY ONE PERSON, HER HUSBAND."[44]

Lady Bird Johnson, as did all first ladies, assumed the unique and unelected role because of her husband, when he became the thirty-sixth president of the United States. It would soon be clear that the Lady Bird's relationship with the president was not only as his helpmate and his most trusted adviser. This relationship would empower her as well to be an active and powerful first lady. Betty Boyd Caroli summed up the importance of her relationship with her husband:

[Lady] Bird had begun to define a new kind of first lady . . . intended to show how a spouse can be a full collaborator. She would continue to privately critique Lyndon's speeches and press conferences, publicly help him court legislators and the press, and act as his sounding board. On her own she would travel the nation's troubled spots to highlight problems and explore solutions. It was a tall order for a presidential partner, but the Texan in her understood that in some quarters a workhorse counted for more than a show horse."[45]

Along with her Texan heritage, her Southern influence pervaded the way she handled issues and projects and how she related to people. With Lyndon, she had evolved from a shy girl in the rural environment of East Texas to a first lady on the world stage, using her podium in an extremely effective way.

Despite her strength, love, and patience, Lyndon remained a complicated and demanding marriage partner. He could be insecure about decisions, become depressed, and anger quickly. Her approach definitely helped him achieve all that he did. In describing Lyndon, the first lady told Gillette her husband was "marvelous, contradictory, [with] great natural intelligence, [a] showman sometimes, hurtful sometimes, very often tender and giving. He was many faceted. . . . He was full of faults, too, and sometimes [made] misjudgments about people. . . . We all got as mad as could be at him from time to time, and hurt. But we also remember how we always turned to him to help us in everything."[46] Indeed, he was often larger than life and always in a hurry. He played Henry Higgins, and she was a willing student. Yes, he had some affairs, and the first lady knew of them, but as she told Barbara Walters in a television interview, it was a different time then. Like other political spouses before and after her, she chose her own way of addressing this situation. In response to Walters's question about LBJ having mistresses, she made the comment, "Oh, Lyndon was a people lover. And that certainly did . . . not exclude half the people in the world—women. Lyndon loved people and women were 50 percent of the population."[47]

To this complicated, accomplished, and demanding man she loved so much, who also loved and valued her, Lady Bird contributed her quiet calmness, poise, careful opinions, deliberateness, strength, and shrewdness. They were a couple of opposites in personality, but there is no doubt each loved the other, and they bettered each other. In reflecting on their relationship later in her life, Lady Bird said: "He was an exciting person to live with, and I consider myself very lucky."[48]

When they first fell in love, Lyndon had written her a prescient letter: "Never have I been so dependent on anyone. . . . Never shall I expect so much of any individual." Time and time again, often tirelessly, she would give him her thoughtful advice and always her support on crucial issues.[49]

As his counselor, Lady Bird used the gentle, kind, and firm persuasion befitting a steel magnolia. In August 1964, LBJ was seriously considering not running for the Democratic nomination for president. Lady Bird later reminisced, "I think one of the few times I was just darned positive [about] what Lyndon ought to do was that he ought to run in August of 1964, and that he ought not to run four years later. That was a firm conviction from which I never did waiver."[50] Late that month she wrote him the following note:

Beloved

You are as brave a man as Harry Truman—or FDR—or Lincoln. You can go on to find some peace, some achievement amidst all the pain. You have been strong, patient, determined beyond any words of mine to express. I honor you for it. So does your country. To step out now would be wrong for your country, and I can see nothing but a lonely wasteland for your future. Your friends would be frozen in embarrassed silence and your enemies jeering. I am not afraid of Time or lies or losing money or defeat. In the final analysis I can't carry any of the burdens you talked of—so I know it's only your choice. But I know you are as brave of any of the thirty-five [preceding presidents]. I love you always. Bird[51]

For President Johnson, this note both stirred his love of country and inspired his courage. His wife was also telling him to ignore his critics. He decided to run.[52] The note shows well Lady Bird's careful, loving, but very firm way of knowing how to appeal to just the right instincts to reach the decision she felt was best.

A demonstration of her loyalty to friends, and her willingness to differ with her husband when she thought necessary, was in her response to an incident that occurred on October 14, 1964. Various news agencies had learned that Walter Jenkins, President Johnson's top aide and a longtime friend of both Johnsons, had been arrested on a morals charge regarding an alleged homosexual encounter at the Washington, DC, YMCA. The first lady called the president the next morning, when he was in New York on a campaign trip. The telephone call lasted more than twelve minutes and depicts well Lady Bird's handling of her husband, her loyalty to their friend, and her steely determination to do something in support of him. She told Lyndon she wanted to do two things to support Jenkins, the first being to offer him the number two job at KTBC radio station (she knew the decision had been made that he would have to leave his White House job). Before she could say anything further, Lyndon immediately responded: "I wouldn't do anything along that line now. . . . I don't think that's right."

She remained firm, however, and insisted that she also wanted to offer a statement of support for Jenkins when asked about him by the press. She let LBJ know she had checked with their friend Abe Fortas, a Washington lawyer (and later Supreme Court justice), who had approved her two-part plan of the job offer and the statement. Her husband then insisted she should talk to Clark Clifford and not get involved in this.

Although the president kept calling her "honey," and the first lady kept calling him "darling" and "my beloved," the conversation was tense and ended with Lady Bird saying, "You are a brave good guy" but still insisting that she would give a statement of support for Jenkins.[53]

Shortly after this call, the first lady, against Lyndon's strong advice, did release to the press a very sympathetic and loving paragraph backing Jenkins, demonstrating her steel magnolia traits:

> My heart is aching today for someone who has reached the end point of exhaustion in dedicated service to his country. Walter Jenkins has been carrying incredible hours and burdens since President Kennedy's assassination. He is now receiving the medical attention which he needs. I know our family and all of his friends—and I hope all others—pray for his recovery. I know that the love of his wife and six fine children and his profound religious faith will sustain him through this anguish.[54]

Jenkins returned to Austin, where he ran a construction and consulting business and worked as an accountant.

A much lighter episode that once again demonstrates Lady Bird's role as close and trusted adviser to President Johnson was a telephone conversation on March 3, 1964, when she offered him her journalist's opinion on how he could improve his performance at press conferences. The conversation started with her asking him if he had a minute. His response "Yes, ma'am"—was an indication that he was bracing himself. She then went on to tell him that although he looked splendid, his statements were a little breathless, he looked down too much, and he should study his text more and read it with greater conviction. She ended by saying she would give his performance a good B+. The president said he thought he did much better than the week before. Lady Bird then changed her voice to a more girly, affectionate tone, said their friends the Thornberrys were coming to dinner, and ended the conversation by telling the president she "loves him very much."[55] There were many other instances of her interaction with Lyndon in which she gave her advice, support, and love but also her honest opinion. As she said about her role on advising her husband, "I sure didn't mind expressing my feeling."[56]

As she ended her role as first lady, her quiet, calm, and effective style had gained many admirers. Eric Sevareid, a *CBS News* journalist, said, "The plain fact is that there has never been a first lady to equal Mrs. Johnson"; author Shana Alexander called her "quite possibly . . . the best first lady we have ever had," and journalist Selwa Roosevelt noted, "She accomplished more with less controversy than any other first lady in history."[57] Many properly credited her with the activism of the Johnson administration on conservation and environmental issues, which resulted in passing more than two hundred laws. President Johnson thanked her for her hard work and gave her a plaque that said "To Lady Bird, who has inspired me and millions of Americans to try to preserve our land and beautify our nation."[58] Throughout her years in public life, as first lady and after, her Southern/Texas heritage was part of her unique style in how she related to people and got things done. She brought this background to the issues she championed and to the way in which she offered her valuable advice and support to her husband, daughters, and friends as she enacted her own meaningful and lasting agenda.

Lady Bird referred to her Whistle-Stop Campaign as a "journey of the heart." This phrase, however, is also applicable to her role as first lady and to her life. She changed greatly from the shy Southern girl from East Texas who spent so much time on her own enjoying nature to a confident and effective first lady who used her national podium to champion beautification and conservation of the environment, education, and civil rights. But no matter how far she traveled from her home and how much her life changed in her "journey of the heart," she never forgot "her people," her roots, and her desire to remain true to herself.

## NOTES

1. "Whistle Stop 10/13–16/64," Folder 3, Transcript, Box 12, Elizabeth Carpenter's Subject Files, White House Social Files, LBJ Library, Austin, Texas (hereafter LBJL).

2. Elizabeth Carpenter Oral History with Joe B. Frantz, December 3, 1968, Interview Transcript 2, LBJL, 5.

3. Bill Moyers, "Transcript of Eulogy of Bill Moyers for Mrs. Johnson," *Austin-American Statesman*, July 15, 2007, https://www.democraticunderground.com/discuss/duboard.php?az=view_all&address=389x1340948.

4. Quoted in Phyllis McKenzie, "Women of Texas: Traits, Qualities, and Characteristics," Great Texas Women, http://texaswomen.housing.utexas.edu/index.html.

5. Quoted in McKenzie, "Women of Texas."

6. Mary Beth Brown, *Condi: The Life of a Steel Magnolia* (Nashville, TN: Thomas Nelson, 2007), xii.

7. Claudia Taylor Johnson (CTJ) Oral History Interview by Michael L. Gillette, Transcript 1, August 12, 1977, LBJL, 5.

8. CTJ Oral History, Interview Transcript 1, 25–26.

9. CTJ Oral History, Interview Transcript 1, 11.

10. CTJ Oral History, Interview Transcript 1, 13.

11. Michael Gillette, *Lady Bird Johnson: An Oral History* (New York: Oxford University Press, 2012), 8.

12. Lady Bird Johnson, "Remarks for the 50th Reunion of Marshall High School Class of 1928," May 27, 1978, Mrs. Johnson's Post-Presidential Files, LBJL.

13. Mrs. Johnson—Speeches, Reference Files, LBJL.

14. CTJ Oral History, Interview Transcript 2, LBJL, 2.

15. Cecille Harrison Marshall Oral History, LBJL, 6.

16. "A National Tribute to Lady Bird Johnson: On the Occasion of Her Sixty-Fifth Birthday," Transcript, December 11, 1977, LBJL, 5.

17. Jodi Kantor, "The Obama Marriage," *New York Times Magazine*, October 26, 2009, http://www.nytimes.com/2009/11/01magazine/01Obama-t-html.

18. "National Tribute to Lady Bird Johnson."

19. Lady Bird Johnson to Rebekah Baines Johnson, letter, February 27, 1942, Lyndon B. Johnson Folder, Box 8, Personal Papers of Rebekah Baines Johnson, LBJL.

20. Gillette, *Lady Bird Johnson*, 142.

21. Betty Boyd Caroli, *Lady Bird and Lyndon: The Hidden Story of a Marriage That Made a President* (New York: Simon and Schuster, 2015), 204.

22. Lewis L. Gould, *Lady Bird Johnson and the Environment* (Lawrence: University Press of Kansas, 1988); Gould, *Lady Bird Johnson: Our Environmental First Lady* (Lawrence: University Press of Kansas, 1999), 25.

23. Moyers, "Transcript of Eulogy of Bill Moyers for Mrs. Johnson."

24. Lady Bird Johnson, *A White House Diary* (New York: Holt, Reinhart, and Winston, 1970), ix–x.

25. Nancy Kegan Smith, "On Being First Lady: An Interview with Lady Bird Johnson," *Prologue* 19, no. 2 (Summer 1987): 136.

26. Moyers, "Transcript of Eulogy of Bill Moyers for Mrs. Johnson."

27. Smith, "On Being First Lady," 136.

28. Carpenter Oral History, Interview Transcript 2, LBJL, 1.

29. Gillette, *Lady Bird Johnson*, 367.

30. Elizabeth Carpenter Oral History interview with Joe B. Frantz, December 3, 1968, Interview Transcript 1, LBJL, 11.

31. Carpenter Oral History, Interview Transcript 1, 11.

32. "Whistle Stop 10/13–16/64."

33. Moyers, "Transcript of Eulogy of Bill Moyers for Mrs. Johnson."

34. See Lady Bird Johnson, "At the Epicenter, November 1963–January 1965: The Whistle-Stop Tour," https://www.pbs.org/ladybird/epicenter/epicenter_report_train.html.

35. Johnson, *White House Diary*, 496.

36. Barbara Klaw, "Lady Bird Johnson Remembers," *American Heritage* 32, no. 1 (1980): 6.

37. Smith, "On Being First Lady," 138.

38. Carpenter Oral History Interview, Transcript 2, 4–5.

39. Gould, *Lady Bird Johnson: Our Environmental First Lady*, 51.

40. Johnson, *White House Diary*, 240.

41. Gould, *Lady Bird Johnson and the Environment*, 157.

42. Russell Roe, "Lady Bird in Big Bend," *Texas Parks and Wildlife* (July 2016), https://tpwmagazine.com/archive/2016/jul/LLL_ladybird/.

43. Press Release: Remarks of Mrs. Johnson at Williams College, Williamstown, Massachusetts, October 8, 1967, Mrs. Johnson—Speeches, Reference Files, LBJL, https://www.discoverlbj.org/item/refe-ctjspeeches-19671008.

44. Lady Bird Johnson Quotes. BrainyQuote.com, 2018, https://www.brainyquote.com/quotes/lady_bird_johnson_114695.

45. Caroli, *Lady Bird and Lyndon*, 233–234.

46. Gillette, *Lady Bird Johnson*, 370.

47. Lady Bird Johnson: Documentary Transcript—Part Four, www.pbs.org/ladybird/shattereddreams/shattereddreams_documentary.html.

48. Gillette, *Lady Bird Johnson*, 370.

49. "National Tribute to Lady Bird Johnson."

50. Smith, "On Being First Lady," 141.

51. Lyndon Baines Johnson, *The Vantage Point: Perspective of the Presidency, 1963–1969* (New York: Holt, Reinhart, and Winston, 1971), 97–98.

52. Johnson, *Vantage Point*, 98.

53. Lyndon Johnson and Lady Bird Johnson, audiotape of telephone conversation, October 15, 1964, LBJL.

54. Statement of Mrs. Lyndon B. Johnson, October 15, 1964, White House Social Files, Alpha Files, Jenkins, Mr. & Mrs. Walter Only, LBJL.

55. http://www.lbjlibrary.org/lyndon-baines-johnson/timeline/lady-bird-evaluates-lbjs-performance-after-a-press-conference/.

56. Smith, "On Being First Lady," 139.

57. Gould, *Lady Bird Johnson and the Environment*, 238.

58. http://www.ladybirdjohnson.org/biography.

# CHAPTER 15

# Diplomacy First
## Rosalynn Carter as Diplomat

Kristin L. Ahlberg

By January 20, 1977, Rosalynn Carter had solidified her image as Jimmy Carter's political partner during both her tenure as first lady of Georgia and the 1976 presidential campaign. It was thus not surprising when, having repudiated the foreign and domestic policies of his predecessors Richard Nixon and Gerald Ford by promoting a more inclusive policy responsive to human rights and other concerns, President Carter sent Rosalynn as his personal envoy on a seven-nation trip to Latin America in May–June 1977 in an effort to reset relations with the region. It was not just a goodwill tour; the first lady held substantive discussions with Latin American leaders on a number of issues. In so doing, she amplified President Carter's foreign policy in these areas. Two years later, the president sent his wife to Thailand in the midst of a humanitarian crisis to assess conditions on the ground in Southeast Asia. The first lady used her stature as a diplomat to advocate for increased food aid and humanitarian assistance to the Kampucheans then living in Thai refugee camps. In both instances, Rosalynn Carter drew upon her lifelong humanitarian activism and political acumen, attributes enhanced in her work as first lady of Georgia, to serve the United States as an effective diplomat.

## REORDERING RELATIONSHIPS: ROSALYNN CARTER'S TRAVEL TO LATIN AMERICA, MAY–JUNE 1977

Jimmy Carter campaigned for the Democratic nomination promising to restore morality to domestic and foreign policy. In speeches delivered throughout 1975 and 1976, the candidate criticized his predecessors' policies, namely those linked to the Vietnam War and the Watergate scandal.[1] Carter's vision of US foreign policy replaced "balance-of-power" politics with trilateral cooperation, increasing emphasis on North-South relations and a commitment to human rights.[2] Speaking before the Chicago Council on Foreign Relations on March 15, 1976, Carter contended that the Ford administration had been "especially neglectful" toward Latin America. He continued, "There is no question that both Africa and Latin America have been ignored since the Presidencies of John Kennedy and Lyndon Johnson. These areas should become, and indeed will become, increasingly important in the next decade. Our relationships with these must abandon traditional paternalism."[3] In an interview several weeks later, Carter connected his intended foreign policy to the efforts he had taken as Georgia governor to promote racial equality and racial justice, noting,

> We have the same kind of opportunity yet unrealized in foreign affairs to treat nations as individuals and to deal with them in a predictable and a compassionate and understanding and respectable way. This will particularly apply to the small nations and the nations whose citizens happen to be brown or black, who in the past were often treated with a lack of respect and sometimes even contempt and certainly insensitivity. As President, I think I can change that dramatically.[4]

Carter stressed that his foreign policy would take into account the attributes and needs of individual nations and would not treat the region as a monolithic bloc.

After he took office, the president and his foreign policy advisers began to review US–Latin American relations. A State Department study conducted at President Carter's request confirmed the administration's fears that relations were poor and in need of revitalization. The study noted deterioration in official contacts over the previous decade, underscoring that the United States had "appeared increasingly out of step with the process of change in either Latin America or the Caribbean, even on matters directly affecting our own interests."[5] It also set forth issues for further discussion by the interagency Policy Review Committee (PRC), including interventions, arms transfers, human rights, and the style of US diplomacy and attention paid toward Latin America. At a March 24 PRC meeting, National Security Adviser Zbigniew Brzezinski challenged the notion of a "special relationship" with Latin America, terming it "ahistorical." He added that relationships with individual nations might become "healthier" if the United States emphasized "bilateral relations" and perceived the area's issues "in a global context."[6] In making these statements, Brzezinski was moving away from the once-paternalistic and often cold war–focused approach in the US relationship with Latin American countries. Brzezinski's deputy, David Aaron, then "suggested joining the two agreed approaches—the movement towards globalism and establishing a closer affinity with democracies—by a Presidential trip to selected democracies, say in Latin America as well as in Africa or Asia."[7] Such a trip held out the promise that President Carter would develop personal connections with individual leaders, signifying a break with the past. It also provided the president an opportunity to explain and justify the changing US positions on human rights, nonproliferation, and other global issues, many of which were intertwined with an improved US–Latin American relationship. Lastly it offered an opportunity to deploy Rosalynn Carter as his emissary. When asked about a role for his wife in his administration in an interview with *Time* magazine shortly before he entered office, Carter had responded: "I'll let her decide what sort of projects she wants to become involved in. But she and other members of my family will probably travel a good bit, both within this country and in foreign countries. I'll use her as an extension of myself."[8]

During the first weeks of his presidency, Carter and his advisers made human rights a priority. The president-elect had made clear during the 1976 campaign that he would place human rights at the center of US foreign policy, a position that reflected his long-standing worldview.[9] Secretary of State Cyrus Vance articulated the beginnings of this initiative when he indicated that the United States would speak out against human rights abuses—both domestic and foreign. Although the administration would not comment on all instances, it would speak out "when we see a threat to human rights, when we believe it is constructive to do so."[10] Wasting no time, Vance announced during his February 24 testimony before the Senate Appropriations Subcommittee on Foreign Operations that the administration had recommended cuts in military assistance to Argentina, Ethiopia, and Uruguay based on their human rights records.[11] Carter described these and other changes, as well as the ideology underpinning them, in a series of addresses made during spring 1977, notably in March at the United Nations (UN) and in May at the University of Notre Dame. At the United Nations, he asserted that the United States had a "historical birthright" to be associated with the "universal demand for fundamental human rights."[12] In the Notre Dame address, Carter claimed that his administration's actions had "reaffirmed America's commitment to human rights as a fundamental tenet of our foreign policy."[13] With regard to Latin America, historian Vanessa Walker contends that Carter "sought to use human rights as the backbone for a new regional policy"—an approach that also reflected a new cognizance of the limits of US policy in an ever-interdependent world.[14]

The Carter administration also moved to make nuclear nonproliferation a foreign policy priority. Earlier, in a May 13, 1976, UN address, candidate Carter had called for "new forms of international action" to limit the spread of nuclear weapons.[15] The expansion of facilities designed to enrich uranium and reprocess spent fuel was a particular concern; in 1975, the Federal Republic of Germany (FRG) sold a nuclear reactor and plutonium technology to Brazil, and, in 1976, France considered selling a uranium reprocessing plan to Pakistan.[16] Late in the campaign, Carter attacked Ford for "fail[ing] to oppose" the West German and French actions.[17] After he was in office, Carter asserted that the US "security objective" was to "prevent the spread of nuclear explosive—or near explosive—capabilities to countries which do not now possess them."[18] To this end, his administration opposed the sale of nuclear technology, especially in the Southern Hemisphere.

In addition to articulating his administration's positions on specific issues that affected US relations with Latin America, Carter sought to contextualize his broader, regional policy. On Pan-American Day, April 14, the president addressed the Organization of American States (OAS) in Washington, DC, to describe the new approach. Peter Bourne recalled, "To the significant appreciation of his audience, he opened his speech in Spanish, and reminded them of the call for cooperation and consultation he had made" when he had hosted the OAS in Atlanta in 1974.[19] Acknowledging that a "single United States policy" toward the region was untenable, Carter asserted that future interactions with each country would "be more suited to each nation's variety and potential."[20] His administration's policy was based on three components: respect for the "individuality and sovereignty" of each nation; emphasis on human rights as a key influence in relationships; and resolution of the "great issues" that had plagued relations between developed and developing nations. The president's statements concerning human rights, nonproliferation, and Latin America policy clearly set him apart from his predecessors. Yet, especially in the area of human rights, the Latin American leaders had expressed some skepticism and concern regarding the administration's approach—perhaps seeing it as another form of US meddling—suggesting that a personal explication of policy might prove useful.

The difficulty in undertaking a presidential visit stemmed from the timing; thus, as the first lady later recalled, the president asked her to "go on a special mission for him. He was so busy setting in motion a host of domestic and foreign policy initiatives, including the national energy program, the Panama Canal treaties, the Middle East peace effort, and the Strategic Arms Limitation Treaty (SALT) II negotiations, he had time for only one major trip at the beginning—an economic summit in London."[21] She continued, "It was necessary for us to show in a dramatic way our commitment to human rights and democracy in our own hemisphere. Jimmy and his security advisers agreed that more than an official State Department visit was necessary; someone close to him should make this carefully structured trip. Would I be willing to go?"[22] On May 10, the White House announced that the first lady would travel to Latin America from May 30 through June 12 and visit Jamaica, Costa Rica, Ecuador, Peru, Brazil, Colombia, and Venezuela.[23]

On the surface, the designation of a first lady as a presidential envoy was not that unusual. First Lady Eleanor Roosevelt had undertaken foreign travel during her husband's administration, although as Kathy Smith writes, her "mission was not to explain American foreign policy to heads of state."[24] In January 1972, First Lady Patricia Nixon had traveled to Liberia, Ghana, and the Ivory Coast; similarly, Gil Troy characterized the visit as a "goodwill tour."[25] What was unprecedented in 1977 was that President Carter relied on his wife to participate in substantive, policy-related discussions with Latin American leaders rather than tour hospitals, schools, and orphanages. The president's decision is unsurprising when viewed from the vantage point of the Carters' mutually respectful personal relationship. Earlier in their lives, Rosalynn Carter had supported her husband when he decided in the early 1960s to run for a Georgia state senate seat; she ran the family peanut business in Plains during the legislative session. She had also championed her own causes while first lady of Georgia in the early 1970s—including support for the Equal Rights Amendment (ERA) and mental health services. In reference to the latter, Governor Carter appointed his wife to his newly established Governor's Commission to Improve Services to Mentally and Emotionally Handicapped Georgians. She had, moreover, campaigned extensively during the 1976 presidential campaign, especially in the Southern primary states. After her husband won the Democratic nomination, Rosalynn not only informed audiences about her husband's positions but also explained that she would advocate for the same initiatives she supported during her time in Atlanta, especially mental health services and passage of the ERA. The president implicitly trusted the first lady, her business acumen, her ability to gauge peoples' intentions and motivations, and her grasp of the issues. As Betty Glad notes, "Carter talked to his wife Rosalynn 'about absolutely everything.'"[26] From her perspective, the first lady characterized herself as her husband's closest adviser, a role she occupied when he served as governor of Georgia. The presidency had not altered his reliance on his wife's counsel, and he believed Rosalynn would excel in communicating the administration's initiatives. In addition, representing the United States in Latin America seemed a natural choice to the first lady, owing to her long-standing interest in the region's culture. Earlier in the 1970s, both Carters had visited Latin America and had arranged for subsequent people-to-people exchange trips.[27] The first lady had made other trips to the region, as recently as December 1976, when the president-elect asked her to represent him at the inauguration of Mexican President Jose Lopez Portillo y Pacheco.[28]

Rosalynn Carter undertook extensive preparations in advance of her departure, including continuation of her Spanish language lessons. On the policy side, State Department and National Security Council (NSC) staff officials briefed her on all aspects of US–Latin American relations. The first lady's press secretary, Mary Finch Hoyt, describing the "exhaustive" briefings, recalled "40 experts in 13 sessions lasting 2 to 5 hours each."[29] Myra Gutin wrote, "Those who briefed the first lady were impressed by her curiosity, her quickness, and also her toughness."[30] In addition to the oral briefings, both the State Department and NSC staff prepared papers that provided historical background, the status of US policy in the region, and comprehensive overviews of the major issues the first lady would raise with foreign leaders. A State Department paper, "Human Rights, May 1977," for example, assessed Latin American human rights records and identified the worst offenders, noting that these nations' leaders had "rejected, as unacceptable, U.S. security assistance tied to good behavior in the area of human rights."[31]

State Department officials also communicated the objectives of the first lady's visit to the US diplomats in the region. In a May 7 telegram to the seven Latin American posts, the Department emphasized that the first lady "is taking this trip very seriously" and that the scheduled conversations with foreign leaders would be "substantive" in nature. Counting on the posts' close coordination, President Carter believed the visit would prove "valuable" both in terms of her ability to explicate policy and her willingness to listen to the leaders' specific concerns.[32]

Initially, the trip's optics gave pause to some within the administration and outside of it, precisely because Rosalynn Carter's objective was to engage leaders in substantive foreign policy discussions rather than fulfilling her "traditional" role. Following the trip announcement, Jane Pisano, a White House fellow assigned to the NSC staff, informed Associate Press Secretary Jerry Schecter that US Representative Dante Fascell (D-FL) had called her to discuss the "press strategy" for the trip in light of "bad vibes" he had received from the US press and other sources. Pisano noted that Fascell attributed this to the first lady's gender and suggested that to overcome these reservations, the administration needed "a decent, definitive media program in the U.S. plus a big USIA [United States Information Agency] effort in Latin America."[33] USIA officials were aware of the messaging difficulties inherent in the visit but believed that they were not insurmountable. Assistant Director for Latin America John Chatten, in a memorandum to Finch Hoyt, explained that USIA must "push through the media and other filters" the reality that the first lady "is one of the President's closest advisors." Her persuasiveness in explaining the administration's human rights policy, Chatten noted, must be the centerpiece of this approach. He concluded, "Mrs.

Carter's instincts are accurate in avoiding the 'lady bountiful' image by down-playing emphasis on children's hospitals and other 'women's' things."[34] Director John Reinhardt of the USIA echoed these points in a memorandum to Brzez-inski, asserting that Carter's capacity to discuss human rights paid dividends in the post-Vietnam era: "There is something to be gained by emphasizing that after the well-publicized foreign and domestic difficulties of the past decade, Americans are eager to stand for something they can be proud of."[35]

Counsel to the Senate Foreign Relations Committee Subcommittee on Foreign Economic Policy Jerome Levinson also perceived more opportunity than concern, sensing that Rosalynn Carter's past experiences as first lady of Georgia made her uniquely qualified to represent what the United States stood for. Following a Senate briefing in early May, the first lady asked Levinson for his thoughts regarding the trip's purpose and nature. Responding in a May 14 letter, Levinson cautioned that if she were to avoid pure symbolism, her interactions with each Latin American leader should hinge on two concepts: "politics and social change." He explained, "After all, you have been your husband's political partner in the most grueling of all American political endeavors, Presidential politics, and you have been a part of perhaps the most fundamental American social transformation of the past generation—the emergence of a new South."[36] Indeed, the Carters had strongly supported the civil rights movement and the development of a more tolerant South. Rosalynn Carter had staked out these positions as first lady of Georgia, E. Stanly Godbold Jr. writes, as part of her advocacy efforts there: "From her position of power, she wanted to help the young, the elderly, the poor, blacks, females, the mentally challenged, and any groups or individuals who could not care for themselves."[37] For his part, Levinson argued that the first lady conferred legitimacy on the administration's human rights policy because of this background. Earlier in her life, Rosalynn had supported the Koinonia community, an interracial farm near Plains, especially after the 1954 *Brown v. Board of Education* decision. Godbold writes that the future first lady "stood up to the Baptist church, the segregationists, and many of the prominent leaders of the county" who wanted the Reverend Clarence Jordan "to close down his farm and leave the area."[38] Both Carters also supported the consolidation and establishment of a county high school in Sumter County, a position that put them at odds with community members, some of whom feared that the consolidation "would be an excuse for racial integration." "Neighbors, relatives, and warehouse customers," Godbold notes, "stopped speaking to Jimmy and Rosalynn."[39]

Cognizant of some remaining concerns, administration officials attempted to clarify the trip's purpose in the days leading up to the departure. Robert Pastor, one of the NSC staff Latin America experts scheduled to accompany the first lady, emphasized during a May 24 White House briefing that she would "discuss serious issues" with the heads of state. The objectives were clear: to explain administration policy, to highlight the "new directions" the president outlined in the OAS address, and to hear the thoughts of Latin American leaders "on where the United States is going right and where it's going wrong."[40] Rosalynn attempted to address any last reservations during her May 29 interview with news service reporters, insisting that although she would not "negotiate" with foreign leaders, she would "explain to them that in the Carter Administration there will be an open and wider foreign policy."[41] In her May 30 departure remarks, the first lady emphasized her "longtime" interest in Latin America. She also recalled her command of domestic issues during the 1976 presidential campaign, which had drawn on her work as first lady of Georgia, asserting that her ability to understand and explain foreign policy was similar.

The official records, reporting cables, and recollections from the trip all illustrate that the first lady, just as any envoy in her position would have, used her meetings with Latin American leaders to outline the administration's reset of US–Latin American relations. She articulated the administration's overall Latin America policy, which the president had underlined in the OAS address, during a news conference in Quito, Ecuador, on June 2. She said that her husband "is taking a 'new approach' to Latin American foreign policy—'not to promise things he cannot deliver.'"[42] Carter reiterated this reconceptualization during her June 3 meeting with President General Francisco Bermudez of Peru. According to Finch Hoyt's notes of the conversation, the first lady began by "stressing an 'open and wider approach'" and reassured him that "her husband's feeling for Latin America was not a new feeling and that she was glad she had been chosen to come."[43]

In many instances, Latin American leaders raised the human rights issue with the first lady. It emerged as the first topic of her May 31 discussions in San José with President Daniel Oduber of Costa Rica. The visit, as Kathy Smith and Scott Kaufman wrote, began auspiciously when Oduber invited his wife, Marjorie, to sit in on his conversations with Rosalynn, although she later departed.[44] According to the memorandum of conversation, the president stated that he was "happy" that President Carter and the United States "are involved in an area [human rights] that Costa Rica has long been fighting for, and expressed hope that both countries can move ahead together."[45] President Oduber added that he and other Costa Rican officials would pursue human rights issues within the context of the United Nations; he acknowledged, however, that "one way" of addressing general human rights concerns "is not to antagonize countries, but rather to be emphatic supporters of countries that are human rights defenders."[46] The first lady returned to the issue later in their conversation, inquiring about political refugees and making a push for Costa Rica to increase investigations of human rights violators through the Inter-American Commission on Human Rights.[47]

Although military issues dominated her meetings in Quito with the Ecuadorian military junta, including its concern over a Peruvian arms buildup, the first lady recalled that the junta had discussed human rights and its intention to sign the American Convention on Human Rights.[48] She later described the meeting as "helpful," continuing, "Not only did Admiral [Alfredo] Poveda pledge to sign and ratify the American Convention on Human Rights, but our support for their move toward democracy was very important. I was beginning to believe that being a woman in Latin America was more an asset than a liability. I could get away with a lot of things another representative of our government couldn't do."[49] Carter might have been both downplaying her own skills and reflecting some of the unspoken sexism she encountered, but in making this statement, she was also marking the new importance of women and women's issues as part of the increasing attention paid to global issues during the 1970s. Just two years earlier, Mexico City hosted the first UN World Conference on Women, where women's rights had been a key human rights concern.

The discussions that took place in Peru focused on arms control and nuclear nonproliferation. Carter, in raising arms control with Bermudez, referred to several points her husband had elucidated in his Notre Dame address. According to Finch Hoyt's notes, the first lady also passed along Ecuadorian concerns about a Peruvian arms buildup, adding: "The spiraling effort concerns us very much."[50] Although Bermudez expressed support for US human rights efforts, he challenged the allegation that his country was engaged in an aggressive arms buildup, asserting: "We have no strategic offensive plans—all are defensive and we must bear in mind our situation is more complicated than others in Latin America."[51] The first lady responded that "it was important for Peru to 'send a clear signal, a demonstration that your intentions are defensive and not aggressive.'"[52]

Nowhere were Rosalynn's conversations more contentious than in Brazil. After President Carter was in office, he had attempted to convince Chancellor Helmut Schmidt of West Germany to cancel the sale of the nuclear fuel cycle to Brazil, but to no avail.[53] During their June 7 meeting, President Ernesto Geisel of Brazil tried to assuage the first lady by telling her that he understood the burdens her husband faced as president. She responded then "that Geisel could well understand President Carter's position on the nuclear issue." Bringing up a more traditional concern for first ladies, she pressed her argument further: "For the sake of our children and grandchildren . . . it was necessary to eliminate reprocessing facilities."[54] Geisel stated that although Brazil was a "peace-loving" nation, "it cannot do without nuclear energy."

Rosalynn Carter lobbied Geisel on other nonproliferation issues, encouraging him to "demonstrate" the nation's "sincerity and commitment to peace" by "waiving the conditions and putting the Treaty of Tlatelolco into effect."[55] The 1967 treaty prohibited and prevented the development, testing, use, or manufacture of nuclear weapons in Latin America; the government of Brazil had signed the treaty but only with reservations. Yet Geisel remained unmoved, according to the first lady, because of Argentina's failure to ratify the treaty.[56] Geisel also stated that his government would not sign the American Convention on Human Rights, given the existence of the UN Universal Declaration of Human Rights (UDHR). Nor would Geisel endorse the work of the Inter-American Commission on Human Rights on the grounds that it "implied an interventionist policy and could promote police states."[57] Human rights continued to be a source of tension between the two countries even after the first lady departed Brasilia. Two US missionaries went to the consulate in Recife before Rosalynn arrived and asked to speak with her so that they could "present her with data on human rights violations."[58] Upon consultation with her husband, the first lady did meet with the missionaries and later with the governor of the state, to whom she expressed her "dissatisfaction with the way the Americans had been treated" by the police prior to their contacts with US officials at the consulate.[59] In a June 11 editorial, the *New York Times* editorial staff noted these meetings with both Geisel and the two missionaries: "The apparent intention is to maintain normal channels of diplomacy and communication with the governments but some contact also with their democratic critics. This marks a radical departure from the practice of recent Administrations and has created a good deal of tension." In meeting with the missionaries, Rosalynn "underscored the message that cooperation with the Brazilian Government will not blind Washington to any inhumane treatment of its legitimate and peaceable political critics."[60] This bridging the gap between people and their governments was also something she had done in Georgia as first lady; moved in those years by the sheer exhaustion of the caregivers she met, she sought to change the mental health care system so that family members of people with mental illnesses could gain state assistance.[61]

For her part, the first lady believed her trip had paid dividends in improving US–Latin American relations. Upon her return to Washington on June 12, she referenced her meeting in Caracas with President Carlos Andres Perez of Venezuela that morning, noting that Perez had indicated that the Carters together "had opened new paths" in US relationships with Latin American countries.[62] A week later, during remarks made in San Jose, California, Rosalynn explained why the trip was undertaken at this time. She emphasized that part of her goal was to reinforce the speeches President Carter had delivered at the United Nations, OAS, and Notre Dame.[63] More than forty years later, Stuart Eizenstat,

Rosalynn Carter on her return from Latin America with Jimmy Carter and Vice
President Walter Mondale, June 12, 1977. Courtesy of the National Archives.

who had served as President Carter's assistant for domestic affairs and policy,
summarized the import of the first lady's visit, writing that she had "planted the
flag of human rights in Latin America in a tangible way and in the president's
name."[64]

In terms of domestic public opinion, the mission received positive notice.
President Carter's pollster, Pat Caddell, provided him statistics that indicated
that 70 percent of Americans rated the visit as "excellent" or "good."[65] Reporter
David Vidal, writing in the *New York Times* on June 14, provided an assessment
of the trip, noting that "Mrs. Carter has achieved a personal and diplomatic
success that goes far beyond the modest expectations of both her foreign policy
tutors at the State Department and her hosts."[66] Writing in the *Washington Post*
that same day, reporter Susanna McBee cited an exchange at the end of the trip,
when a reporter asked the first lady if she saw "any significance" in the role she
had assumed, based on her gender. Rosalynn responded,

> "If it has not been done before, maybe it's significant." She added, "I don't
> know. I've always worked. I worked in a peanut warehouse, and I didn't
> think about being a woman working in a peanut warehouse. I campaigned
> for Jimmy. I campaigned because we didn't have any money, and everyone

in my family had to go and campaign. I'm doing this because I really think it can be helpful to Jimmy." She paused and added, "I'm glad I'm a woman."[67]

Yet the very fact that she undertook this mission in her capacity as the president's wife—and not an elected official—prompted other US journalists such as Judy Woodruff and Meg Greenfield to question—but not dismiss—the practice of using a first lady as a presidential emissary.[68] In her June 15 *Washington Post* column, Greenfield claimed that the questions raised by the Latin America trip were not related to the first lady's capability to serve as envoy "but rather whether she should. That's the hard one—the question lurking beneath all those layers of pink whipped-cream prose in which we traditionally discuss the role of a President's wife."[69] Rosalynn Carter, a first lady from the South, had succeeded in breaking the expectations Northern journalists had for her position, surely a result of the kind of active involvement she had pursued already as first lady of Georgia.

## ASSESSING A HUMANITARIAN CRISIS: ROSALYNN CARTER'S TRAVEL TO THAILAND, NOVEMBER 1979

Throughout the remainder of 1977, 1978, and 1979, Rosalynn Carter undertook a number of foreign trips, often accompanying her husband. In other instances, specifically to represent her husband at presidential inaugurations and state funerals, she traveled with their daughter, Amy, and other US officials. None of these visits garnered the sort of recognition and press coverage that her 1977 trip to Latin America had until the first lady again served in a diplomatic capacity in November 1979, when she made an abbreviated visit to Thailand to assess the humanitarian tragedy unfolding in Southeast Asia. On the surface, the 1979 trip bears little resemblance to the earlier one. The president did not send the first lady to Thailand in an attempt to articulate and communicate a new US policy for the region. Nor did she enjoy the extensive and in-depth briefings she had in May 1977. Much of her contribution to shaping policy came after she returned to the United States. Yet, similarities do exist. The president again dispatched his wife to serve as his envoy, in meetings with high-ranking Thai officials and representatives from voluntary agencies. He depended on her assessment of the situation on the ground as he and administration officials continued to develop the US response. President Carter also relied on his wife's stature among the American people to convince them to contribute to relief efforts. The first lady, as she had in 1977, demonstrated the ability to represent the United States at the highest levels.

She had, of course, remained active throughout the presidential term on the domestic stage. Many of her activities again reflected the advocacy role she had played as first lady of Georgia, especially her commitment to securing essential mental health services and her empathy for individuals suffering from depression. In late February 1977 President Carter issued Executive Order 11973, establishing the President's Commission on Mental Health (PCMH). Although the 1967 Postal Revenue and Federal Salary Act prohibited the first lady from serving in an appointed cabinet position, President Carter appointed his wife honorary chair. Gerald Grob asserted that Rosalynn's role was an outgrowth of her earlier mental health activism in support of her fellow Georgians.[70] The first lady attained significant visibility in February 1979 when she testified before the Senate Subcommittee on Human Resources in support of the administration's Mental Health Systems Act. The first lady's success during the 1977 Latin America mission, in addition to her ability to advocate for others experiencing trauma, meant that she would be able to draw significant global attention and push other countries and the United Nations to respond to a humanitarian crisis.

The worsening situation in Southeast Asia prompted US intervention and influenced the decision to send the first lady to Thailand. In 1978, Vietnamese forces invaded Kampuchea (Cambodia). The invasion, combined with already poor harvests, exacerbated famine conditions there. Seeking food, some Kampucheans fled to refugee camps along the Kampuchean-Thai border. Those who remained in Kampuchea suffered from severe malnourishment. Initially, the administration's response came in the form of relaxed refugee requirements. At the June 1979 Group of 7 (G-7) Tokyo economic summit, President Carter announced that the United States would accept 17,000 refugees from Indochina each month, bringing the yearly total to 168,000 refugees.[71] On October 15, he announced a US pledge of $7 million to the larger UN International Children's Fund (UNICEF)/International Committee for the Red Cross (ICRC) effort.[72] Following further appeals from these agencies, the president on October 24 offered an additional $3 million and requested further congressional action on a supplemental Food for Peace (PL-480) appropriation to speed needed commodities to the region.[73]

President Carter also requested that Senator James Sasser (D-TN), Senator Max Baucus (D-MT), and Senator John Danforth (R-MO) travel to Southeast Asia in October 1979 to convince the Heng Samrin regime and the government of Vietnam to allow ICRC and UNICEF truck convoys from Thailand across the border to Kampuchea to bring needed food and supplies. They toured three refugee camps on the Thai-Kampuchea border as well as Phnom Penh. Upon their return, they took part in a White House press briefing on October 26, at which Sasser asserted that if the government in Phnom Penh failed to act, "tens of thousands of people, we believe, will die and perish over the next 30–60–90 days."[74] Their recommendations included a forceful call for national and international relief.[75]

Yet by early November, Aaron and Brzezinski pressed the president to undertake additional efforts; the relief effort was getting lost "in the bureaucracy."[76] Aaron reported that he, Brzezinski, and NSC staff member Henry Owen had discussed a series of needed steps, including the dispatch of the first lady, accompanied by other US officials such as Surgeon General Julius Richmond and Director of the Centers for Disease Control and Prevention (CDC) William Foege to Thailand to visit refugee camps as well as meet with the king and queen of Thailand and Prime Minister Chamanand Kriangsak.[77]

On November 7 Rosalynn Carter, Richmond, Foege, and the other members of the delegation departed Washington.[78] Their preparations were necessarily rushed, but Kaufman wrote that the first lady did receive pre-trip briefings by both State Department and NSC officials "specifically about the causes of the refugee crisis."[79] Finch Hoyt, describing it as a "trip to Hades," noted that while en route to Bangkok for twenty-two hours "in an ancient aircraft custom-designed for Lyndon Johnson," Rosalynn spent her time largely in meetings and reviewing what she had learned from the briefings.[80] Nevertheless, the first lady later wrote, "Nothing had prepared me for the human suffering I saw in the refugee camps when I arrived."[81]

In contrast to the 1977 Latin America trip, the delegation spent only about forty hours on the ground in Thailand. In her arrival remarks in Bangkok, Carter underscored the dire nature of the crisis: "We are filled with alarm when we contemplate the possibility that the Cambodian people are facing extinction as a result of war and famine."[82] The first lady went to three camps and the Lumpini refugee transit center in Bangkok. She met with King Phumiphol Aduldet and Queen Sirikit, along with Kriangsak, in addition to other Thai officials and representatives from the voluntary agencies.[83] Recalling her visit to the newly constructed Sakeo Camp, administered by the UN High Commissioner for Refugees (UNHCR), she wrote: "Swallowing hard and blinking back tears, my reaction was to move, not just stand there—to do something, to talk to someone. I leaned down to touch the brow of one of the refugees and spoke quietly, 'Hello,' but there was no reaction. I kept moving, kept speaking to them, but most just stared into space with blank looks on their faces."[84] Carter found the emaciated children hardest to take; holding a baby girl, she reflected, "I had been thinking to myself, as the television cameras followed me through the camp, that if Americans could see and understand this unbelievable suffering they would surely respond."[85]

In her meeting with the king and queen, the first lady found the king somewhat reluctant to commit additional resources to resolve the issues. She noted that he was "very displeased that his own prime minister had opened the borders. He remained convinced that Thailand was doing too much to help with not enough assistance from others."[86] In her departure remarks, she graciously acknowledged the efforts the Thai government had taken to meet the crisis, adding, "I came as a personal representative of my husband, the President of the United States. I return to America a devoted friend to Thailand with a renewed sense of mission."[87]

In her formal report to the president, the first lady summarized camp conditions and the position the Thai government faced. The decision to allow additional refugees had come at a cost, she noted, and the absence of third country support "could undercut their current humanitarian approach. We must give Thailand our support and understanding."[88] Rosalynn praised the efforts of the international organizations and voluntary groups but insisted that the coordination of aid should be "improved."[89] To that end, she included a number of recommendations, ranging from airlifting more foodstuffs and increasing the numbers of US volunteers to encouraging other nations to increase their contributions. On November 13, President Carter approved several of these initiatives, including the airlift of "vegetable oils and special foods for children" to Thailand as well as a $6 million authorization for the purchase of rice.[90]

The first lady also briefed UN Secretary-General Kurt Waldheim after she returned to the United States. She called him to broach the idea of designating a single coordinator for relief efforts, a recommendation she had heard during her conversations with aid workers. Waldheim agreed and appointed Sir Robert Jackson, who had coordinated relief efforts during the 1971 famine in Bangladesh.[91] Carter and Waldheim met at the UN headquarters building in New York prior to her December 12 address before the Council on Foreign Relations. The first lady's handwritten notes from the meeting indicate that she advocated for an early donor conference as soon as possible and for a strengthening of Jackson's role. She also noted, "Would be helpful if you *expressed concern* for 600,000 *who are on border*—speaking out on international relief."[92]

During her address to the Council on Foreign Relations, Rosalynn underscored the dire conditions, stating: "The plight of the Cambodian people is truly one of the gravest humanitarian issues that the world has ever witnessed. Like the Holocaust, it is a tragedy of indescribable dimension. . . . The world cannot stand by—silently—in a moral lapse, as we did thirty-seven years ago."[93] The first lady highlighted the efforts the Carter administration had undertaken as a result of her report, including an additional $2 million donation to UNICEF and airlifting baby food. Continuing into the new year, she addressed the National Cambodian Crisis Committee (NCCC), meeting at the White House on

January 29, 1980, acknowledging that both the Iranian hostage situation and the Soviet invasion of Afghanistan had the potential to "push Cambodia off the front pages and out of the public's mind." She insisted that more must be done to ensure that this did not happen.[94]

Some twelve years later, Kathy Cade reflected on the first lady's efforts regarding the Cambodian crisis, asserting that her response illustrated her "ability to mobilize people, her capacity to inspire them, and her talent in drawing on resources in both the public and the private sectors to bring about significant change."[95] Carter's trip aided the NCCC in raising some $70 million from Americans outside the government, and she continued her involvement in public initiatives throughout 1980.[96]

Although not garnering the same volume of positive notice as the 1977 Latin America trip, Rosalynn's visit and her subsequent initiatives did elicit praise. Syndicated columnist Jack Anderson characterized the trip as a "mission of mercy to publicize the Cambodian's [*sic*] desperate need of food and medicine."[97] The first lady's efforts were not above criticism, however. A *Christian Science Monitor* editorial noted that some refugee workers had intimated that her trip was "politicking" for the president; yet, the editorial continued, "The charge seems belied by her heart felt [*sic*] concern for victims . . . [and] will unquestionably be belied if, after her highly visible journey, she put in the hard, patient work necessary to follow through on her pledge delivered while among the refugees," which indeed, she did.[98] An all-female congressional delegation also took umbrage at Rosalynn's work. In early November 1979, six members of the House of Representatives—Elizabeth Holtzman (D-NY), Patricia Schroeder (D-CO), Margaret Heckler (R-MA), Lindy Boggs (D-LA), Barbara Mikulski (D-MD), and Olympia Snowe (R-ME)—made a one-day trip to Phnom Penh to discuss aid issues with the regime. The delegation—prior to departing for Phnom Penh—met with the first lady in Thailand to review her tour of the camps and their impending visit.[99] Despite this meeting, *Los Angeles Times* reporter Keyes Beech wrote that several of the representatives "were privately critical of Rosalynn Carter's visit to Thai refugee camps last week, complaining that the First Lady was 'out to steal our thunder.'"[100]

Their concerns might say more about the limited space then afforded women in US diplomacy. Regardless, Rosalynn Carter effectively remade the image of the American first lady, as this chapter has shown, to include the role of diplomat. Her political experience had made her an invaluable asset to her husband both while he was governor of Georgia and later as president of the United States. Because of his implicit trust in his wife's political instincts and intellect, President Carter did not hesitate to send her to Latin America to communicate his "reset" of US–Latin American relations and to Thailand to assess famine conditions. In so doing, he opened his administration up to criticism from various sides: from those who believed that a first lady would not adequately or competently represent the interests of the United States to those who believed that the first lady's marital status (not her own accomplishments) served as the sole criterion for her selection in this capacity. President Carter ignored these judgments and continued to use Rosalynn's many talents just as he would those of other members of his administration. Her talents would lend themselves to numerous causes after they returned to Georgia, and their marriage of nearly three-quarters of a century still fosters their activism as this book goes to press.

## NOTES

The views expressed in this chapter are my own and not necessarily those of the Department of State and/or the US government. All sources used are unclassified and available to the public. I would like to thank my Office of the Historian colleagues Adam M. Howard, Laura R. Kolar, and Kathleen B. Rasmussen for their helpful comments. JCL archivists Ceri McCarron, Brittany Parris, and Keith Shuler provided invaluable assistance during the researching of this chapter. David Langbart of the National Archives and Records Administration also offered guidance regarding AAD citations.

## ABBREVIATIONS USED IN NOTES

| | |
|---|---|
| AAD | Access to Archival Databases, National Archives and Records Administration |
| CFPF | Central Foreign Policy File |
| FLO | First Lady's Office |
| FLPO | First Lady's Projects Office |
| *FRUS* | *Foreign Relations of the United States* |
| GPO | Government Printing Office |
| JCL | Jimmy Carter Presidential Library, Atlanta, Georgia |
| NSC | National Security Council |
| *PPPUS* | Public Papers of the Presidents of the United States |
| PRC | Policy Review Committee |
| RG | Record Group |
| USNA | United States National Archives and Records Administration |

1. Jimmy Carter also made similar statements in interviews. When asked by the editors of *U.S. News & World Report*—in an interview published in the September 13, 1976, issue of the newsmagazine—what the "single most important issue influencing voters" in the presidential campaign was, Carter indicated that it was the "desire to restore respect for and trust of" the federal government. The interview is printed in *Conversations with Carter*, ed. Don Richardson (Boulder, CO: Lynne Rienner, 1998), 21.

2. For more on Jimmy Carter's worldview, see Jerel A. Rosati, "Jimmy Carter, a Man Before His Time? The Emergence and Collapse of the First Post–Cold War Presidency," *Presidential Studies Quarterly* 23, no. 3: *The Domestic and Foreign Policy Presidencies* (Summer 1993): 459–476; David Skidmore, "Carter and the Failure of Foreign Policy Reform," *Political Science Quarterly* 108, no. 4 (Winter 1993–1994): 699–729.

3. Jimmy Carter, "Our Foreign Relations," remarks before the Chicago Council on Foreign Relations, March 15, 1976, in *FRUS, 1977–1980*, vol. 1: *Foundations of Foreign Policy*, ed. Kristin L. Ahlberg (Washington, DC: GPO, 2014), doc. 4.

4. Jimmy Carter, interview, *Encore American and Worldwide News*, April 5, 1976, in *The Presidential Campaign 1976*, vol. 1, pt. 1 (Washington: GPO, 1978), 136.

5. "Review of United States Policy Toward Latin America," n.d., in *FRUS, 1977–1980*, vol. 24: *South America; Latin American Region*, ed. Sara Berndt (Washington, DC: GPO, 2017), doc. 4. Robert Pastor sent a copy of the review to Zbigniew Brzezinski under a March 14 memorandum, in Berndt, *FRUS, 1977–1980*, vol. 24, doc. 5.

6. Minutes of a PRC Committee Meeting, March 24, 1977, in Berndt, *FRUS, 1977–1980*, vol. 24, doc. 7. As Zbigniew Brzezinski later recalled, the United States now had to "deal with the region as a collection of mature states with whom we had diverse relationships." Brzezinski, *Power and Principle: Memoirs of the National Security Adviser, 1977–1980* (Boston: Farrar, Straus, and Giroux), 135.

7. Minutes of PRC meeting, March 24, 1977.

8. Richardson, *Conversations with Carter*, 64.

9. As Jimmy Carter noted in his memoirs, "Our country has been strongest and most effective when morality and a commitment to freedom and democracy have been most clearly emphasized in our foreign policy." Carter, *Keeping Faith: Memoirs of a President* (New York: Bantam, 1982), 142. For additional assessments on Carter's views on human rights, see Barbara A. Keys, *Reclaiming American Virtue: The Human Rights Revolution of the 1970s* (Cambridge, MA: Harvard University Press, 2014); Joseph Renouard, *Human Rights in American Foreign Policy: From the 1960s to the Soviet Collapse* (Philadelphia: University of Pennsylvania Press, 2016); Robert A. Strong, *Working in the World: Jimmy Carter and the Making of American Foreign Policy* (Baton Rouge: Louisiana State University Press, 2000); Mary E. Stuckey, *Jimmy Carter, Human Rights, and the National Agenda* (College Station: Texas A&M University Press, 2008). See also Hauke Hartmann, "U.S. Human Rights Policy under Carter and Reagan, 1977–1981," *Human Rights Quarterly* 23, no. 2 (May 2001): 402–430; David F. Schmitz and Vanessa Walker, "Jimmy Carter and the Foreign Policy of Human Rights: The Development of a Post–Cold War Foreign Policy," *Diplomatic History* 28, no. 1 (January 2004): 113–145.

10. Cyrus R. Vance made these remarks in response to a question posed at his January 31, 1977, press conference. Telegram 24394 to multiple diplomatic and consular posts, February 3, 1977, in *FRUS, 1977–1980*, vol. 2: *Human Rights and Humanitarian Affairs*, ed. Kristin L. Ahlberg (Washington, DC: GPO, 2013), doc. 8. See also Ahlberg, *FRUS, 1977–1980*, vol. 1, doc. 18. Vance later reflected that he favored this use of quiet diplomacy because it allowed officials to "sav[e] public pressure for those occasions that called for a strong and forthright public statement." Vance, *Hard Choices: Critical Years in America's Foreign Policy* (New York: Simon and Schuster, 1983), 46.

11. Ahlberg, *FRUS*, 1977–1980, vol. 2, doc. 23, fn. 2. For an excerpt of Vance's statement, see Ahlberg, *FRUS*, 1977–1980, vol. 1, doc. 22.

12. Jimmy Carter, address to the UN General Assembly, March 17, 1977, in Ahlberg, *FRUS*, 1977–1980, vol. 1, doc. 29.

13. Jimmy Carter, address at the University of Notre Dame, May 22, 1977, in Ahlberg, *FRUS*, 1977–1980, vol. 1, doc. 40. Zbigniew Brzezinski said that Carter used the address to explain "the premises on which his foreign policy would be founded" and to present "the goals we had developed with him." Brzezinski, *Power and Principle*, 56.

14. Vanessa Walker, "At the End of Influence: The Letelier Assassination, Human Rights, and Rethinking Intervention in US–Latin American Relations," *Journal of Contemporary History* 41, no. 1: *Conflict and Cooperation in the Cold War* (January 2011): 115.

15. Jimmy Carter, "Address on Nuclear Energy and World Order," May 23, 1976, in *The Presidential Campaign 1976*, vol. 1, pt. 1 (Washington: GPO, 1978), 185.

16. Winston Lord to Henry Kissinger, memorandum, "Implications of FRG-Brazil Nuclear Sale," June 16, 1975, and Telegram 58655 to Paris, March 11, 1976, in *FRUS*, 1973–1976, vol. E-15, pt. 2: *Documents on Western Europe, 1973–1976*, ed. Kathleen B. Rasmussen (Washington, DC: GPO, 2014), docs. 289 and 334, respectively. Regarding the FRG sale, Gaddis Smith wrote that the episode "bruised American relations with both countries." He noted, "The problem of how to apply pressure and what pressure was delicate. The United States, with relatively abundant access to uranium and substantial non-nuclear sources of energy, was vulnerable to the charge of being the dog in the manger—denying to others something which it did not need itself. And how far did Washington want to go in damaging bilateral and alliance relations in pursuit of this one goal?" Smith, *Morality, Reason, and Power: American Diplomacy in the Carter Years* (New York: Hill and Wang, 1986), 61.

17. Jimmy Carter, "Address on Nuclear Weapons Proliferation," September 25, 1976, in *The Presidential Campaign 1976*, vol. 1, pt. 2 (Washington, DC: GPO, 1978), 817. Carter alleged that the United States had done "nothing" after the West German sale was announced and that Secretary of State Henry Kissinger had practiced "briefcase diplomacy" only after the Italian and Pakistani governments had completed negotiations.

18. PD/NSC 8, "Nuclear Non-Proliferation Policy," March 24, 1977, in *FRUS*, 1977–1980, vol. 26: *Arms Control and Nonproliferation*, ed. Chris J. Tudda (Washington, DC: GPO, 2015), doc. 330.

19. Peter Bourne, *Jimmy Carter: A Comprehensive Biography from Plains to Postpresidency* (New York: Scribner's, 1997), 391.

20. Jimmy Carter, "Address to the Organization of American States," April 14, 1977, in Ahlberg, *FRUS*, 1977–1980, vol. 1, doc. 33.

21. Rosalynn Carter, *First Lady from Plains* (Boston: Houghton Mifflin, 1984), 185.

22. Carter, *First Lady from Plains*, 185.

23. "First Lady Going Abroad," *Washington Post*, May 11, 1977, B6; US Department of State to the Embassies in Kingston, San José, Quito, Lima, Brasilia, Bogota, and Caracas. Telegram 104903, May 7, 1977, D770161–0958, CFPF, 1973–1979 Electronic Telegrams, RG 59: General Records of the Department of State, USNA (accessed through AAD). Betty Glad explained that the first lady toured "only countries approved by the State

Department as having a positive or substantially improving human rights record." Glad, *An Outsider in the White House: Jimmy Carter, His Advisors, and the Making of American Foreign Policy* (Ithaca, NY: Cornell University Press, 2009), 242.

24. Kathy B. Smith, "The First Lady Represents America: Rosalynn Carter in South America," *Presidential Studies Quarterly* 27, no. 3 (Summer 1997): 542.

25. Gil Troy, *Mr. and Mrs. President: From the Trumans to the Clintons*, 2nd ed. (Lawrence: University Press of Kansas, 2000), 195, 254. Jill Abraham Hummer notes that the purpose of the trip was for Patricia Nixon to represent the United States at the inauguration of President William Tolbert of Liberia. In contrast to Troy, Abraham Hummer asserts that Nixon did engage in some substantive discussions with foreign leaders, but these were mostly limited to briefing them on President Nixon's upcoming February 1972 visit to the People's Republic of China. Abraham Hummer, *First Ladies and American Women: In Politics and at Home* (Lawrence: University Press of Kansas, 2017), 132–133.

26. Glad, *Outsider in the White House*, 11. In an earlier work, Betty Glad wrote of Rosalynn Carter, "She was one of her husband's closest political confidantes. Relishing politics, she came to play a gate-keeper role—screening Carter's associates for their loyalty to him, warning Jimmy about whom he could and could not trust." Glad, *Jimmy Carter: In Search of the Great White House* (New York: Norton, 1980), 142. Robert P. Watson made a similar claim; he wrote that President Carter "publicly admitted that his wife, Rosalynn, was his most trusted adviser. Rosalynn, for her part, readily admitted to influencing her husband's decisions as well as those of high-ranking government officials." Watson, *The President's Wives: Reassessing the Office of First Lady* (Boulder, CO: Lynne Rienner, 2000), 29. See also Scott Kaufman, *Plans Unraveled: The Foreign Policy of the Carter Administration* (De Kalb: Northern Illinois University Press, 2008), 25; Barbara Kellerman, "The Political Functions of the Presidential Family," *Presidential Studies Quarterly* 8, no. 3 (Summer 1978): 305.

27. Jimmy Carter, *Why Not the Best? Why One Man Is Optimistic about America's Third Century* (Nashville, TN: Broadman, 1975), 124–125; Glad, *Jimmy Carter*, 147; E. Stanly Godbold Jr., *Jimmy and Rosalynn Carter: The Georgia Years, 1924–1974* (Oxford, UK: Oxford University Press, 2010), 246–248. Peter Bourne wrote that the April 1972 trip included stops in Brazil, Mexico, Costa Rica, Colombia, and Argentina, adding: "In Brazil, where Georgia had a sister-state relationship with the state of Senora, the Carters were particularly well received." Bourne, *Jimmy Carter*, 239.

28. Susanna McBee, "Mrs. Carter's Trip Carefully Crafted to Make Policy Points," *Washington Post*, May 29, 1977, 6.

29. Mary Finch Hoyt, *East Wing: Politics, the Press, and a First Lady* (Philadelphia: Xlibris, 2001), 145–146. According to the *Washington Post*, Finch Hoyt "said that the First Lady was already receiving substantive briefings regarding her trip from various advisers. Some of these were taking the place of her three weekly Spanish classes, which Mrs. Carter has been taking for several months." "First Lady Going Abroad," *Washington Post*, May 11, 1977, B6.

30. Myra G. Gutin, "Rosalynn Carter in the White House," in *The Presidency and Domestic Policies of Jimmy Carter*, ed. Herbert D. Rosenbaum and Alexej Ugrinsky (Westport, CT: Greenwood, 1994), 520.

31. Department of State Briefing Paper, "Human Rights," May 1977, Records of the Office of the National Security Advisor, Staff Material, North-South Files, Bob Pastor's Subject Files, Carter, Mrs.—Visit to Latin America (5/30/77–6/13/77), Folder Country Book B [III] 5/77–7/77, Box 51, JCL.

32. US Department of State to the Embassies in Kingston, San José, Quito, Lima, Brasilia, Bogota, and Caracas. Telegram 104923, May 7, 1977, P840070-0632, CFPF, 1973–1979 Electronic Telegrams, RG 59, USNA.

33. Jane Pisano to Gerald Schecter, memorandum, May 16, 1977, Records of the Office of the National Security Advisor, Zbigniew Brzezinski Material, Schecter/Friendly (Press) Files, Trips/Visits File, Folder 5/30/77–6/12/77, Mrs. Carter Trip to Latin America, Box 12, JCL.

34. John Chatten to Mary Finch Hoyt, memorandum, May 19, 1977, in *FRUS, 1977–1980*, vol. 30: *Public Diplomacy*, ed. Kristin L. Ahlberg (Washington, DC: GPO, 2016), doc. 53.

35. John Reinhardt to Zbigniew Brzezinski, memorandum, "Mrs. Carter's Trip to Latin America," May 20, 1977, Records of the Office of the National Security Advisor, Zbigniew Brzezinski Material, Schecter/Friendly (Press) Files, Trips/Visits File, Folder 5/30/77–6/12/77, Mrs. Carter Trip to Latin America, Box 12, JCL.

36. Jerome Levinson to Rosalynn Carter, memorandum, May 14, 1977, FLO, Mary Hoyt's Foreign Trips Files (Press), Folder Foreign Trips Background Material, 1977–1980, Box 24, JCL.

37. Godbold, *Jimmy and Rosalynn Carter*, 213.

38. Godbold, 88–90.

39. Godbold, 91.

40. Susanna McBee, "'Substantive' Talks Are Slated for Mrs. Carter on Latin Trip," *Washington Post*, May 25, 1977, A24.

41. Laura Foreman, "Mrs. Carter Leaves on Latin Tour Today: She Will Confer with Leaders of 7 Nations During 12-Day Visit," *New York Times*, May 30, 1977, 4.

42. Susanna McBee, "Carter's Latin Approach: No Undelivered Promises," *Washington Post*, June 2, 1977, A23.

43. Notes of a meeting, FLO, Mary Hoyt's Foreign Trips Files (Press), Folder Peru, June 3, 1977, Box 24, JCL (emphasis in original).

44. Smith, "First Lady Represents America," 544; Scott Kaufman, *Rosalynn Carter: Equal Partner in the White House* (Lawrence: University Press of Kansas, 2007), 67.

45. Embassy in Quito to US Department of State, Telegram 3606, June 2, 1977, D770196-0337, CFPF, 1973–1979 Electronic Telegrams, RG 59, USNA.

46. Embassy in Quito to US Department of State, Telegram 3606.

47. Smith, "First Lady Represents America," 544.

48. Embassy in Quito to USIA, Telegram 3637, June 3, 1977, transmitting text of June 2 press conference, FLO, Mary Hoyt's Foreign Trips Files (Press), Folder Ecuador, June 1–3, 1977, Box 24, JCL; Stuart E. Eizenstat, *President Carter: The White House Years* (New York: St. Martin's, 2018), 110. On June 1, President Carter signed the American Convention

on Human Rights on behalf of the United States. For the text, see Department of State *Bulletin*, July 4, 1977, 28.

49. Carter, *First Lady from Plains*, 201.

50. Notes of a meeting, FLO, Mary Hoyt's Foreign Trips Files (Press), Folder Peru, June 3, 1977, Box 24, JCL.

51. Notes of a meeting, FLO, Mary Hoyt's Foreign Trips Files (Press), Folder Peru, June 3, 1977, Box 24, JCL.

52. Carter, *First Lady from Plains*, 203.

53. Kaufman, *Plans Unraveled*, 103; Carter, *First Lady from Plains*, 204.

54. Embassy in Bogota to US Department of State, Telegram 5392, June 10, 1977, P840086-0764; N770003-0677, CFPF, 1973–1979 Electronic Telegrams, RG 59, USNA.

55. Embassy in Bogota to US Department of State, Telegram 5392.

56. Carter, *First Lady from Plains*, 206.

57. Embassy in Bogota to US Department of State, Telegram 5392.

58. Glad, *Outsider in the White House*, 242.

59. Carter, *First Lady from Plains*, 207.

60. "Balancing in Brazil," *New York Times*, June 11, 1977, 14. In assessing the visit to Brazil, Rosalynn Carter stated that it "was the most difficult of all. We were quite concerned because the military regime was not happy with my husband." Laura Foreman, "Mrs. Carter Keeps Stress on Rights," *New York Times*, June 8, 1977, 2.

61. See Kristin L. Ahlberg, "Eleanor Rosalynn Smith Carter," in *A Companion to First Ladies*, ed. Katherine A. S. Sibley (West Sussex, UK: Wiley-Blackwell, 2016), 574.

62. "Remarks of the President and Mrs. Carter on Her Return," June 12, 1977, in Jimmy Carter, *PPPUS, 1977*, Book 1 (Washington, DC: GPO, 1980), 1098.

63. Rosalynn Carter's remarks in San Jose, California, June 21, 1977, transcript, FLO, Mary Hoyt's Foreign Trips Files (Press), Folder Foreign Trips Background Material 1977– 1980, Box 24, JCL.

64. Eizenstat, *President Carter*, 110.

65. Faye Lind Jensen, "An Awesome Responsibility: Rosalynn Carter as First Lady," *Presidential Studies Quarterly* 20, no. 4 (Fall 1990): 770. See also Lind Jensen, "These Are Precious Years: The Papers of Rosalynn Smith Carter," in *Modern First Ladies: Their Documentary Legacy*, ed. Nancy Kegan Smith and Mary C. Ryan (Washington, DC: National Archives Trust Fund Board, 1989), 145–146. Gutin and Kaufman also cite this specific poll data; see Gutin, "Rosalynn Carter in the White House," 520–521; Kaufman, *Rosalynn Carter*, 74.

66. David Vidal, "Ambassador Rosalynn Carter: First Lady Confounds the Skeptics and Makes a Striking Success of Her Latin American Tour," *New York Times*, June 14, 1977, 18.

67. Susanna McBee, "First Lady Stresses Journey Was Her Show," *Washington Post*, June 14, 1977, A11.

68. For more detailed overviews of this criticism, see Smith, "First Lady Represents America," 546; Abraham Hummer, *First Ladies and American Women*, 148–149.

69. Meg Greenfield, "Mrs. President," *Washington Post*, June 15, 1977, A17.

70. Gerald N. Grob, "Public Policy and Mental Illnesses: Jimmy Carter's Presidential Commission on Mental Health," *Milbank Quarterly* 83, no. 3 (September 2005): 429. There is some inconsistency with the commission's title; some sources refer to it as the Presidential Commission on Mental Health, whereas other sources and the executive order refer to it as the President's Commission on Mental Health.

71. Vance, *Hard Choices*, 126.

72. Jimmy Carter, *PPPUS, 1979*, Book 2 (Washington, DC: GPO, 1980), 1925. The $7 million included $2 million from the US Emergency Refugee and Migration Fund and $5 million worth of Food for Peace (PL-480) commodities.

73. Carter, *PPPUS, 1979*, Book 2, 2011–2012. The president also requested another $9 million for refugee funding, indicated that the administration would support a congressional proposal to earmark $30 million in relief, asked the President's Commission on World Hunger to recommend additional steps, and appealed for Americans to increase their individual donations. The undated PCWH report is printed in Ahlberg, *FRUS*, 1977–1980, vol. 2, doc. 266.

74. "Press Briefing," October 26, 1979, Department of State *Bulletin*, December 1979, 4.

75. "Senators' Report," October 26, 1979, Department of State *Bulletin*, December 1979, 10.

76. David Aaron to Jimmy Carter, memorandum, "Kampuchea Relief," November 3, 1979, in *FRUS*, 1977–1980, vol. 22: *Southeast Asia and the Pacific*, ed. David P. Nickles and Melissa Jane Taylor (Washington, DC: GPO, 2017), doc. 66.

77. Nickles and Taylor, *FRUS*, 1977–1980, vol. 22, doc. 66. President Carter approved the recommendation that the first lady travel to Thailand, writing on the first page of Aaron's memorandum: "Zbig, Let Rosalynn go w/Richmond. Warren [Christopher] agrees. J." In addition to Richmond and Foege, Assistant Secretary of State for East Asian and Pacific Affairs Richard Holbrooke, Deputy Assistant Secretary of State for East Asian and Pacific Affairs Michael Armacost, former Iowa governor Harold Hughes, and others accompanied the first lady to Thailand.

78. Steven R. Weisman, "Mrs. Carter Off Today on a Trip to Refugee Camps in Thailand," *New York Times*, November 7, 1979, A3.

79. Kaufman, *Rosalynn Carter*, 83.

80. Finch Hoyt, *East Wing*, 191.

81. Carter, *First Lady from Plains*, 295.

82. Marlene Cimons, "Mrs. Carter Says Trip Shows U.S. Concern," *Los Angeles Times*, November 9, 1979, 8.

83. "Mrs. Carter in Thailand for Visit," *New York Times*, November 9, 1979, A2; Henry Kamm, "Mrs. Carter Visits Thai Camp: 'It's Like Nothing I've Seen,'" *New York Times*, November 10, 1979, 2.

84. Carter, *First Lady from Plains*, 295.

85. Carter, 295–296.

86. Carter, 297.

87. Embassy in Bangkok to US Department of State and USIA, Telegram 46196, November 12, 1979, D790521-0386, CFPF, 1973–1979 Electronic Telegrams, RG 59, USNA.

88. "Report of Mrs. Rosalynn Carter on Cambodian Relief," November 8–10, 1979, FLO, FLPO, Kathryn Cade's Project Files, Folder Cambodian Relief-Rosalynn Carter's Report, 11/79, Box 6, JCL.

89. "Report of Mrs. Rosalynn Carter on Cambodian Relief."

90. Steven R. Weisman, "Carter Asks Relief Groups to Avoid Criticism over Aid to Cambodians," *New York Times*, November 14, 1979, A8; "Carter Orders Aid, Airlift for Cambodian Refugees," *Washington Post*, November 14, 1979, A5.

91. Carter, *First Lady from Plains*, 298.

92. Undated handwritten notes from December 12 Waldheim meeting, FLO, FLPO, Kathryn Cade's Project Files, Folder Cambodian Relief-Today Show-Rosalynn Carter Handwritten Notes, Reports and Remarks, 12/79, Box 6, JCL (emphasis in original).

93. "Mrs. Carter's Remarks on the Record," press release, December 12, 1979, FLO, FLPO, Kathryn Cade's Project Files, Folder Cambodian Relief-Address to the Council on Foreign Relations, New York, 12/12/79 [1], Box 2, JCL.

94. Press release, January 29, 1980, FLO, FLPO, Kathryn Cade's Project Files, Folder Cambodian Relief-National Cambodia Crisis Committee Meeting 1/29/80 [1], Box 5, JCL.

95. Quote is from Cade's remarks as a discussant at the Hofstra University Presidential Conference on the domestic politics of the Carter administration. See Rosenbaum and Ugrinsky, *Presidency and Domestic Policies of Jimmy Carter*, 531–532.

96. Cade's remarks in Rosenbaum and Ugrinsky, *Presidency and Domestic Policies of Jimmy Carter*, 533–534.

97. Jack Anderson, "Many Hands Help in Mission of Mercy," *Washington Post*, November 22, 1979, 21.

98. "Cambodia: 'Do All We Possibly Can,'" *Christian Science Monitor*, November 13, 1979, 32.

99. Embassy in Bangkok to US Department of State, Telegram 46875, November 15, 1979, D790526-0206, CFPF, 1973–1979 Electronic Telegrams, RG 59, USNA.

100. Keyes Beech, "Cambodia Welcomes Aid, Visitors Told," *Los Angeles Times*, November 13, 1979, 5.

# CHAPTER 16

# The Lone Star Yankee as First Lady
## Barbara Bush of Texas

Myra G. Gutin

The historian Herbert S. Parmet wrote of George Herbert Walker Bush in his well-respected biography of the forty-first president that Bush was a "Lone Star Yankee," a man reared and educated among Eastern elites who decided to seek his fortune in the oilfields of West Texas.[1] Parmet's narrative follows the financial success and political ascendancy of Bush as he and his family put down roots in Odessa, later in Midland, and finally in Houston, Texas.

At the age of twenty years, Bush made a fateful decision when he asked Barbara Pierce, another Eastern elite daughter, to be his wife. Both had been raised with similar values and attitudes, but a life in politics and living in Texas could never have been in Pierce's plans. Texas, however, was her lot, and the Bushes lived in the state for seventy-one of their seventy-three years of marriage. It was a challenging environment in which to live in the late 1940s, but it became home, and she adapted to the South.

When the former first lady died in 2018, historian Timothy Naftali observed that in her long life, she had learned about flexibility; if she were wrong, she could change her opinions. He wrote, "Barbara Bush never ceased questioning, learning, and adapting—changing along with the nation that she and her family served."[2]

Barbara did not discuss or write a great deal about her life in the South, but some conclusions can be drawn from her behavior and some of her writings that provide a clearer picture of her time in Texas and the ways in which it affected her. It was a lengthy journey from Rye, New York, to Texas, to Maine, to Washington, DC, and back again to Texas, but "the first lady of the greatest generation" was loved and admired in her adopted state and by her country.[3]

Barbara is broadly classified as a Southern first lady even though she was born and raised in New York; she lived in Texas far longer than she ever lived in the North. Her Southern narrative is not that of Lady Bird Johnson or even her daughter-in-law, Laura Bush. Though not born in the Southern part of the country, like many others described in this book, Barbara Bush was affected by Southern clime and culture. Moreover, she wholly embraced the Southern notion of the importance of family, and she learned Southern graciousness. While campaigning for her husband, she also ingratiated herself with Texas voters, who in those early races when a poll tax still fell most heavily on Black voters, were nearly all white. She became a political wife; she did what was necessary to be social, to get along, and to be accepted. Some of her attitudes and values were not those held by Southerners, however. In the 1950s, she opposed segregation, and later she was pro-choice, but she kept these controversial opinions to herself.

A Southern influence can be discerned in the selection of her White House initiative, literacy. Her love of reading was nurtured by her mother but amplified by the Southern love of literature and storytelling. Her growing willingness not only to read but to speak out was perhaps bolstered by the examples set by the larger-than-life Texas women of her generation: Johnson, Barbara Jordan, Ann Richards, and Liz Carpenter.

Despite living mainly in the South, for almost six decades Barbara spent six months of the year, from April to October, at Walker's Point, in Kennebunkport, Maine. There she recharged her Northern batteries. Still, at the end of every summer she returned to Houston, and until shortly before her passing, she was actively involved in philanthropy and volunteerism in her adopted hometown. Houstonians grew used to seeing the Bushes at social events, at restaurants, and endorsing various causes. Barbara continued to advocate for literacy, and George was involved with his presidential library and various philanthropic endeavors, notably working with former president Bill Clinton in trouble spots around the world.

Although George H. W. Bush spent less of his year in Maine, there is no evidence that either Bush was seen as a Northern interloper; indeed, they were integrated into the fabric of Texas life. Barbara arrived in the Lone Star State as a visitor, but over time, she was accepted as a Texan. To the end of her life, she was a study in contradictions. She was part of the community and accepted its Southernness but retained East Coast sensibilities and polish. Like her husband, she, too, was a Lone Star Yankee.

## AN UNEXPECTED POLITICAL—AND SOUTHERN—LIFE

The third of four children of Pauline Robinson Pierce and Marvin Pierce, Barbara Pierce was born in New York City on June 8, 1925. She had an impressive

First Lady Barbara Bush, January 8, 1989. Photo by David Valdez. Courtesy of the Library of Congress Prints and Photographs Division. Reproduction Number: LC-USZ62-98303 (b&w film copy neg.) LC-USZC4-1701 (color film copy transparency).

lineage; her great-great-great uncle was President Franklin Pierce (1853–1857), and her mother was the daughter of James Robinson, an Ohio Supreme Court justice. Marvin Pierce was the assistant to the publisher of *McCall's* and in later years would rise to become president of the company.

Pauline Pierce was a cultured, if somewhat distant, woman known to have many enthusiasms, including gardening and collecting antiques. Later, Barbara Pierce Bush would write that she was not among her mother's enthusiasms, and the two had a respectful but tepid relationship. Pauline doted on her older daughter, Martha, an attractive young woman whose photo once adorned the cover of a *Vogue* magazine college issue. Friends thought that Pauline Pierce could be mean to her younger daughter, who would spend a lifetime battling weight issues. At mealtimes, Pauline would say to her girls, "Eat up, Martha— not you, Barbara."[4]

The occasional caustic comment Barbara suffered from her mother caused her to develop a thick skin and an acerbic tongue. One of her childhood friends commented that she could freeze out other children or saddle them with the kind of nickname that hurt.[5] Her relationship with her father was the opposite of her relationship with her mother, however. Father and daughter were close, and there was great warmth in their relationship. Later, Barbara would write of her father that he was the "fairest man I knew, until I met George Bush."[6] Perhaps because of the yin and yang of the two different relationships she had with her parents, she developed a life philosophy early on that would serve her well: "You can like what you do, or you can dislike it. I have chosen to like it."[7]

Barbara attended the Milton School, a public school, through sixth grade and then the Rye Country Day School through ninth grade. The following year, she was sent to her sister's alma mater, Ashley Hall, in Charleston, South Carolina. In her autobiography, Barbara wrote she believed part of the reason she was sent there was because it was cheaper than a Northeastern school, but Ashley Hall probably appealed to Pauline Pierce as a fashionable boarding and finishing school that would make her daughters more marriageable.[8]

The South Carolina Barbara encountered in the early 1940s enforced segregation. South Carolina, of course, had been the first state to vote for secession from the Union in 1860 and was and continues to be politically conservative and deeply religious. Women did not win the right to vote in South Carolina until the nineteenth amendment was passed in August 1920. In 1921, the state passed a law allowing women to vote in statewide elections but prohibiting them from jury duty until 1957, and the state itself did not ratify the nineteenth amendment until 1969.

Perhaps in defiance of what she considered benighted attitudes, Mary Vardrine McBee founded Ashley Hall in 1909, with the motto of *Possunt Quae*

*Volunt* [Girls who have the will have the ability], although of course, no Black girls were welcome. McBee was still head of the school during the Pierce girls' tenure. This was Barbara's first exposure to elite Southern norms, and though she was likely oblivious of other aspects of Southern culture that surrounded the school in Jim Crow Charleston, she responded well to the school's strict rules and demanding curriculum. One of her classmates observed, "Being bad meant taking off your hat and gloves when you got out of sight of the school."[9] The girls were certainly expected to uphold high standards of decorum.

Barbara loved Ashley Hall. She was a member of the student council, the swim club, and the drama club (when she visited the school in 1993, she saw a blown-up photo of herself acting in *Much Ado about Nothing*).[10] Though popular, she wrote, "I was so shy at the time and never could have gotten up and given a speech." One of her classmates held a different view and recalled her as "just the prettiest thing and very outgoing and athletic."[11] Tall, with reddish-brown hair, she had also slimmed down by that time.

On Christmas break 1941, during her junior year at Ashley Hall, she attended a dance at the Round Hill Country Club in Greenwich, Connecticut. She was introduced to George H. W. Bush, known as "Poppy," a senior at Phillips Academy in Andover, Massachusetts.[12] She would later recall that young "Poppy" Bush was so attractive and charismatic that when he was in the room, she had difficulty breathing. When she returned home, she told her mother, who demanded details, that she had met a nice boy named Poppy Bush. Before Barbara awoke the next morning, Pauline had gathered intelligence on the new young man in her daughter's life. She learned that the Pierce and Bush families belonged to many of the same clubs. Barbara was irritated that her mother had made inquiries, but she would have been pleased to know that Poppy had told his mother, Dorothy Walker Bush, that he had met "the niftiest girl at the dance, the most terrific person."[13] Years later he would observe, "I never felt toward another girl as I do towards her."[14] Barbara, for her part, she commented, "When I tell my children that George Bush was the first man I ever kissed, they just about want to throw up!"[15]

After Christmas vacation, she returned to Ashley Hall with stories about him. The two began a regular and ardent correspondence. Occasionally, Barbara and her classmates would get together and write prank letters to him. Later that spring, he invited her to be his date to his senior prom.

There is little evidence to suggest she or any of her Ashley Hall classmates were aware of world events, but Barbara's romantic idyll was about to have a collision with the war. Poppy Bush graduated from Phillips Academy and joined the US Navy in June 1942. He had been accepted to Yale but decided to delay matriculation and enlisted on his eighteenth birthday; enrolling in flight training school, he became the youngest fighter pilot in the navy. They continued their correspondence, and George invited Barbara to spend his predeployment leave with him at his family's summer home in Kennebunkport, Maine. While there, the pair became secretly engaged.

Barbara was convinced his family would hate her, but the Bushes instead embraced her—they had done their own intelligence work and knew she, too, came from a socially prominent family (George's father, Prescott Bush, was known to be just as snobby as Pauline). Shortly after the young couple's sojourn in Maine, George Bush headed off to join his squadron in the Pacific.

Barbara, once again following in the footsteps of her sister, set off for her first year at Smith College. Years later, she would say she would not have wanted anyone to look at her grades, far from stellar. She captained the first-year soccer team and was well liked but not especially interested in the classroom. Her father spent time that year explaining his daughter's poor academic performance to Smith's dean of first-year students. He indicated that she was worried about her fiancé serving in the South Pacific, which, as it turned out, she had good reason to be.[16] The couple became formally engaged in December 1943.

Though Barbara returned to Smith for her sophomore year, she dropped out a few weeks into the semester because she was preoccupied with wedding plans; the ceremony was set for December 17, 1944. But George's plane was shot down over Chichi Jima, in the Bonin Islands, on September 2, 1944. Miraculously, even as other American pilots in that assault either drowned in the ocean or were executed on a nearby island, he was spared. He was listed as missing for a time before his parents were informed he had been rescued by a US submarine; he spent a month on that submarine and had no contact with his parents or Barbara. He then returned to his squadron, but his leave was pushed back several times, and he only arrived in Rye on Christmas Eve. He had missed his wedding, but his fiancée scratched out the original date on their invitations, and they were married instead on January 6, 1944. One of her Ashley Hall classmates offered this somewhat cynical assessment: "It was a real storybook romance. They married and went off to New Haven, and she worked her tail off for the rest of her life."[17] As this chapter details, Barbara's life with George would indeed have its challenges, underlined by the expectations of wives of her generation and complicated by living as a transplanted Yankee in Texas for much of every year. However, she continued to follow her own philosophy, deciding to like her life.

Before that, however, the war raged on, and for the next eight months the couple moved around the country as his new squadron was formed and trained for what they assumed would be the invasion of Japan. The Bushes lived in navy quarters in three locations in Michigan, Maine, and Virginia. However, things changed when the United States dropped atomic bombs on Hiroshima and Nagasaki; on September 2, 1945, Japan formally surrendered, and World War II came to an end. Because George had been in the navy for three years and had served overseas, he was one of the first men in his squadron to leave the service. The couple could finally leave for New Haven and his long-delayed college education.

George did well at Yale. He majored in economics and was inducted into Phi Beta Kappa. He played on the baseball team and captained the squad during his senior year. Also during that year he was tapped for the exclusive and secretive Skull and Bones senior society. The men he met in Skull and Bones would help him attain financial success and later would be critical to his success in politics. During their time in New Haven, Barbara gave birth to their first child, George W. Bush.

As George neared graduation, he began to ponder his future. He felt that after three years of war service, he had a lot of catching up to do. He wrote, "I came back to civilian life feeling that I needed to get my degree and go into the business world as soon as possible. I had a family to support."[18] George was reasonably sure he did not want to work in investment banking with his father. He applied for but did not get a job with Procter & Gamble; he was offered a job in the advertising department at Bates Fabrics in New York but declined the position. For a time, the couple considered farming in the Midwest after reading Louis Bromfield's book *The Farm*. As they explored this prospect in more detail, they realized that agriculture required a background and knowledge neither possessed.

Instead, George Bush, like other well-connected and affluent young Easterners he knew, became enamored of the idea of working in the burgeoning oil and gas industry in Texas. His father's Yale classmate and fellow Bonesman Neil Mallon headed Dresser Industries, with a subsidiary, International Derrick and Equipment Company (Ideco), headquartered in Odessa, Texas. Mallon offered Bush a job with Ideco, and he accepted.

Barbara Bush never spoke about her feelings regarding the move to Texas. It is safe to assume she thought her husband would join his father's investment banking firm, and they would build a life in Connecticut or some other Northeastern state. Without any consultation with his wife, however, George decided they would go to Texas.

Barbara might have felt as Lady Bird Johnson did when she married Lyndon Baines Johnson (LBJ), "This was your husband, this was your life."[19] To both young Bushes, going to Texas might have seemed like a great adventure. To Pauline Pierce, it was puzzling, and she asked, "Who had ever heard of Odessa,

Texas?" Barbara Bush would later observe, "As far as my mother was concerned, we could have been living in Russia." George was much more pragmatic: "We all just wanted to make a lot of money quick."[20]

Texas offered that opportunity, and George drove his new red Studebaker coupe, a Yale graduation gift from his parents, to Odessa ahead of his family. In June 1948, he wrote to his friend FitzGerald "Gerry" Bemiss, "Texas would be new and exciting . . . hard on Bar perhaps—and heaven knows many girls would bitch like blazes about such a proposed move. Bar's different though. . . . She lives quite frankly for Georgie and myself. She is wholly unselfish, beautifully tolerant of my weaknesses and idiosyncrasies and ready to faithfully follow any course I choose."[21] He was an equipment clerk at Ideco, earning $375 a month to clean out warehouses and paint fixtures. He rented half of a duplex (with a shared bathroom) and sent for his wife and son to join him. Life in West Texas, however, was harsh; the summers were miserably hot, the rain could be torrential, and the region occasionally had sandstorms. Their one bathroom was also in high demand because they shared the duplex with two sex workers, a mother and daughter. Pauline Pierce, meanwhile, was convinced that her daughter would not be able to buy nice things, so she sent her packages crammed full of cold cream, tissues, and soap. Barbara and George Bush grew up quickly. Although she adapted well, he worried about her and wrote to his mother, "She is happy, I know, but anyone would like to be around her own friends, be able to take at least a passing interest in clothes, parties, etc. She gets absolutely none of this. . . . She is here in this small apartment."[22] For her part, Barbara rarely if ever complained about her circumstances. Indeed, she told a biographer, "I was glad to get away, to move to Texas."[23] She would come to see the move, almost halfway across the country, as her personal declaration of independence, as Susan Page reflects: "On the East Coast, [she] had a critical mother in Rye, and a forceful mother-in-law in Greenwich and a prettier sister down the road. Now, for the first time in her life, she was on her own."[24]

George was soon promoted to become a salesman, and if he was not an especially talented one, he nonetheless prospered with Ideco. In 1949, however, he wrote to his friend Gerry that he had another interest: "I have in the back of my mind a desire to be in politics, or at least to do something of service to this country."[25] Again, one wonders if he shared his early political aspirations with Barbara and if she supported and encouraged him. Perhaps, harkening back to the life philosophy she had adopted, she was going to choose to enjoy whatever politics would bring.

George was sent to a number of locations in California to continue learning the oil and gas business, gaining important experience and contacts along the way. His peripatetic life took the family to Whittier, Ventura, Bakersfield, and

Compton; along with his later political postings, they might have moved close to thirty times in the course of their marriage.

Barbara was seven months pregnant with her second child when she learned that her mother had been killed instantly in a freak auto accident. Marvin Pierce, injured in the tragic crash, prevailed on his youngest daughter not to attend the funeral because of her condition. She obeyed but years later confided to her daughter, Dorothy "Doro" Bush Koch, that she always regretted her decision to remain in California. She told Koch, "My mother and I loved each other, but I was not her favorite."[26] Two months later, Pauline Robinson "Robin" Bush, named in memory of her maternal grandmother, was born.

Shortly after Robin Bush's birth, George was summoned back to Texas, but this time he was assigned to work in Midland, "the heart of the Permian Basin" as well as the money center of that region; it was a rapidly expanding financial boomtown.[27] Before long, George left Ideco to form his own oil and gas company. The family, meanwhile, continued to expand; John Ellis "Jeb" Bush was born in 1953. Historian Jeffrey Engel has observed that to understand Barbara Bush's life, "one needs to appreciate that she was really a product of her times . . . raising a family, and . . . being a good and loyal wife to her husband over the course of his varied careers. In many senses, he was an active [but] absentee father for many years."[28]

Unlike Rosalynn Carter, Barbara did not play a formal role in her husband's businesses. However, she was his partner in civic activities and later his political pursuits. The Bushes helped to start their local YMCA, established three banks, and raised funds for the United Way and the Cancer Crusade. Both taught Sunday school at the local Presbyterian church. Barbara also reached out on her own, networking and establishing friendships. The Bush family became well known for their Sunday evening barbecues, which attracted a diverse group of "neighbors, friends, coworkers, and strays."[29] They would continue this practice years later in Washington, DC.

Unfortunately, another tragedy soon befell the Bush family. One morning in 1953, young Robin seemed lethargic and did not want to play. Barbara took her to the pediatrician, who did some tests. The doctor called Barbara later in the day and asked her to return to the office that evening with her husband. When the worried parents met with the doctor, she told them as gently as possible their daughter had leukemia. Years later, George recalled, "The doctor said this child has leukemia, and we didn't know what the hell the doctor was talking about back in those days, and I said, 'What does that mean? And she said, 'Well, it means that it's not likely she can live many more weeks longer.'"[30] The physician recommended that the Bushes take their daughter home and let her slip away, but they decided to have her treated at New York's Sloan-Kettering Hospital.

She rallied at first but died seven months later. The Bushes were devastated. Barbara's grief was intense, and although she had been the strong one of the pair during their daughter's illness, George was his wife's mainstay in the months following the little girl's death.

Barbara recounted a story about her young son George W. Bush that took place as she was grieving for Robin. Some of the neighborhood children had come to the Bush home to ask him to come out and play, but George responded that he could not join them because his mother needed him. That chance comment started Barbara on the path to recovering her life. She commented, "I was too much of a burden for a seven-year-old boy to carry."[31] She emerged from this terrible time a more compassionate and understanding person. Later the Bushes founded the Bright Star Foundation to support leukemia research. Their spirits were lifted by the births of Neil Mallon Bush in 1955, Marvin Pierce Bush in 1956, and Dorothy "Doro" Walker Bush in 1959.

Barbara's neighbors and friends thought she was "Super Mom." Hers was the home where the neighborhood children congregated. With her husband away a great deal, she was constantly driving carpools, attending Little League games, and administering discipline to her large and boisterous family. Later, when she was the wife of the vice president, an interviewer lauded her for her success in childrearing, but Barbara stated frankly that she was exhausted much of the time, and some days it was all she could do to keep her head above water. She commented, "I tried my best, but I don't think I did very well."[32]

In 1959, the Bushes left Midland for Houston; although more cosmopolitan, it was still very much a Southern city. Despite the time Barbara had spent earlier in both Midland and Charleston, she had not accustomed herself to the social attitudes of this region, as an archivist at the George H. W. Bush Library in College Station, Texas, recalled. One afternoon, she was hosting a luncheon at her home attended by some prominent white women in Midland. She heard one of the women repeatedly use a racial slur in referring to African Americans. She confronted the woman and was reported to have said, "We do not speak like that in this house, and we do not use that word."[33] Gradually, perhaps encouraged by the examples of other Texas women, Barbara was willing to speak out even more. She especially admired then-first lady Lady Bird Johnson, who eloquently advocated for the environment and the importance of her husband's Great Society programs as well as his civil rights initiatives. Years later, Barbara Bush developed a warm friendship with Lady Bird Johnson, who wrote her beautiful letters and would send the Bushes Texas pralines at Christmas.[34] One might also surmise that US Representative Barbara Jordan's pronouncements on the Watergate scandal and Ann Richards's outspokenness as governor of the Lone Star State (though not her pronouncements about Barbara's husband) might have had an influence on her. The admiration and respect she had for these women did not nudge her into politics or advocating for certain issues, but she was a good listener and absorbed a great deal of what went on around her.

George Bush was certainly not so reticent. In 1962, Barbara was surprised when local Republicans asked him to run for chair of the Harris County Republican Party, and he accepted. Although George had told friends of his political bent years earlier, it seems he had not fully shared this with his wife. She told an interviewer that she had not expected her husband to go down this path: "No, he was not into politics, and we never thought about that way, really."[35]

Even though she might not have anticipated a political life, Barbara campaigned enthusiastically for George. Together, they visited all of Harris County's 210 precincts. She did not speak at the time but sat on stage and listened to her husband's stump speech over and over again; to ward off boredom, she began to needlepoint. This new hobby turned out to be a conversation starter with other rally attendees who also enjoyed this craft.[36] Barbara enjoyed the give-and-take with voters. She was adept at small talk, always seemed to remember names, and was comfortable with the many people she met as an adopted Texan. Moreover, she "helped her husband 'read character,' judging who would and would not serve him well."[37] In addition, she would relay what she heard to the candidate.[38] One friend observed, "It is hard to imagine George going as far as he did without Barbara."[39]

Barbara might have been shy during those early years in politics, but she was forced to speak out when she became the focus of a controversy. In a race both rough and dirty, a rumor circulated that she was a Cape Cod heiress whose father published a communist magazine. Neither charge was helpful to candidate George. She did respond: Marvin Pierce had confirmed she was most definitely not an heiress—and she had never even visited or vacationed in Cape Cod. The second part of the rumor grew out of her father's publishing the popular women's magazine *Redbook*, which some thought had a communist bent. Despite the rumors about Barbara Bush (who was surprised how hard it could be to run for county chair)[40] and the demanding campaign, George Bush was elected.[41]

Bush was not as fortunate in 1964, when he lost a US Senate race during LBJ's landslide presidential victory. Barbara Bush went door to door trying to make the case for her husband, wearing a badge that only read "Barbara." She felt that omitting her last name might encourage people to speak more freely. Realistically, she reflected, "with Johnson at the top of the Democratic ticket, we did not have a chance." Still, she took the loss hard. Molly Wertheimer observed, "Her use of the pronoun 'we' here shows that she considered herself very much in the race with her husband as his political partner."[42] This theme would carry through their future political races.

The midterm elections were more favorable, and George Bush was elected to the US House of Representatives in 1966 and reelected in 1968. He made another attempt at winning a US Senate seat in 1970 but was rebuffed once again. The losses did nothing to discourage the Bushes, and their resilience was rewarded. Over the next decade, George, who had been a stalwart and dependable soldier for the Republican Party, was appointed to a variety of posts in the Richard Nixon and Gerald Ford administrations, including ambassador to the United Nations, chair of the Republican National Committee (RNC), US envoy to China, and director of the Central Intelligence Agency (CIA). These positions kept the Bushes on the road, living in Washington, DC, New York, Beijing, and DC again, with frequent trips home to Houston and longer sojourns in Maine.

George was positioning himself for a run for the presidency in 1980, and his wife was an enthusiastic supporter, though she admitted to being afraid of public speaking. To prepare herself for the upcoming race, she perfected a slide show about the gardens of Washington, DC, which she delivered to Texas constituents and other groups; later she would also present a slide show about China. Her friend Marion Chambers recalled that as Barbara rehearsed for a speech, the two women began to laugh because they could hear Barbara's knees knock. Chambers continued, "That was the last time I ever heard them knock."[43] The enthusiastic responses she garnered increased Barbara's confidence.

She understood that she would be asked about which major cause she would champion if her husband were elected president. As a potential first lady, Barbara, who had always been a devoted reader, chose literacy. Her mother had encouraged the Pierce children to become readers, her father had edited magazines, and because both reading and storytelling were part of the Southern culture, literacy seemed a natural choice. Years later, she would tell the graduating class of Wellesley College, "I chose literacy because I honestly believe that if more people could read, write, and comprehend, we would be that much closer to solving so many of the problems that plague our nation and our society."[44] Additionally, Barbara had a particular interest in literacy because she had worked for years on reading with son Neil Bush, diagnosed with dyslexia.

Barbara recalled her first major presentation on the topic. She and a campaign aide had been invited to Cardinal Stritch College in Milwaukee, Wisconsin, and George Bush's presidential campaign had informed the college of her interest in literacy. When she arrived in Milwaukee, the president of the college told Barbara she had assembled forty experts in literacy to hear her comments about the topic. At this point, Barbara was still learning about literacy and was shocked she would be facing an audience of experts. Demonstrating quick thinking, she asked the group, "If you were married to the President of the United States and had the chance to make an impact on illiteracy, what would you do?"[45] The experts rose in turn to present their ideas, and when about half of the participants had spoken, she was informed time was up and they had to leave. It was a narrow escape, but she resolved to learn all she could about literacy.

The year 1980 was not George Bush's year, and he lost the Republican presidential nomination to Ronald Reagan, who surprised many people by asking the runner-up to run as his vice president. Before he could come onboard as the vice-presidential nominee, however, George had to agree to support a pro-life plank in the Republican platform. This proved a difficult issue for the Bushes, who had supported Planned Parenthood. George went along with the platform, but Barbara felt abortion was a personal issue, not a presidential matter. She later wrote that she and her husband differed in their opinions but respected each other's views.[46]

She continued her political education during the hectic vice-presidential years, which she remembered later as "the busiest of my life." She participated in almost five hundred literacy events and established a reputation as a strong advocate for reading-oriented programs. The impeccable manners Barbara had learned from her mother, reinforced at Ashley Hall, came in handy in dealing with first lady Nancy Reagan; although she silently suffered slights from the first lady, Barbara never commented on them. As Susan Page wrote, "Nancy Reagan seemed determined to include the Bushes at White House social events only when she had no other choice," such as when Princess Diana and Prince Charles were in town. But she never had the Bushes to Camp David and invited them only a few times to the White House family quarters. Barbara Bush would later observe graciously that they were friends but never great friends. Their husbands, however, were closer, as Parmet notes; as culturally different as could be, they "shared similar jokes."[47]

Nevertheless, Barbara campaigned vigorously for the Reagan-Bush ticket in 1984. Though popular and well liked by both the press and the audiences who came to see her, an incident confirmed the limits to her bonhomie. During one of the presidential debates, Democratic presidential nominee Walter Mondale needled President Reagan about his rich, elitist vice president. This comment did not sit well with Barbara, and during a supposedly "off-the-record" discussion with reporters, she noted that Geraldine Ferraro, the Democratic nominee for vice president, was a wealthy woman. She said, "That rich, well, it rhymes with rich, could buy George Bush any day." The story generated national coverage. Later, Barbara would say that the word she referred to was *witch* (the comment was made just prior to Halloween), but she apologized to Ferraro, saying she had only been kidding when she made the comment. At this point, Barbara Bush had been in politics for many years, and it would have been naive for her to assume the comment was "off the record" unless she stated this explicitly. More likely, she was expressing her opinion in a way she had learned from her mother-in-law; make your point, then step back and claim it had been made in jest. Peggy Noonan, who worked for the Bushes during the vice-presidential years, commented about Barbara, "Those merry eyes, the warmth, the ability to get the help cracking in a joyful way, and then not so jolly. A lack of pretension, a breeziness, but underneath, she is Greenwich granite."[48] As first lady, Barbara Bush would pursue a somewhat different policy. She told her press secretary, Anna Perez, "If I said it, I said it." Her statement meant that she was taking full responsibility for her comments and did not want anyone explaining, apologizing, or rationalizing any of them.[49]

In 1988, George Bush again ran for president in his own right, and his wife and the rest of their family were fully caught up in his campaign. Barbara gave scores of speeches and met thousands of people as she spoke about her husband. George soundly defeated Democratic challenger Michael Dukakis at the polls. Still, the campaign was roundly condemned for a racist political ad that blamed Dukakis for a prison furlough program. In her autobiography, Barbara Bush defended their effort this way: "One weekend, convicted murderer Willie Horton raped a woman and stabbed a man in Maryland. George used this heinous incident to illustrate that Dukakis was not tough enough on crime. Then a pro-George independent committee—not our campaign—decided to turn the example into a campaign ad, using the image of a sinister-looking Willie Horton, who was black, as the focus. We got blamed for dirty politics and racism. The ad was not ours, and the truth of the matter is, Willie Horton should not have been out of prison."[50] Her explanation does not touch on how the ad appealed to certain voters. Over the years, "Willie Horton" has become synonymous with stoking racial fear. Even if the ad was not conceived and disseminated by the Bush campaign, neither the new president nor his first lady ever denounced its racist message.

As she entered the White House as first lady, Barbara said literacy would be her major issue and volunteerism her minor.[51] Her message had not changed since her early days working with the issue, and she had high hopes for its efficacy: "Literacy fits in with so many other things. If more people could read, fewer people would have AIDS. There would be less homelessness. I am absolutely convinced of that."[52] Shortly after beginning her tenure at 1600 Pennsylvania Avenue, she established the Barbara Bush Foundation for Family Literacy, a private entity that solicited funds to support literacy programs. The foundation celebrated its thirtieth anniversary in March 2019.

A few months later, Barbara began hosting a ten-part Sunday evening radio

show, *Mrs. Bush's Story Hour*. Broadcast over the ABC network, the program attracted thousands of listeners. The first lady read books to children; later the
audiotaped performances were made available for sale by Walmart and other
large retailers. The programs enjoyed great success, and the profits from all sales
also went directly to the foundation.

In 1984, during her time as second lady, Barbara had written (with a ghost-
writer) *C. Fred's Story*. In this book, she told the story of her springer spaniel,
C. Fred, and his life in the vice president's residence. All profits were donated to
charity. In 1990, using the same formula, she wrote *Millie's Book*, which looked
at life in the White House from the viewpoint of Millie (who followed C. Fred),
the first family's second springer spaniel. The book earned a million dollars for
the foundation.

Barbara Bush also used television to further her cause. She spoke about literacy on the *Oprah Winfrey Show*, drawing a wide audience. Additionally, she wrote
a piece for *Reader's Digest* titled "Parenting's Best Kept Secret: Reading to Your
Children." The article appeared in the October 1990 issue and reached millions
of readers. Even after leaving the White House, Barbara continued to advocate
for this cause. Whenever she attended a literacy event, she was always sure to
introduce one or two new readers, calling attention to their accomplishments as
a way of keeping momentum going for learning to read.

As part of his eulogy for the former first lady upon her death in April 2018,
presidential historian and Bush family friend Jon Meacham recalled an incident
that provided evidence of her commitment to literacy and her keen understanding of its importance:

> At a televised event commemorating the bicentennial of the Constitution,
> Mrs. Bush met a man named J. T. Pace, a 63-year-old son of a former
> sharecropper. Mr. Pace, who had only recently become literate, was sched-
> uled to read the Constitution's preamble aloud. Backstage, he was nervous.
> Mrs. Bush asked if it would help if they read it together on the broadcast.
> Mr. Pace agreed. Soon, the two of them stood on stage, reading in unison.
> As Mr. Pace grew comfortable, Mrs. Bush lowered her voice, and lowered
> it again, and then again, until at last J. T. Pace was reading entirely on his
> own. He wept, and he read, supported by Barbara Bush, who stood to his
> side, now silent. Her work was done when his voice spoke of the unending
> search for a more perfect union. J. T. Pace had found his voice, not least
> because Barbara Bush had lent him her heart.[53]

If Barbara inspired others to find their voices, she had also found her own. One
of her White House–era speeches deserves special attention because it demonstrates the confidence she had developed in sharing her views.

In early 1990, she was invited to give the commencement address at Wellesley College. She accepted, never expecting the controversy that would develop. One hundred fifty of Wellesley's six hundred soon-to-be graduates presented the president of the college a petition protesting her appearance. The petition read in part, "To honor Barbara Bush as commencement speaker is to honor a woman who has gained recognition through her husband, which contradicts what we have been taught over the last four years at Wellesley."[54] A Wellesley senior explained, "Barbara Bush was selected because of her *husband's* accomplishments and notoriety, not those of her own. So it is not the validity of her choices in life that we are calling into question but rather the fact that we are honoring not Barbara Bush, but Mrs. George Bush."[55]

Barbara Bush told an interviewer that she never seriously considered withdrawing as commencement speaker.[56] After a period of extensive editorial comment; television appearances; a sour comment by President Bush, who told reporters that the Wellesley seniors "have a lot to learn from Barbara Bush"; and an exchange of telephone calls, the Wellesley seniors came around to believe that she had wisdom to share.[57]

The title of Barbara's speech was "Choices and Change," and in the course of her remarks she encouraged the graduates to make three choices: to pursue a commitment to something larger than themselves (she mentioned this was the reason she had chosen to advocate for literacy), to enjoy life, and to value human connections with family and friends. In one of the memorable passages in the annals of first lady rhetoric, Barbara told the audience: "And who knows? Somewhere out in the audience may even be someone who will one day follow in my footsteps and preside over the White House as the President's spouse—and I wish him well."[58] With graciousness and aplomb, she won over the Wellesley College class of 1990.

Interestingly, however, she was distinctly unsupportive of a professional woman named Anita Hill the following year, when the law professor who had worked with Supreme Court nominee Clarence Thomas at the Equal Employment Opportunity Commission accused him of sexual harassment. Instead, Barbara found Thomas "the most extraordinary man," who was being unfairly treated by "the women's group NOW and the Black Caucus." She did not once mention Hill in her memoir.[59]

Several assessments of Barbara Bush's legacy and effectiveness as first lady provide differing views of the Yankee who went south. John F. Kennedy once observed that Washington, DC, was a Southern city that functioned with Northern efficiency, and this observation could be extended to the first lady: she had been imbued with Southern manners and graciousness, but her time in the White House was a model of efficiency and accomplishment, just as her time as second lady had been. Members of her staff commented that Barbara was one of the busiest first ladies ever, delivering several hundred informal and formal speeches and entertaining thousands of guests at the White House.[60] Diana Carlin lauds her for opening up a discussion about choices and change, most notably in her Wellesley speech, and observes, "Her greatest legacy is her work with literacy, which impacts countless underprivileged individuals."[61] Lewis Gould noted, "Few first ladies can match [her] sustained popularity. . . . Mrs. Bush will probably be regarded as a successful first lady because she fulfilled the several roles of the position so smoothly."[62] Wertheimer added, "All must agree that her achievements have far exceeded what anyone could have expected from a career homemaker and college dropout."[63]

Barbara Bush was more well liked and was perceived as a more successful first lady than George H. W. Bush was as a president, and she certainly was eager for another four years, but a recession and her husband's broken tax pledge sealed their fate. However, her popularity lived on. In 1993, having just left the White House, she ranked eighth out of thirty-seven presidential spouses in the Siena College Research Institute First Ladies Study. More than twenty years later, she was still holding her own, ranked eleventh out of thirty-nine first ladies, one behind Rosalynn Carter and one ahead of her daughter-in-law, Laura Bush. The presidential spouses were rated by scholars, researchers, and historians who evaluated background, value to country, integrity, leadership, and being your own woman, among other elements. Barbara was highly praised for advancing her issues and functioning as a political asset.[64]

As stated earlier, Barbara Pierce Bush's Southern narrative is not the same as that of other women who hail from south of the Mason-Dixon Line. Still, she made Texas her adopted home and made herself part of the communities in which she lived. If she disagreed with local sentiment, she either papered over the differences or kept her opinions to herself. She was able to leave Texas regularly—with summers in Kennebunkport and extended periods of time in New York, China, and Washington, DC. She was accepted and loved by her Southern friends and was an indispensable partner to George.[65] Over time, she gained the confidence to speak out, and she and her husband functioned as an efficient political team. In the White House and in her dealings with people, Barbara was always known for her graciousness. Her greatest legacy was the literacy initiative she endorsed, which continues to enjoy success today. Though Barbara was not a daughter of the South, her experiences there were responsible for some of her sensibilities and informed some of her choices. She always had one foot firmly planted in Texas and another planted in the Northeast.

When she died in 2018, Barbara Bush's humanity, decency, commitment to literacy, and position as matriarch of a distinguished political family were celebrated by a wide swath of Americans. Her death received the type of attention usually reserved for very influential figures. Scores of media representatives reported on her final days, and her funeral was televised live to an international audience. "The first lady of the greatest generation," as Meacham called her, the Southern first lady who hailed from Rye, New York, would be laid to rest in Texas; like her husband, she was a Lone Star Yankee.

NOTES

1. Herbert S. Parmet, *George Bush: The Life of a Lone Star Yankee* (New York: Scribner's, 1997).

2. Timothy Naftali, "Barbara Bush Changed with Her Country," *Atlantic*, April 18, 2018, https://www.theatlantic.com/politics/archive/2018/04/a-visit-with-barbara-bush/558362.

3. Jon Meacham, "Eulogy of Barbara Pierce Bush," April 21, 2018, C-SPAN, https://www.c-span.org/video/?c4725840/jon-meacham-eulogy.

4. Barbara Bush, *A Memoir* (New York: Scribner's, 1994), 7.

5. Myra G. Gutin, *Barbara Bush: Presidential Matriarch* (Lawrence: University Press of Kansas, 2008), 2.

6. Bush, *Memoir*, 7.

7. Bush, 9.

8. Bush, 13.

9. Gutin, *Barbara Bush*, 3.

10. Barbara Bush, *Reflections: Life after the White House* (New York: Scribner's, 2003), 314.

11. Both quotes are from Pamela Kilian, *Barbara Bush: A Biography* (New York: St. Martin's, 1992), 31.

12. Barbara Bush explained George H. W. Bush's nickname, "Poppy": "No. 41 was called Poppy for the first eighteen years of his life. That was because his namesake, George Herbert Walker, was called 'Pop' by his family (at least behind his back). So when George was born, his uncles immediately started calling him 'Little Pop' or 'Poppy'." Bush, *Reflections*, ix.

13. Gutin, *Barbara Bush*, 4.

14. Jon Meacham, *Destiny and Power: The American Odyssey of George Herbert Walker Bush* (New York: Random, 2015), 41.

15. Barbara Bush, interview with Carl Sferrazza Anthony, "The Role of the First Lady," George Washington University, C-SPAN, October 9, 1994.

16. Bush, *Memoir*, 21.

17. Gutin, *Barbara Bush*, 10.

18. Meacham, *Destiny and Power*, 73.

19. Lady Bird Johnson, interview with Barbara Walters, ABC-TV, March 8, 1995.

20. Meacham, *Destiny and Power*, 88.

21. Gutin, *Barbara Bush*, 11–12.

22. Meacham, *Destiny and Power*, 88; Pamela Colloff, "The Son Rises," *Texas Monthly* (June 1999), https://www.texasmonthly.com/politics/the-son-rises/.

23. Susan Page, *The Matriarch: Barbara Bush and the Making of an American Dynasty* (New York: Hachette, 2019), 82.

24. Page, *Matriarch*, 82.

25. Meacham, *Destiny and Power*, 86.

26. Gutin, *Barbara Bush*, 13.

27. Parmet, *George Bush*, 78.

28. Jeffrey Engel, quoted in Susan Swain, *First Ladies: Presidential Historians on the Lives of 45 Iconic American Women* (New York: Public Affairs, 2015), 404.

29. Page, *Matriarch*, 95.

30. George H. W. Bush, interview in "Barbara Bush: First Mom," Arts and Entertainment Television Network, 2002.

31. Bush, *Memoir*, 47.

32. Barbara Bush, interview with Rexalla Van Impe, *Rexalla: One-on-One*, ca. 1982, Van Impe Video.

33. An archivist at George H. W. Bush Presidential Library, College Station, Texas, shared this recollection ca. 2000. The recollection was shared on the condition of anonymity.

34. Kate Anderson Brower, *First Women: The Grace and Power of America's Modern First Ladies* (New York: HarperCollins, 2016), 45, 77.

35. Barbara Bush, interview with author, April 25, 2005, College Station, Texas.

36. Bush, *Memoir*, 57.

37. Molly Meijer Wertheimer, "Barbara Bush: Her Rhetorical Development and Appeal," in *Inventing a Voice: The Rhetoric of American First Ladies of the Twentieth Century*, ed. Molly Meijer Wertheimer (Lanham, MD: Rowman and Littlefield, 1994), 392.

38. Diana B. Carlin, "Barbara Pierce Bush: Choosing a Complete Life, I: 1925–1988," in *A Companion to First Ladies*, ed. Katherine A. S. Sibley (West Sussex, UK: Wiley-Blackwell, 2016), 616.

39. Ludlow Ashley, quoted in Kati Marton, *Hidden Power: Presidential Marriages That Shaped Our Recent History* (New York: Pantheon, 2001), 281.

40. Page, *Matriarch*, 93.

41. Bush interview with Anthony, October 9, 1994.

42. Wertheimer, "Barbara Bush," 392.

43. Marion Chambers, quoted in Donnie Radcliffe, *Simply Barbara Bush* (New York: Warner, 1989), 158.

44. Barbara Bush, "Choices and Change: Your Success as a Family," *Vital Speeches of the Day* 56, no. 18 (July 1, 1994): 549.

45. Bush interview with author. This anecdote appears in a number of sources about her.

46. Gutin, *Barbara Bush*, 23.

47. Bush, *Memoir*, 166; Gutin, *Barbara Bush*, 24; Page, *Matriarch*, 138–140; Parmet, *George Bush*, 259.

48. "Bush's Wife Assails Ferraro, but Apologizes," *New York Times*, October 9, 1984, 29; Peggy Noonan, quoted in Gutin, *Barbara Bush*, 30.

49. Anna Perez, telephone interview with author, July 10, 1994.

50. Bush, *Memoir*, 242–243.

51. Bush interview with author.

52. Myra Gutin, "Barbara Pierce Bush," in *American First Ladies: Their Lives and Legacy*, 2nd ed., ed. Louis L. Gould (New York: Routledge, 2001), 416.

53. Meacham, "Eulogy of Barbara Pierce Bush."

54. Gutin, *Barbara Bush*, 49.

55. Gutin, 49.

56. Bush interview with author.

57. Gutin, *Barbara Bush*, 51.

58. Bush, "Choices and Change," 549.

59. Bush, *Memoir*, 418–419.

60. Gutin, "Barbara Bush," 417.

61. Carlin, "Barbara Pierce Bush," 632.

62. Louis L. Gould, *American First Ladies: Their Lives and Legacy*, 2nd ed. (New York: Routledge, 2001), xii.

63. Wertheimer, "Barbara Bush," 413.

64. Siena College Research Institute First Ladies Study, https://www.siena.edu /centers-institutes/siena-research-institute/social-cultural-polls/first-ladies-study/.

65. Page, *Matriarch*, 346.

# CHAPTER 17

# A Southern Primer
## Hillary Goes to Arkansas

Janette Kenner Muir

> I had my own opinions, interests, and profession. For better or worse, I
> was outspoken and represented a fundamental change in the way women
> functioned in our society.[1]

First lady, senator, secretary of state, and presidential candidate Hillary Rodham
Clinton. Much is known about this remarkable woman and the life she built
over the past thirty years in public service, which in some way nearly always
involved intensive political campaigns. Given what we know, there would seem
to be nothing left to tell that could provide more insight into her life and her
long-standing relationship with her husband, Bill Clinton.[2] However, there is
more to be learned because a volume on Southern first ladies provides an opportunity to consider the influence of the South in shaping Hillary as she navigated
the intersections of gender and culture, building her early career and partnership with her husband. She transplanted her life to the South during a time of
vast societal change, in which women were beginning to build their own careers
and show greater independence. By way of her Arkansas experience, Hillary became a significant symbol of her generation, learning how to balance her moral
convictions and identity with the pragmatics of living a successful political life,
and this positioned her well for the national stage.

In 1974 an independent Hillary Rodham followed her love, Bill Clinton, to
his native home in Arkansas; she would stand by his side through various political quests—from his beginning as state attorney general in 1976 to presidential
victory in 1992. The Clintons, young and well educated, navigated Arkansas

Hillary Rodham Clinton at a campaign rally in 1992 on her husband's final day of campaigning in St. Louis, Missouri. Photo by Joseph Sohm, Shutterstock. Used by permission. Photo ID: 107335979.

culture and politics, forging bonds that would frame their political futures and build them financial success along the way. Yet, this also was a formidable time for the Clintons as they learned how to work as a political team and function as a married couple, both with strong career goals that called for clear orchestration and long-term commitment. Their sometimes uncertain personal relationship, meanwhile, would complicate these goals.

This chapter reflects on those early days, when Hillary Clinton was still Hillary Rodham, a bright-eyed young lawyer ready to take on political challenges such as the Watergate hearings and to be an example to women coming of age in the 1970s—women also learning to juggle career, family, and personal identity. During her initial experience of living in the South, Hillary made many assumptions and mistakes, but these missteps helped her to shape a powerful political future. In navigating Southern culture, she discovered how to acclimate her identity, cultivate power structures, and separate the personal from the political to move forward into her deep commitment to making a national impact.

In effect, the Southern experience served as an important primer for Hillary as she learned how to manage the expectations of being a first lady and establish her role as part of a political team. The state of Arkansas, her relationship with the golden boy raised there, and the many campaigns she directly experienced all provided lessons that would last and were the foundation for building a public life with her political partner in evolving times.

## ARKANSAS: THE EARLY DAYS

Against the better judgment of family and friends, Hillary Rodham announced in 1974 that she was going to Arkansas to marry Bill Clinton.[3] The two met while attending Yale Law School, where, after some persistence, he finally persuaded her to go out on a date with him. It did not take long for them to discover their strong political ambitions and to see how together they might begin to build their political futures. He was gregarious and smart. From her perspective, he was not like other men, many of whom she easily intimidated. She also saw him as someone who could listen to a woman's viewpoint and treat her ideas as equally valid.[4] Hillary found his outgoing, friendly manner contagious, and his political goals mirrored many of her own. Upon completion of law school in 1973, Bill returned to his home state to teach law at the University of Arkansas in Fayetteville. Realizing that he had won her heart and shared her political vision, Hillary soon joined him on the Arkansas faculty.

She described this as a time of great trepidation—going to a place where she had never lived and had no friends or family, but as Hillary reflected in her autobiography, *Living History*, "My heart told me I was going in the right direction."[5] From a young age, Bill had also been impelled by his own direction, aspiring to a life of public service; he would now begin his foray into Arkansas politics with a run for Congress in 1974, during the time of Watergate. While he campaigned for office, Hillary taught criminal and constitutional law, ran a legal services clinic, and engaged in child advocacy work. She also built personal and professional friendships, and throughout the decade she would learn how to be a politician and how to manage the expectations that came with being a feminist first lady in a traditional, Southern state.

### The Intersections of Politics and Culture

Many who have written about Bill and Hillary Clinton know that to understand them, one must start with the geography, history, politics, and culture of Arkansas, the state where they polished their craft. Half of the state is largely mountains and forest; the other half consists of the Mississippi River Delta. Journalist James Morgan described early settlers as "fiercely independent," heading to the hills and forming groups in "tight little knots of independence" and with a general "disdain for authority."[6] These were not the land barons of Southern plantations. Despite, or perhaps because of, this independence, there remains a strong interconnectedness among people. The state's small size cultivates deep personal networks and a sense of belonging. Given the small population with its deeply embedded culture, strong family networks and political connections going back many generations are the norm. There are also big personalities with old money and their own close ties. It was not unusual for Bill to fly around in chicken mogul Don Tyson's airplane or have a meal with Sam Walton, Walmart's founder. This connectedness was commonplace for the Clintons, yet often misunderstood on the national scene. In a 1992 *Washington Post Magazine* article about Arkansas, Morgan described this phenomenon: "Everything in this state—including its politics, which you can't really separate from everyday life—is intensely personal. Everybody's on a first-name basis, including Bill and Hillary, even though Bill went off to Georgetown and Yale and Hillary's an out-of-stater all the way. And it means that political talk is personal talk, and personalities are more important than issues. People here hone their personalities."[7]

Big personalities have long made Arkansas politics into a sophisticated game, played by people with long-held statewide connections. Described as "big-city toughness" in a place where small-town people know each other's past and their current associations, the intersections of politics, family, and culture are pronounced; as Morgan described, "There's a limited number of people who're involved, and you're going to have to be involved with them in the church, the schools, in politics, in business. You have to think it all through and know the unwritten rules."[8]

The unwritten rules were especially challenging for Hillary, who came to Arkansas ready to jump into political campaigns and begin the steady climb toward national recognition for Bill and, ultimately, for herself. Upon arrival in Fayetteville, she wanted to help with his campaign for congressional office. As his girlfriend she jumped into an aggressive campaign mode and pushed him to make connections with the voters in his district. Hillary engaged her family in the work, bringing them down from her home state of Illinois to campaign, posting "Clinton for Congress" signs and going door to door on his behalf. At this time, she was aware that he had a growing reputation as a womanizer, but she tried to put this out of her mind, believing that with her very presence in Arkansas, he would shift his focus to her, and she could help him achieve his political ambitions.[9] As history would eventually show, his various flirtations continued, at times leaving Hillary to wonder about the long-term survival of their marriage.[10]

As the congressional campaign ended, rumors about the couple abounded. Many of the rumors, coming out of Little Rock bars frequented by wealthy businesspeople, described her as a lesbian, reflecting "a deep-dyed cultural prejudice against a woman who didn't wear panty hose, sexy sandals, or fit the southern male's image of how a woman should behave," which basically meant "to keep her mouth shut."[11] There were also deep tensions in the campaign, particularly between Hillary and Paul Fray, Bill's campaign manager. Fray was a Southern lawyer and a close friend of Bill's who understood the politics of the South and never fully appreciated her. Fray described her as arrogant and as an "uppity, Puritanical, Ivy League women's-libber." For her part, she did not fully trust Fray and generally disagreed with his campaign strategies. Whereas she wanted the campaign to be aggressive, Fray argued for a subtler approach. Mary Lee Fray, Paul's wife and one of Hillary's early Arkansas friends, noted the tensions in working with her: "Down here, they give you the peach pie first, then they throw acid on it. Hillary did the opposite."[12]

Mary Lee Fray described how, in the early days, Hillary sought her advice on how to adjust to Arkansas life. Fray told her to consider that the dirt farmer in coveralls driving a beat-up truck could be millionaire Sam Walton and that opinions she expressed on the campaign trail had to be attributed to Bill. Yet although Walton could look like a hillbilly, Hillary was much more constricted by her gender. When asked about appearance, Fray confirmed what others were saying; she should "look like a Southern belle. She needed to wear dresses, hose, delicate sexy sandals, fix her hair, and wear brightly colored nail polish." As Fray observed, Hillary would not make these changes.[13] She struggled with the challenges in staying true to herself and her identity in an environment that had specific opinions about how a political wife should look and behave. As Hillary recalled, it was becoming increasingly clear that she would find it difficult to establish an equal political partnership in Arkansas and, though she deeply loved Bill, doubts about the relationship and her ability to live in Arkansas loomed.[14]

Bill Clinton lost that congressional campaign, but he captured 48.5 percent of the vote despite being inexperienced and up against a strong incumbent. This result brought him a lot of attention in Democratic circles and began to silence some of the early naysayers who rejected his youthfulness. This election also helped Hillary to see his true political potential and to reason that Bill would likely need her help to be successful in reaching his long-term political goals.[15] She also began to see the challenges she would face in addressing his many indiscretions with other women. She learned to compartmentalize this side of him, providing excuses and rationalizations for his behavior, mostly putting up boundaries between public life and private actions.

Following his congressional run, as several biographers note, Bill realized that he very much needed Hillary in his life. Marrying her could squelch the womanizing rumors and help him stay on track, maintaining a more disciplined and steady routine. Seeing Arkansas as his focus, Hillary was uncertain that she could survive in the state; yet, when she returned to Arkansas after an East Coast visit, Bill dispelled doubts by surprising her with a Fayetteville home and a proposal she immediately accepted. On October 11, 1975, they were married in their new house by a Methodist minister; during the reception at the home of prominent Democratic organizers, she announced her name would remain Hillary Rodham, which was not well received by Bill Clinton's mother, Virginia Kelly.[16]

### Building a Political Life

Using his campaign for Congress as a starting place, Bill Clinton focused on state-level politics, winning his first statewide election as attorney general in 1976. This election was hardly contested, and although the salary was low, it served as a way for him to break into state politics. His wife gave up her teaching position in Fayetteville and moved with him to the state capital, where she was invited to join the Rose Law Firm, becoming the first woman hired by that prestigious practice. During her years there, Hillary developed close ties with several people who would later help with Bill's campaign for president. Her work as an attorney and on corporate boards put Hillary at the top among professional women at the time, earning her a six-figure salary and making her the primary wage earner in the family, thereby underscoring again how much Bill needed her in order to succeed in his political goals.[17] She also presented a new model for a political spouse. Hillary was not just a wife who sat silently on the sidelines. She held the family together financially and was actively engaged in her husband's subsequent political campaigns. Her role was often behind the scenes, helping him with speeches and preparing for political events while also trying to focus on her own evolving career.

While working on lawsuits at the Rose Law Firm and taking on pro bono child advocacy cases, Hillary was learning about the constant scrutiny political wives experience. Messages about her appearance began to surface, and she would resist the push to make changes, preferring a comfortable style that fit her life, with a flourishing career and a husband with big political aspirations and soon a daughter, too, joining the family. The pressures for any young woman juggling these roles would have been significant enough, but because Hillary was a transplant from the North, they carried additional characteristics that exacerbated the public's negative perceptions.[18]

## POLITICAL LESSONS: LIFE IN THE GOVERNOR'S MANSION, PART 1

In 1978 the Clintons exploded onto the Arkansas political scene when Bill was elected the youngest governor in the state's history at age thirty-four. Winning 63 percent of the state vote, he promised a youthful perspective and political purity for a state long embroiled in political controversy and entrenched in old ways. Introducing a progressive look for Arkansas, a parade of his "long-haired, Ivy League friends" were hired as legislative assistants, which created a separation with many of his Arkansas friends. Many were uncomfortable with what seemed an elite image—perpetuating the notion that Bill was a liberal intellectual with too many highfalutin' ideas despite his Southern upbringing.[19]

### Southern Expectations and Political Loss

In Bill Clinton's first term as governor, the first lady of Arkansas became the lightning rod for much of the resentment people were feeling about him. Southerners, as Mary Lee Fray reminded Hillary, had different expectations for the first lady. Her rejection of makeup, use of thick reading glasses, and wearing of shapeless clothing and clunky shoes challenged the beliefs of many that the first lady of the state should dress and behave in a certain manner or risk seeming disrespectful to the office.[20] Most importantly, the fact that she had kept her name was magnified after the election, when the press started to write about the first lady named "Hillary Rodham," underscoring the image of a woman who wanted to put her own career first and appear as an equal to her husband rather than be the submissive partner most people preferred to signal proper spousal support. Hillary's appearance led to greater public dislike of her and her Northern, East Coast ways, creating a larger chasm between Hillary and the Arkansas people.[21]

Several biographers have discussed the ongoing challenges she faced in adapting to such a different world in Arkansas. Hillary had trouble making close friends, and many people described her as arrogant and standoffish. When compared with her gregarious husband, she came across as unapproachable and aloof. Whereas Bill thrived on the energy of crowds, Hillary would work more behind the scenes, following polling results and determining the next strategic moves. Though she did have a few close friends, most were from her husband's business relationships or her work with the Rose Law Firm. In reflecting on this time in Arkansas, Hillary talked about the pressures to conform, feeling as if she were "thrown into an unblinking spotlight," and she came to understand for the first time "how my personal choices could impact my husband's political future."[22]

For other reasons, it was not easy for her to balance her career goals with her husband's political goals. As a lawyer at the Rose Law Firm, eventually making partner, Hillary was viewed as one of the most influential lawyers in the country, twice recognized by the *National Law Journal*, and she was labeled as half of Arkansas's "first power couple."[23] Her success bred increasing concerns about her influence and suspicions about potential conflicts of interest. Her law firm, of course, had clout long before she appeared on the scene, especially at critical junctures in Arkansas history. Although it was difficult to separate high-powered lawyers from the economic power of the state, her prominent role as the governor's wife drew even greater skepticism.[24]

Hillary was conscientious about the potential conflict of interest concerns and tried to separate herself from issues her husband faced as governor; however, given the close-knit nature of Arkansas politics, it was challenging to distance herself completely. Through her work at Rose and her various board positions, she was able to build wealth and make investments for the future. One venture named "Whitewater" would come back to haunt the Clintons after they moved to the White House. Hillary also became a mother, giving birth to Chelsea in February 1980, providing another role she had to juggle.

At that time in Arkansas, governors served only two-year terms, and Bill Clinton thus spent a lot of time on the road campaigning for the next election. Despite his initial popularity among both Black and white people, voters were unhappy with decisions he made during that first term, such as his willingness to bring Cubans to Arkansas and his position on increasing the cost of car tags. Some people claimed Bill's biggest problem in his first term was that he "forgot who his friends were." Many were annoyed that they had supported him, and yet when they called on him for something, he would not remember their names or return phone calls.[25] As chair of the Democratic Governors Conference, Bill was seen as a rising star in national politics, but Arkansas citizens were concerned about who was minding the store in his absence.[26]

His loss in the 1980 gubernatorial race was a surprise for both Clintons. Bill

Clinton's opponent, Republican Frank White, criticized his positions, along with his connections to the highly unpopular president, Jimmy Carter, also defeated for his second term. Hillary blamed the loss on the amount of negative advertising run against him, especially because of his links to Carter.[27] Frank White, drawing distinctions between the two potential first ladies, highlighted his wife, Gay White, a homemaker, with stories of her lunching at country clubs and attending regular bible studies. Historians indeed attribute this gubernatorial loss to the fact that Hillary did not change her name or fit other Southern gender expectations after she married Bill.[28] Although it was becoming more common for women to keep their maiden names after they married in the 1970s, the practice was still rare in many parts of the country, including Arkansas. Some people were notably upset when they received invitations to events at the governor's mansion from "Governor Bill Clinton and Hillary Rodham," and the formal announcement of Chelsea's birth included both of those names. Some people equated the first lady's decision to keep her name with Bill Clinton's ineffectuality. If he "could not do better at controlling his wife, how could he run the state government?"[29] In her autobiography, Hillary addressed this dilemma and her early rationale for deciding not to change her name:

> It was a personal decision, a small gesture to acknowledge that while I was committed to our union, I was still me. I was also being practical. This would help avoid the appearance of conflict. . . . [Yet,] people in Arkansas reacted to me much as my mother-in-law had when she first met me. I was an oddity because of my dress, my Northern ways, and the use of my maiden name.[30]

The 1980 loss was a devastating awakening for the Clintons. Voters had turned their backs on the couple, noting in exit polls that they wanted to teach Bill Clinton a lesson—that his arrogance and his wife's independence did not sit well with them and did not show an appreciation of the inherent value of Arkansas voters. The defeat was especially difficult for Bill—it marked his first big political loss as an incumbent, and he was deflated.[31] Even on election night, when he was supposed to meet an assembled crowd at the state capitol, he never showed—instead he attended an election party at a local hotel, where he made a five-minute statement, refused to take questions, and quickly departed. In the end, Hillary was left to speak for her husband in his defeat.[32]

The loss of the office shook the very foundation the Clintons had built. The intensity of the 1980 defeat affected the family because long-term political goals now seemed harder to reach.[33] Bill would not talk with reporters, and this once outgoing and energetic young man spiraled into depression and lethargic behavior. Stories about this time in his life note his extramarital relationships with women and his lack of direction as major contributors to his inability to seriously consider next steps. Meanwhile, Hillary continued to build her law career and personal influence, amassing wealth, and remaining the major financial support for the family.

### Restoring Confidence and Running for Governor, 1982

Former Arkansas Governor Bill Clinton, a rising Democratic star shot down by Republican Gov. Frank White in 1980, has emerged from political exile to try and regain his old job. Clinton has launched a television campaign apologizing for his mistakes as governor; his feminist wife, Hillary Rodham, is giving up her law practice to emphasize she is "Mrs. Bill Clinton," and his bearded young aides have disappeared—or gotten shaves.[34]

In one sweeping statement, a United Press International (UPI) reporter had captured the gist of the transformation already under way as the Clintons attempted to make their way back into the political power circles. The political lessons of this time would contribute to shaping Hillary's political life with him for years to come. Although his laid-back style created doubts about his ability to one day be president, she was insistent it was possible, and she went about her own transformations to bolster his campaign.

One lesson Hillary learned during the 1980 campaign was that she had to be strong to compensate for Bill's lack of aggressiveness. There was criticism that he appeared weak, was not good at fighting for what he wanted, and waffled on issues. As a result, he did not take on his political enemies in the way Hillary thought he should. Former Clinton campaign manager Dick Morris describes the point at which she realized her husband's shortcomings and how she must develop a strategy to save his political career: "She decided he lacked the discipline and toughness. . . . He was too idealistic. His head was in the clouds. He wasn't a pragmatist. He needed a tough-as-nails manager. . . . In 1978 they were a two-career couple; in 1981, Hillary became the manager of their joint political career."[35] She could better manage their future campaigns, she realized, by paying more attention to the advice about appearance and behavior her early Arkansas acquaintances had given her. Making a conscious decision to respond to those Southern expectations, Hillary learned that appearances were essential to one's success, especially in a part of the country with a culture that emphasized more traditional roles for women. She lightened her hair, began to wear contact lenses, and started to show an interest in fashion. And, on Chelsea's second birthday, when Bill announced his decision to run for another term as governor, she embraced the importance of naming conventions and began to refer to herself as Hillary Rodham Clinton.[36]

In adapting to Arkansas cultural and social expectations, Hillary made significant changes. Shifting her legal identity was not an easy one and took time to be fully reflected in the documents.[37] As women nationally were attempting to blaze their own paths, separate from their spouses, she was blending her career, political life, and personal identity. Hillary's choices carried many consequences—for herself, for her husband, for her daughter, Chelsea, and for the many women who saw her as an example for positive change.

To get elected again in Arkansas, the Clintons had to run an aggressive campaign that showed the value of getting two people who would work together as active partners in making positive change.[38] After the primary season ended, Hillary stood in for Bill at public events, which started some of the early rhetoric that they were "two for the price of one."[39] At several political events, she acted as his surrogate, directly attacking her husband's opponent, Governor White. Noting the cultural challenge of attacking the former first lady, White commented, "You couldn't win, confronting the former governor's wife. She was a woman, and this was the South. You'd look like a bully. . . . I knew whenever she showed up that I needed to leave. She'd put the trial lawyer face on and chop me up."[40] Whether White resented most his obligation of exaggerated chivalry in the face of an "ambush," or tolerating what he perceived as a shrill female voice, or enduring her "mannish" ways (perhaps emasculating him), it is difficult to imagine a bigger mashup of misogyny.

Despite White's viewpoint, on many occasions Hillary would appear as the supportive political wife by Bill's side, helping him to stay focused on his message. She realized the importance of establishing connections with the people of Arkansas, so she joined the First United Methodist Church of Little Rock, provided free legal services in the community, and cut back her time in pursuing her own career to support her husband.[41] By shifting her commitment to Bill's political viability, Hillary gradually transitioned from her separate identity to a partnership candidacy in which she created greater power for the couple as a political team.[42] In other words, by effectively engaging with Southern expectations even as men such as White assailed her for violating them, Hillary boosted the Clintons' joint political future.

Another lesson Hillary learned in Arkansas was the necessity to shift to a more centrist ideology to accomplish the couple's mutual goals. Although her early career work reflected her commitment to the teachings of Saul Alinsky and Martin Luther King Jr., as a pragmatist she realized that she had to put aside some of her long-held liberal beliefs and shift to a more centralized stance to move issues along and directly change attitudes. One way she demonstrated this shift was by getting to know reporters and helping them to see what her husband had to offer as a leader. Hillary developed a relationship with John Roberts Starr, editor of the conservative local paper, the *Arkansas Democrat*, especially critical of Bill Clinton during the previous campaign. Seeing the press as essential to her effort to remake his image, the former first lady spent significant time cultivating a relationship with Starr. Not only did this work in Bill Clinton's favor but also it built a friendship between Hillary and the editor that resulted in their working together on education reforms during the Clintons' second term. Later Starr would encourage Hillary to consider running for governor herself. Laying aside political differences and finding common ground in a way that seemed genuine meant she was often better received than her husband. "The difference between Bill and Hillary," the editor said rather bluntly in retrospect, "is that deep down Hillary is a good person."[43]

In the end, the lessons she learned and manifested in the 1982 campaign helped Bill to reclaim the governor's mansion with 55 percent of the popular vote and put Hillary in a position to be better accepted. But there was still much to learn as she continued to navigate complex cultural and political worlds.

RECONCILING POLITICAL LIFE: THE GOVERNOR'S MANSION,
PART 2

After the 1982 gubernatorial campaign, the Clintons settled into the issues facing Arkansas voters, teaming up on public policy issues, particularly education. Bill Clinton's broad promise to improve education throughout the state resulted in his naming Hillary as the chair of a committee designed to study the state's educational system and make recommendations for substantive changes. The first lady went throughout Arkansas talking with citizens and learning about challenges within the public school system. She convinced her husband to support a coaching program for parents on how to school their children, which subsequently became one of the largest in the United States.[44] She also chaired a state task force that designed Arkansas's landmark educational standards, requiring basic skills tests for teachers, a controversial plan. Hillary developed other recommendations that included requests to lower student-to-teacher ratios, add more math and science units, and make kindergarten mandatory.[45] This work highlighted reform that would begin to make slow improvements to a system long suffering from the legacies of Jim Crow laws, more than two hundred years of slavery, and the lasting inequities in public education in a state famous for the Little Rock Nine's attempt to integrate the capitals' Central High School in 1957. In the 1980s, like today, Arkansas was one of the poorest states in the country, with the Mississippi River Delta, then and now, viewed as the most economically depressed region in the nation.[46] These recommendations were important ways to address school systems suffering from low graduation rates and nonattendance; they targeted efforts to help the poorest communities, often empowering parents to engage in literacy education and to better prepare their children for school.[47] The first lady's earlier work with the Children's Defense Fund provided good experience for helping her understand the intersections of poverty, race, and education in Arkansas, and she traveled throughout the state drawing attention to critical education needs.

One of Hillary's jobs was to present educational reform recommendations to the legislators. A notable example was a ninety-minute presentation that outlined the potential policies. With a slight Southern accent reflecting her nearly decadelong residence in the state and a lawyerlike professional demeanor, she articulated to the legislators the educational needs of Arkansas's children, leading one state senator to note: "The good ol' boys weren't threatened. Usually in legislative hearings there are a lot of exits and reentrances. She talked, it seemed like forever—no notes—but she had us all mesmerized."[48] At the end of her lengthy presentation, Representative Lloyd George remarked: "Well, fellas, it looks like we might have elected the wrong Clinton!"[49] The next few years were a popular time for her, which biographer Gail Sheehy described as the "Rodham Regency."[50]

Following a series of such successes and recognition for Hillary, another campaign created new struggles for the Clintons. After he enjoyed an easy re-election in 1984, two combative former governors ran against Bill Clinton in the gubernatorial race in 1986, and the Clintons "braced ourselves for a messy campaign."[51] White, the opponent who faced Hillary as her husband's surrogate in 1982, came back with a vengeance, going after her personal integrity and her influence with her powerful husband, used, as White put it, to "benefit her private legal clients and reap profits for herself."[52] This time, the strategy was to let Bill go after the challenger for attacking his wife, using the Southern chivalry ethos to their advantage, but it did leave Hillary vulnerable to further ethics attacks about her financial and political dealings.

Another line of attack involved Bill's extramarital affairs. A string of women claimed relationships with the governor, and people could support their claims. Whatever her private misgivings, the first lady stayed by the governor's side, illustrating how she could compartmentalize this aspect of his life. Whether she was in denial or rationalized his behavior based on his upbringing, Hillary was able to separate the public from the private in a state where the private can be very public.[53]

Bill Clinton's victory in 1986 was proof of his staying power, and he was transformed at the age of forty into a leading Democrat on the national stage. With the Arkansas legislature's decision to make gubernatorial terms four years, he was considered "king of the mountain." However, as a result, the power

Hillary had experienced during the four years of the Rodham Regency seemed to dissolve, and Bill appeared to need her less.[54] He also gained more national attention, and his presidential ambitions became clear to many people on the political scene. He was even expected to run for president in 1988. However, after Gary Hart (D-CO) had to abandon his campaign because of his sexual indiscretions, Bill decided not to run that year, much to his wife's dismay.[55]

### FINAL DAYS IN ARKANSAS

As the Clintons approached the final days of his leadership in Arkansas, Hillary began to seriously consider her own run for governor. She talked with friends, making it clear that if Bill would not run again, she would. He seemed to support this decision as well, and she asked pollster Dick Morris to test her chances of running as an independent. Hillary had won over skeptics through "years of dogged public service on hospital boards, education reforms and children's projects," as Karen Ball wrote; people could see how hard she worked and how much she cared about the issues. One Arkansas friend, Joan Campbell, best summed up this transformation for Hillary: "Many people in the South are still fighting the Civil War. . . . Anybody who is from the outside—North or East or whatever—is going to have problems. . . . It's even worse if you're female and you went to some fancy school in the East. . . . But I don't know anybody who doesn't think she's a crackerjack."[56] Sadly, after her travels across the state and despite her contributions to Bill's leadership, Arkansas voters still saw Hillary primarily as the governor's wife.[57] He decided to run again, winning his sixth and final term as governor in 1990.

Within months of beginning his new four-year term in 1991, Bill delivered one of the most significant speeches of his political life at the Democratic National Convention, clinching his position as a fresh thinker. In this speech, written with Hillary's help, he laid out the themes that would distinguish the approach of the New Democrats. In August of that year, with his wife's strong support, Bill decided to run for president of the United States, announcing his candidacy in October; he thus would not complete his last term as governor.

As Kati Marton has discussed, Hillary alternated between jeopardizing and saving her husband's political life. She seemed most effective when helping Bill with his campaigns, yet she was then least able to pursue her own agenda, thus creating a challenging paradox that foreshadowed her own later run for national office.[58]

There were soon to be other challenges for Hillary. On January 26, 1992, Gennifer Flowers publicly claimed a long-term extramarital relationship with Bill. A press hearing and a fuzzy recording of a phone call between Flowers and the governor attracted great interest, and there was speculation about whether he could manage the national press on this issue. Many writers recognized Hillary for saving her husband's career at that moment, with a *60 Minutes* interview just after the 1992 Superbowl. When asked directly about his infidelities, she looked directly at the camera and, confronting the rumors of problems in their marriage, commented: "We think that's between us. . . . We don't owe anyone else besides each other. . . . And you know, it is something that we are just not going to go any further into. . . . If that's not good enough, don't vote for him."[59]

In this brief interview, Hillary emerged on the national scene standing by her man but also taking a tough stance and showing the paradoxes of living private lives in public spaces. Other interviews followed that showed her feistiness and her feminist challenge as she defended her choice to become a "professional [and] public advocate" rather than having "stayed home, baked cookies, and had teas," a comment that stirred up a tempest in the press as the nation saw that a different kind of first lady might be entering the White House.

Further challenges in shifting to the national stage required new adjustments for Hillary. The familiarity with Arkansas life and ways of interacting with people, even Bill Clinton's "buy one, get two" rhetoric, did not translate as well nationally as it had in the small state.[60] She shifted between descriptions of a "tough-talking super-lawyer and an apron-clad-cookie-baker during the '92 campaign," and her first lady makeovers created shifting images that showed uncertainty, as Sheehy wrote, demonstrating "confusion or lack of confidence about who she really is or worse, an effort to hide her true self from the public."[61]

The 1992 campaign asked voters to consider something close to home— the duties of a wife, the importance of family values, and generational politics. George H. W. Bush's campaign had effectively emphasized some of these themes, noting the president's World War II service in contrast with Bill Clinton's record of avoiding the draft. First Lady Barbara Bush, moreover, highlighted issues of women and work in a famous commencement speech at Wellesley College in 1990. Hillary's role in the campaign forced people to consider what might happen next: What does a modern woman do outside the White House? Would she have to step back from the limelight? What would a feminist be like as first lady? These were all questions reporters and pundits had not really considered before but served to create important dialogues for that political year.[62]

## EARLY WHITE HOUSE YEARS

Ultimately, as her time as first lady would demonstrate for the nation, Hillary was a pioneer. She came of age working in Arkansas politics and carefully managing her husband's political career aspirations as well as her own, effecting change

Hillary Rodham Clinton addresses the crowd at a DNC fundraiser in New York City, 1992. Photo by Joseph Sohm, Shutterstock, used by permission. Photo ID: 107335991.

in that state for its citizens that would have national implications. Although she served in many ways as a symbol of the 1970s women's movement, Hillary had to struggle to build a political partnership with Bill while maintaining her own identity in a region that had fixed ideas about women's place inside and outside the home.

The lessons she learned while living and campaigning in Arkansas helped to significantly shape her role in the White House. Early on, Hillary learned that she had to soften her appearance, highlight her roles as a wife and mother, and do whatever was needed to showcase the partnership she shared with her husband. Her ability to transform her style, taking a passive role to support her husband's success when necessary and an aggressive stance when advantageous, helped her to navigate Arkansas politics and moved her well into the national scene. Her pragmatic focus on long-term political success would be one of the ways she could rationalize her actions; she was doing what was required to secure Bill's political future and to build her own career in public service.

In "The Choice," a 2016 PBS documentary telling the background stories of Hillary Clinton and Donald Trump, producer Gabrielle Schonder explained why she made the editorial decision to focus on the former first lady, senator, and secretary of state's life in Arkansas as a turning point for her political future:

> Early in our reporting, it became clear that almost everything you need
> to know about Hillary you learn during the lead-up to the 1982 race.
> Her tenacity in the face of defeat is a defining skill she first learned at this
> moment. She does not hunker down after the 1980 loss. . . . She campaigns
> tirelessly through a state in which she is personally disliked to ensure Arkan-
> sans know Bill has learned his lesson. This is a battle for his future and hers,
> and it's a 'high-stakes, do whatever it takes' attitude that she will repeat for
> the next three decades—a permanent campaign stretching all the way to
> her own candidacy in 2016.[63]

This "do whatever it takes" philosophy shaped many attitudes about Hillary during her early years in the White House, and these attitudes remained with her throughout her political career. Many people who appreciated the idea that a political couple could work well together embraced Hillary and Bill Clinton's political partnership, and they were excited to see a woman in the White House who truly reflected societal changes regarding women's roles. Others, however, chafed at the notion that there might be a "copresidency," with the first lady as-suming a stronger role than traditionally expected. Despite various protestations, Hillary forged ahead, taking her position seriously, setting up an office in the West Wing to be closer to the center of policymaking, and working on complex social issues that would require much negotiation and advocacy.[64]

Perhaps her most ambitious high-stakes initiative came just five days after Bill took the oath of office, when he announced the formation of the presi-dent's Task Force on National Health Care Reform, naming Hillary the chair. Many in Washington questioned this decision as well as her expertise on such a vital issue—a shortcoming to which she admitted. Nonetheless, she pushed forward, with the goal of seeing a health-care bill submitted to Congress within a hundred days.[65] Given the complexity of such policy making, though, it would take time to bring congressional members to heel—a lot of analysis, compro-mise, and deliberation, an important contrast with Arkansas politics, where the Clintons knew all the players and power centers. The first lady thus made several appearances at Senate hearings in which she applied her growing ex-pertise to passionately present the administration's position on health-care pol-icy, much as Rosalynn Carter had done on behalf of mental health services (but reaching that moment had taken most of the Carters' time in the White House).

Indeed, Hillary Clinton moved too fast for Capitol Hill. Despite her in-creasingly deep awareness of health-care problems in the United States, her role engendered polarizing perspectives, echoing an aspect of what she had faced earlier as the Arkansas governor's wife: overstepping the bounds of what counted as appropriate for a first lady.[66] Years later, Hillary would admit that her biggest mistake was not the policy itself but rather her failure to fully understand Washington politics, "what was possible and what wasn't possible."[67] Biographers noted a recurring theme; namely, her missteps in trying to do too much too fast and in not recognizing the resistance she would face as a first lady dealing directly with critical policy issues. She also failed to acknowledge that her approach might have been flawed in part by perceptions of its secrecy.[68]

Hillary had greater success in more modest but nonetheless significant initiatives, shepherding programs that drew directly from her work earlier in Arkansas, such as the Adoption and Safe Families Act, signed in 1997, as well as the Office on Violence Against Women at the Department of Justice. Additionally, she traveled the world as an ambassador for President Clinton and for the country, often making two to three speeches a day on children's rights and women's roles and becoming the most traveled first lady by 1996.

A year earlier, Hillary had been invited to speak at the UN Fourth World Conference in Beijing, China. Her speech, "Women's Rights Are Human Rights," addressed the importance of women's social and economic development and was highly praised, even by her critics.[69] Her book *It Takes a Village* (1996) was a culmination of her travel experiences and provided an analysis of what the United States should do to address children's rights around the world. This work was an extension of the interests she developed when helping out Marian Wright Edelman years before in Washington, as well as her work on legal services, child advocacy, and education in Arkansas from the 1970s through the early 1990s. Although such "maternal" emphases might have seemed more fitting for a traditional first lady, Hillary's commitment to women's rights around the globe was pioneering. These were themes she would continue to amplify later as US secretary of state.

Just before Hillary became first lady, in 1992, Gloria Steinem spoke at a Democratic Women's Caucus meeting in New York, specifically honoring the challenges Hillary Clinton faced as she promoted the idea that men and women could be equal partners. Recognizing those accomplishments and sacrifices, Steinem concluded her remarks:

> Like all pioneers, Hillary Clinton has been asked to pay a price, from giving up her own name, something a male political spouse would never be asked to do, to seeing her strengths as weaknesses by some of our blind and biased media, as if partnership were a zero-sum game in which one partner's strength were the other's loss. . . . I regret she has to put up with the most

traditional of all ways in which a male-dominant society reinforces itself:
punishing women for our strength. . . . I regret she had to leave her own
name back there in Arkansas. But I know that her sacrifice on one front will
lead to a future in which all wives can have whatever position they wish inside the home or outside the home, and perhaps lead us to a time in which
the husband of a president can keep his own name . . . most of all, we want
to send Hillary a message today that we recognize her pioneering of this
deepest form of equality, because it's at the start of any barrier-breaking in
the professional world.[70]

Hillary Clinton had indeed left her name back in Arkansas; but she brought
out of the state savvy political skills and rich experience in advocacy work. These
factors would continue to shape her involvement in the White House, the Senate, the State Department, the campaign for US president, and across the globe.

## NOTES

1. Hillary Rodham Clinton, *Living History* (New York: Simon and Schuster, 2003), 110.

2. As I discuss later in the chapter, there is much power in a name. For purposes of
clarity, I will refer to Hillary and Bill, their first names, throughout.

3. Many biographers have written about the early days of the Clinton courtship, and
Hillary Rodham herself talked about how her friends discouraged her from moving to
Arkansas. One discussion about this period, including specific interviews with Hillary
Rodham and others around her, can be found in Gail Sheehy's biography *Hillary's Choice*
(New York: Random House, 1999), 85–91. For other relevant descriptions, see Christopher
Anderson, *Bill and Hillary: The Marriage* (New York: Morrow, 1999); Carl Bernstein and Dick
Rodstein, *A Woman in Charge: The Life of Hillary Rodham Clinton* (New York: Vintage, 2007).
For scholarly treatments of her early life, see Anne F. Mattina, "Hillary Rodham Clinton:
Using Her Vital Voice," in *Inventing a Voice: The Rhetoric of American First Ladies of the Twentieth
Century*, ed. Molly M. Wertheimer (Lanham, MD: Rowman and Littlefield, 2004), 417–433;
and Janette Kenner Muir's historical description in "Hillary Rodham Clinton," in *A Com-
panion to First Ladies*, ed. Katherine A. S. Sibley (West Sussex, UK: Wiley-Blackwell, 2016).

4. David Brock talks in some detail about these initial encounters and how the blossoming relationship was grounded in a strong sense of equality from the beginning, in terms
of both their public and personal commitments. Hillary was equal, if not slightly more
dominant, in the relationship, and at many times their roles were reversed. See *The Seduction
of Hillary Rodham* (New York: Simon and Schuster, 1996), 40–42. For an understanding
of feminist theory and the making of political spousal partnerships, Janette Kenner Muir
and Anita Taylor's discussion of the Clinton relationship shows the complexities in understanding the intersections of gender and politics; see "Navigating Gender Complexities:
Hillary and Bill Clinton as a Political Team," in *Gender and Political Communication in America*,

ed. Janis L. Edwards (Lanham, MD: Lexington, 2009), 1–22; see also Muir and Taylor's specific focus on Hillary Rodham Clinton's 2008 campaign in "The Clinton Political Team: Marriage, Gender, and the Presidential Quest," in *Cracked but Not Shattered: Hillary Rodham Clinton's Unsuccessful Campaign for the Presidency*, ed. Theodore F. Sheckels (Lanham, MD: Lexington, 2009), 69–98.

5. Clinton, *Living History*, 70.

6. For discussions on Arkansas culture and politics, James Morgan's "An Arkansas State of Mind" in the *Washington Post Magazine* (July 12, 1992) and Nicholas Goldberg's depiction of Clinton's home state, "Bill Clinton's Arkansas" in *Newsday* (October 18, 1992) provide rich examples of the close, personal connections Arkansans experience and the importance of this location to both Clintons.

7. Morgan, "Arkansas State of Mind," W4.

8. Morgan, W4.

9. Clinton, *Living History*, 70.

10. Clinton, 75.

11. Brock, *Seduction of Hillary Rodham*, 63.

12. Fray, quoted by Brock, *Seduction of Hillary Rodham*, 64. Karen Ball also discussed the ways in which Hillary was transformed during her time in Arkansas and how she learned to temper her behavior for stronger political gains. See "Hillary Clinton: Doesn't Back Down from a Fight," Associated Press, July 8, 1992.

13. Brock, *Seduction of Hillary Rodham*, 58.

14. Clinton, *Living History*, 75.

15. Kati Marton, *Hidden Power: Presidential Marriages That Shaped Our History* (New York: Random House, 2002), 310.

16. Historians report that when Hillary announced her decision to keep her maiden name, Virginia Kelly burst into tears. See Brock, *Seduction of Hillary Rodham*, 68; Sheehy, *Hillary's Choice*, 119–122.

17. Betty Boyd Caroli, *First Ladies: From Martha Washington to Michelle Obama*, expanded ed. (New York: Oxford University Press, 2010), 296.

18. Ball, "Hillary Clinton."

19. Sheehy, *Hillary's Choice*, 125.

20. Sheehy, 126.

21. David Maraniss's biography of Bill Clinton provides useful insight into the early times in Arkansas and the challenges the couple faced as Hillary adjusted to living in that state and helping him achieve his political goals. See Maraniss, *First in His Class: A Biography of Bill Clinton* (New York: Simon and Shuster, 1996), 246–264.

22. Clinton, *Living History*, 91.

23. Candy Crowley, "Hillary Clinton Answers Her Critics," *CNN News*, April 2, 1992.

24. Martin Weisskopf and David Maraniss, "The Uncertain Intersection: Politics and Private Interests—Hillary Clinton's Law Firm Is Influential with State," *Washington Post*, March 15, 1992, A1.

25. Morgan, "Arkansas State of Mind," W6.

26. Kenneth Bredemeier, "The 1982 Elections: The Arkansas Governor's Race—a Chastened Rising Star Seeks Comeback in Razorback Politics," *Washington Post*, October 28, 1982, A16.

27. Clinton, *Living History*, 90–92.

28. Many discussions of Hillary's choice to keep her name have been written; for one of the most recent, see Muir, "Hillary Rodham Clinton," 641–642.

29. Ellen Debenport, "Hillary Clinton Has a Large Role Quietly," *St. Petersburg Times*, July 16, 1992, D92.

30. Clinton, *Living History*, 93.

31. Clinton, 90.

32. Sheehy, *Hillary's Choice*, 138.

33. For a discussion on how the Clintons handled the public scrutiny via the media, see James E. Mueller, *Tag Teaming the Press: How Bill and Hillary Clinton Work Together to Handle the Media* (Lanham, MD: Rowman and Littlefield, 2008), 2–6.

34. Clay F. Richards. "Political Notebook," United Press International, March 7, 1982.

35. Dick Morris, quoted in Sheehy, *Hillary's Choice*, 143.

36. Clinton, *Living History*, 93.

37. There was a lot of confusion inherent in Hillary's naming preferences and the changing times. Whether referred to as Hillary, Mrs. Bill Clinton, or Hillary Rodham Clinton, she was recognized by her many roles and identities associated with these preferences. See Mattina, "Hillary Rodham Clinton," 422–424.

38. Clinton, *Living History*, 105.

39. Clinton, 105.

40. Frank White, quoted in Sheehy, *Hillary's Choice*, 147.

41. Brock, *Seduction of Hillary Rodham*, 147–148.

42. Muir and Taylor, "Navigating Gender Complexities," 13–14.

43. Starr, quoted in Sheehy, *Hillary's Choice*, 150.

44. Ball, "Hillary Clinton," 4.

45. Ball, 2.

46. Friends Committee on National Legislation, "Top Ten Poorest States in the U.S.," https://www.fcnl.org/updates/top-10-poorest-states-in-the-u-s-1630.

47. Nicolas Goldberg, "Bill Clinton's Arkansas," *Newsday*, October 18, 1992, 3–5.

48. Jerry Bookout, quoted in Brock, *Seduction of Hillary Rodham*, 153.

49. Bookout, quoted in Brock, *Seduction of Hillary Rodham*, 153.

50. Sheehy, *Hillary's Choice*, 151–155.

51. Hillary Rodham Clinton, *It Takes a Village* (New York: Simon and Schuster, 1996), 150.

52. Sheehy, *Hillary's Choice*, 168.

53. Ball, "Hillary Clinton," 3–4.

54. Brock, *Seduction of Hillary Rodham*, 170–171.

55. The decision not to run was a result, in large part, of conversations with advisers about the irrefutable evidence of Bill's sexual encounters. In particular, close adviser Betsey Wright's conversations with him about the women who could directly tarnish his image

likely contributed to his conclusion that running for president at that time would be bad for his family and for his political future.

56. Ball, "Hillary Clinton," 1.

57. Mueller, *Tag Teaming the Press*, 2–4.

58. Marton, *Hidden Power*, 312.

59. This defining moment is discussed in many chapters on Hillary Rodham Clinton. See Mattina, "Hillary Rodham Clinton," 423; Muir and Taylor, "Navigating Gender Complexities," 8. For a closer account of the preparation that went into this interview and the level of control she exhibited throughout the entire process, see James Carville, with Mary Matalan, *All's Fair: Love, War, and Running for President* (New York: Random House, 1994), 106–110.

60. Mattina, "Hillary Rodham Clinton," 423.

61. Sheehy, *Hillary's Choice*, 155.

62. John Balzar, "Hillary's Role Resurrects an Old Arkansas Dilemma," *Los Angeles Times*, October 4, 1992, 26.

63. Gabrielle Schonder, "The Choice 2016," PBS *Frontline*, transcript, https://www.pbs.org/wgbh/frontline/film/the-choice-2016/transcript/.

64. For more discussion of Hillary's adjustment in the White House and her strategies as first lady, see Muir, "Hillary Rodham Clinton," 645–647.

65. Jeff Gerth and Don Van Natta Jr., *Her Way: The Hopes and Ambitions of Hillary Rodham Clinton* (Boston: Little, Brown, 2007), 118; Susan K. Flinn, ed., *Speaking of Hillary: A Reader's Guide to the Most Controversial Woman in America* (Ashland, OR: White Cloud, 2005), 62.

66. See Peggy Noonan, *The Case Against Hillary Clinton* (New York: HarperCollins, 2000).

67. Gerth and Van Natta, *Her Way*, 121.

68. See Brock, *Seduction of Hillary Rodham*; Bernstein and Rodstein, *Woman in Charge*.

69. Flinn, *Speaking of Hillary*, 228.

70. Gloria Steinem, quoted in Debenport, "Hillary Clinton Has a Large Role Quietly," 3A.

# CHAPTER 18

# Laura Bush

## Texan by Nature

Anita B. McBride

On January 17, 2001, George W. Bush and Laura Bush stood on a platform in Centennial Plaza in Midland, Texas, bidding adieu before moving to Washington, DC, to begin their life in the White House. Eight years later, and just hours after the Obama inauguration, they were back in Midland, where their White House journey had begun.[1] They would live in Dallas, but the stop in Midland was an indication of how much the heart of the city and their deep Texas roots meant to them. As President Bush observed in his memoir, *Decision Points*, "Many of the faces in the crowd were the same, a reminder of true friends who were with us before politics, during politics, and after politics."[2]

The setting was equally resonant for Laura Bush, whose character and values were shaped by the people and plains of West Texas. Her experiences as a child of the "boom-and-bust" town of Midland helped inform her choices and her worldview over the course of her life, particularly as first lady of Texas and then first lady of the United States. The woman who became a truly global first lady was constantly guided by the lessons she first learned in West Texas.

Laura Bush's own words about her childhood convey the quiet strength and resilience for which she is so well known. Her calm and soft-spoken manner, characteristics she has exhibited throughout her life, have especially provided the direction—or compass—for her historic journey in the tumultuous world of politics and life alongside her more outspoken husband. As she wrote in her memoir, *Spoken from the Heart*, "It helped to be fearless if you lived in Midland. It wasn't so much an insular world as an isolated one. Aside from neighboring

Laura Bush with bluebonnets. Photo by Grant Miller. Courtesy of the George W. Bush Presidential Center.

Odessa, any town of consequence was at least a two-hour drive away."[3] As an only child (her younger brother died days after birth), she learned to be resourceful.

"In West Texas," Laura recalled, "the wind and the sand were things you lived with. If you were born there, you never knew anything else. But if you moved there, it must have seemed sometimes to be a land forsaken."[4] The landscape in West Texas could be austere, but the wide-open sky was inspiring, especially at night. The potential was equally entrancing. The Midland spirit, she noted, "really has something to do with the landscape because the sky is so huge. There is a real feeling of unlimited possibilities here."[5]

The way Laura Bush wrote about one her favorite memories in *Spoken from the Heart* conveys her sense of wonder for a world beyond Midland:

> Mother and I loved the sky. From almost as far back as I can remember, on a particularly spectacular summer night, Mother would gather a blanket and we would go outside to lie on the ground and gaze up at the sky. . . . So complete was the darkness that all we saw were the stars and the inky blackness. Above us, the constellations hung like strands of Christmas lights waiting to be plucked, and I would lift my little-girl arms to try to touch the glowing orbs. Lying beside me on the blanket, my mother pointed out Orion, the Little Dipper, Cassiopeia, and the planets, the glowing pink of Venus or the distant fire of Jupiter, as her mother had done for her. And she would say, "Laura, look at the sky, because it won't look like this again for another year."[6]

Laura was shaped by the surroundings in which she was raised, but even more, she was influenced by the character of the people she knew. To her, Texas makes people what they are. "There's a certain wide openness about the space and the landscape, but also about the people," she observed.[7] According to Laura, "There is a plainness to the way West Texas looks that translates into how people act and what they value. Those who live there are direct and blunt to the point of hurt sometimes. There is no time for artifice; it looks and sounds ridiculous amid the barren landscape."[8] As she commented on *Good Morning America* in 2002, "Texans are risk takers. All the businesses there, the oil business[,] . . . the cattle business, cotton . . . all depend on other things than your own hard work. . . . Texas is a very difficult landscape, it's pretty unforgiving. It's difficult to settle for women as well as men. I think that's why Texas is known for so many strong women."[9]

As first lady, Laura Bush was first and foremost a woman from West Texas: fearless, in love with the land where she was born and its people, open to the unlimited possibilities beyond the horizon, a risk taker, and a woman of great strength, though her quiet demeanor and Southern graciousness did not always allow the public to think of her that way. Her formative years in Texas forged her agenda to benefit conservation, historic preservation, and literacy, first in her home state and later for all Americans when she became first lady in 2001. This role also enabled her to pursue unexpected opportunities to advocate for women around the world.

It is perhaps easiest to see Laura Bush's West Texas roots in her interest in the conservation of its landscape, a passion that extended from Texas to Washington, and in this she followed the lead of another strong first lady from Texas— Lady Bird Johnson. "I had always admired Lady Bird, the first Texas first lady," Laura wrote, noting that she "recognized the great natural beauty of our home state and nation. When we drive our vast highways, past waving grasses and blooming flowers, acres of bluebonnets or black-eyed Susans or Queen Anne's lace, that is the legacy of her touch, of how she worked to beautify America with native plants and wildflowers."[10]

Lady Bird's legacy inspired Laura's conservation agenda. "In West Texas . . . you really do need to conserve—there's very little water," she explained. "It's drought. And the only plants and trees that do well are the ones that are native, that are used to that kind of arid, dry landscape."[11] Her love of nature and the outdoors has included annual hiking trips, which she began in 1986 at the Grand Canyon with friends, many from Midland. In 2005 these same friends returned as a group to the Grand Canyon, and every year they still get together and hike in various national parks, just as Lady Bird did in the 1960s with Interior Secretary Stewart Udall.[12]

As first lady, Laura worked closely with Secretary of the Interior Dirk Kempthorne to launch the National Parks Centennial Initiative, designed to develop programming to commemorate the upcoming anniversary of the National Park Service and to ensure that US national parks, over a ten-year period, were "on track for another century of conservation, preservation, and enjoyment." The idea was to create a partnership between "increased government investment and private philanthropy [to] fund significant improvements to our National Parks."[13] Laura also took her love of nature and passion for education to a position as honorary chair of the National Parks Foundation in her second term as first lady. She became actively involved in the Junior Ranger program to encourage young people to explore the national parks. In 2007 she also launched an initiative in honor of Lady Bird Johnson called First Bloom, to inspire kids to connect with nature, especially in urban settings.

Upon returning home to Texas after eight years in the White House, Laura Bush helped found Texan by Nature in 2011 to amplify and encourage existing conservation projects and bring conservation groups, communities, and businesses together. The organization, with fifty-seven conservation partners across the state, has already had an impact: "In its role as a connector and catalyst," wrote the *Valley Morning Star*, "Texan by Nature is working to build a culture of conservation and partnership that benefits all Texans."[14] Closer to home, the Bushes have worked to restore a natural prairie at their ranch in Crawford, Texas, and have planted native, wild grasses in the area around the George W. Bush Library and Presidential Center in Dallas.

Having grown up in Midland, Laura knew how important it was to strengthen small communities not only through conservation but also through historic preservation. As first lady of Texas, she made it a priority to visit the Texas Main Street cities, a program launched by the Texas Historical Commission in 1980. She remembered "visiting those towns, and in many cases walking the actual main street around their courthouse, and seeing those cities that tried in many ways to revitalize their small downtowns as people moved out and mom-and-pop stores closed."[15]

At the center of life for many of these communities in the South is the county courthouse, and the Midland Courthouse held a special place in Laura's childhood memories, for in its basement was the Midland County Public Library, where she often went with her mother. "We would come home with lots of stories to read, and that made it even more fun," she recalled. But the significance of this building, and others like it, was even greater. "Everyone who's my age really remembers the courthouse in their town. In fact, [when I was younger] people used to drive around the county courthouse square on Friday nights. That's just what kids did, especially in smaller towns that didn't have a drive-in restaurant like we did in Midland."[16]

Not long before Governor Bush took office, a historic courthouse burned down in a small town called Hillsboro. Consequently, preserving courthouses became a higher priority for which Laura Bush strongly advocated based on her childhood memories and love of recordkeeping as a librarian. For each county, these buildings are "where the births are recorded, and where the marriages are recorded, and where the deaths are recorded. . . . It's really important to restore those archives and make sure they're protected," she pointed out in a 2013 interview with the National Trust for Historic Preservation.[17]

Courthouses are of special importance in Texas, which has more of these historic buildings than any other state; in 2018, 235 were still in active use. Some, dating from the mid-nineteenth century, were the first permanent structures built in their counties.[18] In 1998, while George W. Bush was governor, Texas county courthouses were added to the National Trust's Eleven Most Endangered

Places list, and the state created a preservation grant program, the Texas Historic Courthouse Preservation Program (THCPP), the largest of its kind.[19]

As of today, the Texas Historic Commission reports, a "total of 136 Texas courthouses are listed in the National Register of Historic Places, 145 are Recorded Texas Historical Landmarks, and 109 are State Archeological Landmarks, and as of 2018, 70 of those have been fully restored through THCPP grants and another 29 have received emergency or planning grants."[20] These courthouses also have a troubling history in a state where it is estimated that seven hundred lynchings of African Americans occurred in the nineteenth and twentieth centuries, and their preservation has accompanied a closer look at the way in which due process was denied to Black Texans.[21]

As someone whose work in libraries and education exposed her to the legacies of Jim Crow, Laura has long been aware of the Southern past, and her concern for preserving courthouses drew on an interest in history that she brought from Texas to the White House. As first lady, she championed the Preserve America Initiative, signed into law by President George W. Bush as an executive order in 2003. The preservation effort dispersed grants to support community efforts to protect US cultural and natural heritage. After Preserve America was announced, Laura immediately traveled to Preserve America sites around the country to award grants—to Dayton, Ohio; Louisville, Kentucky; Portland, Maine; and Mobile, Alabama. More than $21 million in matching grants was awarded to 280 projects throughout the country from 2006 to 2010.[22]

Laura Bush also continued to support Save America's Treasures (SAT), an initiative First Lady Hillary Rodham Clinton began in 1999 on the eve of the millennium to protect key historic sites as well as artifacts such as the Smithsonian's Star-Spangled Banner, the flag that flew over Fort McHenry during the Battle of Baltimore in 1814 and inspired the verses that eventually became the national anthem. During her tenure as honorary chair of SAT, Laura Bush directed funding to protect President John Quincy Adams's papers as well as the Mount, the home of noted author Edith Wharton, and the endangered roof of the Centennial Baptist Church in Helena, Arkansas, whose pastor once led the largest African American organization in the United States in the nineteenth century, the National Baptist Convention. The Preserve America Initiative and SAT would ensure the US government's continued ability to protect historic places, objects, and collections for years to come. Inheriting the bipartisan legislation proposed by the Bush administration, President Barack Obama signed it into law in March 2009, coinciding with the tenth anniversary of SAT.

Laura Bush also undertook a significant restoration of the White House when she became first lady and, again, her life in Midland was instrumental. As she explained to *Architectural Digest* in March 2008, she always had a love of houses and design. "I like houses, and I like decorating," she said.

> My father . . . built spec houses for all those people in the oil business, and when we drove around Midland, he would point them out and say, "I built that one, and I built that one." And, of course, he built all the houses we lived in. Whenever he would open a new development in Midland, we'd have another house. He worked at home—all his plans were there—and I was very aware of what he was doing.[23]

Laura had had an opportunity to get to know the White House before she moved there, as a daughter-in-law of a president and first lady. During President George H. W. Bush and Barbara Bush's time there, Laura and George W. Bush often visited the Executive Mansion, staying in various rooms. One of Laura's fondest memories was when she "had the opportunity to walk around on the State Floor at night after dinner when no one else was there. With my mother-in-law, we would go from room to room, turn on the lights and really have a chance to study them."[24]

When she set out to restore the Lincoln Bedroom, on the second floor, Laura along with the White House curator, the Committee for the Preservation of the White House, and the White House Historical Association knew it should accurately reflect its time, the 1850s and 1860s, rather than be furnished with items from the twentieth century. The first lady and her team used documentary evidence to restore period details. For example, they installed window cornices, wallpaper, carpeting, and a mantel that represent the room's history as President Abraham Lincoln's office.

Laura Bush's love of history and historic places was bolstered by her love of reading and learning, and she is perhaps best known for her lifelong advocacy of literacy and education reform. Books held for her a sense of wonder, and even at the age of five, as Laura Welch, she has told her friends, she lined up her dolls and pretended to be their teacher. Reading was for her an escape from her isolated hometown, and she found a world awaiting her in books. Later, as a teacher and then a librarian in economically disadvantaged and segregated areas of Houston, Austin, and Dallas, she recognized that literacy and education are more than an escape into a faraway world; they are the means by which children can survive and overcome obstacles. Still later, as first lady, she advocated for education as a civil right for every child, but she had seen its importance long before.

Indeed, Laura Welch came of age just as the turbulent civil rights era was beginning, graduating from Midland's all-white Robert E. Lee High School in 1964, and the images she saw on the news ignited in her a wish to foster change:

> The scenes from the Alabama marches or the riots that left Detroit and Newark in flames cemented my desire to do what I could, and that was to teach in an inner-city, minority school. I wanted to work with children who had been left out and, too often, left behind, simply because of the color of their skin. When I taught, I always asked to be placed in what were called "minority schools."[25]

The students in the Dallas and Houston elementary schools where Laura taught fourth grade after graduating from Southern Methodist University in 1968 were primarily African American, some bused from other neighborhoods, some living in what she described as "small, run-down houses behind the school building on narrow side streets, which eventually dead-ended alongside warehouses and the train tracks."[26] Once, in Houston, she arranged for a field trip. As the class stopped at one house, though, to pick up a boy, when he opened his door his mother would neither come to the door nor give permission for him to get on the bus. Laura never forgot that moment. It broke her heart to leave him as they drove away. She described this experience as a pivotal point for her, a haunting face-to-face encounter with a child who did not have a chance to experience life and to learn.[27]

Laura's time as a teacher in Texas public schools opened her eyes to "a part of the world she had not seen in segregated Midland," said historian Betty Boyd Caroli. Having been "shocked" by "barriers she had not previously understood or noticed," she decided to become a librarian to promote "literacy and books as a way to improve students' lives."[28]

After getting her library science master's degree from the University of Texas in 1972, Laura Welch worked in a branch library in an impoverished African American section of Houston. There, as she recounts, "I helped families find books, and as soon as school ended, we were overrun with children who had no place else safe to go; I was their de facto caregiver."[29] Also in Houston, her library colleagues introduced her to a consciousness-raising group; she would continue to call herself a feminist throughout her life. Soon missing Austin, however, and her work at a school, she moved back in 1977 to work at an elementary school library in a largely Spanish-speaking neighborhood. Thus, "in a very dedicated fashion," Ann Gerhart writes, "she deliberately chose [to work] where she thought she could have an impact helping kids learn to read, and she felt as if they were being exposed to other parts of life they weren't getting."[30] She met George Bush at a Midland backyard barbecue the year she returned to Austin;

they were engaged within weeks, and in 1978, she helped George in a close race for Congress. His next state campaign, sixteen years later for Texas governor, when their twins were already in their teens, would be more successful.

Those earlier experiences in Texas public schools and libraries informed Laura's role as first lady of Texas. Her first act after moving into the Texas governor's mansion was to invite Texas authors to read from their books as part of an inaugural week celebration. She soon traveled throughout the state to promote literacy and reading programs for children.[31] In November 1996 she founded the first Texas Book Festival. The proceeds from the three-day event were earmarked for Texas public libraries, and over the course of the festival's first four years, grants totaled nearly $1 million.[32] The money was designated to help expand library collections, including books in foreign languages and in large print as well as books on tape, with grants awarded to libraries in every geographical region of Texas.[33] Today the festival is a lasting legacy of this former librarian who arranges her personal collection of books according to the Dewey Decimal system. Since the festival's founding, it has also donated more than 100,000 books to students in low-income Texas schools.[34]

Called on by Governor Bush's education policy advisers to help develop education reform initiatives in the Lone Star State, Laura also convened a summit on early childhood development and brain research. Remembering the students she had taught and wondering how their lives might have been different if they had been better prepared for school, she invited experts to explore family literacy and the importance of reading from infancy. The summit examined the ways in which children's "physical environment—what they eat, how they play, what they do with the adults around them—molds their school years and their lifelong learning." Laura cited the summit as contributing to sweeping education reforms in Texas: "The summit helped convince legislators to create reading readiness programs for preschoolers and, for the first time, to add to the federal Head Start program."[35] Governor Bush's education aide, Margaret Spellings, recalled that the researchers had been "dazzled" by Laura Bush's understanding of the subject, and the *Austin American-Statesman* credited her with pushing "her own legislative agenda."[36] Senate Bill 955 directed $17 million in funding to the state's preschools.[37]

Laura also made it her cause to help children in the care of Texas Child Protective Services. Having learned that caseworkers often purchased supplies for children on their own, she worked to establish resource centers called Rainbow Rooms statewide, where "caseworkers could find anything from clothing to car seats, coloring books, and crayons, whatever they needed to assist families in dire financial straits and children who had been left dirty, hungry, and horribly neglected."[38]

Prior to moving into the White House in 2001, Laura said her goal as first lady would be "introducing children to the magic of words."[39] It was a natural step from her work as first lady of Texas. "If I'm going to be a public figure," she once said, "I might as well do what I've always liked doing, which meant acting like a librarian and getting people interested in reading."[40] She immediately set to work partnering with the Library of Congress to adapt the Texas Book Festival model to a national stage. Initially held on the Washington Mall, the National Book Festival has continued and now draws more than 200,000 book lovers to the convention center in Washington from all across the country who mingle with more than a hundred authors. In 2020, in response to the COVID-19 pandemic, the National Book Festival marked its twentieth anniversary with a virtual event.

Laura also launched a series of literary events at the White House called Salute to America's Authors. The second program, In March 2002, celebrated the writers of one of the richest literary and cultural periods in US history, the Harlem Renaissance. Opening the gathering, Laura noted that these men and women "celebrated their culture in poetry and prose while capturing the stark realities of being Black in America." Author James McBride marveled that Harlem Renaissance writers could not have imagined they would be mentioned in the White House, but as it turned out, one of Laura Bush's favorite poets is Langston Hughes.[41] A third event in the series, in February 2003, on American poetry, was more controversial; the imminent war with Iraq attracted an angry response from some of the invitees, who declared they would instead publish a book of antiwar poetry to present to the first lady. Laura cancelled the event, noting her respect for free speech but also her desire, as she put it, to not "turn . . . a literary event into a political forum." She garnered support on both sides in this controversy, and her support of the war did not seem to hurt her as she maintained a higher approval rating than her husband; campaign events she led in swing states raised significant funds and narrowed the gender gap between the elections of 2000 to 2004 significantly.[42] In 2007, her love for artists influenced by the Harlem Renaissance was again apparent when she installed a painting by Jacob Lawrence, *The Builders* (1947) in the Green Room, where it still hangs; Laura noted how it reminded her of her father's work in Midland. "I guess I had sort of an unconscious connection to it, that made me like it—the strength of the people, the angles, for instance, of the people working. It reminded me of him and the houses he built."[43]

When George and Laura Bush had first entered the White House, they expected to focus on domestic initiatives. Although the United States had experienced several terrorist attacks during the Clinton administration, with the World Trade Center bombing in 1993, the embassy bombings in Kenya and Tanzania in 1998, and the attack on the USS *Cole* in Aden in 2000 (not to mention the Oklahoma City bombing of 1995), the Cold War had been over for more than a decade. The new first lady had jumped right in to promote her goals, and thus on the morning of September 11, 2001, she was headed to Capitol Hill to brief the US Senate Education Committee on findings from an early childhood conference she had hosted in July. By the time she arrived on the Hill, however, planes had struck first the North and then the South Tower of the World Trade Center, making it clear that an orchestrated attack was under way. With the event cancelled, she took the opportunity to speak to the press who had assembled for her briefing and to offer words of comfort to the victims and rescue workers in New York as well as to the country: "Parents need to reassure their children everywhere in our country that they're safe."[44] Minutes later, she and everyone else in the Capitol Hill complex would be evacuated after a third plane struck the Pentagon.

The events of that day changed history as well as her life as first lady. Laura wrote in her memoir:

> I was anxious, but I was never fearful. And I received so many forms of unsolicited comfort. My old roommate from Houston, Janet Heyne, told me on the phone that "the whole time you've been in Washington, I've been so glad that I wasn't you and that I didn't have to do what you're doing." She went on, "Now I'm jealous for the first time because you can do something after this horrible tragedy." And I *could* do things, things that could make a difference. That was my solace, even as the roar of Air Force fighter planes flying cover patrols echoed through the walls and Secret Service details conducted new rounds of evacuations because there were reports of a truck bomb waiting to detonate on a nearby street.[45]

As the country's outlook changed, so did the first lady's agenda. Her West Texas strength fortified her to be open to new possibilities of activism for which nothing in her Midland childhood could have prepared her. "I think American women were shocked after September 11 when the spotlight turned on Afghanistan," she recalled, "and we saw a country where women were brutalized, really, and were marginalized. And what we saw in a country where half of the population is left out, is a failed country."[46] Yet there had been a foreshadowing in Midland of Laura's new global awareness, for her books had taken her to faraway places, and in a remarkable coincidence, she recalled a report on Afghanistan she had written as a sixth grader. She chose Afghanistan because she wanted "to pick a country that sounded completely exotic and remote compared to anything I knew in Midland, Texas."[47] She could not have predicted that she would travel there and certainly not while her country was in an active state of war.

On November 17, 2001, Laura did something no first lady had ever done. She delivered, solo, the weekly presidential radio address, telling the world about what life was like for women in Afghanistan under the Taliban.[48] She spoke forcefully and bluntly:

> When I had put on the headphones and bent over the microphone to read the address, I had thought of those Afghan women, weighted down under their burkas, with nothing more than tiny mesh slits to uncover their eyes, hidden away from the world and having the world hidden away from them. They were truly powerless. At that moment, it was not that I found my voice. Instead, it was as if my voice had found me.[49]

Condoleezza Rice, President Bush's first national security adviser, noted that "9/11 was a turning point for Laura, when she became more involved in foreign policy. It was Laura's idea . . . to fully and completely expose what the Taliban regime was doing to women, emphasizing violations of women's rights prior to the U.S. invasion of Afghanistan."[50] Presidential historian Mark Updegrove explained to Susan Swain and C-SPAN for its *First Ladies* series that "instead of getting deeply involved in education or literacy, as she would have liked, she had to do other things. She did find her voice in that issue." When Middle Eastern women Laura encountered thanked her, "she realized at that moment what a profound difference that she could make."[51] She made a surprise trip in March 2005 to Afghanistan, one of three visits she made to the country in the second term of the administration to champion the rights of women and children and to help launch multiple programs to improve their lives.

Among her projects, Laura worked to try to provide textbooks to Afghan schools and encouraged all Americans, especially children, to send money through America's Fund for Afghan Children, which raised more than $9 million.[52] "I am fortunate to have been able to help," she said. Her assistance was wide ranging and drew upon her history as a teacher, librarian, and advocate for people in impoverished and neglected parts of Texas. Among other initiatives, she noted,

> I have met with Afghan women who are teachers, lawyers, judges, human rights workers, and parliamentarians. . . . I have traveled to Kabul to help with the opening of the American University of Afghanistan and the creation of the Women's Teacher Training Institute to train female teachers from rural provinces. . . . I serve as an honorary co-chair of the U.S.-Afghan

Women's Council, a unique public-private partnership to improve the education, health, economic, and leadership status of Afghan women and children.[53]

She was still serving as honorary cochair, along with Hillary Rodham Clinton and Rula Ghani, first lady of Afghanistan, as this book went to press. Thus, Laura Bush's passion for books and commitment to improved educational outcomes, well known at home, became the focus of her work around the world. Her foreign travel itinerary focused on education and literacy programs for women and children, especially girls, and took her to seventy-seven countries. When the United States reentered the UN Education, Scientific and Cultural Organization (UNESCO) in 2003, the UN secretary general asked Laura to help lead a literacy initiative and serve as the honorary ambassador for the UN Decade of Literacy. In this capacity, she hosted the first-ever White House Conference on Global Literacy at the annual meeting of the UN General Assembly in New York in 2006, bringing leaders and innovators in the field of literacy and education in front of a global audience.

Laura's concerns for promoting education and health also included her work with the largest international health initiative ever directed at a single disease: the President's Emergency Plan for AIDS Relief (PEPFAR), established in 2003. She visited twelve countries—most of them in Africa—that were recipients of the program's assistance in combatting HIV/AIDS; she also promoted the work of the US–Middle East Partnership for Breast Cancer Awareness and Research, including meeting breast cancer patients in Saudi Arabia.

As first lady, she also demonstrated a deep commitment to addressing political and humanitarian crises in Burma, then under the control of a military junta. She met with Burmese exiles and refugees at camps on the Thai-Burma border, and after the devastating Cyclone Nargis in 2008, which killed 140,000 people and displaced almost a million more, she became the first first lady to conduct a press conference from the White House Press Briefing Room. There she called on the Burmese regime to allow aid to enter the country. "The more I've seen," Laura told the press, "the more critical I see the need is for the people in Burma to be—for the world to pay attention to the people of Burma, and for the world to put pressure on the military regime."[54] She was a consistent critic of the junta.[55]

Such wide-ranging endeavors also illustrated her friendly nature and natural ability to reach across the aisle. She was able to work with people who, although they might not have shared her politics, recognized and appreciated her depth of knowledge and commitment to the issues with which she was involved. In the aftermath of Hurricane Katrina in 2005, she worked with Lieutenant Governor

Mitch Landrieu, a Democrat, among others on the Gulf Coast to help rebuild the many schools and libraries damaged or destroyed by the hurricane, making more than twenty trips to the region; her Gulf Coast School Library Recovery Initiative raised more than $6 million, an effort that drew on her history in impoverished and struggling school libraries in Houston and Austin.[56] In another bipartisan effort, in May 2007 she stood alongside Senator Dianne Feinstein (D-CA) and Senator Kay Bailey Hutchison (R-TX) to express solidarity with Burmese opposition leader Aung San Suu Kyi before the Senate Women's Caucus on Burma.

Nearly four years after the Bushes left office, on September 19, 2012, Laura won the Alice Award, named for early twentieth-century suffragist Alice Paul, bestowed by the Sewall-Belmont House and Museum and the National Women's Party in Washington, DC. Her nomination for this award had not been without controversy; many feminists insisted she was not attentive enough to American women's issues. However, others supported her strongly, including *Washington Post* columnist Kathleen Parker, who noted earlier that summer that if Laura Bush did not press the issue of "reproductive freedom," she did use "her bully pulpit . . . to great effect, not just by advancing women's rights in far corners of the world but also by literally saving lives" with her work in women's health care in the Middle East and elsewhere.[57]

Although a popular image has yet persisted of her as a "profoundly traditional first lady," Laura's high-profile efforts abroad have been well recognized by key US leaders and activists.[58] At her own Senate confirmation hearing while the Bushes were in their last days in office, secretary of state nominee Hillary Clinton stated, "Mrs. Bush has been outspoken on behalf of the plight of Afghan women . . . and other women facing oppression around the world."[59] Michelle Bernard, president of the Independent Women's Forum, agreed:

> Whether with her work in Africa or Southeast Asia or in the Middle East, we have seen this first lady go out and tackle huge issues that are of grave importance to women not only at home, but abroad. With AIDS and HIV and breast cancer awareness, I think her legacy, when the history books are written, will be that she has been a graceful advocate for women's rights and democracy-promotion through education in countries all over the world.[60]

It was a bold move for the former teacher-librarian from the plains of West Texas. In her journey, Laura drew on that formative Texas strength to forge an agenda that made a difference for people in her home state, her country, and around the world. And wherever she went, the Midland spirit, with its "real feeling of unlimited possibilities," sustained her.

This was surely clear in an experience I witnessed firsthand on a beautiful day in Petra, Jordan, in late October 2007, as we traveled on camels with the US ambassador to Jordan. Laura later recalled "the twisting, narrow gorge that surrounds the ancient city and its rose-colored walls. Much of the city has lain largely silent since the 300s, when an earthquake struck, but it is still possible to imagine the people who once made their homes amid this cavernous stone." As she rounded one final bend, she came across a group of US tourists from her beloved home state. Immediately, upon seeing her, they made the sign of "hook 'em horns" and began singing "The Eyes of Texas Are upon You."[61]

A half a world away, she was still Laura Bush from Midland, Texas.

## NOTES

1. Geoff Folsom, "Bush Reflects on Presidency, Future," *Odessa American*, January 21, 2009.

2. George W. Bush, *Decision Points* (New York: Crown, 2010), 475.

3. Laura Bush, *Spoken from the Heart* (New York: Scribner's, 2010), 21.

4. Bush, *Spoken from the Heart*, 19–20.

5. Quoted in Ann Gerhart, *The Perfect Wife* (New York: Simon and Schuster, 2004), 31.

6. Bush, *Spoken from the Heart*, 47–48.

7. Laura Bush, interview with Claire Shipman, *Good Morning America*, ABC, May 1, 2002.

8. Bush, *Spoken from the Heart*, 121.

9. Bush interview with Shipman.

10. Bush, *Spoken from the Heart*, 348.

11. Emily Donahue and David Brown, "Laura Bush Wants You to Help Preserve Texas' Natural Beauty," *KERA News*, October 14, 2015, http://keranews.org/post/laura-bush-wants-you-help-preserve-texas-natural-beauty.

12. Bush, *Spoken from the Heart*, 402.

13. "Mrs. Laura Bush's Leadership," Fact Sheet, Bush Record, White House Archive, https://georgewbush-whitehouse.archives.gov/infocus/bushrecord/factsheets/leadership.html.

14. "Laura Bush Celebrates Newest Texan by Nature Conservation Wrangler," *Valley Morning Star*, December 7, 2017, http://www.valleymorningstar.com/coastal_current/news/laura-bush-celebrates-newest-texan-by-nature-conservation-wrangler/article_73d00912-dac8-11e7-8082-5f4f43f54d3b.html.

15. Quoted in Lauren Walser, "Former First Lady Laura Bush's Vision for Historic Preservation," National Trust for Historic Preservation, September 30, 2013, https://savingplaces.org/stories/interview-laura-bush-value-history#.Wo02toJG0ci.

16. Quoted in Walser, "Former First Lady Laura Bush's Vision."

17. Quoted in Walser, "Former First Lady Laura Bush's Vision."

18. "Texas Historic Courthouse Preservation," Texas Historic Commission, http://www.thc.texas.gov/preserve/projects-and-programs/texas-historic-courthouse-preservation.

19. "About the Texas Historic Courthouse Preservation Program," Texas Historic Commission, http://www.thc.texas.gov/preserve/projects-and-programs/texas-historic-courthouse-preservation/about-texas-historic.

20. "About the Texas Historic Courthouse Preservation Program."

21. "Harris County Takes Steps to Face a History of Racial Lynchings," Houston Public Media, September 9, 2019, https://www.houstonpublicmedia.org/articles/news/in-depth/2019/09/09/345203/harris-county-takes-steps-to-face-a-history-of-racial-lynchings/; also see Sam Houston State University's archive on Texas lynchings, http://www.lynchingintexas.org/.

22. Fact Sheet, "Preserve America Program," Preserve America, http://www.achp.gov/docs/preserve-america-fact-sheet-2016.pdf.

23. Quoted in Gerald Clarke, "At Home with President George W. Bush and Laura Bush in the White House," *Architectural Digest* (March 2008), https://www.architecturaldigest.com/story/white-house-article.

24. Quoted in Clarke, "At Home with President George W. Bush and Laura Bush."

25. Bush, *Spoken from the Heart*, 79.

26. Bush, 82–83, 87.

27. "Former First Lady Laura Bush Addresses Women for OSU Event," *Red Dirt Report*, http://www.reddirtreport.com/slice-o-life/former-first-lady-laura-bush-addresses-women-osu-event.

28. Betty Boyd Caroli, *First Ladies: From Martha Washington to Michelle Obama* (New York: Oxford University Press, 2010), 323.

29. Bush, *Spoken from the Heart*, 92.

30. Quoted in Susan Swain, *First Ladies* (New York: Public Affairs, 2015), 430.

31. Skip Hollandsworth, "Reading Laura Bush," *Texas Monthly* (November 1996), https://www.texasmonthly.com/politics/reading-laura-bush/.

32. Molly Meijer Wertheimer, "Laura Bush: Using the 'Magic of Words' to Educate and Advocate," in *Leading Ladies of the White House*, ed. Molly Meijer Wertheimer (Lanham, MD: Rowman and Littlefield, 2005), 641–642.

33. Fact Sheet, "2000 Texas Book Festival Fact Sheet," from Laura Bush's archived materials.

34. Texas Book Festival, "Mission and History," http://www.texasbookfestival.org/mission-history/.

35. Bush, *Spoken from the Heart*, 142.

36. Quoted in Ronald Kessler, *Laura Bush* (New York: Broadway, 2006), 90–91.

37. Phillips Brooks, "First Lady Stakes Out Political Ground; Laura Bush Finds Success," *Austin American-Statesman*, June 23, 1999.

38. Bush, *Spoken from the Heart*, 143.

39. Quoted in Elaine Sciolino, "Laura Bush Sees Everything in Its Place, Including Herself," *New York Times*, January 15, 2001, http://www.nytimes.com/2001/01/15/us/laura-bush-sees-everything-in-its-place-including-herself.html.

40. Quoted in Hollandsworth, "Reading Laura Bush."

41. "White House Letter; Quietly, the First Lady Builds a Literary Room of Her Own," *New York Times*, October 7, 2002; https://www.nytimes.com/2002/10/07/us/white-house-letter-quietly-the-first-lady-builds-a-literary-room-of-her-own.html; "First Lady Celebrates Harlem Renaissance," *Los Angeles Times*, March 14, 2002, https://www.latimes.com/archives/la-xpm-2002-mar-14-mn-32825-story.html; "Opening Remarks by Mrs. Bush at the Harlem Renaissance Event," https://georgewbush-whitehouse.archives.gov/firstlady/initiatives/harlemrenaissanceremarks.html.

42. See Anita McBride, "Laura Welch Bush: Strength and Serenity in Turbulent Times," in *A Companion to First Ladies*, ed. Katherine A. S. Sibley (West Sussex, UK: Wiley-Blackwell, 2016), 664–665.

43. https://www.whitehousehistory.org/photos/the-builders-by-jacob-lawrence; "Green Room Makeover Incorporates a Colorful Past," *Washington Post*, September 19, 2007, https://www.washingtonpost.com/wp-dyn/content/article/2007/09/19/AR2007091902423.html.

44. Bush, *Spoken from the Heart*, 199.

45. Bush, 212.

46. Quoted in Susan Page, "Laura Bush on Afghan Women, U.S. Interests, and 2016," *USA Today*, March 17, 2016, https://www.usatoday.com/story/news/politics/elections/2016/03/17/laura-bush-afghan-women-us-interests-2016/81868130/.

47. Bush, *Spoken from the Heart*, 232.

48. Laura Bush, radio address, November 17, 2001, George W. Bush Presidential Center, https://www.bushcenter.org/publications/articles/2013/02/radio-address-by-mrs-laura-w-bush-crawford-tx-november-17-2001.html.

49. Bush, *Spoken from the Heart*, 238.

50. Quoted in Kessler, *Laura Bush*, 141.

51. Mark Updegrove, quoted in Swain, *First Ladies*, 436.

52. "Ask the Free Press," *Detroit Free Press*, November 20, 2002.

53. Laura Bush, Introduction, in *We Are Afghan Women*, ed. George W. Bush Institute (New York: Scribner's, 2016), xviii–xix.

54. "Mrs. Bush's Statement and Press Briefing on Burma," May 5, 2008, White House archives, https://georgewbush-whitehouse.archives.gov/news/releases/2008/05/20080505-5.html.

55. Hannah Beech, "Laura Bush's Burmese Crusade," *Time*, September 5, 2007, http://wwwcontent.time.com/time/world/article/0,8599,1659170,00.html.

56. Julie Walker, "The Calm AFTER the Storm: An Interview with Laura Bush about the Caring Power of the Gulf Coast School Library Recovery Initiative," *Knowledge Quest* 40 (May 1, 2012), 70–75.

57. "Laura Bush's Fight for Women," *Washington Post*, June 19, 2012; McBride, "Laura Welch Bush," 670–671.

58. Lionel Shriver, "Why Americans Love Laura Bush," *Telegraph*, November 15, 2008, https://www.telegraph.co.uk/news/worldnews/northamerica/usa/3465244/Why-Americans-love-Laura-Bush.html.

59. US Senate Committee on Foreign Relations, Nomination of Hillary R. Clinton to Be Secretary of State, 111th Cong., 1st sess., January 13, 2009.

60. Quoted in Andrea Billups, "Laura Bush's Legacy Emerges," *Washington Times*, June 15, 2008, https://www.washingtontimes.com/news/2008/jun/15/laura-bushs-legacy -emerges/.

61. Bush, *Spoken from the Heart*, 399–400.

# CHAPTER 19

# Reflecting on the Activism of Twentieth- and Twenty-First-Century First Ladies

Katherine A. S. Sibley

Living on the rocky northern Massachusetts coast in the 1950s, poet Charles Olson observed, "Geography lean[s] in on me."[1] Just like that granite and sedimentary rock in New England, piney woods and Southern mountains also leave their impression. As we have seen in the preceding chapters in Part II, when confronted by the cultural and social geography they experienced, modern Southern first ladies often responded with activism. Whether they took their advocacy in the direction of conserving the environment; addressing racial prejudice; or attempting to improve education, health, and safety for women and children at home or abroad, these first ladies all had witnessed such problems firsthand in the South, and were first pushed to respond by those experiences.

Southern climes indelibly shaped the women in this book; as Part I detailed, these influences are clear in the actions of early first ladies such as Martha Washington, Dolley Madison, Julia Tyler, and Sarah Polk. Along with the standards of proper behavior demanded by notions of Southern white womanhood, some of which they successfully resisted or subverted, these elite women were also shaped by gender- and race-based societal and cultural norms typical of the eighteenth and nineteenth centuries.[2]

In the era covered by Part II, women North and South saw their opportunities widening. Many began to successfully break from those earlier confines, just as the Progressive Era's reformist ethos encouraged their speaking out and the strictures of Southern womanhood were undergoing increasing scrutiny.[3] The work of Cincinnati native Nellie Taft, first lady from 1909–1913, illustrates this important transition for women's activism. Although not a Southern first lady, her inspiration sprang in part from her exposure to Southern problems, including the plight of workers in rural textile factories as well as government offices in the District of Columbia and her earlier experiences in the US occupation of the Philippines, with its climatic and cultural features much like the South. She spent three years there with her husband, William Howard Taft, when he was governor general of the islands (1900–1903). A brief exploration of her work helps underline the kinds of motivations and inspirations that propelled the activism of her Southern successors, the focus of this concluding chapter.

In the Philippines, Nellie Taft's interests in promoting social welfare were fired by the class, race, and gender inequalities she well recognized. Defying the racial prejudices of other Americans in the colony, she reached out energetically to the islands' people. She noted especially the ill health of babies and the (understandable) distrust of Filipino mothers toward the US administration's offers of assistance—after all, the Spanish-American-Filipino War had spurred the advance of such diseases as "cholera, malaria, dysentery, beriberi, rinderpest, tuberculosis, smallpox, and bubonic plague," as Daniel Immerwahr noted. Taft encouraged better nutrition among poor women and started the Drop of Milk program, which offered assistance on the safe handling of this product.[4]

Then, in late 1908, just three months before entering the White House, Taft traveled to Spray, North Carolina, to investigate conditions among children working in textile mills there; soon after, she spoke of her concerns about labor at the National Civic Federation's annual meeting in New York City. After she arrived in Washington as first lady, she threw herself into assisting women working in dim, unhealthy departments of the federal government, and under her influence, President Taft signed an executive order in 1912 calling for monthly inspections of all executive branch offices.[5] Nellie's exposure to social and economic conditions in the Philippines and in Southern mills prompted her to act, and she continued this advocacy in the White House, not only clearing the air for office clerks but also hiring more African American staff.

Scholars have long underlined the Progressive Era's impetus for women's "municipal housekeeping," whether in the cities or in the battlefields of the broader US empire.[6] Historian Natalie J. Ring noted how at this time and in analogous fashion, the South, too, "was figured as the tropical Other," as "a diseased and degenerative place" much like the Philippines and other US possessions such as Puerto Rico.[7] Akin to Nellie's experiences, modern Southern first ladies' witnessing firsthand racial injustice, poverty, illness, gendered expectations, and illiteracy in their Southern "tropical Other" during the Jim Crow era, when every one of them came of age, would draw them to speak out on just such issues as well.

Ellen Wilson, the first Southern first lady of the twentieth century, was profoundly influenced by the reformist ethos of the Progressive Era, and she set an example for the activism five of her Southern successors—Lady Bird Johnson, Rosalynn Carter, Barbara Bush, Hillary Clinton, and Laura Bush—all emulated. Certainly, Northern first ladies in these decades, from Florence Harding to Michelle Obama, were also prominent in their advocacy. But the South offered a different and particularly compelling canvas for engagement, and the chapters in Part II have shown how these six women were both goaded and inspired by their Southern experiences, even as gender conventions and a pronounced culture of white supremacy complicated their responses. The following pages will highlight the activism of the modern Southern first ladies profiled in Part II, bringing in new sources and illuminating additional aspects of their involvement to further emphasize the significance of their work both for the nation and for its impact on the position of first lady.

There was, of course, a seventh Southern first lady of the twentieth century, Ellen Wilson's successor and Woodrow Wilson's *second* Southern wife, Edith Bolling Wilson, featured in Valerie Palmer-Mehta's chapter. Edith Bolling, who married Woodrow Wilson in 1915, was also a Progressive Era Southerner, an independent woman with a number of passions, the Lost Cause and her husband among them. However, even as she is still miscast as "running the Executive Branch of government" during the illness that shrouded much of her husband's last years in office, she will not feature in this chapter's coverage of social activism because she had so little interest in it, despite (or perhaps because of) the suffragists she saw picketing around the perimeter of her White House grounds.[8]

## ELLEN AXSON WILSON

Brilliant and talented, Ellen Axson was an internationally acclaimed artist on the way to making her own living as a young woman. She had little time for dating; her friends humorously called her "Ellie, the Man Hater."[9] The men she was meeting were "complete bores" who were "not strong enough in the upper extremity," she icily observed.[10] Her father, Edward Axson, a Presbyterian minister in their hometown of Rome, Georgia, suffered from deep and chronic depression; her mother, Janie Axson, had died when Ellen was just twenty-two.

Woodrow Wilson, visiting Edward Axson's church in 1883, was a different sort of man. Upon meeting Ellen, he quickly recognized her unique brilliance and noted she fit his "ideal": she had "acquired a genuine love for intellectual pursuits without becoming bookish, without losing her feminine charm"; her "mind had been cultivated without being stiffened or made masculine; [she] could enter into men's highest pleasures without becoming at all like men in any other respect," he remarked.[11] Ellen was also inspired by his intellect and worked to improve her own knowledge of languages, especially German, so that she could assist him. Her art, as it turned out, would take a backseat to such endeavors and to raising their three girls, but she would return to it later.

Although her appropriately feminine yet scholarly qualities developed with marriage to Woodrow Wilson, her racial attitudes remained, as Kristie Miller noted, "a work in progress," if arguably more progressive in their trajectory than his. Unlike many Southerners, she had pursued her further education in a large Northern city. In 1884, she attended the New York Art Students League alongside African American students and taught art to a multicultural group of children.[12] She loved her time in New York, where she felt "great satisfaction" and told her fiancé, "It was just what I had been wishing to do."[13]

These experiences made Ellen more aware of her racial views, although reports on their evolution are inconsistent. In 1886, shortly after she had returned South to deliver her first daughter, she patted herself on the back for "hav[ing] gotten rid of [racial prejudices] to a greater extent than I thought." She told her husband, "I am always trying to shake them off."[14] In the late 1880s, she read George Washington Cable's *The Negro Question*, a critical analysis of racism. With grandparents who enslaved people, Ellen felt that her Christian religion and her gender compelled her to alleviate the poor conditions African Americans faced, as Miller suggests, and even if she did not demonstrate a belief in racial equality, these Northern experiences forced her to confront her prejudices.[15] This history certainly seems to have driven her later concerns about the substandard housing of Blacks living in alleys in Washington, DC, as Lisa Burns illustrates in Chapter 12.

Yet Ellen's daughter, Jessie Wilson Sayre, insisted in 1925 that her mother was more rigid on "drawing the color line" than even Woodrow Wilson.[16] Ellen has, indeed, been blamed for the renewed segregation that followed another one of her investigations, where she took on Nellie Taft's work in probing working women's conditions in federal offices. But there were others in President Wilson's Southern-leaning cabinet who would have put pressure in a similar direction, as several scholars have noted.[17]

Indeed, the president himself, despite his activism on other fronts, grew increasingly intransigent on the race issue. Though he had once "endorsed" the idea of a National Race Commission, developed in conversations with editor Oswald Garrison Villard, a founding member of the National Association for the Advancement of Colored People (NAACP), he quickly ditched it. Privately, Villard lamented, "There is no use dilating on it; he has simply bowed down before the powers that be. Booker T. Washington reports what we all know, that never before have the colored people been so embittered or incensed as they are towards Wilson and his Administration."[18] President Wilson's attitude was

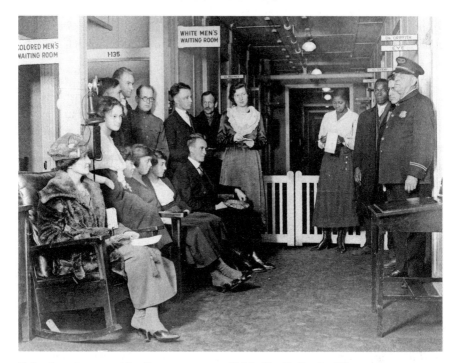

Federal employees waiting for treatment at a Public Health Service Dispensary (1909–1932). Courtesy of the Library of Congress Prints and Photographs Division. Reproduction Number: LC-USZ62-108282 (b&w film copy neg.).

evident when he invited filmmaker D. W. Griffith to screen his paean to white supremacy, *Birth of a Nation*, at the White House in 1915; the president gushed: "It's like writing history with lightning."[19]

Regardless of her husband's approach, in the summer of 1914, as Ellen lay dying of Bright's disease, *Outlook* magazine declared that "in her intervals of consciousness . . . her concern was for the betterment by Congressional action of the slums in Washington."[20] Indeed, she was the first first lady to be "publicly involved in policymaking and in lobbying for legislation," as Burns noted; the Alley Bill passed upon her death, though it was never implemented for lack of funds.[21] In her attempts to help impoverished African Americans, Ellen Wilson did not forget poor Southern whites, either. One of her other legacies was the Ellen Wilson Fund for the Christian Education of Mountain Youth. She had long supported "the mountain boys and girls" and bought furniture and other items for them.[22] This first twentieth-century Southern first lady was deeply influenced by her background and driven thereby to do something for the impoverished people of both races, setting a clear pattern for her successors.

## LADY BIRD JOHNSON

After Ellen Wilson, it would be a half century before another activist Southern first lady was in the White House. And like her, Lady Bird Johnson, too, would work to improve Washington, DC's, neighborhoods. Johnson would also draw on earlier work in her home state in her promotion of such causes as environmental protection, education, health, and literacy, as Nancy Kegan Smith shows in Chapter 14.

Claudia Alta "Lady Bird" Taylor grew up in the small East Texas town of Karnack; she spent her summers with relatives in Billingsley, Alabama. She was well educated and curious, and like Ellen Wilson, she, too, lost her mother but at the much younger age of five. Lady Bird found that the beauty of the outdoors, including the cedar trees and magnolias in her garden, gave her relief and solace. Also providing her support there was her African American nursemaid, Alice Tittle, and her playmates, both Black and white; as Smith notes, she also enjoyed attending church with her Black neighbors.[23]

Shortly after her graduation from the University of Texas–Austin in 1934, with double degrees in history and journalism, Lady Bird Taylor met Lyndon Baines Johnson (LBJ); his proposal of marriage came almost immediately. Far more impoverished in background than she, he was interested in serving struggling Texans, as his early post in the New Deal's Youth Administration confirmed, but her money enabled his initial run for Congress in 1936 as well as their later purchase of a radio station. Lady Bird's inheritance and hard work were largely responsible for the Johnsons' growing financial success, even as she raised their two daughters and simultaneously supported LBJ's successive campaigns for the US House and Senate.

In 1960, when John F. Kennedy called him to be his vice-presidential running mate, Lyndon and his wife were "central in the appeal to southern voters," as Lewis Gould notes. Lady Bird Johnson would serve in the campaign while Jackie Kennedy was pregnant.[24] But not until LBJ's campaign for the presidency in 1964 did Lady Bird get a chance to reach out to the South on her own, when she launched the Lady Bird Special Whistle Stop Campaign—the first solo campaign trip ever led by a first lady. She was also well known for promoting on a national scale the beauty she had experienced in her Texas surroundings with such initiatives as the Highway Beautification Act, which thanks to her efforts became Lady Bird's Bill, and closer to home, the Committee for a More Beautiful Capital. Her hope was to address "civic ugliness . . . and the decay of our cities and countryside."[25]

Perhaps most memorable, however, were her journeys to national parks. It was an auspicious moment, with the recent publication of Rachel Carson's *Silent*

*Spring* (1962) and great interest in conservation; nine parks and sites were dedicated in summer 1964, with the Wilderness Act and the Conservation Fund Act enabling further preservation. As Interior Secretary Stuart Udall noted, "With [the Johnsons'] interest in parks and park preservation I thought I saw a wind at our backs."[26] He invited Lady Bird that summer to dedicate the Flaming Gorge Dam along the Utah-Wyoming border, "knowing of your interest in the out of doors and in the land and people problems of the West," and added to the agenda visits to parks such as the Grand Tetons and Yellowstone as well as some Indian reservations.[27] This was the Land and People Tour of August 14–17, 1964, and it was the first time a first lady had come to visit Native Americans to see their problems directly.[28] At the same time, Lady Bird's press secretary, Liz Carpenter, wondered how they might be able to use the trip into Goldwater-leaning areas most effectively—senators such as Frank Moss (D-UT) had specifically asked for the first lady to come—without it seeming too political.[29]

Interior Secretary Udall and his staff worked hard on the speeches Lady Bird Johnson gave, yet he contended, "I don't think we did anything very blatant, you know, trying to use her. . . . I can't think of an instance where we used her as a kind of battering ram." However, he acknowledged, "With the Redwoods—when I got the President to have that first meeting in the White House—I made sure that she was there."[30] As Udall's points suggest, Lady Bird's Southern-bred love and concern for the environment had great influence.

Interior Secretary Udall speculated that this Western expedition bolstered Lady Bird Johnson for her solo "Southern train trip" that fall, adding, "I think it gave her a lot of confidence."[31] She was more steely a magnolia than he imagined. She had long been involved in her husband's political campaigns, and having grown up in a segregated South, she was also aware that she could be an effective asset in that part of the country, where the recent Civil Rights Act was highly unpopular among whites. At some personal risk, Lady Bird took to the rails from Alexandria, Virginia, to Mobile, Alabama, to New Orleans, Louisiana, that October along with a large staff and more than two hundred journalists. She expected she would encounter some anger, and she did—from hecklers in Columbia and Orangeburg, South Carolina, to bomb threats from the Ku Klux Klan (KKK). But she refused to demonize her fellow Southerners. She touched only lightly on the civil rights issue, instead speaking of new jobs the federal government had created in the region.[32] A the end of the trip, in New Orleans, where Lyndon joined her, she said somewhat idealistically that she "d[id] not believe that the majority of the South wants any part of the old bitterness."[33] As her husband won three of the eight Southern states she visited, her journey seems to have had some effect in that landslide election.[34]

Brent Eastman, Lady Bird Johnson, and Stewart Udall rafting on the Snake River in Grand Teton National Park, Wyoming. Courtesy of the Lyndon B. Johnson Presidential Library. Serial Number S33026–17.

The trip itself would have been impossible without the help of Southern women, including staffers, senators' wives, and local supporters. Liz Carpenter noted their importance: "I will match the political talents of Southern women against any others, anytime and anyplace," she wrote. "They have the uncanny ability to look fragile and lovely as a magnolia blossom, and still possess the managerial ability of an AFL-CIO organizer."[35] Liz could have well been describing Lady Bird herself; her Southern sensibilities gave her the ability to precisely navigate the constraints of Southern womanhood but never drop her firm resolve.

Some of these women became instrumental in other Johnson administration measures, including the establishment of Southern outposts of the new Head Start program of educational and medical assistance for underprivileged children; Lady Bird called its initiatives "the most exciting, productive, and practical any government can embark on."[36] Although not experiencing it herself, she had witnessed great poverty growing up in the South, and an early visit as first lady to Kentucky's Cumberland County, in Appalachia, only underlined its persistence. "When you look into the faces of the children . . . you know that hope for the future in this area must be found in education, job training, and eventually

opportunities for employment from industry, some way of making a living besides clinging to the mortally ill coal industry in this beautiful part of the world,"
she pointed out on May 21, 1964.[37]

While poor white Appalachians struggled to find jobs, African Americans in
the South continued to pursue their right to vote. Two days after Selma's Bloody
Sunday march, when Alabama state troopers fractured John Lewis's skull as he
and other voting rights protesters attempted to cross the Edmund Pettus Bridge
on March 7, 1965, Martin Luther King Jr. planned another march from Selma
to Montgomery across the same bridge, one which Lady Bird had frequently
crossed herself when visiting relatives as a child. In her diary, she applauded
King's decision to turn around on the bridge that day, Turnaround Tuesday,
honoring a judge's order. As she wrote, this was "a temporary restraining lid on
the volcano to grant time for the good sense of the Nation and a strong Voting
Rights Bill in Congress to save us from catastrophe." Tragically, the turnaround
did not avert additional violence; a Northern protester, Unitarian minister James
Reeb, was viciously beaten on March 9 and died two days later.[38]

As these events in Selma weighed on her that day, Lady Bird was busy in
Washington with one of the other causes also closely identified with her history,
traveling to some of the 761 different parks in the capital city and calling for their
renewal and rescue from such blights as "scabrous grass."[39] This second meeting
of her beautification committee included a stop at Greenleaf Gardens, a housing development in an African American neighborhood, alongside Director of
Public Housing for the District of Columbia Walter Washington, with whom
she hoped to encourage the residents' involvement in their own gardens. As one
of her staffers recalled, "Mrs. Johnson attracted quite a crowd of residents and
youngsters," including a "Negro high school band that was very colorful and
snappy and bright. . . . It was a glorious, memorable, wonderful day." Her years
in Washington, just like her early years in Karnack, were infused with this love of
enhancing the natural environment and transcending racial barriers.[40]

Two months later, the first lady took to the roads in a Landscapes and Landmarks tour of Virginia's Interstate 95 segment near Monticello.[41] Udall came
along, as did philanthropist Laurance Rockefeller and a large group of journalists. She would dedicate a wayside shelter in Dumfries, Virginia, as well as see
new road-building techniques.[42] As reflected in her solo campaign trip, too, part
of her success in these endeavors was her close working relationship with the
press, facilitated by her press secretary, Carpenter, the first professional news-
woman ever hired by a first lady. As Burns emphasizes, Lady Bird's own journalist training enabled her understanding of "reporters' needs" and allowed for
"largely positive" coverage.[43]

Lady Bird Johnson carried her Southern-bred concerns into her life as first lady and beyond. After she left the White House, her work went on, as it does now more than a decade after her death in 2007. The Lady Bird Johnson Wildflower Center, in Austin, for instance, continues the cultivation of wildflowers, and programs that bear her imprimatur such as Head Start have benefited millions.[44]

## ROSALYNN CARTER

Less than a decade after Lady Bird Johnson left office, Rosalynn Carter brought her own stamp of Southern activism to the White House. Born in 1927 in Plains, Georgia, the eldest of four children and the daughter of automotive mechanic Wilburn Smith and dressmaker Frances Murray Smith, Rosalynn grew up on her family's farm. Her father died of leukemia when she was just thirteen, requiring her to help her mother with both the tailoring work and with raising her three younger siblings. She would meet her neighbor Jimmy Carter as a teenager; the two married when she was eighteen and he twenty-one. Though she was deep in Jim Crow Georgia, Rosalynn confessed that not until ninth grade did she fully reckon with racial segregation; reading something written by a Black neighbor, she realized how unequal her town's segregated schools were, but at that time it seemed to her that "challenging the status quo was inconceivable."[45] Rosalynn Smith's own education was also abbreviated; she enrolled at Georgia Southwestern College after high school, but her family's financial situation did not permit her to stay.

As a young wife she eagerly experienced life in locales as varied as Pearl Harbor, San Diego, and New London, Connecticut, while Jimmy pursued a career in the US Navy after World War II; when his father's death in 1953 brought them back to Plains to run the family peanut warehouse, Rosalynn took this disappointment gracefully and threw herself back into Southern living. She would have to wait some time for another opportunity for foreign travel—when she became her husband's human rights emissary while first lady, a topic Kristin Ahlberg closely examines in Chapter 15.

Back in Georgia in 1954, Rosalynn noted a change in the landscape: the *Brown v. Board of Education* decision meant that "whenever two or more were gathered together, integration was the primary, and more often than not, heated topic of conversation." Jimmy Carter refused to join the segregationist White Citizens Council; his mother, Lillian, had crossed racial lines as a nurse, and his navy years had also exposed him to a different reality. Rosalynn recalled that she was "influenced" by her husband to broaden her thinking, and this stance cost them support from white friends in the community.[46] In 1962, during Jimmy Carter's first electoral bid for the state senate, such liberal views on integration drew anger among some white Georgians, and he had to fight for his victory against an unscrupulous opponent. Accusations flew that the Carters had "been to a camp run by communists in Alabama to train integration workers."[47] At times, they worried about their business being boycotted, and Rosalynn was driven to barricade her doors. Jimmy was elected, though, and reelected in 1964, but lost his next race, for the governorship, to arch-segregationist Lester Maddox in 1966. Four years later, Jimmy Carter was more successful, but he had felt compelled to campaign by pandering to white voters himself, as E. Stanly Godbold Jr. noted.[48] After Carter was in the governor's mansion, however, he attacked segregation, while Rosalynn Carter decided to pursue her own causes as well.[49] As first lady of Georgia, with four children ranging from three to twenty-three years old, she wanted to make an impact. As she knew, "a first lady can pick and choose her projects and do almost anything she wants because her name is a drawing card, she is influential, and although legislators may not always support her, she can always get their attention, as well as the attention of other powerful people."[50] Her chief domestic cause would be mental health.

Rosalynn remembered seeing her cousin Tommy at the state institution in Georgia when she was a small child.[51] This left "a deep impression" on her, and later, she learned that two of Jimmy's cousins had bipolar disorder and schizophrenia. One of them, Linton Slappey, would berate Plains citizens in such unfiltered and insulting language he had to be sent back to the state mental hospital.[52] This facility, the Georgia State Lunatic, Idiot, and Epileptic Asylum in Milledgeville, operated for more than a century and a half. Blacks and whites occupied separate buildings (and cemeteries) until the 1950s, and the institution practiced sterilization until 1963. Ellen Axson's father had been sent to Milledgeville in 1883—the same year she met Woodrow Wilson—and it remained a bleak and scary place until it closed in 2013.[53]

Rosalynn Carter served on the Governor's Commission to Improve Services to the Mentally and Emotionally Handicapped and volunteered weekly at a mental hospital. Thanks to the efforts of her commission, the number of community mental health centers quintupled during the Carters' time in office, from 23 to 124.[54] After Jimmy Carter was elected president, her work in Georgia would lead her to be honorary chair of the President's Commission on Mental Health, which he established in 1977.[55] This work was much more than "honorary," but federal law prevented her, as the president's spouse, from holding certain appointments.[56] She managed to take her activism abroad nonetheless, as a presidential emissary to both Latin America and Thailand, as Chapter 15 relates, in a significant expansion of the first lady's role in both foreign policy and international human rights. In 1979, moreover, she testified before Congress in favor of the Mental Health Systems Act of 1980 (MHSA)—only the second first lady to testify, after Eleanor Roosevelt. Although the MHSA was designed to support a broader network of community mental health facilities, it was jettisoned within a year under the Reagan administration.

Rosalynn Carter, now in her nineties, continues her work, chairing the Carter Center's Mental Health Task Force and the Board of Advisors for the Rosalynn Carter Institute for Caregiving at Georgia Southwestern State University. Her career as a first lady would have been far different without the priorities etched upon her by her life in the South. Her opportunities to expand her activism from a domestic to a global stage were enabled both by her era and her husband's ready recognition of her abilities.

## BARBARA BUSH

Barbara Bush's story differs somewhat from the others here, given her origins in New England, her annual sojourns in Maine, and the many far-flung posts she shared with her husband over the years. Nevertheless, despite being neither a native nor a first lady of any Southern state, she was not untouched by her Southern exposure, fitting Myra Gutin's description in Chapter 16 that she was a "Lone Star Yankee," like her husband.

Born in New York City in 1925 to Pauline Pierce, a homemaker, and Marvin Pierce, an executive at *McCall's* magazine, she grew up in the suburb of Rye, New York. She attended high school in the South, however, at Ashley Hall, a boarding school in South Carolina. It was on a trip home that she met George H. W. Bush at a Christmas dance in Greenwich, Connecticut, soon after the events of December 7, 1941. He joined the war six months later, when he turned eighteen, while she returned to Ashley Hall. They married in early 1945. After the war, they moved to New Haven, Connecticut, so he could attend Yale University; Barbara, meanwhile, started but never completed her studies at Smith College. After George Bush's graduation from Yale, they moved to West Texas, where he went to work in the oil industry, eventually settling in Midland. Both of them worked hard; the task of raising six children (including one who died as a three-year-old) mostly fell upon her. The struggles with dyslexia of her son Neil, at a time when few Southern schools did much about learning disabilities, may have influenced her interest in literacy.[57]

Despite those early years in the South, Barbara seems to have been only made fully aware of the Jim Crow world she occupied when she and her nanny, Otha Fitzgerald, crossed the country on a trip to Maine in 1958. Barbara Bush was appalled when Fitzgerald was refused service at restaurants and hotels on the trip and forthrightly refused to go into the establishments where her nanny was turned away.[58]

As a full-time mother and supporter of her husband during his business and political careers, beginning with his early run for Harris County Republican Party chair in 1962, Barbara appeared firmly in the domestic sphere, appealing to the ideals of Southern womanhood that two decades later would bedevil Hillary Rodham in Little Rock, Arkansas. Yet in 1990, at Hillary Rodham's alma mater, Wellesley College, a number of students protested First Lady Barbara Bush being the choice for their commencement precisely because of her position as George's wife. She was invited anyway (her appearance with Russian first lady Raisa Gorbachev was no doubt a draw) and gave a speech in which she spoke of her own life choices.[59] The Wellesley women found themselves charmed, and the next year she crossed boundaries in a different way, working with US Representative Paul Simon, a Democrat, to ensure the passage of the National Literacy Act of 1991, the first such bill ever signed, with an impact from preschools to the penitentiary.[60] Her Barbara Bush Foundation for Family Literacy, which she established while in the White House, continues following her death and that of her husband in 2018, and a Southern issue it remains: ten of the bottom fifteen states as measured by literacy rates are in the old Confederacy.[61]

## HILLARY CLINTON

Like Barbara Pierce, Hillary Rodham was born outside the South, in Chicago. Yet she spent many years as a young woman in Arkansas, where she wrestled with its problems and was herself personally shaped by its culture, as Janette Kenner Muir has pointed out in Chapter 17. As with other first ladies' efforts explored in Part II, her work as her state's first lady closely predicted a number of her later concerns in the White House in such areas as education, children's health, and legal reform.

A Goldwater girl in the early 1960s, Hillary became an outspoken and increasingly liberal member of her Wellesley class and the school's first student commencement speaker, graduating in 1968. Three years later, at Yale Law School, she met the Arkansas-born Bill Clinton, and there, too, she connected with South Carolinian Marian Wright Edelman, who would launch the Children's Defense Fund in 1973. Both Southern friends were important for her; she would of course marry Bill in 1975 in Little Rock, and the work she did with Edelman would shape her future calling as an activist for children and families. In 1972, Hillary and Marian investigated all-white academies still in operation almost twenty years after *Brown v. Board of Education*. In Dothan, Alabama, Hillary pretended to be a mother enrolling her child at one of these academies, exposing the continuing segregation.[62]

After law school, Hillary had gone briefly to Washington to work on the

Watergate investigation with the House Judiciary Committee, but she soon returned to Arkansas to teach at the University of Arkansas Law School, where Bill was also teaching and pursuing political office. From the moment she arrived in Fayetteville, she was drawn to the problems of children who had been abused or neglected. She also set up a rape crisis hotline and argued for a number of "urgently needed legal reforms" in prestigious law reviews. In addition, she ran Fayetteville's legal aid clinic, eventually being appointed to the federal Legal Services Corporation by President Jimmy Carter and raising its funding significantly.[63]

By 1976, having lost a close race for Congress, Bill was elected the state's attorney general, and Hillary took a position at the Rose Law Firm in Little Rock. Well paid at this influential firm, she nonetheless continued her work for children and was instrumental in founding the Arkansas Advocates for Children and Families in 1977. Bill was elected Arkansas governor the following year and appointed his wife to another position, chair of the state's Rural Health Advisory Commission. His second run for governor ended in failure two years later, however. Many Clinton advisers zeroed in on the first lady for this loss, calling for her to adopt a "new look," suggesting she did not meet the "Southern womanhood" ideal.[64] Shedding her thick glasses and streaking her hair, she became Hillary Rodham Clinton; Bill Clinton was reelected in 1982. Compelled to do this reinvention, she was forcefully reminded of the South's particular cultural attributes, as Chapter 17 has also underlined.

Arkansas was a state "historically among the poorest in the nation," and there was much work to be done in the Clintons' second term.[65] At one point, carrying her new baby, Chelsea Clinton, in her arms on a visit to the small town of Bald Knob, Hillary met mothers reluctant to actually talk to their babies, thinking it a waste of time.[66] She attempted to persuade them otherwise, and in part to address such gaps for the youngest Arkansans she would introduce a program initiated in Israel by a US Head Start researcher, Alvima Lombard—the Home Instruction Program for Preschool Youth (HIPPY)—where teachers trained parents in literacy. HIPPY continues to this day.[67]

Perhaps the most important initiative Hillary Rodham Clinton pursued in Arkansas, however, was education reform. After their return to the governor's mansion, she chaired the Arkansas Educational Standards Committee for a decade, addressing such topics as curricular standards and teacher competencies. This involved exhaustive travel for her and her staff to different counties to gather information and feedback, where they learned of teachers at risk for burnout and heard from those also excited about the possibility of reforms.[68] People also complained in unvarnished detail to the governor about the deficiencies of individual teachers they knew.[69] Overall, many Arkansans appreciated her efforts, although she also faced much resistance, especially in rural districts that lost their smaller schools.[70]

This initiative, like that of the Arkansas Advocates, greatly influenced her work in Washington later. After her husband's election to president in 1992, Hillary took her concerns about health, education, and child welfare to a much larger platform as first lady, most controversially with her stewardship of the administration's health-care proposal.[71] She had more success in working with Congress to pass the State Children's Health Insurance Program (SCHIP), in 1997.[72] The same year, she was instrumental in passing the Adoption and Safe Families Act, which enabled closer monitoring of foster care. Hillary's work was also visible internationally while she was first lady; at the 1995 Fourth World Conference on Women in Beijing, she prominently highlighted concerns of women and children, attacking policies in China that had led, for example, to murdering girl babies as well as selling women and girls into prostitution.[73]

Later, as a Democratic senator from New York, Hillary continued her efforts for children. She introduced the Medically Fragile Children's Act of 2008, which amended the Social Security Act to establish a program for qualified children under Medicaid. Then, as US secretary of state from 2009 to 2013, she created the Hillary Doctrine, which emphasized that global violence against women was a "security issue," making empowerment for women and girls a pressing priority.[74] Her work drew, she wrote, on lessons "that I learned in Arkansas."[75]

During Hillary Clinton's unsuccessful presidential campaign of 2016, Attorney General Leslie Rutledge from Arkansas declared, "Secretary Clinton just never embraced Arkansas . . . and therefore I think that's why Arkansas is not embracing her."[76] Actually, her embrace of Arkansas lives on long after she moved away. As Ron Fournier noted, "Her advocacy led to new state school standards, a nationally recognized early childhood education program, and Arkansas' first neonatal intensive care unit."[77] Her stamp on the plight of abused and neglected children and adults in need of legal aid started there and continues to the wider world, and these initiatives show the legacy of Hillary Clinton's time in the state.

## LAURA BUSH

Laura Welch and Hillary Rodham came of age at nearly the same moment, although in different parts of the country. Midland, Texas, was a Jim Crow town where African Americans lived separately from whites. Later Laura recalled that its racism might have been "subtler" than in the deep South, but it was there nonetheless, "inflicted behind closed doors" even as it was emblazoned on her

Robert E. Lee High School. In her memoir, the former first lady reflected that her hometown was at least diverse in its mixing of socioeconomic classes and noted that "my friends and I watched the civil rights movement unfold, and we embraced it."[78] Indeed, this background spurred her to work in majority-minority schools as a librarian later, as Anita McBride relates in Chapter 18. Also growing up in her town was the wealthy George W. Bush; however, he was away at Phillips Academy in Andover, Massachusetts. The two did not meet until Laura was thirty, when friends introduced them at a barbecue in Midland.

In the meantime, she would spend close to a decade learning about and working in the fields of education and literacy in Texas. At Southern Methodist University, where she graduated with a degree in education in 1968, she attended a school still much removed from the ethos of its time, where girls wore dresses and protests were unheard of; certainly a different place from Wellesley, where Hillary Rodham graduated the same year. Unlike many of her classmates, however, Laura Welch did not have any immediate plans of marriage and briefly considered law school.[79]

Laura's growing feminist consciousness was stirred further when during a brief sojourn in Washington, DC, after college, she was offered a typing job by her Texas Congressman, who seemed unmoved by her bachelor's degree. She quickly returned to Texas to become a second-grade teacher in Houston, where for the first time a full awareness of racial disparities jumped out at her at the John F. Kennedy Elementary School. It was 1970, and she was shocked at the deficits in resources and learning opportunities she saw at the poor, largely African American institution. Inspired to earn a degree in library science to advocate for "literacy and books" to help needy students, Laura earned her master's degree at the University of Texas–Austin and eventually landed a job at Mollie Dawson Elementary, located in an impoverished Hispanic neighborhood of Austin. She had become increasingly convinced that the ability to read was "the new civil right," as her biographer Anne Gerhart noted.[80] Although she stopped working as a librarian after meeting George W. Bush in 1977 and raising their twin daughters, she never gave up her passion for expanding literacy. It was an issue for her long before she knew her mother-in-law.[81]

In 1995, following George's election as governor of Texas, she became the state's first lady. In this role, Laura launched the Texas Book Festival, which helped "put Texas on the Literary map."[82] Like Hillary Clinton, she was concerned about children's welfare and in Texas worked on prenatal care and teacher training, promoting Head Start's effectiveness for preschoolers.[83] As she told *People* magazine on the eve of the presidential election in 2000 about her plans for her possible new post, "I'd see myself as an activist, working on issues I know something about: education, libraries, and literacy."[84] She followed up in the White House, promoting such programs as Ready to Read, Ready to Learn, part of the more controversial No Child Left Behind Act as well as inaugurating the National Book Festival. Laura's Southern exposure in Texas beginning as a school librarian in the 1960s, where she witnessed the still heavy hand of segregation on the young students who came to her library, and later, as first lady of Texas, strongly influenced her role as first lady. Her efforts to broaden literacy might be seen as well in her work in Afghanistan on women's education, at schools in Africa, and also with the UN Decade of Literacy, as detailed in Chapter 18.

Like Hillary, Laura Bush departed from the other Southern first ladies in Part II by taking her activism to an international level, where she also focused on the importance of women's rights. She invited a group of Afghan women to the White House, sharing with them her conviction that "human rights include the rights of women and children." As she pointed out, "It's also very important . . . to make sure every child there is offered an education—not just the boys."[85] In March 2005, she went to Afghanistan—only the second first lady to travel to an active war zone after Patricia Nixon—and visited the Women's Teacher Training Institute in Kabul, a school she had helped establish.[86] In a trip to Liberia, Ghana, and Nigeria in 2006, she further amplified her concerns regarding education as well as health care. In Accra, Ghana, she visited a teacher training college to launch the Africa Education Initiative and the Korle-Bu Treatment Center, a medical facility concerned with the treatment of AIDS patients, supported by the Bush administration's President's Emergency Plan for AIDS Relief (PEPFAR).[87] Later that spring she traveled to India and Pakistan, where she promoted efforts to address education, AIDS (the administration extended $43 million to India for that malady), and women's issues, including problems ranging from genital mutilation to sex trafficking.[88]

Her emphasis on education and health care, especially for women and children, echoed Hillary Clinton's earlier message about the connections between international peace and security and women's empowerment. It was a message of global significance that reflected the civil rights struggle that began much closer to her home. Laura Bush's work continues today with the George W. Bush Institute, which remains active in education reform and other concerns, as well as her international Women's Initiative.[89]

Like all the women in Part II of this book, Laura had seen from a young age grave injustices and social ills that ranged from the aftermath of slavery to the oppression of Jim Crow to widespread poverty, illiteracy, and mental illness; like them, she too had witnessed striking rural beauty she wanted to preserve. Although not all Southern first ladies responded to these compelling issues—Edith Bolling Wilson had her mythmaking to attend to, regarding both her husband

Laura Bush, James Billington, and authors at the National Book Festival. Courtesy
of the Library of Congress Prints and Photographs Division. Reproduction Number
LC-DIG-ds-10200.

and the Lost Cause—for the others discussed here, these Southern experiences
helped focus their activism, involvement that would have both national and international implications and influence.

As we have seen throughout this book and the lives of its seventeen Southern
first ladies, the tenacious if wilting tendrils that notions of Southern white womanhood still presented challenged the activist roles and initiatives these women
undertook in the White House. As Nancy Beck Young notes in her conclusion
to Part I, Southern worldviews had helped shape the scope of first ladies' roles,
often making their power limited and contingent. To varying degrees, all the
women discussed in this book had to contend with the proprieties of Southern
womanhood as well as the constraints of its expectations, which continued to
push back against them, driving them at times to keep their engagement and
initiatives wrapped up in more "ladylike" activities—such as the entertaining
Dolley Madison and Julia Tyler did so effectively—or to mask their agency in
other ways. Even after women obtained a greater voice during the Progressive
Era, their activism might have either been downplayed, as happened to Ellen
Wilson, or, as with Lady Bird Johnson, they might have found it necessary to

adopt the persona of a steel magnolia to get their agenda implemented, or, as Hillary Rodham Clinton did, even feel compelled to conduct a cosmetic do-over to be effective. More recently, Laura Bush's activism has been minimized amid portrayals of her as a "quiet librarian" concerned with "ladies' things."[90]

Just as for these Southern women, Northern first ladies as well, white or Black—from Lou Henry Hoover to Michelle Obama—also have faced such expectations, and especially for Michelle Obama, their associated racist invective. Thus, Southernness and its cultural and historic resonances, including particular gender conventions, notions of white supremacy, and contested views of activism, have all left a strong stamp on the position of first lady. These women's roles in the White House, and those of their non-Southern counterparts, have been shaped by this heritage in deep, complicated, and sometimes contradictory ways. All of this has imparted a particularly Southern flavor to the White House that has clung to the office and expectations of the first lady to this day. Regardless of those constraints, however, these women were more than willing to act and did so well before reaching Washington, and sometimes well beyond it. Like Sarah Polk, they defied the shadows.

## NOTES

1. Charles Olson, "Maximus to Gloucester, Letter 27 [Withheld]," in *The Maximus Poems* (Berkeley: University of California Press, 1985).

2. See, for instance, Margaret Ripley Wolfe, *Daughters of Canaan: A Saga of Southern Women* (Lexington: University Press of Kentucky, 1995), 59.

3. See Jane Turner Censer, *The Reconstruction of White Southern Womanhood, 1865–1895* (Baton Rouge: Louisiana State University Press, 2003), 9.

4. Daniel Immerwahr, *How to Hide an Empire: A History of the Greater United States* (New York: Farrar, Straus, and Giroux, 2019), 102; Carl Sferrazza Anthony, *Nellie Taft: The Unconventional First Lady of the Ragtime Era* (New York: Morrow, 2006), 155; Jolyon Girard, ed., *Presidents and Presidencies in American History: A Social, Political, and Cultural Encyclopedia and Document Collection* (Santa Barbara: ABC Clio, 2019), 824.

5. Anthony, *Nellie Taft*, 250–251; Rafaele Fierro, "Helen Herron Taft: The Forgotten Impact of a Memorable First Lady," in *A Companion to First Ladies*, ed. Katherine A. S. Sibley (West Sussex, UK: Wiley-Blackwell, 2016), 330; "First Lady Biography: Helen Taft," First Ladies Library, http://www.firstladies.org/biographies/firstladies.aspx?biography=27.

6. Mark E. Kann, *On the Man Question: Gender and Civil Virtue in America* (Philadelphia: Temple University Press, 1991), 297; Kristin Hoganson, *Fighting for American Manhood: How Gender Politics Provoked the Spanish-American and Philippine-American Wars* (New Haven, CT: Yale University Press, 1998).

7. Natalie J. Ring, *The Problem South: Region, Empire, and the New Liberal State, 1880–1930* (Athens: University of Georgia Press, 2012), 84. Residents of both Puerto Rico and North

Carolina, for instance, were plagued by hookworm. See Immerwahr, *How to Hide an Empire*, 140.

8. "Edith Bolling Galt Wilson," https://www.whitehouse.gov/about-the-white-house/first-ladies/edith-bolling-galt-wilson/.

9. Frances Wright Saunders, *Ellen Axson Wilson: First Lady Between Two Worlds* (Chapel Hill: University of North Carolina Press, 1985), 4.

10. Saunders, *Ellen Axson Wilson*, 23; Ellen Wilson to Margaret Jane Hoyt Axson, letter, April 8, 1878, quoted in Saunders, *Ellen Axson Wilson*, 20.

11. Woodrow Wilson to Ellen Axson, letter, July 16, 1883, Box 14, Folder 1, Woodrow Wilson Papers, Seeley Mudd Library, Princeton University.

12. Ellen Axson to Woodrow Wilson, letter, October 15, 1884, Box 15, Folder 1, Woodrow Wilson Papers, Seeley Mudd Library, Princeton University; Kristie Miller, *Ellen and Edith: Woodrow Wilson's First Ladies* (Lawrence: University Press of Kansas, 2010), 18, 76–77.

13. Axson to Wilson, letter, October 15, 1884.

14. Ellen Wilson to Woodrow Wilson, letter, April 27, 1886, in Arthur Link, *Papers of Woodrow Wilson* (Princeton, NJ: Princeton University Press, 1968), 5: 177; Ellen Wilson to Woodrow Wilson, letter, May 22, 1886, in Link, *Papers of Woodrow Wilson*, vol. 5, 251, cited in Miller, *Ellen and Edith*, 18.

15. Miller, *Ellen and Edith*, 74.

16. Miller, 77. Also see manuscript of an interview with Jessie Wilson Sayer, December 1, 1925, Ray Stannard Baker Papers, Seeley Mudd Library, Princeton University; Arthur Link confirms this assessment in Link, *Wilson: The Road to the White House* (Princeton, NJ: Princeton University Press, 1947), 502.

17. See Miller, *Ellen and Edith*, 76–77; Sina Dubovoy, *Ellen A. Wilson: The Woman Who Made a President* (New York: Nova, 2011), 242; Carl Sferrazza Anthony, *First Ladies: The Saga of the Presidents' Wives and Their Power, 1789–1961* (New York: HarperCollins, 1992), 346; Lisa Burns, "Ellen Axson Wilson," in *A Companion to First Ladies*, ed. Katherine A. S. Sibley (West Sussex, UK: Wiley-Blackwell, 2016).

18. Oswald Garrison Villard to R. H. Leavell, letters, May 15, 1913, August 27, 1913, Box 5, Woodrow Wilson Papers, Additional Material, Seeley Mudd Library, Princeton University.

19. Although Woodrow Wilson's exact quote has been controversial, this part at least seems accurate, according to Mark E. Benbow, "Birth of a Quotation: Woodrow Wilson and 'Like Writing History with Lightning,'" *Journal of the Gilded Age and Progressive Era* 9 (October 2010): 527.

20. Link, *Papers of Woodrow Wilson*, vol 30: *1914*, 471n1, quoting *Outlook* 107, August 22, 1914, 953–954.

21. Burns, "Ellen Axson Wilson," 349. Woodrow Wilson himself also supported the bill; he noted he wanted "redemption for the slums of this city (the so-called alleys). I am deeply concerned that the bill on the subject should be taken up at this session, while the interest in its subject matter is still fresh and vivid." See Wilson to Oscar Wilder Underwood, letter, January 23, 1914, quoted in Link, *Papers of Woodrow Wilson*, vol. 29: *1913–1914*, 164.

22. Virginia Daughters of the American Revolution, "Ellen Wilson Memorial Report,"

in Daughters of the American Revolution, Proceedings of the Nineteenth Virginia State Conference, 86–87, Seeley Mudd Library, Princeton University.

23. Adrian Benepe, "How the White House Went Green: The Environmental Legacy of President Lyndon B. Johnson and Lady Bird Johnson," November 1, 2015, https://www.thenatureofcities.com/2015/11/01/how-the-white-house-went-green-the-environmental-legacy-of-president-lyndon-b-johnson-and-lady-bird-johnson/; Michael Gillette, quoted in Lisa Burns, "Lady Bird Johnson," in *A Companion to First Ladies*, ed. Katherine A. S. Sibley (West Sussex, UK: Wiley-Blackwell, 2016), 517.

24. Lewis Gould, *Lady Bird Johnson: Our Environmental First Lady* (Lawrence: University Press of Kansas, 1999), 18.

25. "White House Conference on National Beauty," May 24–25, 1965, White House Secretary's File [hereafter WHSF], Liz Carpenter's Files, 1963–1969, Box 15, LBJ Library, Austin, Texas.

26. Stewart L. Udall, Interview 5 with Joe B. Frantz, December 16, 1969, oral history transcript, LBJ Library, http://discoverlbj.org:443/item/oh-udalls-19691216-5-74-259-e.

27. Stuart Udall to Lady Bird Johnson, letter, July 29, 1964, WHSF, Liz Carpenter's Files, Box 10, LBJ Library.

28. White House Press Release Draft, WHSF, Liz Carpenter's Files, Box 10, LBJ Library; Stuart Udall to Liz Carpenter, memorandum, April 23, 1964, WHSF, Liz Carpenter's Files, Box 10, LBJ Library.

29. Liz Smith to Walter Jenkins, letter, June 24, 1964, WHSF, Liz Carpenter's Files, Box 10, LBJ Library; Frank E. "Ted" Moss to Mike Manatos, letter, June 1, 1964, WHSF, Liz Carpenter's Files, Box 10, LBJ Library.

30. Stewart L. Udall, Interview 2 with Joe B. Frantz, May 19, 1969, oral history transcript, LBJ Library, http://discoverlbj.org:443/item/oh-udalls-19690519-2-74-259-b.

31. Udall Interview 2 with Frantz, 7–8.

32. Gould, *Lady Bird Johnson*, 41.

33. Meredith Hindley, "Lady Bird Special: Mrs. Johnson's Southern Strategy," *Humanities* 34 (May/June 2013), https://www.neh.gov/humanities/2013/mayjune/feature/lady-bird-special.

34. Margaret Truman, *First Ladies* (New York: Random House, 1995), 177; Myra G. Gutin, *The President's Partner: The First Lady in the Twentieth Century* (Westport, CT: Greenwood, 1989), 118.

35. Hindley, "Lady Bird Special."

36. Office of the White House Press Secretary to Mrs. Johnson, press release, March 15, 1966, WHSF, Liz Carpenter's Files, Box 20, LBJ Library; Lady Bird Johnson, Statement, June 30, 1965, WHSF, Liz Carpenter's Files, Box 16, LBJ Library.

37. Lady Bird Johnson, May 21, 1964, White House Diary Collection, LBJ Presidential Library, 142.

38. As Lady Bird Johnson presciently wrote about this tragedy, it would "ma[k]e infinitely more dangerous the forces of tension." Johnson, March 9, 1965, White House Diary Collection, LBJ Presidential Library, http://discoverlbj.org:443/item/ctjd-19650309. No

one was ever sent to jail for James Reeb's murder, but the culprits were uncovered in the 2019 "White Lies" podcasts, https://www.npr.org/podcasts/510343/white-lies.

39. Johnson, March 9, 1965, White House Diary Collection, LBJ Presidential Library, http://discoverlbj.org:443/item/ctjd-19650309.

40. Nash Castro, interview with Joe B. Frantz, February 25, 1969, oral history transcript, LBJ Library, https://www.discoverlbj.org/item/oh-castron-19690225-1-84-9.

41. Now Box 15, Liz Carpenter's Files, WHSF, 1963–1969, May 11–12, 1965.

42. Press Release, April 29, 1965, WHSF, Liz Carpenter's Files, Box 15, 1963–1969.

43. Burns, "Lady Bird Johnson," 523–524.

44. Burns, 527–528.

45. Rosalynn Carter, *First Lady from Plains* (Boston: Houghton Mifflin, 1984), 14.

46. Carter, *First Lady from Plains*, 44–45.

47. Carter, 56.

48. E. Stanly Godbold Jr., *Jimmy and Rosalynn Carter: The Georgia Years, 1924–1974* (New York: Oxford University Press, 2010), 133.

49. Carter, *First Lady from Plains*, 77.

50. Carter, 95.

51. Rosalynn Carter and S. K. Golant, *Helping Someone with Mental Illness* (New York: Times, 1998), 7.

52. Carter and Golant, Helping Someone with Mental Illness; Godbold, Jimmy and Rosalynn Carter, 25; see also Jimmy Carter, An Hour Before Daylight: Memories of a Rural Boyhood (New York: Simon and Schuster, 2001), 143.

53. Alan Judd, "Asylum's Dark Past Relived as Cycle Ends," *AJC Today*, January 20, 2013, https://www.ajc.com/news/state--regional/asylum-dark-past-relived-cycle-ends/uq20K0dgHCeynhFUGba360/.

54. Robert Watson, ed., *White House Studies Compendium*, no. 5 (Hauppauge, NY: Nova, 2008), 68.

55. Kristin Ahlberg, "Eleanor Rosalynn Smith Carter," in *A Companion to First Ladies*, ed. Katherine A. S. Sibley (West Sussex, UK: Wiley-Blackwell, 2016), 575; Gerald Grob, "Public Policy and Mental Illnesses: Jimmy Carter's Presidential Commission on Mental Health," *Milbank Quarterly* 83, no. 3 (September 2005): 429, cited in Ahlberg, "Eleanor Rosalynn Smith Carter," 583.

56. Ahlberg, "Eleanor Rosalynn Smith Carter," 581.

57. "First Lady Spells Out Top Cause: Literacy," *Chicago Tribune*, February 19, 1989, http://articles.chicagotribune.com/1989-02-19/features/8903060540_1_white-house-mrs-bush-lady-bird-johnson.

58. Barbara Bush, *A Memoir* (New York: Scribner's, 1994), 51.

59. The speech's significance is analyzed further in Diana B. Carlin, "Barbara Pierce Bush: Choosing a Complete Life, 1988–2015," in *A Companion to First Ladies*, ed. Katherine A. S. Sibley (West Sussex, UK: Wiley-Blackwell, 2016), 627–629.

60. Myra G. Gutin, *Barbara Bush: Presidential Matriarch* (Lawrence: University Press of Kansas, 2008), 85–87.

61. Evan Comen, "Most and Least Literate States," September 7, 2018, https://247 wallst.com/special-report/2018/09/07/most-and-least-literate-states/9/.

62. Janette Kenner Muir, "Hillary Rodham Clinton," in *A Companion to First Ladies*, ed. Katherine A. S. Sibley (West Sussex, UK: Wiley-Blackwell, 2016), 639; Marian Wright Edelman, "It's Not over in the South: School Desegregation in 43 Southern Cities 18 Years after *Brown*," cited in "How Hillary Clinton Went Undercover to Examine Race in Education," *New York Times*, December 27, 2015, https://www.nytimes.com/2015/12/28/us /politics/how-hillary-clinton-went-undercover-to-examine-race-in-education.html.

63. Allida Black, "Blazing a Trail: Hillary Clinton, Advocate for Children and the Indigent," *Huffington Post*, July 22, 2014, https://www.huffpost.com/entry/blazing-a-trail -hillary-clinton_b_5610884.

64. Hillary Clinton, *Living History* (New York: Simon and Schuster, 2003), 92.

65. "Clinton Remakes Home State in Own Image," *New York Times*, March 31, 1992, 1.

66. Clinton, *Living History*, 93.

67. "Israeli-Begun Program for Preschoolers Gains Attention in Arkansas: Mrs. Clinton Leading Effort, Conference Held," *Pine Bluff Commercial*, Box 5, Folder 1, Hippy Clippings (Home Instruction Program for Preschool Youngsters), Butler Center, Little Rock, Arkansas, Bill Clinton Gubernatorial Record Group II, Education Series, Ann Kamps Subseries; Hippy USA Locations at https://www.hippyusa.org/state-offices-staff.

68. Don Ernst to William Borah, form letter, June 7, 1983; Helen Ruth Teague to Hillary Clinton, letter, July 14, 1983; Carol Teague to Bill Clinton, letter, July 30, 1983, all in Group II, Education Series, Don Ernst Subsubseries: Education Standards, Box 7, File 3, Butler Center, Little Rock, Arkansas. See also Constance Dardin to Beverly Coney, letter, September 16, 1987, Group II, Education Series, Connie Dardin Subseries, General Education, Box 11, File 20.

69. Bill Clinton to Terri Jones, letter, January 5, 1988, Group II, Education Series, Connie Dardin Subseries, General Education, Box 11, File 25, Butler Center, Little Rock, Arkansas.

70. Richard E. Cadieux, Sylvan Learning Center, to Governor Clinton, letter, April 25, 1987, Group II, Education Series, Connie Dardin, Subseries, General Education, Box 11, File 10, Butler Center, Little Rock, Arkansas.

71. Muir, "Hillary Rodham Clinton," 646.

72. Scott Conroy, "In Arkansas, Hillary Clinton's Legacy Remains Potent," *Huffington Post*, May 11, 2015; https://www.huffingtonpost.com/2015/05/11/hillary-clinton-arkan sas_n_7258956.html.

73. Amy Chozick, "Hillary Clinton's Speech on Women Resonates Twenty Years Later," https://www.nytimes.com/politics/first-draft/2015/09/05/20-years-later-hillary -clintons-beijing-speech-on-women-resonates/.

74. Quoted in Valerie Hudson and Patricia Leidl, *The Hillary Doctrine: Sex and American Foreign Policy* (New York: Columbia University Press, 2015), 3.

75. Hillary Clinton, *It Takes a Village*, 10th anniversary ed. (New York: Simon and Schuster, 2006), 241.

76. Ron Fournier, "Hillary Clinton's Faded Footprint in Arkansas," May 12, 2016, https://www.theatlantic.com/politics/archive/2016/05/hillarys-faded-footprint/482259/.

77. Fournier, "Hillary Clinton's Faded Footprint in Arkansas."

78. Laura Bush, *Spoken from the Heart* (New York: Simon and Schuster, 2010), 72–73.

79. Anne Gerhart, *The Perfect Wife: The Life and Choices of Laura Bush* (New York: Simon and Schuster, 2004), 35.

80. Gerhart, *Perfect Wife*, 43.

81. "Reading Laura Bush," *Texas Monthly* (November 1996), in Andrea Ball Papers, Box 1, George W. Bush Library and Museum, Dallas, Texas.

82. "Laura Bush: A Quiet Source of Strength," *People Weekly*, October 9, 2000, Andrea Ball Papers, Box 1, George W. Bush Library and Museum, Dallas, Texas.

83. Deborah Orin, "Stepping Out from Behind the Bushes," *New York Post*, June 16, 1999, Andrea Ball Papers, Box 1, George W. Bush Library and Museum, Dallas, Texas.

84. "Laura Bush: A Quiet Source of Strength."

85. Sandra Sobieraj to James R. Wilkinson, email, November 27, 2001, P_5XQU4004 and P_7ZFU4004; Brian Bravo of White House to Daniel J. Bartlett, reports, November 27, 2001, Pool report P_DTFU4004: 2014-0527-F: Records on Laura Bush's Meeting with Afghan Women on November 27, 2001, George W. Bush Library and Museum, Dallas, Texas.

86. Anita McBride, "Laura Welch Bush: Strength and Serenity in Turbulent Times," in *A Companion to First Ladies*, ed. Katherine A. S. Sibley (West Sussex, UK: Wiley-Blackwell, 2016), 665.

87. Visit to Korle-Bu Treatment Center, memorandum, January 17, 2006; Laura Bush to Pamela Bridgewater, letter, February 6, 2006, Office of Laura Bush, Chief of Staff Anita McBride, George W. Bush Library and Museum, Dallas, Texas.

88. Laura Bush to Jorge Sequeira, March 24, 2006, Mrs. Laura Bush's Trip to India, March 2006, White House Office of Records Management, Box 1, Subject Files PP005-01, First Lady, Folder Title 690526, FOIA 2014-0532-F, George W. Bush Library and Museum, Dallas, Texas.

89. See Education Reform Initiative, https://www.bushcenter.org/explore-our-work/issues/education-reform.html.

90. McBride, "Laura Welch Bush," 672, 668.

# About the Contributors

Kristin L. Ahlberg is a historian in the Office of the Historian, US Department of State, where she compiles and reviews volumes in the *Foreign Relations of the United States* series. She earned her PhD in diplomatic history from the University of Nebraska. Ahlberg is the author of *Transplanting the Great Society: Lyndon Johnson and Food for Peace* (University of Missouri Press, 2009). She has also published articles in *Diplomatic History,* the *Public Historian*, and *Agricultural History* and chapters in the Wiley-Blackwell *Companions* series and the *Oxford Research Encyclopedia*.

Catherine Allgor is president of the Massachusetts Historical Society. She was formerly a presidential chair at the University of California–Riverside. She received her PhD in history from Yale University and has written about women and politics in the Early Republic. She is the author of *A Perfect Union: Dolley Madison and the Creation of the American Nation* (Henry Holt, 2006).

Lisa M. Burns is professor of media studies at Quinnipiac University in Hamden, Connecticut. She holds a PhD in communication from the University of Maryland–College Park. Her publications include *Media Relations and the Modern First Lady: From Jacqueline Kennedy to Melania Trump* (editor), *First Ladies and the Fourth Estate: Press Framing of Presidential Wives*, and multiple journal articles and book chapters on first ladies. She frequently serves as a media expert on topics including first ladies/political spouses, women in politics, and presidential campaign coverage.

Diana Bartelli Carlin is professor emerita of communication and a former associate provost at Saint Louis University. She has taught and lectured extensively on the rhetoric of first ladies and has published book chapters on Lady Bird Johnson, Barbara Bush, Hillary Clinton, and Michelle Obama. Carlin has taught Osher Lifelong Learning courses on first ladies and their impact on the presidency and US society along with regular academic courses on first ladies. She has also participated in symposia at the National First Ladies Library in Canton, Ohio, and at the Southern Methodist University Center for Presidential History.

Teri Finneman is associate professor of journalism at the University of Kansas. Her research focuses on news coverage of American first ladies and women politicians. She also conducts research related to media ethics, journalism history, and oral history. She is the author of *Press Portrayals of Women Politicians, 1870s–2000s: From "Lunatic" Woodhull to "Polarizing" Palin*, which was named a 2016 finalist for the Frank Luther Mott–Kappa Tau Alpha book award for best research-based book about journalism or mass communication.

Louie P. Gallo is a historian at the Ulysses S. Grant Presidential Library and Museum. He is coeditor of *The Personal Memoirs of Ulysses S. Grant: The Complete Annotated Edition* (Harvard University Press, 2017) and coauthor of *Hold on with a Bulldog Grip: A Short Study of Ulysses S. Grant* (University Press of Mississippi, 2019).

Myra G. Gutin is professor of communication and journalism at Rider University, where she teaches courses on the American first ladies and political communication. She is the author of two books, *The President's Partner: The First Lady in the Twentieth Century* (Praeger, 1989) and *Barbara Bush: Presidential Matriarch* (University Press of Kansas, 2008), and numerous book chapters, articles, and op-eds about the first ladies and women in politics. A frequent media commentator, she is writing a biography of Betty Ford.

Sylvia D. Hoffert is professor of history emerita at Texas A&M University. The author of five books, including *Alva Vanderbilt Belmont: Unlikely Champion of Women's Rights* (Indiana University Press, 2012), *Jane Grey Swisshelm: An Unconventional Life, 1815–1884* (University of North Carolina Press, 2004), and *When Hens Crow: The Woman's Rights Movement in Antebellum America* (Indiana University Press, 1995) as well as many articles, she focuses on the history of American women in the nineteenth and early twentieth centuries.

Christopher J. Leahy is professor of history at Keuka College, in the Finger Lakes region of New York. He is the author of *President without a Party: The Life of John Tyler* (Louisiana State University Press, 2020) and is writing a biography of Julia Gardiner Tyler with his wife, Sharon Williams Leahy.

Sharon Williams Leahy is an independent scholar and author of the article "Not a Model: First Lady Julia Gardiner Tyler and New York City's Print Culture," *New York History* 99 (Summer/Fall 2018): 331–355. She is writing a biography of Julia Gardiner Tyler with her husband, Christopher J. Leahy.

Laura Mammina is assistant professor of history at the University of Houston–Victoria, where she teaches courses on gender and sexuality and race and ethnicity in the United States. Her work appears in *Tennessee Women: Their Life and Times*, vol. 2 (University of Georgia Press, 2015), and *The World of the Civil War* (ABC-Clio, 2015), and she coedited, with Megan L. Bever and Lesley J. Gordon, *American Discord: The Republic and Its People in the Civil War Era* (Louisiana State University Press, 2020). She is working on a book examining the interactions of Union soldiers and Southern women during the Civil War.

John F. Marszalek is executive director of the Ulysses S. Grant Presidential Library at Mississippi State University's Mitchell Memorial Library. Along with Tim Smith, he is coeditor of the book series *The World of Grant*. He is the author or editor of many books, including *Sherman: A Soldier's Passion for Order* (Free Press, 1992) and *Lincoln and the Military* (Southern Illinois University Press, 2014).

Anita B. McBride is executive in residence at the Center for Congressional and Presidential Studies in the School of Public Affairs at American University, where she directs programming and national conferences on the legacies of American first ladies and their influence on politics, policy, and global diplomacy. McBride's public service spans two decades and three US presidential administrations, with appointments in the US Department of State and the White House including as assistant to the president and chief of staff to First Lady Laura Bush, directing the first lady's domestic and international initiatives. She cofounded the RAND African First Ladies Initiative, serves as an advisor to American University's Sine Institute of Policy and Politics and the Laura Bush Women's Initiative at the George W. Bush Presidential Center, and is on the board of several organizations including the White House Historical Association. She is a frequent speaker, print source contributor, and news commentator on presidential transitions and the operations and history of the White House and its occupants.

Janette Kenner Muir is associate provost for Academic Initiatives and Services at George Mason University. She is coeditor of *Readings on Political Communication* (Strata, 2007) and has been featured in the *Harvard International Review*, writing about media, politics, and citizen participation. She edited *Coming to Terms: The*

*Collected Works of Jane Blankenship* (Lexington, 2011), and her most recent work focuses on Hillary Clinton in Katherine A. S. Sibley, ed., *A Companion to First Ladies* (Wiley-Blackwell, 2016).

Valerie Palmer-Mehta is professor of communication in the Department of Communication, Journalism, and Public Relations at Oakland University in Rochester, Michigan. Her research has been published in a variety of journals such as *Communication and Critical/Cultural Studies*, *International Journal of Communication*, *Text and Performance Quarterly*, *Women's Studies in Communication*, and *Communication, Culture & Critique*. She also published an essay, "Sarah Polk: Ideas of Her Own," in Sibley, *A Companion to First Ladies*.

Merry Ellen Scofield is associate editor with the Papers of Thomas Jefferson at Princeton University. Her research centers on nineteenth-century social Washington, DC, and includes work on Jefferson's dinner parties, the reign of Dolley Madison, and the first ladies of the Grover Cleveland and Benjamin Harrison administrations.

Katherine A. S. Sibley is professor of history and director of American Studies at Saint Joseph's University in Philadelphia. She edited *A Companion to First Ladies* (Wiley-Blackwell, 2016), authored *First Lady Florence Harding: Beyond the Tragedy and Controversy* (University Press of Kansas, 2009), and will soon begin writing a biography on Michelle Obama. She has published four other books on US-Soviet relations, including *Post–Cold War Revelations and the American Communist Party: Citizens, Revolutionaries, and Spies*, with Vernon L. Pedersen and James G. Ryan (Bloomsbury, 2021), *Red Spies in America: Stolen Secrets and the Dawn of the Cold War* (University Press of Kansas, 2004), and *Loans and Legitimacy: The Evolution of Soviet-American Relations, 1919–1933* (University Press of Kentucky, 1996). Sibley received her PhD from the University of California–Santa Barbara and served for more than a dozen years on the Historical Advisory Committee for the US Department of State.

Nancy Kegan Smith was an archivist at the National Archives and Records Administration from 1973 to 2012, retiring as director of the Presidential Materials Division, which deals with the White House and the presidential libraries on records and artifact issues. She lectures and writes on first ladies and does archival consulting. She is coeditor of the book *Modern First Ladies: Their Documentary Legacy* (National Archives Trust Fund Board, 1990) and has written or coauthored articles and book chapters on presidential records, first ladies, Lady Bird Johnson, and Michelle Obama.

Mary Stockwell received her PhD in history from the University of Toledo and was a professor and department chair of history at Lourdes University. She has been a research fellow at the New York Public Library and the William L. Clements Library and is a full-time writer. She is the author of *Unlikely General: "Mad" Anthony Wayne and the Battle for America* (Yale University Press, 2018); *Interrupted Odyssey: Ulysses S. Grant and the American Indians* (Southern Illinois University Press, 2018); *The Other Trail of Tears: The Removal of the Ohio Indians* (Westholme, 2016); *Woodrow Wilson: The Last Romantic* (Nova, 2008); *The American Story: Perspectives and Encounters to 1865* (Bridgepoint Education, 2012); and books for young people including *Ohio Adventure* (Gibbs Smith, 2006); *A Journey Through Maine* (Gibbs Smith, 2006); and the prize-winning *Massachusetts: Our Home* (Gibbs Smith, 2004).

Nancy Beck Young is professor of history at the University of Houston. She is author of multiple books, including three published by the University Press of Kansas: *Two Suns of the Southwest: Lyndon Johnson, Barry Goldwater, and the 1964 Battle Between Liberalism and Conservatism* (2019); *Why We Fight: Congress and the Politics of World War II* (2013); and *Lou Henry Hoover: Activist First Lady* (2004). She has also held residential fellowships at the Woodrow Wilson International Center for Scholars and the Clements Center for Southwest Studies at Southern Methodist University, and she has won multiple book prizes and teaching awards.

# Index